THE METHUEN D

GUIDE TO CONTEMPORARY

AMERICAN P

Martin Middeke is Profes
the University of Augsburg
University of Johannesburg,

Peter Paul Schnierer is Professor and Chair of English Literature at the
University of Heidelberg, Germany.

Christopher Innes is Professor of English at York University, Canada,
and holds the Canada Research Chair in Performance and Culture.

Matthew C. Roudané is Professor and Chair of English at Georgia
State University, USA.

DISCARD

THE METHUEN DRAMA GUIDE TO CONTEMPORARY AMERICAN PLAYWRIGHTS

Edited and with an introduction by Martin Middeke, Peter Paul Schnierer, Christopher Innes and Matthew C. Roudané

B L O O M S B U R Y

LONDON · NEW DELHI · NEW YORK · SYDNEY

Bloomsbury Methuen Drama
An imprint of Bloomsbury Publishing Plc

50 Bedford Square
London
WC1B 3DP
UK

1385 Broadway
New York
NY 10018
USA

www.bloomsbury.com

Bloomsbury is a registered trade mark of Bloomsbury Publishing Plc

First published 2014

British Library Cataloguing-in-Publication Data
A catalogue record for this book is available from the British Library.

ISBN: HB: 978-1-4725-2007-4
PB: 978-1-4081-3479-5
ePub: 978-1-4081-3481-8
ePDF: 978-1-4081-3480-1

Library of Congress Cataloging-in-Publication Data
The Methuen drama guide to contemporary American playwrights/edited and
with an introduction by Martin Middeke, Peter Paul Schnierer,
Christopher Innes and Matthew C. Roudan?.
pages cm
Includes bibliographical references and index.
ISBN 978-1-4081-3479-5 – ISBN 978-1-4725-2007-4 – ISBN 978-1-4081-3481-8 –
ISBN 978-1-4081-3480-1 1. American drama–20th century–History and criticism.
2. American drama–21st century–History and criticism.
I. Middeke, Martin, 1963– editor of compilation.
PS350.M38 2013
812'.509–dc23
2013033622

Typeset by Deanta Global Publishing Services, Chennai, India
Printed and bound in India

CONTENTS

INTRODUCTION

Christopher Innes, Martin Middeke, Matthew C. Roudané, Peter Paul Schnierer

This collection surveys 25 representative playwrights of contemporary American drama, with an emphasis on those whose work first appeared in the 1970s or later. The chapters are written by a team of internationally renowned specialists from the United Kingdom, United States, Canada, Italy and Germany. Each chapter has a four-part structure: an introduction which includes a short biographical sketch of each playwright; a concise analysis of the major work of the respective author in chronological order; a summary of the playwright's particular contribution to contemporary American theatre, including an assessment of their characteristic themes, stylistic features and the critical reception of their work; and, finally, a bibliography of primary texts and a selection of critical material. The 25 chapters in this volume discuss a total of more than 140 plays in detail (while many more are mentioned on the way) – an abundant body of work, which enables conclusions to be drawn about the development as well as the state of affairs in contemporary American playwriting and provides helpful suggestions for further research. With Arthur Miller and Edward Albee American drama features two acclaimed figureheads with worldwide impact, who have been productive over the entire second half of the twentieth century. In the immediate context of this volume, however, emphasis has been placed on Miller's and Albee's post-1970 work. More than a third of the plays discussed in detail in this volume were premiered in the first decade of the twenty-first century.

* * *

American dramatists since 1970 have progressed towards the centre of the national artistic consciousness. The best, including those featured in this volume, have done so by making significant and original contributions to the rhetoric of nationhood, to the language of the stage, and to the symbology of the self. The plays discussed here, indeed, capture selected public issues of the nation as those issues are reflected within the private anxieties of the individual. Perhaps one of the most distinguishing shifts in recent American drama concerns its relationship to Broadway. When Eugene O'Neill, Susan Glaspell and Thornton Wilder first conferred upon the American stage its modernity, Broadway in New York City was *the* site of dramatic originality and vitality. Broadway was the launching site for playwrights who defined the scope and range of serious American theatre. When O'Neill's *The Hairy Ape* opened the same year as the appearance of James Joyce's *Ulysses* and T. S. Eliot's *The Waste Land* – 1922 – the Mayor of New York City, troubled by the play's themes, tried, unsuccessfully, to close the production. The public flocked to see the show that is considered one of the first successful Expressionistic plays staged by an American. When at mid-century Lillian Hellman, William Inge, Tennessee Williams, Arthur Miller and Lorraine Hansberry extended as they refreshed notions of American theatrical modernity, Broadway was still a vibrant source of dramatic energy. Four plays in a 4-year span confirm the point: *The Glass Menagerie* (1945), *A Streetcar Named Desire* (1947), *All My Sons* (1947) and *Death of a Salesman* (1949) together ran for 2,466 shows.

As the twenty-first century unspools before us, however, Broadway has changed. The earlier Broadway was an initiating theatre. This is where key plays played. Today, many of the best American playwrights open their shows both geographically and symbolically well beyond Broadway. The decentralization is unmistakable. Edward Albee opened *Counting the Ways* (1976) in London and *Marriage Play* (1987) and *Three Tall Women* (1992) in Vienna. David Mamet staged *Glengarry Glen Ross* (1983) and *The Cryptogram* (1994) in London. Sam Shepard staged his recent plays *Kicking a Dead Horse* (2007) and *Ages of the Moon* (2009) in Dublin. Tony Kushner's *Angels in America, Part One: Millennium Approaches* was first staged in Los Angeles in 1990, in San Francisco in 1991, in London and then back to Los Angeles in 1992, and, finally in New York City in 1993. Iris Bahr's one-woman show, played by Bahr herself, *DAI enough* (2008) premiered in Edinburgh. And on and on. Further, many playwrights began directing their own works, exercising authorial control rarely seen during the mid-twentieth-century glory days of such directors as Elia Kazan and José Quintero.

Broadway is now a showcase theatre. It is a place where musicals, classic revivals or guaranteed contemporary sensations animate the stage. To be sure, works by major playwrights featuring entertainment stars, who ensure packed houses, occasionally open on Broadway, as was the case with Mamet's *Speed-the-Plow* (1988), which starred Madonna, or the 1988 revival of Samuel Beckett's *Waiting for Godot,* which showcased Steve Martin and Robin Williams. Today the practice continues as producers and playwrights sometimes transfer their works from regional theatres to New York City, at other times going directly to Broadway, and, box office receipts in mind, sometimes, again, do so with popular stars in lead roles, as occurred when Mos Def acted in Suzan-Lori Parks's *Topdog/Underdog* (2002) at the Ambassador Theatre and when Chris Rock performed in Stephen Adley Guirgis's *The Motherfucker with the Hat* (2011) at Broadway's Gerald Schoenfeld Theatre.

Despite both the importance and, ironically, decentralized status of Broadway, the United States today continues to see a healthy number of 'major' and lesser-known but important playwrights who, like their plays themselves, hail from all parts of the country. Their works are often first staged in the regional theatres – in Louisville, Omaha, Minneapolis, Chicago, Houston, Atlanta, Seattle, San Francisco and so on – and in the numerous university theatres from coast to coast. As seen in the works of the contemporary playwrights in this collection, the central subjects of their plays are as varied as the plays themselves, but patterns emerge. The American dramatists' preoccupation with the status of the imagination, the primal family unit, questions of gender and race, the role of truth and illusion, the compromise of self-reliance, and the collapse of physical, mental and moral space remain vital concerns for playwrights, actors, directors, producers and set designers in the twenty-first century.

Since 1970 America's exemplary playwrights seem to implicitly agree with Judith Malina and Julian Beck, leaders of the Living Theatre, who defined their artistic vision in an essay entitled 'Storming the Barricades' as one committed to increasing consciousness, stressing the sacredness of life and to breaking down the walls. Although Malina's and Beck's idealism and pronouncements may seem like a trip down memory lane from the 1960s, their belief that the theatre increases consciousness, celebrates the sacred and politically may produce change remains as true for Lynn Nottage, Naomi Wallace and Neil LaBute as it did for Susan Glaspell, Arthur Miller and Tennessee Williams. If yesterday's revolution has been appropriated by today's mainstream theatre, the work of Malina and Beck, of O'Neill and Miller and many others, foretold the social confrontations and personal commitments that so characterize recent American drama.

And American audiences remain eager to receive new theatre. Despite considerable cultural, financial and artistic blockades that to this day inhibit American dramatists, they are in a key position to move the American stage from the margins to the centre of American cultural life. This generative process is ever on the verge of collapse, of course. Yet the dramatists in this volume have learnt from the past. They have transcended the circus, the carnival, the minstrel show, the farce and the vaudeville. They have learnt from their European counterparts. With an eye towards the future, American dramatists have embedded in their plays a kind of moral seriousness that the novelists and poets long ago interleaved within their artistry, and audiences continue to appreciate the staging of such issues.

It would be fanciful to suggest that since 1970 American drama has attained the highest ranking within American culture. In the United States, while Broadway thrives, a surprising number of people throughout the country rarely go to the theatre. Further, too many talented actors, unable to support themselves financially, wait tables between shows. Too many playwrights, unable to find producers willing to take chances on their new plays and lured by the megabucks of Hollywood, take their talents to the film industry. The effects of technological and electronic culture have even altered the fundamental ways in which one receives a theatrical performance. The power of cinema and DVDs continue to lure the theatregoing public.

Too little national support in the form of grants and fellowships for the American stage also contributes to the precarious state of American theatre and drama. Performance artist Karen Finley discovered another difficulty. In 1990, Finley became involved in a political struggle over funding for a National Endowment for the Arts (NEA) award. She and three other performance artists, who became known as the NEA Four, had applied for NEA grants, but their applications, though favourably reviewed, were vetoed by the chairman John Fronmayer after Senator Jesse Helms condemned Finley. Something about a nude woman smeared in chocolate railing against the conservative culture upset Helms and others. Helms fomented a McCarthyish hunt over Finley and her art, and a legal battle lasting for years ensued. Finley won at the circuit court level, receiving the grant money and legal fees but, ultimately, lost the first amendment claim at the Supreme Court. NEA versus Finley raised fundamental issues regarding artistic freedom, censorship and 'decency.' The NEA, under pressure from conservatives in Congress, has since stopped funding individual artists whose works are deemed offensive. In the context of the global financial meltdown in recent years, the NEA's decision over two decades ago hampers theatres whose financial struggles are the *donnée* of life in the theatre.

Then there is television. Indeed, the lure of television drama has proven irresistible to many playwrights. It is scarcely surprising that the enormously popular Broadway hit *The Book of Mormon: The Musical of the Church of Latter-day Saints* (2011–12) was written by the creators of television's equally popular *South Park* for Comedy Central. Originally scheduled for Off Broadway production, Trey Parker, Robert Lopez and Matt Stone, its creators, decided to stage it at the Eugene O'Neill Theatre in the heart of Broadway. In *Viewing America: Twenty-First Century Television Drama*, Christopher Bigsby suggests that the twentieth century 'had been in many ways been an American century as far as theater was concerned. Of course, America still produces major talents which command interest of audiences around the world but there is a degree to which some writers of drama, along with novelists, have shifted their attention to television. Once that seemed unthinkable. A decade and a half into the twenty-first century some of the finest dramatic work is now to be seen on a medium that had tended to be dismissed, rather as the novel once was, as an inconsequential form of entertainment, as if entertainment had not always been an objective of the artist. In 2011, seven of the nine writers on HBO's *Big Love* were playwrights and theatre a route into television.' Television dramas from *The Sopranos, West Wing* and *The Wire* to *Mad Men* and *Treme* beamed to millions of households attest to the notion that we are in the midst of a golden age of television drama.

* * *

Various elements help to single out the contemporary generation of American dramatists from earlier playwrights in America – and indeed from their contemporaries elsewhere. Most obvious is the new inclusion of gay, American-Indian and Hispanic or Japanese-American writers, where for an earlier period it was the emergence of Black dramatists – leading to the 'Century' cycle of August Wilson, documenting the changing racial situation in each decade. A second element is, of course, the focus on subjects of the times, whether AIDS or 9/11 (as most notably in Tony Kushner's *Angels in America* 1993, or Neil LaBute's *The Mercy Seat* 2002). A third, and perhaps most crucial element, since it had a strong stylistic impact as well as affecting subject matter, is the burst of new energy flowing partly from the re-discovery of Antonin Artaud and his 'Theatre of Cruelty' theories from the 1930s that emerged with the mid-1960s avant-garde.

Up to then, theatrical developments in America, through the 1940s and on, had been mainly fuelled by dramatists, although their work was promoted by directors like Elia Kazan or actors such as Marlon Brando. However, fuelled by the anti-Vietnam movement and the 'flower-power' liberation, as well as the translation of Artaud's writings that was published in the mid-1950s, collectives – most notably The Living Theatre – emerged: largely a director- and actor-led movement that included Richard Schechner's ritual-based Performance Group or Joseph Chaikin's improvisational Open Theatre, in addition to experimental groups that had started slightly earlier, such as Ellen Stewart's La MaMa, or others who followed on, like Elizabeth LeCompte's Wooster Group. Few well-known playwrights were involved, although Sam Shepard later collaborated with Chaikin.

Having started as a promoter of American experimental drama – William Carlos Williams, and Paul Goodman, Gertrude Stein's *Dr Faustus Lights the Lights* or Jack Gelber's *The Connection*, as well as introducing key European writers such as Pirandello, Cocteau, Lorca and Brecht – The Living Theatre became politicized by the 1968 European student rebellion, promoting an anti-textual theatre of graphic images and physically intense audience involvement. The Living Theatre was still active and influential into the 1980s, while the Wooster Group, with their theatrical deconstruction of technology, remains a major force in American theatre into the new millennium.

But there are also other commonalities that are sometimes overlooked. A number of the contemporary male American playwrights, including Sam Shepard, Tracy Letts, Neil LaBute and Wallace Shawn, started their careers in England and Sam Shepard continued his career in England – indeed, all four are linked to a very specific theatre, the Royal Court, known not only for its championing of John Osborne and new British drama in the 1950s and 60s, but also as the home of later path-breaking dramatists including Howard Brenton, David Hare, David Edgar, Timberlake Wertenbaker and Caryl Churchill, and in the 1990s for the promotion of 'in-yer-face' dramatists like Sarah Kane. Indeed Shepard's 1973 *The Tooth of Crime* served as a catalyst for this movement, while Letts's *Bug* (1996) formed an American equivalent. This context not only created an international reach for their work – and indeed LaBute's plays are generally first staged in London, rather than New York – but also exposed them to the more political as well as more absurdist trend in British theatre, which can be clearly traced in their works. The search for socialist and politically outspoken theatre models is primarily what led young American playwrights to London – as it also led Arthur Miller there when his political criticism of America became more open. While the stage traffic is of course a two-way street, English exports to America are almost all plays by well-established authors, Broadway bound, while young British playwrights whose work is too politically edgy or stylistically daring get their work first performed, like Simon Stephens, in Germany. At the same time, Mamet and LaBute are both heavily influenced by Harold Pinter – who produced Mamet's *Oleanna* in London, while Mamet directed Pinter in Beckett's *Catastrophe*.

Another distinguishing feature of the younger contemporary playwrights, which is very different from the earlier generation, even those still writing such as Edward Albee or (up to his death in 2005) Arthur Miller, is their involvement in the whole range of theatrical activities. Where the earlier generation were primarily or solely writers, the younger generation tend to be performers and directors, both on film and stage, and to write both for theatre and the movies. In a sense Robert Wilson is the iconic example here: while generally considered a director (which is what he has come to focus on), most of his earlier stage work was also developed and scripted by him; and Wilson also acted in many of his shows. Parallel to this, Shepard began writing screenplays (including Antonioni's 1970 *Zabriskie Point*) almost as soon as his first stage works, and from the 1970s on, has directed many of his own plays, as well as acting on stage with Joseph Chaikin and having an extensive parallel career in film acting (winning several nominations and awards). He also both wrote and directed two films (*Far North* 1988, *Silent Tongue* 1994); and his multifaceted career is well illustrated by a snapshot of the year 1986, when *A Life of the Mind* was playing off-Broadway, *Fool for Love* was being filmed in Hollywood and he was acting in *Crimes of the Heart*. Similarly Letts began his career as an actor with Steppenwolf and founded his own acting company – Bang Bang Spontaneous Theatre (which included other playwrights like Greg Kotis or the screenwriter and director Reggie Hayes) – and has continued to act extensively, playing in David Mamet (*Glengarry Glen Ross* 2001; *American Buffalo* 2009), Albee (*Who's Afraid of Virginia Woolf?* 2006 and 2010) and Tony Kushner (*Homebody/Kabul* 2003) as well as British and Irish playwrights like Pinter or McDonagh, as well as appearing in films and TV serials. Marsha Norman too has turned to writing screen plays or librettos for musicals.

The dominance of Hollywood in American culture means that the interplay between stage and screen is far more significant than elsewhere. Miller or Albee might have treated overtures from Hollywood with suspicion. Certainly Miller wrote the script of *The Misfits* in 1961 for his then wife Marilyn Monroe, as well as the film adaptations of his own plays (*All My Sons* 1947, *Everybody Wins* 1984, *Death of a Salesman* 1985, *The Crucible* 1995). But these are not only few in relation to the large number of plays for the stage, but all versions of his own writing in other literary forms. By contrast, increasingly, their younger contemporaries not only regularly adapt their own plays for film, but – like Mamet – are far more likely to create work specifically for film and television. Film stars are frequently cast in their stage work – which brings a particular focus to characters – while the action of their plays tends implicitly towards cinematic structures. While Mamet and LaBute have not appeared as actors, they both have an extensive career in directing films, while Mamet has also published books of theoretical essays.

This points to another distinguishing feature of the new American dramatists: several of them teach drama, thus creating close connections with students and directly influencing the development of American drama. The clearest example is the relationship between Paula Vogel and Sarah Ruhl. But Shepard has also taught extensively, as have key American directors such as Peter Sellars. A sign of this close network is the number of plays dedicated to another contemporary playwright: thus LaBute has dedicated plays to both Shepard and Mamet.

* * *

A survey of the 25 chapters illustrates major thematic and aesthetic trends in contemporary American drama. A common denominator of all the plays at issue is their ambivalence towards the process of modernization. This attributes to the plays an unmistakable social background which, however, is always seen through a more psychological and individualistic lens than, for instance, contemporary British drama. The topics of contemporary American drama corroborate an often almost psychoanalytical interest in such issues as love and hate, sexuality and violence, human drives and desires as opposed to Puritan bigotry. Many plays revolve around the difficulties of human relationships, failed communication in the face of a perennial craving for love and understanding, the desire for but inability of forging meaningful relationships in a meaningless world characterized by important oppositions such as lies versus truth and illusion versus reality. Key to these oppositions is a specifically American illusion which goes far beyond personal ones: the myth of the American Dream, which constitutes a thread implicitly or explicitly running through many plays, albeit in often distorted form. Not only is the American Dream indicative of an often materialistically alienated, subjective perspective, it is also a leitmotif which comments on the social framework of modernization: the works of contemporary American drama seek to lay bare the individuals' entanglement in a collective dream which has turned out a nightmare for many of them. In plays such as *What of the Night?* María Irene Fornés, for instance, presents a pessimistic vision of American civilization in terms of moral, material as well as spiritual decline that brings humanity to the brink of extinction. Many other playwrights have highlighted an American society in transition, caught in vast sociopolitical upheavals, and permeated by greed and violence. Donald Margulies's plays have pointed to the corroding force of material greed on personal friendship; John Patrick Shanley's *Danny and the Deep Blue Sea* deals with the (self-)destructive forces of loneliness and social isolation; Arthur Miller's later drama centres on the split of personal selves and their concern for society. John Guare's *Six Degrees of Separation* investigates the correlation between the American Dream and the illusory world of celebrity; Sarah Ruhl's *Dead Man's Cell Phone* grapples with human disconnectedness in a digital age; Wallace Shawn's *The Designated Mourner* confronts audiences and readers with a nightmarish vision of a permissive society, market cannibalism and American 'dog-eat-dog'-capitalism; Shawn's *The Fever* and David Mamet's *Speed-the-Plough*, *American Buffalo* or, most ostensibly, *Glengarry Glen Ross* have cast icy looks at commodity fetishism and simulacra; the entire work of Neil LaBute has been questioning the way American society today substitutes surfaces for substance, personal appearance for principle, accentuating wrong values of American society for which there is no future but the plunge into animal brutality.

Thematically, there is an ongoing tradition among contemporary American playwrights on family, which has distinguished American drama throughout the twentieth century, and still continues with countless contemporary writers and their plays. While the functional breakdown of the family unit is almost synonymous with that of Western (post-)capitalist society, it is still worth mentioning that it is not only society to which individuals have lost their connection, but also the centre of the family-community does no longer hold. Clearly enough, the family frame is strongly connected to topical issues such as marriage, betrayal, sex, sexuality, gender, and – especially – the performativity of gender. Shanley's plays, for instance, examine the psychological depths of human relationships, and plays such as his *dreamer examines his pillow* or Shawn's *Grasses of a Thousand Colours* delve into the uncontrolled human unconscious. Sarah Ruhl's *In the Next Room* (*Or the Vibrator Play*) is concerned with sexual pleasure but also with characters' repression of or failure to understand potential (sexual) experience. Suzan-Lori Parks's *In the Blood* or *Fucking A* centres on the social over-determination of the black female subject, while Wendy Wasserstein's comedies depict women characters as trapped between conventions and modernity. Likewise, plays such as Naomi Wallace's *One Flea Spare* accentuate the performative act of identity exploration (Judith Butler) and show characters caught between social norms and a transgression of gender and class differences. Paula Vogel has also devoted much of her work to issues like class differences and female desire, when she, by way of example, radically rewrites Shakespeare's pre-text in *Desdemona: A Play About a Handkerchief* or connects female desire to economics in *The Oldest Profession*. A feminist interest in exposing the correlation between the confines of male-dominated hierarchies and hegemonies and women's fight for discovering their individual selves is also addressed in Marsha Norman's *Getting Out*. David Henry Hwang's *M. Butterfly* turns this problem ethnic and deconstructs stereotypes of Asian women (as delicate, passive and submissive). Hierarchies, gender-relations, gender construction (in and out of marriage) involve the topic of betrayal, which is omnipresent in plays such as Albee's *The Goat or, Who is Sylvia?* David Mamet's *Oleanna* also turns to the issue of betrayal in an even more destructive way as this involves sexual harassment. In both cases, though, the sense of betrayal is accompanied by the breakdown of communication. Neil LaBute's plays (i.e. *bash*; *In A Dark Dark*

House, The Distance From Here) lay open brutal and destructive sexual relationships where men prey on women, women use their sex(uality) for manipulative purposes and where characters do not even shrink from child abuse.

The questions of human relationships also concern the issues of homosexuality, gay life and ensuing topics such as homophobia and AIDS. Terrence McNally's *Corpus Christi* imagines Jesus's disciples as gay, and plays such as *Love! Valour! Compassion!* point to the way gay and straight people can live together. Christopher Shinn's *Four* relates the question of how African Americans have difficulties in getting integrated even into a predominantly white gay subculture. The play, thus, makes questions of sexuality coalesce with issues of race, pain and alienation. The entire work of Tony Kushner is an exploration of late-twentieth-century attitudes about gay life, American history, sexuality, race, religion and the conflicting poles of conservative and liberal politics.

Perhaps less widespread, but still a defining characteristic, is the religious element in plays by younger American writers. This may be an attack on witch-hunting orthodoxy, as in Miller's 1953 transposition of McCarthyism into Protestant fanaticism in *The Crucible*, or Kusher's satiric view of Christian fundamentalism in his depiction of Mormons – and indeed God and Heaven – in *Angels in America*. Most obviously there is LaBute, a one-time member of the Mormon Church of Jesus Christ of Latter Day Saints, whose strong religious background echoes directly in his work. This is very unlike English-language playwrights of other nationalities: Indeed, the only specifically religious modern playwright in England was T. S. Eliot; and he too was American by birth. Jewish culture, Jewish identity and a post-Holocaust world are addressed by Wendy Wasserstein's *The Sisters Rosensweig* and many of Donald Margulies's and Tony Kushner's plays, which psychologically depict Jewish roots and the inescapability of memories and their lasting impact on life.

America's multiethnic society is reflected in many plays and various issues: William Yellow Robe's plays offer a differentiated perspective on ethnicity and strive to liberate indigenous identity as they refuse to take sides with either the strategies of separatist essentialism or with the harmonizing lure of assimilationism. Suzan-Lori Parks's plays allegorically render African-American history and identity formation, but clearly deconstruct preconceived, projected and fixed images of black self-definition or a normative understanding of what 'black experience' is. August Wilson's cycle plays likewise counteract normative expectations of what black experience is as they make personal experience, African-American history, the fight for survival and cultural memory interact. Much in this vein, Adrienne Kennedy's *Funnyhouse*, for instance, represents intimately personal investigation next to a foregrounding of colonial history, independence, gender oppositions and contradictions between black and white races including crucial political issues such as sex, identity, history and their relationship to human creativity. Luis Valdez and his Teatro Campesino have been dedicated to the analysis of the sociopolitical problems that concern the Chicano and Mexican communities of the United States. Valdez's answer – just like Yellow Robe's, Wilson's, Parks's and Kennedy's – is an aesthetic one when he sets out to make hybrid structures of his plays – which include elements from realism, surrealism and expressionism – interrogate and, ultimately, transform the way in which Chicanos and Chicanas view themselves in the context of American society. From a Chinese-American perspective, David Henry Hwang's plays also challenge issues of racism, sexism and imperialism. David Mamet's *Race* makes the same diagnosis. All these examples constitute attempts at, in words of the Italian philosopher Giorgio Agamben, the 'coming community', in which – given a present alienation, lack of communication, manipulative use of language and obfuscated truth and a blurred sense of reality – individuals in a multiethnic and multicultural society need to embrace the other and accept difference.

American politics are seen through individual perspectives touching largely on issues such as liberalism or major ensuing topics like war. Tony Kushner's plays are characterized by their boldly political style; Wallace Shawn has addressed the often deluded stances of intellectual liberalism; Wendy Wasserstein (in *An American Daughter* and *Third*) challenged hardened feminist views by pointing to their eventual bigotry and laid bare a liberal self-righteousness and intellectual arrogance as a twenty-first-century American malaise. Terrence McNally has written about military service, authoritarianism and third world problems; Naomi Wallace's plays have explored various conflicts in the Middle East (such as the Israeli-Palestinian one). The plays are merciless responses to American politics in that they focus on the devastating psychological as well as physical effects of war and their traumatic effects on human life. Margulies's *Time Stands Still* is a war play that also explores how the trauma seeps through to the everyday life of a partnership. Likewise Sam Shepard's plays often connect their depiction of domestic strife to the experience of war trauma. Surprisingly few plays, however, tackle the trauma of 9/11. Notable exceptions are Shinn's *Where Do We Live*, Shanley's *Dirty Story*, LaBute's *The Mercy Seat*, and, rather implicitly, Greenberg's *The Violet Hour*. The wars in Iraq and Afghanistan have likewise been treated by a handful of plays only: Wasserstein's *Third*, Wallace's *Fever Chart* and *Not Such Cold Thing*, Shinn's *Where Do We Live*, Sam Shepard's *States of Shock* (which is a general castigation of a culture of war) and Kushner's *Homebody/Kabul*.

As regards the formal developments of contemporary American drama, the plays hover between a heightened realist mode and more experimental, open forms of drama even though the vast majority of plays are recognizably grounded in real life. Christopher Shinn's dramatic realism turns out as an episodic chronicling of small, yet significant details in the everyday events of a life; Shanley's realism in *Doubt* still involves philosophical and epistemological questions; Wendy Wasserstein's plays hover between realistic, mainstream well-made plays (*An American Daughter*) or a more open episodic structure (*The Heidi Chronicles*); Arthur Miller's (psychological) stage realism is interconnected with symbolic underpinnings and individual perspectives; David Mamet's *American Buffalo* is a characteristic hybrid that juxtaposes realist and anti-realist features; Neil LaBute is an interesting case in this respect as his drive for realistic credibility (i.e. in *The Shape of Things*) has led LaBute even to remove curtain calls. It is also interesting to notice that experimental playwrights like María Irene Fornés in their later works have taken their plays to more realist realms.

While most plays discussed here acknowledge the audience's right to be entertained, very few are outright comedies. David Henry Hwang and Wendy Wasserstein as well as the early Terrence McNally have used the genre repeatedly; the other playwrights mostly weave comic strands into otherwise bleak fabric. Situational comedy and farce, the staple of television, are rare – possibly exactly because of their ready availability on big and small screens. Comic relief tends to be produced by verbal means, witty one-liners and come-backs that themselves can shade into the confrontational and agonistic.

On the whole, it is fascinating to witness an abounding interest in experimental deviations from realist conventions such as linear plotlines, teleological action and character development, formal chronology or closure. An overwhelming number of plays are characterized by highly intertextual writing, juxtaposing past and present (texts), metadramatically and metatheatrically breaking up their historical and aesthetic unities (i.e. in works by Wallace, Vogel, Shawn, Shepard, LaBute, Kennedy, McNally, Parks, Ruhl, Fornés or Guare) and relating the present text to numerous influences (among them, most notably, to O'Neill, Wilder, Brecht, Beckett, Chekhov, Strindberg, Maeterlinck and Shakespeare). The juxtaposition of past and present is also visible in such bio-plays as McNally's *Master Class*. While some plays adhere to traditional plotlines, many others by Shawn, Fornés, Shepard and especially Mamet, however, are virtually plotless. Episodic and fractured collage structures in Wasserstein (*The Heidi Chronicles*) or Margulies's *Sight Unseen* reflect the psychological effects of displacement and dismemberment. The epic moment of audience address in Sarah Ruhl's (i.e. *Eurydice*) or even Wallace Shawn's plays function as theatrical alienation effects distorting realist illusions metadramatically. Self-reflexive, metadramatic elements further characterize the plays by Fornés, Naomi Wallace, Suzan-Lori Parks, John Guare, Wallace Shawn and Marsha Norman. For instance, Norman's predilection for *mise-en-abyme* structures, Guare's collage-technique (*Six Degrees of Separation*), the multi-layered, non-linear plot structure of Parks's *Imperceptible Mutabilities in the Third Kingdom*, the Brechtian elements in and the recursive structure of Paula Vogel's *How I Learned to Drive*, the polymorphism of language in Naomi Wallace or the surrealism of Adrienne Kennedy highlight the performative quality of language and, thus, the performative side of human identity formation and the double-sidedness of any conception of the self that is at the same time generated as well as split in often irreconcilable private and public/social parts. Wallace Shawn's complex interlacing of different layers of monologue and dialogue, his use of narrative and the dissolving of temporal unities have laid bare the illusion of a stable self in a changing and bewildering world in much the same way as Adrienne Kennedy or Sam Shepard have pointed to the fragility of human existence. William Yellow Robe has juxtaposed native storytelling, linear and cyclical plot developments and thereby destroyed the notion of naïve kitchen-sink naturalism. Most of the experimental writing in contemporary American drama is concerned with the close relationship between body language and dramatic form (i.e. in works by Vogel, Wallace and many more). All of these plays almost relish their structural as well as ethical inconclusiveness.

Though this might sound pessimistic, the playwrights considered in this volume suggest that there is genuine reason for hope. The source of optimism stems from the fact that there are a healthy number of excellent playwrights who, despite a culture that tends to distance itself from its own live theatre and dramatic literature, continues to enrich the American stage. From Edward Albee, Adrienne Kennedy and Sam Shepard to Marsha Norman, August Wilson and Paula Vogel, American drama continues to resonate, entertain, disturb and enlighten audiences both here and abroad. Indeed there is a common denominator of an appeal structure that the vast majority of the writers and their plays have – often openly – acknowledged and that bestows an, all in all, redeeming function to the theatre that follows a motto of 'healing through disturbing' realist aesthetic securities as well as readers and audiences alike. For Suzan-Lori Parks, the stage is an incubator of new personal experience and cultural as well as personal history; Wallace Shawn sees the shock potential of a play as a means to change the world through changes of perspectives; in a Shklovskyan fashion, Christopher Shinn adheres to a productive strategy of defamiliarizing the familiar as does Richard Greenberg; Edward Albee has always emphasized the dual obligation of a playwright to comment on the condition of man and to advance the nature of the art form 'drama'. None of the plays dealt with in this volume defends or even glorifies a status quo.

Bibliography

Adler, Thomas P., *Mirror on the Stage: The Pulitzer Plays as an Approach to American Drama* (West Lafayette, IN: Purdue UP, 1987).

—, *American Drama, 1940–1960: A Critical History* (New York: Twayne, 1994).

Bigsby, Christopher W. E. (ed.), *Modern American Drama: 1945-1990* (Cambridge: Cambridge UP, 1992).

—, *Modern American Drama: 1945–2000* (Cambridge: Cambridge UP, 2000).

—, *Viewing America: Twenty-First Century Television Drama* (Cambridge: Cambridge UP, 2013).

Brater, Enoch, *Feminine Focus: The New Women Playwrights* (New York: Oxford UP, 1989).

Brown-Guillory, Elizabeth, *Their Place on the Stage: Black Women Playwrights in America* (New York: Greenwood P, 1988). Contributions in Afro-American and African Studies 117.

Burke, Sally F., *American Feminist Playwrights: A Critical History* (New York: Twayne Publishers, 1996).

Case, Sue Ellen, *Performing Feminisms: Feminist Theory and Theatre* (Baltimore: Johns Hopkins UP, 1990).

Cohn, Ruby, *Anglo-American Interplay in Recent Drama* (Cambridge: Cambridge UP, 1995).

—, *Dialogue in American Drama* (Bloomington: Indiana UP, 1971).

Davis, Walter A., *Get the Guests: Psychoanalysis, Modern American Drama, and the Audience* (Madison, WI: U of Wisconsin P, 1994).

Demastes, William W., *Beyond Naturalism: A New Realism in American Theatre* (New York: Greenwood P, 1988). Contributions in Drama and Theatre Studies 27.

Dolan, Jill, *The Feminist Spectator as Critic* (Ann Arbor: U of Michigan P, 1988).

Freedman, Morris, *American Drama in Social Context* (Carbondale: Southern Illinois UP, 1971).

Harris Smith, Susan, *American Drama: The Bastard Art* (Cambridge: Cambridge UP, 1997). Cambridge Studies in American Theatre and Drama 5.

Hart, Lynda (ed.), *Making a Spectacle: Feminist Essays on Contemporary Women's Theatre* (Ann Arbor: U of Michigan P, 1989).

Hart, Lynda and Peggy Phelan (eds), *Acting Out: Feminist Performances* (Ann Arbor: U of Michigan P, 1993).

Hay, Samuel A., *African-American Theatre: An Historical and Critical Analysis* (Cambridge: Cambridge UP, 1994). Cambridge Studies in American Theatre and Drama 1.

Keyssar, Helen, *Feminist Theatre and Theory: Contemporary Critical Essays* (New York: St. Martin's Press, 1996).

King, Kimball (ed.), *Hollywood on Stage: Playwrights Evaluate the Culture Industry* (New York: Garland, 1997). Garland Reference Library of the Humanities 2057.

Kintz, Linda, *The Subject's Tragedy: Political Poetics, Feminist Theory, and Drama* (Ann Arbor: U of Michigan P, 1992).

Krasner, David, *American Drama: 1945–2000: An Introduction* (Malden, MA: Blackwell, 2006). Blackwell Introductions to Literature 14.

Lahr, John, *Up Against the Fourth Wall: Essays on Modern Theater* (New York: Grove P, 1968).

Lewis, Allan, *American Plays and Playwrights of the Contemporary Theatre* (New York: Crown, 1965).

Marranca, Bonnie (ed.), *American Dreams: The Imagination of Sam Shepard* (New York: Performing Arts Journal Publications, 1981).

McDonough, Carla J., *Staging Masculinity: Male Identity in Contemporary American Drama* (Jefferson, NC: McFarland, 1997).

Murphy, Brenda (ed.), *The Cambridge Companion to American Women Playwrights* (Cambridge: Cambridge UP, 1999).

Nadel, Alan, *May All Your Fences Have Gates: Essays on the Drama of August Wilson* (Iowa City: Iowa UP, 1994).

Porter, Thomas E., *Myth and Modern American Drama* (Detroit: Wayne State UP, 1969).

Robinson, Marc, *The Other American Drama* (Cambridge: Cambridge UP, 1994). Cambridge Studies in American Theatre and Drama 2.

Roudané, Matthew, *American Drama Since 1960: A Critical History* (New York: Twayne, 1996).

Saddik, Annette J., *Contemporary American Drama* (Edinburgh: Edinburgh UP, 2007). Edinburgh Critical Guides to Literature.

Schlueter, June (ed.), *Feminist Rereadings of Modern American Drama* (Rutherford: Farleigh Dickinson UP, 1989).

—, *Modern American Drama: The Female Canon* (Rutherford: Farleigh Dickinson UP, 1990).

Schroeder, Patricia R., *The Feminist Possibilities of Dramatic Realism* (Madison: Fairleigh Dickinson UP, 1996).

Vorlicky, Robert, *Act Like a Man: Challenging Masculinities in American Drama* (Ann Arbor: U of Michigan P, 1995).

Watson, Charles S., *The History of Southern Drama* (Lexington, KY: UP of Kentucky, 1997).

Weales, Gerald, *American Drama Since World War II* (New York: Harcourt, Brace & World, 1962).

Wilmeth, Don B. and Christopher Bigsby (eds), *The Cambridge History of American Theatre*. 3 vols. (Cambridge: Cambridge UP, 1998–2000).

1 EDWARD ALBEE

Thomas P. Adler

All Over; Seascape; Three Tall Women; The Play About the Baby; The Goat or, Who is Sylvia?

Introduction

A solid case can be made that Edward Albee is the only American playwright to emerge in the second half of the twentieth century who has any claim to be ranked alongside the triumvirate of Eugene O'Neill, Arthur Miller and Tennessee Williams. When *The Zoo Story* first appeared off-Broadway on a double bill with Beckett's *Krapp's Last Tape* at the Provincetown Playhouse early in 1960, it garnered him immediate acclaim and ushered in a career of sustained creativity – although not always of critical approbation or popular success – highlighted by such pivotal and enduring works as *Who's Afraid of Virginia Woolf?* (1962), still his most famous play, *A Delicate Balance* (1966) and *Three Tall Women* (1993), the last two of which, along with *Seascape* (1975), won him the Pulitzer Prize for Drama. Never knowing his biological parents, he was adopted two weeks after his birth on 12 March 1928 by the socially prominent New Yorkers Reed and Frances Albee – he owner of the Keith Albee vaudeville theatres, she a former high-fashion mannequin. This finds reflection in motifs of the child abandoned and rejected, often psychologically if not physically maimed, that recur almost obsessively in his original plays as well as the works of others he has chosen to adapt. After his primary education at the Rye Country Day School, he attended a succession of prep schools, before enrolling at Trinity College in Hartford, Connecticut, where he lasted just a year and a half. In 1953, Albee was living in New York's bohemian Greenwich Village and working at a variety of odd jobs when with the encouragement of Thornton Wilder, he committed himself to writing for the theatre, to which he would contribute over 30 plays of enormous variety, while also promoting the development of young dramatists as a university teacher and stage director.

Albee expresses his artistic credo in the introduction to two of his most experimental works, the one-acters published together as *Box and Quotations from Chairman Mao Tse-Tung* (1968), asserting the dramatist's dual obligation to comment on 'the condition of "man"' and to advance 'the nature of the art form with which he is working': 'In the first instance—since very few serious plays are written to glorify the status quo—the playwright must try to alter his society; in the second instance—since art must move, or wither—the playwright must try to alter the forms with which his precursors have had to work.'[1] Ever the innovator, refusing to repeat himself even when he seems to have hit upon the formula for immense critical and commercial success, Albee's oeuvre is marked by virtually every imaginable form and style: from the surrealism of *The Sandbox* (1960) to the allegory of the ritualistic *Tiny Alice* (1964) to the expressionism of *Tall Women*; from the Strindbergian battle-of-the-sexes in *Virginia Woolf* or *Marriage Play* (1987) to the black comedy of *The Play About the Baby* (1998); from the quasi-religious drawing room play (*Delicate Balance*) to the evolutionary fable (*Seascape*); from the picaresque journey in *Malcolm* (1966) to the Pirandelloesque deathwatch in *The Lady from Dubuque* (1980); from the vaudeville-like *Counting the Ways* (1977) to the metatheatrical *Lolita* (1981); from the cinematically structured *The Death of Bessie Smith* (1959) and *Finding the Sun* (1983) to the monodrama for a disembodied voice in *Box* or the dramatized lecture in *The Man Who Had Three Arms* (1983). Albee is not primarily a social playwright, although he has always been acutely disturbed by the seeming victory of crass materialism over more substantive values and the downward spiral and paralysis of will that have led to the spiritual aridity of contemporary civilization. As he wrote concerning another of his short works, *The American Dream* (1960), which he intended as a 'private howl' and 'picture of our time' meant to offend audiences: 'The play is an examination of the American Scene, an attack on the substitution of artificial for real values in our society, a condemnation of complacency, cruelty, emasculation and vacuity; it is a stand against the fiction that everything in this slipping land of ours is peachy-keen.'[2] In a 2005 article, Albee differentiates between the 'two ways plays get written': the 'didactic' intention of social problem dramatists like Ibsen and Miller who have an idea and then must 'find a situation that will encompass the idea,' as opposed to his own methodology that he likens to Chekhov and Williams, a 'process' of 'writ[ing] my plays to find out why I'm writing them'.[3] The company he chooses to keep with Chekhov and Williams is an apt one, for like them he is essentially a liberal humanist and compassionate moralist who registers modern man's anxieties without sacrificing astute, even at times acerbic, criticism of his failures.

The Plays

All Over (1971)

Originally conceived as a one-act play to be titled 'Death,' *All Over* had its Broadway premiere on 27 March 1971 and is one of several coming-of-death works in the Albee canon. An unnamed man attended by the Doctor and Nurse lies dying behind a screen upstage in an elegantly appointed masculine bed-sitting room, while others identified only by their relationship to him are gathered downstage: the Wife, the Mistress, the emotionally estranged Son and Daughter who have become so little living in the shadow of their famous father, and the Best Friend, a lawyer whose firm employs the Son and who had a brief affair with the Wife. Still others from the media are offstage outside – though they invade the room at one point – confirming the dying man's prominence. Albee's handling of stage space clearly separates foreground from background, rendering the man both present and absent, the latter helping to universalize the experience. The fact that the unseen man demanded to be brought back home rather than hooked up to a hospital machine indicates his control over the process of dying and his readiness for death, which he sees as a vast emptiness. The play begins, in fact, with a linguistic dispute over an ontological question of being and nothingness, since the man had always insisted that one cannot '*be* dead'. Despite what might be expected, those occupying this 'deathscape' spend little time talking about the life of the man, focusing rather upon themselves. To help establish the tone of a metaphysical drawing room play as might have been written by T. S. Eliot, Albee echoes a Prufrockian line, 'that is not what we meant at all'[4] in order to underscore the condition of these people, inhabiting what the Wife calls 'a sad and shabby time' (p. 328), made that way by their own behaviour. As C. W. E. Bigsby writes, 'the crucial deaths have happened before the play begins'.[5] Self-absorbed and careless of others, the Wife comes to realize they have undergone deaths of the heart: all they have ever *done* is think about themselves', worry over 'what will become of *me*', and love to *be* loved' (p. 366). And so, although they fail to realize it at first, the real lament must be for themselves.

With deceptively little happening, *All Over* is more a play of language than overt action, a composition of monologues (pointing to the characters' separateness and isolation) and duets, oftentimes cattily biting verbal skirmishes. What some commentators have criticized as the studied preciosity, even pretentiousness of, particularly, the Wife's language might more accurately be seen as a carefully controlled veneer to keep at bay what David Jones accurately diagnoses as her 'earlier unresolved trauma of loss to the Mistress'.[6] On the one hand, language can be deliberately formalized and ritualized, to cover over one's dis-ease or disguise one's vulnerability. On the other, as the Mistress cautions the Daughter, language deployed primarily to wound can become so debased that one might no longer be able to summon up the necessary vocabulary for expressing an emotion like love.

When the Doctor announces the man's death in the curtain line, 'All over', the finality does not apply to the survivors, since their pasts can never 'be dead' but remain alive in memory. The Wife's plaintive refrain, 'the little girl I was when he came to me' (p. 321), punctuates the play. And both she and the Mistress retreat into extended reveries of Edenic moments, the Mistress recalling an idyllic sexual awakening when she and a 'beautiful' adolescent boy were like 'an uncorrupted man and woman' (p. 352) in their summer love, and the Wife nostalgically remembering the garden of 'such profusion,' 'a world . . . of . . . floration' (pp. 358–9) at the Paris home she inhabited early in her marriage. Albee establishes a hierarchy among his women here: neither the Daughter, mired in an affair with a married man of disreputable character, nor the Mistress, twice divorced, can lay claim to being both wife *and* mother. And now to those two roles the Wife will add that of widow, reclaiming the husband, the only person whom she still professes to have always loved, and who in death will belong only to her. Yet she is 'UNHAPPY' in her sole possession of him now, for she cannot forget the moment when she was betrayed and happiness died. Memory, it turns out, is a double-edged sword.

Seascape (1975)

Originating in a one-act play called 'Life', Albee's *Seascape* in many ways forms a diptych with *All Over*. If the earlier play was set in an almost claustrophobic room, the latter occurs on an open and expansive stretch of sunlit beach, where the middle-aged and long-married Charlie and Nancy debate the virtues of settling in and doing 'nothing' for the rest of life (he), embracing the possibilities for an ever fuller existence (she). If he wants to make do with what they have, she insists that it is much too early to throw in the towel and welcome 'purgatory *before* purgatory'.[7] As if to challenge Charlie's willed inertia and give support to Nancy's belief that they have been 'married far too smoothly for far too long' (p. 420), from over the sand dunes suddenly appear a younger saurian couple, Leslie and Sarah, who will give a much-needed jolt to Charlie's oppositional relationship to Nancy while, in a pattern similar to what happens in *Who's Afraid of Virginia Woolf?*, they afford the older couple an opportunity to help them move onwards after having outgrown life in the sea. For, as Charlie recognizes, the younger couple – perhaps, as several commentators have suggested, projections of the unconscious – are now like what he and Nancy once were (since 'once upon a time [they] lived down there' [p. 438]), just as Leslie and Sarah might one day become what the older couple now are.

Significantly, Charlie was not always the complacent creature he now is. With some nostalgia for a lost innocence, he tells Nancy of wanting to 'live in the sea' (p. 377) when he was little, and he remembers a time as an adolescent when he would strip off his clothes and 'go down' under the water and let himself sink to the bottom, becoming 'part of the undulation and the silence. It was very good' (p. 379). In his present situation, however, he doubts he would find joy in doing that any longer. Archetypally the source of life, the sea is also a reminder of death, seen by Charlie as a kind of release back into a pre-conscious, pre-moral condition free from the imperative to make right choices. The jet plane that roars overhead periodically, a machine intruding upon pristine nature, might then symbolize the compromises that so-called civilizing forces demand. In a more nuanced reading of the symbol, Liam Purdon claims the 'jets are representatives, *par excellence*, of controlling rationality—for they are non-natural machines created through reason in order to satisfy and, hence, channel the primordial, imaginative urge to fly'.[8] So their sound particularly unsettles the not-yet-fully human Leslie and Sarah, who felt a discomfiting sense of no longer being fully at home or belonging in the sea and so came up to land, and yet will be constrained by the complexities of making the conscious choices that will now be required of them. For evolution in Albee is a willed process, one that is ongoing even for Charlie and Nancy: dissatisfied with stasis, it is never too late to reject passivity, to embrace change and make it happen; in fact, if the opportunity is not seized, the moment may be lost forever. As even Charlie comes to express it in counselling Leslie and Sarah to take the next step on the evolutionary ladder, either 'Mutate or perish' (p. 441).

Toby Zinman argues that 'Gender roles are crucial to this play',[9] and the female of each species does, indeed, seem to have evolved to a higher level than the male, with the former more gently prodding and intuitively compassionate than the latter. Nancy understands that using tools and making art and awareness of death are peculiar to human beings; as is the ability to express abstract feelings through language. But formulating concepts like 'love' must be based on experience, and so the only way that Charlie can further Leslie and Sarah's transformation from beast to man is to make them feel truly human emotions: playing upon Sarah's fear of Leslie's leaving her and never returning, he deliberately makes her cry which, in turn, so arouses Leslie's defensiveness and anger that he hits and chokes Charlie. But Charlie understands that one sometimes must break down in order to build up and hurt in order to heal. Having been forced to acknowledge such dark passions as sorrow and wrath, Leslie and Sarah want more than ever to return to their less dangerous if lesser life in the sea, and so the older couple must beg them to stay, extending a hand in mutual communion to encourage them. Their assent is signalled by Leslie's curtain line, 'Begin'. About that conclusion, Albee has stated in interview: 'It's a threat. . . . Leslie turns around and says, "OK, buddy, begin." Meaning, "and if you don't succeed, I'll rip you to pieces." That's the whole intention of that last line. If you misunderstand that, then it's a misunderstanding of the play as profound as many misunderstandings of *Our Time* [that read Wilder's play as simplistically optimistic]'.[10] The 'Begin' is cautionary, since Albee's characters are always balanced on the precipice of falling for the temptation of admitting 'All over.' So for him, in one of his most comedic plays, the light is dark enough.

Three Tall Women (1991)

A *coup de theatre* even more startling than the appearance of Leslie and Sarah in *Seascape* marks the opening of the second act of *Three Tall Women* – which premiered at the English Theatre in Vienna in 1991 and finally reached off-Broadway in 1994 – when the woman named A, whom the audience sees lying in a coma on an upstage bed after suffering a stroke, suddenly walks out onto the stage, marking a stylistic shift from a realistic to an expressionistic drama. The play begins as a potent look at aging and its indignities – the lack of mobility, the incontinence, the memory lapses, the isolation as friends die off – that enrage the 92-year-old A – and as an unsentimental consideration of the fact of death. Her somewhat brusque and yet finally solicitous and kindly caretaker, the 56-year-old B, in bluntly Beckettian terms tells C, the 28-year-old representative from the office of A's lawyer, 'you start . . . and then you stop,' shocking the younger woman even further by remarking that, by age six, everyone should be made conscious of 'what it means' to be 'dying'.[11] There is much about A that C finds hard to tolerate, particularly her verbally repellent prejudices against Jews and blacks that are so ingrained the old woman is hardly aware of them. Yet it is understandable why A has become hard and defiant for, like so many Albee women, she has had to be 'strong', forced to deal with a sister's alcoholism, a mother's dementia and a husband's long decline from cancer.

Albee's inspiration for the dramaturgical strategies of Act Two, where B and C become embodiments of A at earlier stages in her life, may be traced to his intense appreciation of visual arts other than the theatre; as John Lahr provocatively suggests in his review, 'What we get is a kind of Cubist stage picture, where the characters are fragments of a single self.'[12] By staging multiple identities, by splitting or tripling the single consciousness as the Cubist painters had done, Albee can show how C changed into B and B into A, how A is the sum of C and B and how she reintegrates those fragmentary selves – acknowledging their deficiencies in the things they either did or left undone – so that as indicated in the play's last word, uttered against the image of A clasping B and C by the hand, she can 'stop'. It is a metatheatrical moment, a close of play equated with the central character's death. And if the second half of *Three Tall Women*, postmodern in its consideration of perception and identity and subjectivity, is seen as occurring in the mind of A, then death means not only the loss of possibility for any further change but is equated as well with the stoppage of memory. In this regard, Albee's literary predecessor appears to have been the Beckett of *Krapp's Last Tape*, which not only features a man of 69 and, through taped voices, two younger selves at age 39 and his late twenties, but contains a line echoed verbally in *Women* about the 'Happiest moment' that A, B and C all muse over: whether it be to come sometime in the future (C), or is 'now' (B) or is 'coming to the end of it [death]' (pp. 108–9). A's equanimity, even longing, arises partly from her more distanced perspective that enables her to understand what Albee regards as a crucial distinction 'between knowing you're going to *die*, and *knowing* you're going to die' (p. 109).

The most fully elaborated memories of Albee's protagonist are linked to the decisive choices made in expressing physical sexuality or in responding to the sexuality of others – all relationships tinged (as are many actions in Albee), by betrayal, which David Mamet sees as the overriding subject of 'most great drama'.[13] Many of these relationships have been built upon a confusion of the material with the immaterial, as if some object could be the measure of love; as C comes to understand, what is desired is 'the big diamond' as 'tangible proof . . . that we 're valuable' (p. 379). A recounts an apparently decisive moment when she was sitting nude at her dressing table, and her husband entered naked except for a diamond bracelet on his erect penis, desiring that she fellate him. She, however, could never 'do that', so he loses his erection and the bracelet drops into her lap: 'Keep it, he said, and he turned and walked out'. After this recollection of this fracture in their marriage, A *'weeps slowly, conclusively'* (p. 347) and turns to B for comfort. If the episode was, in one sense, 'a crass exchange of sex for money' as Brenda Murphy terms it,[14] it was also something more: a failure in tolerance for a sexual proclivity different from her own, resulting in rejection – and not the only such rejection she has committed.

Just as striking as the surprising moment when the elegantly dressed A enters with the manikin of her dying body in bed upstage is another entrance late in the play. When A suddenly admits for the first time, 'I have a son' (p. 369), he materializes to sit wordlessly at her bedside, dressed in the same preppy clothes he was wearing at age 23 when B had demanded that he leave her sight when she discovered he was gay. Albee himself confesses to experiencing 'complete surprise' at the boy's sudden appearance: 'I remember stopping and saying, "Well, isn't that interesting? How did you ever figure *that out?*"'[15] So if, as Mel Gussow makes abundantly clear, *Three Tall Women* is an undeniably biographical portrait of the adoptive mother with whom Albee was never reconciled, it must be seen as well as an autobiographical refashioning of himself as a stage character. In a premonition of her death, A claims she saw the unnamed son kiss her forehead, but concludes that he did this devoid of any feeling and simply to comply with the expectations of those who would observe it. Yet immediately after she recounts that accusatory vision and demands that he feel the coldness of her hand, the son – who otherwise remains totally silent and without voice, just as he had been silenced and made absent through rejection – *'shudders, weeps'* in a genuine outpouring that recalls A's after she told of turning her husband away. The mother's death is an experience *before* the experience, as close as the son can come to understanding death before he faces his own. And so, while the act of writing *Three Tall Women* perhaps exorcises the mother, it materializes the dramatist as unequivocally present on the stage of his own play.

The Play About the Baby (1998)

The image of the baby – real or illusory, wanted or unwanted, that has been so potent in Albee's dramas from *The American Dream* and *Who's Afraid of Virginia Woolf?* onwards – reaches its culmination in *The Play About the Baby*, which premiered in London in 1998 and was performed in a playwright-directed production at Houston's Alley Theatre in 2000 before being seen by New York audiences in 2001. In it, Boy and Girl (actually young adults in their early twenties) have a baby, and then have it taken from them, by Man and Woman, whose relationships to one another and to Boy and Girl (perhaps embodiments of remembered younger selves) are left ambiguous. In a brightly lit nursery setting that seems a contemporary Eden, Boy and Girl frolic naked amidst a giant pacifier and oversized alphabet blocks, unashamed of their sexuality and its boisterous satisfaction, with Boy gorging himself on breast milk after the baby has been fed. Man and Woman, however, seem intent on putting a damper on the younger couple's antics and untested innocence. Like Albee's earlier *Counting the Ways* (1977), *Play About the Baby* might also have borne the subtitle 'A Vaudeville', for Man and Woman are performers; as Linda Ben-Zvi tellingly remarks, 'The entire play approximates a Marx Brothers' act',[16] replete with running jokes, linguistic misunderstandings, dance routines to the tune of 'Yessir, where's the baby?' and 'Roll me over in the clover' and even a baby-in-the-blanket trick performed by a carnival barker. The older pair address the audience directly, improvise dialogue when they are answered, and call for applause; they engage in metatheatrical games, welcoming the audience back from the intermission and announcing expository moments, a la Thornton Wilder, a favourite precursor of Albee. They greatly disturb the Boy by intimating earlier sexual encounters with him, though he adamantly denies even knowing them. Man also muses on philosophical questions: about the nature of reality and its relation to experience; about whether forgetting and not remembering are the same; about the escape into a fantasy realm to make life bearable. If they are like a playwright in their manipulation of onstage action, they also play at being God, expelling Boy and Girl from their idyllic existence. Professing to help or assist the younger couple, whom they address as 'Children', they seem determined to rile, even anger, them, finally announcing they 'have come to take the baby'.[17]

Revealingly, the Man has been plagued by feelings of regret and diminishment over how things fade and dissolve. He has a sense of human limitation, of 'what we cannot do, who we cannot be' (p. 521), including a personal awareness of what he 'can never . . . undo. That's the worst' (p. 523). To imbue Boy and Girl with this same reality-check, he and Woman set out with apparent cruelty to break them down until they have 'Nothing', for, in a quintessentially Albeesque formulation: 'If you have no wounds, how can you know you're alive? If you have no scar, how do you know who you are?' (p. 508). The Girl is prescient enough to guess at the older couple's motivation in taking the baby from them – 'To *hurt* us? To injure us beyond salvation?' – though the Boy objects, 'Aren't we too young?' (p. 487). For he resists growth from innocence to experience, insisting that they deserve to live in continued happiness for a while longer and so pleads for a delay: 'If there's anybody out there wants to do this to us—to hurt us so—ask *why*? Ask what we've *done*? I can take pain and loss and all the rest *later*—I *think* I can, when it comes as natural as . . . sleep? But . . . now? We're *happy*; we love each other; I'm hard all the time; we have a baby. We don't even under*stand* each other yet!' (p. 488). The Girl, however, is less recalcitrant and thus, in the Man's assessment, braver and wiser; her resistance, therefore, to accepting the outcome of the test ends somewhat more readily, if still painfully, with her resignation that 'Maybe later? When we're older . . . when we can take . . . terrible things happening? Not now' (p. 534), it will be time finally to have another child.

That the play ends with Boy and Girl both 'hear[ing] it [the baby] crying' (p. 534) undergirds Albee's insistence that the baby must be seen as real and not imaginary; and that, as he says somewhat cryptically in interview, 'The young couple realize that they *cannot have* the baby, and therefore it must disappear'.[18] What Albee appears to be suggesting here is that there must be not just a single but rather successive losses of Eden in an individual's life. These losses, however, or falls from grace if you will, are educative and indispensable to engaging in a fuller life. So here, unlike in *All Over* and more decisively than in *Seascape*, any nostalgic wish that lost Edens may be reclaimed is ripped asunder.

The Goat or, Who is Sylvia? (2002)

Albee won the Tony Award for Best Play of the year for *The Goat or, Who is Sylvia?*, which opened directly on Broadway – a rarity for his works after the mid-1970s – in 2002. The second part of the play's title, as well as its subtitle, 'Notes Toward a Definition of Tragedy', are rich in literary allusiveness. 'Who is Sylvia?' is a well-known song from Shakespeare's *The Two Gentlemen of Verona*, a romantic comedy ending, unlike *The Goat* will, in forgiveness and renewal after treachery and betrayal. Yet an unsettling note, appropriate to Albee's purpose, creeps subtly into two lines near the end of the song, 'She excels each mortal thing/ Upon the dull earth dwelling' (IV, ii, 51–2), hinting that traversing the distance between the this-worldly and an idealized image not be easily accomplished. The subtitle, too, might more accurately have pointed to an exercise in '*re*-definition of the tragic genre, since the tragedy in Albee's *Goat* resides not primarily in an individual's fall from a lofty position after violating a taboo, but rather in the narrow strictures of a society which will not accept following the vagaries of the human heart.

Goat begins with the casual sexual bantering of an astringent Noël Coward comedy as Martin, recently turned 50 and an architect at the pinnacle of his career , and his wife Stevie await the arrival of his long-time friend Ross and a team of cameramen to film an interview with him. The occasion is his winning of the Pritzker Prize and the award of a commission to design a 'dream city of the future'[19] for the grain fields of the Midwest. Martin, as Stevie attests, is virtually perfect in every way – 'decent, liberal, right-thinking, talented, famous, gentle' (p. 572) – and their marriage has been near idyllic: she cherishing the man she 'rose' into love with, and he, an oddity among his buddies for never wanting another woman. They are even planning to build a second home in the countryside, perhaps in part to recuperate a connection with nature that Martin's futuristic structures have risked violating. He was 'after Utopia. . . . Verdancy, flowers and green leaves against steel and stone' (p. 585). As Stevie remarks, however, everything going so right forebodes something going terribly wrong, as it does when Martin confides in Ross that he has fallen unaccountably yet desperately in love with Sylvia, a goat, and been having an affair with her; Ross, in turn, feels compelled to reveal this in a letter to Stevie, complete with a picture of the 'other woman'. During the no-holds-barred confrontation that ensues between husband and wife (akin to the lacerating 'total war' between George and Martha in *Who's Afraid of Virginia Woolf?*), Martin tries to explain, against the orchestrated sounds of Stevie symbolically smashing their treasured *objets d'art*, how he was smitten by Sylvia's gaze, signifying an absolute love unlike anything he ever experienced. He refuses to reduce what he and Sylvia have between them to solely the sexual level, claiming that Sylvia possesses a 'soul' with which he fell ecstatically in love. Albee's earlier characterization of Martin prevents this from being seen as empty rationalization; instead, it comes across as a re-connection with something primal in nature that has been lost in modern civilization's privileging of head over heart.

Despite Martin's protestations to the contrary, Stevie cannot credit his claim that he still loves her 'when he loves [something] so much less' (p. 575). Rather, she feels 'destroyed', diminished to 'nothing'. In a play even more rife with instances of betrayal than *Three Tall Women*, Martin's betrayal of Stevie is not, however, categorically as bad as Ross's betrayal of his friend. In failing Martin, who could never confess to Stevie but believed he could end the affair, given the support of his closest friend, Ross becomes the play's real villain. Although Martin refuses to believe his relationship with Sylvia is morally wrong, he does realize the damage his compulsive behaviour has done to Stevie and their son Billy and accepts his culpability for it. Billy, openly gay though still experimenting with his sexuality, has always been accepted despite his difference and been blessed beyond measure to have parents who loved one another; now, however, that stability seems shattered. Billy's closeness to Martin adds another level to the play's endorsement of the unpredictability of human emotional response when the son's kissing of his father becomes – to Ross's horror and disgust – momentarily passionate. In the same way, Martin suggests that other actions, like a father's having an erection as he bounces his infant on his lap, or martyrdom for religious belief or even crucifixion, might 'click over' to involve an undeniably erotic element and yet must still be regarded non-judgmentally, because they are complex *human* responses less open to rational control than society would like to think.

If audiences at *Seascape* and *Three Tall Women* were pleasantly startled by Albee's *coups de theatres*, spectators at *The Goat* are likely to be shocked and unsettled (as they perhaps have not been since *Zoo Story's* violent climax) when a bloodied Stevie enters dragging the goat Sylvia whom she has killed out of revenge. The innocent goat has been sacrificed as if doing so could purge what society deems abnormal. Audience members attuned, nevertheless, to the allusiveness of the work's subtitle might feel that in the killing of the goat, something sacred has been destroyed. For the word 'tragedy', designating plays performed at the festival of the god Dionysus (whose attendants wore goats' ears) originates in the word 'goat song', and the satyr plays performed along with the tragedies in parody of them, are named after gods half-human and half-goat. Furthermore, the prize awarded to the winning tragedian at the annual festival was a goat that was then sacrificed; Albee intends to make his audiences uncomfortable, for what he demands of them here is nothing less than absolute tolerance for sexual otherness, questioning whether there can be any limitation on what we will tolerate from those we claim to love. As Ellen Gainor writes, 'Martin's transcendence of that repression [the taboo of bestiality], his acting on that desire, reflects the agony of [a] cultural division of man and nature, the ecstasy of the reunion, and yet also its impossibility for those who would simultaneously reside in the society that has fostered their separation.'[20] So Albee's subversive challenge here is nothing less than to recognize that in matters of the heart, the Other may turn out to be the Self. His viewers, therefore, are called upon to 'imagine themselves in the predicament the play examines', since it 'is about . . . who, indeed, we really are'.[21]

Summary

By the 1970s, the fickleness of critics who wanted nothing more from Albee than that he write *Who's Afraid of Virginia Woolf?* over and over again meant he had long since lost his position as the fair-haired boy of the American theatre – his second Pulitzer-winning play, *Seascape*, ran for only 63 performances, not to be given a major New York revival until 2008. Although his critical reputation may eventually have bottomed out, with reviewers treating him as if his work as a serious dramatist were all in the past, his dramatic output never faltered. It took, nevertheless, almost a quarter century before he experienced a critical renascence with the masterstroke of *Three Tall Women*. And yet, during all that time, his central thematic concerns, while deepening, remained essentially of a piece. He continues to write about alienation and lack of communication, about how the imposition of stereotypical gender roles demeans and dehumanizes, and about the way that language can be used to obfuscate truth and distort reality. Increasingly, however, in his later plays from *Three Tall Women* and *Play About the Baby* to *Occupant* (2002) – a biographical work about his sculptor-friend Louise Nevelson – and *Me, Myself & I* (2008), Albee turns to more metaphysical and epistemological issues: the inability of memory to accurately retrieve the past; the modernist concern with the nature of artifice and the making of fictions; and such postmodern notions as the fragmentation of personality and the attempt to fashion an identity, polyvocality and indeterminacy, the multiplicity of perception, the disruption of linear time and the resistance of closure.

From his earliest plays, a major recurrent pattern finds Albee's characters facing a test to become more fully human, from Jerry's arrival in Central Park in *Zoo Story*, determined to jar Peter out of his passivity and complacency, to Harry and Edna's arrival at the home of their dearest friends in *Delicate Balance* to test the limits of friendship and question the quality of Agnes and Tobias's life. The pattern continues, as has been seen, from Leslie and Sarah's coming up out of the sea to prod Charlie to renewed activity – just as the lizards are challenged to continue their evolutionary progress – through Man and Woman's test of the naiveté of Boy and Girl in *Play About the Baby*, forcing them to see that a life without suffering is no life at all. What is implied in the latter is something that Albee's Jerry, and others like George and Martha, Charlie, and Man and Woman, had known all along: to reach the other may require hurt, that if 'kindness' does not work, then 'cruelty', as paradoxical as it might seem, may be the necessary antidote. What stands in the way of taking

15

the step beyond one's present condition, no matter how life-denying that existence might be, is fear of change – the *sine qua non* for growth – and of facing the unknown (something that Albee has never let stop him from risking failure to develop as an artist). That unknown may be a universalized meaninglessness or void at the very core of existence, or it may be an individualized fear of the loss of physical control and erosion of mental capacity that come with time, or of the inevitability of death.

In assessing when character growth can occur, Albee subscribes to what seems a peculiarly American conception of the intersection of fate and free will. Acceptance of change means a concomitant awareness that with every choice one makes, however apparently trivial, all future possibilities are halved, since the road not taken can never be traversed, meaning that the character one creates gradually becomes one's fate and opportunities for fruitful change diminish over time. Increasingly, Albee focuses on the idea that innocence must be lost, or at least risked, before there exists any hope of a paradise regained, moving from the nostalgia for lost Edens of the past in *All Over* and *Seascape*, to the denial in *Play About the Baby* that a continuing state of innocence should be sought, since it stands in the way of human growth and moral maturity, to the undercutting of the possibility for any idyllic condition in the present in *The Goat* – be it Martin's love for Sylvia or a more mundane recovery of nature from the clutches of unbridled environmental damage. Finally, Albee's handling of the need to embrace the Other and accept difference, particularly sexual difference – and the way that this pushes people's tolerance to its very limits – becomes much more explicit in the works from the latter half of his career, beginning with his first openly gay character in *Finding the Sun*, through the silent son in *Three Tall Women*, culminating with Billy and Martin in *The Goat*.

Because of the multiple betrayals of human love that distinguish them, Albee's works since 1970 – with the exception of *Seascape* and *Finding the Sun*, and despite the luminosity that characterizes the oftentimes lyrical writing of *Three Tall Women* – may seem more dark than light. And, indeed, his plays tonally have often had an autumnal, if not wintry, chill about them, not pessimistic in their outlook but certainly unsentimental as they prod audiences into questioning whether the answers that characters put forward in the face of the human dilemma may be (as in later O'Neill) simply illusions to squelch their fears. Not that salvific acts do not occur, but they are often, from the knife thrust in *Zoo Story* to Man and Woman's 'destruction' of the baby for the 'good' of Boy and Girl, desperate, hurtful (if redemptive), and hard to compass. But then, as Albee believes, 'a good play' is full of unpleasant truths, 'an act of aggression against the *status quo*—the psychological, philosophical, moral, or political status quo. A play is there to shake us up a little bit, to make us consider the possibility of thinking differently about things'.[22]

Primary Sources

Works by Edward Albee

The Collected Plays: 1966–1977 (Woodstock, NY: Overlook Duckworth, 2008).
The Collected Plays: 1978–2003 (Woodstock, NY: Overlook Duckworth, 2008).

Secondary Sources

Albee, Edward, 'Aggressing Against the Status Quo', Interview by Lester Strong in *The Harvard Gay and Lesbian Review* 4, 1 (Winter 1997), 7–9.
—, 'Introduction'. In *Box and Quotations from Chairman Mao Tse Tung* (New York: Pocket Books, 1970).
—, 'Introduction'. In *The Plays: Volume One* (New York: Coward, McCann & Geoghegan, 1981).
—, 'Borrowed Time: An Interview with Edward Albee'. In *The Cambridge Companion to Edward Albee* (Cambridge: Cambridge UP, 2001).
—, *Stretching My Mind* (New York: Caroll and Graf, 2005).
Ben-Zvi, Linda, '"Playing the cloud circuit": Albee's vaudeville show'. In *The Cambridge Companion to Edward Albee* (Cambridge: Cambridge UP, 2005).
Bigsby, C. W. E. (ed.), *Edward Albee A Collection of Critical Essays* (Englewood Cliffs, NJ: Prentice-Hall, 1975).
Bloom, Harold (ed.), *Edward Albee* (New York: Chelsea House, 1987).
Bottoms, Stephen (ed.), *The Cambridge Companion to Edward Albee* (Cambridge: Cambridge UP, 2005).
De la Fuente, Patricia (ed.), *Edward Albee: Planned Wilderness* (Edinburg, TX: Pan American University, 1980).

Gainor, J. Ellen, 'Albee's *The Goat*: Rethinking tragedy for the 21st century'. In *The Cambridge Companion to Edward Albee* (Cambridge: Cambridge UP, 2005).

Gussow, Mel, *Edward Albee: A Singular Journey, a Biography* (New York: Simon & Schuster, 1999).

Lahr, John, 'Sons and Mothers', *The New Yorker*, 16 May 1994, pp. 102–5.

MacFarquhar, Larissa, 'Passion Plays: The Making of Edward Albee', *The New Yorker*, 4 April 2005, pp. 68–77.

Mamet, David, *Three Uses of the Knife: On the Nature and Purpose of Drama* (New York: Columbia UP, 1998).

Murphy, Brenda, 'Albee's Threnodies: *Box-Mao-Box, All Over, The Lady from Dubuque* and *Three Tall Women*'. In Stephen Bottoms (ed.), *The Cambridge Companion to Edward Albee* (Cambridge: Cambridge UP, 2005).

Purdon, Liam O., 'The Limits of Reason: *Seascape* as Psychic Metaphor'. In *Edward Albee* (New York: Chelsea House, 1987).

Schvey, Henry I., 'At the Deathbed: Albee's *All Over*', *Modern Drama* 30, 3 (September 1987), 352–63.

Staub, August W., 'Public and Private Thought: The Enthymeme of Death in Edward Albee's *Three Tall Women*', *Journal of Dramatic Theory and Criticism* 12, 1 (Fall 1997), 49–57.

Wasserman, Julian (ed.), *Edward Albee: Interview and Essays* (Houston, TX: University of St. Thomas Press, 1983).

Zinman, Toby, *Edward Albee* (Ann Arbor: University of Michigan Press, 2008).

Notes

1. Edward Albee, 'Introduction' to *Box and Quotations from Chairman Mao Tse-Tung*, p. 9.
2. Albee, 'Introduction' to *The Plays: Volume One*, p. 9.
3. Albee, quoted in: Larissa MacFarquhar, 'Passion Plays: The Making of Edward Albee', p. 76.
4. Albee, *All Over* in *Collected Plays: 1966–1977*, p. 312. Further references appear within parentheses in the text.
5. C. W. E. Bigsby, 'To the Brink of the Grave: Edward Albee's *All Over*', p. 170.
6. David Richard Jones, 'Albee's *All Over*', p. 95.
7. Albee, *Seascape* in *Collected Plays: 1966-1977*, p. 375. Further references appear in parentheses in the text.
8. Liam O. Purdon, 'The Limits of Reason: *Seascape* as Psychic Metaphor', p. 124.
9. Toby Zinman, *Edward Albee*, p. 82.
10. Albee, 'Borrowed Time: An Interview with Edward Albee', p. 245.
11. Albee, *Three Tall Women* in *Collected Plays: 1978–2003*, p. 316. Further references appear within parentheses in the text.
12. John Lahr, 'Sons and Mothers', p. 104.

13. David Mamet, *Three Uses of the Knife: On the Nature and Purpose of Drama*, p. 161.
14. Brenda Murphy, 'Albee's Threnodies: *Box-Mao-Box, All Over, The Lady from Dubuque* and *Three Tall Women*', p. 103.
15. Albee, 'Aggressing Against the Status Quo', p. 9.
16. Linda Ben-Zvi, 'Playing the cloud circuit': Albee's vaudeville show', p. 184.
17. Albee, *The Play About the Baby* in *Collected Plays: 1978–2003*, p. 495.
18. Albee, 'Borrowed Time', p. 246.
19. Albee, *The Goat or, Who is Sylvia?* in *Collected Plays: 1978–2003*, p. 553. Further references appear in parentheses in the text.
20. J. Ellen Gainor, 'Albee's *The Goat*: Rethinking tragedy for the 21st century', p. 210.
21. Albee, 'About This Goat,' in *Stretching My Mind*, pp. 262–3.
22. Albee, 'Aggressing Against the Status Quo', p. 9.

2 MARÍA IRENE FORNÉS

Scott T. Cummings

Tango Palace; Promenade; Fefu and Her Friends; Mud; The Conduct of Life; Abingdon Square; What of the Night?

Introduction

In the last four decades of the twentieth century, María Irene Fornés pioneered an innovation in playwriting that had great influence on two generations of American playwrights. Her plays present a series of brief, enigmatic and sometimes wordless scenes that constitute isolated moments of being for her central characters. In performance, these fragments add up to a portrait of desire and disappointment, a composite marked by emotional honesty, austere lyricism and vivid imagery. The plays often focus on naive, unschooled characters caught up in a movement from ignorance to knowledge and innocence to experience. While they vary in tone from outright whimsy to grinning irony to romantic tragedy, they are always characterized by a tremendous depth of feeling that pushes up from beneath the surface of events to produce dynamism within stillness. In her characters' effort to learn how to be and how to survive in a harsh, inhospitable world, they encounter forces of resistance or oppression that draw attention to how race, class and gender mark the formation of identity.

María Irene Fornés was born on 15 May 1930 in Havana, Cuba, the youngest of six children raised by loving, eccentric parents of limited means. With only a few years of formal education, she nevertheless developed an intellectual curiosity and love of learning that lasted a lifetime. In 1945, months after her father died of a heart attack, she emigrated to New York City with her mother and two sisters. As a young woman, she gravitated to the bohemian counter-culture of Greenwich

Village in the 1950s and 1960s. For most of her adult life, she lived in an apartment on Sheridan Square in the West Village. Early on, her artistic temperament led her to study painting with abstract expressionist Hans Hoffman, and in 1954, she travelled to Europe to pursue the life of an artist, settling in Paris for three years. While there, she happened to attend Roger Blin's world-premiere production of Samuel Beckett's *Waiting for Godot*, which left a lasting impression on her even though she understood little French. Back in New York, she held a series of odd jobs and continued to paint, but a lack of enthusiasm led her to give it up before 1960.

Eventually, she turned to writing, on a lark initially, and soon with an urgency and passion that her painting never had. As a playwright and occasional costume designer, she became a key figure in the off-off-Broadway theatre movement centred in Greenwich Village in the 1960s. She was affiliated with the Judson Poets Theater and the Open Theatre, but she also had work produced at La MaMa ETC and other experimental venues downtown. The 1965 Judson production of her musical *Promenade*, directed by Lawrence Kornfeld and with an extensive score by Al Carmines, set the tone for the counter-cultural off-off-Broadway musical, paving the way for *Hair*, *Godspell*, and other similarly earnest-yet-irreverent shows. When *Promenade* was expanded and re-mounted in a 1969 off-Broadway production uptown, it ran for almost a year, providing Fornés with the one and only commercial hit of her career. A few years earlier, in 1966, her quirky comedy *The Office* was about to open on Broadway, directed by Jerome Robbins and staring Elaine May and Jack Weston, when the producers closed it in previews, anticipating negative reviews.

Fornés' early frustration with watching others direct her plays led her to take full artistic control of her work around 1970 and proceed to direct the first (and often the second) productions of each new play from then onwards. Playwriting and directing became such radically integrated processes for her that she often began rehearsals without a complete script in hand, relying on the rehearsal process and the pressure of opening night to bring a new play to fruition. Her directing was heralded in its own right for its compositional rigour, painterly precision and evocative imagery, and over the years, in addition to her own plays, she directed classics by Garcia Lorca, Calderon, Ibsen and Chekhov, as well as several new works by Latina playwrights who were her students.

In 1973, Fornés banded together with other off-off-Broadway playwrights to form New York Theatre Strategy, a production company dedicated to staging new plays. Fornés took on much of the administrative work for the group, and her playwriting took a backseat until she wrote and directed the premiere of *Fefu and Her Friends* in 1977. A breakthrough for Fornés into a more personal form of writing, it became a landmark of feminist theatre and her most celebrated work. For the next two decades, she maintained a prodigious pace of writing and directing at least one new work per year, a project that benefitted from her association with the Padua Hills Playwrights Festival in southern California and with Theater for the New City, INTAR and Women's Project and Productions in New York City.

At Padua Hills and at INTAR, Fornés also flourished as a popular teacher of playwriting. Starting in 1978, she taught for many summers at the Padua Hills Playwrights Workshop, and from 1978 to 1991, she led INTAR's Hispanic Playwrights-in-Residence Laboratory, where she guided and inspired a generation of Latino/a playwrights, including Eduardo Machado, Migdalia Cruz, Caridad Svich, Cherríe Moraga and Nilo Cruz. Fornés' pedagogy was based on an ever-evolving series of playwriting exercises that used guided visualization, chance operations and free association to help a writer gain access to her creative unconscious.[1]

Fornés herself followed the prompts she gave her students, and on numerous occasions the raw material generated in class became the seed of a new play. Thus did the collateral practices of teaching playwriting and directing her own work enable Fornés to create her own idiosyncratic system for taking a new play from initial impulse all the way to opening night and beyond. The body of work that resulted is notable for its protean variety, its deceptively simple, often telegraphic dialogue and its abiding interest in probing the psyche of ordinary characters caught up in the effort of bringing themselves into being.[2]

The Plays

Tango Palace (1963)

Fornés' first play, an hour-long one-act, received its world premiere on 29 November 1963 at the San Francisco Actors Workshop, where it was directed by Herbert Blau. The play presents a head-to-head battle between two eccentric antagonists: Leopold, 'an earnest youth' in a business suit born into the play out of a canvas sack, and Isidore, 'an androgynous clown' who would be his absolute master and teacher. The play takes place in Isidore's elaborately furnished, hermetic lair, which includes an ornate recessed shrine filled with an exotic miscellany of masks, costume pieces and weapons. In a series of playful yet violent confrontations over three scenes, Isidore subjects Leopold to painful object lessons that prompt him to fight back and try to escape. But the action reveals there is no easy way out of either the cell or their symbiotic relationship. They are locked in a cycle of trust and betrayal, of vicious hurt and tender reconciliation, that goes beyond their tutorial bond as student and teacher to suggest the passion of intimate, possessive lovers.

Fornés gives the play a strong metatheatrical twist by stipulating that each time Isidore says something that he considers profound he flips an index card into the air. Leopold learns that these cards, intended for him, contain the actual lines of dialogue in the play. 'Study hard, learn your cards and one day, you too will be able to talk like a parrot', instructs Isidore (p. 135), but Leopold resists the authoritarian pedagogy of rote learning in favour of listening to the voices in his head. This makes him the first in a series of Fornés characters – mainly female over time – who have intimations of knowledge and ways of knowing that they struggle to realize.[3] *Tango Palace*'s self-conscious theatricality is further revealed in what Isidore calls his 'unconventional pageantry', manifest in his flamboyant, drag-queen persona, a ritualistic dance featuring beetle masks and various role-playing games, most importantly, one in which he plays the 'fearless, confident and dominant' matador to Leopold's charging bull.

While no other Fornés play depicts such a direct head-to-head conflict between two warring opposites, *Tango Palace*'s emphasis on the hierarchy of power in social relationships remains constant, if not always as explicit, in Fornés' subsequent work. While it is easy to see echoes of Beckett's Pozzo and Lucky or Hamm and Clov or Ionesco's *The Lesson* in Isidore and Leopold, they are not mere, absurdist clones. However antic the action, the passion in their give-and-take demonstrates a consuming temperament that is as fierce as in Racine or Strindberg and that surfaces again in such Fornés characters of the 1980s as the title character *Sarita*, Orlando in *The Conduct of Life* and Marion in *Abingdon Square*.

Promenade (1965, 1969)

Promenade became Fornés' signature piece of the 1960s. It premiered in 1965 at the Judson Poets' Theatre as a one-act musical directed by Lawrence Kornfeld and featuring a nimble, energetic score by Reverend Al Carmines. A full-length off-Broadway version was produced in 1969 at the new, eponymous Promenade Theatre at 76th and Broadway, where it drew high praise from critics and ran for 259 performances. 'More a choreographed oratorio than a conventional musical', the show's success was due in large part to the 'perfect mating of two voices that speak the same boldly simplistic language: Mr. Carmines' protomelodies, which borrow their inflections from Gilbert and Sullivan, Kurt Weill, George M. Cohan and a dozen other sources . . . and Miss Fornés' lyrics [which] eschew polished verses for direct, blunt statements about the human condition'.[4]

Promenade presents the comic adventures of two prison inmates, known only as 105 and 106, who dig their way out of prison and hit the streets in search of evil. In scene after scene – at a banquet, in the park, on a battlefield, at city hall – they cross paths with a half dozen high-society types (Misses I, O, U and Misters R, S, T) who are so preoccupied with their hedonistic pursuits that they don't notice their pockets getting picked and their jewellery being stolen. Along the way, these two innocents abroad team up with a female sidekick (Servant) and later re-unite with their long-lost mother before returning of their own volition to the shelter of their prison cell, where Mother tucks them in and sings a mordant lullaby that includes the lyric:

> There are many poor people in the world,
> Whether you like it or not.
> There are many poor people in the world.
> But I'm not one of them.
> I'm not one of them.
> Someone's been stealing my apples
> But I'm not one of them,
> I'm not one of them. (p. 265 in Winter House anthology)

With urban poverty, racial unrest and anti-Vietnam War sentiment on the rise in the United States, *Promenade* captured something of the zeitgeist of the late-1960s without resorting to overt satire or bitter recrimination. In a rave review in the *New York Times*, Clive Barnes wrote, 'There is a Dada zaniness here that creeps up on you where you least expect it, and a topsy-turvy Brechtian morality that is most attractive. . . . The style is the perfect reflection of the show, wickedly amusing, joyously blithe, and yet with a serious if lightly touched layer of protest and social comment beneath'.[5] The play's achievement, as Stephen Bottoms argues, is to balance disapproval and delight so that 'apparent contradictions are held in tension, without allowing the one perspective to cancel out the other, or permitting the spectator to take refuge in the reassuring simplicity of an unambiguous statement'.[6] This delicate, paradoxical blend of tones and attitudes – winsome irreverence mixed with cocky exuberance, moral outrage leavened by carefree insouciance – is summed up in a lyric often cited as quintessentially Fornesian:

> To walk down the street
> With a mean look in my face,
> A cigarette in my right hand
> A toothpick in the left.
> To alternate between the cigarette
> And the toothpick

Ah! That's life.
Yes, I've learned from life.
Every day I've learned some more.
Every blow has been of use.
Every joy has been a lesson.
What surprises me
Is that life
Has not learned from me. (p. 226)

Fornés' other plays of the 1960s, notably the picaresque one-act *The Successful Life of 3* and the mock-lecture *Dr. Kheal*, are governed by the same ludic spirit as *Promenade*. They are filled with comic non sequiturs, slapstick violence, antic wordplay and theatrical routines that have led some to perceive them as mere silliness. But the seeming nonchalance is the mask of a genuine concern with the inequality of rich and poor, the tyranny of the powerful and a decay of moral principles, themes which surface again and again in Fornés' body of work.

Fefu and Her Friends (1977)

Fornés' 1960s' characters are two-dimensional types known only by a generic pronoun, letter of the alphabet, number or job title, but *Fefu and Her Friends* marked a shift in her approach. Characters became more realistic without being defined by an individual personal psychology rooted in a complicated family history. And more and more the central characters were female, a shift signalled by *Molly's Dream*, first produced in 1968. The consciousness of women is the explicit focus of *Fefu and Her Friends*, a radical choice of subject when the play premiered in 1977 and one that put Fornés at the centre of the women's theatre movement at that time. Its unorthodox, provocative and joyous celebration of women being together as women made it a landmark of feminist drama and one of the most important American plays of the twentieth century.

Written in three acts, *Fefu and Her Friends* takes place in the New England country home of Stephany Beckman, known to her friends as Fefu, who is hosting a luncheon meeting for eight middle-class women to plan a fundraising event for an educational cause. In the first act, the women arrive in Fefu's living room one or two at a time and make small talk before heading in to socialize over lunch. The second act presents four intimate two-person scenes that take place in different locations around the house – the kitchen, a bedroom, the study and on the lawn – and then the whole group reconvenes for the third act back in the living room. The gathering is coloured by the mystery surrounding one of them, Julia, who is wheelchair-bound and still recovering from a bizarre accident in the woods in which she was struck and paralyzed by a hunter's stray bullet. She is subject to seizures and bouts of delirium in which she is persecuted by 'the Judges', unidentified figures who seem somehow to be after Fefu as well. The action ends on a profoundly unresolved note when Fefu takes a shotgun, steps outside, fires a shot into the yard and then returns with a dead cat in hand as Julia collapses onstage bleeding from the head. The others look on aghast.

While these events can bewilder an audience in the onward rush of performance, a close look at the text makes clear that Julia's medical condition – paralysis, hallucinations of torture, loss of will and spirit – is a complex metaphor for the ways in which women have internalized the forces of patriarchy and oppression over the centuries, robbing them of their humanity and their power to shape the world. In her fever dream, Julia thrashes in bed and wards off the blows of the Judges by reciting their prayer:

> The human being is of the masculine gender. The human being is a boy as a child and grown up he is a man. Everything on earth is for the human being, which is man. . . . Woman is not a human being. She is: 1—A mystery. 2—Another species. 3—As yet undefined. 4—Unpredictable; therefore wicked and gentle and evil and good which is evil. (p. 35)

Without resorting to simplistic rhetoric, the play is a call to the collective unconscious of women to recognize the tremendous potential of being and acting together as women. The action of the play's third act offers a suggestive case in point. The women gather in the living room to finalize plans for their big meeting. Christina expresses 'the concern of the educator—to teach how to be sensitive to the differences in ourselves as well as outside ourselves, not to supervise the memorization of facts' (p. 44). Emma performs an interpretative dance and recites the allegorical prologue from a book on *Educational Dramatics*. They outline their remarks, rehearse their appeal for pledges and play around with the order of events until it feels right, and then the meeting gives way to doing the lunch dishes, serving coffee and reminiscing about college days. Some of them sing the chorus of a popular tune. A water fight breaks out, dies down and then resumes with increased fervour. An irrepressibly playful community spirit prevails until it is overshadowed by the final confrontation between Fefu and Julia.

The potent collectivity of this experience is reinforced by a staging convention inspired by the play's first production. The script was incomplete when Fornés visited a makeshift performance space in lower Manhattan as a possible venue for the premiere. A small auditorium with a stage suitable for Fefu's living room was surrounded by other rooms in the building – a kitchen, a dressing room, a lounge – which struck Fornés' imagination as other rooms in Fefu's house. She finished the play with this in mind and then staged it so that in performance each short scene of the second act takes place in a separate location away from the main playing area. The audience is divided into groups and led in turn to each site until all four sub-groups have seen all four scenes, albeit in a different sequence. For the individual spectator, this kinesthetic reconfiguration of the audience-to-actor and audience-to-audience relationship invites a recognition of being part of a collective that parallels the recognition of women being together as women that the play pursues. In 1977, *Fefu and Her Friends* marked an early experiment in the evolution of site-specific performance in the United States, one that helped to make the feminism of the play profound and enduring.

Mud (1983)

If *Fefu and Her Friends* focuses on women collectively – on women as 'another species' – then *Mud* is a prime example of Fornés plays from the 1980s centred on a single female protagonist caught up in an effort to bring herself into being. These pieces include *Evelyn Brown*

(A Diary) (1980), Fornés' ruminative staging of the 1909 diary of a New Hampshire housekeeper; *A Visit* (1981), a ribald coming-of-age story inspired by Victorian pornographic novels; *Sarita* (1984), a romantic tragedy about a Cuban-American girl's uncontrollable passion for her abusive lover; and *The Trial of Joan of Arc in a Matter of Faith* (1986), a theatrical rendering of the French national heroine's interrogation by the Bishop of Beauvais on charges of heresy.

In *Mud* (1983), the heroine is Mae, an illiterate rural woman in her twenties who lives with an oaf named Lloyd, an orphan her father took in as a boy. They are, as Mae says, 'like animals who grow up together and mate', living in utter poverty in a plain wooden shack atop a promontory of red earth. She takes in ironing, he tends to the pigs. But Mae dreams of a better life, and towards that end she is going to school to learn how to read. When Mae brings home an older man named Henry to help her read a medical pamphlet, she falls in love with him and invites him to move in with them because 'sometime I feel hollow and base. And I feel I don't have a mind. But when I talk to you I do. I feel I have a mind' (p. 24). Lloyd is forced to sleep on the floor, Henry soon has some kind of stroke and the unending squabbles between the two needy men eventually prompt Mae to abandon them and 'look for a better place to be . . . a place where the two of you are not sucking my blood' (p. 39). This prospect is unimaginable for Lloyd, and as soon as Mae leaves, he chases after her with a rifle, shoots her and brings her back home to die in his arms as he and Henry look on helplessly.

As Bonnie Marranca pointed out, *Mud* is the most austere instance of Fornés' move into a spare, unadorned realism that lifts 'the burden of psychology, declamation, morality, and sentimentality from the concept of character. She has freed characters from explaining themselves in a way that attempts to suggest interpretations of their actions, and put them in scenes that create a single emotive moment, as precise in what it does not articulate as in what does get said'.[7] More and more, she constructed her plays out of a series of short, simple, fragmentary scenes, some of them like a tableau only seconds long, which she then juxtaposed one after the other to create a complex portrait of yearning or despair. Susan Sontag called it 'a theater of heartbreak'.[8]

Fornés followed *Mud* with two plays – *Sarita* and *The Conduct of Life* – that offer a metaphysics of sexual desire. Sarita is a typical Fornés Innocent, young, naive, desperate to become the person she senses she should be, but her undeniable attraction to Julio thwarts her best intentions and leads her to betray her husband Mark. She ends up in a mental hospital, a martyr to her desire. Orlando in *The Conduct of Life* is just the opposite. In the play's first scene, he recognizes that 'I must no longer be overwhelmed by sexual passion or I will be degraded beyond hope of recovery', but his inability to control his demonic lust makes him an absolute villain, perhaps the only Fornés character unworthy of compassion.

Abingdon Square (1987)

Abingdon Square represents Fornés at her zenith. It was workshopped at the Seattle Repertory Theatre in 1985, premiered in New York in 1987 by Women's Project and Productions and directed by Fornés again a year later at Studio Arena Theatre in Buffalo. A 1989 production directed by Nancy Meckler for Shared Experience and the Soho Poly Theatre was remounted in 1990 at the National Theatre in London, giving Fornés her highest profile production outside of the United States. Fornés staged a bilingual production of the play at the San Diego Repertory Theatre in 1992. An exquisite two-act drama of 33 scenes, *Abingdon Square* is one of Fornés' longer plays and well-suited for the repertoire of the resident regional theatre.

Abingdon Square tells the coming-of-age story of a girl named Marion, a child bride who matures into a woman torn between her older, caring husband and a lover who she creates out of her own imagination. The action spans the years 1908–17, and most of it takes place in the living room of an elegant townhouse on 10th Street near Abingdon Square in New York's West Village. For Marion, orphaned at 15, this house represents a form of salvation, and she looks forward to wedding its owner, a widower businessman of 50 named Juster. 'In this house', she says, 'light comes through the windows as if it delights in entering. I feel the same. I delight in entering here' (p. 11). She yearns to achieve the nobility of spirit she associates with her new family and household and 'to conquer this vagueness I have inside of me. This lack of character. This numbness' (p. 20). Towards this end, as a sort of catechism, she sneaks up to the attic, stands on her toes and recites passages from Dante until she collapses in exhaustion. But this effort at self-discipline is countermanded by a sexual awakening that starts off as a schoolgirl fantasy of romance that she scribbles in her diary. To her surprise, she spots her imaginary lover in a bookstore one day, and he turns out to be 'as real as someone exists'. A love affair ensues – with the usual melodramatic complications. The play ends tragically with Marion cradling Juster in her arms as he succumbs to the effects of a stroke while Michael, Juster's son and Marion's devoted friend, looks on.

Like many other Fornés play, *Abingdon Square* grew out of images, characters and fragmentary dialogue that surfaced in writing that she did in her own playwriting classes. Once again, they coalesced into a portrait of an unschooled, naive woman who aspires to a dignity and a knowledge that she can only vaguely conceive and who experiences erotic desires that are threatening to her ideals. The early twentieth-century setting of *Abingdon Square* has led some to see the play as a simplistically feminist critique of oppressive gender roles, but the setting actually serves to abstract the dramatic situation from contemporary social discourse around sexual politics in order to focus on a tormented soul torn between two absolutes. Here again, Fornés uses visual, linguistic and directorial controls to present a heroic suffering of feeling – that is, a passion, both sexual and spiritual – which does not become sentimental or maudlin.

What of the Night? (1989)

Fornés' plays of the 1990s shifted away from a central female figure caught in a crucible of emotion to focus on communities of characters looking for ways to survive in the face of disease, widespread poverty and a world that seems to be coming to an end. *Enter the Night* (1993) is a melancholy portrait of three friends who are defined by illness: one is a hospice nurse, another has a life-threatening heart condition, and the third is convinced he has AIDS. *Manual for a Desperate Crossing* (1997) is Fornés' libretto for an opera composed by Robert Ashley and re-titled

Balseros/Rafters for its depiction of economic refugees from Cuba making the dangerous 90-mile journey by sea to a new life in the United States. *Terra Incognita* (1997) generates a complex metaphor of disorientation by using the occasion of three young Americans travelling in Spain to harken back to Columbus and the bloody European encounter with the native peoples of the Caribbean. Not all of Fornés' later plays strike such an ominous chord – *The Summer in Gossensass* (1998) is about the joy of discovering *Hedda Gabler*! – but there is a current of concern about the desperate state of the world that is as sharp as ever. In 1969, when Fornés expanded *Promenade* for its off-Broadway incarnation, she added a song with this tell-tale refrain:

> I know what madness is.
> It's not knowing how another man feels.
> A madman has never been
> In another man's shoes.
> Madness is lack of compassion,
> And there's little compassion
> In the world. (p. 254)

At the end of her career, Fornés continued to identify lack of compassion as a human failing that leads to injustice and catastrophe.

What of the Night? is Fornés' most ambitious work. Written in the late 1980s, it is comprised of four separate, short plays which were first performed together as a suite under Fornés' direction at the Milwaukee Repertory Theatre in 1989 and then again at Trinity Repertory Company in Providence in 1990. The action spans more than half a century, and most of the characters are drawn from one extended family. Many appear in more than one of the four plays, but there is no grand, overarching narrative tying them together. They fall out in different directions; several have been performed or published independent of the others. The first play, *Nadine*, depicts a mother's struggle to provide for a family so poor that they live outdoors in an empty lot with furniture picked up off the street. Twenty years later, *Springtime* chronicles the tender and sad romance between Nadine's daughter Rainbow and her lover Greta, bedridden with tuberculosis and needing medicine. *Lust* is a portrait of runaway greed that focuses on Nadine's son Ray, abandoned at birth and now a fast-rising corporate executive married to the boss's daughter. The final play, *Hunger*, takes place in the not-too-distant future after an economic apocalypse has left most of the population, including several of Nadine's older adult children, living in bureaucratically managed shelters for the homeless.

The four plays of *What of the Night?* presents Fornés' 'vision of a difficult but relatively compassionate past, a rapacious present, and an apocalyptic future'.[9] Taken as a whole, the tetralogy depicts a process of moral, material and spiritual entropy that ends with civilization on the brink of extinction. In this regard, the play recalls *The Danube*, just as the concern with the widening gap between rich and poor harkens all the way back to *The Successful Life of 3* and *Promenade*. But the sanguine whimsy and cheerful ironies of the 1960s have given way to a darker mood:

> What inspired me to write this play is the overwhelming number of homeless, destitute, and ill who inhabit the streets and undergrounds of our cities and my state of confusion as to why this is happening. I fear for our future. I feel that we are becoming greedy and heartless. I don't understand what is leading us to these feelings and I can't imagine anything but disaster being the outcome of our mindlessness and heartlessness.[10]

What of the Night is Fornés' attempt to capture that fear and confusion.

Summary

In 1999, Fornés became the ninth contemporary American playwright to be celebrated by New York's Signature Theatre with a full season devoted solely to her work. Previous Signature honorees included Edward Albee, Horton Foote, Adrienne Kennedy, Sam Shepard and Arthur Miller. The Fornés season included a revival of *Mud* paired with the short play *Drowning*, the New York premiere of *Enter the Night*, and a world-premiere commission titled *Letters from Cuba*, which turned out to be the last play Fornés ever wrote or directed. Over the next several years, cognitive issues worsened into dementia and she became unable to work. Not at all by design, her Signature season turned out to be the capstone on a brilliant playwriting career that spanned four decades.

After her momentary flirtation with Broadway in 1966 and the commercial success off-Broadway of *Promenade* in 1969, that career took place outside of the American theatrical mainstream, a situation that Bonnie Marranca, Fornés' publisher and critical champion, found outrageous:

> It is one of the scandals of the American theatre, obsessed as it is with "development," whether of the playwright or funding sources or subscribers . . . that at the age of sixty-two, after three decades of a richly committed life in the theatre, Fornés is still working on the margins. . . . At her age, and with such a long record of distinguished achievement entirely within the medium of theatre, a fully elaborated directorial style, and a grand reputation as a teacher, Fornés should be given all that the American theatre has to offer in terms of resources—choice of actors, technicians, designers, access to larger audiences, longer runs. Imagine what other artists might learn from Fornés. Imagine how her own work might grow under new artistic conditions.[11]

As it was, over four decades, Fornés 'created more than fifty works for the stage, including comic sketches, one-act plays, full-length dramas, musical plays, site-specific pieces, devised works, libretti for opera, and adaptations of modernist classics'.[12] She was awarded a total of nine Obies, more than any other downtown theatre artist except for Sam Shepard, as well as numerous career achievement awards and two honorary doctorates. The variety of her work stems in part from her experimental approach to playwriting. She never set out to repeat herself or to satisfy an audience's expectations or to make a particular statement. 'It's not that she's just a ruthless experimenter', observed Steven Drukman. 'It's more that she reinvents the Fornés play each time she writes one. No major playwright who has lasted so long can make the same claim'.[13] Her work was always driven by images and not ideas, and her creative process depended on making contact with the reservoir of the unconscious and bringing forth what she discovered there without questioning its meaning or logic. In that, she was a model and inspiration to hundreds of aspiring and emerging playwrights, particularly women, Latino/as and others just finding their voice in the American theatre. She embodied the off-off-Broadway aesthetic long after its heyday in the 1960s, always determined to create as full a production as possible with whatever resources were at hand, always committed to a process of perpetual discovery and to the autonomy of her vision as an artist.

Primary Sources

Works by María Irene Fornés

Promenade and Other Plays [*Promenade, The Successful Life of 3, Dr. Kheal, A Vietnamese Wedding, Tango Palace, The Red Burning Light, Molly's Dream*] (New York: Winter House, 1971).

Plays [*Mud, The Danube, The Conduct of Life, Sarita*] (New York: PAJ Publications, 1986).

Fefu and Her Friends (New York: PAJ Publications, 1992).

Letters from Cuba and Other Plays [*Letters from Cuba, Terra Incognita, Manual for a Desperate Crossing*] (New York: PAJ Publications, 2007).

What of the Night?: Selected Plays [*Abingdon Square, The Summer in Gossensass, What of the Night?, Enter the Night*] (New York: PAJ Publications, 2008).

Secondary Sources

Alker, Gwendolyn, 'Teaching Fornés: Preserving Fornesian Techniques in Critical Context', *Theatre Topics* 19, 2 (2009), 207–21.

Barnes, Clive, 'Theater: 'Promenade,' Wickedly Amusing Musical', *New York Times*, 5 June 1969, p. 56.

Bottoms, Stephen J., '"Language Is the Motor": María Irene Fornés' *Promenade* as Text and Performance', *New England Theatre Journal* 8 (1997), 45–71.

—, *Playing Underground: A Critical History of the 1960s off-off-Broadway Movement* (Ann Arbor: The University of Michigan Press, 2004a).

—, 'Sympathy for the Devil?: María Irene Fornés and the Conduct of Life,' *The Journal of American Drama and Theatre* 16, 3 (2004b), 19–34.

Cole, Susan Letzler, *Directors in Rehearsal: A Hidden World* (New York: Routledge, 1992).

—, *Playwrights in Rehearsal: The Seduction of Company* (New York: Routledge, 2001).

Crespy, David A., *off-off-Broadway Explosion: How Provocative Playwrights of the 1960s Ignited a New American Theater* (New York: Backstage Books, 2003).

Cummings, Scott T., 'Seeing With Clarity: The Visions of María Irene Fornés,' *Theater* 17, 1 (Winter 1985), 51–6.

—, 'Notes on Fefu, Fornés, and the Play of Thought,' *Ideas and Production* 8 (1988), 91–103.

—, *María Irene Fornés* (Abingdon: Routledge, 2013).

Delgado, María M. and Caridad Svich (eds), *Conducting a Life: Reflections on the Theatre of María Irene Fornés* (Lyme: Smith and Kraus, 1999).

Drukman, Steven, 'Notes on Fornés (With Apologies to Susan Sontag)', *American Theatre* 17, 7 (1988), 36–9, 85.

Fornés, María Irene, '"I Write These Messages That Come"', *The Drama Review* 21 (December 1977), 25–40.

Geis, Deborah R., 'Wordscapes of the Body: Performative Language as Gestus in María Irene Fornés' Plays', *Theatre Journal* 42, 3 (1990), 291–307.

Holden, Stephen, 'Stage: Promenade, Carmines-Fornés Work', *New York Times,* 25 October 1983, p. C8.

Kent, Assunta, '*And What of the Night?*: María Irene Fornés' Apocalyptic Vision of America at the Millennium', *Journal of Dramatic Theory and Criticism* 7, 2 (Spring 1993), 132–47.

—, *María Irene Fornés and Her Critics* (Westport CT: Greenwood Press, 1996).

Koppen, Randi, 'Formalism and the Return to the Body: Stein's and Fornés' Aesthetic of Significant Form', *New Literary History* 28, 4 (1997), 791–809.

Marranca, Bonnie, 'Interview: María Irene Fornés', *Performing Arts Journal* 2, 3 (1978a), 106–11.

—, 'The Real Life of María Irene Fornés', *Performing Arts Journal* 8, 1 (1978b), 29–34.

—, 'The Aging Playwright and the American Theater', *Village Voice,* 16 June 1992a, 94.

—, 'The State of Grace: María Irene Fornés at Sixty-Two', *Performing Arts Journal* 14, 2 (1992b), 24–31.

Moroff, Diane Lynn, *Fornés: Theater in the Present Tense* (Ann Arbor: University of Michigan Press, 1996).

O'Malley, Lurana Donnels, 'Pressing Clothes/Snapping Beans/Reading Books: María Irene Fornés' Women's Work', *Studies in American Drama, 1945-Present* 4 (1989), 103–17.

Robinson, Marc, *The Other American Drama* (Baltimore: The Johns Hopkins University Press, 1996).

—, (ed.), *The Theater of María Irene Fornés* (Baltimore: The Johns Hopkins University Press, 1999).

Ruhl, Sarah, 'Six Small Thoughts on Fornés, the Problem of Intention, and Willfulness', *Theatre Topics* 11, 2 (September 2001), 187–204.

Schuler, Catherine A., 'Gender Perspective and Violence in the Plays of María Irene Fornés and Sam Shepard'. In June Schlueter (ed.), *Modern American Drama: The Female Canon* (Rutherford: Fairleigh Dickinson University Press, 1990).

Sofer, Andrew, 'María Irene Fornés: Acts of Translation'. In David Krasner (ed.), *A Companion to Twentieth-Century American Drama* (Malden: Blackwell, 2006).

Sontag, Susan, 'Preface'. In María Irene Fornés (ed.), *María Irene Fornés: Plays* (New York: PAJ Publications, 1986).

Svich, Caridad, 'The Legacy of María Irene Fornés: A Collection of Impressions and Exercises', *PAJ* 93 (2009), 1–32.

Wetzsteon, Ross, 'Irene Fornés: The Elements of Style', *Village Voice* 29 April 1986, 42–5.

Wolf, Stacy, 'Re/Presenting Gender, Re/Presenting Violence: Feminism, Form and the Plays of María Irene Fornés', *Theatre Studies* 37 (1992), 17–31.

Worthen, W. B., 'Still Playing Games: Ideology and Performance in the Theater of María Irene Fornés'. In Enoch Brater (ed.), *Feminine Focus: The New Women Playwrights* (Oxford: Oxford University Press, 1989).

Notes

1. For more on Fornés' exercises, see Caridad Svich, 'The Legacy of María Irene Fornés: A Collection of Impressions and Exercises' and María M. Delgado and Caridad Svich, *Conducting a Life: Reflections on the Theatre of María Irene Fornés*.
2. This essay draws from my recent book-length study of Fornés for Routledge's Modern and Contemporary Dramatists series. Efforts have been made to avoid verbatim repetitions.
3. My Routledge study traces the development of this figure, who I call the Fornés Innocent, in detail.
4. Stephen Holden, 'Stage: Promenade, Carmines-Fornés Work', p. C8.
5. Clive Barnes, '"Promenade", Wickedly Amusing Musical', p. 56.
6. Stephen Bottoms, '"Language is the Motor"', p. 58.
7. Bonnie Marranca, 'The Real Life of María Irene Fornés', p. 30. For more on these dramatic units, which are so distinct to Fornés' work that I have labelled them 'emotigraphs', see Scott T. Cummings, *María Irene Fornés*.
8. Susan Sontag, 'Preface', p. 9.
9. Assunta Kent, '*And What of the Night?*: María Irene Fornés' Apocalyptic Vision of America at the Millennium', p. 134.

10. Excerpted from Fornés' programme note for the 1990 production of *What of the Night?* at Trinity Repertory Company.
11. Bonnie Marranca, 'The State of Grace', p. 27. For further consideration of the Fornés legacy, see Alker, Drukman, and Ruhl.
12. Scott T. Cummings, *María Irene Fornés*, p. xviii.
13. Steven Drukman, 'Notes on Fornés', p. 37.

3 RICHARD GREENBERG

Jochen Achilles, Ina Bergmann

The Author's Voice; Three Days of Rain; The Dazzle; Take Me Out; The Violet Hour

Introduction

Richard Greenberg was born in East Meadow, Long Island, New York, in 1958. He graduated magna cum laude from Princeton, did graduate work in English and American literature at Harvard for a while, and was finally accepted in the Yale playwriting programme,[1] starting his career as a dramatist with *The Bloodletters* (1984).[2] Greenberg received a number of prestigious awards for his dramatic work: the New York Drama Critics, Drama Desk, Outer Critics Circle, Lucille Lortel and Drama League Awards, and the Tony Award for *Take Me Out* (2002). He was a finalist for the Pulitzer Prize in Drama twice, for *Three Days of Rain* in 1998 and for *Take Me Out* in 2003.[3]

The Plays

The Author's Voice (1987)

The Author's Voice (World Premiere: 13 May 1987, Ensemble Studio Theater, Los Angeles) is a one-act play, consisting of nine scenes. It is a dramatic reflection on authorship and its discontents. First, it unfolds the relationship between Todd, a young and extremely handsome author, and his admiring and equally attractive editor Portia, who strives to unravel the secret of Todd's creativity. She is disappointed by the gloominess of Todd's 'House of Usher' (p. 174) and by the blandness of Todd, who has nothing to say when he is not quoting from his own, quite melodramatic, text. Portia is nevertheless enthusiastic about Todd's talent and the promise of his writing. In rapture, she even offers a close and erotic relationship. But hardly has she left, her playful guess that behind a door in the back wall of Todd's apartment 'there's some horribly twisted gnome who does all your writing for you—' (p. 176), comes true. The psychology of authorship – the dual task of writing a book in solitary confinement and selling it to publisher and public in communicative and attractive ways – is exteriorized in *The Author's Voice* in the split between Todd, who looks 'more like a model for cologne than like Herman Melville' (p. 201), and the third character of the play, Gene, the dwarfish, horribly disfigured actual author. The relationship of the two men evokes not only Victor Hugo's novel *The Hunchback of Notre Dame* (1831) but also a whole tradition of doubles and revenants from the beauty and her princely beast in *La Belle et la Bête*, Roderick and Madeline Usher in Edgar Allan Poe's 'The Fall of the House of Usher' (1839), Jekyll and Hyde in Robert Louis Stevenson's *The Strange Case of Dr. Jekyll and Mr. Hyde* (1886) to beautiful Dorian and Basil Hallward's increasingly less handsome portrait of him in Oscar Wilde's *The Picture of Dorian Gray* (1890). The contrast between Todd's manicured appearance and the deformity of his poet-in-residence also suggests the discrepancy between the public personae of flamboyant Yuppie authors of the 1980s' Brat Pack such as Jay McInerney and Bret Easton Ellis and the sinister dissipation and despair depicted in their novels. Like Patrick Bateman of Ellis's *American Psycho* (1991), Greenberg's Todd may have to grapple with demons of writer's block as well as feelings of emptiness and aggression, which manifest themselves in the distorted shape and superior mental capacity of Gene, his alter ego. The relationship between Todd and Gene can thus be understood as illustrating and acting out performatively problems of authorship. By being based on a whole tradition of doubles, this relationship is as much a product of literature as it is a comment on it.

Beyond its initial surprise effect, this constellation yields less insight into the creation of art than might be wished for. Gene and Todd act out in miniature the dialectics of the experience of the world and its artistic reconstruction. Gene complains of the isolation Todd forces on him, the forlorn Bartleby existence in his 'cupboard' from which he stares 'out at an airshaft' (p. 181). Against Todd's wish and in Todd's clothes, he ventures out in the streets for a brief moment to experience life and to buy some books to have his 'vocabulary replenished' (p. 182). Conversely, Todd is unconfined in his movements but also unable to assess his own experiences himself. Empty shell that he is, he cannot make sense of them and needs Gene in his confinement to explain them for him. The symbiosis of the beautiful author and the demon living with him seems to work. Todd's book written by Gene appears to rave reviews and huge sales. On publication day, Gene has a present for Todd, an out-of-print novel by an obscure Canadian. When Todd begins to read, he learns that his own just successfully published work is a plagiarized version of this Canadian novel. Once it is republished, allegedly as the work of an extremely handsome young writer, the overwhelming success of a forgotten novel by an unknown author with '(u)nfortunate looks' (p. 203) confirms Gene's disillusionment and justifies his vindictiveness.

The Author's Voice is a successful satire on the simulacral aspects and vanities of contemporary literary publishing. Although saturated with allusions to the literary tradition of doubles, it is not quite as successful as a dramatization of the inner divisiveness of authorship. The distinction between Todd and Gene as separate characters in a realistic play is never challenged and too one-dimensional for a truly dialectic treatment of the return of the repressed. The play's conventional structure restricts the convincing unleashing of psychological forces. This would have required more phantasmagoric scenic experimentation as can be found in the drama of Adrienne Kennedy or Suzan-Lori Parks, for example.

Three Days of Rain (1997)

Three Days of Rain (World Premiere: South Coast Repertory, Costa Mesa, CA, 1997) is Richard Greenberg's best known and most noteworthy play. It was a finalist for the Pulitzer Prize in 1998. Since its premiere, the play enjoyed quite a number of subsequent productions in the United States and abroad. The most outstanding of these are its British premiere at the Donmar Warehouse in London in 1999, starring Colin Firth, Elizabeth McGovern and David Morrissey, and its Broadway

41

revival at Bernard B. Jacobs Theatre, starring Paul Rudd, Julia Roberts and Bradley Cooper in 2006.

Three Days of Rain consists of two acts, which are not subdivided by scenes. It is set entirely in a 'loft space in downtown Manhattan' (p. 3). While the first act is set in 1995, when the loft is untenanted, the second act is set in 1960, when the loft is occupied, and therefore a 'happier' (p. 3) place. Because it evolves around two generations of the members of the same two families and their secrets, the play has been labelled a 'generational drama'[4] or a 'generational mystery'.[5] The adult children, a brother and sister and their childhood friend, explore the secrets of their parents' lives in the first act, while the second act, set 35 years earlier and presenting the older generation in their youth, unravels those secrets in unexpected ways.

The first act revolves around Nan and Walker, siblings and the children of a prominent architect, as well as Pip, their childhood friend and son of their father's business partner. Nan meets with her brother and Pip in the unoccupied flat that belonged to their late father. The reason why the three come together is to attend a reading of his will. While Nan has found peace in marriage and motherhood and Pip has become a successful soap opera actor, Walker, still haunted by the memories of his tormented childhood with a distracted father and a mentally unbalanced, meanwhile institutionalized mother, has become a 'hopelessly neurotic ne'er-do-well',[6] an 'unstable drifter',[7] a 'self-styled flâneur'.[8] Walker's is essentially a telling name. Greenberg is drawing on the literary figure of the flâneur, well-known from Poe's 'The Man of the Crowd' (1840) to Walter Benjamin's *Das Passagen-Werk* (1927–40). Pip's name, on the other hand, which, of course, points to Charles Dickens's *Great Expectations* (1861) and seems particularly laden with symbolism regarding the topic of inheritance, is, according to the playwright himself, really a 'blind alley'.[9]

Eventually it becomes clear that the threesome also form a love triangle. Nan and Pip had an affair years ago as young adults, which they kept secret from Walker ever since, because he was in love with Pip, too. Nan, who is surprised that her brother had no idea of her past relationship with Pip, asks: 'do things really stay secret that long?' (p. 37) This question can be seen as programmatic of the play. Walker is very interested in his father's journal, which he has found in the loft. While it mainly confirms Walker's impression of his father as a detached and non-compassionate character, the very first entry, '1960, April 3rd to April 5th—Three days of rain' (p. 20), puzzles him. He cannot make sense of what he takes to be '[a] weather report. *A fucking weather report!*' (p. 20) When the will has been opened, it is revealed that Pip will inherit the 1960s 'Janeway House' (p. 16). It is the building that has made Nan's and Walker's father's fame and can be seen as his legacy. Walker is outraged, but ultimately he believes to have found evidence for his father's surprising last will in his journal. He takes the entry 'Theo dead. Everything I've taken from him . . .' (p. 43) as evidence that his father's architectural merits ultimately belonged to Theo, Pip's father, who died young. Nan remains doubtful about Walker's assumption that he now knows the truth about the past and so does the audience.[10]

The second act goes back to the 1960s and proves Nan right. Theo Wexler, a handsome womanizer, and Ned Janeway, a lonely stutterer, are young architects who share a loft. They have just been commissioned by Ned's parents to build what will become known as the Janeway House. Theo, supposedly the artistic and creative head of the team, fails to come up with original ideas for the house. After a fight with Ned, who has discovered that Theo's initial plans plagiarize existing structures, Theo leaves the house to return only three days later. When the overstrung Southern belle Lina, Theo's girlfriend, turns up at the flat during a rainstorm, she and Ned, who is 'struggling for his professional and personal identity',[11] realize their attraction to and affection for each other, or rather, find each other in their frustration over the unfulfilled and/or unsatisfying love for Theo. When Theo returns, it becomes clear that now Ned and Lina have become an item over the last 'three days of rain'. When Theo leaves again, Ned, with Lina as his muse, conceives of the first draft for his original masterpiece, the Janeway House.

Ultimately, the play leaves it to the audience to draw conclusions about the past and the present. In Greenberg's play, the sons repeat the sins of their fathers, not able to learn from the past and the 'romantic triangles and rivalries of the first act echo in the second act'.[12] This is nicely supported by the provision that each single actor plays two corresponding roles, Walker/Ned, Pip/Theo and Nan/Lina, respectively.

The play also affirms the notion that one can never know the truth about the past, even if seemingly authoritative documents exist. After all, the truth of the past is only a subjective interpretation of it. And although Greenberg, in an interview, affirms that he is 'not a natural postmodernist', the underlying concept of mistrusting any text as the origin of meaning is a poststructuralist concept.[13]

The title of the play is supposedly derived from poet laureate W. S. Merwin's 'For the Anniversary of My Death' (1967), a poem about death, love and infamy. And, indeed, these topics are also addressed in *Three Days of Rain*. It is a play about the 'existential enigmas and conundrums of faith',[14] or, in short, about love and betrayal.

All the characters in *Three Days of Rain* are 'analytical, acutely literary types, given to academic name-dropping and the sort of lyrical, brittle and purely theatrical speech that is Mr. Greenberg's signature'.[15] This is especially true for the characters' highly articulate monologues, mixing 'information and humor'[16] but also pathos and self-deprecation. As the hyper-articulateness and the many intertextual devices become almost overwhelming, this 'surfeit of glibness . . . threatens to drown Mr. Greenberg's larger themes'.[17]

The Dazzle (2000)

(World Premiere: New York Stage and Film Company and the Powerhouse Theatre at Vassar, July 2000. New York City Premiere: Roundabout Theatre Company, March 2002.)

In his author's note Greenberg states right away that '*The Dazzle* is based on the lives of the Collyer brothers, about whom I know almost nothing' (p. 3). Though the play can be appreciated by an uninformed audience, certain foreknowledge about these historical characters is without a doubt helpful:

Homer Lusk Collyer (1881–1947) and Langley Wakeman Collyer (1885–1947) came from a privileged family. After the death of their parents, the brothers inherited a Gilded Age mansion on upper Fifth Avenue. By and by, the Harlem neighbourhood around them changed inexorably, and so did the Collyers, who eventually became recluses and compulsive hoarders. Their life in secrecy aroused public interest and they became known as the 'Hermits of Harlem'. In 1947, the police found Homer dead in the house, and, after three weeks of clearing it, they finally also found Langley there, dead by a trap he had constructed himself to keep burglars away. The authorities ultimately had to clear 180 tons of junk objects the Collyers had hoarded in their house.[18] The life story of the Collyers has since inspired quite a number of cultural products, the earliest of these being Marcia Davenport's novel *My Brother's Keeper* (1954). Since the premiere of Greenberg's play, there have been further cultural reverberations.[19] The most noteworthy of these are Franz Lidz's urban history *Ghosty Men: The Strange But True Story of the Collyer Brothers, New York's Greatest Hoarders* (2003) and E. L. Doctorow's novel *Homer & Langley* (2009).

Greenberg's play takes the known facts about the life of the brothers only as a starting point. The most outstanding fictitious addition is certainly that of a third character besides the two Collyers, a woman named Milly Ashmore, who functions as love interest to both brothers and becomes a catalyst for their reactions[20]: '[Y]ou're our *enzyme*. In your presence, reactions take place' (p. 43). *The Dazzle* consists of two acts with five scenes each. It is set entirely in the claustrophobic space of the Collyer Mansion, which, with the insanity of the siblings and the parallel decay of house and family, reminds one of Poe's 'The Fall of the House of Usher'.[21] *The Dazzle* is a history play or period drama that covers a time period of several decades, from the early until the mid-twentieth century.

The first act presents the Collyers as young men, who already exhibit mild mental ticks. Langley, Homer and Milly Ashmore are at the Collyer Mansion, – already slightly over-stuffed with '[b]ric-a-brac' (p. 5) –, after one of Lang's piano concerts. Lang is introduced as a perfectionist and a musical genius, whose eccentricity is admired by Milly but scorned by his brother Homer. Milly, an obviously bored rich girl, is fascinated by the Collyers' otherness and behaves like a groupie. Lang seems to be interested in her only as an object of scrutiny and observation, similar to his bizarre interest in a thread in the antimacassar. Milly, on the other hand, falls in love with him, or, rather, with the bohemian lifestyle of the Collyers. While Lang yearns to lead a 'normal' life like his neighbours, Milly wants to break free from the upper-class society she is confined in. She is trying to rebel against her upbringing, her family and social conventions in general. Homer is introduced mainly as 'Langley's straight man',[22] as his brother's keeper. He is a manipulative and rude character, who treats Milly in an ungentlemanly manner and bosses around Lang. Despite his own sentiments towards her, he and Milly become conspirators in planning her and Lang's wedding, after having spent together 'the first really traditional Christmas . . . in years' (p. 40). On their wedding day, however, when Milly boasts about the realty that will be her dowry, Lang comprehends that he will have to leave behind his life with his brother, and especially their house and his daily, pathological routine of contemplating minute details of objects. Lang consequently refuses to marry Milly, despite the Collyers' bad financial prospects.

The second act, set many years after the first act, presents the Collyers in decaying surroundings. The house is now filled with all kinds of stuff, 'impassable mountains of bric-a-brac' (p. 5), identifying them as compulsive hoarders. The pathological mutual dependence of the brothers, spiced up by their hostility towards each other, has increased greatly. Oddly enough, it again needs the reappearance of Milly to make Lang realize that his brother has gone blind. Milly appears again at the door of the Collyers on Christmas Eve, indeed as a Dickensian 'Ghost of Christmas Past' (p. 74). She relates to Homer how she has fared since the 'wedding-that-never-was' (p. 78). Apparently, she has subsequently been abused by her own father, the resulting pregnancy has been aborted and she has, in a development parallel to that of the Collyers, turned into, in her own words, a 'well-dressed madwoman' (p. 79). First locked away in a public facility, she was then disowned, ended up on the streets and then eventually at the threshold of the Collyer mansion, obviously more dead than alive. Here the harsh criticism some reviewers elicit with regard to Milly's character seems justified.[23] The last scene of the play is set some years later, and once again, it is Christmas Eve. The brothers have become even more withdrawn and desperate. In the moment of Homer's death, the two seem to finally acknowledge their fraternal love for each other. On the whole, the second act lacks the coherence and density of the first one and seems 'strained'.[24]

The Dazzle tells a strangely enthralling tale in which glamor and dazzlement intertwine and which allows the audience to revel in nostalgia and voyeurism. Mainly, the play has been praised for its refined dialogue, which has been compared to Oscar Wilde's, George Bernard Shaw's and Tom Stoppard's.[25] *The Dazzle* showcases Greenberg's talent as a wordsmith[26] and is a cornucopia of memorable lines, such as 'Tragedy is when a *few* people sink to the level of where *most* people always *are*' (p. 31). But all in all, one may agree with reviewers, who have called *The Dazzle* a 'fascinating and frustrating . . . play', 'as eccentric, obsessive and ultimately as messy as the Collyers themselves', although exhibiting 'flashes of . . . daring originality'.[27] It is 'wonderful entertainment' and a 'masterful piece of writing',[28] but not exactly a masterpiece.

Take Me Out (2002)

Take Me Out (World Premiere: 21 June 2002, Donmar Warehouse, London) is the first play that deals with homosexuality in professional baseball.[29] While in real life major league players made their homosexuality public only after they finished their careers, the protagonist of *Take Me Out* has his coming out while he is still playing and at the height of his popularity. Against this background Greenberg's Tony Award-winning three-act play negotiates personal identity, sexual orientation and sports enthusiasm. More concretely, it probes into baseball as an allegory of social life in America. All the play's characters are men, all are involved in Major League baseball, a quintessentially masculine world. The play's World Series-winning team of the Empires resembles the New York Yankees and several of the characters of Greenberg's play have been associated with real-life players: the divinely gifted, mixed-race protagonist Darren Lemming with Yankee player Derek Jeter, his bigoted antagonist Shane Mungit with pitcher John Rocker and central intelligence Kippy Sunderstrom with Yankee pitcher David Cone.[30] *Take Me Out* is organized achronologically in scenes which comment on each other and are sometimes organized by Kippy Sunderstrom, who most of the time functions as a stage manager, filling in blanks by informing the audience about important events not shown on stage. The play's central character is homosexual centre fielder Darren Lemming, who publicly came out to the amazement of his teammates.

Kippy, the other players and also the Empires' team manager William R. Skipper accept Darren's coming out with more or fewer reservations. By his superior intelligence paired with sarcastic humour, Darren puts those of his teammates who object and claim to have become self-conscious about sharing showers and locker rooms in their place. Kippy, a highly intelligent former scholarship student at Stanford University ardently seeking Darren's approval, tries to soften the prejudices of their mostly dim-witted teammates. Unaware of Darren's sexual orientation, Darren's best friend Davey Battle, who, although equally gifted as Darren, plays on a different and inferior team, advises Darren to shed his aura of mysterious remoteness, to explore 'his true nature' and to make 'his whole self known' (pp. 24–5). As a closet homosexual unsure of himself and his mission in life, Darren's financial agent Mason Marzac admires Darren's candidness and self-confidence despite his inner contradictions. Mason himself is the opposite of both Darren and ostentatiously happy Davey – a man full of doubt and uncertain loyalties. In his belated but all the more wholehearted enthusiasm for baseball, he resembles Greenberg himself, who discovered his love for the game in general and the New York Yankees in particular in 1999.[31] Despite their differences as family men like Kippy and Davey or gay people without stable partnerships like Darren and Mason, these men share ambivalences which undermine stereotypical self-definitions.

Only Shane Mungitt, the newly acquired relief power pitcher, does not seem to fit into this group of discreetly ambivalent men. When his pitches begin to save the Empires' season, he is interviewed on TV and uses the opportunity for crude racial slurs and homophobic remarks. He is suspended and makes an enemy of Darren. When Shane writes a public letter of apology his suspension is lifted and he is allowed to return to the team. Shane's return precipitates the play's catastrophe in a series of episodes, whose climactic sequence can only be reconstructed in hindsight with Kippy as narrator. Shane's first game after his suspension is against Davey's team. Before this game Davey seeks a private conversation with Darren. With disgust and loathing he lets Darren know that he did not mean Darren's homosexuality, which he considers a perversion, when he recommended that Darren reveal his true nature. Apparently infuriated by Davey's insults, Darren sexually harasses Shane by embracing and kissing him during a pre-game shower both men take. Shane faces Davey at bat and hits him vehemently by his first pitch – 'beans him,' in baseball phraseology. Davey does not survive his injuries. Shane is suspended from baseball for life although it is not clear whether 'this was . . . wildness' or '*murder*' (p. 95). In a final conversation between Shane, Kippy and Darren it transpires that Shane may be an illiterate redneck with a traumatic childhood but that both Kippy and Darren are largely responsible for his fatal throw that killed Davey: Kippy wrote the letter of apology for Shane which brought him back into the team. Shane overheard the pre-game quarrel of Darren and Davey during which Darren shouted 'DROP DEAD!' (p. 105). And Darren infuriated Shane by making a mock-pass at him in the shower. Without these interventions Davey might still be alive. Baseball not only as a profession and a spectator sport but also as a national pastime and even as a metaphor or allegory of life unites the play's characters. When the Empires win the World Series after all, Darren invites Mason to the team's championship party at the end of the season, tosses him a baseball and gives him one of his championship rings to wear, maybe as a sign for their future more intimate partnership. Mason, standing alone in the ballpark with ball and ring, yearningly pronounces the play's final line: 'What will we do till spring?' (p. 116)

Take Me Out is an immensely witty treatment of serious issues to which it may perhaps not quite do justice. The nation's love relationship with baseball is very convincingly conveyed. As the game it celebrates, the play works foremost as 'an unconditional, all-American epiphany', as one critic has remarked.[32] What is less convincing is the fact that human tragedies play second fiddle to the celebration of baseball. After a glimpse into the abyss of racial discrimination, latent homophobia as well as homophilia, childhood trauma, educational deficits and familial disruption, the game must go on, as Mason makes clear at the end. As opposed to an authentic tragedy like 9/11, baseball provides 'a representation of tragedy, so it allows for catharsis', as Greenberg has said in an interview.[33] In *Take Me Out* the catharsis tends to obliterate the tragedy it should result from.

The Violet Hour (2002)

The Violet Hour (World Premiere: South Coast Repertory, 8 November 2002) is a historical play, set on 1 April 1919, in Manhattan's Flatiron district.[34] It metadramatically deals with both the production and impact of artworks like itself. John Pace Seavering, its central character, is a Princeton University graduate in his twenties with an affluent family background who wants to establish himself as a publisher. He has hired Gidger as an assistant in publishing and punch lines. His Princeton buddy Denis McCleary has written an extremely meandering and disorganized novel, which shares the play's title. It derives from Seavering's, McCleary's, and presumably Greenberg's sharing of a romantic fascination for the violet hour, 'that wonderful New York hour when the evening's about to reward you for the day—. . . The violet light you walk between that hastens you places . . .' (p. 21). McCleary will only be able to convince the family of Rosamund Plinth, a Chicago meatpacking heiress, to accept him as Rosamund's husband, if he can present himself as a published novelist. But Seavering hesitates to publish McCleary's sprawling novel, since he has another manuscript under consideration and does not want to take the financial risk of publishing two books at once. The other manuscript is the memoir of Jessie Brewster, a black singer 20 years Seavering's senior, with whom he has a clandestine love affair. Stylistically, Jessie's memoir seems to be the reverse of Greenberg's voluble play full of witticisms, McCleary's convoluted novel and Gidger's predilection for the sprung rhythms of Gerard Manley Hopkins's poetry. By contrast, Jessie claims that her life writing is authentic, produced without a ghost writer in a straightforward, realistic style which is dedicated to nothing but the truth. The rivalry between the two authors and Seavering's wavering between them propels the play's plot. Jessie wants Seavering to commit himself to publishing her memoir and accuses him to be willing 'to fuck a nigger but you don't want to be a nigger press' (p. 49). In support of McCleary's project, Rosamund Plinth threatens to throw herself out of a hotel room window, if Seavering does not comply. Seavering remains undecided between the equally unattractive options of either losing Jessie or killing Rosamund. Then there is a new development that beats these not altogether probable turns of plot: a mysterious machine, a somewhat surreal printing press, is producing excerpts from books published at the end of the twentieth century. These books deal with the protagonists of the play, reveal their secrets and publish their correspondence.

The second act of *The Violet Hour* oscillates between 1 April 1919, and later periods, evoked by the books which the machine dishes up. By this device Greenberg turns the dialogue between time periods and the changes of perspective and evaluation resulting from it into the dominant theme of the play's second act. This interrelation opens up both a perspective on American cultural history in the twentieth century and, more importantly, an existential dimension. As some of Greenberg's other plays (*Three Days of Rain* and *Everett Beekin* [2001]) and less elegantly than Stoppard's *Arcadia* (1993) and *Indian Ink* (1995), *The Violet Hour* exposes the erosion of expectations and hopes over time in the minds of those who cherish them. Conversely it explores the ironies resulting from the retroactive application of the normative assumptions of a later generation to such hopes. As some reviewers have noted, the device of the mysterious machine that prints out future comments on the present is reminiscent of time travelling techniques in science fiction.[35] While this technique structurally resembles the merging of the beginning and the end of the twentieth century in *The Violet Hour*, the function of the dialogic evocation of the author's and audience's present in Greenberg's play is different from the creation of sci-fi fantasy worlds. In *The Violet Hour* the future perspective of late-twentieth century book excerpts provides a more realistic assessment in hindsight of both the professional and artistic hopes of the protagonists as well as their love relationships. From the angle of 1 April 1919, the norms and evaluations valid at the end of the twentieth century conversely appear in an ironic light. Seavering considers himself a member of a lost generation, who experienced the Great War but, for all its disorientation, is propelled by the conviction that 'the century's still so young . . . and all the worst things have already happened in it' (p. 44). This is the first instance of the irony deriving from historical distance, which determines the second act. In Seavering's statement Greenberg also implies a potential parallel between the post-World War I Jazz Age and the post-9/11 situation a century later.

The play's protagonists seem to be loosely modelled on celebrities of the 1920s: John Pace Seavering resembles Scribner's editor Maxwell Perkins (1884–1947), who promoted Scott Fitzgerald, Ernest Hemingway and Thomas Wolfe. Seavering's lover Jessie Brewster appears as a variation of transnational singer and dancer Josephine Baker (1906–75). Denis McCleary and Rosamund Plinth evoke Scott (1896–1940) and Zelda Fitzgerald (1900–48). And the editorial problems Seavering has with McCleary's sprawling first novel are reminiscent of the problems Perkins faced with Thomas Wolfe's famous first novel *Look Homeward, Angel* (1929).[36] Despite their discussions about more or less ornate literary styles and their respective truth value, these associations are not sufficiently concrete to turn the interaction of these characters into a recreation of the lost generation and the Jazz Age. By the same token, the comments from the future do not chiefly amount to an assessment of modernism from the vantage point of a century later but rather reveal some touching existential truths.

When Seavering and Jessie uncomprehendingly read about their own lives as represented in the poststructuralist jargon of the 1990s, Greenberg's irony subverts the self-importance of present-day intellectuals which has not yet been exposed to the same historical deconstruction as that of Seavering's generation. Texts, both fictive and real, tend to render questionable both the determinants of the lives they deal with and their own and other books' constructions of these lives. It is on this note that the play ends when all five characters in it leave for the theatre with tickets printed by the mysterious anteroom machine. As the curtain of the play, whose characters they are, falls, they worry about missing the curtain of the play they wish to attend. The metadramatic and metafictional aspects of *The Violet Hour* emphasize the simulacral qualities of art works, biographies, critical studies as well as the lives depicted and discussed in them. The evocation of the exciting avant-gardism of the Jazz Age, the Lost Generation and High Modernism as well as its ironic reassessment through the lens of contemporary poststructuralist and gender theory by means of sci-fi techniques of time travelling reinforce the hyper reality of what is presented on stage. That *The Violet Hour* is set on April Fools' Day may be a less than subtle further indication of this Baudrillardian constructedness of the real. What shines through *The Violet Hour's* nostalgic conjuring up of a more glamorous but vanished art scene and its playful exposure of the illusionary nature of the real is Greenberg's existential concern with problems of madness, homosexuality, ethnic identity, drug and alcohol addiction. Yet in Greenberg's drama stylistic pyrotechnics and flights of the imagination tend to drown out weightier matters. In *The Violet Hour* the evocation of weaknesses and tragedies as well as fame and glamour prevents this and balances intellectual wit and emotional depth.

Summary

With more than 30 plays staged, Greenberg's prolific productivity has often been noted. The pace of this productivity has been applauded but also raised criticism 'that he has been churning out too much too carelessly'.[37] It is surprising that despite Greenberg's high visibility on Broadway, scholarly interest in his work has been extremely scarce to date.[38] Only about a third of his plays have been published so far. Greenberg has similarly been both praised and criticized for the 'searing intellect and lightning wit'[39] that informs his plays. Critics note admiringly Greenberg's 'almost Stoppardian love of language'[40] and 'linguistic richness and playfulness', only matched by Tony Kushner.[41] But critics also foreground the artificiality, generated by this intellectualism, when some characters speak 'pure Greenberg'.[42] Such psychologically unconvincing language affects character delineation.

It is possible to single out topics which Greenberg addresses repeatedly in his oeuvre. He is concerned with authorship, or, more generally, with forms of representation in *The Author's Voice*, *Hurrah At Last*, *Jenny Keeps Talking* (1992), *Night and Her Stars* (1997) and *Naked Girl on the Appian Way* (2005). Gender and homosexuality are dealt with in *Eastern Standard* (1988), *Hurrah At Last*, *Naked Girl on the Appian Way*, *Take Me Out* and *The Violet Hour*. Jewishness (*The American Plan* [1990] and *The Author's Voice*), wealth and power (*Life Under Water* [1985], *The Maderati* [1987], and *Injured Party* [2007]), and madness (*Vanishing Act* [1986], *Three Days of Rain*, and The *Violet Hour*) also seem to be recurring issues. But indisputably most prominent is his obvious interest in history and the past. Greenberg has a pronounced tendency to draw on historical characters or events – the Lost Generation, the Collyer Brothers, the New York Yankees. The period most covered is the first half of the twentieth century, starting with the 1920s (*The Dazzle, The Violet Hour, The House in Town* [2006], but also including the 1940s (*Everett Beekin*), the 1950s (*Night and Her Stars*) and the 1960s (*The American Plan* and *Three Days of Rain*). Often, this historicity is combined with or juxtaposed to a second storyline set in the present. Greenberg's occasional adaptations (*The Hunger Artist* [1987; from Kafka] and *The Dance of Death* [2003; from Strindberg]) seem to tie in with this concept of bringing together the past and the present by modernizing and updating pre-existing material. Both his extremely intellectual, witty use of language as well as the historical and literary models Greenberg uses appear as so many distancing techniques. It is as if Greenberg needed defamiliarization to express himself. The Stoppardian technique of juxtaposing two time periods allows for philosophical insights into the passing of time but tends to detract from the emotional impact of individual fate.

Primary Sources

Works by Richard Greenberg

Night and Her Stars (New York: Dramatist Play Service, 1997).
Take Me Out (New York: Faber and Faber, 2003).
Three Days of Rain and Other Plays (New York: Grove, 1999).
The Dazzle and Everett Beekin: Two Plays by Richard Greenberg (New York: Faber and Faber, 2003).
The House in Town (New York: Dramatist Play Service, 2008).
The Violet Hour (New York: Faber and Faber, 2004).

Secondary Sources

Anon., 'Richard Greenberg', *The New York Times*, 8 April 2012.
Brantley, Ben, 'Theater Review; Prolonging the Punch of a Lone Punch Line', *The New York Times*, 22 May 1999.

—, 'Theater Review; At Home with the Collyer Brothers', *The New York Times*, 6 March 2002.

—, 'Theater Review; For Love of the Games Men Play', *The New York Times*, 6 September 2002.

—, 'Love Affair With Baseball and A Lot of Big Ideas', *The New York Times*, 28 February 2003.

—, 'Jazz Generation Sees the Future: It's not Cool', *The New York Times*, 7 November 2003.

—, 'Enough Said About "Three Days of Rain", Let's Talk Julia Roberts!' *The New York Times*, 20 April 2006.

Burns, Gail M., 'The Violet Hour', *GailSez*, July 2008. http://gailsez.org/2008/07/the-violet-hour/ [30 July 2012].

Drukman, Steven, 'Life Flows Through It', *American Theatre* 15, 3 (March 1998), p. 20.

—, 'Greenberg's Got Game: A Master Playwright Swings for the Fences with a Socially Conscious Baseball Play', *Theatre Communications Group—American Theatre* (October 2002). http://www.tcg.org/publications/at/oct02/gotgame.cfm [4 April 2012]

Erskine, Helen Worden, *Out of this World: A Collection of Hermits and Recluses* (New York: Putnam, 1953).

Gholson, Craig, 'Richard Greenberg', *BOMB* 21 (Fall 1987), 36–9.

Greenberg, Richard, 'The Author's Voice'. In Richard Greenberg (ed.), *Three Days of Rain and Other Plays* (New York: Grove, 1999), pp. 169–203.

Gross, Robert F., 'Richard Greenberg's *Everett Beekin*: Trauma, Forgetting, and Mannerism', *Hungarian Journal of English and American Studies* (HJEAS) 45, 1 (2011), 45–57.

Kakutani, Michiko, 'How Did They End Up That Way?', *The New York Times*, 1 September 2009.

Lidz, Franz, 'The Paper Chase', *The New York Times*, 23 October 2003a.

—, *The Strange but True Story of the Collyer Brothers, New York's Greatest Hoarders: An Urban Historical* (New York: Bloomsbury, 2003b).

Lohrey, David, 'A Curtain Up Los Angeles Review: *Three Days of Rain*', *CurtainUp*, 2001. http://www.curtainup.com/3daysofrainla.html [25 June 2012].

—, 'A Curtain Up Review: *The Dazzle*', *CurtainUp*, 2002. http://www.curtainup.com/dazzle.html [25 May 2012].

Marks, Peter, 'Parents' Secrets Cry Out, But Children Don't Hear', *The New York Times*, 12 November 1997.

McKinley, Jesse, 'Broadway Debut for Julia Roberts', *The New York Times*, 29 July 2005.

McNulty, Charles, 'Theater Review: *Three Days of Rain* at South Coast Repertory', *Los Angeles Times*, 22 May 2011.

Morsberger, Robert E. and Katherine M., 'Falling Stars: The Quiz Show Scandal in Steinbeck's *The Winter of Our Discontent*, Richard Greenberg's *Night and Her Stars*, and Robert Redford's *Quizshow*', *Steinbeck Yearbook I* (2000), 47–76.

Sommer, Elyse, 'Some Facts About the Real Collyer Brothers', *CurtainUp*, 2002a. http://www.curtainup.com/dazzle.html [25 May 2012].

—, 'Postscript.' *CurtainUp*, 2002b. http://www.curtainup.com/dazzle.html [25 May 2012].

—, 'A CurtainUp Review: *The Violet Hour*', *CurtainUp*, 2003. http://www.curtainup.com/violethour.html [4 April 2012].

—, 'A CurtainUp Review: *Three Days of Rain*', *CurtainUp*, 2006. http://www.curtainup.com/3daysofrainny.html [25 June 2012].

Weber, Bruce, 'Throwing a Curve in a Supposedly Straight Game', *The New York Times*, 1 September 2002.

Witchel, Alex, 'A Dramatic Shut-In', *The New York Times*, 26 March 2012.

Young, Harvey, '*The Violet Hour* by Richard Greenberg', *Theatre Journal* 56, 1 (March 2004), 117–19.

Notes

1. Anon., 'Richard Greenberg'.
2. Gholson, Craig, 'Richard Greenberg'.
3. Anon., 'Richard Greenberg'.
4. Marks, Peter, 'Parents' Secrets Cry Out, But Children Don't Hear' and McKinley, Jesse, 'Broadway Debut for Julia Roberts'.
5. McNulty, Charles, 'Theater Review: *Three Days of Rain* at South Coast Repertory'.
6. Brantley, Ben, 'Enough Said About "Three Days of Rain", Let's Talk Julia Roberts!'.
7. Lohrey, David, 'A Curtain Up Los Angeles Review: *Three Days of Rain*'.
8. McNulty, Charles, '*Three Days of Rain*'.
9. Drukman, Steven, 'Life Flows Through It'.
10. Lohrey, David, '*Three Days of Rain*'.
11. McNulty, Charles, '*Three Days of Rain*'.
12. Marks, Peter, 'Parents' Secrets Cry Out'.
13. Drukman, Steven, 'Life'.
14. Brantley, Ben, 'Enough'.
15. Ibid.
16. Sommer, Elyse, '*Three Days of Rain*'.
17. Marks, Peter, 'Parents' Secrets Cry Out'.
18. See Brantley, Ben, 'At Home with the Collyer Brothers', Erskine, Helen Worden, *Out of this World: A Collection of Hermits and Recluses,* Kakutani, Michiko, 'How Did They End Up That Way?', Lidz, Franz, *The Strange but True Story of the Collyer Brothers, New York's Greatest Hoarders: An Urban Historical* and 'The Paper Chase', Sommer, Elyse, 'Some Facts About the Real Collyer Brothers'.
19. See Kakutani, Michiko, 'How Did They End Up That Way?' and Lidz, Franz, 'The Paper Chase'.
20. Brantley, Ben, 'At Home'.
21. Lohrey, David, '*The Dazzle*'.
22. Brantley, Ben, 'At Home'.

23. Ibid.
24. Ibid.
25. See Brantley, Ben, 'At Home', Lohrey, David, '*The Dazzle*', Sommer, Elyse, 'Postscript'.
26. Lohrey, David, '*The Dazzle*'.
27. Brantley, Ben, 'At Home'.
28. Lohrey, David, '*The Dazzle*'.
29. Drukman, Steven, 'Greenberg's Got Game', Weber, Bruce, 'Throwing a Curve in a Supposedly Straight Game'.
30. See Brantley *For Love*, Drukman, Steven, 'Greenberg's Got Game', Weber, Bruce, 'Throwing a Curve'.
31. Weber, Bruce, 'Throwing a Curve'.
32. Brantley, Ben, 'Love Affair With Baseball and A Lot of Big Ideas'.
33. Weber, Bruce, 'Throwing a Curve'.
34. Burns, Gail M., 'The Violet Hour', Sommer, Elyse, '*The Violet Hour*'.
35. See Brantley *Jazz*, Sommer, Elyse, '*The Violet Hour*'.
36. See also Brantley, Ben, 'Jazz Generation Sees the Future: It's not Cool', Burns, Gail M., 'The Violet Hour', Sommer, Elyse, '*The Violet Hour*'.
37. Witchel, Alex, 'A Dramatic Shut-In'.
38. See Drukman, Steven, 'Life Flows Through It', Gross, Robert F., 'Richard Greenberg's *Everett Beekin*: Trauma, Forgetting, and Mannerism', Morsberger, Robert E., and Katherine M., 'Falling Stars: The Quiz Show Scandal in Steinbeck's *The Winter of Our Discontent*, Richard Greenberg's *Night and Her Stars*, and Robert Redford's *Quizshow*', Young, Harvey, '*The Violet Hour* by Richard Greenberg'.
39. Witchel, Alex, 'A Dramatic Shut-In'.
40. Burns, Gail M., 'The Violet Hour'.
41. Brantley, Ben, 'Jazz Generation Sees the Future'.
42. Brantley, Ben, 'Theater Review; For Love of the Games Men Play'.

4 JOHN GUARE

Ken Urban

The House of Blue Leaves; Landscape of the Body; Lydie Breeze;
Six Degrees of Separation; A Free Man of Color

Introduction

John Guare's war against the kitchen sink continues into its sixth
decade. While the plays of Marlowe and Chekhov inspired the young
Guare, it was a performance of Lorraine Hansberry's *A Raisin in the
Sun* in 1959 that crystallized Guare's decision to fight against the
conventions of naturalism. Hansberry's play, following the struggles
of an African-American family living in Chicago's Southside, is on
the surface a classic piece of dramatic realism. Its setting contains
both a kitchen sink and naturalism's other hallmark, a couch. Yet,
what excited Guare about the play was the moment when Beneatha
and her brother Walter dance to a 'Nigerian melody' and the pair are
transported 'back to the past'.[1] For Guare, 'it was an extraordinary
moment when Beneatha imagined her African past. That was the play
I wanted to see. It showed me you could take naturalistic theatre and
break it open'.[2]

His argument against the kitchen sink is that 'naturalism believes by
just replicating a thing you give the truth, rather than earning the truth'.[3]
Guare's own work breaks the fourth wall, dismantles verisimilitude
and in doing so, seeks to 'earn the truth'. To both the delight and
consternation of critics and audiences, Guare's plays feature naturalistic
scenes that always tear at the seams. He incorporates direct address and
music as well as radical shifts in tone, all in an attempt to 'get the play
out of the kitchen sink and hurl it into the Niagara Falls of life'.[4] His
goal as a writer is to 'strive for emotional understanding' of the 'invisible
forces' at work in the lives of his characters.

The subjects of Guare's plays range in scope, from the intimately domestic to the epically historical, and yet his work embraces the unexpected or what Viktor Shklovsky terms 'defamiliarization', the making strange of the familiar and everyday. 'The purpose of art', in Shklovsky's view, 'is to impart the sensation of things as they are perceived and not as they are known', 'to make the stone stony' once again by rendering it 'strange' or unfamiliar.[5] Guare's revolt against naturalism 'defamiliarizes' the American dream and its obsession with celebrity, revealing the cost of a belief in perpetual progress or fame. His characters, from Artie Shaughnessy to Lydie Breeze to Jacques Cornet, are all dreamers. The theatricality of Guare's plays reveals both the possibilities and ultimate price of such dreams.

Born on 5 February 1938, Guare was raised in the Jackson Heights neighbourhood of Queens, New York. The theatre was in his blood. His great-uncles were former vaudevillians and one went on to become the head of casting at Metro-Goldwyn-Mayer. His parents began taking him to the theatre weekly by age 7. He wrote his first dramatic work, a trilogy of short plays, at age 11 and though modestly staged in the garage of his friend's parents' home, the boys convinced reporters from *Newsday* to cover the event. During his undergraduate years at Georgetown University, Guare continued to write plays and after graduation in 1960, he attended the Yale Drama School, partially out of a desire to avoid the draft. His time at Yale studying under John Gassner was, in his words, 'painfully dull'. Guare found Gassner's ideas about playwriting stifling, with his teacher's adherence to the 'well-made play', but in his classes on theatrical design with Donald Oenslager and Ernest Bevan, Guare learnt a tremendous amount about 'the air between stage and audience' where a play lives. This allowed him to develop his own ideas about playwriting beyond Gassner's model. After a brief stint west as a screenwriter, Guare returned to New York and became part of the off-Broadway theatre movement in the mid-1960s. His early one-acts, including *Something I'll Tell You Tuesday, To Wally Pantoni, We Leave a Credenza* and *Muzeeka,* were produced at famed venues like Caffe Cino and Provincetown Playhouse. Two of these short one-acts, *Cop Out* and *Home Fires,* appeared as a double bill at Broadway's Cort Theatre in 1969, but only played four performances. Though the harsh reviews wounded Guare, he had a Broadway option on his full-length play *The House of Blue Leaves*, whose first act he finished in 1966. Guare found the second act difficult to write, but after many drafts, completed the play in 1970. It would be produced off-Broadway in February 1971. Though the critics were divided, the play ran for over 300 performances. Mel Shapiro, who directed *Blue Leaves*, asked Guare to help him adapt *Two Gentleman of Verona* as a musical for that summer's Shakespeare in Central Park, and the resulting show was a huge commercial success, eventually transferring to Broadway, playing over 600 shows, and winning a number of awards, including the New York Drama Critics' Circle Award for Best Musical of 1971–72. The financial success of the musical changed Guare's life, allowing him to pursue his playwriting in the enviable position as an experimental writer with a degree of mainstream acceptance.

The 1970s and the 1980s were a productive time for Guare. Like many new plays, Guare's new creations premiered outside of New York, away from the glare of the critics. *Marco Polo Sings a Solo* premiered at the Nantucket Stage Company in 1973, before a revised script premiered at the Public Theatre in New York four years later. *Landscape of the Body* and *Bosoms and Neglect* were both produced in Chicago, before their New York premieres, and in both cases, New York did not reciprocate Chicago's positive notices. The 1979 Broadway production of *Bosoms and Neglect*, for instance, closed after just four performances. In the 1980s, Guare focused on writing a historical tetralogy of plays set during the tumultuous end of the American nineteenth century. All the while, Guare supported his playwriting by working as a screenwriter, penning *Atlantic City* for director Louis Malle, as well as teaching at Yale Drama School. In 1990, Guare had his biggest critical and commercial success with his play *Six Degrees of Separation*, which opened at Lincoln Center in May, with Stockard Channing playing Ouisa. She would revisit the role for the 1993 film adaptation, which Guare adapted from his play, and which also stars a young Will Smith. *Six Degrees of Separation* remains the play that defines Guare as a writer.

In 1998–99, the Signature Theater in New York devoted its season to Guare's work, producing *Marco Polo Sings a Solo*, a revised *Bosoms and Neglect* and a new play, *Lake Hollywood*, which incorporated material from Guare's early one-act *Something I'll Tell You Tuesday*. The Signature would produce a new Guare play in 2002, *A Few Stout Individuals*, his historical re-imagining of Ulysses S. Grant and Mark Twain, as well as a revised *Landscape of the Body* in 2006. Guare's adaptation of *His Girl Friday*, incorporating material from both the 1940 film and the stage play *The Front Page* that inspired the film, premiered at the National Theatre in London in 2003 with Zoe Wanamaker playing the role of Hildy. *A Free Man of Color*, scheduled to open in 2009 at the Public Theatre but delayed because of financing, ran at Lincoln Center from December 2010 until January 2011. Guare remains prolific. In May 2012, *Are You There, McPhee?* premiered at the McCarter Theatre in Princeton, NJ, though following the production, Guare substantially rewrote the text because 'he finally figured out the play'. A year later, *Three Kinds of Exile*, a meditation on three Eastern European artists, opened at the Atlantic Theater Company in New York. This play is written in a presentational style not so unlike Martin Crimp's *Attempts on Her Life* or Simon Stephens's *Pornography*, a new development in Guare's work. Yet, Guare's preoccupation with fame remains; in the dialogue about Elzbieta Czyzwewska that comprises the play's second part, the Polish actress utters the very Guarian lines, 'Everyone in Poland knows who I am. And you don't? What a refreshing feeling'.[6]

The Plays

The House of Blue Leaves (1971)

Guare's first major play contains a number of autobiographical elements. Like Guare's parents, Artie and Bananas Shaughnessy live in a shabby apartment in Sunnyside, Queens, and their son Ronnie details a humiliating 'audition' in front of his parents' friend, the famed film director Billy Einhorn, that comes straight from Guare's own childhood. A lapsed Catholic, Guare sets his play on the day of the Pope's historic visit to New York to speak to the United Nations in October 1965. Rather than a piece of childhood nostalgia, the play is a dark parody of a *Künstlerroman*, the story of an artist's maturation. Artie, who works at the zoo, dreams of being a songwriter. At open mic nights at a local bar, the audience ignores his songs. Yet, his mistress Bunny convinces Artie of his talent, assuring him, 'I didn't work in Macy's music department for nix' (p. 12). Artie fears he is becoming 'too old to be a young talent', and plans to put his mentally ill wife Bananas in a hospital. Once Bananas is out of the picture, he and Bunny will head to California, where, with the help of Billy Einhorn, they will get Artie's songs into the movies.

The characters are obsessed with celebrity. Bunny sees the world through the lens of films. When Artie tries to calm Bananas's fears about the hospital, Bunny interrupts,

> I know these sick wives. I've seen a dozen like you in movies. I wasn't an usher for nothing. You live in wheelchairs just to hold your husband and the minute he is out of the room, you're hopped out of your wheelchair doing the Charleston. (p. 21)

Bananas describes the day her 'troubles' began two years ago as a ludicrous vision when she acts as a gypsy cab driver for Cardinal Spellman, Jackie Kennedy, Bob Hope and Lyndon Johnson. When Bob Hope and Cardinal Spellman are guests that evening on *The Tonight Show*, the men mock Bananas-the-cab-driver. This imaginary incident, watching Johnny Carson and his audience laugh at her, drives Bananas to the roof of the apartment during a fierce snowstorm, for, in her mind, nothing could be worse than being derided by the famous. In Guare's universe, even the Pope is a celebrity who inspires insanity. The three nuns from New Jersey that take refuge in the Shaughnessy's apartment are more like paparazzi stalking a star than devoted on a pilgrimage to see His Holiness.

The play's second act becomes a farce, but the explosion that punctuates the end of the act's first scene leads to tragedy for Bananas and Artie. Ronnie, who has gone AWOL from the Marines, plans to blow up the Pope, not out of animosity towards the Pope, but because he will 'be on headlines around the world' (p. 37). In the chaos that ensues, Ronnie's bomb goes off in the elevator, killing two of the nuns and Billy's actress girlfriend Corrinna who has come to visit the Shaughnessy family. The aftermath of that death means that Billy finally returns to Queens.

Instead of his big break, Bunny leaves with Billy to go to Australia and be his cook. Artie remains trapped in Queens with his crazy wife Bananas who mocks his talent. Unlike Bunny who claimed Artie's songs were 'perfect for Oscar-winning medleys', Bananas points out that his song 'I Love You So I Keep Dreaming' steals its melody from Irving Berlin's 'White Christmas'. Artie strangles Bananas to death, and only then can he imagine performing his songs for an appreciative audience.

A 2011 Broadway production, directed by David Cromer, re-imagined the play. Cromer's directorial style aims for a gritty hyper-realism. His stagings of *Our Town* and *Brighton Beach Memoirs* emphasized more sombre elements than usually found in productions of Thornton Wilder and Neil Simon. The 2011 revival brought the 'kitchen sink' back to Guare's play and the cast, featuring Ben Stiller as Artie, played the text's more absurd elements 'straight'. While this style angered some of the critics, including the *New York Times*'s Ben Brantley, the overall effect created poignancy in the journey of Bananas, played by Edie Falco. The moment of direct address also took on new resonance, feeling like 'confessionals' on reality-TV programmes, scenes when the 'real' people speak directly to the camera in monologue. Though these moments are meant to feel like private revelations, the more astute TV viewers know how carefully choreographed such 'candid' moments are. In Cromer's revival, the characters in Guare's play all acted as if they were trying to be cast in the next big reality show, their world permeated with the idea that they are all performers for some unseen audience, making the 1971 play feel especially prescient.

Landscape of the Body (1977, revised 2006)

Like Artie, Betty, the protagonist of *Landscape of the Body*, is a dreamer who finds her world falling apart when her son is murdered in New York City. The play opens and closes with the only scene in the present. On the ferry to Nantucket, the disguised Police Captain Marvin Holahan confronts Betty. No longer on the force, Holahan cannot stay away from her because he 'know[s] more about [her] than anyone [he] know[s]' (p. 53). Betty is in the midst of writing her confession, jotting down 'everything that happened'. She stuffs these notes in bottles then hurls them into the sea. In essence, the play is a dramatization of those sea-tossed confessions, a series of flashbacks detailing the previous two years. Scenes at the precinct show Betty interrogated by Holahan, who is convinced that she murdered her 14-year-old son Bert. Other scenes show earlier moments in Betty's life in New York as well as the occasional scene featuring Bert that 'contains information completely unknown to the boy's mother' (p. 16). Betty's deceased sister Rosalie introduces scenes, acting as the audience's guide through the outrageous series of events.

Betty arrived in New York two years ago to find her sister Rosalie and bring her back home to Bangor, Maine. Entranced with her sister's life working for a dubious travel agency and making mafia-financed porno film, Betty stays. A wayward bicyclist, however, strikes Rosalie dead. Betty steps into Rosalie's life and works for Raulito's travel firm. Bert, unbeknownst to his mother, spends his days luring closeted gay men looking for sex at the docks behind Rosalie's apartment. His friend Donny, hiding in the tub, surprises the men and knocks them unconscious with a wrench. The boys rob the men, dragging them like trash into the hallway, confident that when the men regain consciousness, they will be too ashamed to pursue justice. Betty's life takes an unexpected turn when Durwood Peach, a man from her childhood, declares his love for Betty and offers her a perfect life at his farm in South Carolina. Betty temporarily abandons Bert in New York, leaving him Durwood's gift of thousand dollars and a promise to collect him once she determines if Durwood's promises are legitimate. During her absence, Bert plays a trick in a bank that results in Raulito being accidentally shot. Bert himself becomes the victim when he hugs Donny and his friend kills him in a fit of homosexual panic. To make Bert's death look like the work of a serial killer, Donny cuts off his head and dumps his body in the Hudson River. Meanwhile, Betty arrives at Durwood's farm only to be sent packing by his family, explaining that Durwood is not of sound mind. Betty eventually returns to New York only to find the last person she loved gone.

The tragic dimensions undercut the play's offbeat sense of humour, for it is a comedy with a large body count. Rosalie's song-and-dance routines playfully punctuate scenes. Yet, Rosalie is a chanteuse only after her untimely run-in with a bicycle; hers are post-mortem performances. Betty's boss Raulito is 'sexually threatening', and yet wears 'a gold lamé evening gown over his business suit' because when he grew up poor in rural Cuba, he would see images in American magazines of women wearing such expensive outfits and assumed all rich people, men and women alike, dressed this way (pp. 21–2). His success in America is dependent upon a con. He targets the recently engaged, promising them a free honeymoon trip, and once he lures them downtown, the couple discovers the trip will cost them. Raulito meets his own death when he is mistaken for a bank robber, thanks to Bert's joke. Betty's journey is the most tragic. If she refused Durwood's offer and stayed in New York, perhaps her son would not have died. 'It bothered me at first not knowing who killed Bert', she tells Holahan near the play's end, 'But then I thought all the things we don't know'. She comforts herself knowing only one thing; 'There's got to be some order in there' (pp. 52–3). The play ends with Betty 'considering' Holahan and then moving towards him. Unlike the dream world that Artie must escape to, Betty might find happiness in the real world with her former interrogator.

The play was first produced Academy Festival Theater in the Lake Forest metropolitan area of Chicago in July 1977 before premiering in New York at the Public Theatre in October of that year. Again, the critical opinion was mixed, and the *Boston Phoenix*'s Don Shewey speculated that the play's morbid streak contributed to that reception. In 2006, the play had a major New York revival directed by Michael Greif at the Signature. Guare revised the text slightly for this production, for instance, moving Bert's song 'Voices of Eagles' from the start of Act Two to the end of Act One. Ben Brantley of the *New York Times* raved about the revival, calling the play a 'delirious heartbreaker of a comedy' and 'a happy reminder that no one puts the sting in whimsy like Mr. Guare'.[7] As a result of such successful revivals, *Landscape of the Body* now is seen as a major work in Guare's canon.

Lydie Breeze (1982, revised 2000)

Guare decided by the time of *Lydie Breeze*'s premiere in February 1982 at the American Place Theater that it was to become part of a four-play cycle. *Lydie Breeze*, set in 1895, follows the aftermath of a Nantucket utopic community founded by four friends who met during the Civil War. *Gardenia*, the second play to be written, takes place 20 years earlier, showing the end of the friendship and the seeds of discontent that fully bloomed in *Lydie Breeze*. After *Gardenia*'s production at Manhattan Theatre Club in April 1982, Guare completed *Women and Water*, the third play in the cycle, which shows the meeting of the four friends and how the experience of war led them to found their Nantucket utopia. Guare imagined a fourth play, which chronologically would occur after *Women and Water* but before *Gardenia*. This play, with the working title *Bulfinch's Mythology*, would eventually become *A Few Stout Individuals*, featuring none of the characters from the *Lydie Breeze* story because in Guare's words, 'Ulysses S. Grant took over that play'. In 1984, Guare saw the New Playwrights Theatre productions of *Gardenia* and *Lydie Breeze* performed in rep. The experience of seeing the plays produced together led Guare to imagine the plays working as a single two-part work, much like Tony Kushner's *Angels in America*. In the 1990s, Guare revised both *Gardenia* and *Lydie Breeze* so the plays could be performed together under the title *Lydie Breeze*. The work was meant to have its premiere at the Signature during the 1998–99 Guare season, but proved too costly. In May 2000, the revised *Lydie Breeze* received its world premiere at New York Theatre Workshop, directed by Itamar Kubovy, featuring Elizabeth Marvel as Lydie.

Though initially seen as a departure from Guare's previous work, *Lydie Breeze* dramatizes Guare's familiar theme: the disparity between the characters' ideals and the actuality of human life. After the Civil War, Lydie, her husband Joshua Hickman, and her lover Dan Grady 'fought a war against false and cruel principles' and with the help of Amos Mason, set up Aipotu ('utopia' spelt backwards) to serve a 'transcendental purpose' (pp. 17, 21). At the opening of *Part One: Bulfinch's Mythology*, Lydie and Joshua despair at the state of their lives. Joshua's manuscript was rejected for publication, and in his grief, he killed Lydie's beloved gardenia plant. Lydie's prospects as a nurse look scarce after she lashes out at a couple for their support of Grant, the corrupt 'butcher of Cold Harbor.' Dan is gone, riding the railways, and unbeknownst to her husband, Lydie is pregnant with Dan's child.

With money scarce, Lydie proposes turning the colony into a 'primitive' resort in order to survive. As Amos points out, their life driven by 'transcendental purpose' appears lost. Dan, however, returns with a bag of cash, which he stole from a dying lobbyist. With the money, the foursome hopes to fulfil their dreams. Amos can pursue an education at Harvard. Joshua can travel to Europe to further his education. With Joshua gone, Dan and Lydie hope to conceive again, after Lydie loses the baby. The newly arrived Beaty will tend to household duties, including watching Dan's son Jeremiah and Lydie's daughter Gussie. But Joshua's jealousy ends that hope. Act Two opens nine years later. Joshua resides in the Charlestown Prison, his punishment for killing Dan. Amos visits Joshua with a demand. During his time in prison, Joshua wrote a memoir of life at Aipotu and the manuscript got into the hands of William Dean Howells, who wants to publish it. Amos, now a lawyer with political aspirations, does not want the book, with its unseemly details of his former life, to see the light of day. Amos brings Lydie, a shadow of her former self, having tried to murder her two children, to convince Joshua to destroy the book. Seeing Lydie, Joshua realizes that 'in all [their] dreaming [they] never allowed for the squalid, petty furies' (p. 58). Amos offers to pay for Joshua's release from prison, and Joshua complies, shredding his manuscript.

The play's second part *The Sacredness of the Next Task*, set in 1895, returns to the Nantucket community. After Joshua's release from prison, Lydie commits suicide. Her youngest daughter, who shares her name, keeps her mother's memory alive with the help of Beatty. Young Lydie lives in fear of her father, who drunkenly staggers around the home. Older sister Gussie is the mistress of Amos, now a US Senator, and the pair returns to Nantucket on the eve of Amos's important campaign speech. The past acts as a literal infection. Dan's son Jeremiah arrives in order to punish Lydie for infecting him with syphilis. It is discovered that his father Dan, infected with the disease, passed it on to Lydie and then Lydie, who, in grief over Dan's murder, raped his son, passed the disease on to Jeremiah, who then infected Beatie, who mistook the boy for Amos during their lovemaking. The play concludes with hope for Lydie's two daughters, who, unlike their mother, find suitors far more pragmatic than Joshua, Dan or Amos. Leaving her childhood Nantucket house, Gussie, full of hope, remarks, 'It's almost 1900. I'm American, by God. It's about to be my century' (p. 108).

The themes of *Lydie Breeze* are familiar, and yet the play's melodrama represents a new battle in Guare's war against the kitchen sink. Guare uses the dominant theatrical form of the nineteenth century to tell the story of these idealists. The play, especially Part Two, features the plot contrivances of melodrama: the revelatory letter, the 'unspeakable' ailment, cases of mistaken identity. Guare signals the importance of melodrama in the character of Jeremiah, who is now an actor in London, playing Frankenstein's monster. Jeremiah even quotes lines from Leopold Lewis's popular 1871 melodrama *The Bells*. The critics of the first production of *Lydie Breeze* in 1982 were hostile towards the play's melodramatic elements, and found *Gardenia* confusing in the absence of its companion play. In 2000, when the two-part revised version was staged, critics felt differently. Wilborn Hampton of the *New York Times* called the play 'haunting and humorous', and the *Village Voice*'s Michael Feingold seconded the praise, calling the revised play

> tight, clarified, sequential—and with enough data flooding through it to make any of Guare's fellow bookmeisters beam with pleasure at his fidelity to historical fact, even when his events or characters are at their most outrageous.[8]

Six Degrees of Separation (1990)

Six Degrees of Separation, Guare's biggest critical and commercial success, was written quickly in 1989, and was produced at Lincoln Center, without any readings or workshop – a rarity in the American theatre. In 1983, two of Guare's friend told him about their encounter with David Hampton, a con artist who convinced the couple he was the son of famed Black actor Sidney Poitier. *The New York Times* reported in October of that same year how Hampton 'pos[ed] as the son of the actor Sidney Poitier to gain access to the homes of prominent New Yorkers', and his victims now included a Columbia University dean and the president of a local television station.[9] Guare used details of the case for his play, which focuses on the fictional Ouisa and Flan Kittredge.

The Kittredges entertain their South African friend Geoffrey in the hope that he will lend Flan, an art dealer, two million dollars in order to purchase a Cézanne he will sell to the Japanese at a profit. Geoffrey tells the couple that he stays in South Africa 'to educate the black workers' and success will come when 'they kill us'. When Geoffrey extends an invitation to his home, Ouisa teases, '[W]e'd visit you and sit in your gorgeous house planning trips into the townships demanding to see the poorest of the poor' (p. 10). An unexpected visitor interrupts the evening. The doorman brings Paul, a young black man, bleeding as a result of a mugging in Central Park, to the apartment. A friend of Ouisa and Flan's children attending Harvard, Paul recognized the building as the Kittredges' home and not knowing what to do, ran into the building after being attacked. Paul reveals he is the son of the famed actor and director Sidney Poitier and charms the threesome, promising them roles in his father's film of *Cats*, and cooking them a feast from assorted items in the kitchen. Geoffrey, so charmed by Paul, tells Flan he can count on him for the money, and Ouisa insists that Paul spend the night before meeting his father at the Sherry Hotel the next morning. Ouisa wakes the next morning to find Paul entertaining a naked hustler in her home. With Paul and his guest thrown out, Ouisa and Flan are relieved they were not murdered in their sleep.

The next day, friends Kitty and Larkin tell a story about their own visit from the son of Poitier and they realize Paul has duped them. The link between Paul's victims, now numbering five, is their children: they all attended the same boarding school. Ouisa's daughter Tess uncovers Paul's identity: a hustler in Boston who conned one of their high-school friends into giving him the details of the lives of the Kittredges and their ilk. Ouisa realizes Paul's brilliance as a con artist and feels sympathy for this man's desire to want to be in their lives. Paul's crimes eventually catch up with him after a young man who he swindled out of money commits suicide. The man's girlfriend presses charges. Reading about the man's death forces Paul to call Ouisa, during which he tells her that the night they spent together 'was the happiest night [he] ever had' and his desire to follow in Flan's career footsteps. Ouisa's own children do not want to be associated with their parents, but here is a young Black man who dreams of being a

Kittredge. Ouisa convinces Paul to turn himself into the police and offers to drive him there. But when Flan and Ouisa go to meet him, he is gone, apparently already arrested. Ouisa can never find Paul; they don't know his real name and have no legal rights to find him in the courts. In one of Guare's best speeches, Ouisa, angry at her husband who has no real feeling for Paul, asks,

> How do we fit what happened to us into life without turning it into an anecdote with no teeth and a punch line you'll mouth over and over for years to come?. . . . How do we keep the experience. (pp. 117–8)

The image of the rotating double-sided Kandinsky reflects Ouisa's dilemma: one side of the canvas is ordered; the other is chaos. Life, it appears, is the tug between the two.

On one hand, the play is a critique of white liberalism. These are the kinds of New Yorkers who do not know Black people, who do not understand the lives of people not in their class strata except as 'anecdotes' at dinner parties. Yet, the play is also part of Guare's continued investigation of the American dream and the false allure of celebrity. Paul seduces Ouisa and Flan with a promise of being extras in a film of the same Broadway musical Ouisa once dismissed as an 'all-time low' in American theatre. Paul believes that in America, he can be anybody he wants, turning his identity into the ultimate form of collage, where 'everything is somebody else's'. There is no real person underneath Paul, or at least, no real Paul that any of the white characters ever discovers. The issue of celebrity would eventually hit home in a real way for Guare. The real-life basis for his character, David Hampton, demanded royalties from the play and threatened Guare. Guare describes how Hampton harassed him over the phone and painted 'John Guare Must Die' on his wife's apartment door. Guare took Hampton to court. In response, Hampton countersued Guare for a hundred million dollars. There was a hung jury in the case and Hampton fled New York before he could be re-tried. Hampton died in 2003 of AIDS-related complications.

A Free Man of Color (2010)

In 2004, director George C. Wolfe approached Guare about writing a Restoration comedy set in America that would star Jeffrey Wright. Wolfe liked Guare's approach to history in *Lydie Breeze* and *A Few Stout Individuals*. The new play would be set in New Orleans during a time of transition, from 1801 to 1806, when the city went from a Spanish possession to a French one until, thanks to the Louisiana Purchase, it became part of the United States. Initially overwhelmed by his research on the topic, Guare found the description of Spain's police force in New Orleans in the late eighteenth century was his way into the material. Spain, too poor to arm its small police force properly, dressed its officers in gold lace brocade in hopes that the citizens, overwhelmed by the uniform's grandeur, would behave. That image made Guare say, 'I want to live in that world'. The play was also inspired by the sexual bawdiness of William Wycherley's restoration comedy *The Country Wife* (1675). The first draft, finished in 2007, was read at the Public Theatre, running over five hours. After another reading and a two-week workshop in which the script was streamlined considerably, Lincoln Center produced the play at the Vivian Beaumont in December 2010.

Guare's play takes place in three worlds: Jacques Cornet and his milieu in New Orleans, the newly elected Jefferson administration and the French court of Napoleon. Jacques Cornet bought his way out of slavery, a legal option in New Orleans during its time as a Spanish colony, and his white father and former owner, so impressed by his actions, made Jacques the heir to his estate, not his white son Pincepousse. Jacques enjoys his monetary power, dressing in the finest silks, commanding his slave Murmur to do his bidding, purchasing maps in hopes of discovering the much-desired direct water route across the continent and having sex with as many of the local prostitutes and wives of his friends as he can. Jacques's genitals are legendary, as the women all attest, but the husbands suffer the cuckolding in silence, wanting to stay in wealthy Jacques's good graces. That changes when news spreads that Spain has given New Orleans to France, bringing the possibility that the *le Code Noir* – slavery – might be reinstated, makes Jacques *persona non grata*. Jacques hatches a scheme to prevent his re-enslavement; he will make these men think a gunshot wound has rendered him a eunuch and that unbeknown to the others, each of these former friends is sole heir of Jacques's estate.

This story unfolds against the backdrop of international politics. France invades its former colony Haiti, imprisoning Toussaint L'Ouverture, but yellow fever decimates the French forces. A ship, carrying hundreds of imprisoned Haitians, sets sail for New Orleans. Hearing of the ship's impending arrival, and its cargo of yellow fever, the townspeople plead with Jacques to bribe the captain to dock the ship elsewhere. Seeing an opportunity, Jacques reasons that 'the world needs New Orleans' and if he 'were the one to save it', 'the world would be indebted to' him (p. 69). Seeing his fellow Blacks treated as vermin forces Jacques to feel the first pangs of racial consciousness. The city, however, discovers Jacques's manhood remains intact. Instead of a hero, he must flee the city. Upon hearing that Jefferson has acquired all of Louisiana, he returns to New Orleans. Instead of finding newer New Orleans a place where 'all men are created equal', Jacques is sold back into slavery.

Guare's trademark intricate plots were sometimes swallowed by the sumptuous Lincoln Center. But the play's closing image of the slave auction set against the backdrop of the American flag was powerful, reminding its audience of the unfinished business of racism in this country.

Summary

Guare's prolific career surprisingly has not been matched with an equally in-depth body of critical literature. Two recent monographs – Gene A. Plunka's *The Black Comedy of John Guare* and Robert J. Andreach's *John Guare's Theatre: The Art of Connecting* – as well as Christopher Bigsby's chapter on Guare from *Contemporary American Playwrights* give a helpful overview of the major plays. Plunka's study characterizes Guare's oeuvre as farce; the 'black comedy' of the plays, Plunka argues, prevents many critics from seeing their 'significant philosophical issues', which connects Guare to writers such as Beckett, Pinter and Stoppard. Plunka sums up Guare's work in this way:

> Although we must realize that our utopian dreams . . . will dissipate due to brutal reality, Guare asserts that one must always strive for the pursuit of the imaginative vision as a means to liberate ourselves from the mundane.[10]

Andreach finds Guare to be O'Neill's heir and his study finds the theme of connection as the common thread of Guare's varied plays. Though published much earlier, and therefore limited to the earlier versions of the play, Bigsby's thorough chapter gives detailed readings of Guare's major plays, devoting extended attention to *Lydie Breeze*, calling it Guare's 'flawed masterpiece'.

More theoretical approaches to Guare's work have focused almost exclusively on *Six Degrees of Separation*. David Zimmerman's essay 'Six Degrees of Distinction' reads the play through the ideas of cultural theorists David Harvey and Pierre Bourdieu, arguing that 'what Paul "kills" is the idea that the cultured class rule the cultural field by some natural or even earned right'.[11] Jennifer Gillian's 2000 essay looks at the play's representation of 1980s masculinity, focusing on Flan and Woody. Her claim is that the play 'dramatizes the shifting of blame for social and economic exploitation and general societal decay onto a "deviant" individual', in this case, Paul.[12] She furthers that analysis in her 2001 essay about the play's film adaptation, which she reads as a critique of the Hollywood 'buddy' picture. Robert F. Gross's '"Life in a Silken Net"' is one of the few scholarly articles to focus on another Guare play, in this case, the 1982 version of *Lydie Breeze*. Unlike Bigsby, who extols the play's 'lyrical language' and its veiled critique of 1980s greed, Gross argues that *Lydie Breeze* 'exhibits the homophobic fears that mark modern Western patriarchy, without, however, critiquing them', and that the play's representations of mourning 'become the basis for a cyclic view of history', a conservative gesture. The 2000 revision of the play invalidates much of Gross's argument.

Guare himself has turned into a critic of sorts in recent years. He has penned incisive introductions to plays by Arthur Miller,

Tennessee Williams and Thornton Wilder, a reminder of what great critics playwrights can be. These writings serve as reminders of Guare's boundless intelligence and imagination, as if the plays were not evidence enough.

Primary Sources

Works by John Guare

The House of the Blue Leaves (New York: Samuel French, 1971).
Six Degrees of Separation (New York: Vintage, 1990).
Lydie Breeze (Revised Edition) (New York: Dramatists Play Service, 2001).
Landscape of the Body (Revised Edition) (New York: Dramatists Play Service, 2008).
A Free Man of Color (New York: Grove Press, 2011).

Secondary Sources

Andreach, Robert J., *John Guare's Theatre: The Art of Connecting* (Newcastle upon Tyne: Cambridge Scholars Publishing, 2009).

Bigsby, Christopher, *Contemporary American Playwrights* (Cambridge: Cambridge UP, 1999).

Bouchard, Larry D., 'Eliza And Rita, Paul And Luke: The Eclipse And Kenosis Of Integrity In *Pygmalion*, *Educating Rita*, And *Six Degrees Of Separation*', *Religion & Literature* 40, 2 (Summer 2008), 25–60.

Brantley, Ben, 'Gold Lamé Dreams Dashed by Polyester Reality in *Landscape of the Body*', *New York Times*, 17 April 2006, http://theater2.nytimes.com/2006/04/17/theater/reviews/17body.html?pagewanted=all.

Brockes, Emma, 'John Guare: "Writing is a bloodsport"' Interview with John Guare, *The Guardian*, 5 January 2010, http://www.guardian.co.uk/stage/2010/jan/05/john-guare-interview.

Cattaneo, Anne, 'Interview with John Guare'. In George Plimpton (ed.), *The Paris Review: Playwrights at Work* (New York: Modern Library, 2000), p. 328.

Curry, Jane Kathleen, *John Guare: A Research and Production Handbook* (Westport: Greenwood Press, 2002).

Feingold, Michael, 'American Madness', Review of *Lydie Breeze* and *The Laramie Project*, 23 May 2000, http://www.villagevoice.com/2000-05-23/theater/american-madness/.

Fowler, Glenn, 'Suspect In Hoax Is Arrested Here In Rendezvous', *The New York Times*, 19 October 1983, http://www.nytimes.com/1983/10/19/nyregion/suspect-in-hoax-is-arrested-here-in-rendezvous.html [23 September 2012].

Gillan, Jennifer, '"No One Knows You're Black!": *Six Degrees of Separation* and the Buddy Formula', *Cinema Journal* 40 (Spring 2001), 47–68.

—, 'Staging a Staged Crisis in Masculinity: Race and Masculinity in *Six Degrees of Separation*', *American Drama* 9 (May 2000), 50–73.

Gross, Robert F., '"Life in a Silken Net": Mourning the Beloved Monstrous in *Lydie Breeze*", *Journal of Dramatic Theory and Criticism* IX, 1 (Fall 1994), 21–42.

Guare, John, *Three Kinds of Exile*, manuscript dated 25 October 2011.

Hampton, Wilborn, 'Guare's Utopia Seems Like Less Than One', *New York Times*, 16 May 2000, http://theater.nytimes.com/mem/theater/treview.html?res=9B0DE4D6103BF9 35A25756C0A9669C8B63.

Hansberry, Lorraine, *A Raisin in the Sun and The Sign in Sidney Brustein's Window* (New York: Vintage, 1995).

Harrop, John, '"Ibsen Translated by Lewis Carroll": the Theatre of John Guare', *New Theatre Quarterly* 3 (May 1985), 150–4.

Plunka, Gene A., *The Black Comedy of John Guare* (Newark: University of Delaware Press, 2002).

Shklovsky, Viktor, 'Art as Technique' in Lee T. Lemon and Marion J. Reis (eds and trans), *Russian Formalist Criticism: Four Essays* (Lincoln: University of Nebraska Press, 1965), 3–24.

Zimmerman, David, 'Six Degrees of Distinction: Connection, Contagion and the Aesthetics of Anything', *The Arizona Quarterly* 55 (Autumn 1999), 107–33.

Notes

1. Lorraine Hansberry, *A Raisin in the Sun and The Sign in Sidney Brustein's Window*, pp. 76–7.
2. John Guare, Interview with author, 14 September 2012. All quotes from Guare come from the author's interview except where noted.
3. Emma Brockes, 'John Guare: "Writing is a bloodsport"'.
4. John Guare, interview with Anne Cattaneo.
5. Viktor Shklovsky, 'Art as Technique', p. 12.
6. John Guare, *Three Kinds of Exile*, p. 13.
7. Ben Brantley, 'Gold Lamé Dreams Dashed by Polyester Reality in *Landscape of the Body*'.
8. Wilborn Hampton, 'Guare's Utopia Seems Like Less Than One'; Michael Feingold, 'American Madness'.
9. Glenn Fowler, 'Suspect In Hoax Is Arrested Here In Rendezvous'.
10. Gene A. Plunka, *The Black Comedy of John Guare*, p. 232.
11. David Zimmerman, 'Six Degrees of Distinction', p. 109.
12. Jennifer Gillian, 'No One Knows You're Black!', p. 51.

5 DAVID HENRY HWANG

Russell Vandenbroucke

FOB; The Dance and the Railroad; Family Devotions; M. Butterfly; Golden Child; Yellow Face

Introduction

As the sun sets in 1978 at the inaugural Padua Hills Playwriting Workshop, David Henry Hwang strolls across a patio playing his violin with professional aplomb. He has travelled 25 miles east of his Los Angeles home to study playwriting with Sam Shepard, Maria Irene Fornes and others. The next spring, before graduating Phi Beta Kappa from Stanford, Hwang will direct his play *FOB* in the lounge of his residence, Asian-themed Okada House. Before he graduates weeks later, *FOB* is selected by Lloyd Richards for the 1979 National Playwrights Conference of the Eugene O'Neill Theatre Center. Twenty years earlier, Richards had directed Lorraine Hansberry's *A Raisin in the Sun,* the country's most important African American play up to then. The O'Neill workshop leads directly to a professional production at the New York Shakespeare Festival's Public Theater led by Joseph Papp, the country's most important producer of new work, and directed by Mako. Hwang is 22 and, before turning 30, Hwang's *M. Butterfly* would win the Tony Award for Best Play.

With the perspicuity of hindsight, Padua Hills and *FOB* reflect many facets of Hwang's artistic spine: music fused with theatre; formative personal relationships with masters of their discipline like Shepard, Richards, Mako and Papp; and the equipoise to balance the psychic geography of the East Coast theatre establishment and the West Coast base of his family, his education, and his first artistic encounters. In Los Angeles, East West Players, which Mako led, was the nation's first theatre focused on Asian Americans; in San Francisco, Shepard had become resident playwright of the Magic Theatre. Perhaps most formative of all, the West Coast is the locus of Hwang's Chinese American community and the crucible of his ethnic identity.

Hwang was born 15 August 1957 in San Gabriel, California, the son of Chinese immigrants – following their marriage, the newlyweds tried to move into Monterey Park but owners would not sell to Chinese Americans. Today this LA suburb is almost completely Chinese, which the playwright cites as 'an example of the old saying that fear creates the thing feared'.[1]

Eager to assimilate, Hwang's parents spoke English at home although he and two sisters enrolled in Chinese classes for a time. He recalls of his father, 'He's never much liked China, or the whole idea behind China or Chinese ways of thinking. He's always been much more attracted to American ways of thinking'.[2] Friction between Christianity and traditional Chinese beliefs provides a dramatic nexus of Hwang's *Family Devotions* and *Golden Child.* Henry Hwang's ebullient embrace of everything American, especially its materialism, is clear in characters modelled after him in *Family Devotions, Rich Relations* and *Yellow Face.* Hwang's mother became a successful piano teacher. The depth of Hwang's own engagement with music, evident on the Padua Hills patio, has deepened from its strategic presence in straight plays like *FOB* and *M. Butterfly* to the centre of opera libretti and his books of Broadway musicals.

The Plays

FOB (1980)

FOB is like many first plays in America: it needs only a simple set; the action occurs in a locale familiar to the playwright, a Chinese restaurant in a Los Angeles suburb; and the cast is limited, just two men and a woman. The basic plot is familiar too: Steve and Dale, young rivals of different backgrounds, compete for Grace. However, *FOB* is far from a typical first play: the characters embody alternative ways to be ethnically and culturally Chinese in America, and each represents a different phase of American assimilation. Grace, an immigrant from Taiwan, must choose, in a sense, between sparring acronyms: Steve the FOB, Fresh off the Boat, or Dale the ABC, American-Born Chinese, like Hwang himself.

FOB mixes Western and Asian styles in utilizing patently theatrical soliloquies and Chinese opera, such as Grace's banging of pots to sound a gong. Hwang writes that the play 'was invaded by two figures from American literature: Fa Mu Lan, the girl who takes her father's place in battle, from Maxine Hong Kingston's *The Woman Warrior*, and Gwan Gung, the god of fighters and writers, from Frank Chin's *Gee, Pop!*'[3] Chin's *The Chickencoop Chinamen* (1972) was the first play by an Asian American to be professionally produced in New York; Kingston's bestseller was published in 1976. Gwang Gun and Fa Mu Lan, alter egos for Steve and Grace, infuse an ordinary Chinese restaurant with myth and heightened theatricality.

The male competition for Grace includes a duel over the amount of hot sauce each consumes. Steve wins, as he does at the end of the play. Grace chooses Steve's easy embrace of his ethnic identity over the westernized ways of Dale. She punctuates her California dreaming by embracing the promise of preserving her Chinese identity, as Steve does, rather than shedding it for Dale's assimilated American self. Grace calls Steve scrawny when she meets him, but he suggests more vital sexuality in winning Grace than is often manifest in Asian characters. Far from being a neutered geek, the FOB heads off to dance and potential romance with a woman he just met.

Hwang's playfulness with language, accents and dialects anticipates future scripts. Steve speaks first in Chinese; later, his English is perfect. Language is also code: Steve assumes a Chinese accent and a mock Chinese one whenever he (or Hwang) desires.

Critics often overlook Hwang's lacerating humour. Grace derides an unseen suitor's threat to kill himself: 'You don't even know when they come—you'd have to lie on those tracks for hours' (p. 15). Hwang subverts melodrama's gender roles, and if the audience overlooks his sly evocation of the tie between Chinese Americans and the railroad, they can hardly ignore the ethnic humour of Grace's twin strategies for obnoxious customers: 'If the customer's Chinese, you insult them by giving forks . . . . If the customer's Anglo, you starve them by not giving forks' (p. 10).

The summer after its National Playwright's Conference workshop, *FOB* premiered at the New York Shakespeare Festival. Papp recalled: '*FOB* reminded me of the 'greenhorns,' the Jews who came from Easter Europe. Even though the cultures were strikingly different, it was the same notion. The principle of someone coming from the old country who didn't know how to behave himself was very much part of my own tradition'.[4] The journey to America had transformed radically since Papp's progenitors: from Europeans landing at Ellis Island on the East Coast to Asians disembarking at Angel Island on the West. The shift is more than another geographical tilt to the American west or the gradual rise of Asia over Europe. The meaning of assimilation and ethnicity had changed profoundly too.

Following its US premiere in 1908, Israel Zangwill's *The Melting Pot* became an eponymous American ideal. By 1980 and *FOB's* premiere, assimilation was no longer an unquestioned ideal. The myth of the melting pot had been supplanted by another image – a salad bowl that preserves the distinct identity of each item it contains.

FOB won the 1980 Drama-Logue Playwriting Award, the 1981 US-Asia Institute Award, and a 1981 Obie for Best New Play.

The Dance and the Railroad (1981)

Hwang says of his next work: 'For some time I had wanted to write a play about the work of Chinese-Americans on the transcontinental railroad, and I wanted to center it around a particular historical incident, the strike of 1867'.[5] He retained the single set, small cast, Western setting, and youthful newcomer to America of his first play. This time the dialogue is perfectly colloquial since Lone and Ma are 'really' speaking Chinese. The new play pushes the theatricality of *FOB* further: instead of using a few discrete elements of Chinese Opera, *Dance* is infused with it to dramatize the gulf between a trained artist's devotion to his craft and a naive admirer's presumption that he could easily become a star. Successful plays with historical settings are always about the present more than the past, which is also true of *Dance*. It asks which requires more dedication: building a railroad or performing on stage? In the course of five scenes the neophyte Ma learns that play is not play at all. He develops a genuine work ethic, not Protestant but Chinese Opera.

Hwang's first period play is set in the nineteenth century, but the historical drama remains largely offstage. Strikes depend on solidarity, but a solitary Lone practises the flowing movement of Chinese Opera until Ma, like a messenger from another world, interrupts him by delivering bits of strike news. Thus begins the wary *pas de deux* between them that constitutes the play's central action.

Despite confinement to a bachelor world bereft of women, Ma and Lone are, at ages 18 and 20, more mature than the boys of *FOB*. Lone is a dancer and Ma aspires to be one. Neither is the emasculated coolie described by Leland Stanford, president of the Central Pacific Railroad laying track east from Sacramento (and founder of Hwang's alma mater) who called the Chinese workers 'quiet, peaceable, industrious, economical—ready and apt to learn all the different kinds of work'.[6] Because their labour was desperately needed, Lone and Ma entered the United States easily, unlike later generations of Chinese routinely excluded by law.[7] Far from being minions of Stanford's continental expansion, Lone and Ma assert themselves in a strike that wins shorter hours and higher pay. They retain their dignity and are not portrayed with unknowing condescension as often happens with characters of lesser economic means than their creator.

In Scene Two, Lone teaches Ma: 'When my body hurts too much to come here, I look at the other Chinamen and think, "They are dead. Their muscles work only because the white man forces them. I live because I can still force my muscles to work for me." Say it. "They are dead"' (p. 66). Lone echoes the image of Auschwitz Muselmänner (inmates on the brink of death) and the words of Camus on Sisyphus: 'A face that toils so close to stones is already stone itself.'[8] Lone's artistic discipline sets him free. After Ma fails his training at being a duck, then a locust, Lone admonishes: 'You think you understand the dedication one must have to be in the opera? You think it's the same as working on a railroad?' (p. 74)

Two years after the historical strike, Eastern and Western railways joined to connect the continent. A century later, Los Angeles-born

David Henry Hwang continued bridging East and West artistically. Commissioned by Henry Settlement House, *Dance* premiered in New York on 21 March 1981 and continued its run at his Manhattan home, the New York Shakespeare Festival Public Theater.

Family Devotions (1981)

As *Dance* moved towards opening, Hwang returned to a script he had already begun. Opening at Papp's Public Theater on 18 October 1981, *Family Devotions* marked his third New York production in 16 months. It was not received as positively as its predecessors. Hwang's first domestic comedy focuses on three generations of a family much like his own: Chinese American, Evangelical, prosperous and little interested in the place of their ethnic past in their worldly present. The family includes a surrogate for Hwang himself, Chester, a young professional violinist. The play's inciting incident is Di-Gou's arrival from 'Communist' China to visit Ama and Popo, sisters he has not seen since the Chinese Revolution. They now live with extended family in a wealthy Los Angeles enclave. Comedy fuels the manic energy driving the play until mistakes about the true identity of a deceased aunt who converted the family to Christianity are revealed. Amidst an at-home revival meeting, *Family Devotions* turns deadly serious when, like scores of American family plays before it, truth shatters a family secret.

The play is dedicated to Sam Shepard, but this whacky family could live as comfortably in Christopher Durang's universe.[9] Ama reveals her geopolitics through the promise of a friend: '"I will send you a picture. If Communists are good, I will stand—if bad, I will sit." . . . . In picture she sent, she was lying down!' (pp. 98–9) Di-gou quashes his sisters' preconceptions of life in the People's Republic of China: he has a servant and a chauffeur. He also speaks better English than they, thanks to his UCLA medical education decades earlier.

Ethnic humour has a long history on stage, but *Family Devotions* offers fresh variations to audiences unfamiliar with Chinese American families. The contortions of Ama's and Popo's English may be familiar, but their prejudice against Japan is not. They resent that the father of Robert, Amo's son-in-law and Chester's father, traded with the Japanese during the war; they are concerned that Seiji Ozawa leads Chester's orchestra; son-in-law Wilbur, who is Japanese-American and owns their Bel Air home, contributes to his own ridicule by wearing his hair permed.

Family Devotions opens with a spotlight on a Chinese face that the audience later recognizes as Di-Gou's. In the play's most poignant moment, he asks Chester to use his violin as a mirror: 'the shape of your face is the shape of faces back many generations—across an ocean, in another soil. You must become one with your family before you can hope to live away from it' (p. 126). Ama and Popo traded their Chinese heritage and identity for Christian ones. Amid the mayhem at the play's end, Hwang hints at an authentic future for himself and the next generation of the family: The audience sees a spotlight on the face of Chester, finally poised to emancipate himself from his family, head East, and begin his career. He bears an Anglicized name but embodies – to a degree his older relatives cannot – the presence of the ethnic past within his American present.

M. Butterfly (1988)

Hwang's recalls that in May 1986: 'A friend asked, had I heard about the French diplomat who'd fall in love with a Chinese actress, who subsequently turned out to be not only a spy, but a man?' (p. 94) How could this be? Hwang imagined the diplomat falling in love with a fantasy stereotype: 'The idea of doing a deconstructivist *Madame Butterfly* immediately appealed to me. This, despite the fact that I didn't even know the plot of the opera! I knew Butterfly only as a cultural stereotype; speaking of an Asian woman, we would sometimes say, "She's pulling a Butterfly"' (p. 95). Two years later, *M. Butterfly* opened on Broadway and earned Hwang a Tony Award for Best Play.

The dramatic potential of the diplomat's mysterious story is self-evident, but as with *Dance*, Hwang was little interested in historical facts. Transcending the restricted time and unified settings of his previous plays, he created an epic tapestry interconnecting racism, sexism and imperialism 'all being manifestations', he says, of an attempt 'to make "the other" less than oneself. I also tried to deal with my discomfort with the perceived "exotic" elements of my work by facing it squarely'.[10] After *Family Devotions* he had not written for two years: 'I hit a period of writer's block and I wondered if I was sort of just creating Orientalia for the intelligentsia . . . repackaging the old stereotypes in more intellectually hip forms'.[11]

Dialectical tensions crisscross *M. Butterfly*: male and female, gay and straight, fantasy and reality, East and West, and colonial power versus colonized people. Above all else it is a love story. Conjured retrospectively by Rene Gallimard, the diplomat, from the cell where he has been imprisoned for treason, *M. Butterfly's* plot jumps freely in time and space as quicksilver as memory itself. One Gallimard flashback sometimes interrupts another. Serving as a raconteur who addresses the audience directly, as a quasi-stage manager who sets scenes and effects transitions and as the central character too, Gallimard is the nexus of almost every scene. Avoiding chronology, he unspools his story in a tantalizing sequence that intensifies the drama. In the first two scenes he reveals that people laugh at him over his apparent sexual confusion, but it is not until 20 scenes later that he visually perceives that his 'perfect woman' is actually a man.

Time is fluid and subjective. It slows when Hwang wants, as in the treason trial. Elsewhere, time accelerates: the earliest scene chronologically is 1947, the latest the Paris trial of 1986. In between, decades go unmentioned (and unmissed). In one sense, the entire play transpires in the five scenes set in Gallimard's cell; the others are imagined from his cell. His many costume changes help the audience follow the time line as he 'escapes' incarceration.

Madame Butterfly (1904) is frequently produced, but Hwang could not assume that his audience knew its central characters or plot any more than he had. In the third, fifth and sixth scenes Gallimard summarizes its plot and conjures characters who speak a libretto updated by Hwang to include modern idioms. These lead to the moment Gallimard's future lover, Song Liling, makes her unforgettable entrance singing the role of Madame Butterfly at a Beijing soiree. Gallimard is immediately smitten even as Song proffers what becomes a major theme: 'It's one of your favorite fantasies, isn't it? The submissive Oriental woman and the cruel white man' (p. 17). The comment applies to both the inner play of

Song portraying a variation on Puccini's *Butterfly* and the outer play Hwang invented to track the equally fatal love affair between Gallimard and Song. Their first meeting, as in so many romances, sets the tone for decades to come. In a *coup de théâtre* marking the play's climax, Gallimard escapes the chrysalis of his cell by transforming from the pursuer of Butterfly into Butterfly herself. He declares 'Death with honor is better than life . . . life with dishonor' (p. 92), then kills himself ritualistically as in Puccini's opera.

Song is trained in Chinese (Beijing) opera, which has a tradition (*dan*) of men portraying women. In seducing Gallimard, Song seems as adept at portraying the *idea* of female seduction as its reality; this works for Gallimard who seems, similarly, as comfortable with the *idea* of masculinity as its reality. Song tells the court, 'it was my job to make him think I was a woman. And chew on this: it wasn't all that hard' (p. 82).

M. Butterfly's voyeuristic appeal appears to be over mistaken anatomy; but what is mistaken at a far deeper level is identity. Gallimard is a kind of everyman (and woman) whose life experience is common: he idealizes the person he loves, is consumed by fantasies so vivid they seem more real than life itself, and suffers grievously following the inevitable shattering of his illusions. In this sense, *M. Butterfly* shares less with memory plays like *The Glass Menagerie* and *Equus* than with Pirandello's dramatic puzzles that obliterate distinctions between illusion and reality. Gallimard deludes himself about far more than his love's gender. Like Roy Cohn, the man and the character in Tony Kushner's subsequent *Angels in America*, he self-identifies as heterosexual, which means that any sexual act he performs is, to him, heterosexual.

Hwang's play is structured, as it were, of Chinese boxes, including a Chinese man who portrays a Japanese woman and pretends to be a Chinese woman. Gallimard calls himself 'a man who loved a woman created by a man'. Which male creator does he mean: Song? Puccini and his librettists who made Butterfly famous? Belasco's play that was the basis for Puccini? The short story by John Luther Long that Belasco adapted? In the experience of live theatre, it is Hwang who created a man who loved a woman created by a man.

Hwang deconstructs the blithe stereotype of Asian women as delicate, passive and submissive in pleasing Western men, their supposed superiors. While praised for dissecting this hyper-feminine stereotype, *M. Butterfly* has been criticized for perpetuating another: effeminate Asian men. In *Yankee Dawg You Die* by Japanese-American playwright Philip Kan Gotanda, a contemporary and friend of Hwang's, a character who is an actor derides the available parts: 'They fucking cut off our balls and made us all houseboys on the evening soaps. *(Calls out.)* "Get your very own neutered, oriental houseboy!"'[12]

Golden Child (1996–8)

Where *M. Butterfly* focuses on a central character enamoured with the 'exotic' East, or at least his (mis)perception of it, *Golden Child* dramatizes the reverse: an Eastern patriarch beguiled by the West converts his extended family to its modern mores. This metamorphosis, like Song's, includes changing clothes, external emblems of the profound transformation from a traditional if restrictive past to an uncertain future. Christianity, monogamy, female education and individual freedom supplant old customs such as ancestor worship, polygamy, foot binding and collective responsibility. At its simplest level, *Golden Child* contextualizes the roots of one Chinese American family.

The play's genesis is the conversion to Christianity of Hwang's great-grandfather, as told to Hwang by his maternal grandmother when he was 10. She had previously appeared as Ama in *Family Devotions;* this time she is Eng Ahn, the golden child of the title. She appears as both a wilful 10-year old in 1918 China and as an old woman returned from the dead, the mother of a contemporary American writer whose dream devolves into the palpable story of his ancestors. This awkward framing device makes the core of *Golden Child* a dream play within a ghost story. Whereas *Family Devotions* lampoons a family's religiosity and rues the denial of its Chinese past, *Golden Child* focuses on the domestic drama of transformation from old ways to new.

Tieng-bin, the family patriarch, is a wealthy businessman. When the land fails and peasants risk starving, he opens his gate to them. His entrepreneurship, resourcefulness and sense of responsibility benefit the collective even if his economics are pre-socialist and his work ethic pre-Protestant. He yearns for a different life and hopes to escape the ghosts of past generations by tearing down the altars of ancestor worship and embracing the freedom of individuality, an apparently new concept to China at the time. The play's central conflict between tradition and modernity is voiced when the only wife Tieng-bin married for love counters his ideal: 'You want me to abandon my parents? Let their spirits wander alone for eternity? . . . . Is that what's best for us? To forget about others, and think only about ourselves?' (p. 45).

Although Tieng-bin converts to Christianity, the life he idealized does not follow. He laments: 'Papa, Mama—this is how you punish a disobedient son? Take from me the wife I love, even the wife I respect, leaving me with the one for whom I feel . . . nothing' (p. 59). His individual enterprise leads to a revolution within his family, but he is twice widowed and faces a solitary future with a duplicitous wife. Despite personal disappointment, his belief in a better life persists: 'There's a whole new generation of men who will want an educated wife. Not some backwards girl hobbling around on rotting feet, filling the room with the stench of death!' (p. 13). The golden child's bound feet are liberated. She will attend school and become devoted to Jesus. For all the play's focus on change and embrace of modernity, its world remains highly patriarchal. The peasants follow their landlord's lead and are baptized too.

Golden Child embodies a version of the culture wars fought in the United States over multiculturalism and diversity. Here it is not a national struggle between political right and left but a single family's divide over preserving the old versus embracing the new. Is equipoise possible? Change is obviously easier to believe in than to effect.

Following workshops and productions at a series of not-for-profit theatres across the country, the play premiered in 1996 at Hwang's first theatrical home, the New York Shakespeare Festival and he received his second Obie. After further development, it opened on Broadway in 1998. Hwang was nominated for a Tony, but the production ran only two months.

Yellow Face (2007)

Face Value (1993) closed before its scheduled Broadway opening, but it gave Hwang a central idea for *Yellow Face*; the echo between their titles is no coincidence. He says, 'The play is a mix of fact and fiction, in a mock stage documentary style, about a character based on me'.[13] In 1990 Hwang had become a leader of opponents to the casting of Caucasian Jonathan Pryce as an Eurasian in the Broadway production of *Miss Saigon*. In what might be called a series of Chinese boxes more than 15 years later, *Yellow Face* ridicules an imagined production of *Face Value* and its author's casting of a white actor to play an Asian character. Hwang says: 'I've been struggling since the *Miss Saigon* incident back in 1990 to make sense of, how do you talk about the nuances of race, both the desire to get past race and the awareness that racism still exists? How do you balance those two?'[14]

He does so by transmuting mistaken (racial) identity – a central device in farce – until identity itself becomes the focus. Racial and ethnic identity, central to the so-called 'identity politics' of American cultural and political discourse since the 1970s, may not sound like a promising focus for comedy, but *Yellow Face* is often hilarious in skewering its subject and characters, especially one called DHH who posits, 'When you write an autobiographical play, no one uses their real name. That would be self-indulgent' (p. 63). Hwang mocks his surrogate repeatedly. DHH calls himself 'the poster child for political correctness' (p. 13), but in college he survived a hunger strike by fasting in shifts. Hwang gives new meaning to the term 'self-abuse' when DHH ends an email chat with a character called Yellowgurl8 by asking, 'So—what are you wearing?' (p. 54) and again when a theatre-loving bookstore owner recognizes the playwright buying Asian porn. Hwang's self-lacerating 'mocumentary'[15] is filled with in-jokes about making theatre, especially casting. Marcus Gee does not instigate the public deception that embroils him. Rather, like all actors, he auditions, is offered a part and does his best to transform himself, going so far as 'becoming' Asian American. Must Hamlet be played by an actual Dane? A college student? A man? DHH articulates a *reduction ad absurdum* when he confers with his agent, 'So long as I help Marcus pass as an Asian, I can still fire him for being white' (p. 29). As *Yellow Face* evolves, Marcus 'plays along' to embrace the Chinese concept of 'face', which he explains as 'the face we choose to show the world—reveals who we really are . . . . I've chosen *my* face. And now I'm becoming the person

I've always wanted to be' (p. 43). DHH echoes Marcus in the play's final words, 'I go back to work, searching for my own face' (p. 70). DHH is trapped by the 'reality' of a construct, race, that does not truly exist.

Yellow Face moves rapidly through scores of characters, half of them representations of real people, and dozens of vignettes including investigations of John Hwang, Wen Ho Lee and Henry Y. Hwang, here abbreviated HYH. The playwright observes, 'The role of my father originally started out as a much more minor character, and, as he tended to do in life, he just kind of took over the play. In a way, the play, for all its dealing with history of the movement and the history of multiculturalism and all these cultural contradictions, is at heart a father-son story'.[16] Hwang skewers HYH almost as sharply as DHH, but the play also pays homage. Gregarious, voluble and like many immigrants utterly uncritical in his embrace of American ideals, HYH dies near the end of a play he infuses with his abiding values. DHH reflects: 'That was Dad's dream: a world where he could be Jimmy Stewart. And a white guy—can even be an Asian. *(Pause.)* That's what you do after your father dies. You start making his dream your own' (p. 69).

Yellow Face premiered in May 2007 at the Mark Taper Forum in Los Angeles. Later that year the Public Theatre produced it in New York, which led to Hwang's third Obie. Still, unlike *M. Butterfly, Face Value, The Flower Drum Song* or *Chinglish* (2011), *Yellow Face* did not have enough popular potential to tempt Broadway producers. George S. Kaufman famously quipped, 'satire is what closes on Saturday night'. Although some of the many parts of *Yellow Face* do not cohere, it is exceedingly funny along the way. Perhaps American audiences have difficulty giving themselves license to be amused by an edgy play's conundrums, enigmas and contradictions when, as Cornel West suggests, race matters.

Summary

Ezra Pound famously urged writers to 'make it new'. Theatre has generally been more pragmatic and earthbound than poetry since playwrights can be constrained by artistic and financial collaborators while making their plays palpable on stage. A more plebeian expectation for theatre writers than Pound's would be: make the new familiar or the familiar new. Hwang's newness has been to expand the range of drama and broaden what holds an audience's attention. Asian and Asian American characters are no longer so novel. In 1990 he observed presciently that 'multicultural plays and multicultural theaters are ultimately the way of the future'.[17] He has contributed to and benefitted from a culture now embracing an increasingly broad perspective. August Wilson's *Ma Rainey's Black Bottom* was developed at the National Playwrights Conference three years after *FOB*. Wilson completed his 10-play cycle nearly 25 years later, a span also marking Hwang's ascendancy.

He says, 'When I first started writing plays I had no particular desire to write about myself as an Asian American or as a person of color'.[18] All characters in his first three plays are Asian or Asian American. In the years ahead he consciously evolved to a multicultural model that includes characters from a range of heritages.

Hwang started college only a few years after America's first ethnic studies programmes began at nearby San Francisco State University (1968) and Berkeley (1969). In an introduction to *Dance*, he writes: 'America has traditionally denied the importance of its minorities, and this denial has been reflected in its theater, which has portrayed a relatively homogenous society, with white males as the centers and prime movers. This is ethnic theater—but the theater of only one ethnic group. The great American temptation is to be suckered into the melting pot. We somehow believe that to be less 'ethnic' is to be more human. In fact, the opposite is true.'[19]

American theatre has a long history of 'ethnic' characters appearing as caricatures in plays, minstrelsy and vaudeville. The rise of realism led to a growing expectation of verisimilitude, and no one is better at creating life-like characters than writers (and actors) working within their own realm of experience. Still, playwrights often experience added pressure from compatriots when popular success led to mainstream consciousness of their plays: Mart Crowley's *Boys in the Band* (1970) cannot represent all gay experience any more than Luis Valdez's *Zoot Suit* (1978) dramatizes every Chicano family. Hwang faced similar second-guessing with *M. Butterfly.*

Stereotypical images of Asians long included sensuous dragon ladies, evil scientists, psychopathic soldiers and malevolent despots. Positive images such as all Asian Americans being excellent in school, deferential to authority and masterful in martial arts are equally clichéd. Charlie Chan, the portly detective spouting pseudo-Confucian wisdom as profound as fortune cookie aphorisms, was once the most popular fictional character in the world. When only a few images exist in the popular imagination, illusion and reality meld, especially in an art like theatre that encourages willing suspension of disbelief.

When pioneering writers like Hwang move past stock imagery, their communities often respond with added expectations. The more popular the work, the stronger the pressure to meet a priori litmus tests such as all representations of ethnicity should be positive. Backlash among the intelligentsia suggests that no work can be financially successful, artistically worthy and politically acceptable all at the same time. When artists are expected to speak for an entire people, they are judged sociologically rather than artistically. After Nancy Kwan starred in *The World of Suzie Wong* she was told, 'You created an image that all Chinese women are prostitutes'.[20] Production of *Mrs. Warren's Profession* had been prohibited, but not because the Lord Chamberlain thought Shaw's former prostitute represented *all* English women.

Hwang's first three plays were produced off-Broadway; his recent plays have moved from major regional productions to Broadway. Viewed narrowly in terms of economics, his career, like his father's, substantiates China's nineteenth-century name of America: *Gam Sam,* Gold Mountain, the place immigrants could earn their fortunes, though most did not.

When Hwang was born, America's Asian American population was about one million, approximately 0.5 per cent. Today it numbers over 15 million, nearly 5 per cent of the whole. During this period Asian Americans also became known as a 'model minority'.[21] Asian Americans are among the fastest growing groups, and the idea of ethnic identity is expanding too. Hwang's personal life reflects this trend. After divorcing Ophelia Y. M. Chong, a Chinese Canadian artist, he married Caucasian actress Kathryn Layng. Their children were first counted in the 2000 census, which was the first that allowed individuals to identify themselves by more than one race. Nearly seven million Americans, 2.4 per cent of the population, selected more than one racial identity that year.

Hwang's collaborators also reflect the growth of multiculturalism. Between *M. Butterfly* (1988) and *Yellow Face* (2007), his only full-length play to open was *Golden Child* (1998).[22] Hwang's writing had not slowed over the two decades; his embrace of musical theatre accelerated. Following his first musical collaboration, with American Philip Glass in 1989, he worked as librettist with Korean Unsuk Chin, Argentine Osvaldo Golijoy, Chinese Bright Sheng, Canadian Howard Shore and two exceedingly popular Britons commissioned by Disney: Elton John for *Aida* (2000), Hwang's second Broadway show inspired by Italian opera, and Phil Collins for *Tarzan* (2006). For his most ambitious musical project, he rewrote *Flower Drum Song* (2002) by Rogers and Hammerstein, Broadway's most illustrious partnership, which earned Hwang his third Tony nomination. Terence McNally and Marsha Norman are the only other contemporary playwrights to swing between straight plays and musicals so readily.

Hwang says, 'all American theater is ethnic theater to some degree, that even if you have Tennessee Williams for instance, writing primarily about whites in the South, that a lot of writers derive their authenticity from focusing on a particular group and then drawing the universality from those particular specifics'.[23] A generation earlier and half-way around the world, South African Athol Fugard had similarly focused on the specificity that attracts playwrights, 'My job is to witness as truthfully as I can the nameless and destitute of one little corner of the world'.[24] Both Hwang and Fugard strive to represent diverse and multicultural human experience in ways that elicit the empathy of audiences around the world. Beyond demographics, sociology or anthropology, this is the reason their plays are so widely produced, revived, published and studied. Hwang's 1999 anthology is named for one of his short plays, *Trying to Find Chinatown*. The emphasis seems to rest on 'trying'. A dozen years later, as Hwang's career and America itself have evolved, Chinatown is more and more likely to be found on Main Street as well as Broadway.

Primary Sources

Works by David Henry Hwang

M. Butterfly (New York: Plume, 1988).
Golden Child (New York: Theatre Communications Group, 1998).
Trying to Find Chinatown. The Selected Plays: FOB, The Dance and the Railroad, Family Devotions, The Sound of a Voice, The House of Sleeping Beauties, Bondage, The Voyage, Trying to Find Chinatown (New York: Theatre Communications Group, 1999).
Yellow Face (New York: Theatre Communications Group, 2009).

Secondary Sources

Benson, Mary, 'Athol Fugard and "One Little Corner of the World"', *yale/theatre* 4 (Winter 1973), 55–64.

Camus, Albert, *The Myth of Sisyphus: And Other Essays* (NY: Vintage, 1955).

Chan, Paul, Frank Chin, Lawson Fusao Inada and Shawn Wong, *The Big Aiiieeeee!: An Anthology of Chinese American and Japanese American Literature,* (NY: Meridian, 1991).

DiGaetani, John L., *A Search for a Postmodern Theater: Interviews with Contemporary Playwrights, Contributions in Drama and Theatre Studies*, No. 41, (NY: Greenwood Press, 1991), 161–74.

Dong, Arthur, *Hollywood Chinese: The Chinese in American Feature Films* (Los Angeles: Deep Focus Productions, 2008).

Gee, Deborah, *Slaying the Dragon* (New York: Women Make Movies, 1988).

Gerard, Jeremy, 'David Hwang: Riding on the Hyphen', *The New York Times Magazine,* 13 March 1988, pp. 44 and 88–9.

Gotanda, Phillip Kan, *Yankee Daw You Die* (New York: Dramatists Play Service, 1991).

Ho, Howard, 'Multicultural Absurdities: An Interview with David Henry Hwang', *Asian Pacific Arts,* 23 October 2010. http://asiapacificarts.usc.edu/w_apa/showarticle.aspx?articleID=16302&AspxAutoDetectCookieSupport=1

Hwang, David Henry, 'Abramowitz Memorial Lecture', 15 April 1994. http.www.mit.edu/arts/abramowitz.html.

—, 'Evolving a Multicultural Tradition', *MELUS* (The Society for the Study of the Multi-Ethnic Literature of the United States), 16, 3. (Autumn 1989–Autumn 1990), 16–19.

—, 'Foreword', In Chay Yew (ed.), *Version 3.0: Contemporary Asian American Plays* (NY: Theatre Communications Group, 2011), pp. ix–xii.

Kim, Elaine H., *Asian American Literature: An Introduction to the Writings and Their Social Context* (Philadelphia: Temple, 1982).

Pace, Eric, 'I Write Plays to Claim a Place for Asian-Americans', *New York Times*. 12 July 1981, 4D.

Piepenburg, Erik, 'He Writes about What He Knows', *New York Times,* 2 December 2007, II, 6:1.

Street, Douglas, *David Henry Hwang* (Boise: Boise State University Press, 1989).

Takaki, Ronald, *A Different Mirror: A History of Multicultural America* (Boston: Little Brown, 1993).

Notes

1. David Henry Hwang, 'Abramowitz Memorial Lecture', (unpaginated).
2. Jeremy Gerard, 'David Hwang: Riding on the Hyphen', p. 88.
3. David Henry Hwang, *Broken Promises: Four Plays*, p. 3.
4. Jeremy Gerard, 'David Hwang: Riding on the Hyphen'.
5. Eric Pace, '"I Write Plays to Claim a Place for Asian-Americans"', 4D.
6. Ronald Takaki, *A Different Mirror: A History of Multicultural America*, p. 196.
7. The Chinese Exclusion Act of 1882, which prevented Chinese from entering the United States and becoming natural citizens, was the first US immigration law based on race. It perpetuated the alien status of 'yellow peril' Chinese living in America until the Chinese Exclusion Repeal Act of 1943.
8. Albert Camus, *The Myth of Sisyphus: And Other Essays*, p. 89.
9. For comparisons with Shepard see Douglas Street, *David Henry Hwang*, p. 26.
10. David Henry Hwang, 'Evolving a Multicultural Tradition', p. 18.
11. David Henry Hwang, 'Abramowitz Memorial Lecture'.
12. Philip Kan Gotanda, *Yankee Daw You Die,* (New York: Dramatists Play Service, 1991), p. 27.
13. Erik Piepenburg, 'He Writes about What He Knows', p. 6.
14. Ibid.
15. Howard Ho, 'Multicultural Absurdities: An Interview with David Henry Hwang'.
16. Howard Ho, 'Multicultural Absurdities'.
17. David Henry Hwang, 'Evolving a Multicultural Tradition', p. 19.
18. Ibid., p. 16.
19. David Henry Hwang, *The Dance and the Railroad and Family Devotions*, p. 7.
20. Interviewed in Deborah Gee, *Slaying the Dragon*. For what Hwang calls 'the official Asian-American syndrome', see Hwang, 'Abramowitz Memorial Lecture'.
21. For more on the history and subtext of this fraught term, see Elaine H. Kim, *Asian American Literature: An Introduction to the Writings and Their Social Context*, p. 177.
22. Hwang has also written many short plays including *The Sound of a Voice* (1983), *As the Crow Flies* (1986), *Bondage* (1992), *Trying to Find Chinatown* (1996), *Bang Kok* (1996),

Merchandising (1999), *Jade Flowerpots and Bound Feet* (2001), *The Great Helmsman* (2007), and *A Very DNA Reunion* (2010). Adaptations include Kawabata's *The House of Sleeping Beauties* (1983), Ibsen's *Peer Gynt* (1998) and *Tibet through the Red Box* (2004) by Peter Sis.

23. Hwang, 'Evolving a Multicultural Tradition', p. 17.
24. Mary Benson, 'Athol Fugard and "One Little Corner of the World"', p. 55.

6 ADRIENNE KENNEDY

Klaus Benesch

Funnyhouse of a Negro; The Owl Answers; A Rat's Mass; A Movie Star Has to Star in Black and White; The Alexander Plays: She Talks to Beethoven; Ohio State Murders; The Film Club (A Monologue by Suzanne Alexander); Dramatic Circle

Introduction

According to Werner Sollors, the editor of the first substantial collection of Adrienne Kennedy's works, Kennedy's plays have not only affinities to the work of American dramatists as formally and thematically wide-ranging as Arthur Miller, Edward Albee, Sam Shepard, Amiri Baraka or Ntozake Shange. They also echo 'the entire dramatic tradition, from Greek tragedy to the theatre of the absurd, from Euripides to Shakespeare, and from Chekhov to Tennessee Williams'.[1] Add to these strikingly wide-ranging formal influences the tendency of many of her plays to act as a kind of prism through which individual characters are fragmented, dissected almost into multiple identities that frequently resist the viewer's/reader's desire to reintegrate or make whole again, and you are also looking at one of the most pronounced 'deconstructivist', postmodern playwrights of contemporary American theatre. Kennedy's obvious complexity has made her, however, a kind of 'academic' writer. Many of her plays are performed in college and university workshops or on European stages rather than on Broadway or in American resident theatres. Her captivating style has sometimes been described as 'hallucinogenic' and mysterious, and critical responses to her dramatic work continued to be divided. *Funnyhouse of a Negro*, the 1964 play that won Kennedy an Obie Award and succeeding international acclaim, had originally been dismissed by reviewers and closed after a total of 46 performances.

Debuting in the 1960s, when she introduced an experimental, visceral style to American off-off Broadway stages that adumbrated aspects of 'performance art' long before the term had been coined, Kennedy continues to blend private and collective experience in dazzling, stream-of-consciousness one-act plays. In her autobiographical *People Who Led to My Plays* (1987), a magical 'scrapbook' of personal vignettes, photographs and images, Kennedy explains how she had come across some of the motley personages that frequent her plays (from Shakespeare, van Gogh and Queen Victoria to Clark Gable, Ingrid Bergman, Paul Robeson, Billy Holiday and Eleanor Roosevelt). Early on, Kennedy, who had been born on 13 September 1931, into a middle-class family, began writing and keeping diaries about her siblings and parents. Her father, a social worker, and her mother, a school teacher, instilled in her a knack for reading and, through her involvement in church activities, provided a stable and protected social environment. Growing up in a largely integrated, culturally diverse neighbourhood of Cleveland, Ohio, as a child Kennedy had not known overt racism. It was only during trips to her grandmother in Montezuma, Georgia, and later in Columbus, where she attended Ohio State University, that she learnt about the impact of 'race' on the lives of black people. As she is a light-skinned 'Negro' with family roots in both the black and white families of Montezuma, the racially tense atmosphere she encountered at Ohio State has left an indelible mark on both herself and her dramatic writing. Like many African American women writers, however, Kennedy's intense engagement with personal experience has not led to the exclusion of social involvement or political issues in her plays. If much of her dramatic work is highly personal, sometimes autobiographical, Kennedy always investigates the personal self in relation with the social and political world from which it unfolds.

The Plays

Funnyhouse of a Negro (1964)

Funnyhouse of a Negro, Kennedy's first and probably her best-known one-act play, was written partly in Accra (Ghana), partly in Rome; the playwright had returned to Europe after a field trip to Ghana with her husband, by then a professor at Hunter College in New York. As she explains in both the postscript to the play, 'On the Writing of *Funnyhouse of a Negro*', and in her memoir, *People Who Led to My Plays*, many of the characters and places are highly autobiographical. The play centres on Sarah, a biracial girl, who agonizes over her mixed racial heritage. The entire play is set in Sarah's room, scarcely furnished with a bed, a writing table and a mirror. While Sarah sits in this private space, which is set at centre stage, the rest of the play unfolds around her. In addition to Sarah the Duchess of Hapsburg, Queen Victoria, Jesus, Patrice Lumumba, Raymond (the white, ghostly 'funnyman of the funnyhouse') and Sarah's mother and her landlady (the 'Funnyhouse Lady') have appearances.

According to Kennedy's meticulous stage directions, the play is designed to evoke an enchanting, mysterious, even ghostly atmosphere. Black and white are the dominating colours [e.g. *the Queen's chambers are set in 'a strong white LIGHT, while the rest of the stage is in unnatural BLACKNESS'* (p. 12) *and there are great black RAVENS flying about, a woman who carries before her a bald head, and faces excessively powdered so that they possess the expressionless quality and stillness as in the face of the dead.*] As in several of her later plays, Kennedy also employs sound as a framing device [in some of the scenes we hear a constant, staggering KNOCKING or the uncanny laughing of the 'mad characters in a funnyhouse' (p. 15)]. Perhaps the most striking feature of the play is its intriguing treatment of space, the ease with which theatrical spaces, often overlapping and in dialogue with each other, are created by way of light and sound. In fact, the play may well be said to turn on Sarah's attempt to explore and make her own the dichotomous, racialized cultural spaces that unfold around her: the history saturated spaces of the White World and the tragic, disaster-ridden spaces of black life, both in America and elsewhere.

Funnyhouse clearly represents an intimately personal investigation of (the author's) self. Yet it also foregrounds issues such as colonialism, independence, gender oppositions and, most prominently, contradictions among the black and white races. By constantly blurring autobiographical experience with world history, e.g. the separation of Kennedy's parents and the Duchess of Hapsburg, the sister of the Belgian King Leopold II and wife of the ill-fated Mexican Emperor Maximilian, *Funnyhouse* questions the boundaries between self and history, male and female, black and white. It also deconstructs the notion of identity as a given, by breaking it down into several selves, wearing masks and speaking (and repeating) the same lines, though with a slightly different twist. Kennedy's eclectic borrowing of theatrical techniques (a Greek chorus, baroque allegories, Shakespearian comedy) and myths (Oedipus, the black Sambo figure, the 'New' Negro) from ancient times to the present is to create a surreal, mythopoetic quality which makes it difficult to sort out the good from the bad, right from wrong. The ensuing effect is, however, not entirely postmodern: in that it explores the issue of racial identity through imagined 'mythologized' spaces, *Funnyhouse* posits the tedious process of coming to terms with one's identity as a painful, frequently traumatic ritual, a continuous rite of passage energized by what critic Paul Bryant-Jackson has called her characters' 'inner dramaturgically fragmented and culturally contradictory restlessness'.[2]

The Owl Answers (1965)

Written in 1963 during Kennedy's confined pregnancy in Ghana and first produced in 1965 at the Whitebarn Theatre, Westport, Connecticut, *The Owl Answers* – like *Funnyhouse* – draws on personal experience. It is centred around the character of Clara Passmore, a Mulatto girl torn between the white and black worlds of her mixed ancestry. Her telling last name suggests the issue of 'passing' which for long had been a taboo among both white and black Americans. Thematically, *The Owl Answers* evokes, as Sollors points out, 'the complex family relations, reminiscent of Langston Hughes' play *Mulatto* (1935) . . . through Clara's changing identities as white man's "blood" daughter, black cook's daughter, black reverend's foster daughter, Virgin Mary, and owl' (p. x). Set on a stage that recalls the interior of a New York subway train, the eight actors take on the roles of many more characters, so that 'SHE who is CLARA PASSMORE' also becomes 'VIRGIN MARY who is the BASTARD who is the OWL' etc. The characters move smoothly in and out of these roles, against the backdrop of lights flashing, gates slamming and feathers falling. Like its predecessor, *The Owl Answers* also features historical figures – Shakespeare, Chaucer, William the Conqueror and sixteenth-century Queen of England Anne Boleyn. Dressed in their historical costumes, their lines are not spoken by one person specifically, but by all or part of them, thus making their interchangeable voices the commentary of a larger community, as in a Greek chorus.

The subway setting recalls another famous African-American one-act play, coeval with the production of *The Owl Answers*, LeRoi Jones' *Dutchman* (1964), in which the public confrontation between a black man and a white woman leads to the highly symbolic sacrificial death of the former. Yet while *Dutchman* is entirely predicated on stereotypical assumptions of black manhood and on the often masochistic elements of black-white relations, Kennedy's play refuses to settle on one stable meaning. Instead it invokes by way of the owl imagery an enchanting, uncanny atmosphere, not unlike Shakespeare's *Midsummer Night's Dream* or Eugene O'Neill's *Emperor Jones*. The effect is one of blurring the everyday experience of black people, with a complex history of race and racial transgressions in the West that can no longer be clearly identified and, therefore, dealt with by the individual alone. What *The Owl Answers* again brings to the fore is thus not only the liminal, precarious status of black identity; it also teases out the complexity and composite nature of human identity at large. Though undeniably personal, the owls Kennedy remembers at night in the trees outside of her home in Ghana or as elements of complex African masks, as in the mask 'of a woman with a bird flying through her forehead',[3] take the action to a level of universal importance that transcends the author's autobiographical experience.

A Rat's Mass (1966)

A Rat's Mass tells the story of two siblings, BROTHER RAT and SISTER RAT, who are half animal half human. Together with ROSEMARY, JESUS, JOSEPH, MARY, TWO WISE MEN and a SHEPHERD, they enact a Catholic mass, including a holy communion and a procession. During the course of the action, the sister and brother increasingly become animal-like, their voices sounding more like 'gnawing' or rat sounds. In its stunning description of humans' regress to the status of rats and in its blurring of different levels of time and place (a holy chapel, the Roman Capitol, Georgia, the Nazi invasion of Europe etc.), the play employs an absurdist aesthetics, often associated in American drama with Edward Albee, Arthur Kopit and Amiri Baraka. At a time when other African American playwrights set out to make a statement in the direction of black nationalism and black pride, Kennedy posits a world view that has lost its centre, a universe without orientation that 'gnaws' at the existence and identity of her frequently multiethnic characters. Abandoning mimetic representation Kennedy's theatre instead offers a 'dream' setting designed to unravel several intertwined myths of racial, sexual and cultural crisis.

In *A Rat's Mass* she pictures an absurd human condition marked by 'a philosophical/psychological/personal/cultural angst and including past, present, and future history, often occurring simultaneously'.[4] As critics have pointed out, the play might be called 'subversive' in that it also gnaws at an American understanding of self and community. The main action again pivots on personal guilt and trauma, BROTHER RAT's and SISTER RAT's childhood incest, which leads to their alienation and estrangement from the white Christian ethos. As Kennedy revealed in an article in *Drama Review*, the main image of *A Rat's Mass* was based on a dream she had while travelling from Paris to Rome: 'I had this dream in which I was being pursued by red, bloodied rats. It was [a] very powerful dream, and when I woke up the train had stopped in the Alps. It was at night. . . . I was just haunted by that image for years, about being pursued by these big, red rats'.[5] In *A Rat's Mass* the regressing siblings are also haunted by their past ('now there will always be rat blood on the rat walls of our rat house', p. 52), and though they yearn to go back to their childhood and redeem their original sin ('I'm praying to be atoned', p. 52), they also realize that the door to the past has been irreversibly closed and that they have to live with the burden of their illegitimate liaison: 'Bombs fall I am alone in our old house with an attic full of dead rat babies' (p. 52).

A Movie Star Has to Star in Black and White (1976)

Originally performed as a work in progress at the New York Shakespeare Festival in New York on 5 November 1976, *A Movie Star Has to Star in*

Black and White stands out among Kennedy's plays in that it consists of three scenes (instead of one act). The play opens (and ends) with an image of the Columbia Pictures Lady and it features well-known movie stars such as Paul Henreid, Jean Peters and Shelly Winters. The scenes mimic key scenes from famous Hollywood movies, but are also set in 'real' places (Bette Davis in *Now Voyager;* Marlon Brando in *Viva Zapata*; and Montgomery Clift in *A Place in the Sun*). Rather than making the actors repeat lines from the respective film with which they are associated, Kennedy has them discuss and sometimes read verbatim from her own earlier plays, especially *A Lesson in Dead Language* and *The Owl Answers*. The effect is quite stunning and also empowering: instead of creating characters that look like movie stars, Kennedy adapted the personality of famous stars to make them – literally – her own.

Thematically, *A Movie Star Has to Star in Black and White* clearly revolves around the cultural iconicity of Hollywood movies and their power to influence – both aesthetically and imaginatively – our own daily lives. The various movie stars re-enact scenes of private trauma and personal conflict (e.g. the separation of families, a miscarriage or the onset of menstruation) against the backdrop of classic Hollywood movies. They are thus turned into spokespersons for the playwright herself, who employs them to revisit her own career as an artist and writer and to foreground themes taken from her earlier plays. The quandary of a mixed racial identity, a theme that haunts many of Kennedy's plays, also reappears in *A Movie Star Has to Star in Black and White*. In response to an argument between two characters, tellingly called MOTHER and FATHER, about the light-skinned, 'yellow' mother's refusal to go back to the south, Kennedy has actor Jean Peters recite from her play *The Owl Answers*: 'I call God and the Owl answers, it haunts my tower, calling, its feathers are blowing against the cell wall, it comes feathered, great hollow-eyes . . . with yellow skin and yellow eyes, the flying bastard' (p. 73). As a blunt counter statement to the movies' underlying 'black-and-white' dichotomy, the quotation not only works to complicate the fantasy lives of Hollywood, it also questions the racial ideology that informs the sense of self in the Western world at large. Though reminiscent of her own mixed racial biography, Kennedy constantly defies the attempt of audiences to draw connections between the plays and her life by de-contextualizing and re-imagining these personal traces in surprisingly new and innovative dramatic forms.

The Alexander Plays: She Talks to Beethoven; Ohio State Murders; The Film Club (A Monologue by Suzanne Alexander); Dramatic Circle (1995)

The four dramas, collectively known as 'The Alexander Plays', mark a turning point in Kennedy's career as an introspective, psychoanalytical playwright. Joined together by the fictive personality of writer Suzanne Alexander, the dramatic style of these plays seems to have mellowed. Denying the characters to openly expose their hallucinations and personal catastrophes on stage, 'The Alexander Plays' instead introduce a softer, more (self-) reflective tone, one that taps into theatre's innate capacity to heal and make whole, rather than to strip bare and publicly display personal drama. The first of the four plays, *She Talks to Beethoven*, originally produced by River Arts in Woodstock, New York, in 1989, is again set in Accra, Ghana. Interspersed with a dialogue between Suzanne Alexander and Beethoven are voices on the radio that comment on the events involving the disappearance of David Alexander, Suzanne's husband; the African American expatriate community in Western Africa; and a projected play on Beethoven that Suzanne supposedly has been working on. As in all four of 'The Alexander Plays', the role of speech and dialogue seems to have significantly increased, to provide an almost epic, multi-vocal account of the burgeoning pan-African milieu in Ghana's capital during the 1950s. Yet despite their more pronounced 'narrative' form of representation, all four dramas also retain characteristics of Kennedy's earlier plays: the fragmentation of an authorial dramatic persona into different, sometimes antithetical selves (such as Beethoven, Frantz Fanon or Thomas Hardy), a strongly felt political undercurrent, the exploration of the role of popular culture and media and the self-reflective investigation of the unfolding of the dramatic work of the playwright herself.

In keeping with the pronounced self-reflective gesture of 'The Alexander Plays', Kennedy's authorial projection Suzanne Alexander tells Beethoven about a remark by her husband David, a university professor, who has felt 'that many scenes [of her play on Beethoven] are too romantic—and that [she] must read more diaries about [him]' (p. 143). In *She Talks to Beethoven* the famous composer acts as a kind of sounding-board for the playwright's alter ego, Suzanne Alexander, who is reading to him both from a Beethoven biography and from her own work. Struggling with the onset of impending deafness and his rapidly deteriorating physical condition, Beethoven also serves to articulate deep personal grief and thus, by proxy, to alleviate the traumatic experiences of Suzanne Alexander and, ultimately, Kennedy herself.

The same is true of *Ohio State Murders*, which had its world premiere at the Great Lakes Theater Festival on 7 March 1992, and had been hailed by some as Kennedy's most powerful play to date. Set at night amid 'hundreds of books on "O" level beneath the library at Ohio State [University]' (p. 152), *Ohio State Murders* revisits the racially tense atmosphere at Kennedy's alma mater during the early 1950s, juxtaposing the plight of a young, talented, aspiring African American writer with an infanticide that shook both the college and the mid-western city of Cleveland. Much of the events are recounted in a monologue by Suzanne Alexander, who returns to Ohio State to deliver a speech, and who performs scenes both in the present and in the past. In the opening scene, while rehearsing her talk, she explains that part of the reason for her being invited to the campus had been to shed light on her often violent, hypnotic aesthetics: 'I was asked to talk about the violent imagery in my work; bloodied heads, severed limbs, dead father, dead Nazis, dying Jesus. The chairman said, we do want to hear about your brief years at Ohio State but we also want you to talk about violent imagery in your stories and plays. When I visited Ohio State last year it struck me as a series of disparate dark landscapes just as it had in 1949, the autumn of my freshman year' (p. 152).

The initial reference to a 'series of dark disparate landscapes' sets the tone for the riveting drama in its entirety. What Suzanne has experienced as the biased, discriminatory treatment of an English professor, who refused – her excellent academic performance notwithstanding – to support her eventual enrolment as an English major, turns out a much less personal incident. Like the shadowy killer in the infanticide case, what blights the lives of Suzanne Alexander and other African American students at Ohio State (and elsewhere) is not so much the personal hatred of individuals, but the demon of racism, what African American writer Charles Johnson has called the plight of 'relative being',[6] of being judged solely on the basis of one's skin colour. Though employing similar techniques as some of the earlier plays, particularly the interspersion of literary para-texts such as quotations from Thomas Hardy's novel *Tess of the D'Urbervilles, Ohio State Murders* may thus well be said to be Kennedy's most straightforward political play, in which personal catastrophe serves to illuminate the larger problem of race relations and racially defined identities. It is perhaps also the play where Kennedy is most explicit about the roots of the often violent imagery in her work and the forces behind her idiosyncratic, sometimes painful dramatic style. As Suzanne states in the final lines of both her talk and the play itself, she had never been able 'to speak publicly' about her dead daughters and 'that is the main source of the violent imagery in [her] work' (p. 173) – likewise, to 'speak publicly' of and have others perform her private tribulations and anxieties and to connect personal experience with larger issues such as race, history and the quandaries of becoming a writer and playwright may also have been a major incentive for Kennedy to pursue and remain true to her own concept of contemporary American drama.

As Werner Sollors has pointed out, *The Film Club* and *Dramatic Circle*, the other two of 'The Alexander Plays', continue Kennedy's exploration of popular culture, particularly the movies; taken together, they represent two different theatrical modes, dramatic monologue (*The Film Club*) and the dramatization of events via performing interlocutors (*Dramatic Circle*). Set in London, in 1961, both turn on the capacity of popular culture to distract from but also express abstract fear and anxiety. Blending the events of Kennedy's trip from Accra to London in 1961 with quotations from *Dracula* and poems by revolutionary African poet David Diop, Suzanne Alexander's dramatic monologue powerfully underwrites the hopes, desperation and fears of postcolonial Ghana and the sympathetic African American expatriate community. Its companion piece, *The Dramatic Circle*, posits the same events, yet does not arrive at the same degree of perturbed anticipation and potential doom conveyed by Suzanne Alexander's voice in the more tightly knit monologue.

Summary

In *Unmaking Mimesis* Elin Diamond writes that 'no contemporary playwright has theatricalized the disturbances of identification with the acuity of Adrienne Kennedy'. To this assessment of Kennedy's singular place within contemporary American theatre, critic Claudia Barnett adds 'not only does Kennedy theatricalize these disturbances, she embodies them'.[7] Taken together, the two statements underwrite Kennedy's obvious obsession with matters of identity and the construction of self. They also point to the frequently quoted autobiographical orientation of Kennedy's oeuvre, of her attempt to translate her own private disturbances of identification into theatrical public performances. True, given the playwright's frankness about personal experiences that have influenced her work and her efforts to shed light on the sources and roots of her dramatic characters (as in *People Who Led to My Plays*), Kennedy's personal investment in almost all of her plays can hardly be overrated. Writing at a time when black theatre pushed for an all-out political, often afro-centric black aesthetic, Kennedy continued to personalize the political and to question smug identifications with either group, white or black. One might even state that her dramatic work is political only insofar as it regards the consequences of politics on the individual and her rapport with the larger world (including crucial issues such as sex, identity, history, creativity etc.). What is more, Kennedy's relentless investigation of how we (per-)form an identity tend to produce ever more complicated (rather than simplified) versions of self. In doing so, she posits a truly postmodern moment of uncertainty about who we are, a wavering between different, at times even antithetical identities.

Kennedy's drama has been repeatedly dubbed 'hypnotic' and 'surreal', and as such, it is indebted to a wide range of theatrical influences from both sides of the Atlantic, from Greek and Shakespearian classical tragedies to contemporary modern (and postmodern) drama, from past and present. Her explorations of liminal stages of existence and a deeply rooted 'angst' about one's own identity are, however, also an indication of Kennedy's understanding of theatre as an existential human art form. While exposing the treacherous dynamics of identity construction under conditions of racism and racial politics, her plays reinstate the fragile, fragmented individual as the centre of a mythical performance based on the dramatic conventions of *anagnorisis* (recognition), *pathos* (suffering) and *catharsis* (purification). 'White society', Kennedy once remarked, 'defines blacks in terms of clichés; I always felt that I'm being defined in terms of a cliché by white society'.[8] Since clichés frequently turn into powerful cultural myths, theatrical performances appear to be the one art form suited best to investigate contemporary myth-making. Contrary to the longer and laborious epic, the dramatic arts are most directly engaged with myths because, as Aristotle points out, they use 'recognition' as a stylistic tool to bring about 'a change from ignorance to knowledge'.[9] To convey meaning, dramatic performances stress the recurrence of types of events and characters already known to the viewer, thereby expressing fundamental human needs that transcend any particular form of society or historical frame of reference. What is more, like archaic myths, the dramatic mode involves the audience in a ritual of participation and identification. In the theatre, as Arthur Miller keenly observes, 'we see what we see on the stage not only with our own eyes but with the eyes of others'.[10]

Modern drama may be tainted, as George Steiner suggests, by the shadow of 'myth emptied of active belief',[11] yet the collective encounter of actors and audience in the theatre still unites the participants in a spectacle that suspends – at least momentarily – the need for rationalization. As we enter the theatre and watch the action unravel on stage, we also enter into an arena larger than our individual lives and our fragmented sense of the real. It is an arena where the spectator is revealed to himself 'so that he may touch others by virtue of the revelation of his mutuality with them'.[12] Likewise, Kennedy's dramatic oeuvre is grounded in a play of illusions about the self, our place in a changing, bewildering world and our ongoing search for meaning. Though bound by specific historical space-time contexts, her plays are also universal in that they posit multiple personae navigating a timeless theatrical universe. It is a universe in which public presentation and visibility always also includes its antithesis, that is, the ultimate effacement of the self as a recognizable and objectifiable entity. The striking charm and enchantment that mark the best of her plays are thus indebted to a paradox: the paradox of a confessional dramatic style that at once creates an arsenal of highly symbolical (personal) imagery, yet also erases the personality of the author/writer from scrutiny. In her best-known play *Funnyhouse of a Negro* this paradox takes the form of a panoply of diverse representations of a fragmented self that deny identification with merely one (real or imagined) personality. Later, in 'The Alexander Plays', it works via the authorial projection of a writer figure who simultaneously connects but also distances the viewer from the imagined self of the playwright.

Finally, it should not go unnoticed that Kennedy's plays frequently reference characters and themes from earlier plays, thus proffering the idea of a closed yet growing dramatic universe in its own right. As critics have pointed out, her constant recycling of earlier material may sometimes work against the autonomy of the individual play, necessitating, as it does, a basic knowledge of her work in its entirety in order to appreciate its allusive quality; or, it may lead to instant gratification for those who are well acquainted with her theatrical universe. As she mentions in a telephone interview with Claudia Barnett in 2002, 'I always had an ambition to write a cycle of plays, like, you know, great poets or something'.[13] The idea of a cycle or series of plays is tempting in part because it suggests a sense of wholeness or unity that transcends the limited meaning of each individual play. Though dismissed by post-structuralist critics as ultimately itself a fiction and myth, the concept of a unified oeuvre seems to live on in the imagination of both critics and writers. In Kennedy's case it may equally point to her being a quintessentially American poet and playwright, one who tries to capture in her grooming of specific images the motley tapestry and complexity of American lives. Kennedy's ongoing modifying and rehashing of the same material and characters may thus be compared to that of great American poets such as Walt Whitman, William Carlos Williams or Ezra Pound, who have kept expanding their poetic universes not to arrive at some form of premeditated wholeness, but to grasp the processual quality and the potential for change and innovation inscribed in the American myth itself. As an African American and a woman, Kennedy embarks on a similar project with a difference. Instead of merely embracing her mixed racial ancestry, she also articulates the psychological downside and trauma of her own Americanness, of what it means for a coloured, aspiring female writer to navigate a social environment frequently marked by misogyny and racism.

Primary Sources

Works by Adrienne Kennedy

The Adrienne Kennedy Reader (Minneapolis/London: University of Minnesota Press, 2001).

Secondary Sources

Aristotle, *On Poetry and Style*, Trans. G. M. A. Grube (New York: Liberal Arts Press, 1958).

Barnett, Claudia, '"An Evasion of Ontology": Being Adrienne Kennedy', *The Drama Review* 49, 3 (2005), 157–75.

Betsko, Kathleen, and Rachel Koenig, 'Interviews with Contemporary Women Playwrights', In Kathleen Betsko and Rachel Koenig (eds), *Adrienne Kennedy* (New York: William and Morrow, 1987), 246–58.

Brown, Lorraine A., '"For the Characters are Myself"': Adrienne Kennedy's *Funnyhouse of a Negro*', *American Literature Forum* 9, 3 (1975), 86–8.

Bryant-Jackson, Paul K., 'Kennedy's Travelers in the American and African Continuum'. In Paul K. Bryant-Jackson and Lois More Overbeck (eds), *Intersecting Boundaries: The Theatre of Adrienne Kennedy* (Minneapolis/London: University of Minnesota Press, 1992), 45–57.

Cummings, Scott T., 'Adrienne Kennedy', *American Theatre* 9, No.3 (June 1992), xxx.

Curb, Rosemary K., 'Fragmented Selves in Adrienne Kennedy's *Funnyhouse of a Negro* and *The Owl Answers*', *Theatre Journal* 32, 2 (1980), 180–95.

Curley, Maureen, 'Kennedy's *A Lesson in Dead Language*', *Explicator* 60, 3 (2002), 170–2.

Diamond, Elin, 'An Interview with Adrienne Kennedy'. In Philip C. Kolin (ed.), *Studies in American Drama 1945–Present* (Columbus, OH: Ohio State University Press, 1989), 143–57.

—, *Unmaking Mimesis: Essays on Feminism and Theatre* (New York/London: Routledge, 1997).

Hartigan, Patti, 'Adrienne Kennedy: A Fragile but Ferocious African-American Playwright', *TheJournal of Blacks in Higher Education* 28 (2000), 112–3.

Hurley, Erin, 'BLACKOUT: Utopian Technologies in Adrienne Kennedy's *Funnyhouse of a Negro*', *Modern Drama* 47, 2 (2004), 200–18.

Johnson, Charles, *Being and Race: Black Writing Since 1970* (Bloomington, IN: Indiana University Press, 1990).

Kennedy, Adrienne, *People Who Led to My Plays* (New York: Alfred A. Knopf, 1987).

Kintz, Linda, 'The Sanitized Spectacle: What's Birth Got to Do with It? Adrienne Kennedy's *A Movie Star Has to Star in Black and White*', *Theatre Journal* 44, 1 (1992), 67–86.

Kolin, Philip C., 'Orpheus Ascending: Music, Race, and Gender in Adrienne Kennedy's *She Talks to Beethoven*', *African American Review* 28, 2 (1994), 293–304.

McDonough, Carla, 'God and the Owls: The Sacred and the Profane in Adrienne Kennedy's *The Owl Answers*', *Modern Drama* 40 (1997), 385–402.

Miller, Arthur, 'Introduction to the Collected Plays'. In Miller Arthur (ed.), *Collected Plays* (London: Secker & Warburg, 1978).

Overbeck, Lois More, 'The Life of the Work: A Preliminary Sketch', in Paul K. Bryant-Jackson and Lois More Overbeck (eds), *Intersecting Boundaries: The Theatre of Adrienne Kennedy* (Minneapolis/London: University of Minnesota Press, 1992), 21–41.

Sollors, Werner, 'Owls and Rats in the American Funnyhouse: Adrienne Kennedy's Drama', *American Literature* 63, 3 (1991), 507–31.

Steiner, George, *The Death of Tragedy* (London: Faber and Faber, 1961).

Wilkerson, Margaret B., 'Adrienne Kennedy', in Thadious M. Davis and Trudier Harris (eds), *Dictionary of Literary Biography. Volume 38. Afro-American Writers After 1955: Dramatists and Prose Writers* (Detroit: The Gale Group, 1985).

Notes

1. *The Adrienne Kennedy Reader*, p. vii.
2. Paul K. Bryant-Jackson, 'Kennedy's Travelers in the American and African Continuum', p. 56.
3. Adrienne Kennedy, *People Who Led to My Plays*, p. 121.
4. Paul K. Bryant-Jackson, 'Kennedy's Travelers', p. 53.
5. Qtd. in Lois More Overbeck, 'The Life of the Work: A Preliminary Sketch', p. 30.
6. Charles Johnson, *Being and Race: Black Writing Since 1970*, p. 21
7. qtd. in Claudia Barnett, '"An Evasion of Ontology": Being Adrienne Kennedy', p. 158.
8. qtd. in Claudia Barnett, 'Being Adrienne Kennedy', p. 160.

9. Aristotle, *On Poetry and Style*, p. 21.
10. Arthur Miller, 'Introduction to the Collected Plays', p. 10.
11. George Steiner, *The Death of Tragedy*, pp. 37–8.
12. Arthur Miller, 'Introduction to the Collected Plays', p. 11.
13. Claudia Barnett, 'Being Adrienne Kennedy', p. 163.

7 TONY KUSHNER

James Fisher

A Bright Room Called Day; Hydriotaphia, or The Death of Dr. Browne; Angels in America. A Gay Fantasia on National Themes; Homebody/Kabul; Caroline or Change; The Intelligent Homosexual's Guide to Capitalism and Socialism with a Key to the Scriptures

Introduction

Tony Kushner rose to prominence on American and international stages in the early 1990s in the wake of uncommon critical acclaim and controversy surrounding his Pulitzer Prize-winning two-play epic, *Angels in America*. This widely produced work depicts a troubled nation in the throes of a profound moral combat over nothing less than the sociopolitical soul of the United States. Set in the midst of Ronald Reagan's presidency, as the horror of the AIDS pandemic is visited on the lives of Americans on both sides of the national political divide, *Angels* was the most discussed play of its era. Critics could hardly fail to grasp the importance of *Angels* or Kushner's skills as a dramatist as the play entered the canon of great American dramas. Alternately referred to as a 'gay', 'political' and 'theological' playwright, Kushner, whose works reflect those labels and much more, finds the well-spring of his plays, *Angels* and otherwise, in dark times and periods of social transition. Great drama, Kushner avers, emerges

> when playwrights, actors and directors are as appalled as everyone else by the world and the misbehavior of our leaders, and dumbstruck, exasperated, flabbergasted. Speechlessness is unavoidable. But we recover, and rage is a good engine for the stage.[1]

In Kushner's hands, however, rage is transmuted into a compassionate view of the experience of ordinary individuals buffeted by the currents of history, politics, religion and human suffering. 'I think', he states,

> that people do go to art in general as a way of addressing very deep, very intimate, very mercurial and elusive, ineffable things in a communal setting. It ends a certain kind of inner loneliness. Or it joins one's own loneliness with the inner loneliness of many other people. And I think it can be healing.[2]

Angels healed, but also disturbed some audiences in the typical ways through its use of strong language, sexual situations and nudity. However, most outrage centred on the play's depictions of homosexuality (all of the major male characters are either 'closeted' or 'out' gays), its indictment of the failures of both conservative and liberal politics to address the true social and political crises of the last decades preceding the new millennium and its blunt assault on the Reagan administration and what Kushner believed it represented. For the majority of critics and audiences, however, *Angels* was and is a bracing immersion in late-twentieth-century American issues. As writer Anna Quindlen stressed at the time of its Broadway premiere, *Angels* is

> a brilliant, brilliant play about love and the human condition at a time when our understanding of what it means to be human and loving has, thankfully, expanded.[3]

Prior to *Angels*, Kushner had already established himself as an adaptor, playwright and sometime director in regional theatres beginning in the mid-1980s, but with his 'Gay Fantasia on National Themes', as *Angels* is subtitled, he won recognition as the most promising American dramatist in decades and as a national spokesman for left-wing and LGBT causes.

Born Anthony Robert Kushner in Manhattan on 16 July 1956, the son of classically trained musicians who encouraged his interest in the arts and literature, Kushner spent his childhood in Lake Charles, Louisiana. His mother performed in local amateur theatre productions, entrancing Kushner with the emotional power of the theatre. As he later recalled,

> I have very strong memories of her power and the effect she had on people. . . . I grew up very, very closeted, and I'm sure that the disguise of theatre, the doubleness, and all that slightly tawdry stuff interested me.[4]

His escape from the closet came when he moved to New York in 1974 to pursue a B.A. degree in English Literature from Columbia University. While in college, he also immersed himself in the New York theatre scene, subsequently completing a Master of Fine Arts degree at New York University's Tisch School of the Arts, where he trained as a director under the guidance of Bertolt Brecht specialist Carl Weber. In this period, Kushner directed his own plays with fellow students. These included an opera, *La Fin de la Baleine: An Opera for the Apocalypse* (1982), an adaptation of Goethe's *Stella: A Play for Lovers* (1987), theatre for youth plays *Yes Yes No No* (1985) and *The Protozoa Review* (1985) and one-act and full-length plays including *The Heavenly Theatre* (1986) and *In Great Eliza's Golden Time* (1986). In these earliest works, Kushner explores themes and techniques still evident in *Angels* and his other full-length plays as well as films including *Munich* (2005) and *Lincoln* (2012), free adaptations of plays by Corneille, Goethe, Kleist, Ansky and Brecht and a slew of one-acts and non-dramatic essays on art, culture and politics.

Prior American dramatists with overt and leftist political aims, Clifford Odets and Arthur Miller, for example, influenced Kushner. He directed Odets' *Golden Boy* in 1986 at the Repertory Theatre of St Louis and has edited two volumes of Miller's plays for the Library of America. However, Kushner descends most directly from Henrik Ibsen, George Bernard Shaw and especially Brecht, whom he greatly admires. Kushner believes that all theatre is political, that drama, like democracy, springs from the 'frazzle, the rubbed raw, the unresolved, the fragile and the fiery and the dangerous'[5] in human circumstances and political discourse. Kushner's political awakening began in college and his Marxist-based politics permeate his work. After reading Ernst Fischer's

The Necessity of Art: A Marxist Approach, Kushner's commitment to the social responsibility of artists came into full focus. At the time of his emergence, most American dramatists with political aims approached their subject with utmost realism; Kushner, however, turned to Brecht's epic theatre and the heightened realism in the lyrical dramas of Tennessee Williams and John Guare. Kushner's powerfully emotional dramas (and memorable American characters) also feature a broader scope suggesting Eugene O'Neill's dramas emphasizing the failure of individuals to live up to their own ideals and spiritual longings, as well as those of the society they live in. The impact of economics, and especially the moral dilemmas Americans faced as materialistic success often defined the 'American Dream', stems from Miller and, to a lesser extent, Odets. But beyond these influences, it is of central significance that Kushner identifies himself as a gay dramatist, though his works extend beyond the experiences of the LGBT community. In his most representative works, Kushner explores characters of all stripes caught up in periods of wrenching cultural transitions and vast sociopolitical upheaval, although in both his historically-based and contemporary works, issues of change are inextricably woven together with the smaller lives of individuals facing parallel upheavals in their personal relationships reflecting those in the society in which they live.

The Plays

A Bright Room Called Day (1985)

A Bright Room Called Day, written during 1984, was first produced as a workshop at New York's Theater 22, followed by an October 1987 staging at San Francisco's Eureka Theater and a January 1991 production at the New York Public Theater, which was largely vilified by critics who found Kushner's equating of Ronald Reagan's election to the US presidency with Adolf Hitler's rise to power in Germany disturbing. *Bright Room* views the cataclysm of the rise of the Nazis through the lives and varied responses of a group of artists and filmmakers in Berlin during 1932–33. Kushner's answer to Brecht's

1938 play, *Fear and Misery of the Third Reich* (also known as *The Private Lives of the Master Race*), he adopts in this drama the episodic structure and breaking of the fourth wall typical in Brecht, but the Brechtian influence is more significantly evident in the dialectics of this highly politicized drama.

Bright Room combines an intimate, largely realistic portrayal of the lives of its characters, particularly protagonist Agnes Eggling, during the first year of the rise of the Nazis with an epic scope merging the prelude to the Holocaust with 1980s American politics. The connection is made through the presence of Zillah Katz, a Jewish political activist and ardent feminist, who is enraged and deeply frightened by Reagan's ascension to power and takes her argument directly to the audience as she observes the moral conundrums facing Agnes and her friends. She rants about the banality of evil (which she sees in Reagan's avuncular persona) and recognizes the feeling of powerlessness leading to deep fears as an individual (and outlier) in a time of vast change.

Bright Room invokes Judaic and other traditional religious imagery, sometimes to enhance the play's dark fantasy (none less than the Devil, calling himself Herr Swetts, makes a chilling, serio-comic appearance), sometimes for humour or to raise the troubling questions of what may be lost as one world, one culture and one faith die. These issues are investigated from a different perspective in Kushner's 1995 free adaptation of S. Ansky's pre-World War I Yiddish theatre play, *A Dybbuk; or, Between Two Worlds*, in which the last vestige of the Old World, a shtetl in Eastern Europe, faces the coming of modernity and of unimaginable horrors. *Bright Room* is a similar prologue to catastrophe, compelling the play's characters to attempt to understand what is happening to their country as the Nazis assume power. Each is tested: Will they stay in Germany and fight against the rising evil? Will they flee? Or will they simply lie low in hopes of weathering the coming storm? Zillah, observing the past and the decisions made by those living in a terrible time, tries to comprehend the new manifestation of political evil she fears in her own time and what her actions should be. Speaking for Kushner, Zillah calls for 'not caution or circumspection but moral exuberance. Overstatement is your friend: use it' (p. 70). Zillah's comparison of Reagan to Hitler is such overstatement. She wants to frighten herself as a means of stiffening her resolve as an activist, a Kushnerian view of the fundamental responsibility of a citizen:

> Don't put too much stock in a good night's sleep. During times of reactionary backlash, the only people sleeping soundly are the guys who are giving the rest of us bad dreams. So eat something indigestible before you go to bed, and listen to your nightmares (p. 71).

As the shadowy spectre of the Nazis spreads over Germany, Agnes hunkers down, immobilized by her fears, wondering if those neighbours passing her on the street are murderers. Alone in a dark corner of her apartment, she is a trapped animal, unable to achieve Zillah's activism, only hoping to survive. Zillah, aware of the restless fear that connects her to Agnes' circumstances, says

> She still can't sleep. Restless, like me. I'm calling to her: across a long dead time: to touch a dark place, to scare myself a little, to make contact with what moves in the night, fifty years after, with what's driven, every night, by the panic and the pain . . . (p. 90).

The few approving critics acknowledged the lyricism of Kushner's language and found *Bright Room* 'an ambitious, disturbing mess of a play'[6] and 'a big, dense play of ideas—a welcome rarity after an era of apolitical American isolationist theatre'.[7]

Hydriotaphia, or The Death of Dr. Browne (1987)

This play was written and first produced at New York's Home for Contemporary Theater and Art in 1987. A decade later, Kushner revised this 'epic farce' for productions at Houston's Alley Theater and California's Berkeley Repertory Theater in 1998. A wild flight of intellectual and theatrical fantasy centred on an obscure historical figure, Sir Thomas Browne (1605–82), a seventeenth-century philosopher, writer, scientist and, in Kushner's imaginings, seminal capitalist, the play is inspired in part by Edward Bond's 1973 play, *Bingo*. Kushner sets the black comedy of *Hydriotaphia* on the day of Browne's death, bringing together various members of his inner circle, all with self-centred dreams of the ways his riches might transform their lives. The much-unloved Browne is indicted as a grasping businessman whose wealth has come to him through a ruthless scheme to throw local peasants off common lands which he converts into a profitable quarry. Pounding quarry machines keep up an incessant beat in the background as Browne's unloving wife, Dorothy, doubts the value of her husband's acquisitive life as he dies. The quarry machines collapse into a great pit at the moment of his death, stopping their eternal pounding as Browne's mercenary heart stops. 'The moments in history that interest me the most are of transition',[8] Kushner explains, and in *Hydriotaphia* he finds in Browne's life an embodiment of the rise of capitalist greed and in his time an opportunity to explore the human price of economic inequity, a subject he would approach in a more realistic, contemporary vein in *The Intelligent Homosexual's Guide to Capitalism and Socialism with a Key to the Scriptures* in 2009.

A primer for appreciating the style and substance of Kushner's more mature works, *Hydriotaphia* establishes his lofty ambitions for a revitalized epic theatre which, as he explains, explores possibilities that 'range from a vastly improved world to no world at all'.[9] Critics disagreed on the balance of farce and seriousness in the play, describing it as 'often amusing, sometimes provocative'[10] and as a 'bubbly, profound, historically rooted Monty Python-meets-Ben Jonson tribute to writing'.[11]

Angels in America. A Gay Fantasia on National Themes (1991–2)

Tragic and comic elements – and a Kushnerian collision of reality and fantasy – define *Angels in America*, in which Kushner captured the late twentieth-century zeitgeist in its merging of the personal problems of two unhappy couples in the months following Reagan's re-election to the US presidency and in the earliest, darkest hours of the AIDS pandemic. Such a description cannot begin to catalogue the broad range of themes found in the two plays, *Millennium Approaches* and

Perestroika, making up *Angels*. US and world history, art and culture, religion and spirituality, sexuality and gender and the fiercely divided poles of post-World War II American politics (seen, in part, through Kushner's inclusion of two historical figures of the post-World War II era, Roy Cohn and Ethel Rosenberg) are front and centre in the play's searing drama and uproarious comedy. Kushner commenced work on these plays in the late 1980s on a commission from San Francisco's Eureka Theater and the National Endowment for the Arts, where the plays were first performed in 1991, following a 1990 workshop at the Mark Taper Forum. Following an acclaimed run at the National Theatre of Great Britain in 1992, *Angels* slowly found its way to Broadway, where *Millennium Approaches* opened at the Walter Kerr Theatre in May 1993, followed by *Perestroika*, which was performed in repertory with it, in November of the same year.

Angels presents a struggle between reactionary and progressive forces in the lives of the characters and the world around them, which also includes a realm of fantasy in which past and present, as well as ideas of the unknowable future, collide. There is a pervasive sense of Greek fatality in *Angels* and its feverish historical drama and the socialist predilections of its author. *Angels* attempts to permit both sides of the political spectrum to be seen and heard at their best and worst; its most lovable character, the play's protagonist, Prior Walter, is dying of AIDS, but so is its most detestable, the rapacious Roy Cohn, whose real life is re-imagined by Kushner with fidelity to the broad facts, freely imagining its specifics. Both conservative and liberal characters are shown to have admirable and reprehensible motives, while the strong become weak and the weak strong as the play moves inexorably towards a guardedly optimistic conclusion.

Set in the mid-1980s shortly after Reagan's re-election, *Millennium Approaches* follows two fictional couples and Cohn, Sen Joseph McCarthy's right-hand man during the Communist 'witchhunt' era of the early 1950s. Now a behind-the-scenes conservative powerbroker, Cohn is fighting for both his professional and personal life in the mid-1980s, facing disbarment and a diagnosis of AIDS. One of the couples, Joe and Harper Pitt, are Mormons recently transplanted to New York and facing a profound test of their unhappy marriage as Joe can no longer deny his homosexual desires. A law clerk for a right-wing judge, Joe has come to Cohn's nefarious attentions. Trying to save his career, Cohn intends to secure a position for Joe as his spy in the Reagan administration's Justice Department. Harper is self-medicating with Valium, which has unleashed her vivid imagination, as she agonizes over her suspicions about Joe's true sexual persuasion. At the same time, Prior and Louis Ironson, a long-time gay couple, learn that Prior is HIV-positive. Louis, a liberal court reporter working in the same building with Joe, fears he cannot live up to the requirements of caring for Prior as the disease takes its toll. When Prior's condition worsens, Louis abandons him and spirals downward into despair and self-recrimination. Left alone and ill, Prior turns to a close friend, Belize, an African American nurse and sometime drag queen. Meanwhile, Joe, finally accepting his sexuality, telephones his repressed mother, Hannah, to confess. He leaves Harper to pursue Louis, as both Prior and Cohn become sicker. The delirious Prior is visited by ghostly ancestors from the Middle Ages and the seventeenth century, who commiserate with him on dying from plague (as they refer to Prior's AIDS) – and warn of a coming Heavenly harbinger. The similarly ailing Cohn is haunted by the spectre of Ethel Rosenberg, whose execution for treason years before resulted from Cohn's strenuous and likely illegal efforts. Cohn vehemently refuses to acknowledge his homosexuality – gay men, in his opinion, are powerless and faceless people – and despite his weakening condition, he seems more concerned about preventing his disbarment. The closet, to Kushner, is populated with the profoundly repressed or those in denial. In either event, as depicted, the closet leads to twisted or miserable lives, and Cohn is the most egregiously twisted, with Joe as the most tortured. The proudly out-of-the-closet Prior intermittently hears the voice of an Angel mysteriously calling him prophet and the play culminates with the Angel crashing through the ceiling of Prior's bedroom to announce: 'The Great Work Begins' (p. 125).

In and around the personal crises of the characters, *Millennium Approaches* explores late-twentieth-century attitudes about American history, sexuality, race, religion and the conflicting poles of conservative and liberal politics. Kushner was influenced in part by Walter Benjamin, whose essay, *Theses on the Philosophy of History*, was, in turn, inspired by

Paul Klee's 'Angelus Novus', a painting depicting the Angel of History being blown into the future by the winds of progress while glancing back at the rubble of history. Using that potent image as an over-arching thematic metaphor, Kushner employs an epic theatre style drawn from his admiration for Brecht's plays, weaving epic techniques with American lyric realism in the manner of Tennessee Williams. Caught between two worlds – one dying and one being born – Kushner's characters are tormented by fear of an unknown future even more harrowing than their present, an uneasy sense of moral uncertainty and profound feelings of inexplicable loss. In one scene, a nameless, homeless woman offers the prediction that 'In the new century, I think we will all be insane' (p. 111). Near the end of *Millennium Approaches*, Kushner offers a *coup de theatre*, as the ghost of Ethel Rosenberg faces off with the frightened but unrepentant Cohn, prompting him to boast, 'I have *forced* my way into history. I ain't never gonna die' to which Ethel ominously replies, 'History is about to crack wide open. Millennium approaches' (p. 118).

Ethel's prediction comes true in *Perestroika*, as great changes occur for all of the play's main characters. The more intellectually and thematically complex of the two *Angels* plays, *Perestroika* stresses the necessity for forgiveness and the acceptance of loss if the characters' lives, and their society, are to progress into a future that may (or may not) be better than the present in which they reside. Kushner depicts this in many ways; for example, at one point, Louis is appalled to find himself at the bedside of Cohn, who, despite persistent denials about his sexuality, is succumbing to AIDS. The ghostly Ethel joins Louis to chant the Kaddish over Cohn's corpse in an act of forgiveness from both his historical and present-day enemies. Transgression can and must be forgiven, Kushner implies, and is the means by which it becomes possible to journey forward, as hopes for a brighter future and society's progress result from facing the hard truths and the spectres of fear and loss. Whereas *Millennium Approaches* depicts faithlessness and selfishness in a time of the retreating conscience of American society, *Perestroika* finds Kushner's characters moving tentatively towards feared realities and changes in their lives and in their country. Is it possible to face ourselves and our failures to live up to our national ideals? Can we change? Is change desirable? These and other questions posed by Kushner invite his audience, like his characters, to examine the great, perhaps unanswerable questions of existence and national identity. Despite the overall grimness of much of *Perestroika*, the play finally brings some of its characters a measure of forgiveness and a settling of accounts. Belize, for example, embraces compassion to nurse the delirious and dying Cohn, despite hateful taunts from his patient. Hannah, Joe's mother, similarly embraces compassion caring for the abandoned, delusional Harper. While working at her newfound job at New York's Mormon Welcome Center, Hannah leaves Harper alone with a diorama of a nineteenth-century Mormon pioneer family. Harper thinks she sees Joe, her errant spouse, in the image of the 'Mormon Father', while pleading for guidance from the resolute 'Mormon Mother'. When the figure comes wondrously to life and advises Harper on facing her suffering and moving on in her personal journey, Kushner achieves a transcendent meeting of past and present, a unique theatrical space in which the fictions of human history and literature converge with contemporary reality and the intimacy of personal lives.

Perestroika's final scene at Central Park's Bethesda fountain, with a statue of a healing angel in its centre, is set five years after the rest of *Angels*, and in which Kushner offers a newly created family made up of Prior, Hannah, Belize and a repentant Louis. In this essential scene, which brings to culmination the complex themes of the two plays, Kushner allows his characters to bluntly state his own guardedly optimistic views. A stronger, wiser Hannah asserts Kushner's mantra the interconnectedness of all humanity – regardless of race or sexual preference – and the primacy of loyalty and commitment to others. Prior points out the angel of the fountain, a figure commemorating death but suggesting 'a world without dying' (p. 279). Louis provides Kushner's metaphor for the scene by recounting the tale of the angel Bethesda who 'descended and just her foot touched earth. And where it did, a fountain shot up from the ground' (p. 279). Belize makes the connection, stressing that if

anyone who was suffering, in the body or the spirit, walked through the waters of the fountain of Bethesda, they would be healed, washed clean of pain (p. 279).

Giving voice to the human longing for transcendence and life-giving affirmation in the face of unspeakable suffering, Kushner's Prior, the prophet, whose AIDS symptoms have stabilized, explains that the healing waters of the fountain are not now flowing, though he hopes to see the day it flows again. In a final statement made directly to the audience, Prior speaks for Kushner, and those who have come before:

> This disease will be the end of many of us, but not nearly all, and the dead will be commemorated and will struggle on with the living, and we are not going away. We won't die secret deaths anymore. The world only spins forward. We will be citizens. The time has come (p. 280).

Critics acclaimed *Angels*, though the play's production in some American and international theatres inspired controversy over its sexual frankness and politics, even as *Millennium Approaches* won a Pulitzer Prize and many critics' awards, including back-to-back Best Play Tony Awards for each part.

Homebody/Kabul (2001)

Kushner's *Homebody/Kabul*, which premiered at the New York Theater Workshop in late 2001, is a significant expansion of an hour-long one-act monologue, *Home Body*, first performed at London's Chelsea Theatre Centre in 1999. Expanded to three-acts, the play is a disturbing drama about an unhappy British family caught up in the wrenching tragedies of Afghanistan under Taliban rule. As they went into rehearsals for its premiere, the terrorist attacks of 11 September 2001 occurred, lending the play increased relevance as critics and audiences recognized Kushner's prescient statement on the tragic conflicts of the Middle East. *Homebody/Kabul* won the Obie Award for Best off-Broadway Play and several critics' prizes.

Kushner stresses in *Homebody/Kabul*, as in earlier works, that social change becomes possible when the unstable dynamism of a chronically chaotic society or the acute turbulence of an important transition period shatters illusions of stability. Few lands have been as unstable as Afghanistan in recent decades and Kushner became interested in the mayhem resulting from the historical legacy of colonization. The crumbling city of Kabul provides the background as a dysfunctional British family is forever changed by an encounter with an unknown, at least to its characters, corner of the world. Kushner's belief in theatre as a transformative force is in full evidence as he proposes immersion in the culture of the 'other' as necessary to find a greater understanding which he sees as the only hope for our redemption. That the family in *Homebody/Kabul* is British matters little – Kushner uses them to explore the particularly Western aversion to bad news, discomfort, difference and instability. The mother of the family, the titular 'Homebody', insists that those living in comparable comfort and safety in the West are in grave danger of 'succumbing to luxury' (p. 1). She concludes that it might be better to live among the oppressed and suffering than to fade into senescence of ease and security. As in *Bright Room*, Kushner calls for engagement and activism, a willingness to aid those without luxury, though this path is fraught with peril.

Kushner's characters are obliged to reap the consequences of choices Western nations have made in response to the complexities of the Middle East. Fascinated by the vast history of Afghanistan, the Homebody concludes a dizzyingly imaginative monologue about other worlds, particularly Afghanistan, as the play shifts from her cozy London living room to the wounded city of Kabul. Milton Ceiling, a repressed, middle-aged British computer specialist, and the Homebody's distant husband, arrives in Kabul in the play's second act with their troubled twenty-something daughter, Priscilla. Milton, paralyzed with fear in the midst of this dangerous and mysterious place, accepts the official explanation that a brutally mangled body of a woman is that of his wife. He sinks into an alcohol- and drug-induced daze with an unofficial liaison for the British government who has remained in Kabul because it provides him easy access to drugs. Priscilla, however, refuses to accept the official scenario and, donning a burka, slips into the harsh, exotic environs of Kabul to find her mother.

Kushner explores the disturbing face of religious fanaticism through Priscilla's eyes, revealing his aversion to the intolerance of religious zealots of any stripe. Kushner assails the Taliban for its misogyny and brutality, but humanizes other Afghani characters trapped under its tyranny. Priscilla finds herself a guide, a poet who shows her the world her mother has either embraced or been destroyed by, a city, Kushner suggests in a powerful metaphor, cursed by the myth that Cain's grave may be located within its environs. Ironically, its purported location is now a Taliban minefield and Priscilla, wandering the figurative minefield that is Kabul, receives the startling news that her mother may be alive and living as the wife of a well-to-do Muslim. This character is never seen, but his Afghani wife, Mahala, is, and her rage at both the Taliban and the West is disquieting. Kushner's globalism takes on a darkly bitter edge as Mahala, a former librarian who, like the Homebody, reveres language and books, and a woman of intellect and dignity, is obliged to beg Priscilla's help in escaping Afghanistan. The constant terror and isolation, she reveals, are causing her to forget the alphabet – an insupportable loss to this intellectual woman. She spews rage in various dialects, demonstrating Kushner's facile manipulation of and appreciation for language. Priscilla grows in wisdom from this encounter, ruefully noting that Mahala 'isn't mad, she's fucking furious. It isn't at all the same' (p. 80). If oppressions are severe enough, Kushner suggests as he does in *Bright Room*, they inevitably lead to either the defeat of total resignation or an unending fury that true survivors require to fight on.

Whether or not the Homebody is dead or alive is never confirmed, but this is not the point engaging Kushner. The violent collision of cultures, as the Homebody explains, is what intrigues him:

> Ours is a time of connection; the private, and we must accept this, and it's a hard thing to accept, the private is gone. All must be touched. All touch corrupts. All must be corrupted (p. 2).

This corrupting touch may eventually bring greater understanding, but in the short term, the shattered lives of both the citizenry of Kabul and the visiting Westerners are the result. Only Priscilla and Mahala ultimately gain from this corruption. Though Priscilla has lost a mother, she has matured on her individual journey into the dark, surreal recesses of Kabul, saving Mahala's sanity and probably her life. Mahala, living in London in the Homebody's home and with the Homebody's husband, enjoys first-hand the luxuries of the West, but appears not to have succumbed to them. Immersion in another world and another life is a leap into a culture at once alien, inviting and appalling, Kushner stresses, and Priscilla's yearning, desperate search for her missing mother expands into a deeper comprehension of difference and for the connection the Homebody insists is essential, both among nations and people.

Homebody/Kabul's haunting timeliness raises questions about love and connection, war, guilt, displacement and the complex maze of history as Kushner asks profoundly important questions about the present moment and illuminates the hard lessons of the past.

Caroline, or Change (2003)

The application of the healing power of theatre is clearly a dramatic goal in Kushner's libretto and lyrics for *Caroline, or Change*, which, with music by Jeanine Tesori, opened at New York's Public Theater under the direction of George C. Wolfe in late 2003, prior to a four-month Broadway run in 2004 at the Eugene O'Neill Theatre, is perhaps the most overtly autobiographical of his works. Set at the height of the Civil Rights movement and in the immediate aftermath of President John F. Kennedy's assassination, *Caroline* addresses not only issues of race and national tragedy, but more particularly the economics of oppression and prejudice. A highly imaginative and, at times, phantasmagoric work, *Caroline* is set at a transition moment in American history, as the conflicts of race, ethnicity and American politics in the early 1960s cause turmoil in the lives of a middle-aged African American maid, Caroline Thibodeaux, who works for a Jewish family in Louisiana, and the eight-year-old son of the family, Noah Gelman, who has recently lost his mother and is emotionally adrift and as spiritually alone as his family's maid. Caroline, a divorced mother of four, cannot negotiate the rapid changes inherent in the times in which she lives, just as Noah cannot comprehend the shattering changes a tragic loss has brought into his young life.

At his most theatrical, Kushner depicts Caroline in the hot hell of the Gelman's basement washing clothes while being serenaded by appliances who sing of the social changes happening around her. He ends *Caroline* on a hopeful note as Caroline's children, led by the optimistic radical Emmie, express a readiness to move into a potentially brighter racial future. Kushner emphasizes the need for his characters to face realities, however harsh, and recognize what can be changed and what must be endured.

Critics applauded *Caroline*, if also finding it uncommonly serious in its dialectics for a Broadway musical. In Kushner's next major play, he also addresses economic concerns, but unlike *Caroline*, he approaches the subject in a more traditionally realistic way.

The Intelligent Homosexual's Guide to Capitalism and Socialism with a Key to the Scriptures (2009)

An unendurable problem of economics is again faced in this play, darker in tone than its title might immediately suggest and, as critic Charles McNulty describes it, a 'thrillingly ambitious' and 'wise, challenging and heartbreaking play'.[12] It premiered at the Guthrie Theater in the summer of 2009 as part of a festival celebrating Kushner's work, and, with revisions, in New York in May 2011 at the Public Theater, where it met with mixed reviews.

The Intelligent Homosexual visits working-class America to examine central themes for Kushner, including most specifically economics, but also the many meanings of American history, confusions of sexuality and gender, spirituality and the pain of loss. The play's protagonist, Gus Marcantonio, a 70-something retired longshoreman and former union representative, has tried to commit suicide and, most disturbingly, plans to try again. His understandably concerned adult children, their various spouses and lovers, and Gus's ex-nun sister return to the family home in Brooklyn to confront him. What family members see as Gus's great achievement, a deal he brokered with management, is now viewed by Gus as the insupportable failure of his life, even though his peers view him as a hero. In his heart, Gus believes he sold out (in the deal, younger workers did not get the benefits that older workers did) even though it seems clear no deal at all would have been possible without his efforts. In addition to this woe, Gus believes (possibly incorrectly) that he has Alzheimer's disease and wants to sell the family home for maximum value before the economic bubble bursts (that the play is set in 2007 makes Gus seem prescient). Gus methodically pursues a means to end his life, including inviting a suicide specialist to his home to provide the means and the know-how. Gus's family members are also dealing with more personal economic concerns (especially the ultimate disposition of the family home) and trying to understand their father's disorienting agonies and their own confused desires.

Gus, much like Zillah in *Bright Room*, is profoundly distressed by the injustices in the world around him, and whereas Zillah turns to hate mailing the President of the United States even as she realizes her craziness in doing so, Gus wants only to end his life. Alienated and depressed, tortured by his self-perceived failure to achieve his ideals, he cannot bear to go on despite his love for his family. The play's complex mix of economic and gender issues, as well as the problems of living in a morally adrift society, are central concerns to Kushner's protagonists. As *New York Times* critic Ben Brantley noted, *The Intelligent Homosexual*, like Kushner's other plays, focuses above all, on one central question: 'How do we live when the old systems of belief and morality that gave form to our existence have fallen apart or proved empty?'[13]

Summary

Despite influences from the classics to modern European theatre, Tony Kushner's ambitious, boldly theatrical and overtly political style has been a revitalizing factor in contemporary American drama. His influence may ultimately equal that of O'Neill and Williams, for while his contemporaries Sam Shepard and David Mamet, among others, present increasingly minimalistic and fundamentally realistic dramas, Kushner provides a model for an American drama boldly mixing fantasy and reality – as well as tragedy and comedy – to explore the history and politics, ideals and morality of the American past, present and future. As gay activist playwright Larry Kramer states, Kushner is 'drunk on ideas, on language, on the possibility of changing the world',[14] and, at the same time, as John Lahr proclaims, Kushner guides his audience to 'that most beautiful, divided, and unexplored country—the human heart'.[15]

Primary Sources

Works by Tony Kushner

Angels in America: A Gay Fantasia on National Themes. Part One: Millennium Approaches. Part Two: Perestroika (New York: Theatre Communications Group, Inc., 1995).

A Backstage Pass to Hell (*New York Times Magazine*, 29 December 1996, Sec. 6), pp. 22–3.

A Bright Room Called Day (New York: Theatre Communications Group, Inc., 1994).

Caroline, or Change (New York: Theatre Communications Group, 2004).

Death and Taxes: Hydriotaphia and Other Plays (New York: Theatre Communications Group, Inc., 1998).

Homebody/Kabul (New York: Theatre Communications Group, 2002; Revised Edition, 2005).

The Intelligent Homosexual's Guide to Capitalism and Socialism with a Key to the Scriptures (New York: Theatre Communications Group, Inc., 2013).

Slavs! Thinking About the Longstanding Problems of Virtue and Happiness (New York: Broadway Play Publishing, 1996).

Thinking About the Longstanding Problems of Virtue and Happiness (New York: Theatre Communications Group, Inc., 1995).

Secondary Sources

Abramovich, Alex, 'Hurricane Kushner Hits the Heartland', *New York Times*, 30 November 2003.

Barrett, Amy, 'The Way We Live Now: 10-07-01: Questions for Tony Kushner', *New York Times*, 7 October 2001.

Bloom, Harold (ed.), *Tony Kushner*. Bloom's Modern Critical Views. (New York: Chelsea House, 2005).

Brantley, Ben, 'Debating Dialectics and Dad's Suicide', *New York Times*, 6 May 2011.

Brask, Per (ed.), *Essay on Kushner's* Angels (Winnipeg, Canada: Blizzard Publishing, 1996).

De La Viña, Mark, 'Kushner's Farce is a Mortal Cinch', *San Jose Mercury News*, 18 September 1998.

Evans, Everett, 'Kushner Hits Highs, Lows in Epic Farce', *Houston Chronicle*, 10 April 1998.

Fisher, James (ed.), *The Theater of Tony Kushner: Living Past Hope* (New York: Routledge, 2001 [hardback], 2002 [revised paperback]).

—, *Tony Kushner: New Essays on the Art and Politics of the Plays* (Jefferson, NC: McFarland, 2006).

—, *Understanding Tony Kushner* (Columbia, SC: University of South Carolina Press, 2008).

Geis, Deborah R. and Steven F. Kruger (eds), *Approaching the Millennium: Essays on* Angels in America (Ann Arbor, MI: University of Michigan Press, 1997).

Kekki, Lasse, *From Gay to Queer: Gay Male Identity in Selected Fiction by David Leavitt and in Tony Kushner's Play* Angels in America I-II. (New York: Peter Lang, 2003).

Lahr, John, 'Angels on Broadway', *The New Yorker*, 23 May 1993.

Mader, Travis, 'Tony Kushner and Dr. Browne', *Alley Theatre Newsletter*, September 1998.

McNulty, Charles, 'The Intelligent Homosexual's Guide to Capitalism and Socialism with a Key to the Scriptures' at the Public Theater, *Los Angeles Times*, 5 May 2011, http://latimesblogs.latimes.com/culturemonster/2011/05/theater-review-the-intelligent-homosexuals-guide-to-capitalism-and-socialism-with-a-key-to-the-scrip.html.

Nielsen, Ken, *Tony Kushner's* Angels in America. Modern Theatre Guides (New York: Continuum, 2008).

Quindlen, Anna, 'Happy and Gay', *New York Times*, 6 April 1994.

Richards, David, 'Tale of One City Set in Two Times – Both Fearful', *New York Times*, 13 January 1991.

Roca, Octavio, 'Kushner's Next Stage', *San Francisco Chronicle*, 6 September 1998.

Savran, David, 'Tony Kushner.' In Philip C. Kolin and Colby H. Kullman (eds), *Speaking on Stage: Interviews with Contemporary American Playwrights* (Tuscaloosa, AL: University of Alabama Press, 1996).

Vorlicky, Robert H. (ed.), *Tony Kushner in Conversation* (Ann Arbor, MI: University of Michigan Press, 1997).

Winer, Linda, 'Evils of Humanity Crowd *Bright Room*' *Newsday*, 8 January 1991.

Notes

1. Alex Abramovich, 'Hurricane Kushner Hits the Heartland', *New York Times*, 30 November 2003, Section 2, p. 5.

2. Amy Barrett, 'The Way We Live Now: 10-07-01: Questions for Tony Kushner', *New York Times*, 7 October 2001, Section 6, p. 230.

3. Anna Quindlen, 'Happy and Gay', *New York Times*, 6 April 1994, p. A21.

4. David Savran, 'Tony Kushner'. In Philip C. Kolin and Colby H. Kullman (eds), *Speaking on Stage: Interviews with Contemporary American Playwrights* (Tuscaloosa, AL: University of Alabama Press, 1996), p. 293.

5. Tony Kushner. *Thinking About the Longstanding Problems of Virtue and Happiness* (New York: Theatre Communications Group, Inc., 1995), pp. 10–11.

6. David Richards, 'Tale of One City Set in Two Times – Both Fearful', *New York Times*, 13 January 1991, p. 5.

7. Linda Winer, 'Evils of Humanity Crowd *Bright Room*', *Newsday*, 8 January 1991, p. 44.

8. Kushner quoted in Travis Mader, 'Tony Kushner and Dr. Browne', *Alley Theatre Newsletter*, September 1998, p. 1.

9. Travis Mader, 'Tony Kushner and Dr. Browne', *Alley Theatre Newsletter*, September 1998, p. 1.

10. Everett Evans, 'Kushner Hits Highs, Lows in Epic Farce', *Houston Chronicle*, 10 April 1998, p. D1.

11. Mark De La Viña, 'Kushner's Farce is a Mortal Cinch', *San Jose Mercury News*, 18 September 1998, p. 29.

12. Charles McNulty, Theatre Review: 'The Intelligent Homosexual's Guide to Capitalism and Socialism with a Key to the Scriptures' at the Public Theater, *Los Angeles Times*, 5 May 2011, http://latimesblogs.latimes.com/culturemonster/2011/05/theater-review-the-intelligent-homosexuals-guide-to-capitalism-and-socialism-with-a-key-to-the-scrip.html.

13. Ben Brantley, 'Debating Dialectics and Dad's Suicide', *New York Times*, 6 May 2011, p. C1.

14. Octavio Roca, 'Kushner's Next Stage', *San Francisco Chronicle*, 6 September 1998, p. 32.

15. John Lahr, 'Angels on Broadway', *The New Yorker*, 23 May 1993, p. 137.

8 NEIL LABUTE

Christopher Innes

bash: latter day plays; *The Shape of Things*; *The Distance from Here*;
In a Dark Dark House

Introduction

Neil LaBute was born March 1963, in Detroit, Michigan, and raised
in an isolated country homestead in Washington State. LaBute has
referred to his father as '"a son of a bitch." He was challenging—the
way Hitler was challenging. So, you never really knew what you were
waking up to'.[1] He was forced to work, unwillingly, on his father's farm,
and his only exposure to art came through watching foreign films – *The
Seven Samurai, The 400 Blows, La Dolce Vita* are ones LaBute picks
out[2] – together with Woody Allen's *Annie Hall*. To escape, he took a
Mormon student counsellor's advice and enrolled at Brigham Young
University in Utah, where in 1981 he converted to the Church of Latter
Day Saints. There, he began directing and writing plays – although
he shocked the religious community by his choice of material: *In
the Company of Men*, written for a playwriting class, was rejected
for performance on grounds of misogyny, while an early version of
his *Friends & Neighbours*, at that point titled *Lepers*, was locked out
of the theatre by the university authorities. His continuing uneasy
relationship with the Mormon Church is shown by his rewriting of
bash to omit all 'latter-day' references – which had led to him being
'disfellowshipped' – and by his marriage to a fellow student at Brigham
Young, also a Mormon, who by 2009 had separated from him due to
'the dark nature of his writings'.[3]

After graduating he eventually took an MFA in Dramatic Writing at
New York University (NYU), spending his final spring semester (1991)
at the Royal Court in London – which he later referred to as 'a very

formative experience'[4] – and where he came in direct contact with the work of Edward Bond, Caryl Churchill and Howard Brenton, which together with Pinter's writings, has as much influence on LaBute's plays as the work of David Mamet (to whom he dedicated *fat pig*) or Sam Shepard (to whom *In a Dark Dark House* was dedicated).

His first play to be commercially produced came less than a year after his graduation from NYU, and was characteristically provocative in its title: *Filthy Talk for Troubled Times: Scenes of Intolerance*. Staged off-Broadway in 1992 (and restaged, directed by LaBute at MCC Theatre in 2010), it also established a characteristic pattern in its form: a series of monologues set in a bar. Over the two decades since, LaBute has had no fewer than 24 plays staged, including several trilogies of short plays. Several of those he also directed. As if that were not extraordinary enough, he also scripted and directed 10 films – four being adaptations of his own plays – plus one film for television.

The extent to which LaBute remains an outsider, in terms of his preference for unconventional dramatic forms and his uncomfortable view of society – which has gained him a reputation as 'American theatre's reigning misanthrope' on both sides of the Atlantic[5] – is indicated by the fact that his first play to reach Broadway was only in 2009. This was *Reasons to be Pretty*, which had premiered at MCC in 2008; and as yet this is the only LaBute play to reach Broadway.

In addition, almost half his total output of plays has been produced first in London, generally at alternative theatre spaces (Almeida Theatre, The Bush, Greenwich Theatre, Southwark Playhouse), even though he has had an ongoing relationship with the New York Off-Broadway MCC theatre since 2002. So LaBute has a strong international reach, despite the way his bleak portrayal of human nature causes recurrent audience discomfort – so much so indeed that spectators have walked out during performances, screamed 'kill the playwright!' (*Filthy Talk for Troubled Times*) or slapped an actor's face after a performance (*The Shape of Things*). In his more recent full-length plays the provocation is more disguised. However, part of the softening of LaBute's acerbic tone is directly due to achieving the public acceptance of Broadway productions. As the *New York Times* review of *Reasons to be Pretty* commented, in the Off-Broadway production, when in a shopping mall the young girl Steph reads out a list of her boyfriend's faults – the tiny size of his penis, his genital hairiness, his habit of eating his toenails – she ends with the declaration that what she has publicly proclaimed is true; rewritten for Broadway, she says 'I made it up . . . it's not true. Any of it'.[6]

The Plays

bash: latter day plays (1999)

This is perhaps the most powerful as well as the most characteristic of LaBute's plays, demonstrating his intrinsic methods while presenting a more nuanced and inter-textual concept than most of his work. The central piece, *a gaggle of saints*, was written (though never performed) while he was at Brigham Young University; it premiered as a trilogy at the Douglas Fairbanks Theatre in 1999.

Like much of his work, there is a deliberate absence of surface detail. *bash* is set on a darkened, empty stage, where the figures of each piece are presented in blank squares of white light with minimal props: an armchair and a water glass; a pair of side chairs; a table, an ashtray, a water glass and a tape recorder. For some critics this avoidance of specific location marks his plays as morality tales – reinforced by the way LaBute tends to name characters 'young man' or just 'woman', as in the bookend pieces of *bash*.[7] However, particularly in this play, it can also be seen as an image of existential displacement, a quintessentially Beckettian progress into the depths of the self.

In this trilogy, the titles of *iphigenia in orem* and *medea redux* emphasize a relation to Greek tragedy, specifically Euripides, who is explicitly mentioned in the final monologue. Since one of the defining characteristics of Classical Greek drama is that violent acts are never performed on stage, but reported by an observer, it provides a powerfully engaging literary justification for these monologues, each of which reveals a murderous act in the recent past. At the same time this overt connection to Greek tragedy gives a mythic level to the play as a whole, combined with Freudian archetypes.

Instead of taking place in Aulis the first play is 'in orem', a small town in Utah – but also playing on the saying *nihil per orem* ('nothing by mouth', an ungrammatical Latin tag, used in medical prescriptions) as against *oremus* (Latin for 'let us pray'), emphasizing the piece's aggressively verbal nature and its un-healing quality, the absence of any salvation. Again, in deliberate variation on Euripides, where at the last minute the goddess Artemis substitutes a deer for the sacrifice and spirits Iphigenia away, here there is no doubt that the child is dead, while the sacrifice is not only purely selfish on the part of the father, but also revealed to have been pointless. Similarly in the last play, while like Euripides' obsessed Medea the unnamed woman has killed her own child to revenge herself on the man who abandoned her, 'redux' (Latin for 'brought back', 'revisited') is a term for films that have been updated and re-released. And indeed, here, the protagonist is a sexually abused, semi-educated, single mother, already arrested for murder, who reveals her own mental confusion: the opposite of Euripides' powerful and vengeful Queen. *a gaggle of saints* has also been seen as a possible analogue to another Euripides play, *The Bacchae*, sharing a similar link between violence and sexual arousal, and using homosexuality as an equivalent of Pentheus' cross-dressing.[8] The centrality of this piece is indicated by the play on the double meaning of *bash* (a party as well as violence) in the opening lines.

Both *iphigenia in orem* and *a gaggle of saints* emphasize the apparent wholesomeness of the speakers. In the first, the protagonist is a business-suited, clean-cut 30-year old. In the central play we are presented with 'a young, attractive couple sitting apart from one another, they are dressed in the popular evening fashion of the day' (p. 35). The original religious references were intended to reinforce their respectability. All designed to intensify audience shock at the revelations of murderous violence, but also to undermine popular assumptions about religion: 'The point was not that they were also blood-thirsty killers, but that going to church, and having a testimony—or being around those who do—is not insurance against having choices in your life that cause you to go the wrong way. . . .'[9] In addition, in *a gaggle of saints* the vicious anti-homosexual feelings have been inculcated by conservative religion, while in all three monologues there is a sense of sexual repression and stereotyped gender roles imposed by such a church.

All three plays of the trilogy are memory tales, explicitly confessions. And while each is a monologue, all three are spoken to an on-stage presence, leaving the audience in the position of literally overhearing. In *iphigenia* this is a passing stranger, picked up in a hotel bar, but unseen; and particularly with this set-up the audience are placed in the position of voyeurs – a morally compromised situation that in some ways echoes the compromises of the speakers. In *medea* this is the tape recorder set there by the police; and in the middle play, the couple, while they never connect, are ostensibly speaking to each other. All three showcase people whose violent acts are truly purposeless, or in the first play turn out (horrifyingly) to be so, leaving them with an unassuaged guilt which they cannot atone for because they can't acknowledge their actions. Like Beckett's plays, the format assumes that these confessions are an infinite series: the salesman will always choose another person each night, since he 'can't tell anyone in the church, or the police, of course . . . so I chose you'; similarly the recorded speech of the female prisoner will be replayed by the police, then by lawyers and in court. And the acts are so horrific that, as witnesses who can provide no absolution (the role spectators are assigned here), we must assume that these stories will be repeated endlessly – as indeed they are, each night, during the run of the play.

The opening salesman's self-justifying tale unintentionally reveals the accidental death of his baby daughter to have been deliberate infanticide. Apparently threatened with losing his job – having got a 'heads up' from a friend at head office – he takes 'this calculated risk for my family that this whole episode would . . . give me that little edge at work and maybe . . . they'd change their minds because of, you know . . .' (p. 27) only to discover much later that his friend was only joking. In *saints*, the bridegroom claims to be morally outraged by a gay couple he has noticed in Central Park, and incites his friends to go after one in a public toilet. But this religiously justified violence is undermined when, alone in the toilet, he makes homosexual advances indicating he too is intimately familiar with gay code; and steals the man's gold ring to give his girlfriend. In *medea*, the prisoner is in denial – not only about the sexual acts with her teacher (all she mentions are hugs and kisses), but also the killing of their child (the tape deck that electrocutes him lands in his bath without apparent agency).

Like LaBute's other plays, *bash* is a powerful attack on the standards of contemporary American society. The valuation of external appearances in combination with repressive religiosity is a recipe for disaster. These speakers not only could be all of us, but three out of the four represent what society defines as the best, while the fourth is a victim of society. As the woman says, (mis)referencing the ancient Greek concept of Adikia, from her experience, the only conclusion is 'the world out of balance'. And their stories are also given a wider frame by LaBute's over-arching connection to classical tragedy. The murder of children (in both opening and closing episodes) is the death of the future, and as in Euripides, fate – the controlling force in Greek tragedy – is a very questionable factor. The salesman, having run out of other excuses, claims 'it was fate' that took his baby daughter, while the woman of the closing play justifies the murder of her son – aged 14, just as she was 14 years old when she became pregnant: indicating the patterning of the whole drama – as punishment for the abusive, abandoning father's belief that 'he'd beaten fate . . . and gotten away with it' so that in her final vision he would be (finally) weeping and screaming at the unfeeling heavens 'why?! why?!' without any answer (pp. 27, 78, 92–4).

The Shape of Things (2001)

In LaBute's first major success – which also provided the script for his first film – *In The Company of Men* (1992), viciously predatory males target women, and through women, each other, in a setting which is carefully designed to be universal. Located in a nameless city, they work for an unidentified corporation, doing undefined executive tasks, and producing unspecified products. Even though their female victim survives (and indeed prospers in the cut-throat world of commerce, signalling an implicit critique of these men), while sympathy is channelled to the female victim, doubly vulnerable because deaf, LaBute's depiction of triumphant masculinity and sexual exploitation was deeply disturbing for the critics and the audiences. Clearly responding to the reviewers' charges of misogyny, LaBute followed up with a gender reversal in *The Shape of Things*. Here the exploiter is a woman, an art student engaged in her MFA project, while the victim is a male undergraduate studying

English literature and working part-time as a museum attendant. But in fact – even though here the woman is dominant – this play is even more misogynistic since sympathies are channelled directly towards the man, and the way the art student is depicted arouses extreme hostility.

Where *bash* implied an attack on appearances, this play makes explicit what can be seen as LaBute's dominant theme, followed up in *fat pig* (2004) and *Reasons to Be Pretty* (2009). Meeting the symbolically-named Adam when setting up to spray-paint a penis on a Greek statue whose genitals have been covered with a fig-leaf, and finding him totally passive and a complete innocent, Evelyn – the Eve of the play whose 'initials, the acronym of her names' spell 'eat' – undertakes to literally sculpt him, physically, emotionally and mentally, into the perfect American male (underlining the title of the play): 'a living, breathing example of our obsession with the surface of things, the shape of them' (pp. 121, 124).

A four-person play, this is as tightly focused as *bash*, and again the revelation comes through monologue: here Evelyn's graduating defence of her art project in an auditorium (doubling as the theatre, so the audience are also her auditors), and she summarizes all that we have watched – but from a destabilizing perspective. His change in hairstyle, switch to contact lenses, and to vegetarianism, adopting a bodybuilding exercise regimen, ceasing to bite his nails, and his surgical nose job – undertaken at her urging in response to her claims of affection and (videotaped) sexual seduction – are all revealed to be completely manipulative. She also manipulates him into breaking with his only friends. She openly acknowledges that she has consistently and deliberately lied about everything: her family background, her claim to herself have undergone cosmetic surgery, even her date of birth and age, and in particular her declared love for Adam, now admitted as 'manufactured emotions'. She labels the old Adam as no more than 'base material' for her '*human* sculpture' seeing the new Adam as 'my creation': a proof of her proposition, 'can i install "x" amount of change in this creature, using only manipulation as my palette knife?'(pp. 118–20, 122)

The audience, who have equally been manipulated and had their 'Cosmo' illusions (the *Cosmopolitan.com* sexual relationship website being repeatedly mentioned) shattered, are likely to cheer Adam's reply that she is 'about two inches away from using babies to make lamp shades and calling it "furniture"'. Yet Adam is aware of literary precedents for his situation:

> **Evelyn**   i gave you a couple of ideas and you're changing your entire life. i'm very proud of you.
> **Adam**   thank you . . . (*cockney*) . . . 'enry iggins. (p. 20)

Adam's reference is of course to *My Fair Lady* (where the newly educated Eliza does end in a romantic relationship with her creator, rather than Bernard Shaw's original more realistic *Pygmalion*; and other still more unpleasant precedents are forecast, as when he refers to Mary Shelley (Frankenstein's monster). Indeed Evelyn's defence, that how we define art is subjective, was raised by Adam in the opening scene: 'they're both pretty subjective: "art". "truth".' And LaBute supports this definition. 'I'm big on what the argument the film (2003) proposes about subjectivity about art itself' (pp. 8, 20, 133).[10]

The Distance from Here (2002)

This bleak picture of Middle America could be seen as a parallel to *bash*, except that these are inarticulate people without any inner life so that the play is all action instead of monologue. They are members of no church and their families are all broken. *The Distance from Here* is also a contrasting companion piece to LaBute's second film: *Your Friends and Neighbours* (1998). Explicitly a contemporary variant on Wycherley's most cynical Restoration comedy *The Country Wife* (a scene from which is performed by characters in the film), this presents a group of wealthy professionals, preoccupied by sexual games and practicing adultery, whose lifestyles have no inner meaning.

In *The Distance from Here* there is no aesthetic appearance to offset the disintegrating reality; and these figures are impoverished, failed by the school system and banished from the American Dream being lived so delusively by *Your Friends and Neighbours*. There is also another, more central contrasting parallel: in the film a gynaecologist is shown lecturing beside a cut-out model of a female reproductive tract holding a model of a foetal baby: in a moment of rage he drop-kicks the plaster model across the room. In *The Distance from Here* a real, living baby in a bag is thrown – '*Darrell pulls it back and lets it fly with a full revolution*' (p. 116) – over a zoo fence into a penguin pool. The parallel shows there is no 'distance' from either group of people to the social context of LaBute's American audience.

In *The Distance from Here* we are introduced to two generations: teenagers and the mother of one (twice-married and now with a boyfriend) together with the daughter of her husband number two (who is both an unmarried mother herself, and the lover of her stepmother's boyfriend). The setting for the home says it all:

> *Well worn and threadbare. . . . Really cheap. . . . TV in the corner, on and loud.*

His mother's lover is ironically named Rich. His one sensible remark to Darrell is, 'Giving you a clue, pal . . . get the fuck outa here, you got the chance'. And that is precisely what Darrell does, having stolen his mother's credit card and the keys to her car, after killing his stepsister's baby, and beating his only friend into unconsciousness. But it is a journey to nowhere: 'Guess I'll just keep driving, you know? Go upstate, maybe, fuck if I know. . . . And I don't give a fuck it's any place I ever even heard of . . .' (pp. 19, 43, 118).

The action demonstrates the inability of these characters to actually do anything. Shari, Darrell's stepsister, who at one point tries to seduce him too (on the basis of fabricated childhood memories), has a perverted fantasy of the American Dream that she imagines playing out with her lover Rich – a relationship fuelled by mutual guilt at deceiving her mother: 'Be so great . . . to be together . . . paint the house . . . right down the middle, where the two front doors are. And use some colour that would drive the whole neighbourhood crazy!' Then, in a retreat from reality that is also a denial of life, she imagines them retreating from an unfriendly world 'We all gotta just stay inside. Food running out. Utilities all been shut off. And so . . . we just make love all the time . . . . 'Cause that's all we got left' (pp. 121–2).

But as LaBute points out: 'The absent fathers that haunt the pages of this play are not the only "Missing Persons" here; emotionally,

Darrell and company went AWOL a long time ago'. Rich clearly seeks only sexual gratification from either woman. Darrell continually and increasingly violently beats up his one and only friend, Tim, and has no remorse about killing his stepsister's baby. Darrell's mother and stepsister always leave the baby to cry without attention because (implicitly referencing the American Dream) they 'don't think you oughta just jump up whenever they start wailing like that . . . just teaches 'em . . . *false* expectations 'a things. 'Cause life isn't like that . . .' (Preface, pp. 8, 22).

The American family ideal is denied. Darrell's father has abandoned the family; and when his mother remarried, it was 'a bad time for me . . . . Lost the kid, . . . and Shari's dad and me at each other a lot. Fighting'. Even Darrell means little to her: 'just you as an individual—you never really made that big an impression'. Tim's family is no better; his father has chased him 'around the neighbourhood with a hammer' (pp. 104, 113).

'The Monkey Cage' – the setting for the opening scene – is a clear symbol of the social situation for these characters, which LaBute describes in the Preface:

> In high school I sat next to a bunch of boys like Darrell and Tim . . . and watched them simmer and burn and consistently pull down a D- in nearly every subject. They knew, even at sixteen, that they had no hope in life. . . . Darrell, his friends, and the other characters of this story are banging their collective heads against the bars of their cage. . . .

In the closing scene, Tim tries to do something good: to retrieve the long dead baby from the frozen pool. But when he asks Jenn, 'you don't think this is, like *stupid*, do ya?', they both know the rescue is pointless (pp. 7–8, 105).

Even with these despairing and irredeemably downmarket characters, LaBute filled all the major parts with well-known film stars: Darrell being played by Mark Webber, whose IMDbPro bio emphasizes his suitability for the role, telling us he was: 'raised by his single mother in the slums of North Philadelphia, . . . homeless, living in cars and abandoned buildings, and struggling to survive during the harsh winters'. While the recognition factor might make the audience identify with the characters – here, figures they would specifically not imagine as their 'friends and neighbours' – it underlines the potential that has been denied to them by their social situation. As in *bash*, but even more explicitly, given the contrast right from the beginning, this star-recognition is designed to bring out LaBute's attack on the false values of American culture.

As a society, America is given no hope for the future. LaBute's own high school was the one these characters have all gone to, and he references

> our own little urban myth, in fact, about a boy and a girl who had dated since junior high. . . . It was whispered that she had gotten pregnant on several occasions and, whenever it happed, the boy would pound the girl in the stomach until she miscarried (Preface, p. 8).

If these youngsters are the abandoned generation, there will be no babies to follow them. Darrell arbitrarily kills his stepsister's baby on discovering that Jenn has aborted his own baby, at age 15, during a summer when he rejected her and left town. Told of a video, showing Jenn sucking the penis of a black ball player who then pounds her in the stomach, Darrell is enraged, and even more disturbed to learn that the man gave his own girl repeated abortions in this way and the blow job is the only payment Jenn could offer. In this (symbolically representative) group the generational sequence has been definitively broken. To reinforce this, LaBute introduces an animal theme. Scenes in the zoo and in a pet shop switch with living room scenes, implying a clear equivalence, while Darrell's father's 'best' memory of the war in Iraq is being on a helicopter that collided with 'big fucking birds . . . went ripping right through 'em at about a hundred and fifty miles an hour . . . feathers, blood, all sorts 'a shit on everybody!' which saves his life by terrifying the insurgents when they land. The contrast with Rich's war memories are telling. As he remembers, in Riyadh, while making a sexual assignation with an underage girl and her mother, he came across a toyshop that stocked wonderful kites – in the shape of white birds; 'Hugh white wings . . . long graceful neck . . . had it up there, oh, at least a good couple hundred feet . . .' (pp. 12, 33, 84). Even the animals are killed or in cages, and the only freedom is represented by a simulacrum on a cord.

In a Dark Dark House (2007)

In a Dark Dark House has an even more personal autobiographical resonance than *bash* and *The Distance from Here*, with LaBute pointing in interviews as well as his Preface to the theme of abuse that runs through this play. Like the repeated 'dark' of the title, this is doubled: a violent father and a homosexual paedophile. It is no accident that this play is dedicated to Sam Shepard, whom LaBute hails as an artistic father figure because of all the 'difficult fathers and brothers at each other's throats' in Shepard's work (p. xiii).

Like most of his other plays, too, this opens in '*Silence. Darkness*' – even though the scene 'in the woods' echoes the title of Sondheim's musical and in the first MCC production the setting was so bright and 'magical realist' that critics described 'a sunny, Never Never Land quality', further indicated as delusive since in the final scene we hear heavy machinery and are told the woods are being built over for condos.[11] Nothing, not even the scenery, can be trusted.

With just three characters, the focus is intense; and again the structure is one of successive revelations, which exposes the fakeness of the setting, where the noise of traffic mingles with sounds of wildlife. Drew, whom we first see in a wheelchair (although he immediately shows he has no need of such prosthetics), claims that he is in this rehab facility to avoid charges of drunk driving; and we finally learn that he has called in his older brother, Terry, to back up his scam that his actions have been caused by the trauma of a psychologically-damaged childhood when he was raped (something Drew had denied at the time) by Todd, who had already made himself Terry's partner. Learning this, Terry vows revenge, even though he is aware that his brother's real reason for being in rehab is to neutralize charges of infidelity that endanger his marriage, and of ethical misconduct likely to get him disbarred as a lawyer.

Terry, a security guard, goes in search of Todd, but instead finds Todd's teenage daughter running a miniature golf course. He picks her up, kisses her, persuades her to go for a car ride with him. She '*pulls an elaborate key chain out of her pocket . . . Twirls her keys and looks at him*' – and at the end of the final scene, when he has managed to dismantle Drew's lies, discovering that Drew could not have had a boyhood relationship with Todd, Terry pulls the same key chain from his pocket '*twists it in the dying light. Watches the glowing splinters dance around him as dusk begins to approach. / Sound of traffic and the woods./Silence, Darkness*'. While reviewers of the first production were confused (commenting, 'Terry retrieves an object from his pocket and holds it up to the light, but one can't be sure exactly what his possession of the object is meant to indicate') (pp. 3, 5, 56, 88).[12] There are only two options: either Terry has become her lover – perverted because of the age difference together with his motivation – and expropriated her car; or, far more likely, he has killed her. And both actions, as with so many other final actions in LaBute's plays, are pointless because they are based on lies.

Summary

LaBute's overarching theme is that of personal appearances. This is paralleled by, and portrayed through his spiritual and ethical focus. And both are intensified or made extremely personal by his particular use of dramatic form.

The titles of two of his plays speak directly to the theme of bodily appearance: *Fat Pig* and *Reasons to be Pretty*. Both – along with *The Shape of Things* – explicitly embody (in a literal and physical sense) the contemporary American obsession with advertising-determined physical ideals. What can be called or seen as beauty – and what should it matter in our estimate of ourselves, or others? Why do we assume that external attributes express the inner reality: does plastic surgery change the personality, or does psychotherapy alter one's physical image? In a land where obesity is almost the norm, who is justified in criticizing anyone?

Indeed, the provocation of LaBute's plays is primarily aimed at making us question the way American society today substitutes surfaces for substance, personal appearances for principle, and – in his view – lacks or even deliberately betrays ethical standards and morality that it so officiously proclaims. This is underlined by the way he characterizes his leading figures. So, while the actions of Chad (*In the Company of Men*) or Guy (*Some Girl(s)*) mark them as the most selfish, immoral and manipulative characters – Chad's opening statement is 'Let's hurt somebody' – they are described as handsome, clean-cut and respectable, their physique, faces and dress representing the male ideal of the popular imagination. This iconography is highlighted by LaBute's habit of having characters played by film stars, starting in *bash* with the TV actor Paul Rudd together with the 'Ally McBeal' star Calista Flockhart, where it was clearly designed to garner respect and approbation, thus making the revelations still more shocking. LaBute himself has commented, 'pretty guys have this glow. No matter how bad they are, people keep going back to them. Being pretty can bring out the worst in people'.[13]

It is primarily women these men exploit, although – like Mamet's *Glengarry Glen Ross* – Chad's predatory and misogynistic stalking of an arbitrarily selected victim, whose deafness makes her doubly vulnerable, is revealed as only a pretence for demolishing his male companion in crime, even if here that male-on-male focus intensifies the insult to the female target. However, while the male characters in his plays are almost always the exploiters, LaBute is careful to level the (im)moral playing field, with female characters such as Evelyn (*The Shape of Things*) who uses her sexuality for completely manipulative purposes, or Steph (*Reasons to be Pretty*) whose diatribes dominate her male partner. Predatory betrayal and egotistical manipulation is an equal opportunity field in LaBute's plays.

The complete normality of the way these figures all speak and LaBute's extraordinarily naturalistic dialogue – one thing that the critics continually praise – makes his characters seem (horrifyingly) normal, while his drive for realistic credibility has led LaBute to remove curtain calls (for instance, in the first production of *The Shape of Things*), as the moment where actors step out of role and the play is revealed to be 'a lie', so that the audience can be taken 'out of the presupposed place . . . and say to them, "I would like you to feel as uncertain as we do, as the story is trying to be"'.[14] No escape is allowed from the depiction of a dysfunctional society; but what he sets against the cold egotism his characters embody is a conviction in the value of spirituality that he sees as absent in everyday American life. As he has commented, 'Whether I'm in organized religion or not, the moral structure that was instilled in me early has always been interested in those larger questions of good and bad, of sin and morality'.[15] In short, the darkness in LaBute's plays can be seen as moralist.

At the same, the spirituality – so absent in his plays – that implicitly stands against the misogynist, egotistical and materialistic figures he portrays, is not associated with organized religion. Nor is it expected to come from instantaneous conversion.

In one of his earliest pieces, *bash*, it is the conservative morality of the Mormon Church that allows and even – in the characters' distorted view – justifies inhumanity and violence. Similarly, in one of his latest pieces, *The Book of Job*, in the 2011 Bush Theatre *66 Books* celebration of the King James Bible, LaBute's focus is on the 'comforters', represented as racists and paedophiles, casual murderers, wife beaters and adulterers without remorse. The pious Job is seen as little more than a fall guy and victim, while his tormentors represent the way contemporary people feel they have licence to behave badly. By comparison, in *The Break of Noon* (2010) the only survivor of an office massacre – by an outraged ex-employee whom he had personally fired – is led by a sense of undeserved salvation to proclaim he has been saved by God to spread the holy word. As we follow him through intrusions on his ex-wife and his mistress (both played in the MCC production by a film and TV personality, Catherine Dent), a prostitute and a talk-show host (each played by the same award-winning film star, Tracy Chimo), the immoral selfishness at the core of his personality becomes plain. As the *New York Times* review commented: 'Mr. LaBute's latest play is the one that most directly takes on an issue that is always, it seems on his mind: the possibility of divine grace in an irredeemably human world'.[16]

These contrasting themes are given bite and depth by LaBute's idiosyncratic use of monologue as his characteristic form of expression. From his very first professional produced piece, *Filthy Talk for Troubled*

Times (1989) through to his one-person horror-play, *The Unimaginable* (2010), LaBute returns continually to monologue. The unsettling voices of *bash* are intensified through the impression of solipsistic isolation and the stream-of-consciousness revelation of the speakers' self-deception. When *Reasons to be Pretty* was originally staged, it included four monologues, one by each character, recounting how ideals of physical attractiveness shaped their lives – although these were cut for the Broadway production, privileging character instead of social theme. Even in plays with conventional dialogue, speeches that are effectively monologues recur, even if within the dramatic context. The opening self-examination by the protagonist of *Break of Noon* trying to come to terms with the massacre around him, functions as monologue; and as Christopher Bigsby has pointed out, most of LaBute's plays 'are marked to indicate overlapping dialogue. This is less because his characters cannot wait for someone to complete a thought or even a sentence before responding than because they believe what they wish to think and say has primacy. They speak out of a self which demands space, attention, centrality'.[17] This is as much as to say that LaBute's figures representing the American scene are all inherent monologists.

Primary Sources

Works by Neil LaBute

Autobahn, a Short Play Cycle (New York & London: Faber & Faber, 2005).

Bash (Woodstock, NY: Overlook Press, 2001).

The Break of Noon (Berkley, CA: Soft Skull Press, 2010).

The Distance from Here (Woodstock, NY: Overlook Press, 2002).

Fat Pig (New York: Faber & Faber, 2004).

Filthy Talk for Troubled Times, and Other Plays (Berkley, CA: Soft Skull Press, 2010).

In a Dark Dark House (New York & London: Faber & Faber, 2007).

In a Forest, Dark and Deep (New York & London: Faber & Faber, 2011).

In the Company of Men (New York & London: Faber & Faber, 1997).

The Mercy Seat (New York & London: Faber & Faber, 2003).

Reasons to be Pretty (New York: Dramatists Play Service Inc., 2009).

The Shape of Things (New York & London: Faber & Faber, 2000).

Some Girl(s) (New York & London: Faber & Faber, 2005).

This is How It Goes (New York & London: Faber & Faber, 2002).

Your Friends and Neighbours (New York & London: Faber & Faber, 1998).

Secondary Sources

Bigsby, Christopher, *Neil LaBute: Stage and Cinema* (Cambridge: Cambridge University Press, 2007).

Brantley, Ben, 'Let's Twist Again, Dude, as the Screws Turn', *New York Times*, 8 June 2007.

English, Mary, 'A Modern Euripides'. In Gerald Wood (ed.), *Neil LaBute: A Casebook* (New York: Routledge, 2006), pp. 23–38.

Jordan, Pat, 'Neil LaBute Has a Thing About Beauty', *The New York Times*, 29 March 2009.

Lahr, John, 'A Touch of Bad: Why is the director Neil LaBute so interested in jerks?' In Gerald Wood (ed.), *Neil LaBute: A Casebook* (New York: Routledge, 2006), pp. 11–22.

Morrison, Alan, 'Neil LaBute', *The Guardian*, 2 November 2003.

Peary, Gerald, 'Neil LaBute', October 2000. www.geraldpeary.com/interviews/jkl/labute.html

Portantiere, Michael, 'In a Dark Dark House', *Theatermania*, 7 June 2007.

Weinert-Kendt, Rob, 'Review of Deirdre O'Connor's *Jailbait*', *The Village Voice*, 8 April 2009.

Welch, Rosalynde, 'An Interview with Neil LaBute', *Times and Seasons*, 19 January 2005.

Wood, Gerald C., *Neil LaBute: A Casebook* (New York: Routledge, 2006).

Notes

1. Christopher Bigsby, *Neil LaBute: Stage and Cinema*, p. 2.
2. Gerald Peary, 'Neil LaBute'.
3. Pat Jordan, 'Neil LaBute Has a Thing About Beauty', *The New York Times*, 29 March 2009.
4. Rosalynde Welch, 'An Interview with Neil LaBute', *Times and Seasons*, 19 January 2005.
5. Rob Weinert-Kendt (a passing comment in reviewing Deirdre O'Connor's *Jailbait*), *The Village Voice*, 8 April 2009. *The Independent* echoed this characterization, calling LaBute 'America's misanthrope par excellence'. 28 May 2008.
6. Pat Jordan, 'Neil LaBute Has a Thing About Beauty'.
7. For instance: Christopher Bigsby. *Neil LaBute: Stage and Cinema*, (Cambridge: Cambridge University Press, 2007), p. 12. John Lahr, 'A Touch of Blind'. In Gerald C. Wood (ed.), *Neil LaBute: A Casebook* (New York: Routledge, 2006), p. 12.
8. Mary English, 'A Modern Euripides', p. 28f.

9. Rosalynde Welch, 'An Interview with Neil LaBute', *Times and Seasons*, 19 January 2005.

10. Alan Morrison, 'Neil LaBute', *The Guardian*, 2 November 2003.

11. Ben Brantley, 'Let's Twist Again, Dude, as the Screws Turn', *New York Times*, 8 June 2007.

12. Michael Portantiere, 'In a Dark Dark House', *Theatermania*, 8 June 2007.

13. Pat Jordan, 'Thing About Beauty'.

14. Rosalynde Welch, 'An Interview with Neil LaBute', *Times and Seasons*, 19 January 2005.

15. Ibid.

16. Ben Brantley, 'Let's Twist Again, Dude'.

17. Christopher Bigsby, *Neil LaBute: Stage and Cinema*, p. 15.

9 DAVID MAMET

Toby Zinman

American Buffalo; Glengarry Glen Ross; Speed-the-Plow; Oleanna; The Cryptogram; Race

Introduction

An extraordinarily prolific and controversial playwright, David Mamet is a presence in contemporary American culture which extends beyond theatre into film and beyond performing arts into fiction, memoirs, children's stories, poetry and essays. In addition to writing, he has directed plays and films, and has established three theatre companies. Since the death of Arthur Miller, Mamet has become America's foremost theatrical social critic, but unlike Miller, who believed that we 'could be better', as Chris tells his father in *All My Sons*, Mamet seems to have no such hope. In his best plays, Mamet reveals again and again that human beings, motivated by greed for money and/or power, lie, cheat, manipulate and, when that doesn't work, resort to violence. Everyone betrays everyone – individually or collectively – and the feeling of having been betrayed – individually or collectively – creates rage.

David Mamet was born in Chicago in 1947; his father was a labour lawyer and his mother a teacher. Their rancorous marriage and divorce shaped his childhood, terrifyingly recounted in his autobiographical essay 'The Rake'. His sister, Lynn Mamet, who shared that childhood, is now a television producer; in Mamet's collection *Writing in Restaurants*, she appears in a piece called *True Stories of Bitches* in which the brother and sister are in a delicatessen; Mamet says of his pastrami sandwich, 'How can we eat this food? This is *heart*-attack food . . . .' Lynn Mamet 'remonstrated' in a riposte Mamet calls an example of her genius: 'Listen, it gave six million Jews the strength to resist Hitler'.

While in Chicago, Mamet started working in the theatre and eventually he, William Macy and Steven Schachter formed the St Nicholas Theatre Company; his association with Macy would become the core of an acting group including Felicity Huffman and Joe Mantegna, referred to as the 'Mamet Mafia'. Young Mamet also hung around Second City, Chicago's famed theatre for sketch comedy and improv; early members of that company were Ed Asner, Elaine May, Mike Nichols, Alan Arkin and Bill Murray.

Mamet began writing plays while at Goddard College in Vermont and spent what he calls his 'Junior year abroad' in New York studying with Sanford Meisner; this would become the basis of much of Mamet's theorizing about acting where theory was discounted as minimal; instead, Mamet believed the actor's task was to: 'learn the lines, find a simply objective, . . . speak the lines clearly in an attempt to achieve that objective' (*True and False*, 57); in other words, 'Get the work done'. It is worth noting that despite this Meisner emphasis on 'The best way to act is to live truthfully', when Mamet directs his own work, the staccato dialogue and his extreme demands of unadorned clarity often create performances that seem robotic.

After graduation from college, Mamet dabbled in acting, and his first play, *Lakeboat*, was produced in 1970 at Marlboro College in Vermont. This success was followed by others; when *Sexual Perversity in Chicago* won the Obie award for Best Play in 1975, Mamet's career was launched, to be followed by the major New York premiere of his first great full-length play, *American Buffalo*. While his theatrical career continued, mounting in excitement and importance, Mamet's film career began with his first screenplay for *The Postman Always Rings Twice* in 1981, to be followed the next year by *The Verdict* (starring Paul Newman) with starry vehicles following, including *Hoffa* (starring Jack Nicholson) and *The Untouchables* (Kevin Costner and Robert De Niro). In 1986 he both wrote and directed *House of Games* starring his then-wife, Lindsay Crouse.

His first marriage was to actress Lindsay Crouse, with whom he has two children. He is currently married to actress Rebecca Pidgeon,

who often performs in his plays and films, and they live with their two
children in Santa Monica, California.

The Plays

American Buffalo (1976)

> 'Cause there's business and there's friendship . . . and what you
> got to do is keep clear who your friends are . . . . Or else the rest
> is garbage . . . . (pp. 7–8)

There is plenty of garbage in David Mamet's fierce and funny play
American Buffalo, which, in 1975, launched Mamet's reputation as one
of America's premiere playwrights. The action takes place in a junkshop
that is clearly a metaphor for America.

American Buffalo is about three inner-city losers: Don, who owns
the junkshop; Bobby, his eager-to-please, not-too-bright protégé who
is a recovering drug addict; and Don's friend Teach. Teach is the high-
voltage role, famously filled first by Robert Duvall, then by Al Pacino
(the performance that launched his career) and, most recently (as of this
writing), by Tracy Letts, actor turned Pulitzer Prize-winning playwright
(*Superior Donuts, August: Osage County, Bug, Killer Joe*) turned actor
again in the 2010 brilliant *Steppenwolf* production. Dustin Hoffman
played Teach in the film version.

The plot turns on a collectible nickel and a ludicrous robbery plot.
The three incompetents are repulsive and pathetic and hilarious and
touching, as they stumble their way through their friendships and half-
baked philosophies, 'action talks and bullshit walks'. *American Buffalo*'s
characters' idea of 'action' is ineffectual violence and cruel betrayals and
flabby apologies; although the play seems to be action-filled, in fact it is
about inaction, ineffectual action and non-event, similar to his early short
plays, *Duck Variations* and *Lakeboat*, which are also eventless. The play's real
action is in the dialogue which requires a startling speed of delivery; ideally
the actors barely pause for breath. Crucial, too, is a director's willingness to

take the pauses and deliver the urgent, tense silences. When one character says to another, 'Wait a minute', the actors should wait that minute.

Mamet's hilarious and breathtakingly fierce indictment of the business ethos is revealed in this exchange:

> **Teach** You know what is free enterprise?
> **Don** No. What?
> **Teach** The freedom . . .
> **Don** . . . yeah?
> **Teach** Of the *Individual* . . .
> **Don** . . . yeah?
> **Teach** To Embark on Any Fucking Course that he sees fit.
> **Don** Uh-huh . . .
> **Teach** In order to secure his honest chance to make a profit. Am I so out of line on this? . . . . The country's *founded* on this, Don. You know this. . . . Without this we're just savage shitheads in the wilderness. . . . Sitting around some vicious campfire. (pp. 72–3)

The set for *American Buffalo* provides the designer with an opportunity to create a fabulously cluttered stage – a floor-to-ceiling array of the detritus of materialism, toying with the play's realism and anti-realism simultaneously – making Mamet's disgust with the American business ethic visible. This disgust will surface again in *Glengarry Glen Ross,* and *Speed-the-Plow.* The pig-sticker, a mysterious and repulsive object that seems constantly to threaten some immanent hideous incident, becomes the play's central prop; it is the inexplicability of this odd object that fuels Teach's high-voltage rage and paranoia. The hat he makes of newspaper sheets to protect his head from the rain functions as the other memorable prop, balancing with grotesque pathos and foolishness the obscene aggression of the pig-sticker.

A note on the title: the American buffalo roamed the western prairies for centuries; estimates are that herds numbered between 30 million and 200 million. Through overhunting for food, hides and sport, using horses and guns and tourist trains (contrary to the conservative way Native Americans hunted), their numbers dwindled to mere hundreds.

Also nearly vanished is the Indian Head Nickel, a five-cent coin that was minted from 1913 to 1938. On one side was an Indian in profile, and on the obverse, a buffalo. The implication of Mamet's title suggests the vanishing of values of an America of the past. The two off-stage women, Ruth and Grace, are, given the values their names imply, significantly absent.[1] We watch this little male society, where love and loyalty are well-laced with violence and mistrust, founder. The nickel is also devalued money, and Mamet's indictment of capitalism, especially notable considering his newest book, *The Secret Knowledge: On the Dismantling of American Culture* (2011) which is a pro-capitalism argument; C. W. E. Bigsby calls *American Buffalo* 'an assault on the American business ethic and an assertion of the collapse of morale and morality in America'.[2]

Glengarry Glen Ross (1982)

Mamet worked in a Chicago real estate office when he was in college: now *that* was a job that paid off in the long run. He would eventually use his experience to write a play about unscrupulous real estate salesmen, and *Glengarry Glen Ross* won the 1984 Pulitzer Prize.

One of Mamet's 'business plays' (this list includes at least *American Buffalo, A Life in the Theatre, Speed-the-Plow* and *Race*), *Glengarry Glen Ross* provides an interesting contrast to Arthur Miller's business play, *Death of a Salesman*, written 33 years earlier, which is also about the high price of doing business to both the individual and society. *Glengarry* is a play about debased values resulting in desperation and betrayal; it is very funny and very sad and reaches to the utmost despair inherent in President Calvin Coolidge's famous slogan, 'The business of America is business'. A variation on this debasement was President George W. Bush's advice to America in 2007 when recession loomed, 'I encourage you all to go shopping more'. It is worth remembering here that Miller's play, *The Price*, has Solomon, its wise old man, tell us,

> Years ago a person, he was unhappy, didn't know what to do with himself—he'd go to church, start a revolution—*something*. Today you're unhappy? Can't figure it out? What is the salvation? Go shopping. (p. 41)

Glengarry is in Pinter's debt, not only for the English playwright's stylistic influence on the younger American playwright, but directly. Mamet had sent the script to Pinter with a note reading, 'There is something wrong with this play. What is it?' Pinter 'wired him immediately. "There is nothing wrong with this play. I'm giving it to the National"'.[3] It premiered at the Cottesloe Theatre at the National Theatre in London in 1983, followed in 1984 by the Chicago premiere and then the New York premiere.

Glengarry Glen Ross is about a group of backstabbing men (one critic called them 'jackals in jackets') who sell suckers worthless, pie-in-the-sky property in Arizona or Florida. 'Glengarry Glen Ross' is the name of the current development they are trying to hustle. Their uneasy friendships hinge on competition, an ongoing crusade to prove, daily, their masculinity in this 'world of men'. At the moment the play opens, they are vying to win a Cadillac (a flashy, expensive American car). Ricky Roma, a pinky-ringed slick talker, is the office's alpha male. Williamson is the slimy, exploitative office manager, written off by the men who work in the field as 'whitebread', i.e. colourless and bland; he is both despised and feared, and his 'Go to lunch' scene is a study in icy power (and an opportunity for a virtuosic performance in an otherwise thankless role). Shelly 'the Machine' Levine is the old-school salesman, a throwback who has lost his touch and is panicked for money. Moss is the nastiest of the bunch, while Aronow is the most decent and – not coincidentally – the most clueless.

The plot revolves around stolen 'leads' – names of prospective buyers. The audience/reader is partly in on the theft, although when we hear Moss suggest to Aronow the idea of stealing the leads, he is 'just speaking' as opposed to 'actually talking' about it. This now-classic distinction emerges as a commentary on the dialogue; in a play about fast and fraudulent talk, this distinction is crucial, and we are likely to discover our assumptions about who did what when are startlingly wrong. Mamet has conned us into believing what he needs us to believe. Thus our sense of betrayal allows us to sympathize with the men we also simultaneously despise. Note that this distinction between talking and speaking, and the idea of the con game – fooling your victim into believing he knows more than you do about the transaction – is the engine of Mamet's tricky and brilliant film, *House of Games* in which a psychiatrist and a cardsharp are pitted against each other in a high stakes game.

Speed-the-Plow (1988)

Revived on Broadway with a high-profile cast in 2009, *Speed-the-Plow* revealed that there is nothing dated about this high-velocity evisceration of the way Hollywood does business: the ethics versus greed wars are lost and won yet again. In his essay, 'A Playwright in Hollywood', Mamet wrote, 'Now we Americans have always considered Hollywood, at best, a sinkhole of depraved venality. And, of course, it is.'[4]

The plot revolves around two men: Bobby Gould, newly promoted to a position of power in a movie studio, and his long-time friend, Charlie Fox. Karen, a young, temporary secretary seduces Bobby Gould in an attempt to create a position for herself in the industry. She uses his insecurities about 'art' and 'being good' to urge him to produce a high-minded, commercially unviable film as opposed to the meaningless buddy-movie moneymaker which would be the making of Charlie's career.

When Karen challenges the status quo with, 'But why should it all be garbage?' Bobby Gould replies, 'Why? Why should nickels be bigger than dimes? That's the way it is'. (p. 29) Thus the garbage aesthetic is not only firmly established but clearly articulated when Bobby Gould confesses to her that he 'prayed to be pure' and that 'the job corrupts'. Although he flirts with the idea of the redemption of making an 'artsy' film, he comes to his senses when he realizes that Karen slept with him only to advance her career. Once again, male friendship and the complex homosocial dynamic of competition and loyalty triumphs as the one female character proves herself to be treacherous, as do so many of Mamet's other women.

Bobby Gould's need for spiritual legitimacy ('I was called to my new job') is overwhelmed by his need for power and money. In the catechism that ends the play, the two producers celebrate their prosperity in an exchange that harks back to an earlier play, *Bobby Gould in Hell*:

> **Fox** . . . And what *if* this fucken' "grace" exists? It's not for you. You know that, Bob. You know that. You have a different thing.
>
> **Gould** She told me I was a good man. . . .
>
> **Fox** I know what you wanted, Bob. You wanted to do good.
>
> **Gould** Yes. (pause) Thank you . . . I wanted to do Good . . . . But I became foolish.
>
> **Fox** Well, so we learn a lesson. But we aren't here to "pine," Bob, we aren't put here to *mope*. What are we here to do (pause) Bob? After everything is said and done. What are we put on earth to do?
>
> **Gould** We're here to make a movie.
>
> **Fox** Whose name goes above the title?
>
> **Gould** Fox and Gould
>
> **Fox** Then how bad can life be? (p. 81)

The play answers Fox's question, and suggests that we, the movie-going public, may well get the movies we deserve. In his essay 'Film is a Collaborative Business' Mamet wrote, 'Hollywood is the city of the modern gold rush, and money calls the turn. This is the first and last rule, as we know, of Hollywood—we permit ourselves to be treated like commodities in the hope that we may, one day, be treated like *valuable* commodities'.[5]

The play's title comes from an English proverb, 'God speed the plough'; the earliest known usage is 1472. It does not mean that God should hasten the plough, but rather prosper the plough.[6] And *Speed the Plough*, a comedy in five acts written by Thomas Morton in 1800, sets a theatrical precedent. Mamet's intention is clearly ironic as a commentary on the very nature of work, juxtaposing farming with movie-making.

Oleanna (1992)

Oleanna is a shocking, stunning play: each revival provokes audiences anew, suggesting that not only is it a strong script, demanding performances of great subtlety and ambiguity, but that its subject – gender warfare – is far from resolved. Consider its likeness to Ibsen or Strindberg, both in content and in unresolved sociopolitical issues. The first production off-Broadway, with Mamet directing William Macy and Rebecca Pidgeon (Mamet's wife), caused audiences – angry feminists, Harvard professors, Coast Guard Academy cadets – to cheer or shout abuse at the characters. In London, Harold Pinter directed *Oleanna* to new effect; as Matt Wolf wrote, 'the catcalls that have littered the history of this play are shown to be secondary to a much more deafening noise—the collective gasp of an audience as it watches a great playwright/director team extinguish civilization's lights'.[7] This is sociopolitical, psychosexual dialectic honed to a razor-sharp edge.

The title comes from a nineteenth-century tune written by a Norwegian whose dreams of freedom led him to try to found a Utopian community in Pennsylvania; in the twentieth century Pete Seeger translated his lyrics ('In Oleanna land is free/The wheat and corn just plant themselves . . . .' The third verse contains these shocking lyrics: 'The women there do all the work/As round the fields they quickly go/ Each one has a hickory stick/And beats herself if she works too slow'), suggesting it is a song about freedom and slavery, and further suggesting that one person's idea of paradise is not another's. Following Seeger's version, the Kingston Trio, a popular folk singing group, recorded their own adaptation where each verse contains a disaster (at sea, mountain climbing, space travel, etc.) and where the singer is each time greeted with the pseudo-merry chorus, 'Ole, oleanna. Ole, oleanna. Ole, ole, ole ole, ole, oleanna'.

This play is about a male professor and his female student, and steps into the arena of sexual harassment when it was having its dreadful heyday on American campuses. Mamet finished writing this during the controversy generated by the Hill-Thomas hearings, although he insists its subject is the abuse of power rather than, specifically, sexual harassment. John's course in theories of education has confused and discouraged his student. Carol comes to him for help with the course material and his response is both preoccupied (he's in the middle of buying a new house and is on the phone with his real estate agent) and willing to help (he offers to abandon the tyranny of a grade if she comes for tutorial sessions) and patronizing (his vocabulary is jargonized and pretentious). His university has voted 'yes' on his bid for tenure, but it is not yet official.

Carol is exasperatingly dense and her seemingly wilfully irrational arguments infuriate him (and us). Her literalism and incapacity to understand the nuances of language create some of the mayhem, but his frustration at not being able to convince her – through language – of his good and noble intentions (what a pompous ass he is) mean that this play, like most Mamet plays, is about communication. The issue is not only who intended what, but who said what and who understood that what to mean what. The frequently repeated line is, 'I don't understand'. That Mamet plays are filled with expert talkers (Teach in *American Buffalo*, Roma in *Glengarry Glen Ross*, Bobby Gold the hostage negotiator in *Homicide*) suggests the exhaustion of language as a human tool and the thematic ambiguity then extends to us: what is the playwright's relation to his audience?

Act One ends with this exchange about John's wife's secret plans for his upcoming tenure party:

> **John**   There are those who would say it's a form of aggression.
> **Carol** What is?
> **John**   A surprise (p. 41).

Act Three provides both surprise and aggression. Once again betrayal is Mamet's theme. And feeling betrayed, as we see in play after play, leads to rage. John and Carol's struggle between male and female, powerful and powerless amounts to witnessing a political revolution as well as a tragedy. Hubris is on the loose again on both sides.

The Cryptogram (1995)

Maybe every American playwright has to write a family drama. *The Cryptogram* is Mamet's, and it is a difficult and deeply disturbing play. And although many of Mamet's plays deal with unpleasant topics and nasty behaviour, they are usually laugh-out-loud funny; *The Cryptogram* lacks this comic element entirely. Initial critical reaction to the premiere in London directed to Geoffrey Mosher followed by the American premiere under Mamet's own direction, was summed up by the Varity review, 'a prime example of style triumphing over content that teeters on the brink of banality'. Subsequent productions, not under Mamet's direction, were far more positive, acknowledging the play's deeply disturbing power to portray the loss of innocence rather than the 'melodrama' of marital betrayal it was first thought to be.

Tolstoy told us in the famous opening line of *Anna Karenina* that 'All happy families are alike; each unhappy family is unhappy in its own way'. Mamet takes this wisdom one step further: 'Aggression has an unlimited vocabulary. The unhappy family has myriad ways in which to be unhappy, in which to torture its members'.[8] Emotional torture is the specialty of the house lived in by Donny and her son John and visited by Del, a long-time family friend. In an remarkable memoir essay called 'The Rake', Mamet wrote about his own shockingly unhappy family, and added, in an interview with John Lahr, that his talent for dialogue probably came from the pressure his father placed on everyone:

> From the earliest age, one had to think, be careful about what one was going to say, and also how the other person was going to respond. In my family, in the days prior to television, we liked to wile away the evenings by making our selves miserable, solely based on our ability to speak the language viciously. That's probably where my ability was honed.[9]

John is a sensitive, insomniac child, troubled by voices. Donny is a self-absorbed, tense, perpetually distraught mother. Del is the family's friend who, it will emerge, is probably in love with Robert, the absent husband/father, who, it will further turn out, has abandoned the family, having manipulated Del into betraying Donny and John. All three adults will betray the child. Mamet's play thus becomes a fable of the loss of innocence, of the terrifying dark at the top of the stairs which John ascends into literal death or the metaphoric death of childhood and the beginning of adulthood.

Robert's German knife, a war memento, is far more than a prop; it increasingly grows in meaning, first as a bribe to Del to aid Robert in his infidelity, then as it is revealed to be a fake, purchased souvenir rather than hero's spoil of war, and, finally, in its horrifying real function as a murderous weapon as the adults send the disturbed boy upstairs, into the dark, with that knife. In Mamet's 'The Northern Novel' in *Make-Believe Town*, we hear this:

> In my beloved novels there is no question of waiting till the final act to see the knife used—the knife is used in every scene. The aura of foreboding is not an effect designed to manipulate the reader's interest. It is the stuff of the novel. It is not added to the narrative, it is the narrative (p. 90).

It is worth noting that Mamet's 1998 book about theatre, titled, significantly, *3 Uses of the Knife*, tells us that there are two kinds of plays: one is intellectually impressive and quickly forgotten, while other leaves the audience unsure but 'something in them comes from the heart, and, so goes to the heart . . . . Tragedy is a celebration not of our eventual triumph but of the truth—it is not a victory but a resignation' (p. 21). *The Cryptogram* is, by this definition, a tragedy.

In *The Cryptogram*, there is repeated reference to a children's book about a wizard and 'three misfortunes' and, following the story's plot, the play's first act begins with the first misfortune, a broken teapot; then there's a ripped blanket, which may be a misfortune but from long ago. Does that mean there are still two misfortunes to happen? If so, the boy's suicide would be the last. Fairy tales often begin with the death of a parent, and it is likely that on a subconscious level, John realizes his father is not going to return. Mamet's insight into childhood is evidenced in his remarkable essay, 'Kryptonite: A Psychological Appreciation' included in *Some Freaks*. Mamet writes, 'Far from being invulnerable, Superman is the most vulnerable of beings, because his childhood was destroyed'. If *Cryptogram* is Mamet's theatrical study of childhood destroyed, this passage from 'Kryptonite' is helpful, especially in relation to the book about the wizard:

> Superman comics are a fable, not of strength, but of disintegration. They appeal to the preadolescent mind not because they reiterate

grandiose delusions, but because they reiterate a very deep cry for help.

Superman's two personalities can be integrated only in one thing: only in death. Only Kryptonite cuts through the disguises of wimp and hero, and affects the man below the disguises. And what is Kryptonite? Kryptonite is all that remains of his childhood home (p. 178).

The play's title could well be 'The Kryptogram'.

The Cryptogram is a cryptogram, and the play is brimming with clues, most of which we understand only in retrospect. John asks hundreds of questions, and his mother's answers are unhelpful: 'Things occur. In our lives. And the meaning of them . . . the *meaning* of them . . . is not clear' (p. 79). Mamet has subverted conventional domestic dialogue by oddly stilted language that sounds like code. Further, Del suggests a game of observation to John, where each person picks up clues to lead him to understand what he has already seen. This becomes the method of watching/reading the play.

The coded message, in all Mamet works, however funny or scathing or both they are, is to reveal the struggle between good and evil. As Del tells the boy, 'But you see, in reality, things unfold . . . independent of our fears of them' (p. 31). Mamet's film, *Homicide,* also concerned with deeply embedded family betrayals, has a brief but horrific scene in which a man who murdered his wife and children asks a policeman, 'Would you like to know how to solve the problem of Evil?' The cop replies, 'No, man, cause if I did, then I'd be out of a job'. As would Mamet.

Race (2009)

Stepping into the national conversation about race – the most difficult conversation Americans can have – Mamet expresses equal-opportunity cynicism; when asked by a young African American female lawyer, 'You think Black people are stupid?' Jack, the smart, slick, blindingly articulate white lawyer says in response, 'I think *all* people are stupid. I don't think blacks are exempt . . . ' (p. 19).

Mamet is not shy of risk-taking, and *Race* takes risk after risk: the story itself is not complicated, but the characters' hidden agendas create highly convoluted moral subplots which assault us with speed as well as daring. The stage becomes a dangerously ambiguous moral universe, exposing, as serious theatre can, our own racism, sexism and the ambiguity of our private systems of justice.

The plot revolves around a law firm and a volatile, high-profile case: Charles, a very, very rich white man is accused of raping a young black woman in a hotel room (and given recent scandals involving Dominique Strauss-Kahn, the play seems weirdly prescient). Jack and his law partner Henry, who is, significantly, a black man, concoct a shrewd defence, only to discover that they have been betrayed by the youngest member of the firm, a black woman. Although we can see what's coming (perhaps too far in advance), the point is, nevertheless, driven home with ferocity. 'Hatred, fear and envy: the trifecta of all law cases', plays itself out with grim inevitability. Charles' innocence or guilt becomes one of several debates the play embroils us in – Mamet is an old hand at making us root for the bad guys (*Speed-the-Plow* depends on that manipulation). Scene One ends with Susan saying, 'This isn't about sex, it's about race'. To which Jack replies, with the most cogent line of the play, 'What's the difference?' (p. 37)

And there is another grim inevitability: in Mamet's view it is always the young woman who, for various ambiguous but always vengeful reasons, undermines the men. Consider this partial list: Karen, the temporary secretary in *Speed-the-Plow;* Glenna, the actress/waitress in *Edmond;* Carol, the student in *Oleanna;* and even the unseen 'Fuckin' Ruthie, fuckin' Ruthie, fuckin' Ruthie, fuckin' Ruthie, fuckin' Ruthie' in *American Buffalo*. Mamet's reputation as a misogynist has been argued over since the beginning of his career: the central issue is whether he is depicting the misogyny of American society or whether he has revealed his own bias. This same issue swirls around the works of Neil LaBute who seems to be Mamet's heir, both in themes and in controversy.

'Guilt', Mamet has Jack point out, 'is a Legal Term'. While shame is a feeling, which, he maintains, is common to all humanity. And the audience – we become the surrogate jury – is swayed and shoved from one side to the other in this Shavian dialectic as the revelations pile up.

As the lawyer tells us, people conjoin into groups, and which way we sway or which way we defend our own beliefs or loyalties depends, in part, on which group we feel part of: black or white, male or female, rich or poor, young or old. As Henry resignedly remarks, 'We all have to put up with a lot from each other'.

In an article for *The New York Times*, Mamet wrote:

> Most contemporary debate on race is nothing but sanctimony—efforts at exploitation and efforts at restitution seeking, equally, to enlarge and prolong dissent and rancour.
>
> The question of the poor drama is "What is the truth?" but of the better drama, and particularly of tragedy, "What are the lies?" . . . My current play does have a theme, and that theme is race and the lies we tell each other on the subject.[10]

Mamet's talent for aphoristic dialogue is riding high in *Race*, and we hear quotable line after quotable line, and each has to be delivered with breathtaking precision, speed and Mametude – as it was by James Spader in the Broadway premiere, directed by the playwright. The cast has to do the playwright justice, so to speak.

Summary

Mamet is best known for his scathing indictments of American culture, in each realm he takes up – real estate, movie-making, the legal system, academia – he reveals American culture to be corrupt and loveless. His male-dominated plays and his stance of cigar-smoking, poker-playing machismo (he has lately relinquished the cigars) informs all the work and frequently contributes to the continuing gender politics debate in contemporary culture. He has become increasingly religious and deeply concerned with being a Jew in America, and several of his works on stage (*The Old Neighborhood*) and screen (*Homicide*) reflect that.

His theories about theatre-making are widely discussed in a variety of his books and essays, and succinctly summarized in a television interview where he explained that 'the whole idea of drama is about three things: Who wants what from whom? What happens if they don't get it? And why now?' He continued by citing Aristotle's dictum 'all character is habitual action', and added 'There is no such thing as character development—everything we can infer about a character we get from the action'. Segueing from the obvious to the surprising, Mamet added: 'Plays are not about nice things happening to nice people. Plays are about conflict. And plays are about the difference between our intentions and the results, or the difference between our self-view and our actual morality, or the difference between our view of the world and God's view of the world. They're about conflict on different levels'.[11]

Most recently (as of this writing) his book *The Secret Knowledge: On the Dismantling of American Culture* (2011) expresses a new anti-liberalism and surprising pro-capitalism views. A *New York Times* interviewer mused, 'this guy is going to infuriate a huge chunk of the people who pay money to see his plays' and then inquired, 'Are you concerned that you're alienating your public?' Mamet's reply was, 'I've been alienating my public since I was 20 years old . . . . Of course I'm alienating the public! That's what they pay me for'.[12] His newest play is due to open in London and then on Broadway in the fall of 2012. Its subject is a prisoner and her parole officer, inspired, Mamet told the *Wall Street Journal,* by a newspaper interview he read in which Bernardine Dorne and Bill Ayers, formerly leaders of the Weather Underground, said they did not regret the bombing in New York in 1970. Mamet read that interview on a plane on 11 September 2001; while he was in the air, the World Trade Center was destroyed by terrorists. *The Anarchist,* the title of this new play, has been developing since that now historic day.[13]

Mamet's style is famously spare and repetitive, reflecting, as so many contemporary playwrights do, the influence of Samuel Beckett. Another clear influence is Harold Pinter who was, himself, deeply influenced by Beckett. And like Pinter, Mamet's attitudes towards women are vexed and his political indictments fierce. And, again like Pinter, Mamet's distinctive rhythms create an often hilarious and unnerving dialogue; his ability to inflect the vernacular reveals him to be, simultaneously, a wizard of obscenity and a commentator on the devaluation of language. Sam Mendes, then artistic director of the Donmar Warehouse, who directed the London production of *Glengarry Glen Ross,* pointed out in a 1994 interview, that the 'commercially successful playwrights of the past ten years' are not 'wordsmiths' as Mamet and Pinter are, playwrights who 'can spin characters out of nothing. It's very narrative-based now'.[14] Mamet's wordsmithing is perhaps amusingly evidenced in his slight, early one-act called *Squirrels*. He wrote the play in 1974, but when he attended a 1990 performance he decided it needed a new closing line. What he added was 'Or words to that effect'. Thus, as I have pointed out elsewhere,[15] it is often style not content that matters most in Mamet. Note the witty epigraph to *Squirrels* where rhythm triumphs:

> The reason I like
> Edna St. Vincent Millay
> Is that her name
> Sounds like a basketball
> Falling downstairs.
> The reason I like
> Walt Whitman
> Is that his name
> Sounds like
> Edna St. Vincent Millay
> Falling downstairs (p. 101).

It is perhaps testimony to his having achieved canonical status that Mamet has become the punch line of a widely told joke: A panhandler asks a prosperous-looking businessman for money, who replies, self-righteously, 'Neither a borrower nor a lender be. William Shakespeare'. The panhandler replies, 'Fuck you. David Mamet'.

Primary Sources

Works by David Mamet

Plays One: The Duck Variations, Sexual Perversity in Chicago, Squirrels, American Buffalo, The Water Engine, Mr. Happiness (London: Methuen Drama, 1994).

Plays Two: Reunion, Dark Pony, A Life in the Theatre, The Woods, Lakeboat, Edmond (London: Methuen Drama, 1996a).

Plays Three: Glengarry Glen Ross, Prairie du Chien, The Shawl, Speed-the-Plow (London: Methuen Drama, 1996b).

Plays Four: Oleanna, The Cryptogram, The Old Neighborhood (London: Methuen Drama, 2002).

Secondary Sources

Bigsby, C. W. E., *A Critical Introduction to Twentieth-Century American Drama, Volume Three: Beyond Broadway* (Cambridge: Cambridge UP, 1985).

—, *The Cambridge Companion to David Mamet* (Cambridge: Cambridge UP, 2004).

Goldman, Andrew, 'David Mamet Explains His Shift to the Right', *The New York Times*, 29 May 2011, p. MM15.

Hudgins, Christopher C. and Leslie Kane (eds), *Gender and Genre: Essays on David Mamet* (New York: Palgrave, 2001).

Kane, Leslie (ed.), *David Mamet: A Casebook* (New York and London: Garland, 1992).

Lahr, John, 'David Mamet's Child's Play', *The New Yorker*, 10 April 1995, p. 33.

—, 'Fortress Mamet', *The New Yorker*, 17 November 1997, p. 70.

Mamet, David, 'A Playwright in Hollywood'. In *Writing in Restaurants* (New York: Penguin, 1986).

—, 'Film is a Collaborative Business'. In *Some Freaks* (New York: Penguin, 1989).

—, 'We Can't Stop Talking About Race in America', *The New York Times*, 13 September 2009, p. AR12.

Nadel, Ira, *David Mamet: A Life in the Theatre* (New York: Palgrave, 2008).

Price, Steven, *The Plays, Screenplays and Films of David Mamet: A Reader's Guide to Essential Criticism* (New York: Palgrave, 2008).

Sauer, David Kennedy and Janice A. Sauer, *David Mamet: A Research and Production Sourcebook* (Westport, CT: Praeger, 2003).

Stevenson, Burton, *The Home Book of Proverbs, Maxims and Familiar Phrases* (New York: Macmillan, 1959).

Weiss, Bari, 'David Mamet's Coming Out Party', *The Wall Street Journal*, 28 May 2011.

Wolf, Matt, 'Oleanna', *American Theatre* 10, 11 (November 1993), pp. 77–8.

Zeifman, Hersh, 'Phallus in Wonderland: Business and Machismo in *American Buffalo* and *Glengarry Glen Ross*'. In Leslie Kane (ed.), *David Mamet: A Casebook* (New York and London: Garland, 1992).

Zinman, Toby, 'Jewish Aporia: The Rhythm of Talking in Mamet', *Theatre Journal* 44, 2 (May 1992), pp. 207–15.

—, 'So Dis Is Hollywood: Mamet in Hell'. In Kimball King (ed.), *Hollywood on Stage: Playwrights Evaluate the Culture Industry* (New York: Garland, 1997).

Notes

1. Hersh Zeifman, 'Phallus in Wonderland'.
2. C. W. E. Bigsby, *A Critical Introduction to Twentieth-Century American Drama*, p. 72.
3. John Lahr, 'Fortress Mamet', p. 75.
4. David Mamet, 'A Playwright in Hollywood', p. 75.
5. Mamet, 'Film is a Collaborative Business', p. 139.
6. Burton Stevenson, *The Home Book of Proverbs, Maxims and Familiar Phrases*.
7. Matt Wolf, 'Oleanna'.
8. Lahr, 'David Mamet's Child's Play', p. 34.
9. Lahr, 'Fortress Mamet', p. 73.
10. Mamet, 'We Can't Stop Talking About Race in America', p. AR12.
11. 'Night Talk: Interview with David Mamet', *Bloomberg Television*, 24 July 2009.
12. Andrew Goldman, 'David Mamet Explains His Shift to the Right', p. MM15.
13. Bari Weiss, 'David Mamet's Coming Out Party'.
14. Leslie Kane, *David Mamet: A Casebook*, p. 248.
15. Toby Zinman, 'Jewish Aporia'.

10 DONALD MARGULIES

Kerstin Schmidt

Sight Unseen; Collected Stories; Dinner with Friends; Brooklyn Boy; Time Stands Still

Introduction

Donald Margulies is one of the most prolific playwrights of contemporary American theatre, even if success on a wider scale came rather late in his career. In 2000, he received the Pulitzer Prize for Drama for his play *Dinner with Friends*. At that time, he had already produced a substantial body of works. His breakthrough play, that perhaps also paved the way for the reception of the prestigious prize, was *Sight Unseen* (1991). In an interview with Jerry Patch, Margulies takes the prize as appreciation for his complete oeuvre:

> I don't think I ever aspired to winning a Pulitzer Prize, but once I became a finalist it suddenly became something that was accessible to me. At this stage of my career, I have a body of work that's been produced on stages across the country, and this kind of national recognition seems to acknowledge not only *Dinner with Friends*, but that collection of plays; for me, it's a validation of all those years working in the theatre.[1]

In contrast to *Dinner with Friends*, Margulies's earlier plays focus more on issues related to Jewish culture and Jewish identity in the United States. The playwright has repeatedly been filed under the rubric of Jewish American theatre. While Jewish-American culture features prominently in many of his works, a too narrow focus would run the danger of skirting the whole array of other topics that also inform Margulies's work and that have spoken to a larger audience of theatregoers. His plays deal with the troubles and tribulations of the East Coast intelligentsia and the well-to-do American middle class. They are appreciated above all for their humour and wit, and the playwright's great talent for dialogue.

Born in Brooklyn on 2 September 1954, as the second son of Charlene and Bob Margulies, Margulies says he grew up in a 'high rise ghetto' of a Jewish neighbourhood.[2] His father was a wallpaper salesman, working long hours and constantly fearing about losing his job. His mother raised their two sons, putting much emphasis on education and success. Whereas his mother encouraged reading and writing, his father was probably more intimidated by his intellectual and artistically gifted son. Due to long working hours, he was also absent from family life for long stretches of time and remained a silent, not unproblematical figure in his son's childhood and later life. Many of Margulies's plays explore troubled father-son relationships and the difficulties in communicating with a silent parent. In light of Margulies's own family life, these plays have subsequently been read as autobiographical. A more positive parental influence lay perhaps in Bob Margulies's fascination with American theatre and musical. He took the family to New York City for weeklong vacations in order to see plays and Broadway musicals. In the Afterword to the collection *Sight Unseen and Other Plays*, Margulies remarks: 'I was the only kid in the sixth grade who knew by heart the entire score of Happy Hunting, an obscure Ethel Merman musical I heard countless times'.[3]

Margulies's interests were not limited to writing and reading. He was also a talented artist and was granted an art scholarship to Pratt Institute. One of his collages is on the cover of *Collected Plays*. He stayed at Pratt only a short while and then transferred to the State University of New York at Purchase, a liberal arts college where he studied art and literature. During that time, he met Julius Novick, a professor of literature who became his lifelong mentor and, together with Herb Gardner, Joseph Papp and others, one of his surrogate father figures.

One of Margulies's first plays was *Pals*, an unproduced piece of work, written in 1978, in which he deals with the problematic relationship with his father. Many shorter plays were produced in the following years before his first full-length play, *Gifted Children* (1983), was staged. The play is about a pregnant woman artist who attempts to come to terms with her mother while trying to decide whether to have an abortion or not. Despite quite unfavourable reviews, the play caught the attention of the impresario of American Theater, Joseph Papp, who then decided to stage Margulies's next play, *Found a Peanut* (1984), at the New York Shakespeare Festival. *Found a Peanut* is about eight children, from age 4 to 14, on the last day of vacation before the new school year begins. That day in a Brooklyn yard, however, turns out to be an important moment in their lives as they lose their childhood innocence and experience the difficulties of growing up and adult life. They sing a children's song about consumption of a rotten peanut (the singer also dies from it), and the song parallels events in the children's lives. While digging a grave to bury a dead bird, they discover a bag with money. The resulting quarrel about the booty provokes greediness, violence and finally leads to the disruption of their friendship. The loot is not the only thing that the children find on that day. They are also confronted with the dead body of the next-door neighbour. When they bury the animal, they can still play being adults, mimicking their burial rituals and behaviour, but the case of the dead neighbour triggers a change in attitude in the children, as they start seeing and understanding death in relation to themselves. On a broader scale, the play can also be seen as a step to introduce his characters to incidents of disruptive violence throughout the world. Critics have seen this as a first attempt to link plots and characters to the post-Holocaust world. The play, however, tends to be rather formulaic; it received mixed reviews, but, all in all, these were more encouraging than previous ones.

A play dealing explicitly with the post-Holocaust world is *The Model Apartment* (1988). In this black comedy, Lola and Max move to a Florida retirement community. As their own condominium is not yet finished, they are put into a fancy studio apartment for the time being. Soon they discover that the chic accessories and modern appliances of the model apartment are fake. Gradually, Margulies unveils their seemingly perfect lives as fake and pretentious as well. The audience finds out that the couple moved to Florida without telling their mentally challenged daughter Debbie. They are embarrassed by their daughter who constantly derides their Holocaust experiences (both parents are Holocaust survivors) with abusive and scurrilous remarks. Debbie knows that she is named after

Max's deceased daughter Deborah to whom Max still feels very closely connected and to whom he talks during imaginary nightly visits. Unable to cope with the burden of their parents' past and the overpowering presence of her deceased half sister, Debbie's protest becomes violent. But Max and Lola also experience the power of the horrific past, the inescapability of their memories and their continuing impact on their lives. As William C. Boles writes, 'the onus of the Holocaust is a devastating and oppressive cloud that damages and consumes all'.[4]

Father figures and Jewish upbringing also characterize the plays *What's Wrong with this Picture?* and *The Loman Family Picnic*. The first play follows the life of Mort and Artie, father and son, after the death of their wife/mother and the problems they have with overcoming their grief and continuing their lives. Due to the earlier negative reviews, Margulies decided not to invite critics to the first performance of the play; its premiere before critics was three years later, in 1988, in Los Angeles. The 1989 play *The Loman Family Picnic* also explores Jewish family life in America, with the explicit reference to Arthur Miller's *Death of a Salesman* in the play's title. In order to escape dull and complicated family life, one of the two sons in the play, Mitchell, decides to write a musical version of *Death of a Salesman* in which his family members become the Lomans in a picnic.

Margulies identifies Arthur Miller and Willy Loman as powerful childhood influences, noticing the many similarities between Miller's play, in which many critics have lamented the merely covert Jewish context,[5] and his own upbringing:

> I was eleven years old when I read *Death of a Salesman*, and I remember the guilt and shame I felt for recognizing in the Lomans truths about my own family . . . . But the play's uncanny reflection of my life and worst fears also exhilarated me and made me feel less alone. I studied it with great fascination, as if it were a key to understanding what was happening to the people I loved . . . . I imagined that our high-rise was one of the buildings that overshadowed the Lomans' modest house. Years later, in *The Loman Family Picnic*, I took that notion and made a play out of it.[6]

Margulies is professor of English and Theater Studies at Yale University. In addition to playwriting, he also develops scripts for film and television. One of his current projects is an adaptation of the novel *Middlesex* by Jeffrey Eugenides for HBO.

The Plays

Sight Unseen (1991)

Sight Unseen generated wide-scale critical interest among theatre critics and the audience alike, garnering a great amount of praise for the playwright. The play is about Jonathan Waxman, a celebrated, media-savvy artist, and his problems balancing fame, celebrity status and rampant artistic consumerism. When he was younger, he cherished more idealistic beliefs in the function and role of art. Reminiscent of Yasmina Reza's 1994 hit *Art*, Margulies's play also investigates the art boom of the 1980s. *Sight Unseen* is one of the first plays to be less focused on the domestic issues of a Jewish family. Waxman has considerably loosened the ties to his Jewish heritage, having become a 'mainstream' American artist instead. In the course of the play, however, he finds himself still grappling with his heritage and the expectations of his Jewish upbringing. When he has a retrospective in London, he uses the opportunity to visit his ex-girlfriend Patricia. Patricia is married to Nick, an English archaeologist, but the marriage is, on her part, more out of necessity than love. Most of the play takes place in Patricia and Nick's cottage in England or in the London art gallery, except for two flashbacks to the scenes when Patricia and Jonathan meet for the first time in the New York art college and when they break up a few years later in his parents' house in Brooklyn.

At the beginning of the play, when Jonathan comes to visit Nick and Patricia, the tension and discomfort is all-consuming. The conversation centres on questions of art and the art market, but also on Jonathan and Patricia's unreconciled past relationship and Jonathan's reasons for his violent break-up. Patricia learns that Jonathan is now married to a non-Jewish wife who is expecting a baby. He also chose to come to

England to supervise the exhibition instead of sitting shiva for his late father. In a flashback, we learn about the younger Jonathan's substantial reservations towards marrying a non-Jewish woman. When they meet for the first time, as college students, Patricia is modelling for a class of art students and offers to sit longer for Jonathan. He is drawn to Patricia, her bold and open behaviour, but is also reticent to act on his attraction and establish a relationship with the non-Jewish young woman. He explains that his reservations are connected to his particular upbringing and to Jewish history:

> **Jonathan**   . . . It's the six million! It's, it's the Diaspora, it's the
> history of the Jewish people! You have no idea, the *weight*.
> You got to remember I come from Brooklyn. People where
> I come from, they don't like to travel very far, let alone
> intermarry. They've still got this ghetto mentality: safety in
> numbers, no matter what. . . . This is the attitude about the
> world I grew up with. It's a miracle I ever left the house!
> (p. 334)

When Patricia replies that: 'We are not talking about the future of the Jewish race', Jonathan retorts: 'See, but I think we are' (p. 334). He thematizes the Holocaust [the six million] and insinuates in his short speech that intermarriage is viewed as a growing threat to the survival of Jewish culture because it runs the danger of loosening the connections to Judaism. A few years after that, Jonathan's mother dies and he deliberately excludes his girlfriend Patricia from the family and from his own emotions as well. He feels immense guilt and retreats into a 'ghetto' mentality, violently rejecting her empathy, consolation and her love. As critic Julius Novick notes, Jonathan nowhere in the conversation mentions religion or God.[7] His reservations and feeling of guilt seem much rather related to an obligation to conform to ideas of Jewish identity and less so to religion proper. His father, for example, is the one to call Patricia and invite her to their home during the period of mourning. Jonathan, though, seems unable to handle the conflicts that he feels so strongly, breaks up with her, putting the blame for his failure on her. At present, in the farmhouse, Patricia reminds Jonathan that he has assimilated into mainstream American culture in the meantime. He has become a stranger to his own world: 'When you married your wife, you married her world. Didn't you? You can't exist in two worlds; you've got to turn your back on one of them. . . . Your wife should thank me. . . . I laid the groundwork. I was the pioneer. . . . The sacrificial shiksa' (pp. 272–3).

The challenge of assimilation also works on the professional level. As a young man, Jonathan is described as a very sincere, dedicated and genuine artist. He has changed considerably and become a 'bankrupt, bereft' figure[8] when he turned into a celebrity and a brand name, often at the expense of artistic content. In a discussion with the young German interviewer Grete, Jonathan describes the process thus: 'Who *are* these people who are suddenly throwing money at you and telling you how wonderful and talented you are? . . . The work loses its importance; the importance is on "Waxman"' (p. 315). Those who can afford to buy a 'Waxman' haven't even seen the painting when they buy it: they buy 'sight unseen'.

Grete proves to be a keen and perceptive interviewer and strikes a nerve when she brings up the sensitive question whether the (Jewish) artist should remain an outsider or integrate into the mainstream American art scene:

Grete   Would you have preferred to remain an outsider?

Jonathan   Preferred? No. It's cold and lonely on the outside.

Grete   And yet being cozy on the inside—

Jonathan   "Cozy"?

Grete (*Continuous*)   —seems to make you uncomfortable as well.

. . .

Grete   . . . the problem Jews face in the twentieth century?

Jonathan   What problem is that?

Grete   The problem of being on the inside while choosing to see themselves as outsiders?—

Jonathan   Is that a Jewish problem?

Grete (*continuous*)   —even when they are very much on the inside?

. . .

> **Grete** All I am suggesting, Mr. Waxman, is that the
> artist, like the Jew, prefers to see himself as alien
> from the mainstream culture. For the Jewish *artist* to
> acknowledge that the *contrary* is true, that he is *not* alien,
> but rather assimilated into that mainstream culture—
> (pp. 315–16)

The conversation becomes a heated argument at the end of which Jonathan angrily insists: 'I am an *American* painter. *American* is the adjective, not *Jewish*, *American*' (p. 316), and upon accusing her of anti-Semitism, he leaves abruptly. Notably cast as a young blonde German woman, Grete asks questions that go to the heart of (ethnic) art in America. The interview may not be entirely fair on both sides, as Grete, too, falls prey to facile and stereotypical preconceptions of Jewish people as sinister outsiders. But Jonathan becomes defensive quite soon, deliberately using his Jewish heritage for glib reproaches of anti-Semitism when it is convenient for him and he can terminate an interview that poses too many painful questions.

Sight Unseen is structured as a collage, a sampling of bits and pieces of Jonathan's life that each illustrates traits of his character as they have changed over time; taken together, these mosaic-like pieces present major issues that Jonathan struggles with. By using the collage as an organizing principle of his play, Margulies deliberately resorted to a visual art form that leaves plenty of room for interpretative ambiguity with regard to the complexities of memory and changing perspectives that make up someone's life: 'The jumbled chronology seemed to suit the sort of memory play that I think it is. I frankly thought it should be ambiguous; it should be mysterious. Pieces should fall into place the way they would if you're analyzing a painting. You scrutinize it and something makes sense in relation to something else, but not immediately. The juxtapositions give it resonance.'[9]

Sight Unseen won the Obie for Best Play and received a Pulitzer Prize nomination. The play had its New York premiere at Manhattan Theatre Club's City Center Stage II on 27 January 1992. It was later moved to the Orpheum Theatre where it ran for 293 performances.

Collected Stories (1996)

The major theme of *Collected Stories* is the betrayal of artistic endeavour. It tells the story of the encounter between Ruth Steiner, established writer and teacher of writing, and her dedicated and overeager student, Lisa Morrison. In the course of the play, Lisa becomes Ruth's assistant, her friend, and gradually develops into a serious and successful writer herself. By the end of the play, both their friendship as well as their working relationship will be in shambles.

The beginning of the play shows Lisa as an insecure, but persistent student, who adores the elder woman in a rather juvenile fashion. Ruth recognizes Lisa's talent, still raw and in need of shaping. Ruth seems edgy and given to moodiness, but the naïve and devoted young student manages, over time, to become not only an assistant, but also a friend, a confidante. In terms of writing, Lisa grows into a serious young literary voice under Ruth's tutelage. Upon Lisa's first success as a writer, a change in their relationship is noticeable. There may also be a whiff of jealousy on Ruth's part when she learns that Lisa is about to have her first story published. But what is more, Ruth perceives a first incident of betrayal, as Lisa has clandestinely submitted her story to a magazine while they had, earlier on, agreed not to send the story to that specific magazine. When Lisa's story is accepted for publication, she is forced to admit having sent the story on her own. The incident may be dismissed as merely a healthy step towards Lisa's independence and maturity, but given Lisa's clumsy and secretive behaviour and in light of the plot of the play as a whole, the slight contretemps becomes significant.

In the scene of the final betrayal, we learn that Lisa has not been around Ruth so much lately, and if she was, Ruth noted her repeated avoiding of eye contact. Interestingly, when Lisa finally does visit Ruth after her first public reading, Ruth has the key chain of the door to her apartment locked, which she usually never does. She explains that she is 'expecting burglars' (p. 67). The theft that Ruth insinuates here is the following: Lisa has written a novel that includes a story based on a real event in Ruth's life. She had told Lisa of her affair as a young woman with the older and more established writer Delmore Schwartz. When Ruth discovers that Lisa has used this story in her novel, she feels betrayed and is enraged. She has opened both her house and her life to a stranger, and now feels robbed by her. Lisa defends herself, arguing that there is no ownership of stories, at least not as soon as they are fictionalized, and claiming that her intention was to honour and pay tribute to her teacher by including details of Ruth's life. In more general terms, *Collected Stories* deals with the problems of being a responsible artist with a 'moral conscience' (p. 74) and the problem of developing an authentic artistic voice of one's own. In this context, the *Los Angeles Times* review of the play speaks of the 'cannibalism' of being an artist.[10]

In New York, the play was produced at Manhattan Theatre Club's City Center Stage I in 1997, at the Lucille Lortel Theatre in 1998, and in the year 2010, it was staged on Broadway at the Friedman Theatre.

Dinner with Friends (2000)

With *Dinner with Friends*, Margulies returns to the domestic realm as he stages the impact of a divorce on two married couples. Gabe and Karen have known Tom and Beth for almost all their adult lives, in fact, they introduced them to each other several years ago and have since then been close friends. When the marriage of Tom and Beth falls apart, Gabe and Karen lose their equilibrium as well. They have nothing to hold on to in this situation, no religiously defined moral code or doting parents, setting an example and trying to provide guidance. The play details the tedious process of separation, uncovering the reasons and deep layers of emotion, in long conversations among the four friends, in varying constellations. There is very little outward action.

Gabe and Karen are genuinely concerned about their friends, but there is also an increasing fear of the dissolution of their own marriage. Karen's question towards the end of the play: 'How do we not get lost?' (p. 71) thus points to the heart of the matter. Gabe and Karen cling to each other more than ever, but the ending is ambiguous and what will happen in their future remains open. Disturbances and dissatisfactions in their own marriage break through the suburban middle-class and well-kept surface like little cracks, barely noticeable and anxiously hushed away, as the following scene from the beginning of the play indicates:

> **Gabe**   Anyway, the *pomodoro*.
> **Karen**   The *pomodoro* was amazing.
> **Gabe**   And simple.
> **Karen**   Amazingly simple. Sauteed garlic . . .
> **Beth**   Yeah . . .?
> **Gabe**   A *lot* of garlic.
> **Karen**   A little onion. Finely diced.
> **Gabe**   That's right. That was interesting: Very little onion.
> **Karen**   Are you gonna let me tell this or what? (p. 10)

Among many other things, Gabe and Karen's preoccupation with food, which they prepare with theatrical expertise and demonstrative adroitness, underlines their concern with sustenance and nurturing that is expected from a stable relationship as well. It is also a further indicator for a typically suburban setting of the play. Karen's observation about herself may be true for the audience as well: Tom and Beth's breakup may be 'too close to home' (p. 31), the loss of safety a shared feeling ('You think you're safe, on solid ground, then all of a sudden the earth cracks open', p. 31). Margulies underlines the sentiment when he writes in the 'Author's Notes' about the 'encroaching sense of loss' towards the end of the play (p. 76). In a comprehensive reading of the play, Udo Hebel explores in depth the repercussions of suburban discontent and what he calls 'marital entropy'. He also suggests calling the play a version of 'comedy of manners'.[11] The play does have witty scenes, but, all in all, as Margulies specifies in the 'Notes', this is 'not really a comedy' (p. 75). The play has no villains; rather, all characters are caught in the sincere attempts of establishing and maintaining relationships, whether friendship or marriage, navigating commitment and stability with passion and love.

Dinner with Friends was awarded the Pulitzer Prize for Drama in 2000. The play was commissioned by the Actors Theatre of Louisville, Kentucky, where it premiered at the 1998 Humana Festival of New American Plays. Later that year, it was produced at South Coast

Repertory (Costa Mesa, CA) and in November 1999, it opened at the Variety Arts Theatre (New York) where it ran for 654 performances. It was produced in cities all over the world, including London, Berlin, Vienna, Stockholm, Tokyo, Mumbai and Tel Aviv.

Brooklyn Boy (2004)

The play's major topic is the relationship between a Jewish middle-class father, Manny Weiss, and his intellectual son Eric as well as the relationship of the son to his Jewish upbringing. Eric has become a successful writer; especially his latest book garnered widespread recognition on a national level and may very well be his breakthrough as a writer. Hollywood film producers are interested in making a movie of Eric's novel.

Interestingly, the book is about a family and context that very much resemble Eric's own. He grew up in a Jewish neighbourhood in Brooklyn, as did the character in the novel. When he learns that his novel will be on the national bestseller list, he also hears about his father's serious illness and goes to visit him in the hospital. The relationship between father and son has always been tense, characterized by mockery and witty derision on the part of Manny Weiss, the father, and despair and vulnerability on the side of the son. Manny simply does not share, and does not even attempt to share, his son's world. Even at his father's bedside, they engage in an argument that illustrates their opposing worldviews and agendas quite well. Manny consistently wants to know whether the father in the book 'is him'; he is also worried over the representation of his wife, who both loved dearly. The difference between a figure in a novel that may be inspired by or modelled after the private experiences of the novelist, but that 'is not' the person of that individual experience keeps puzzling the father. Eric tries, in vain, to expound on the complicated relationship between truth and fiction in novelistic writing. There is mockery in his father's reaction, but there is also a slight contempt, at least a possibly deliberate misunderstanding.

Manny's difficulties are shared by Eric's childhood friend Ira Zimmer whom Eric accidentally meets in the hospital's cafeteria. The surprise meeting is not altogether happy, as childhood rivalries surface and misconceptions about each come to the fore. Even though Eric and Ira grew up in the same neighbourhood, the different paths that they chose as adults clash in the play. Ira married a Jewish girl, they have several kids, he observes Jewish customs and he has taken over his father's business (a deli), living, with his family, in the house that he grew up in. Eric, by contrast, has resigned his Jewish heritage, has married (and is about to get divorced from) a non-Jewish woman who shares his writing ambitions, but also feels left out and inhibited by the success of her husband. She has not been able to publish a story in years.

After Eric's father dies, Ira comes, at first kindly offering, then pushing Eric to sit shiva and say Kaddish with him. Thinking that Eric may have forgotten the words, he has already prepared a piece of paper with a phonetic description of the prayer. A debate ensues which brings out opposing views of and experiences with Jewish religion. 'Judaism has *never* helped me feel better. I've always found it sorrowful, guilt-provoking. There was never any comfort. Not for me', Eric objects (p. 64). Eric felt a necessity, an urgency, to get away from the Jewish context of his upbringing: 'I chose to *escape* from all this; you chose to stay' (p. 64). After Ira leaves, Eric's father appears as a ghost figure and finally explains himself to his son, something that Eric had craved for so long. He gives the son the long-awaited recognition, and when he leaves again, Eric takes Ira's phonetic writing of Kaddish and begins to read. Only after the reconciliation with his father, Eric is able to rediscover and develop a sound relationship to his heritage.

Brooklyn Boy was produced at the Pacific Playwrights Festival in 2003 and at South Coast Repertory; on Broadway, it was staged by Manhattan Theatre Club at the Biltmore Theatre. The play was an American Theatre Critics Association New Play Award finalist, an Outer Critics' Circle Nominee and a Burns Mantle Best Play of 2004–05.

Time Stands Still (2009)

The famous war photojournalist Sarah Goodwin recovers from a near-fatal battlefield injury in the New York loft apartment that she shares with her partner James, also a war correspondent. The play explores the moral conflicts and ambiguities of journalists/artists working in war zones and living off the victims of combat and deprivation. At the same time, it negotiates the ways in which Sarah and James can survive as a couple at a point where their personal and professional paths seem to diverge. The title of the play, *Time Stands Still*, capitalizes on photography's ability to stop time and capture a moment in time on the photographic plate.

As the play begins, we see an overeager James trying to take care of the ailing Sarah, compensating for the guilt he feels for having left her in the war in order to cure his depression at home. A long-term friend of the couple, Richard, comes to visit, bringing his new, and much younger, girlfriend Mandy. A rather naïve but good-natured person, Mandy becomes immediately subject to Sarah's devastatingly cool reactions and thorny asides. The uneasy, but trying relationship of Sarah and James contrasts with the more natural interaction between Mandy and Richard who, despite intellectual differences, enjoy life together, far away from the dangers of war journalism. Whereas James, in the course of the play, shares the desire for a comfortable life and has substituted horror movie reviews for war journalism, Sarah is unable to join him and, at the end of the play, accepts another dangerous appointment.

The play raises the philosophical question whether or not it is justifiable to take pictures of wounded civilians instead of coming to their rescue. In fact, Mandy is chirping away the question. Put differently, how can one accept the artistic beauty of some of Sarah's photographs while they show the atrocities of war? While the photos may help to raise public opinion, they also become a marketable commodity, ending up on the coffee tables of affluent New Yorkers. Sarah, too, is aware that she capitalized on the impoverished victims of war: 'I live off the suffering of strangers' (p. 69). The pain of others is not a sentiment that she unflinchingly accepts; during her work, she claims that 'all I see is the picture', feeling a parental attachment to her product: 'I am their mother' (p. 33). Defending herself and the medium, she says 'the camera's there to *record* life. Not change it' (p. 40). Stepping into the frame to change whatever one doesn't like, is not an option for her. This may also ring true with regard to her personal life; by taking a picture, she is able to master time and chaos by fixing them on the photographic plate. This seems less true in personal affairs.

Critics were quick to label *Time Stands Still* a war play, reflecting on the power of the media during times of military combat. Margulies, by contrast, takes the play to be mainly a 'love story'.[12] Sarah and James are no strangers to horror, violence and pain, so New York Times theatre critic Charles Isherwood may be correct in saying that the play shows 'how much pain and trauma are involved in the everyday business of two people creating a life together, one that accommodates the mistakes of the past, the reality of the present and the changes that the future may bring'.[13]

The play was commissioned by the Geffen Playhouse in Los Angeles where it also had its world premiere. It opened on Broadway on 28 January 2010, at the Manhattan Theatre Club for a limited engagement and later ran at the Court Theatre. The play received a 2010 Tony Award Nomination and was chosen a Burns Mantle Best Play of 2009–10.

Summary

Margulies's oeuvre offers a variety of theatrical styles. While most plays are written in a realistic mode (e.g. *Sight Unseen*; *Collected Stories*; *Dinner with Friends*), some follow more naturalistic tendencies (*The Model Apartment*); in yet others, he experiments with free verse (Act I of *Resting Place*), plays with musical sections (*The Loman Family Picnic*) or resorts to elements of the Epic Theater (*Shipwrecked! An Entertainment – The Amazing Adventures of Louis de Rougemont (as Told by Himself)*). And yet, Margulies's strength is writing dialogues, providing fully rounded characters, thus allowing the audience a profound glimpse at these figures' relationships, their troubles and tribulations.

Situated at the intersection of art and society, morality and responsibility, all of his plays deal with the experience of loss in some ways and cover the grey area between the life that one aspired to and the life that one leads. In virtual fireworks of wittily crafted dialogue, he explores emotional interaction, the impact of past failures on present life and the often desperate attempts to cope with future uncertainties.

The critic William C. Boles identifies as the single, most powerful quality of Margulies's work the playwright's 'ability to use little details and small moments to suggest the hollowness of life, especially in regard to personal failures, loneliness, economic struggles, familial conflicts, the numbing repetition of daily existence, and the elusive nature of love'.[14]

Critical attention has been given to his significance as a Jewish-American playwright.[15] Especially his earlier plays are explorations of Jewish culture and, in particular, his Jewish upbringing. He has also written an adaptation of Sholem Asch's eminent *God of Vengeance*. Many of his characters attempt to distance themselves from that background as well as come to terms with it. Even though Margulies does not think of himself exclusively as a Jewish writer, his subject matter often brings Jewishness to the foreground.[16] As a 'post Holocaust baby boom Jew who grew up in a Brooklyn ghetto', Margulies knew many Holocaust survivors and heard their stories.[17] He watched footage from the liberated camps at an early age and sections from the trial of Adolf Eichmann on NBC's Huntley-Brinkley report. Margulies himself grew up in a secular household, as his parents did not go to synagogue, but to Broadway shows. The mix of Jewishness, Jewish traditions and American musicals let Margulies develop a keen sense of Jewish identity while not being limited by it. The status of the outsider that Jonathan Waxman is so worried about in *Sight Unseen* does not seem to be a pressing personal problem for the playwright: 'Some writers are very interested in being an outsider. I am not. . . . It has always made me uncomfortable, and set me on forays into the larger world'.[18] During the 1990s, he found more acceptance in a mainstream audience; especially his Pulitzer Play *Dinner with Friends* hit the nerve of a large group of people across ethnic lines. Challenges that he may have become too mainstream, neglecting Jewish issues, are brushed away by him, even though the dilemma between remaining marginal or assimilating into mainstream culture is a quintessentially American one, with Hester Prynne to Huckleberry Finn being but two iconic examples.

New York theatre critic John Simon praised the work of the adroit wordsmith Margulies: 'Margulies is remarkable because he's not simplistic. The trend now is to couch a very simplistic point of view in a sort of symbolic, absurdist, fantastical garb. Margulies cloaks things in nothing. He gives them to you as he sees them, but as he sees them very carefully and conscientiously and thoughtfully observed, from all sides'.[19]

Primary Sources

Works by Donald Margulies

Brooklyn Boy: A Play (New York: Theatre Communications Group, 2005).

Collected Stories: A Play (New York: Dramatists Play Service, 1998).

Dinner With Friends (New York: Theatre Communications Group, 2000).

God of Vengeance (New York: Theatre Communications Group, 2004; adapted from the play by Sholem Asch).

July 7, 1994 (New York: Dramatists Play Service, 1997).

The Loman Family Picnic (New York: Theatre Communications Group, 1989).

Luna Park: Short Plays and Monologues (New York: Theatre Communications Group, 2002).

Misadventure: Monologues and Short Pieces (New York: Dramatists Play Service, 2004).

Shipwrecked!: An Entertainment: The Amazing Adventures of Louis de Rougemont (As Told by Himself) (New York: Theatre Communications Group, 2009).

Sight Unseen and Other Plays (New York: Theatre Communications Group, 1995).

Time Stands Still: A Play (New York: Theatre Communications Group, 2010).

What's Wrong With This Picture? (New York: Broadway Play Publishing, 1988).

Secondary Sources

Ben-Zvi, Linda, 'Generational Shifts in American Jewish Theatre'. In Edna Nahshon (ed.), *Jewish Theatre* (Leiden, Boston, MA: Brill, 2009), pp. 215–38.

Boles, William C., 'Donald Margulies'. In Christopher J. Wheatley (ed.), Vol. 228 of *Dictionary of Literary Biography: Twentieth-Century American Dramatists*, Second Series, (Detroit et al.: Gale, 2000), pp. 193–203.

Dubner, Stephen J., 'In the Paint: Donald Margulies Scores with a Play about the Art Hustle', *New York* (9 March 1992), pp. 48–52.

Geis, Deborah R., 'In Willy Loman's Garden: Contemporary Re-visions of *Death of a Salesman*'. In Enoch Brater (ed.), *Arthur Miller's America: Theater & Culture in a Time of Change* (Ann Arbor: University of Michigan Press, 2005), pp. 202–18.

Hebel, Udo J., '"Not Really a Comedy": Donald Margulies's *Dinner With Friends* as a Scaring Game of Marital Entropy and Suburban Discontent'. In Helge Nowak (ed.), *Comedy and Gender: Essays in Honor of Dieter A. Berger* (Heidelberg: Winter, 2007), pp. 183–97.

Herman, Jan, 'Drawing on Familiar Obsessions: "Former Artist" Writes Play for SCR that Parallels His Life—in Some Ways', *Los Angeles Times*, 17 September 1991, http://articles.latimes.com/1991-09-17/entertainment/ca-2820_1_sight-unseen.

Isherwood, Charles, 'What's Really Fair in Love and War?', *New York Times*, 29 January 2010, theater.nytimes.com/2010/01/29/theater/reviews/29time.html.

Mitchell, Sean, 'Donald Margulies Raises More Moral Questions in *Time Stands Still*', *Los Angeles Times*, 8 February 2009, www.latimes.com/entertainment/la-ca-donald-margulies8-2009feb08,0,4002462.story.

Nahshon, Edna (ed.), *Jewish Theater: A Global View* (Leiden, Boston: Brill, 2009).

Novick, Julius, *Beyond the Golden Door: Jewish American Drama and Jewish American Experience* (New York: Palgrave Macmillan, 2008).

Patch, Jerry, 'Donald Margulies: From *Boitschick* to Man'. In Joan Herrington (ed.), *The Playwright's Muse* (New York: Routledge, 2002), pp. 279–92.

Schiff, Ellen, 'On Arriving Front and Center: American Jewish Identity on the American Stage'. In Edna Nahshon (ed.), *Jewish Theatre*, pp. 199–214.

Notes

1. Jerry Patch, 'Donald Margulies', p. 279.
2. Qtd. in Stephen J. Dubner, 'In the Paint', p. 51.
3. Donald Margulies, Afterword by the Playwright, *Sight Unseen and Other Plays*, p. 339.
4. William C. Boles, 'Donald Margulies', p. 198.
5. For articles on Arthur Miller's *Death of a Salesman* as a (covert) Jewish play, see Deborah R. Geis, 'In Willy Loman's Garden' and Linda Ben-Zvi, 'Generational Shifts'.
6. Margulies, Afterword, *Sight Unseen and Other Plays*, p. 340.
7. Julius Novick, *Beyond the Golden Door*, p. 119.
8. Boles, 'Donald Margulies', p. 200.
9. Jan Herman, 'Drawing on Familiar Obsessions'.
10. Sean Mitchell, 'Donald Margulies'. The play apparently was inspired by the David Leavitt/Stephen Spender controversy: Spender sued author Leavitt for allegedly using details from his personal life in his 1994 novel *While England Sleeps*. A settlement was reached to withdraw the book from publication, and Leavitt had to make changes for a revised edition.
11. Udo J. Hebel, 'Not Really a Comedy', p. 193.
12. Mitchell, 'Donald Margulies Raises More Moral Questions in "Time Stands Still"', n.p.
13. Charles Isherwood, 'What's Really Fair in Love and War?', n.p.
14. Boles, 'Donald Margulies,' p. 194.

15. On the debate over the definition of Jewish Theatre, see Edna Nahshon's introduction to *Jewish Theatre: A Global View*, pp. 1–11.
16. Mitchell, 'Donald Margulies Raises More Moral Questions in *Time Stands Still*', n.p.
17. Patch, 'Donald Margulies: From *Boitschick* to Man', p. 280.
18. Ibid., p. 281.
19. Qtd. in Dubner, 'In the Paint', p. 51.

11 TERRENCE MCNALLY

Peter Paul Schnierer

The Ritz; Frankie and Johnny in the Clair de Lune; The Lisbon Traviata; Master Class; Corpus Christi; Some Men

Introduction

Terrence McNally was born on 3 November 1938, in St Petersburg, Florida, and grew up in Corpus Christi, Texas. In 1956, he enrolled at Columbia University, New York, where he graduated in English in 1960. He began writing and working for the theatre immediately afterwards, first as stage manager of New York's Actors Studio and soon as a playwright who was (and is) at home both in theatre and musical shows. A long and distinguished career was to follow, unbroken by McNally's successful battle against lung cancer. He is married to Thomas Joseph Kirdahy, a civil rights attorney and theatre producer.

McNally is the author of some 50 plays, opera libretti and books for musicals, the latter including *Kiss of the Spider Woman* (1992), *Ragtime* (1996) and *The Full Monty* (2000).[1]

He also wrote the screenplays for the film versions of three of his own plays: *The Ritz* (1976), *Frankie and Johnny* (1991) and *Love! Valour! Compassion!* (1997).

Throughout his career, he has been a highly visible figure, through his willingness to talk and write about his craft but also through public service for the Dramatists Guild of America, as whose vice-president he served from 1985 to 2001.

Popular acclaim, particularly when it translates into commercial success, does not necessarily win over the critics; it is a tribute not just to McNally but equally to his reviewers that he has garnered a long string of awards and nominations from 1974 onwards, for some 15 different plays and books for musicals. These include four Drama Desk Awards, an

Emmy, two Obies and four Tony Awards, a Citation from the American Academy of Arts and Letters and two Guggenheim Fellowships. In 2011, he was the recipient of the Dramatists Guild Lifetime Achievement Award.

An oeuvre of this magnitude is impossible to summarize fully in a few pages; yet McNally has developed his portfolio akin to a musical score, repeating themes, extending them and transposing them, as it were, into other keys. The six plays introduced below, spanning almost four decades, therefore may be seen as representative of McNally's craft and concerns.

The Plays

The Ritz (1975)

The Ritz is not McNally's best play, but it was one of his early critical successes, and it is an excellent specimen of its genre: a pure farce which ought to be read and performed accordingly, without too much effort expended on 'meaning'. Like many of McNally's plays, it generates its dramatic energy by juxtaposing self-confident gay protagonists and straight antagonists profoundly disturbed by them. The plot is either simple or almost impossible to paraphrase, depending on the importance one attaches to its ramifications. Simply put, the play shows the adventures of one Gaetano Proclo, a heterosexual, middle-aged, essentially harmless man, who has made the mistake of marrying into a mafia family whose dying *capo* enjoined his men to 'get Proclo', evidently for no other reason than that marriage. Proclo deems it a good idea to hide out in a bathhouse, that is a place specifically designed to facilitate homosexual encounters *en masse*:

> *The main thing we see are doors. Doors and doors and doors. Each door has a number. Outside all these doors are corridors. Lots and lots of corridors. Filling these corridors are men. Lots and lots of men. They are prowling the corridors. One of the most important aspects of the production is this sense of men endlessly prowling the corridors*

*outside the numbered doors. The same people will pass up and down
the same corridors and stairways over and over again. After a while,
you'll start to think some of them are on a treadmill. Most of them
are dressed exactly alike, i.e., they are wearing bathrobes. (p. 272)*

Such a set-up offers a range of dramatic possibilities, because it either
enables a sufficiently imaginative creative team to come up with a
Dantesque vision of eternal, mirthless repetition or alternatively may
serve as a frame for an absurdist play that highlights the pointlessness
of the characters' existence. Either way there would be metaphysical
heightening, and characteristically McNally eschews all such references,
opting instead for a manic farce. Proclo's initial act of hiding generates
confusion, particularly once his pursuers (and his wife) enter the
bathhouse, not all of them being aware of its purpose and patrons.

Much of the play is taken up with the usual staples of farce: high-speed
pursuits, sexual innuendo, near misses, mistaken identities and loss of
garments, a gallimaufry of action that is evident from the proliferation
of stage directions:

> *Carmine goes into his room, starts to undress. We will see him take
> out a revolver, a stiletto, and a pair of brass knuckles. From
> offstage, Claude calls.*
> **Claude**   Vespucci! (*Proclo appears on the third level and races
> into a room. Claude runs past the room and sees a patron.*) Say,
> have you seen a Vespucci go by? (*Proclo leaves his hiding place
> and heads down to the second level. Claude yells as he follows
> him down the stairs and they disappear.*) Vespucci! Vespucci!
> (*Googie appears and pokes her head into Proclo's room.*)
> **Googie**   Where are you hiding, Mr. Vespucci? (*She disappears.
> Proclo appears and starts down the stairs to his own room on
> the first level. Midway he crosses paths with Tiger and Duff.*)
> **Tiger**   There you are!
> **Duff**   Why did you run away? (*Proclo escapes and continues
> down to his room. Tiger and Duff disappear, looking for
> Googie. Meanwhile Googie appears in a corridor, now looking
> for Claude.*) (p. 299 f.)

The dialogue, on the other hand, is evidently of less prominence here. One-liners and verbal double-takes are more important than reasoning, debate or characterization; this is adequate for a farce such as this, but also a hallmark of other early McNally plays from his anti-war satire *Bringing It All Back Home* (1966) onwards.

Portraying homosexual characters and acts on stage is no particular challenge any more, but in 1975 a play such as *The Ritz* had the power to disturb as well as to educate. Like his English predecessor Joe Orton, whose 1960s plays *Entertaining Mr Sloane*, *Loot* and *What the Butler Saw* also privileged farce over a serious engagement with gay emancipation, McNally opted for the grotesque; the result is that *The Ritz*' 'outlandish representations of gay private life',[2] while entertaining enough for a 'straight' audience, also serves to reinforce stereotypes of gay behaviour. Later in his career, McNally would be far more subtle in his portraits of homosexual characters, culminating in the *dramatis personae* of *Corpus Christi*.

Frankie and Johnny in the Clair de Lune (1987)

If *The Ritz* marks one end of McNally's spectrum as a dramatist, *Frankie and Johnny in the Clair de Lune* sits at the other. Where the earlier play presented a large cast in frantic but ultimately static activity, in this two-hander the plot is almost non-existent but the protagonists experience momentous changes. Frankie and Johnny are well past their first youth when they meet, and the play charts their journey towards each other. This journey is a mental, maybe even spiritual one, for physical closeness is only the starting point – literally so, since the play begins in spectacular fashion:

> *At rise: We hear the sounds of a man and woman making love. They are getting ready to climax. The sounds they are making are noisy, ecstatic and familiar. Above all, they must be graphic. The intention is a portrait in sound of a passionate man and woman making love and reaching climaxes together.*
> *The real thing.*
> *They came.*

> *Silence. Heavy breathing. We become aware that the radio has been playing Bach's Goldberg Variations in the piano version.*
> *By this point, the curtain has been up for at least two minutes. No light, no dialogue, just the sounds of love-making and now the Bach.* (p. 7)

But that remains the total extent of outward action; the rest of the play presents a double movement, away from that sexual encounter towards a more reasoned basis for the beginning relationship, and from flippancy and distance towards a growing intimacy that offers the opportunity for injury – and the chance to demonstrate affection by not taking it. McNally achieves an immediacy that is perfectly suited to the subject matter and intimate form of this play by almost never resorting to dramatic irony (the main device he used in *The Ritz*, both verbal and situational). In *Frankie and Johnny*, we as the audience are witnesses and participants in the characters' gradually growing acquaintance; every twist of behaviour takes us as much by surprise as the dramatic figure, so that Johnny's displays of slightly manic exhibitionism earlier on in the play put Frankie on her guard as much as the audience:

Johnny What people see in one another! It's a total mystery. Shakespeare said it best: "There are more things in heaven and on earth than are dreamt of in your philosophy, Horatio." Something like that. I'm pretty close. Did you ever read *Hamlet*?

Frankie Probably.

Johnny I like him. I've only read a couple of his things. They're not easy. Lots of old words. Archaic, you know? Then all of a sudden he puts it all together and comes up with something clear and simple and it's real nice and you feel you've learned something. This Horatio was Hamlet's best friend. He thought he had it all figured out, so Hamlet set him straight. Do you have a best friend?

Frankie Not really.

Johnny That's okay. I'll be your best friend.

Frankie You think a lot of yourself, don't you? (p. 29f.)

If dramatic irony is to be found in the play, it is in the way McNally offers metadramatic triggers that misfire, as it were. The extended Hamlet reference suggests parallels between the two plays: Johnny and Frankie as the close friends Hamlet and Horatio, as the doomed lovers Hamlet and Ophelia, even as Claudius and Gertrude, the mature couple with issues. But none of these parallels work even reasonably well, and we are thrown back to accepting Johnny's speech at face value: as a piece of braggadocio that is intended to convey cultural cachet, nothing more. Similarly, the 'clair de lune' of the title, the moonlight associated with late nineteenth-century French poetry and music, with Verlaine, Debussy and Fauré, ends the play's two acts in Debussy's version and allows a range of associations to emerge rather than indicate or privilege a particular reading. The most striking instance of what one might call intertextual dead ends is, of course, the name of the couple. 'Frankie and Johnny', the traditional murder ballad that tells the story of two lovers, his infidelity, her deadly revenge on him and her subsequent trial, serves to invite a set of clear expectations, and these are disappointed in every respect. Far from growing alienation and hatred, Frankie towards the end feels secure enough to show Johnny her wounds, both physical and emotional:

> **Frankie** I want to show you something, Johnny. (*She pushes her hair back.*) He did that. The man I told you about. With a belt buckle. (*Johnny kisses the scar.*)
> **Johnny** It's gone now.
> **Frankie** It'll never go.
> **Johnny** It's gone. I made it go.
> **Frankie** What are you? My guardian angel?
> **Johnny** It seems to me the right people are our guardian angels. (p. 60)

That is about as far as McNally moves towards the melodrama of the eponymous ballad; throughout his work, he is attracted by the pathos of his material and simultaneously goes to great lengths to undercut any grand gestures. *The Lisbon Traviata* is another play that signals its intertextual indebtedness in its very title and similarly avoids the melodramatic implications one ought to expect.

The Lisbon Traviata (1989)

The Lisbon Traviata dramatizes the shifting relationships of four gay characters: Stephen, who shares a flat with Mike, Mike's new lover Paul and Stephen's fellow opera fanatic Mendy. The first act sees Stephen exiled in Mendy's flat because Paul is with Mike. They spend the evening discussing fantastically arcane points of opera history, particularly the performances of Maria Callas and specifically her Lisbon *Traviata*, a recording of which Stephen has left behind with Mike; Mendy desperately wishes to hear it. Much of the comedy of the play is generated by the obsessiveness with which he attempts to obtain the recording, but in the second act, the play takes a darker turn. It is essentially a dialogue between Mike and Stephen that spells out their break up. Although the part of Stephen is the longest in the play by far, the fact that Mike takes the initiative again results in the balance of power (or powerlessness) that is so typical for McNally's democratic theatre.

Democratic, that is, in the sense of even-handedness vis-à-vis the protagonists; the later McNally never simply chooses one spokesperson, with the possible (and justifiable) exception of the Jesus figure in *Corpus Christi*. His mature theatre is a forum for debate, not for propaganda. It can, however, be elitist as far as accessibility is concerned: the links between this play and Verdi's *La Traviata* only become evident if one is quite familiar with the opera; there are no plot correspondences to speak of, no high-class prostitution, no noble sacrifice, not even an intruding father figure. It is rather the sense of helplessness in the face of decline that the two pieces have in common, a remix of *La Traviata*'s themes of fatal illness, failure of loyalty and fear of pain:

> **Stephen** Don't tell me what I think. I'll tell you what I think and what I think is this: you're leaving me at a wonderful moment in our long, happy history of queerness to seek a new mate to snuggle up with right at the height of our very own Bubonic Plague.
>
> **Mike** You'll find someone.
>
> **Stephen** I don't want someone. No, thank you. I'll stay right here. Those are dark, mean and extremely dangerous streets

> right now. You can say all you want against Maria, no one's
> ever accused her of causing AIDS. Renata Scotto, yes;
> Maria, no.
>
> **Mike**   Why can't you be serious?
>
> **Stephen**   It hurts too much, okay? Asshole. Self-centered, smug,
> shit-kicking, all-his-eggs-in-one-basket, stupid asshole.
> (*He goes to the stereo and moves the needle to Callas singing the
> recitative leading to "Sempre libera" beginning with "Follie,
> follie!"*)
>
> **Mike**   That's not going to make it hurt any less. (p. 124)

Stephen's choice of music is significant: The recitativo Callas delivers
is a complaint by Violetta Valéry, the 'traviata', the fallen 'woman who
left the path', in which she foresees with terrible clarity the future in
store for her, loneliness amidst an uncaring crowd, 'abbandonata in
questo popoloso deserto'. Here and elsewhere an audience will see the
full force of a scene only if they know what Callas is singing – the
coloratura demanded by the recitativo even before the aria begins means
that careful listening will not be sufficient to realize that Stephen lets
Callas/Violetta express his fear of becoming lonesome in the middle of
New York.

One might argue that this does not really matter; the characters'
'folly' in assuming continuing happiness becomes clear enough. Yet
the impression persists that McNally reserves the full range of authorial
subtlety for those in the know, spectators as sophisticated as his
protagonists where opera is concerned and who similarly might feel that
even musical theatre deserves a little disdain:

> **Mendy**   . . . I wouldn't expect an insensitive faggot whose
> idea of a good time is sitting around listening to Angela
> Lansbury shrieking on about "The Worst Pies In London,"
> like yourself, to understand what I'm talking about. I'm not
> surprised you don't like life. (p. 38)

The reference is to the original recording of Stephen Sondheim's *Sweeney
Todd, the Demon Barber of Fleet Street* (1979), about as melodramatic a

musical as one could hope to find. Even at this arcane level, McNally's anti-melodramatic agenda holds firm. *The Lisbon Traviata*, rather than celebrating operatic pathos, shows its limitations. Verbal wit, even if many of the play's one-liners are spoken in uneasy self-defence, seems to be the better option.

Master Class (1995)

Master Class represents a departure for McNally, although it is in some sense a sequel to *The Lisbon Traviata*. The earlier play showed the obsession of two average men with Maria Callas, this play puts her centre stage. Again, there is no real plot: Callas conducts the eponymous class, making life miserable for the succession of sopranos (and one tenor) who come to learn from her. She is rude, self-centred, reminiscing and cajoling in turns, and gradually (and involuntarily) reveals a complex and damaged personality that has been more sinned against than sinning:

> Ari always said, They're not coming to hear you, no one comes to hear Callas any more. They've come to look at you. You're not a singer. You're a freak. I'm a freak. We're both freaks. They've come to see us. You're a monstre sacré now. We are both monstres sacrés. And we are fucking.
> I don't like that word, Ari. (p. 20)

The way she slides from narrating the past cruelties of her lover Aristoteles Onassis to his literal presentation in direct address is characteristic of this memory play; Kalogeropoulou the young hopeful, Callas the *primadonna assoluta* and the Maria of the master class all blend into the portrait of a contradictory, many-facetted, self-obsessed and courageous artist. Like any memory play, *Master Class* offers no external corroboration to speeches such as the one above, even though Callas' biography is well-documented. We do, literally, have to take her word for Ari's; did he prompt her to see themselves as the holy freaks she speaks of, or does she conveniently make him take responsibility for what is, 'really', her own terrifying insight? Not to be able to resolve such ambiguities is one of the pleasures this play has to offer; the semantic openness paradoxically adds to the presence of an overpoweringly honest artist who can move even at the nadir:

> *She begins to sing the first lines of Lady Macbeth's recitative. What comes out is a cracked and broken thing. A voice in ruins. It is a terrible moment.* (p. 39)

Those lines are 'Ambizioso spirto tu sei Macbetto' – you are an ambitious mind, Macbeth (McNally writes 'spirito'); the *a cappella* attack of these words after a spoken prologue make the passage difficult to sing at the best of times; to fail at this point is to fail spectacularly, and this is quite of a piece with the Callas presented here: on the wane, slightly risible, but with an ineluctable grandeur that is unpretentious but still operatic.

   Master Class is McNally's masterpiece. Although, in the last analysis, the play fails to account for the 'divinity' of Callas, it lays open the conditions under which such adulation and self-fashioning are absolutely necessary for artistic and indeed physical survival. When Callas quotes Cherubini's *Medea* (and the real Callas at a celebrated occasion), saying 'Ho dato tutto a te' (50 *et passim*; 'I have given everything to you'), she may mean Ari, her master class, her opera audiences, the theatre audience, music, life. We need to decide; not many plays give us this privilege.

Corpus Christi (1998)

While the play was widely seen as shockingly deviant even before it received its premiere at the Manhattan Theatre Club, the format of *Corpus Christi* is traditional; it continues a genre that was developed in Europe from the late Middle Ages onwards: the passion play, originally embedded in larger cycles of playlets that dramatized important segments of the entire biblical canon from Genesis to the Resurrection and beyond. Most of these plays depended for their effectiveness on the sequential structure of a day-long performance; only the story of the passion and, to some extent, the nativity achieved a measure of independence. The cycles, four of which survive, were originally performed on Corpus Christi day; just one of the layers that make up McNally's title. He is not the first contemporary playwright to make use of the formula; in Britain alone, Howard Barker, Edward Bond and Tony Harrison have modernized the pattern. But it was left to McNally to add a notorious twist: His Jesus (called Joshua in the play) and some, if not all, of his disciples are gay. The play narrates his life from the nativity to his death on the cross, significantly omitting the resurrection that was the focus and origin of the old cycles. Thus the last image of the play is the crucified body of Joshua, the *corpus Christi* accompanied by one kneeling actor/disciple.

In line with McNally's strategies of defamiliarizing the biblical story so as to emphasize the fictionality of his version, he sets the events of the play in his home town Corpus Christi, the third frame of reference for the title but not one that turns the play into a satire. McNally allows himself the occasional dig:

> **Joseph** What are we gonna call Him?
> **Mary** I told you. Jesus.
> **Joseph** I told you no. This is Texas. It sounds like a Mexican.
>   (p. 14 f.)

But by and large, the importance of the setting is that it is not Jerusalem, not Golgotha. Joshua is, to identify another medieval strain in the play's genetics, an Everyman figure, merely a good man who will not compromise his capacity for love. McNally makes an even bolder claim:

> The purpose of the play is that we begin again the familiar dialogue with ourselves: Do I love my neighbor? Am I contributing good to the society in which I operate or nil? Do I, in fact, matter? Nothing more, nothing less. The play is more a religious ritual than a play. (p. vi)

This may be somewhat overambitious, particularly since any ritual, whatever one's personal beliefs and practices, surely requires immersion and not meta-theatrical musings such as this:

> **Thomas** I'm an actor. I mean Thomas is an actor. I'm an actor, too, of course, but you know that or you wouldn't be paying good money or even no money to sit there and listen to me tell you I'm someone else, in this case the ever popular and appealing Thomas. It's called the willing suspension of disbelief—or in certain cases the unwilling suspension of disbelief. I've seen audiences fight a play for an entire performance. (p. 4)

Such passages of direct audience address are intercut with acted scenes, quotes from the Scriptures and liturgical material. When Joshua teaches his disciples to pray, he recites the entire Lord's Prayer to them, with no deviation or addition (cf. p. 59). This may be deemed a ritual, but in this case it is not the play that is ritualistic but that which it ingests and quotes. It is tempting to employ post-dramatic notions of fragmentation and deconstruction here, but in fact this is exactly the way the old Corpus Christi cycles operated, intermingling canonical material, fictional dialogue, jokes and asides *ad spectatores*. McNally, ever the craftsman, shows a profound grasp of these techniques; in the strongest passages of the play, they synthesize into moving moments, even if some were moved to repulsion:

> **James** Bartholomew and I had wanted our union blessed for a long time—some acknowledgment of what we were to each other.
> **Bartholomew** We asked, Josh. They said it was against the law and the priests said it was forbidden by Scripture.
> **James** "If a man lies with a man as with a woman, both of them have committed an abomination; they shall be put to death, their blood is upon them."
> **Joshua** Why would you memorize such a terrible passage? "And God saw everything that He had made, and behold

it was very good," I can quote Scripture as well as the next man. God loves us most when we love each other. We accept you and bless you. Who's got a ring? (p. 61)

That is the central message of the 'King of the Queers' (p. 75); it was too much for many. In the uproar that accompanied productions of the play the world over, McNally was routinely accused of blasphemy, a charge that needs to be addressed. Theatres, directors and actors were threatened; I remember my first encounter with the play when some 200 police had to escort us into the theatre through an angry picket line – in a small German university town almost two years after the play's American premiere. The scandal made McNally a household name; it helped to eclipse, however, for years to come, his earlier work.[3]

It is of little help to say that those who protested against productions of *Corpus Christi* were unsophisticated fundamentalists who normally would not notice a theatre at all. McNally chose to link homosexuality, anathema to many, with the human incarnation of the godhead, revealed truth to many more. The overlap between those two groups could not have come as surprise to the playwright; the *Corpus Christi* scandal was made to measure. But it would be equally of little help to accuse McNally of mere publicity-seeking. The play is a serious meditation on the limits of love. This Jesus/Joshua has none – that is the very attribute that makes him divine. From McNally's point of view, the son of God has to be gay, among all the other forms love, charity and compassion can take. If this is blasphemy, then it is close to what T. S. Eliot had in mind when he said: 'no one can possibly blaspheme in any sense except that in which a parrot may be said to curse, unless he profoundly believes in that which he profanes'.[4] Among many other things, McNally is a religious dramatist, much as he strives to contain that.

Some Men (2007)

McNally continued to write for the stage in the 2000s. He neither managed to repeat the critical success of *Master Class* nor the furore around *Corpus Christi*; his recent plays have met with mixed reviews at best. The most noticeable feature of McNally's late period is the return to the subjects and settings of earlier texts. In *Some Men* this revisiting can be seen in almost every scene, most strikingly in the one set in a bathhouse in 1975 – a direct reference to and reworking of that year's *The Ritz*.

Some Men charts 85 years of gay life and culture in New York, starting in 1922 and ending in the present of 2007. A total of 54 characters, performed by a minimum of nine actors, go through every conceivable relevant topic, from the clandestine freedom found in early speakeasies via Stonewall to the AIDS crisis and, particularly, the struggle for legal recognition of gay marriages. It consists of 14 scenes that are arranged achronologically, starting and ending in the present.

There is something of a tradition here: McNally clearly is indebted to Noël Coward's *Cavalcade* (1931).[5] At the same time, *Some Men* finds more than just an echo in Jonathan Harvey's *Canary* (2010), a play that follows 50 years of gay history in Britain. The need to take stock, to evaluate one's history, seems to have taken precedence over calls to action in contemporary gay drama.

The first and last of McNally's scenes depict the same wedding, thus creating a frame that characteristically rounds off a play concerned with the need for achieving harmony. Not only are we let in on a successful, loving long-term relationship (between Bernie and Carl), we also see self-confident characters, functioning social networks and intergenerational family solidarity.

The upbeat messages the play incessantly sends constitute its central problem, though. There is nothing wrong with presenting positive role models, but the neatness with which McNally operates here moves the play dangerously close to an exercise in wishful thinking, even, at times, sentimentality. The text itself in one passage moves towards acknowledging this, when the mature couple Scoop and Aaron find themselves patronized by two students:

Scoop What is this interview for again?
Pat We're gender studies majors at Vassar. Our professor said
we should talk to some elder queers and find out what it
was like to be part of the pre-Stonewall oppressed and non-
liberated generation.
Scoop And we fit the bill?

Fritz Exactly! As a queer theorist, I find the oral history of an elder queer in his fifties or sixties – or late forties even! – is worth more than a whole library full of sociological studies. Who else is going to tell us who we were or where we've been better than guys like you?

Aaron Thank you . . . ?

Fritz Fritz. And this is my friend, Pat.

Aaron Pat! I was wondering. It's a good name for gender studies.

Pat Men like you are the keepers of the flame. Our very own Dead Sea Scrolls. You lived through the years of secrecy and oppression that would have decimated a lesser people.

. . .

Aaron I hate to break it to you but we did okay for ourselves.

Fritz You were oppressed by the straight white male patriarchy.

Aaron We were?

Scoop When you put it like that, it sounds terrific. (pp. 71–3)

Pat and Fritz may be caricatures of insensitivity, and thus the laughing stock of audiences, but they do have a point in recalling past injustices, and that point is weakened when all our sympathies lie with the quick-witted campness of their interviewees: Once the students are gone, Scoop and Aaron actually break into a song and dance routine. Dancing, in fact, is the dramaturgical panacea for this play; it even ends in a collective dance scene that has little of the ambiguity of the one erupting in Brian Friel's *Dancing at Lughnasa* (1990) and much of the concluding number of a musical show.

One critic called the play 'an uneven assembly of symmetrical blackout sketches',[6] another 'fine . . . play that's filled to the brim with compelling ideas'.[7] In a way, both assessments are justified: as a play, *Some Men* lacks structure and coherence; as an anthology of gay and emancipatory *topoi*, it represents a summary of what was possible on and off stage in the past.

Summary

Like his near namesake, the Roman dramatist Terence, McNally is first and foremost a comedian, even though his later work, and particularly *Corpus Christi*, moves away from the farcical frenzy of *The Ritz* and the shower of one-liners of *The Lisbon Traviata*.[8] Although his career was more constantly successful than that of most of his contemporaries, he created his best work in the 1990s, a period of intense productivity: 'I like to write plays. As I get older, I'm getting more prolific'.[9]

Many of his plays are all but plotless: They consist of long, carefully observed and masterfully composed dialogues that almost imperceptibly alter the relation between the speakers. They may grow more intimate (as in *Frankie and Johnny*) or estranged (as in *The Lisbon Traviata*). As a corollary, these plays do not have one central character but either balance a couple (*Frankie and Johnny* again), a quartet (*The Lisbon Traviata*) or a larger group (*Love! Valour! Compassion!*). A further implication of McNally's polylogues is the equable distribution of arguments and rebuttals; in his disinterestedness he would make an ideal thesis dramatist, but this is not what he sets out to do. His plays (with a few early exceptions) are undidactic; they do not preach.

This is not to say they address no political issues. Military service, authoritarianism, Third World problems all make an occasional appearance; McNally's central concern is the way gay and straight individuals and groups can live together. The hostile treatment meted out to homosexuals is never far away in McNally's writing. Even *A Perfect Ganesh* (1993), a play about two elderly American women travelling in India, is held together by references to and memories of Walter, the son of one of them, killed by a posse of six African Americans for being a 'faggot'. India, for all its presence in this sprawling play, is merely a place whose colours, smells and sometimes revolting sights trigger sorrow, self-accusations and reveries that revolve around the parental love Walter ought to have had. Even the earliest of the plays reviewed here, *The Ritz*, for once suspends the frantic jostling to make room for this exchange:

> **Proclo** What about Tiger and Duff?
> **Chris** What about them?

Proclo I thought they were normal.

Chris They are normal. They've also been lovers for three years.

Proclo I'm sorry. I didn't mean it like that.

Chris Yes, you did.

Proclo Yea, I did.

Chris I'll tell you something about straight people, and sometimes I think it's the only thing worth knowing about them. They don't like gays. They never have. They never will. Anything else they say is just talk. (p. 293)

There is enough evidence that the later McNally moved away from such desperation; *Corpus Christi* is not the work of a cynic. Thus a certain irony can be found in the fact that McNally's most outrageous offerings, from the mechanical mass couplings of *The Ritz* to the extended sexual act presented acoustically at the beginning of *Frankie and Johnny*, were taken by audiences in their stride, whereas the reticent, traditionally composed *Corpus Christi* generated a wake of theatre scandals across the globe.

But it would be wrong to reduce McNally's range to a trademark concern with the social consequences of homosexual partnerships in a heterosexually dominated world. His remit is wider than that of Jonathan Harvey or Kevin Elyot, two British dramatists, and his treatments are less grotesque than that of Mark Ravenhill, the third iconic gay playwright on the British scene. Perhaps the best analogue is another American, Tony Kushner. Their oeuvre is very different in many respects, with Kushner the more 'political' author, but the insistence on dignity and the right to love and be loved that is grounded neither in sexual orientation nor on social bonds but in the mere fact of one's humanity, makes them fellows.[10]

So does the simultaneous fascination with the holy and the hieratic; McNally, like Kushner, time and time again approaches the idea of the sacred. Kushner's canvas is wider, but McNally achieves a precision that can almost reconcile the human with the divine: Maria Callas and Joshua stop just short of apotheosis. The former admits to her limits, having given all she had to give, the latter dies on the cross in the play's final moments, with his resurrection only a conjectural possibility after the curtain has come down: metaphysics, like melodrama, must not be given in to. In his best moments, McNally achieves a subtlety that is rare both in his earlier work and that of his fellow mainstream dramatists.

Primary Sources

Works by Terrence McNally

McNally, Terrence, *Frankie and Johnny in the Clair de Lune* (New York: Dramatists Play Service, 1988).

—, *The Lisbon Traviata* (New York: Fireside Theatre, 1990).

—, *15 Short Plays* [Includes *Bringing It All; Back Home; Noon; Botticelli; Next; Cuba Si!; Sweet Eros; Witness; Whiskey; Bad Habits; The Ritz; Prelude & Liebestod; Andre's Mother; The Wibbly, Wobbly, Wiggly Dance That Cleopatterer Did; Street Talk; Hidden Agendas*] (Lyme: Smith and Kraus, 1994).

—, *Love! Valour! Compassion!* and *A Perfect Ganesh* (New York: Plume, 1995).

—, *Master Class* (London: Methuen Drama, 1997).

—, *Corpus Christi* (New York: Grove Press, 1998).

—, *Some Men* and *Deuce* (New York: Grove Press, 2007).

Secondary Sources

Brantley, Ben, '8 Decades of Gay Men, at the Altar With History'. *New York Times*, 27 March 2007. http://theater.nytimes.com/2007/03/27/theater/reviews/27men.html

Denton, Martin, 'Some Men'. 24 March 2007. http://www.nytheatre.com/Review/martin-denton-2007-3-24-some-men

Eads, Martha Greene, 'Conversion Tactics in Terrence McNally's and Paul Rudnick's Gay Gospels', *Modern Drama* 48, 1 (2005), 163–85.

Eliot, T. S., *After Strange Gods: A Primer of Modern Heresy* (London: Faber and Faber, 1934).

Fisher, James, 'Terrence McNally'. In Christopher Wheatley (ed.), *Twentieth-Century American Dramatists, Third Series* (Detroit: Thomson Gale, 2002), pp. 216–37.

Hodges, Ben (ed.), *Out Plays. Landmark Gay and Lesbian Plays of the Twentieth Century* (New York: Alyson Books, 2008).

McNally, Terrence, 'A Blueprint for the House', In Robert Viagas (ed.), *The Alchemy of Theatre: The Divine Science. Essays on Theatre and the Art of Collaboration* (New York: Playbill Books, 2006), pp. 39–47.

Schultz, Ray, 'Not Just a Monolith: Gay "Class" Divisions in Terrence McNally's *Love! Valour! Compassion!*, *ANQ: A Quarterly Journal of Short Articles, Notes, and Reviews* 23, 2 (2010), 96–104.

Zinman, Toby Silverman, 'The Muses of Terrence McNally', *American Theatre* 12, 3 (1995), 12–17.

–(ed.), *Terrence McNally: A Casebook* (New York: Garland, 1997).

Zinoman, Joy (principal interviewer), 'Terrence McNally'. In Jackson R. Bryer (ed.), *The Playwright's Art: Conversations with Contemporary American Dramatists* (New Brunswick, NJ: Rutgers UP, 1995), pp. 182–204.

Notes

1. McNally frequently defends his keen interest in musical theatre; see, for example, Terrence McNally, 'A Blueprint for the House'.
2. Hodges, Ben (ed.), *Out Plays. Landmark Gay and Lesbian Plays of the Twentieth Century*, p. xxi.
3. For more information on the controversy, cf. James Fisher, 'Terrence McNally', pp. 216–37, 235f.
4. Eliot, T. S., *After Strange Gods: A Primer of Modern Heresy*, p. 52.
5. Brantley, Ben, '8 Decades of Gay Men, at the Altar With History'.
6. Ibid.
7. Denton, Martin. 'Some Men'.
8. Zinman, Toby Silverman, 'The Muses of Terrence McNally', p. 13.
9. McNally, Terrence, *15 Short Plays*, n.p.
10. Cf. Ray Schultz, 'Not Just a Monolith', p. 96.

12 ARTHUR MILLER

Susan C. W. Abbotson

The Archbishop's Ceiling; The American Clock; The Ride Down Mt. Morgan; Broken Glass; Resurrection Blues; Finishing the Picture

Introduction

Arthur Miller continues to be one of American's most important playwrights, whose drama is produced and studied worldwide. With more than 20 major plays, alongside screenplays, fiction and non-fiction, his oeuvre stretches over 60 years, well into the twenty-first century. Miller has been both hailed and scorned as 'America's conscience', and his works are rooted in a profoundly humanistic philosophy that is fiercely patriotic, just as it is determined to bring attention to American and human flaws. His later works have also revealed a rich streak of humour, ever present in his earlier drama, but grown increasingly emphatic, perhaps as a sign of his growing frustration and disillusionment with world events. Miller, however, never gave up hope that people could be better. His driving concern was to make a difference, convinced that theatre was a public art that could accomplish this; at his memorial service in 2005, Edward Albee declared that Miller had done just that. Kurt Vonnegut has spoken of how Miller's plays 'speak movingly about America to almost all Americans, while telling the truth about America',[1] but in Miller's later plays, especially, his target extends beyond American shores, with works like *The Archbishop's Ceiling* (1977), located in Eastern Europe, and *Resurrection Blues* (2002), set on an unnamed South American island.

Arthur Asher Miller was born 17 October 1915 in Harlem, New York, to an immigrant father and first-generation mother. This Jewish family seemed to have achieved the American Dream of comfort and wealth, living in a beautiful apartment overlooking Central Park, but it all fell apart with the social changes of the 1920s. The Great Depression forever haunted Miller, and he confronts these memories in *The American Clock* (1980). The clothing business his father, Isidore Miller, had created went bankrupt, and the family relocated to Brooklyn. Working for nearly two years at an auto parts warehouse to finance college, Miller attended the University of Michigan from 1934 to 1938. He switched his major from Journalism to English after winning a university prize for playwriting. Under the tutelage of Professor Kenneth Rowe, he became entranced by the social realism of Henrik Ibsen.

Miller returned to New York after graduation, during a period when Clifford Odets was showing the theatre world a new kind of drama, both poetically infused and politically motivated. First hired by the Federal Theater Project, until it was closed down in 1939, Miller then wrote plays for the radio networks, further honing his craft. In 1940 he married his college girlfriend, Mary Slattery, with whom he would have two children, Jane and Robert. His first publication was a book of reportage, *Situation Normal . . .* (1944), recounting his experience touring army camps; that same year he also had his first full-length play produced on Broadway – *The Man Who Had All The Luck* – which, unluckily, closed three days after opening. Miller considered giving up the theatre and turned to fiction, publishing a novel about American anti-Semitism: *Focus* (1945). Allowing drama another chance, he achieved success in 1947 with *All My Sons*, and swiftly followed this with the now seminal *Death of a Salesman* (1949).

Miller followed the phenomenal success of *Salesman* with plays like *The Crucible* (1953) and *A View from the Bridge* (1956), which helped redefine the concept of 'modern tragedy' for the American stage. In 1956 he would divorce his wife to marry Marilyn Monroe, for whom he wrote the screenplay, *The Misfits* (1961). In 1956, he was also called to testify before the House Un-American Activities Committee. He refused to name names, and found in contempt; but Miller appealed and the conviction was overturned as unconstitutional. After his marriage to Monroe collapsed, he wed the Austrian photographer, Inge Morath, with whom he would have two children, Rebecca and Daniel, and live happily for the next 40 years. His relationship with Morath was to draw Miller into a more cosmopolitan milieu, leading him to explore Russia, China, Cuba and parts of South America, as well as much of Europe. Getting politically involved on a global level, in 1965 Miller accepted the presidency of International P.E.N., the international literary organization, and would continue to advocate for writers' rights throughout the century. While Miller's reputation in America suffered for decades following his marriage to Monroe and an ill-received production of *After the Fall* (1964), he continued to be lionized abroad, with his dramas being regularly produced around the world. Although *The Price* (1968) was fairly popular, Miller's plays would be given short shrift by American critics for many years. Miller's disappointment in these critics is reflected in his decision to premiere works, like *The Ride Down Mt. Morgan* (1991), in England rather than America. The Holocaust-inspired *Broken Glass* (1994) seemed to invoke a renewed interest in the power of Miller's drama in his native land, and his final two plays, *Resurrection Blues* and *Finishing the Picture* (2004), were both premiered in the United States.

While Miller's reputation is often evoked through his early successes from the 1940s and 1950s, he produced as many plays in the latter quarter of the twentieth century as in that earlier period. While constant, successful revivals of his earlier plays keep them well in the public consciousness and conscience, Miller's influence as a playwright and commentator on the human condition can only be fully assessed through a consideration of his later work, which extends and complicates many of the nascent themes and concepts encapsulated in the earlier pieces, and also illustrates the continuing innovation and self-reinvention of a writer too often wrongly pigeonholed as a realist. Aside from an early Pulitzer for *Death of a Salesman*, and numerous drama awards for other individual plays, Miller won many major awards acknowledging his lifetime achievement in American theatre: in 1959, he received the Gold Medal for Drama from the National Institute of Arts and Letters; in 1984, the Kennedy Center Honors; in 1995, the William Inge Festival Award; in 1996, the Edward Albee Last Frontier Playwright Award; and in 2003, the Jerusalem Prize. He died at his Connecticut home in 2005, a few months short of his 90th birthday.

The Plays

The Archbishop's Ceiling (1977)

On 30 April 1977, *The Archbishop's Ceiling* premiered in a limited production at the Kennedy Center in Washington. Attacked by critics, plans were scrapped for New York, but Miller did extensive rewrites. The play reappeared in England at the Bristol Old Vic, in 1985, followed by a successful Royal Shakespeare Company production the following year. Miller eradicated a whole character, simplified the setting and reworked several scenes. Audiences now got the sense that the play was about something more than Eastern dissidents; it was also a reflection of life in the West, as well as a treatise on the nature of art, power and how reality could be perceived. Miller had moved into the realm of the universal on a far broader level.

The setting is an ornate apartment, once owned by an Archbishop, in an unnamed European capital modelled on Vaclav Havel's Prague in the 1970s. While visiting friends about whom he has been writing a book, an American writer, Adrian, gets caught up in a political quagmire. The apartment may or may not be bugged by a sinister government, for whom its owner, Marcus, another writer, may or may not be working. Local writer, Sigmund, appears to have had the only copy of his latest manuscript taken by the police and arrives to plead for assistance. All the men seem in love with a local beauty, Maya, who demands Marcus assist Sigmund. As he strives to get a party going, Marcus admits the government wants Sigmund to leave the country, and argues for compromise. Sigmund refuses to leave, standing firm on principle, and, by the close, will apparently have his manuscript returned.

In *The Archbishop's Ceiling* reality is ever in question, partly to explore what place morality might have in such a world. The play may take place in Eastern Europe, but the setting symbolizes conditions Miller considers universal. The idea of this room being bugged is less paranoia than a reasonable possibility, even within America after the Watergate scandal. We can never be certain if Miller's ceiling does contain microphones, but believing they exist gives the characters an audience and a role to play, allowing them to view their lives as significant. Miller perceives surveillance and censorship as a worldwide problem, and one that goes beyond politics. He uses a political metaphor to address deeper concerns regarding people's relationship to power, the function and nature of reality, truth, compromise and art.

The heavy, chaotic furnishings of the room convey its potential as a trap and the complexities of contemporary life. The titular ceiling with its religious mural, along with the surrounding detritus, emblematize beliefs that have ceased to have real meaning in such a world, yet remain a continuous and haunting presence and possibility. The constant evasions and difficulty of trust between these characters is conveyed by their consistently cautious speech and movement, which are carefully orchestrated by the playwright. Miller allows us to observe how people react when they are faced with unending uncertainty. Each character creates a world from their personal perspective, formed by the lies they decide to accept, and the realities they choose to recognize. The only success is to be in control of your own role, as it seems Sigmund finally manages to be. He and his fictions become a fixed point around which all the characters can coalesce to find hope for the future.

The American Clock (1980)

The American Clock was first produced on 24 May 1980, at South Carolina's Spoleto Festival, and transferred, in a modified form, to New York. An ambitious play, with 21 songs and more than 50 characters, it took time to find the right director and format, but by its 1986 production at London's National Theatre, directed by Peter Wood, its mural spirit, balancing the epic against intimate psychological portraits, was evocatively conveyed. An amalgam of Miller's own memories of the Depression era, and episodes related in Studs Terkel's *Hard Times*, the play creates a diorama of life in America in the 1930s, in all of its hardship and glory. In 1980, Miller saw American society hurtling towards a repetition of these conditions, with none of the supporting optimism to lift her out. His play was intended as a voice of warning and as a reminder of past survival techniques worthy of reconsideration.

Miller interlinks an autobiographical family tale of excess followed by increasingly desperate poverty with scenes that include a bootblack at work, the President of General Electric, a veteran hobo riding the rails, a farm auction, the welfare office, and a small Southern café. A fluid collage of characters and scenes is punctuated by a plethora of period songs that offer subtle commentary on the action. The episodic structure is loosely tied by overlapping characters, thematic links and two narrators: the cautious financier, Arthur Robertson, and the youthful Lee Baum, son of the central family whom we follow from youth to adulthood. Both participants in, and commentators on, the events of the play, with often contrasting interpretations, these narrators guide us to the conclusion. From the devastation of the Wall Street Crash, through the dustbowl years, to the onset of World War II, exploring and dismissing the possibilities of a communist solution along the way, we finally determine that belief in American democracy and its inherent possibilities is what will give people the strength to continue.

Terry Otten describes the play as 'both experimental and a reiteration of seminal Miller themes'.[2] In this lies its strength. Miller re-addresses perennial concerns over materialism, public and private integrity, guilt and responsibility, and the relation between family and society, but with a lighter touch, underscored by the play's vaudevillian approach, upbeat songs, and the gentle humour of the Baum family episodes. The central image of the clock ticking away indicates that nothing lasts forever and all must change. In this constant change, hope can be found, for although change can be for the worse, it can just as equally be for the better. For example, although the father, Moe Baum, feels humiliated at being reduced to having to borrow a quarter from his son, Lee is able to feel great pride in being able to help his father. Miller uses the three Baums to illustrate the different reactions he perceived people had to the Depression: Moe responds practically, Lee ideologically and the mother, Rose, emotionally. In combination, they offer a comprehensive picture of the overwhelming impact of the Depression on the American psyche and disposition. Thus, the play acts as both history lesson and, through its uplifting final chorus, a beacon of hope for the future. Unsurprisingly, there has been an increase in productions of this play as many, once again, face leaner years in the twenty-first century.

The Ride Down Mt. Morgan (1991)

The Ride Down Mt. Morgan opened 23 October 1991 at the Wyndham Theatre, London, but was not produced in America until 1996. Despite a comic veneer, this is an uncomfortable tale of bigamy and deceit, in the tradition of *Death of a Salesman*'s Willy Loman, and Quentin from *After the Fall*. Here we view events from 'inside the head' of the central protagonist, Lyman Felt, whose perspective inevitably colours what we witness. Filled with dream sequences and conflicting versions of events, reality can never be more than subjective. Lyman Felt appears to be what Willy Loman always wanted to be: handsome, successful and well-liked, if only Willy had been more confident and irresponsible. What Lyman's story shows is the cost of such a life, while addressing the difficulties of living in an amoral, postmodern society far more chaotic than the world Willy faced. Lyman ends the play abandoned and in anguish: when you live for yourself alone, then that, we discover, is with whom you are finally left.

The play begins with Lyman heavily injured in a hospital bed, having driven his car down a mountain. We later discover this 'accident' to have been the latest act of hubris in the life of Lyman, who has been living a life of increasing excess. Hospital notifications to families bring to light the fact he has two wives: Theo with whom he has a daughter, Bessie, and Leah, with whom he has a son, Benjamin. His double marriage has allowed him to explore the riskier side of his nature; with Theo he continued to play the cautious family man, but with Leah he led a more vital and exciting existence. While horrified at the prospect of them meeting, Lyman fantasizes that their regard for him may overwrite their anger. Once they actually meet, while they initially fight over who can claim him, they both end up deciding to leave, recognizing that Lyman's over-whelming self-concern leaves no room for a proper relationship with either one. Lyman is not wholly villainous, and seems to reach an epiphany at the close, beginning to acknowledge the selfish implications of his behaviour.

It is our guilt, Miller suggests, that connects us to other human beings, and by ignoring his conscience, Lyman has effectively cut himself off from his own humanity. His marriage to Leah occurred the same year Ronald Reagan became President, and Miller intended Lyman's bigamous behaviour to reflect the values and type of leadership he saw America subsequently experiencing. Lyman is not alone in being found to have lived dishonestly as both wives admit they, too, have manipulated the truth. It is Bessie who quietly provides the moral centre of the play, telling her father one must live for others as much as for oneself.

Broken Glass (1994)

First performed on 1 March 1994 at the Long Wharf Theatre in Connecticut, *Broken Glass* later transferred to Broadway. With a realistic, straight drama, Miller once again found critical approval on both sides of the Atlantic, and won Britain's Olivier Award for best new play after its London premiere. On a 2011 revival of the play, starring Anthony Sher, *The Guardian*'s Michael Billington declared, 'Arthur Miller's 1994 play towers over the dismal lowlands of current West End theatre like a majestic mountain peak . . . far and away the best of Miller's late plays'.[3]

Set in 1938 Brooklyn, *Broken Glass* addresses issues of anti-Semitism and the kind of bigotry and self-hatred that helped fuel the atrocities of the Holocaust. Obsessed with work, and his own desire to assimilate, Phillip Gellburg has little time for his wife, Sylvia, until she demands his attention by falling prey to a mysterious paralysis after seeing the events of Kristallnacht in the newspaper. Sylvia has been a quiet housewife, but this violence against Jews has provoked her to express her buried fears and longings. Dr Harry Hyman is called in to help, and though no specialist, decides the case is a psychiatric one, proceeding to treat Sylvia despite the increasing hostility of her husband, who confesses to the doctor his own impotency. Hyman draws out Sylvia's hidden fears of Phillip, and leads Phillip to face his own inadequacies as a Jew. At the play's close, we witness Sylvia symbolically struggle to her feet towards her husband who has collapsed in bed, possibly dead, while recovering from a heart attack brought on by the callous dismissal of his WASP boss, Stanton Case, over a deal gone bad.

Though predominantly realistic, the play contains a symbolic underpinning. Sylvia's physical paralysis represents the moral paralysis of many Americans in the face of the Holocaust, and her husband's appearance, with his pale face and black garb, depicts the sheer lack (and fear) of life with which his character is afflicted. The doctor's contrasting potency becomes ironic, given his barren marriage and blindness to the realities of German racism. The glass of the title conveys not just its connection to the broken windows of Kristallnacht, but also the glass broken at Jewish weddings as a symbol of the world's imperfection to remind us of our need to get involved, and the Gellburgs' need to break out of the glass bell-jars in which each has been living. Their constricted lives connect them to those Jews being frozen into ineffectuality in the ghettos and everyone else around the world who refused to admit the Holocaust was happening.

Written in the shadow of atrocities in Rwanda and Bosnia, the play conveys the necessity of a humanistic response to a violent world. Miller believed something like the Holocaust involves everyone, and there can be no turning away without cost. Denial, resignation or ignorance, all reactions we see in *Broken Glass*, are tantamount to complicity. All forms of non-action become destructive when they allow other actions to occur. The issue of potency versus impotency is central to the play, and spills into every aspect of life. What use is the Doctor's sexual potency when he is incapable of true commitment or fidelity to his culture or his wife? What value is Phillip's commercial success when he understands so little of who he is and what he does? What use is even Sylvia's compassion when she has lost touch with her own selfhood so much that she no longer retains even the capacity to stand? The play explores the difficulties faced by those who neglect that important balance between self-awareness and connection to others, for it is through such neglect that other Holocausts can occur.

Resurrection Blues (2002)

Resurrection Blues premiered at the Guthrie Theater in Minneapolis on 3 August 2002. In the early 1980s Miller travelled to Venezuela and Colombia, giving him the idea for a play based on a fictitious South American banana republic that would satirize their kind of government, and the hypocrisy of American involvement. Miller also wanted to highlight the growing vulgarity and amorality of the media and so created the ultimate bad taste reality show scenario: an American film crew's intention to film a real-life crucifixion, interspersed with advertisements for medical products. The controversy over filming the execution of Timothy McVeigh around this time, even while the courts blocked the idea, unintentionally made the conceit more believable.

Facing despair, Jeannine Schultz tries to commit suicide, but gains a renewal of hope through a mysterious Christ-like figure, Ralph. However, her uncle, Felix Barriaux, the military dictator against whom she fought, has arrested Ralph and plans to have him crucified, to scare his people into submission and make a fortune from the American television company. Complications ensue as Jeannine's father (who had withdrawn into a life of philosophy over action) decides to take her side; the director argues with her producer over whether they should film such a horrendous thing; Felix falls in love with Emily and rediscovers his lost potency, and Ralph keeps disappearing (although he sends his hippy disciple Stanley to negotiate with the dictator and keep his options open). As they wrangle to and fro regarding whether the crucifixion should proceed or not, these farcical events – and the humour is deliberately broad and biting – conclude with Ralph (now called Charley) disappearing in a cloud of light. Rather than a serious drama revealing the vacuousness of modern life with its soul-destroying accommodations and dissolution of moral value, Miller surprises his audience with a darkly comic satire.

While the uncomfortable connection between religion and violence, the banal unfeeling bureaucracy of dictatorships and the crass greed of a materialist culture without restraint obviously colour the play, it ends up less a critique of religion, politics or the media, than an exploration of the possibility of faith in an evidently cynical world. That no one questions an audience's desire to watch a crucifixion says as much about the characters' lack of humanity as those people who will tune in. People play roles and have lost touch with their authentic selves. Just the possibility of Ralph/Charley, who is never actually seen on stage, allows most of them, at least momentarily, to look beyond themselves, and rediscover core values they had forgotten. But their Messiah finally retreats, for this is a blues lament, and salvation cannot be assured; the fakeness of existing 'ideals' has been exposed, but these people still need to fashion new ones by which to redeem themselves.

Finishing the Picture (2004)

On 21 September 2004, *Finishing the Picture* opened at the Goodman Theater, Chicago. The title of Miller's final play is unintentionally apposite; it was one on which he had begun working decades earlier, but set aside. With the death of Inge Morath, in 2002, Miller was given space to readdress and possibly exorcise the spirit of Marilyn that had long haunted him: we see ghosts of her presence in much of his writing in the latter quarter of the twentieth century. The title partly refers to Miller's effort to complete the story behind events that took place during the filming of his 1961 film *The Misfits* but the play turned out to be less about Monroe than the power that surrounded her iconic status and the price and pitfalls of creativity. Just as some seeds need fire to germinate, so does art demand a sacrifice.

The play's first director, Robert Falls, suggested the inclusion of video images before each scene and a cinematic technique in the second act which displayed a live feed of the actors speaking to Kitty. Though initially uncertain, Miller saw how this idea helped underline those aspects of the movie-industry he was attempting to expose – both its artifice and the self-centred nature of many of those involved – and agreed to make these part of his play. The main action of the play revolves around various characters trying to get Kitty out of bed to complete the movie in which she is the star. The inauthenticity of this star status is ironically conveyed by Kitty's somnambulant and predominantly silent presence throughout the play. All manipulate Kitty for their own selfish reasons and few show any regard for her as a human being. She ceases to be truly human, becoming a mirror that reflects the needs and desires of those cajoling at her bedside. These characters display the same lost sense of positive purpose we saw in *Resurrection Blues*, playing roles in which even they no longer believe. Thus Miller exposes the distorted self-involved and self-promoting artistry of Kitty's acting coaches, Jerome and Flora Fassinger (based on real-life couple Lee and

Paula Strasberg), the coldness of the product being created by director Derek Clemson and cinematographer Terry Case, who both mouth sympathy for Kitty, but nonetheless see her as a creature to be controlled in order to complete their movie, and husband Paul, who is emotionally stiff and unable to give Kitty the love she so desperately needs, though he at least acknowledges his shortcoming. Unlike *Broken Glass*'s Sylvia Gellburg, Kitty does not have the strength to break out of her paralysis and reclaim responsibility for her own life, apparently too far drained by the leeches that surround her.

Satirizing an industry he views as determined to turn everyone and everything into a product, Miller comically skewers nearly everyone associated with making the movie; a movie we are never sure will be completed or would be worth the effort. The opening news of fire encroaching on the hotel provides an apocalyptic ambience. However, the play is framed by the hopeful romance of producer Phillip Ochsner and secretary Edna Meyers, two people who unexpectedly find a void filled by the other's presence, and potential love even on the edge of the abyss. Although Ochsner is centred on business, it is with a decency that makes him more appealing than many of the artists on display. He is not the stereotypical power-hungry philistine, but a sensitive, level-headed decision maker. It is hard not to see in this couple something of Miller's unexpected late-life relationship with the much younger Agnes Barley at the time he was completing this play. This allows for a glimmer of hope as we also learn that the fire has burned itself out. Like so much of Miller's work, this play is ultimately underpinned with a concern for responsibility to one another, suggesting that a failure to take responsibility will always have a severe cost.

Summary

Perhaps persuaded by the dismissive views of critics such as Robert Brustein, who in 1991 declared Miller's sensibility so outdated that it relates to 'the eighteenth century, which is the age of Newton, rather than to the twentieth, the age of Einstein',[4] production reviews of Miller's later plays reveal a perception of Miller as a playwright in decline, writing works that are 'disappointingly unpersuasive', 'quite horrible' and 'riddled with problems'.[5] Miller's earlier plays are strong works, and deserve the attention they have received for their craft, social engagement and burgeoning humanism. The later plays, however, should not be so readily dismissed, but rather seen as developing and even refining those earlier works. The case is, as fellow playwright David Rabe points out: 'People act like his early plays are the only ones he wrote . . . the critics have praised him for a certain kind of play and dramaturgy of moral ideas and then they have maligned him for not growing when in fact what has happened is that they have refused to admit he has grown'. Rabe concludes: 'What is really insane is not to recognize the value of the later plays, the development of the writer, the evolving struggle of his relationship to the idea of a moral position'.[6] By the turn of the century, with a resurgence of scholarly interest in Miller and more successful productions of his later plays, critical opinion has begun to reassess his stature and recognize that Miller remains as forceful in the twenty-first century as he was during those early days of success.

Throughout Christopher Bigsby's 1990 collection of commentaries, *Arthur Miller & Company*, various artists and critics speak of Miller's commitment to democracy, truth, morality and humanity. Directors see his plays as complex and difficult to put on due to their many levels and fine balance. Actors find his work challenging and exhilarating. All realize that his plays demand audience involvement to be fully effective. As a kind of prophet, a role prescribed to him by several critics, Miller uncovers humanity's flaws and tries to enlighten people as to the harsh realities of their existence, in the hope that they might strive to improve their behaviour and lives. He approaches this task not as a saint but as a fellow sinner, in search of his own answers.

Committed to theatre by a sincere belief that it can change people for the better, Miller felt his responsibility as an artist was to encourage such change. With Miller's agreement, Steven Centola summed up the playwright's work as deriving from a 'vision of the human condition as a kind of existential humanism—a vision that emphasizes self-determinism and social responsibility and that is optimistic and affirms life by acknowledging man's possibilities in the face of his limitations and even sometimes in the dramatization of his failures'.[7] Miller's plays display an inherent humanism, which insists that our creative will is sufficient to provide us with a sense of human values. He believes we have the capability to define ourselves, the society we inhabit, and what we will stand for, because we have freewill. 'My effort, my energy, my aesthetic', he once stated, 'is to find the chain of moral being in the world, somehow. It's moving in its hidden way through all my work'.[8] The balance between individual and social interests and needs, which Miller's work promotes, is achieved by asserting moral responsibility towards self and others.

Miller offers us a revitalized and flexible humanism growing out of existentialist principles, as opposed to the confident and imperialistic humanism of the past: the same 'revitalised humanism' that Alan Wilde advocates for 'our postmodern age', which does not elitistically defend individualism, although it does recognize the worth of individuals and such individuals' need and capacity to realize their own potential for being.[9] Miller's plays exemplify this mode by provoking audiences into feeling that humans are worth something, and therefore, deserving of attention and respect, despite all their flaws.

While Miller's best known plays were from the earlier part of his career, his later plays offer extensions of these early successes to effect an even wider and more complex vision of human dilemma and potential. The self-involved and self-deluded protagonists of *All My Sons* and *Death of a Salesman* (Joe Keller and Willy Loman), combine to create *The Ride Down Mt. Morgan*'s supremely amoral tyrant, Lyman Felt, while further developing the experimental stylism of both *Death of a Salesman* and *After the Fall*. Where *The Crucible* boldly spoke to the vagaries of power throughout American history from the Salem witch trials to the McCarthyism of the 1950s, *The Archbishop's Ceiling* and *Resurrection Blues* offer more global visions, while *Finishing the Picture* completes the self-examination of responsibility begun in *After the Fall*.

With their concomitant connection to the moral realm of guilt, blame and responsibility, which directs his entire canon, the Great Depression and the Holocaust remain key influences on Miller's perspective. Both colour earlier works, though often only peripherally, except for his 1964 *Incident at Vichy*, which takes place at a Nazi detention centre in Vichy, France. However, by the 1980s, Miller seems more able to embrace and explore the fuller implications of both events. While his 1980 screenplay adaptation of Fania Fenelon's memoir, *Playing for Time* takes us right inside the camps, presenting a controversial humanized depiction of Nazis, *Broken Glass* addresses how these events impacted the American public. *The American Clock* is the fullest and most telling exploration of the trials and lessons of the Depression years, offered in the hope that a country heading down the same path might learn a lesson and alter course.

Miller moved on from the realistic dramas of his past and as Bigsby points out: 'experimented with form, disassembled character, compressed and distended language'.[10] Miller disliked definitions of almost any of his writing as realistic, because he saw himself as not attempting to create reality, but rather interpret it. Constantly trying out new techniques, he created works whose artistic form was part of their message. Brenda Murphy rightly suggests that Miller's whole career since *Death of a Salesman* has been a continual experimentation with realistic and expressionistic forms to uncover an effective means of conveying the bifurcation of a human experience which he sees as split between a concern for the self and a concern for society as a whole.[11] Miller's later works are perceptive, critical commentaries on contemporary society, written in a style which reflects the confused and fragmentary nature of that society, while offering hope that an alternate mode of living remains possible.

Primary Sources

Works by Arthur Miller

Echoes Down the Corridor. Edited by Steven R. Centola (New York: Viking, 2000).

Miller Plays: 1: All My Sons, Death of a Salesman, The Crucible, A Memory of Two Mondays, A View from the Bridge (London: A&C Black, 2009).

Miller Plays: 2: After the Fall, Incident at Vichy, The Price, Creation of the World, Playing for Time, The Misfits (London: A&C Black, 2009).

Miller Plays: 3: The American Clock, The Archbishop's Ceiling, Two-Way Mirror (London: A&C Black, 2009).

Miller Plays: 4: The Golden Years, The Man Who Had All the Luck, I Can't Remember Anything, Clara (London: A&C Black, 2009).

Miller Plays: 5: The Last Yankee, The Ride Down Mount Morgan, Almost Everybody Wins (London: A&C Black, 2009).

Miller Plays 6: Broken Glass, Mr Peter's Connections, Resurrection Blues, Finishing the Picture (London: A&C Black, 2009).

On Politics and the Art of Acting (New York: Viking, 2001).

The Theater Essays of Arthur Miller. Rev. ed. Edited by Robert A. Martin and Steven R. Centola (New York: Da Capo Press, 1996).

Timebends: A Life (New York: Grove, 1987).

Secondary Sources

Abbotson, Susan C. W., *Critical Companion to Arthur Miller* (New York: Facts on File, 2008).

Adam, Julie, *Versions of Heroism in Modern American Drama: Redefinitions by Miller, O'Neill, and Anderson* (New York: St. Martin's, 1991).

Ali, Syed Mashkoor (ed.), *Arthur Miller: Twentieth Century Legend* (Jaipur, India: Surabhi, 2006).

The Arthur Miller Journal 1, 1 (Spring 2006).

Bigsby, Christopher (ed.), *Arthur Miller and Company* (London: Methuen, 1990).

—, *Modern American Drama 1945–1990* (Cambridge: Cambridge University Press, 1992).

—, *Arthur Miller: A Critical Study* (Cambridge: Cambridge University Press, 2005a).

— (ed.), *Remembering Arthur Miller* (London: Methuen, 2005b).

—, *Arthur Miller 1915–1962* (London: Weidenfeld & Nicolson, 2008).

— (ed.), *The Cambridge Companion to Arthur Miller.* 2nd edn (New York: Cambridge University Press, 2010).

—, *Arthur Miller 1962–2005* (London: Weidenfeld & Nicolson, 2011).

Brater, Enoch (ed.), *Arthur Miller's America: Theater and Culture in a Time of Change* (Ann Arbor: University of Michigan Press, 2005).

— (ed.), *Arthur Miller's Global Theater* (Ann Arbor: University of Michigan Press, 2007).

Brustein, Robert, *Reimagining American Theatre* (New York: Hill, 1991).

Centola, Steven (ed.), *The Achievement of Arthur Miller: New Essays* (Dallas, Tex: Contemporary Research, 1995).

Centola, Steven and Michelle Cirulli (eds), *The Critical Response to Arthur Miller* (Westport, CT: Praeger, 2006).

Christiansen, Richard, 'Arthur Miller Opens New Play in London for Good Reason'. *Chicago Tribune*, 13 November 1991, sec. 1: 24.

Coe, Richard L., 'Miller's *The Archbishop's Ceiling*; Arthur Miller's Ceiling'. *Washington Post* 2, May 1977, B1, B7.

Gussow, Mel, *Conversations with Miller* (London: Nick Hern, 2002).

Koorey, Stefani, *Arthur Miller's Life and Literature: An Annotated and Comprehensive Guide* (Boston: Scarecrow Press, 2000).

Langteau, Paula T. (ed.), *Miller and Middle America: Essays on Arthur Miller and the American Experience* (Lanham, MD: University Press of America, 2007).

Marino, Stephen, *A Language Study of Arthur Miller's Plays: The Poetic in the Colloquial* (New York: Mellen, 2002).

Martine, James J., *Critical Essays on Arthur Miller* (Boston: Hall, 1979).

Mason, Jeffrey, *Stone Tower: The Political Theater of Arthur Miller* (Ann Arbor: University of Michigan Press, 2008).

Murphy, Brenda, 'Arthur Miller: Revisioning Realism'. In William W. Demastes (ed.), *Realism and the American Dramatic Tradition* (Tuscaloosa: University of Alabama Press, 1996), pp. 189–202.

—(ed.), *Critical Insights: Arthur Miller* (Hackensack, NJ: Salem Press, 2010).

Nanda, Silima, *Faces of Miller Women* (New Delhi, India: Mittal Publications, 2007).

Otten, Terry, *The Temptation of Innocence in the Dramas of Arthur Miller* (Columbia: University of Missouri Press, 2002).

Polster, Joshua E., *Reinterpreting the Plays of Arthur Miller* (Lewiston, NY: Mellen, 2010).

Roudané, Matthew C., *Conversations with Arthur Miller* (Jackson: University Press of Mississippi, 1987).

Teachout, Terry, 'View: First-Rate Second City; Chicago's Thriving Theater Scene Has a Few Lessons to Teach Broadway'. *Wall Street Journal* 8 October 2004, W1.

Wardle, Irving, 'American Patron Saint of the English Stage: Arthur Miller'. *Independent,* 28 January 1990, 36.

Watt, Douglas, 'Another Round of Miller Light'. *Daily News* 19 February 1987. *New York Theatre Critics' Review* 48 (1987), 344–5.

Weber, Bruce, 'It's Gloves-Off Time for an Angry Arthur Miller'. *New York Times,* 15 August 2002, E1.

Welland, Dennis, *Miller: The Playwright*. 3rd. edn (New York: Methuen, 1985).

Wilde, Alan, *Middle Grounds: Studies in Contemporary American Fiction* (Philadelphia: University of Pennsylvania Press, 1987).

Notes

1. Christopher Bigsby (ed.), *Arthur Miller and Company*, p. 10.
2. Terry Otten, *Temptation of Innocence*, p. 179.
3. Michael Billington, 'Stage: *Broken Glass*', *Guardian Online*, 18 September 2011.
4. Robert Brustein, *Reimagining American Theatre*, p. 24.
5. *The Archbishop's Ceiling*'s New York production was cancelled after a disastrous try-out in Washington DC, and Richard Coe declared this to be 'good news both for New York

and Miller', p. B7. Terry Teachout called *Finishing the Picture* 'quite horrible', p. W1, and Bruce Weber's response to *Resurrection Blues* was a 'disappointingly unpersuasive work', E1. Be it the gentler dismissal of *The Ride Down Mt. Morgan* by Richard Christiansen as 'riddled with problems . . . an artistically unresolved play in a profoundly unsettled production', p. 24, or Douglas Watt's reference to *The American Clock* as 'bloodless', p. 345, it is clear that Miller's later work struggled to please the critics. Irving Wardle marks *After the Fall* as the turning point in the American public's attitude towards Miller: 'Almost overnight, the image of a heroic public spokesman was replaced by that of a confused private man: and thereafter Miller was punished in the only way America knows how to punish a fallen idol. *Death of a Salesman* and *The Crucible* remained great national classics, but in the work he has written since the sixties he was treated as a bankrupt trying to pick up the pieces', p. 36.

6. Christopher Bigsby (ed.), *Arthur Miller and Company*, pp. 144–6.

7. Matthew C. Roudané (ed.), *Conversations with Arthur Miller*, p. 343.

8. Christopher Bigsby (ed.), *Arthur Miller and Company*, p. 179.

9. Alan Wilde, *Middle Grounds*, p. 6.

10. Christopher Bigsby, *Modern American Drama 1945–1990*, p. 117.

11. Brenda Murphy, 'Arthur Miller: Revisioning Realism', pp. 189–91.

13 MARSHA NORMAN

Annalisa Brugnoli

Getting Out; Third and Oak: The Laundromat and The Pool Hall; 'night, Mother; Loving Daniel Boone

Introduction

Marsha Norman is a playwright, novelist, librettist and screenwriter. She is a Pulitzer Prize winner, and, at the same time, a rebel against a profession that makes her 'feel very used by the theater, discarded by the theater'.[1] Norman is also an artist passionate about the drama of ordinary people, 'people you would never see',[2] who then grows tired of domestic situations and doesn't 'want to see kitchens onstage anymore'.[3] Again, she is a writer obsessed by mother-daughter relationships, until she becomes herself a mother, which 'makes it a lot more complicated to write about'.[4] In short, Marsha Norman appears as a well-rounded portrayal of complexity: the complexity of being a woman and artist at the present time. Her work reflects her developing vision of the world as a place 'of guesses and instincts, and coincidence and accidents' where life is 'a constantly unfolding mystery'.[5]

Marsha Norman was born in Louisville, Kentucky, in 1947, the first of four children. Her parents were Methodist fundamentalists who kept her away from radio and television and did not let her socialize. In reaction, she invented her first character, an imaginary friend named Bettering. Her parents hoped she 'would work for the airlines for a few years and then marry a doctor'.[6] But Norman had different plans. A gifted writer and piano player, she won first prize in a local literary contest with an essay entitled 'Why Do Good Men Suffer' and considered studying composition at Juilliard. She then majored in philosophy at Agnes Scott College in Decatur, Georgia. Back in Kentucky, she undertook teaching disturbed children at the Kentucky State Central

Hospital. This experience, her isolated childhood and the creation of an imaginary friend, provided the main sources of inspiration of her debut play *Getting Out* (1977). Norman said she never at first seriously considered writing as a career.[7] The success of *Getting Out* changed her mind. With prizes and acknowledgements still pouring down on her first work, Norman quickly wrote the twin one-act plays *Third and Oak: The Laundromat* and *The Pool Hall* (1978), which were also well received. Yet her subsequent play, *Circus Valentine* (1979), drew negative reviews. Norman describes its premiere as 'a night of humiliation and failure so complete as to almost destroy [her] ability to remain in the theater'.[8] Ironically, the play is about a crumbling family circus 'learning how to fall'. On the one hand, its fiasco aroused the playwright's enduring anger at the theatrical world and at its temperamental critics; on the other hand, it also triggered a reaction out of which came her best-known work, *'night, Mother* (1982). Hailed as Norman's masterpiece, *'night, Mother* won the Pulitzer Prize for Drama in 1983, ran for 11 months on Broadway in 1983–84, and was successfully revived in 2004–05. In 1986 it became a film starring Sissy Spacek and Anne Bancroft. Norman's next play, *The Holdup*, devised for a workshop in 1980 and first produced in its full version in 1983, was another debacle. A tragicomic romance featuring an ageing outlaw, a former frontier beauty and two brothers coming of age in the wheat-fields of 1914 New Mexico, *The Holdup* disappointed the critics, who expected another domestic drama. Next to *The Holdup* came *Traveler in the Dark* (1984), soon labelled as Norman's 'worst play yet'.[9] Nor was *Sarah and Abram* (1988) much more successful. Described by the author as the ideal continuation of her high-school composition 'Why Do Good Men Suffer'[10] and as her personal reaction to the spiritual needs triggered by her religious background,[11] *Sarah and Abram* displays the metatheatrical taste that will also inform Norman's subsequent works, *Loving Daniel Boone* (1992) and *Trudy Blues* (1995). Marsha Norman has also worked as a librettist and lyricist in musicals. Her 1990 adaptation of *The Secret Garden* ran for 709 performances and won a Tony Award in 1991. By contrast, *The Red Shoes*, for which she wrote the libretto and co-authored the lyrics, was 'a disaster of unheralded proportions',[12] closing after only five performances. She was then the librettist of the musical version of

The Color Purple. The musical was first produced on Broadway in 2005 and has been touring the United States and Europe ever since. Marsha Norman also authored the novel *The Fortune Teller* (1988), and worked as a screenwriter in films and television series.

The Plays

Getting Out (1977)

Getting Out is about the rebirth of Arlene, a 'thin, drawn woman in her late twenties' (p. 3),[13] who has just been released from prison after serving eight years for murder. In the play the hardships Arlene has to face in order to overcome her nightmarish past and to reinvent herself in her new life take the form of a series of obstacles – external and internal alike – that keep coming between Arlene and her regained freedom. These include Bennie, the prison guard whose attitude turns from friendly to sexually abusive; Arlene's undemonstrative and manipulative mother; and Carl, her former lover and pimp. But Arlene's deadliest enemy is clearly herself. In *Getting Out*, Arlene's callous, cynical and destructive *persona* becomes itself a character, named Arlie. Engendered by the trauma of Arlene's violent and ruthless life before and during her confinement, Arlie is visually portrayed onstage as a younger double of Arlene whom no one else can see. According to Norman's stage directions,

> Arlie, in a sense, is Arlene's memory of herself, called up by fears, needs, and even simple word cues. The memory haunts, attacks and warns. But mainly, the memory will not go away (p. 3).

Arlie acts in the play as a secret saboteur, at least until Arlene meets her new neighbour, Ruby, who approaches her without physical, sexual or psychological violence.

The plot of *Getting Out* originates in Norman's own experience as a teacher in the psychiatric ward of Kentucky Central Hospital. Norman wrote she got the core idea of the play from a particularly troublesome patient, who seemed able to escape whenever she wanted. 'What I wanted to write about, was what would happen if a girl like this was ever really locked up, locked up someplace she could not get out of' (p. 2) In *Getting Out*, Arlene cannot get out of jail ahead of time; still, on the metaphorical level, the place Arlene cannot really get out of is the inner prison of her past life and its visible incarnation in the play, her former self. Conceived as a stage device to solve the problem of the protagonist's abulia, Arlie is also an homage Norman pays to Modernist theatre, where doubles and states of mind were typically staged as actual characters.[14] Moreover, in *Getting Out*, Norman already foreshadows the meta-theatrical and meta-literary approach that will be typical of her later plays. According to Christopher Bigsby, the meta-literary quality of *Getting Out* shows at its most visible in the scene of Arlene's meeting with her mother.

> The fact remains that if she [Arlene] has to re-invent herself, become the protagonist of another drama of her own construction, she has to free herself of her author, the mother who seems effectively to have written her life for her. . . . Her mother accuses her of "playin," acting out sexual roles in prison, of "actin" worse with every passing day, when in fact she has been desperately trying to discover her true self.[15]

Getting Out is a rich and complex play that combines Modernist influences, meta-literary reflection and experimental techniques. Reminiscent of Tony Morrison's *Beloved* (1987) both in its use of the *topos* of the ghost exorcism in a contemporary setting and in privileging not logical but analogical patterns, *Getting Out* explores the theme of historical, familial and even biological determinism and the possibility to break free from it. Unlike Deedee and Alberta, the protagonists of Norman's subsequent one-act play, *The Laundromat*, Arlene will finally succeed in 'getting out' of her self-imprisonment by developing from a predetermined character into a self-determined human being.

Getting Out was first produced in 1977 by Actors Theatre of Louisville. The following year it premiered in the West Coast under the production of the Center Theater Group of Los Angeles. Its 1979 production by Lester Ostreman, Lucille Lortel and Mac Howard became an off-Broadway hit. *Getting Out* was the co-winner of Actors Theatre of Louisville's Great American Play Contest and received numerous awards and recognitions, including the Newsday Oppenheimer Award and the John Gassner Medallion.

Third and Oak: The Laundromat and The Pool Hall (1978)

Rigidly realistic and steadfastly observant of the classical unities, *Third and Oak*, Norman's set of two one-act plays, *The Laundromat* and *The Pool Hall*, addresses the question of whether someone's life can be redeemed by recounting it. 'Not that the plays answer this question', Norman remarks in the introduction, 'Plays don't answer questions, they simply preserve them, they pass them on'.[16] Patent symmetries connect the twin one-act plays that make up *Third and Oak*. In *The Laundromat* two white women who have never met before talk away the time it takes to do the laundry. In *The Pool Hall* two black men who have known each other for a lifetime talk away during a game of pool. In both plays, the younger co-protagonists are in their 20s, while the older are about 30 years their seniors, which also activates familial dynamics such as love-hate relationships and power struggles, although no character in either play is blood-related. Characters even migrate from one play to the other. Shooter, the younger co-protagonist of *The Pool Hall*, appears first as a voice on the radio and then in person in *The Laundromat*. In exchange Deedee, the younger co-protagonist of *The Laundromat*, pays him a visit in *The Pool Hall*. The two plays can be staged either separately – without these cameos – or together in a double bill. In both the unities of action, place and time are so scrupulously observed that one could suspect that *The Laundromat* and *The Pool Hall* are one-act plays just because such is the time it takes to do the wash and to play a nine-ball match. And yet, despite the obvious analogies and parallelisms that may cause *Third and Oak* to appear more like clockwork than artwork, the play is by no means cold or phony or artificial. On the contrary, its rigid structure serves the purpose of framing and, indeed, containing the compelling issue that stands at its core: Can human sympathy and reciprocal understanding heal the inner scars and open wounds everybody conceals? If, for some reason, for a moment, we were able to tell the truth about ourselves, expose the hidden secrets we jealously conceal as, day by day, we put on our masks and play out our parts, would we be saved? Doesn't the truth become itself an act of fiction in the instant we recount ourselves, and, by so doing, we dramatize ourselves, thus resuming our parts again? To further complicate things, the answer is different in each play.

In *The Laundromat*, the answer is: no, we would not be saved. In the play, two women who could not be more diametrically opposed for age, upbringing and character meet in a laundromat at the corner of Third and Oak in the middle of the night, and get into a conversation. Alberta is an educated, withdrawn, inhibited middle-aged woman. Her reserve and obvious incongruity with the time and place of the setting make her appear a somehow mysterious character. Deedee is a volcanic, chatty, simple young woman. As they wait for their laundries to get done, the two women open up with one another. Solitude, childless marriages and troubled parental relationships soon stand out as the common elements of this impromptu friendship. Meanwhile, the exchange between Alberta and Deedee increasingly mimics the forms of a mother/daughter relation.

> **Deedee** I wish Mom were more like you
> **Alberta** Stuck up?
> **Deedee** Smart, Nice to talk to. . . . Mom's just got me and
> a giant-size Cheer. And she don't say two words while I'm
> there. Ever. I don't blame her I guess (p. 78).

Yet this parental make-believe triggers not only the intimacy but also the power struggle that is inherent in families. Alberta, clearly the smarter of the two, is initially in control. But when Shooter shows up in the laundromat and makes advances to Deedee, the latter becomes dominant. As Deedee's cheerfulness grows more and more into bantering and inquisitive attitudes, the play comes to resemble a mystery game, at which Alberta observes 'You've been reading Sherlock Holmes' (p. 76). With clues adding up, the final release is near. Hurt by a remark of

Alberta's, in a twist of unsuspected insightfulness, Deedee blurts out Alberta's secret, and her own. With their mysteries unravelled, the two women stand unarmoured in front of each other, their make-up as if laundered away. All the lies and the tricks and the self-defensive strategies are gone, and Alberta and Deedee are given a chance to reach out to one another, which they do, but just for a moment. Thankful for the time they spent together, the two women walk out of their extemporary friendship and back again into their solitudes as the play comes to an end.

In *The Pool Hall* the answer to the seminal question that connects the two one-act plays is, instead: yes, maybe human sympathy and reciprocal understanding can save us.

In *The Pool Hall* two men play billiards next door to the laundromat. Shooter, the younger, brags about his talent as a pool player and a radio star. Willie, the elder, is a close friend of Shooter's father and the proprietor of the rundown pool hall they are in. Willie tries to talk Shooter out of his present lifestyle and into choices that are more loyal to his wife and of himself. As it will turn out, Willie knows the truth about the suicide of Shooter's father and namesake, who killed himself believing he had lost his talent as a pool player, and is currently trying to sell the pool hall to help George, a crippled and dying friend.

The Pool Hall is less explicit than *The Laundromat* about its central issue. Here, the two men's talk is intermingled with asides and anecdotes that at first seem inconsequential. Plus, Shooter and Willie know each other well, and share a life experience that is mostly unfamiliar to the reader. Still, in terms of content, *The Pool Hall* succeeds where *The Laundromat* had failed: here human friendship and reciprocal understanding really make the difference. However initially rebellious against what he calls 'The Gospel According to Willie' (p. 104), Shooter will eventually endorse his elder friend's morals. Significantly, this coincides with the successful fulfilment of the parental metaphor that stands as a major issue in both works. As *The Pool Hall* comes to an end, Shooter replaces his idolized father image with the fond memory of his father's friendship with Willie and George and of the way this is perpetuated by the latter. Remarkably, this is the only Norman play where male sensibility is not only compared to, but even implicitly regarded as superior to sympathy among women. As the analysis of Norman's masterpiece, *'night, Mother*, will show, female relationships, especially when blood-related, are invariably regarded as problematic and tainted by rancour and competitiveness.

Third and Oak was originally produced in 1978 by Actors Theatre of Louisville. In 1989 it was presented in New York City as part of Ensemble Studio Theatre's One-Act Marathon. In 1984 Robert Altman filmed *Third and Oak: The Laundromat*. *The Pool Hall* was filmed in 1989 by Fielder Cook and produced by Gladys Nederlander.

'night, Mother (1982)

Like *The Laundromat* and *The Pool Hall*, *'night, Mother* is a play for two. Unlike them, Thelma and Jessie Cates are mother and daughter. One only will survive. *'night, Mother* is a play about suicide.

The play opens in a living room that, according to Norman's stage directions, should avoid specific connotations. The time is the present. Clocks have to be visible onstage. Mama and Jessie appear. Mama is a plain woman in her late 50s or early 60s. Jessie is in her late 30s or early 40s. Epilepsy, which Jessie has managed to conquer only in the last year, makes her look 'pale and vaguely unsteady, physically' (p. 4).[17] Jessie is making lists and searching for her father's gun. As it will soon turn out, the gun is to kill herself. The lists will help her mother in the daily routine once she is gone. Initially incredulous, Thelma embarks in a race against the time that ticks inexorably on the clocks onstage in her attempt to talk her daughter out of suicide; the audience awaits to know if Jessie will fulfil her purpose. Explanations, recriminations, clarifications pour onstage, framing the theatrical technique of the anticipation of the outcome Norman masterfully deploys and filling what Robert Brustein has called 'an extended death scene'.[18] As Jessie explains, she is not acting out of anger. She is not showing off. She is not mad at her mother. She just feels 'tired', 'hurt', 'sad' and 'used' (p. 22). Jessie has not accomplished anything in her life ('I'm what was worth waiting for and I didn't make it' p. 50). She is divorced, and her only son is a crook. She is not in control of herself. She has no prospects. There is nothing she really likes. She makes her case in the following terms:

> **Jessie** Mama, I know you used to ride the bus. Riding the bus, and it's hot and bumpy and crowded and too noisy and more than anything else in the world you want to get off and the only reason in the world you don't get off is it's still 50 blocks from where you're going? Well, I can get off right now if I want to, because even if I ride 50 more years and get off then, it's still the same place when I step down to it. Whenever I feel like it, I can get off. As soon as I've had enough, it's my stop. I've had enough. (p. 24)

Throughout the play, Jessie's logic is incontrovertible. Her vision of suicide as a means not to kill oneself but to end the pain is so cogent as to leave Thelma dumbfounded. Thelma is the type of woman who, when her time comes, will have to be dragged 'screaming and . . . screeching into [her] grave' (p. 51). Still she has to sit in on her daughter's self-inflicted death. Jessie's suicide is compared to a performance nobody but Thelma is invited to attend (p. 15). In this, 'night, Mother stands as the culmination of Norman's sustained reflection on the power of words, hence, of fiction, to save our lives. As in *The Laundromat*, words fail again in 'night, Mother. Taking the bedroom door in the background, 'a point both of threat and promise, . . . an ordinary door that opens into absolute nothingness' (p. 6), Jessie locks herself in as a shot is heard.

Praised as a 'scrupulously realistic' and 'chastely classical'[19] playwright, Marsha Norman has accustomed her audience to works that leave no room for inconsistency or wasted emotions. And yet, just as in *Third and Oak*, most of the power of 'night, Mother lies not in the questions it answers, but rather in those it leaves open.

First and foremost, there are the ethical and philosophical issues aroused by Jessie's suicide and by its paradoxically affirmative nature. Jessie repeatedly contends that death is the only means left to her to claim back her life. Adrift as a wife and as a mother and unnaturally regressed to a state of perpetual childhood, Jessie is not in control of anything in her life but of the moment when she can stop it. As

Laurin Porter puts it, Jessie 'is making a decision, and that decision is "no"'.[20] Marsha Norman explicitly emphasizes the affirmative nature of Jessie's act, too. In her words, 'night, Mother is 'a play of nearly total triumph' where 'Jessie is able to get what she feels she needs'.[21] The conundrum of Jessie's reclaiming her life through death is the conundrum of suicide itself.

Disturbingly fascinating, 'night, Mother has not ceased to compel audiences and scholars, many of whom have kept searching for hidden motives that go beyond what Jessie so cogently explains. Christopher Bigsby and Louis Greif have argued that absence – and, in specific, the missing male figures in Jessie's life – could be as significant as presence in understanding Jessie's decision. Men are missing both in the play and in Jessie's and Thelma's lives. Indeed, men have abandoned them. Unconcerned or perhaps unable to cope with his daughter's disease, Jessie's father 'could've had that Gone Fishing sign around his neck in that chair' (p. 32); Jessie's former husband, Cecil, has left her for another woman; as to Ricky, her son, he is a thief in his own house. But Jessie has no bad feelings. On the contrary, according to Bigsby, she summons the memory of her father time and again 'as if he were indeed the gravitational pull of her universe and this is a love story after all'.[22] It is not coincidental that Jessie carries out her suicide using her father's gun, in what appears to be a ritual death. According to Greif, the escapism Jessie has inherited from a father she idolizes lies behind her plan to reunite with him through suicide.[23]

There is then Jessie's illness, and the issue of control that ensues. For Jessie, epilepsy is a matter of losing control. In seizures, Jessie is not in control of herself. The fear of them prevents her from leading a normal life. Jessie's need for control, moreover, goes beyond epilepsy. Throughout the play, she keeps making lists. She even gives herself a deadline for shooting herself. Thelma tries to gain more time in trivia, at which Jessie replies, 'I can't. It's too late' (p. 57). Jessie is evidently overcontrolled in her emotions and never loses her temper, which reflects on her logical skills and on the chilling attitude she displays on the verge of her own death.

But it is the mother-daughter relationship between Jessie and Thelma that stands as the central mystery of 'night, Mother. In order to achieve the self-fulfilment she craves, Jessie has to get away with her symbiotic relationship with Mama. Critics have argued that the question of orality and of food preparation and intake stands as a central metaphor of this. Throughout the play, Jessie keeps rejecting the junk food Thelma offers. As Linda Ginter Brown noticed, she dislikes milk in particular.[24] Accordingly, *'night, Mother* can be seen as the narrative of Jessie's coming of age by cutting the bonds with perpetual childhood and the familial place. *'night, Mother* is, after all, a play about leaving. The process is not only painful but also tainted with revenge. Throughout the play, Jessie keeps denying that Thelma is to blame for her decision until, towards the end, she slightly but significantly changes her version.

> **Jessie** (*Exasperated at having to say this again.*) It doesn't have anything to do with you!
>
> **Mama** Everything you do has to do with me, Jessie. . . .
>
> **Jessie** Then what if it does! What if it has everything to do with you! What if you are all I have and you're not enough? What if I could take all the rest of it if only I didn't have you here? What if the only way I can get away from you for good is to kill myself? What if it is? I can *still* do it! (p. 47)

Ironically, what can be regarded as the most ferocious revenge of a daughter upon her mother results in a unique moment of pure understanding. Jessie and Mama exchange roles as actors on a stage (who is mothering whom? Who will prevail? Who is in control?), but their power struggle gives way to moments of deep affection.

'night, Mother is as compelling in form as it is in content. The action begins with the clocks onstage set at 8:15, as by Norman's stage direction. But 8:15 is also the average starting time of evening performances. With the time in the play and the time of the audience coinciding, reality and fiction overlap, as the play's unbending realism activates a *trompe l'œil* that overcomes the boundaries between the action unfolding onstage and the life of the audience unfolding in the stalls. Time and rhythm are founding elements in Norman's art, ostensibly on account of her

musical background. In a speech she delivered in 1987, Norman has argued:

> If you are going to write for the theatre, you must come to terms with time. Novels are about place. Movies are about action. The theatre is about time. Two hours, give or take ten minutes, is how long you have to play. Two hours of audience time, two hours of characters time.[25]

'night Mother was originally produced by the American Repertory Theatre in Cambridge, Massachusetts, in 1983. The same year it opened on Broadway at the John Golden Theatre under the direction of Tom Moore. It won the Pulitzer Prize for Drama, the Dramatists Guild's Hull-Warriner Award and the Susan Smith Blackburn Prize.

Loving Daniel Boone (1992)

Loving Daniel Boone celebrates the triumph of Norman's bent for *mise en abîme* techniques and meta-fictional reflection. Here the realism of the early plays gives way to daring experimentation, as a new playful mood replaces the taut and incisive tones of before. All these elements recur as a common feature of what Linda Ginter Brown calls the 'mythic approach'[26] that is typical of Norman's later endeavours: *The Holdup*, *Sarah and Abraham* and *Loving Daniel Boone*.

The protagonist of *Loving Daniel Boone* is Flo, a museum cleaning woman who has casually found a passage that allows her to travel back in time to 1778 Kentucky, where Daniel Boone is getting ready for his final battle against the Shawnees. Torn between her shallow everyday reality and the exciting perspective of a romance with Daniel Boone, Flo will nevertheless choose the former when Hilly, her new colleague and suitor, goes all the way to 1778 Kentucky to bring her back. In *Loving Daniel Boone* Norman explores a number of new themes. Like Flo, the playwright is admittedly '[n]ot interested in domestic dramas' and in 'see[ing] kitchens onstage any more'.[27] In *Loving Daniel Boone* Norman barters realism for whim, seriousness for comic relief. This also inhibits the identification process. Here the gap between reality and fiction comes to be replaced by the tension between two dimensions, the past and the present, that are both real and fictitious. In both, Flo is a protagonist and a character at the same time, which is what, in our respective realities, we all are. In *Loving Daniel Boone*, the audience does not identify with the characters emotionally, but ontologically.

Yet the potential of the play is spoilt by inner flaws, mainly connected to character and plot development. For instance, all male characters in *Loving Daniel* are in love with Flo, the only exceptions being Mr Wilson, the homosexual curator of the museum, and the Indian chief Blackfish, who doesn't know her. Two-dimensional as they are, all the figures in the play immediately recognize Flo's outstanding depth somehow. Without doing anything extraordinary, Flo is constantly perceived as extraordinary. *Loving Daniel Boone* looks more like a feminist empowerment fantasy than like a humorous comedy at times.

Commissioned for the 200th anniversary of the Kentucky, *Loving Daniel Boone* premiered at the Humana Festival of Actors Theatre of Louisville in 1992. Despite the initially favourable reviews, it did not enjoy many productions afterwards.

Summary

Marsha Norman's career path shifts from the unbending realism of the early works to the mythic turn that is typical of her plays after *'night, Mother.*

In Norman's early plays, human relations are portrayed in terms of conflict *versus* understanding: love/hate relationships, familial dynamics, power struggles and the issue of control of both oneself and others stand out as the playwright's chief concerns. They all converge in what Norman has called the need to 'redefine survival' as 'the ability to carry on your life in such a way that it fulfils and satisfies you. With this definition of survival, Mother looms large'. According to Norman, redefining survival means shifting values from the patriarchal concept of fulfilment as the achievement of material success to the idea of fulfilment as the realization of personal hopes and needs, 'all things with which Mother is connected'.[28] In this sense, all Norman's early characters are survivors, including Jessie in *'night, Mother*. Correspondingly, in her plays Norman is uncompromisingly hard on the mothers that fail to equip their children for this idea of redefined survival.

At this stage Norman privileges a realistic approach and complies with the classical unities. The result she achieves through this symmetric treatment of form and content is a fictional dimension that parallels and, indeed, overtakes the real. She recounts how she became aware of the potential of the narrator to recreate a make-believe reality through formal constraint. While recording a production of *Third and Oak*, she realized that the climax of each one-act came right when she had switched the recorder off to turn the tape over.

> There it was, the big scene, right at forty-five minutes. I had written it there out of instinct or ignorance, or both, but it became, from that time on, a hard and fast rule for me. One of the two or three I never break.[29]

The meta-theatrical reflection that can be observed in the early works becomes overpowering in the late plays. Here, Norman dismisses her former realistic approach to the advantage of experimental forms that privilege *mise en abîme* and *trompe l'œil* techniques. Norman never disavowed her unsuccessful plays. On the contrary, she insists that the faults of her later plays stem from the same root from which her best-known works originate. For instance, she writes that through 'another critical disaster, *The Holdup*', she 'learned how to contain the action of a play, to cause the piece to erupt and resolve without bringing in a character from the outside. That technique was at the heart of *'night, Mother*, too'.[30]

Norman's plays have been studied from feminist (Brown, Dolan, Keyssar, Spencer, Smith, Hart), psychoanalytic (Kane, Reuning, Schroeder) and comparative (Demastes, Greiff, Kachur, McDonnel, Porter) standpoints. Ironically, what Matthew Roudané calls Norman's 'less than fulsome embrace of the feminist movement'[31] prompted an ambivalent reaction from feminist scholarship, part of which saw in Norman's plays a surrender to the male-dominated values of the patriarchal society.

Hailed by Robert Brustein in 1983 as an emerging 'universal playwright' in the tradition of Anton Chekhov and Eugene O'Neill,[32] Marsha Norman has progressively stepped away from the limelight.

In the speech she delivered at a luncheon honouring Pulitzer Prize winners in 1987, Norman lamented the condition of American dramatists, whom she described as 'under siege' by financial hardships, on the one hand, and by the psychological pressure of critics, on the other hand. Here Norman vindicates the right to write unsuccessful plays, because, she says, 'writers take a lifetime to develop'.

> Now if you think we will always write plays just because we like to do it, you are wrong. When it stops being merely impossible, and becomes absolutely insane, we will quit. We don't want to quit, and we won't give a press conference saying we've quit. No, when the day comes, we just won't have any more ideas . . . What we need, in order to keep writing, is to live in a world, in a theatrical community where it is still possible to believe these things.[33]

Primary Sources[34]

Works by Marsha Norman

'night, Mother (New York: Dramatist Play Service, 1983).
Four Plays (New York: Theatre Communications Group, 1988a).
The Fortune Teller (New York: Bantam: 1988b).
Collected Works. Vol. 1. (Lyme: Smith and Kraus, 1998).

Interviews

Beard, Sherilyn, 'An Interview with Marsha Norman', Southern California Anthology 3 (1985), 11–17.
Betsko, Kathleen and Koenig, Rachel, Interviews with Contemporary Women Playwrights (New York: Beech Tree Books, 1987).
Brustein, Robert, 'Conversations with. . . . Marsha Norman', Dramatists Guild Quarterly 21 (September 1984), 9–21.

Guernsey, Otis, 'Five Dramatists Discuss the Value of Criticism', *Dramatists Guild Quarterly* 21 (March 1984), 11–25.

Norman, Marsha, 'Articles of Faith: A Conversation with Lillian Hellman', *American Theatre* 1 (May 1984), 10–15.

Secondary Sources

Bigsby, Christopher, *A Critical Introduction to Twentieth Century American Drama: Beyond Broadway*. Vol. 3 (Cambridge: Cambridge UP, 1985), pp. 420–40.

—, *Contemporary American Playwrights* (Cambridge: Cambridge UP, 1999), pp. 210–51.

Browder, Sally, '"I Thought You Were Mine": Marsha Norman's 'night, Mother'. In Mickey Pearlmann (ed.), *Mother Puzzles: Daughter and Mothers in Contemporary American Literature* (New York: Greenwood Press, 1989), pp. 109–19.

Brown, Janet, *Taking Center Stage: Feminism in Contemporary U.S. Drama* (Metuchen: Scarecrow, 1991), pp. 60–70.

Brown, Janet and Stevenson, Catherine Barnes, 'Fearlessly "Looking under the Bed": Marsha Norman's Feminist Aesthetic in *Getting Out* and *'night, Mother'*. In Karen Laughlin and Catherine Schuler (eds), *Theatre and Feminist Aesthetics* (Madison: Fairleigh Dickinson UP, 1995), pp. 182–99.

Brown, Linda Ginter (ed.), *Marsha Norman: A Casebook* (New York/London: Garland, 1996).

Burkman, Katherine, 'The Demeter Myth and Doubling in Marsha Norman's *'night Mother'*. In June Schlueter (ed.), *Modern Drama: The Female Canon* (Rutherford: Farleigh Dickinson UP, 1990), pp. 254–63.

Craig, Carolyn Casey, *Women Pulitzer Playwright* (Jefferson: McFarland, 2004), pp. 166–83.

Demastes, William W., *Beyond Naturalism: A New Realism in American Theatre* (New York: Greenwood Press, 1988), pp. 125–54.

Dolan, Jill, *The Feminist Spectator as Critic* (Ann Arbor: UMI, 1988), pp. 19–40.

Greiff, Louis K., 'Fathers, Daughters and Spiritual Sisters: Marsha Norman's *'night, Mother* and Tennessee Williams's *The Glass Menagerie'*, *Text and Performance Quarterly* 9 (1989), 224–8.

Kachur, Barbara, 'Women Playwrights on Broadway: Henley, Hove, Norman and Wasserstein'. In Bruce King (ed.), *Contemporary American Theater* (London: Macmillan, 1991), pp. 15–39.

Kane, Leslie, 'The Way Out, The Way In: Paths to Self in the Plays of Marsha Norman'. In Enoch Brater (ed.), *Feminine Focus: The New Women Playwrights* (New York: Oxford UP, 1989), pp. 255–74.

Kauffmann, Stanley, 'More Trick than Tragedy', *Saturday Review* 9, 10 (September 1983), 47–8.

Keyssar, Helene, *Feminist Theatre: An Introduction to Plays of Contemporary British and American Women* (New York: St. Martin's, 1984), pp. 148–66.

Kerr, Walter, 'The Joy of the Unexpected', *The New York Times* (10 April 1983), pp. 15–19.

Kilgore, Emile S. (ed.), *Landmarks of Contemporary Women's Drama* (London: Methuen, 1992).

Krasner, David (ed.), *A Companion to Twentieth Century American Drama* (Malden: Blackwell, 2005), pp. 393–7.

McDonald, Ronan and Rohrer-Paige, Linda, *Southern Women Playwrights* (Tuscaloosa and London: The University of Alabama Press, 2002), pp. 103–23.

McDonnel, Lisa J., 'Diverse Similitudes: Beth Henley and Marsha Norman', *Southern Quarterly* 3 (1987), 95–104.

Morrison, Tony, *Beloved* (New York: Vintage, 1997).

Morrow, Laura, 'Orality and Identity in *'night, Mother* and *Crimes of the Heart'*, *Studies in American Drama, 1945-Present* 3 (1988), 23–39.

Murray, Timothy, 'Patriarchal Panopticism, or the Seduction of a Bad Joke: *Getting Out* in Theory', *Theatre Journal* 35 (1983), 376–88.

Patrarka, Vivian M., 'Staging Memory: Contemporary Plays by Women', *Michigan Quarterly Review* 26 (1987), 285–92.

Porter, Laurin, 'Women Re-Conceived: Changing Perceptions of Women in Contemporary American Drama', *Conference of College Teachers of English Studies* 54 (1989), 53–9.

Prunty, Wyatt (ed.), *Sewanee Writers on Writing* (Baton Rouge: Louisiana UP, 2000), pp. 138–44.

Reuning, Sara, 'Depression: The Undiagnosed Disability in Marsha Norman's 'Night, Mother'. In Thomas Fahi and Kimball King (eds), *Peering Behind the Curtain: Disability, Illness, and the Extraordinary Body* (London: Routledge, 2002), pp. 55–67.

Roudané, Matthew C., 'Marsha Norman'. In Christopher Bigsby and Don B. Wilmeth (eds), *The Cambridge History of American Theatre:Post World War II to the 1990s*, Vol. 3 (Cambridge: Cambridge UP, 2000), pp. 373–8.

Schoreder, Patricia R., 'Locked Behind the Proscenium: Feminist Strategies in *Getting Out* and *My Sister in the House'*, *Modern Drama* 32 (1989), 104–14.

Simon, John, 'Theater Chronicle: Kopit, Norman and Shepard'. *Hudson Review* 32 (1989), 77–8.

Smith, Raynette Halvordsen, *''night, Mother* and *True West*: Mirror Images of Violence and Gender'. In James Redmond (ed.), *Violence in Drama: Themes in Drama* (Cambridge: Cambridge UP, 1989), pp. 147–65.

Spencer, Jenny S., 'Norman's *'night, Mother*: Psychodrama and the Female Identity', *Modern Drama* 30 (1987), 364–75.

—, 'Marsha Norman's She-Tragedies'. In Linda Hart (ed.), *Making a Spectacle: Feminist Essays on Contemporary Women's Theatre* (Ann Arbor: Michigan UP, 1989), pp. 147–65.

Wattenberg, Richard, 'Feminizing the Frontier Myth: Marsha Norman's *The Holdup'*. *Modern Drama* no. 33 (1990), 507–17.

Wertheim, Albert, 'Eugene O'Neill's *Days Without End* and the Tradition of the Split Character in Modern American and British Drama'. *The Eugene O'Neill's Newsletter* 6 (Winter 1982), 5–9.

Notes

1. Linda Ginter Brown, 'Update with Marsha Norman'. In Linda Ginter-Brown (ed.), *Marsha Norman: A Casebook*, p. 169.
2. Ibid., p. 176.
3. Ibid., p. 171.
4. Ibid., p. 194.
5. Ibid., p. 187.
6. Marsha Norman, 'Articles of Faith: A Conversation with Lillian Hellman', p. 11.
7. Ibid., p. 11.
8. Marsha Norman, *Collected Works*, p. 110.
9. Ibid., p. 222.
10. Ibid., p. 274.
11. Linda Ginter Brown, 'Update with Marsha Norman', In Linda Ginter-Brown (ed.), op. cit., p. 174.
12. Ibid., p. 197.
13. All the quotations from Norman's works except *'night Mother* are from *Collected Works. Vol. 1* (Lyme: Smith and Kraus, 1998).
14. For further reference, see Albert Wertheim's essay 'Eugene O'Neill's *Days Without End* and the Tradition of the Split Character in Modern American and British Drama', which compares Norman's *Getting out* to O'Neill's *Days Without End*.
15. Christopher Bigsby, *Contemporary American Playwrights*, p. 216.
16. Marsha Norman, *Collected Works*, p. 60.
17. All the quotations from *'night Mother* are from Marsha Norman, *'night Mother* (New York: Dramatist Play Service, 1983).
18. Robert Brustein, 'Don't Read This Review!' repr. in Linda Ginter-Brown (ed.), op. cit., p. 160.
19. Robert Brustein, op. cit., p. 159.
20. Laurin Porter, 'Women Re-Conceived: Changing Perceptions of Women in Contemporary American Drama', p. 56.
21. Kathleen Betsko and Rachel Koenig (eds), *Interviews with Contemporary Playwrights*, p. 339.
22. Christopher Bigsby, op. cit., p. 236.
23. Louis Greiff, 'Fathers, Daughters, and Spiritual Sisters: Marsha Norman's *'night, Mother* and Tennessee William's *The Glass Managerie*'.
24. Linda Ginter Brown, 'A Place at the Table. Hunger as Metaphor in Lillian Hellmann's *Days to Come* and Marsha Norman's *'night, Mother*'. In Linda Ginter-Brown (ed.), op. cit., p. 78.
25. Marsha Norman, 'Honor is not Enough', Transcr. in Marsha Norman, *Collected Works*, p. 400.
26. Linda Ginter Brown, 'Update with Marsha Norman', in Linda Ginter-Brown (ed.), op. cit., p.171.

27. Ibid., p. 171.
28. Kathleen Betsko and Rachel Koenig (ed.), op. cit, p. 339.
29. Marsha Norman, 'Time and Learning How to Fall', Transcr. in *Marsha Norman, Collected Works*, p. 402.
30. Ibid., p. 408.
31. Matthew Roudané, 'Marsha Norman', p. 378.
32. Robert Brustein, op. cit., p. 163.
33. Marsha Norman, 'Honor is not Enough', Transcr. in Marsha Norman, *Collected Works*, pp. 410–2.
34. I am indebted in this bibliography to Robert Conklin, who collected and commented on a comprehensive bibliography of Marsha Norman's works in Linda Ginter Brown, op. cit., pp. 221–35.

14 SUZAN-LORI PARKS

Ilka Saal

Imperceptible Mutabilities in the Third Kingdom; In the Blood;
Fucking A; Topdog/Underdog; The America Play

Introduction

Parks was born on 10 May 1963 in Fort Knox, Kentucky.[1] Due to her
father's career as an army colonel, the family moved frequently, throughout
the United States and abroad, including a four-year stay in Germany.
According to Parks, 'moving around had an influence on my writing',[2]
providing her, among other things, with a critical perspective of the
function of language, along with a keen sense of the meaning of longing
'for home, for the missing, for the distant and the dead'.[3] Another strong
influence was exerted by Parks's vivid imagination, which she expressed
throughout her childhood by making up songs, drafting novels and
editing a family newspaper.[4] Yet, despite such early poetic aspirations, at
Mount Holyoke College in South Hadley, Massachusetts, Parks at first
majored in chemistry – allegedly having been discouraged from writing
by a high school English teacher because of poor spelling skills. The
discovery of Virginia Woolf's *To the Lighthouse*, however, soon pulled
her 'from the science lab into the literature lab'.[5] A creative writing class
with James Baldwin at the neighbouring Hampshire College brought
the turning point. Reading out a piece of her fiction to the class, Parks
started to enact her characters, prompting Baldwin to encourage her to
pursue playwriting.[6] For her senior project in English, Parks wrote her
very first play *The Sinner's Place* (1984). After graduating from college
in 1985, she spent a brief stint studying acting at the Drama Studio in
London but soon returned to the United States to pursue a career in
playwriting. In 1987 her play *Betting on the Dust Commander* opened
at The Gas Station, a makeshift bar in a garage in the East Village; only

two years later *Imperceptible Mutabilities of the Third Kingdom* opened in Brooklyn to nationwide acclaim, prompting Mel Gussow of the *New York Times* to hail her as 'the year's most promising new playwright'.[7] The production won Parks the 1990 Obie Award for Best New American Play. More plays and awards followed in quick succession: *Death of the Last Black Man in the Whole Entire World* (1990), *Devotees in the Garden of Love* (1992), *The America Play* (1994), and *Venus* (1996) – the latter garnering Parks a second Obie Award for Playwriting. In 2000, she received a Guggenheim Fellowship in Playwriting and in 2001 the MacArthur Foundation 'Genius' Grant. 2002 brought her the Pulitzer Prize for Drama for *Topdog/Underdog* and 2008 the NAACP Theatre Award for her musical play *Ray Charles Live! A New Musical*. Recent dramatic works include the collection *365 Days/365 Plays* (produced simultaneously in over 700 theatres nationwide from 13 November 2006 to 12 November 2007), the epic cycle *Father Comes Home from the Wars* (of which parts 1, 8 and 9 premiered in 2009) and *The Book of Grace* (2010).

The Plays

Imperceptible Mutabilities in the Third Kingdom (1989)

Imperceptible Mutabilities opened on 14 September 1989 under the direction of Liz Diamond at BACA Downtown in Brooklyn, New York. With its episodic character, layered and non-linear plot, abstract figures and inventive deployment of language, leaving the text open to multiple interpretation, it poses one of the most challenging plays of Parks's repertoire. Together with the subsequent *Death of the Last Black Man*, it also establishes key themes of her overall dramaturgy: the experience of displacement, dismemberment and misrecognition, along with the desire for re-membering, the restaging and rewriting of one's identity in the performative use of language.

Imperceptible Mutabilities consists of five parts, three mini-plays interlinked by the repeated choral section 'Third Kingdom'. In the first part 'Snails', we encounter the roommates Mona, Chona and Verona, whose home is infested by a giant cockroach, placed there by a so-called 'Naturalist' as a sort of 'fly on the wall' (p. 27) to observe and study the three African American women as specimen of a *mundus primitivus* (p. 29). At the same time, the women's sense of alterity is made apparent in Mona's ongoing struggle with standard American English, which has been the reason for her expulsion from school. A Dr Lutzky, a professional exterminator (the Naturalist in disguise), called up for help, complicates the situation by misaddressing the women as Charlene and Molly and turning his squirt gun against them rather than the insect. Insisting on being called 'Wipe-em-Out' (p. 32), he echoes not only the Naturalist's sardonic demand that 'them roaches' 'somehow be – taken care of for there are too many of them' (p. 29) but also the actions of the host of Verona's favourite TV show 'Wild Kingdom' who, despite his claims of love and respect 'for all the wild things' (p. 37), ends up shooting them.

Part 2, 'Third Kingdom', functions similar to a choral poem, interweaving, in the tradition of Greek tragedy, the voices of five figures called Kin-Seer, Us-Seer, Shark-Seer, Soul-Seer and Over-Seer into a sort of commentary and lament on the preceding action. The figures give voice to a general sense of displacement and alienation brought about by their violent abduction from their home continent and the endurance of the middle passage. The 'Third Kingdom' refers here not only to the space in-between a world 'cleaved inthu 2' (p. 37) but also to the fragmentation of the self under the trauma of displacement. Shark-Seer's and Kin-Seer's frantic attempts to retrieve a holistic notion of self repeatedly culminate in a chorus of strange throat sounds – 'Gaw gaw gaw gaw-eeh uh. Gaw gaw gaw gaw-eeh uh' (p. 57) – evocative, as Geis suggests, both of 'African dialect (the world on one side of the cliff)' and of 'being choked or strangled or lynched and thus silenced, suffocated (the world on the other side of the cliff)' (p. 50). This is the language of the third kingdom simultaneously connecting them to, but also liberating them from, hegemonic language.

Part 3, 'Open House', continues these reflections on the violent and traumatic effects of misrecognition, displacement and alienation in the figure of Miss Aretha Saxon, a former slave whose work with the white Saxon family has been discontinued. 'The book says you expire. No option to renew', a Miss Faith informs her (p. 45). According to 'the book', Aretha is also scheduled for the extraction of all her teeth, so that they can be 'chronicled' for the record (p. 46). When Miss Faith insists that its 'contents are facts' (p. 47), Aretha begins to suspect that they 'got different books' (p. 51). Where Aretha believes to be able to accommodate three guests in her small flat, Miss Faith insists on squeezing in 600, citing the precedence of the slave ship *Brookes* as historic evidence. At the same time, however, her book contains no record of the nine million Africans abducted by force from their homeland, prompting Aretha to protest, 'Buchenwald! Buchenwald!' (p. 52). With this she not only interlinks the African American and the Jewish holocaust but also draws an implicit link between the extraction of her teeth and the extermination of a people. As Master Charles Saxon warns her, 'You let them take out the teeth you're giving up the last of the verifying evidence. . . . We won't be able to tell you apart from the others. We won't even know your name. . . . People will twist around the facts to suit the truth' (p. 53). The discrepancy between an official 'historical' record and the lived experience of its subjects is illustrated most poignantly in a slide show at the start of Part 3. The pictures of ever-wider smiling Saxon children have little to do with the reality of Saxon family life or with Aretha's relationship to them. At the end, however, despite her experience of mistreatment and misrecognition by the Saxons and Miss Faith, Aretha insists on establishing her own historical record/memory/identity: 'Don't care what you say you done, Charles. We're making us uh histrionical amendment here, K? Give us uh smile. Uh big smile for the book' (p. 54).

Following a reprise of the choral part 'Third Kingdom', *Imperceptible Mutabilities* concludes with Part 4, 'Greeks (Or the Slugs)'. Here Parks continues to explore the themes of recording, dismembering and remembering in the context of a 1950s military family, whose father is away on duty on a far-off island. While Mrs Smith is trying to uphold the image of the picture-perfect American family and while the children are fidgeting over whether or not the household ledger recording father's letters is correct, Sergeant Smith feels isolated from his family, forever awaiting the 'Distinction' that might return him home. When it, at long last, arrives, it does so ironically not thanks to some heroic deed but as compensation for an accident during which Smith loses both legs. Upon his return home, he encounters a family that barely recognizes him and a wife that has gone blind, presumably from trying too hard to see her dream of assimilation come true. 'Greeks' stands out for its repetition and lyrical integration of various previously mentioned motifs: the sense of being stranded in the Third Kingdom ('A big rock in the middle of the ocean', p. 61), the struggle with a hegemonic language ('Say "why is that," Muffy, not "how come", p. 62), the anxiety of misrecognition ('We needs documentation. Proof. . . . There's lots of Smiths', pp. 69–70), the unreliability of language ('Certain ways that are plain to us could, for Sergeant Smith, spell the ways of betrayal', p. 64), the threat of dismemberment ('The mine blew his legs off', p. 70) as well as the possibility for remembering ('A mine is a thing that remembers', p. 70). Most importantly, however, this concluding part gathers up these various repetitions into a fresh revision, once more bringing into focus how 'meanings mutate of necessity' in the third kingdom'.[8]

For Parks, *Imperceptible Mutabilities* presents an allegorical rendition of 'African-American history in the shadow of the photographic image'.[9] With this she points out the discrepancy between a fixed, preconceived image and actual people trying to relate to it. Projected and fixed against an overwhelming white background, Parks's black figures struggle to define themselves, constantly aware of its effect on their own self-perception. Yet, in the end, these black figures are able to create their own 'histrionical amendment', such as Aretha shooting her own '[s]craps uh graphy for my book' (p. 54) or Smith resignifying the story of his dismissal as a revised Icarus myth. Insisting on having been wounded while catching a man falling from the sky, he not only accomplishes his hoped-for noble deed but also appropriates the high-soaring dreams and ambitions of white mythology. His final words, 'no, we ain't even turtles. Huh. We'se slugs. Slugs. Slugs' (p. 71), should therefore be read as hopeful: The inhabitants of the third kingdom might lack the protective shields of turtles, they might not even be able to retreat into their (home) shells like snails, but as slugs they have developed other defence mechanisms. Mutable by necessity, they are gradually and (im)perceptibly refiguring themselves through language.

The Red Letter Plays: In the Blood (1999)
and Fucking A (2000)

The year 1999 saw the production of two new Parks plays, which – though usually produced separately – are commonly referred to as *The Red Letter Plays* for their joint riffing on Nathaniel Hawthorne's *Scarlet Letter*. According to Parks, *In the Blood* came to her while sitting down to write *Fucking A* and realizing that her female protagonist Hester might require another play.[10] The *Red Letter Plays* thus illustrate how Parks submits not only the historical and literary canon to a radical process of repetition and revision – 'Rep & Rev', as Parks calls it[11]– but her own work as well, refiguring characters and tropes by inserting them into new situations and constellations. *In the Blood* opened at the Papp Public Theatre in New York on 2 November 1999 under the direction of David Esbjornson; *Fucking A* followed on 24 February 2000, in a production directed by Parks herself at the Diverse Works Art Space in Houston, Texas.

With the *Red Letter Plays* we begin to notice a decisive shift in Parks's deployment of form – a switch to a more classic, Aristotelian conception of drama. The shift away from a highly experimental to a more conventional dramaturgy does not, however, mean that Parks has forfeited her initial concern with re-membering dis(re)membered black bodies, nor that theatre has now become a purely mimetic medium for her. On the contrary, with the *Red Letter Plays* as well as the subsequent *Topdog/Underdog* and *365 Days/365 Plays*, she continues her explorations of African American identities, histories, and experience – in particular, with regard to the 'intersection of the historical and the now'.[12]

Occupying centre stage in the *Red Letter Plays* is the marginalized and abused black woman. With Hester La Negrita and Hester Smith, Parks creates two contemporary descendants to Hawthorne's Hester Prynne – two African-American women shunned by a hypocritical society on the basis of their race, class, education and gender. Like their Puritan ancestor, both Hesters take great pride in their children, cherishing them as their 'treasure' (IB, p. 7) and 'angel' (FA, p. 134), even as they bear the social stigma of their fatherlessness and outcast status. In both plays, however, this unconditional maternal love turns, under the persistent pressure of an abusive society, into an instinct to kill. Parks here inscribes her heroines in a rather complex literary genealogy of infanticide, evoking alongside Hester Prynne Euripides's Medea, the motherhood of slave narratives (notably Sethe in Toni Morrison's *Beloved*) and Brecht's Mother Courage. As Verna Foster comments, when profound love for one's children turns to murderous rage against them, then we ought to read these acts of violence as directed not so much against the child 'but at what the child represents, what society has made of the child or will do to the child'.[13]

In the Blood's Hester La Negrita ends up killing her oldest son Jabber when he repeats the word 'slut', scrawled on the wall of her makeshift shelter under the bridge, once too often – a word that she herself cannot read but that brands her existence as the unemployed, homeless, illiterate mother of five children by different fathers throughout the play. Similar to Hawthorne, Parks opens her narrative by exposing Hester to the prejudice and vicious judgement of public opinion. Hurling abuse, even spitting at her, the chorus makes clear that they consider her a burden to society: 'somethings gotta be done to stop this sort of thing/Cause I'll be damned if she gonna live off me' (p. 7). Ironically, it is this 'Puritanical' society that is shown to be living off Hester, repeatedly subjecting her to social, emotional and sexual abuse. Thus, Reverend D. (a version of Dimmesdale), specializing in empathy for the poor, has no qualms about abusing Hester sexually and emotionally as he continues to deny his fatherhood of her youngest child. Welfare provides Hester with 'hard honest work' in form of underpaid needlework but deliberately neglects to teach her how to sew, thereby keeping Hester dependent on her repeated requests for physical (a backrub) and sexual favours (a *ménage-à-trois* with her husband). The 'free' medical check-up offered Hester by the Doctor in the manner of a hurried car inspection similarly turns out to be but a preparation for a hysterectomy – his response to 'the Higher Ups' (p. 38) demanding of him solutions to the public sore and health hazard they consider Hester to be. In the end, even Hester's one friend Amiga steals from her every opportunity she gets, while contemplating how to market Hester's body most profitably. Given this constant regime of abuse by a society that claims to know what is best for her, even as it persistently deprives her of the right to make her own choices,[14] Hester's impulsive striking out against Jabber for mimicking in a childlike manner the one word that consigned her to this abject position follows logically from this plot development. Throughout the play, we can sense her penned up frustration, humiliation and anger. Twice she warns Welfare 'Don't make me hurt you' (pp. 57–8), and once she unsuccessfully strikes out against Reverend D. with a baton Jabber had stolen from a police officer earlier in the play. Not incidentally, the baton becomes the very same weapon with which she bludgeons her son to death. Yet, ironically, Hester's appropriation of the symbol of paternal authority does not set her free but, on the contrary, subjects her even further to its power. The play thus ends in the manner it began: with Hester standing, just as her Puritan ancestor, at 'The Prison Door', once again exposed to the vicious ostracism of her community.

While *In the Blood* is set in the 'Here' and 'Now' (p. 3), *Fucking A* presents an 'otherworldly tale involving a noble Mother, her wayward Son, and others' (p. 113). Once again, it is the persistent ostracism, administrative indifference and outright hostility of these 'others' that prompt Hester Smith to murder her own son, her former 'angel' who in the hands of this society has been turned into a 'Monster' to be hunted down, tortured and killed. In this dystopian society, the individual human being is reduced to a mere body to be administered, disciplined and misplaced by an extensive prison system and an indifferent welfare system called 'Freedom Fund', respectively, to be subjected to rigorous biopolitics, in which the mandatory reproduction in married couples goes hand in hand with prostitution and abortion. Hester herself has become part of this machinery in her profession as an Abortionist, making a living off the misery of others. For most of the play, she is shown in a bloody apron; and yet, just like her friend and lover Butcher, she also takes pride in her professional skills, bearing the mark branded on her left breast with both shame and distinction: 'my A is also like a shingle and a license, so nobody in need'll ever get suckered in by a charlatan' (ibid). In a way, she has accommodated herself to her role in society. As she sings together with her friend, the whore Canary Mary, 'We dig our ditch with no complaining/ . . . We'll say:/ 'Here is a woman/ Who does all she can" (pp. 122–3). Just as in Brecht's *Mother Courage*, we bear witness to a mother fighting for her child, saving money, enduring humiliations and setbacks to be at long last, after 30 years, able to visit him in prison. When encountering her son on the run, her final decision to deliver the fatal blow herself (before the Hunters have a chance to capture and torture him) likewise bespeaks her assertion of agency. As her son puts it, 'Us killing me is better than them killing me' (p. 219). Parks here picks up a prominent trope of slave narratives: the black woman's wresting of the right over life and death from white society.

Parks's investigation into the social overdetermination of the abused black female subject differs slightly from that of her sister play *In the Blood*. While Hester La Negrita is in the final tableau shown to stretch forth her blood-stained hands towards the sky, rebelling in Greek tragic fashion against a fate reserved for her ('Big hand coming down on me', p. 110), we see Hester Smith picking up her bloody tools, tying on her bloody apron, determined just like Mother Courage to get back into business. Yet, regardless of the degree of their complicity in an abusive system (Hester La Negrita, too, seems to go along rather willingly with her frequent degradation to sexual object), ultimately both plays prompt us to question a social system that in delimiting the choices for black women forces them either into complicity or radical rebellion. We are asked, as Carol Schaffer puts it, to consider to what extent they are 'products of a social structure that alienates them from themselves and their history as well as from any form of nurturance, a society that forces them to become animals who inherit bloody instincts for survival'.[15]

Topdog/Underdog (2001) and *The America Play* (1994)

Parks's Pulitzer Prize-winning *Topdog/Underdog* opened at the Papp Public Theater in New York on 26 July 2001 under the direction of George C. Wolfe, relocating to the Ambassador Theatre on Broadway the following spring. Similar to the *Red Letter Plays*, *Topdog/Underdog* evolved from a previous work of Parks's, *The America Play* (opening at the Papp Public on 22 February 1994 under the direction of Liz Diamond). Yet, once again they are entirely different plays, even as the later borrows one of the former's central tropes (the professional black Lincoln impersonator) and continues its thematic probing into questions of inheritance and remembering, commodification and authenticity, and finally, violence. 'Rep & Rev'-ing on these continuing concerns of Parks's, *Topdog/Underdog* arrives at answers very different from that of its older companion piece.

At the centre of both plays stands the figure of a black man earning his living by impersonating Abraham Lincoln – more specifically, his assassination. The presidential wound signifies for Parks on various levels. To begin with, it refers to a dominant, nationalist historiography, in which Lincoln has been enshrined as the Great Emancipator of African Americans and subsequent martyr at the hand of a southern rebel. This master narrative entails, however, not only the erasure of more complex readings of Lincoln, considering for instance his assertions of white supremacy but also, and more traumatically, the pre-empting of alternative, black historiographies. In *The America Play*, history is represented as a Great Hole, in which a protagonist, who bears 'a strong resemblance to Abraham Lincoln' (p. 159) but calls himself the Lesser Known, re-enacts the presidential death. While aspiring to be 'of interest to posterity' himself (p. 162), he remains condemned to work out his life in the shadow of the Great Man. Parks marks his sense of insignificance and inferiority by also naming him 'The Foundling Father'. *Topdog/ Underdog*, too, presents us with the 'foundlings' of history: two black brothers forsaken in their teenage years by their parents, attempting to cope with the legacy of abandonment throughout their lives. That this personal trauma stands for a larger collective trauma is evident not only in the irony of the older brother's occupation as a white-face presidential impersonator in a penny arcade but also in their ominous given names: Lincoln (Link) and Booth – their absconding father's sense of a joke. According to Parks, Lincoln's legacy continues to affect African American lives: 'Everything that happens, from 1865 to today, has to pass through that wound'.[16] As she demonstrates in both plays, this legacy proves to be an ambiguous one: simultaneously nourishing (literally, enabling a living) as well as stifling his black progeny.

Parks's protagonists attempt to find out who they are by digging at their past. *The America Play* realizes this trope quite literally: the Foundling Father, a grave digger by profession, imagines to have been called upon to dig the Great Man's grave but is instead confined to digging the Great Hole of History, a sort of historical theme park, in which he is to re-enact the latter's spectacular death, while his son Brazil digs within this 'inheritance of sorts' (p. 185) another hole in an attempt to retrieve his father's bones. The protagonists of *Topdog/Underdog* likewise engage in archaeological work by repeatedly rehearsing childhood memories, flipping through their 'raggedy' family album (p. 13), imitating routines of home life and pondering the meaning of their inheritance (they received $500 each from their parents). Yet, the history they are able to recover remains ambiguous at best, not always asserting clear distinctions between 'what is' and 'what 'ain't' (p. 73). Thus, their childhood memories tend to be based on idealized versions of a picture-perfect home, which have little to do with the impoverished circumstances of their actual home. Fake memories are, along with received and commodified versions of history, however, just as relevant to Parks as real ones. Her historian-impersonators readily cater to the public demand for a reified Lincoln myth. To their clients it hardly matters that the iconic stovepipe hat was seldom worn indoors, or that a black man is putting on whiteface. Lincoln's politics, too, remain at best secondary to the melodrama of his assassination. In the Foundling Father's rendition, 'the freeing of the slaves' is but a hurried reference squeezed in between 'the slipping of Booth into the presidential box' and 'the pulling of the trigger'.[17] Moreover, Parks's protagonists are not always able to tell 'thu truth from thu hearsay' (AP, p. 175). The Foundling Father becomes 'confused', dying a lonely death (ibid). Link, who initially insists on his own separate identity – 'Fake beard. Top hat. Don't make me into no Lincoln. I was Lincoln on my own before any of that' (TU, p. 30) – eventually erases the distinction between himself and his impersonation, when he begins to wear the Lincoln outfit on the way home, to fall asleep in his costume and increasingly to identify with the death scene: 'And for a minute, with him [the assassin] hanging back there behind me, it's real' (p. 50).

In *Topdog/Underdog* the inability to distinguish between 'what is' and 'what ain't' ultimately proves to be fatal. The brothers' given names turn out to be more than a personal joke, indexing instead the melancholic re-enactment of a traumatic history: Booth, once again, ends up killing Lincoln. Indeed, the naturalist form and setting of Parks's play allows for no other denouement. The brothers' 'seedily furnished rooming house room' (p. 7), containing but one bed, one armchair, one wooden chair, literally allows for only one inhabitant. Una Chaudhuri describes it as 'a room with a vengeance' (p. 289), as the 'very emblem of limits and boundaries' imposed on black masculinity by a white, patriarchal, capitalist economy (ibid.). Hence, the brothers' relationship is not merely fraternal (sharing the trauma of abandonment) but also a highly competitive one – the latter evident not only in the binary logic of the play's title but also in the 3-card-monte motif punctuating the plot. The hustling game offers a viable alternative to 'the demeaning lack of resources African-American males generally have in order to gain a foothold in the capitalist economy and to assert themselves as patriarchs'.[18] Booth, who throughout the play shies away from the 'real thing', preferring the simulation of work (shoplifting), sexual relations (masturbation) and social status (clothes, telephone) to concrete personal interaction, is eager to acquire Link's hustling skills, sensing in them not only an alternative 'economic opportunity' (p. 21) but also a way of asserting his masculinity. Yet, when their *agon* over access to the game culminates in a 3-card show-down, Booth's faith that the fake is 'just as good as the real thing' (p. 9) prevents him not only from distinguishing 'what is' from 'what ain't' in this key moment but also from entertaining the possibility that his older brother, given the naturalist topography of their lives allowing for only one top dog, might actually be capable of conning him. Having staked and lost his much cherished maternal 'inheritance' (which he had saved through every fiscal crisis, not even taking a peek at it, while Link had long blown his father's share), he is now unable to face the possibility of final defeat (as a hustler, as a son, as a brother), shooting his brother before the latter can open the stocking to uncover whether the treasured inheritance is of any substance at all. Historical overdetermination (the legacy of black post-emancipation abandonment) thus leaves the brothers with little room for choice and agency. They remain, as Joshua Shenk writes, 'wrapped up in a history of trauma and violence the origins of which they do not fully understand'.[19]

Such fatalistic denouement stands in marked contrast to the conclusion Parks works out in *The America Play*. The 'openness and diffused spatiality'[20] of its *mis-en-scène* ('A great hole. In the middle of nowhere', p. 159) along with an experimental dramaturgy, heavily relying on Rep & Rev, enables the production of an alternative historiography (rather than the traumatic re-enactment of a canonical one). Although the Lesser Known's son, Brazil, is able to retrieve from his archaeological digs not history as such but merely its artifacts (e.g. the blond beard his father was fond of donning as Abe Lincoln), he is nonetheless able to open up the meaning of these commodified versions of history through radical re-signification. For just like his father, Brazil combines his knack for 'diggin' with that of 'fakin' (p. 179). In this manner, he is able to retrieve the story of the Lesser Known from the Great Hole of History and to reconfigure the latter into his own Hall of Wonders, in which the resurrected ghost of his father receives, at long last, his 'designated place' (p. 176): 'To my right: our newest Wonder: One of thu greats Hisself!' (199). The different formal approaches thus allow for a very different assessment of black history and experience. If Parks peruses such different strategies, then, however, not merely to demonstrate the interdependence of form and meaning[21] but, above all, to show her audiences that 'There is no such thing as THE Black Experience' but that 'there are many experiences of being Black'.[22]

Summary

Parks demonstrates this credo most prominently in her subsequent *365 Days/365 Plays*: a loose collection of plays varying widely in length, form and themes. A 'black play' is, for her, no longer one that engages blackness only in its response to whiteness[23] but one in which '[b]lack characters, like all characters, ask the fundamental questions of 'who am I and what am I doing here?'[24] While Parks thus opens up the possibilities for engaging black experience and identity in its 'beautiful and powerful infinite variety',[25] her work nonetheless repeatedly returns to key themes, crucial to the production of such variety – in particular, digging and faking.

Many of Parks's characters dig, often in the most literal sense – from her first college play with 'a lot of dirt on stage which was being dug at',[26] to the Faulknerian effort of an entire family to unearth the maternal remains in the novel *Getting Mother's Body* (2003). Digging serves as one of the central tools in Parks's archaeological endeavour of locating what she calls 'the ancestral burial ground', of unearthing an African American past that she considers 'unrecorded, dismembered, washed out'.[27]

Not incidentally, Parks's protagonists tend to be possessed by a past that has forsaken them. Through digging (literally and figuratively) they attempt to locate and retrieve a form of inheritance, which – even as it does not turn out to be exactly a treasure – can nonetheless provide them with a sense of historical continuity and recognition. Digging then becomes a means of converting haunting into possession. The relationship between 'possessor and possessed', however, remains 'like ownership . . . , multidirectional' for Park.[28] At times, characters are able to resolve it into genuine inheritance; at other times, however, their attempts at recovery merely exhaust themselves in compulsive re-enactment of their own 'fabricated absence'.[29] Parks's resignified historiography is in this regard rather complex and open-ended. Hers is not necessarily a cathartic progression from melancholy to mourning, nor is it simply a victim-centred revision of history. In fact, for Parks the Great Hole of History holds forth several possibilities: as a cave, it might unleash the monsters lurking in the dark; as a lacuna it is waiting to be discovered and inscribed; and as a void it is capable of generating, similar to the Big Bang, its own proleptic meaning. As Brazil says, 'in thu beginning there was one of those voids here and then 'bang' and then *voilà*! And here we is' (AP, p. 184). The hole becomes a stage on which faint voices, echoes, ghosts from the past can enact and speak themselves into existence. This capacity for genesis, or rather *poiesis*, is, however, very much contingent on a second capacity: faking.

Most of Parks's characters prove to be self-conscious performers (Brazil, Venus), even conmen (Booth and Link), or, at least, people who realize that in the end they have to create their own 'scraps of graphy' (Aretha Saxon, Colonel Smith). Through their particular use of language they do not so much reflect as actively create reality. Playfully reworking tropes, images, discourses of power, they not only destabilize reified notions of identity but also unearth the very discursive structures that have interpellated black people within the prevailing notion of history – or more precisely, which have written them out of history, as Hegel notoriously proclaimed. Parks persistently reworks meanings through Rep & Rev, her trademark technique that she borrows from the signifying tradition of the black vernacular (cf. Gates). Riffing and punning, deploying homonyms and chiasms, onomatopoeia and neologism, she doubles, inverts and defers established and accepted meanings to the point that they become destabilized, detached from their customary referents and, ultimately, freed up for new possibilities of signification. Just as a founding father is haunted by his double, the Foundling Father, so forefathers can easily morph into faux fathers and foe fathers. In this manner, Parks packs all the meaning she can into her words, charging them with what she calls 'plutonic' power[30] so that, eventually, they must explode into new significations. 'KERBANG-KERBLAMMO! And now it all belongs to us', Brazil aptly describes this Rep & Rev (AP, p. 185). Moreover, if variation and resignification is possible on the level of language, then it is also possible on the level of narrative and, hence, historiography. As in a jazz score (a major source of inspiration for Parks), the playwright moves her narrative not directly from A to B, but lets it evolve from A>A>A>B>A.[31] Through such revised repetitions, she challenges the very idea of forward progression and, thus, the very basis of Aristotelian linearity as well as of a teleological conception of history – perhaps Parks's ultimate dig at Hegel's notorious erasure of black history. 'He digged the hole and the whole held him', Parks states at the beginning of *The America Play* (p. 159). In a way, this chiasm, which turns absence into presence and lack into plenitude by sheer virtue of Rep & Rev, serves as a perfect motto for much of her oeuvre.

All this underlines Parks's faith in the performative capacity of poetic language. She means to do things with words, taking up J. L. Austin's assertion that words not only have the capacity to describe but also the power to perform, to bring about the thing they say. Notably, Austin had denied this performative power to literature, maintaining that poetic speech acts remain invalid outside the conventions of the text. Parks disagrees; clearly she means what she says on stage and intends her words to take effect outside the play they are embedded in. Poetic language is to her just as valid in this regard as legal language, reminding us of drama's etymological roots in the verb 'doing'. For Parks, the stage is an 'incubator' for the creation of new historical events and personae, for *making* history. '[A]s in the case of artificial insemination', she insists, 'the baby is no less human'.[32] This is not to say that Parks no longer distinguishes between 'what is' and 'what ain't'. On the contrary, she remains intensely aware of the actuality of wounded, dismembered and misrepresented bodies. But she does contend that just as one can dig up fresh material for inclusion in the canon of history, one can also unearth the specific codes and discursive structures with which existing canons have been constructed. As we change these codes and structures, so will our experience of the past and our self-understanding in the present change. Drawing our awareness to the inherent performativity of language and signification, particularly to that deployed on behalf of hegemonic historiographies and identity discourses, Parks thus invites us to change these processes of signification.

Primary Sources

Works by Suzan-Lori Parks

The America Play and Other Works: Imperceptible Mutabilities in the Third Kingdom, The America Play (New York: Theatre Communications Group, 1995).

The Red Letter Plays: In the Blood, Fucking A (New York: Theatre Communications Group, 2001a).

Topdog/Underdog (New York: Theatre Communications Group, 2001b).

Secondary Sources

Austin, J. L., *How to Do Things with Words*, 2nd edn (Cambridge: Harvard University Press, 1975).

Bush, Jason, 'Who's Thu Man?! Historical melodrama and the performance of masculinity in *Topdog/Underdog*'. In Kevin J. Wetmore Jr. and Alycia Smith-Howard (eds), *Suzan-Lori Parks: A Casebook* (New York: Routledge, 2007), pp. 73–88.

Chaudhuri, Una, 'Review of *Topdog/Underdog* at the Public Theater', *Theatre Journal* 54 (2002), 289–90.

Drukman, Stephen, 'Suzan-Lori Parks and Liz Diamond: Doo-a-diddly-dit-dit. An Interview', *TDR* 39, 3 (Fall 1995), 56–75.

Foster, Verna, 'Suzan-Lori Parks's Staging of the Lincoln Myth in *The America Play* and *Topdog/Underdog*', *Journal of American Drama and Theatre* 17, 3 (Fall 2005), 24–35.

—, 'Nurturing and Murderous Mothers in Suzan-Lori Parks's *In the Blood* and *Fucking A*', *American Drama* 16, 1 (Winter 2007), 75–89.

Frank, Haike, 'The Instability of Meaning in Suzan-Lori Parks's *The America Play*', *American Drama* 11, 2 (Summer 2002), 4–20.

Garrett, Shawn-Marie, 'The Possession of Suzan-Lori Parks', *American Theatre* 17, 8 (October 2000), 22–6, 132–4.

Gates, Henry Louis Jr., *The Signifying Monkey: A Theory of African American Literary Criticism* (Oxford: Oxford University Press, 1988).

Geis, Deborah, *Suzan-Lori Parks* (Ann Arbor: University of Michigan, 2008).

Jiggetts, Shelby, 'Interview with Suzan-Lori Parks', *Callaloo* 19, 2 (Spring 1996), 309–17.

Parks, Suzan-Lori, 'From Elements of Style'. In *The America Play and Other Works* (New York: Theatre Communications Group 1995a), pp. 6–18.

—, 'An Equation for Black People Onstage'. In *The America Play and Other Works* (New York: Theatre Communications Group 1995b), pp. 19–22.

—, 'Possessions'. In *The America Play and Other Works* (New York: Theatre Communications Group 1995c), pp. 3–5.

Pearce, Michele, 'Alien Nation', *American Theatre* 11, 3 (March 1994), 26–7.

Saal, Ilka, 'The Politics of Mimicry: The Minor Theater of Suzan-Lori Parks', *South Atlantic Review* 70, 2 (Spring 2005), 57–70.

Schaffer, Carol, 'Staging a New Literary History: Suzan-Lori Parks's *Venus, In the Blood*, and *Fucking A*', *Comparative Drama* 42, 2 (Summer 2008), 181–203.

Shenk, Joshua Wolf, 'Beyond a Black-and-White Lincoln', *New York Times,* 7 April 2002, A 5.

Solomon, Alisa, 'Signifying on the Signifyin': The Plays of Suzan-Lori Parks', *Theater* 21, 3 (1990), 73–80.

Wetmore, Jr., Kevin J., 'It's an Oberammergau Thing: An Interview with Suzan-Lori Parks' In Kevin J. Wetmore, Jr. and Alycia Smith-Howard (eds), *Suzan-Lori Parks: A Case Book* (London and New York: Routledge, 2007), pp. 124–40.

Notes

1. Some critics, such as Geis, list Parks's year of birth as 1964. In an interview with Kevin Wetmore, Parks however asserts it as 1963. Cf. Wetmore Jr., Kevin J., 'It's an Oberammergau Thing', p. 128.
2. Quoted in Shelby Jiggetts, 'Interview with Suzan-Lori Parks', p. 310.
3. Shawn-Marie Garrett, 'The Possession of Suzan-Lori Parks', p. 24.
4. Deborah Geis, *Suzan-Lori Parks*, p. 3.

5. Quoted in Shelby Jiggetts, 'Interview', p. 310.
6. Shawn-Marie Garrett, 'The Possession', p. 22.
7. Quoted in Shawn-Marie Garrett, 'The Possession', p. 24.
8. Alisa Solomon, 'Signifying on the Signifyin': The Plays of Suzan-Lori Parks', p. 75.
9. Quoted in Alisa Solomon, 'Signifying', p. 76.
10. Shawn-Marie Garrett, 'The Possession', p. 134.
11. Suzan-Lori Parks, 'From Elements of Style', p. 8.
12. Quoted in Kevin J. Wetmore Jr., 'Oberammergau Thing', p. 134.
13. Verna Foster, 'Nurturing and Murderous Mothers in Suzan-Lori Parks's *In the Blood* and *Fucking A*', p. 75.
14. Deborah Geis, *Suzan-Lori Parks*, p. 133.
15. Carol Schaffer, 'Staging a New Literary History: Suzan-Lori Parks's *Venus, In the Blood*, and *Fucking A*', p. 199.
16. Quoted in Joshua Wolf Shenk, 'Beyond a Black-and-White Lincoln', p. 5.
17. *The America Play*, p. 188. Cf. Haike Frank, 'The Instability of Meaning in Suzan-Lori Parks's *The America Play*', pp. 15–16.
18. Jason Bush, 'Who's Thu Man?! Historical melodrama and the performance of masculinity in *Topdog/Underdog*', p. 78.
19. Joshua Wolf Shenk, 'Beyond', p. 5.
20. Una Chaudhuri, 'Review of *Topdog/Underdog* at the Public Theater', p. 289.
21. Suzan-Lori Parks, 'Elements', p. 7.
22. Suzan-Lori Parks, 'An Equation for Black People Onstage', p. 21.
23. Suzan-Lori Parks, 'An Equation', p. 19.
24. Quoted in Kevin J. Wetmore Jr., 'Oberammergau Thing', p. 138.
25. Suzan-Lori Parks, 'An Equation', p. 22.
26. Quoted in Shelby Jiggetts, 'Interview', p. 310.
27. Suzan-Lori Parks, 'Possessions', p. 4.
28. Ibid., p. 3.
29. Stephen Drukman, 'Suzan-Lori Parks and Liz Diamond: Doo-a-diddly-dit-dit. An Interview', p. 67.
30. Quoted in Stephen Drukman, 'Interview', p. 58.
31. Suzan-Lori Parks, 'Elements', p. 9.
32. Suzan-Lori Parks, 'Possessions', p. 5.

15 SARAH RUHL

Deborah Geis

Eurydice; The Clean House; Passion Play; Dead Man's Cell Phone; In the Next Room (Or the Vibrator Play)

Introduction

> *I come into the theater wanting to feel and think at the same time, to have the thought affect the emotion and the emotion affect the thought. That is the pinnacle of a great night at the theater.*[1]

Sarah Ruhl was born in 1974 and grew up in Wilmette, an affluent suburb on Chicago's North Shore. From an early age, she was a precocious writer, claiming to John Lahr in the *New Yorker* that when in third grade she received a 'poison-pen letter' from a classmate, 'I corrected the punctuation and sent it back'.[2] She received her BA and her MFA in playwriting from Brown University, and also studied at Pembroke College in Oxford. Before she was a playwright, she was a poet, and she had a book of poems, *Death in Another Country*, published at age 20.[3]

At Brown, her mentor was Paula Vogel (author of *The Baltimore Waltz, How I Learned to Drive* and many other works; see discussion in this volume). Vogel says that when Ruhl showed up, as a sophomore, in her advanced playwriting course, 'I thought at first she was a senior: she was quiet and serious, but so obviously possessed a mind that came at aesthetics from a unique angle'.[4] One can see the influence of Vogel in Ruhl's interest in unconventional relationships and in the willingness to subvert conventions of theatrical realism while maintaining a certain level of psychological realism. While under Vogel's tutelage, Ruhl began work on several pieces that were later produced professionally, including *Melancholy Play, Virtual Meditations #1* and adaptations of two Chekhov stories, *Lady with the Lap Dog* and *Anna around the Neck*. An early workshop version of her play *Eurydice* was produced at Brown University in January 2001, and this piece went on to receive another workshop production at the Children's Theatre Company in Minneapolis that September, then premiered in a full production form at Madison Repertory Theatre in September 2003.

Another key early pair of mentors for Ruhl were Joyce and Bernard Piven of the Piven Theatre Workshop in Evanston, Illinois (they also worked with such artists as David Mamet and John Cusack early in their careers), and the Pivens helped to shape some of Ruhl's earliest professional stage productions such as *Melancholy Play* in June 2002. The Goodman Theatre in Chicago also produced the early versions of some of Ruhl's plays such as *The Clean House* (first commissioned by the McCarter Theatre in Princeton in 2000), and she continues a strong affiliation with that company.

At the same time, her work began to generate interest on the West Coast and off-Broadway (*Late: A Cowboy Song* was produced at the Ohio Theatre in New York in April 2003 and her adaptation of Virginia Woolf's *Orlando* opened at New York's Classic Stage Company that same year; *Eurydice* received a major production by the Berkeley Repertory Theatre in October 2004). She received national recognition when *The Clean House*, after premiering at Yale Repertory Theatre in September 2004, moved to the Goodman Theatre that May and then to Broadway (Lincoln Center) in October 2006, the same year that her play *Demeter in the City* was produced. *Passion Play*, which Ruhl has drafted, reworked and remounted many times over the course of her career, was produced in a workshop version at the Tristan Bates Theatre in London in July 2002, had its world premiere at Arena Stage in Washington, D.C. in September 2005, was produced at the Goodman Theatre in September 2007 and Yale Repertory Theatre in September 2008 and again by the Epic Theatre Ensemble in Brooklyn in May 2010. *Dead Man's Cell Phone* premiered in June 2007 at the Woolly Mammoth Theatre Company in Washington, D.C., had its New York premiere at Playwrights Horizons in March 2008 and was produced by Steppenwolf (Chicago's other major repertory company) that same month and year. Ruhl's second play to make it to Broadway was *In the Next Room (Or the Vibrator Play)*, which premiered at Berkeley Repertory Theatre in February 2009 and opened that November at the Lyceum Theatre on Broadway in a Lincoln Center Theatre production. Her most recent play, *Stage Kiss* – a theatrical satire that draws upon Noel Coward's *Private Lives* – opened at the Goodman Theatre in Chicago in May 2011. Her works have also been translated into Spanish, Arabic, Russian, Polish and Korean, and have been performed internationally, including in Germany, Israel, New Zealand, Poland and Australia.

Ruhl has won many major grants and awards for her work, including a Helen Merrill Emerging Playwrights Award, a Whiting Writers' Award and a PEN/Laura Pels Award, all in 2003 alone. In 2004, *The Clean House* won the Susan Smith Blackburn Award and was a 2005 finalist for the Pulitzer Prize. In 2006, Ruhl won the prestigious MacArthur Fellowship. Her unpublished play *Demeter in the City* was nominated for nine NAACP awards. *Passion Play* won the Kennedy Center's Fourth Freedom Forum Playwriting Award. And in 2010, *In the Next Room (Or the Vibrator Play)* won the Glickman Prize, was a finalist for the 2010 Pulitzer Prize and earned a Tony nomination for Best Play. Ruhl was married in 2005 to Tony Charuvastra, a child psychiatrist, and has a daughter, Anna.

The Plays

Eurydice (2004)

Eurydice is a contemporary update of the Greek myth and while it is one of Ruhl's more overtly magical or surreal plays, the characters (especially Eurydice and her father) are depicted in a manner that still generates psychological empathy for them. The piece maintains some of the trappings of Greek drama such as a Chorus, represented here by a set of semi-human characters called Stones. As in classical drama, these Chorus members both comment on the action and at times fail to understand it; they can be comic, ignorant and at times a bit vindictive. And as in the classical version of the myth, Orpheus is a musician and Eurydice his loved one, though in Ruhl's representation of the characters, they are an innocent, quarrelsome young couple a little like the characters of her earlier play *Late: A Cowboy Song*.

Although the bare-bones version of the play's plot is similar to the mythological one – when Orpheus comes to fetch Eurydice back from the underworld, he disobeys the order not to look back at her and thus they are lost to one another – Ruhl's version is less interested in the character of Orpheus, devoting far more of its focus to the other two male characters who are interested in Eurydice, the Devil character and Eurydice's long-dead father. The most charismatic character in the play is Ruhl's version of 'A Nasty Interesting Man/The Lord of the Underworld', who appears first as a seducer who goes after Eurydice when she leaves her own wedding reception and who appears later as a child on a tricycle. Reviewer Roger Malone aptly calls his character 'the disconcerting catalyst to the tragedy'.[5] Eurydice, who has walked out of her reception from apparent boredom, is intrigued by the Nasty Interesting Man's seeming attention to her, whereas Orpheus is portrayed as somewhat self-absorbed. Of course, it is all a ruse, but Ruhl implies that the Devil knows her secret wishes and has him capitalize on being older, richer, more sophisticated (he offers her champagne and has a spectacular apartment), as well as promising to show her a letter from her dead father. When Eurydice arrives in the underworld (via a raining elevator), the surreal quality of her surroundings is accentuated by her comically everyday reaction to them as, not understanding where she is, she attempts to get regular porter service at the hotel. The man whom she thinks is the hotel bellman, though, is her dead father, and their reunion becomes the key point of the play. They use the workings of the imagination – an inherently theatrical process wherein we, like Eurydice and her father, must pretend (for instance) that the string around them is her room – and begin to tell one another stories, attempting to piece together their memories to create some kind of a present bond even though the Stones insist, 'Father is not a word that dead people understand' (p. 363).

One of the major tropes of the play is the connection between language and memory, particularly as embodied in the sending of letters between the present and the afterlife/underworld. As mentioned above, the letter that fell into the Devil's possession was one that Eurydice's father wrote to her from the underworld on her wedding day; after Eurydice has gone to the underworld herself, Orpheus writes and says that he loves her, but Eurydice doesn't understand the letter (she has the amnesia of the underworld) when her father reads it to her, until the very end of it when the name Orpheus suddenly resonates for her. When Orpheus sends her a book – the *Collected Works of Shakespeare* – she tries to read it but again, can't understand, and her father takes over and quotes from King Lear: 'We two alone will sing like birds in the cage' (p. 377). Forgetting the past, including past history or literature, is a kind of death in itself, and if Shakespeare (theatre, imagination) is divine, it is forbidden in the underworld, as the Stones insist. Yet the father, like King Lear, seems happier to have his daughter to himself than to share her with any husband. Eurydice begins to articulate both a new empathy for Orpheus and a reason for her feelings that he was always distant from her; she says that as an artist, 'he is always going away from you. Inside his head there is always something more beautiful' (p. 385). Yet it is his art – his music – that enables Orpheus to find Eurydice in the underworld, by singing her name (until the Devil intercedes and says he can't turn around and look at her, knowing full well he will be unable to resist). While the father, in his grief, dips himself in the river of forgetfulness, Eurydice (as she prepares to become the Devil's bride) sends a last letter to Orpheus offering loving instructions to Orpheus's next wife – but when he comes back down to the underworld to fetch her again, the rainwater makes him forget everything and he's unable to read the letter; the play ends with '*The sound of water. Then silence*' (p. 411). For Ruhl, language/writing and song/music are intricately tied up with the acts of memory, which itself is the basis of continued love. It's not until the later *Dead Man's Cell Phone* that a different way of renewing the faith in communication between the living and the dead returns.

The Clean House (2004)

The Clean House continues Ruhl's interest in some of the language issues in *Eurydice*, particularly that of translation. Here, though, she uses joke-telling as one of the play's major tropes; in fact, Ruhl notes at the end of the cast list that '[e]veryone in this play should be able to tell a really good joke' (p. 7). 'Lightness isn't stupidity', Ruhl tells interviewer John Lahr. 'It's actually a philosophical and aesthetic viewpoint, deeply serious, and has a kind of wisdom—stepping back to be able to laugh at horrible things even as you're experiencing them'.[6] The play indeed begins with the protagonist, the cleaning lady Mathilde, telling a joke, only it is in Portuguese: the audience is supposed to be able to tell, even if unable to understand her, that this is what she is doing. Ruhl says, 'I think that at the most primal level, the intention to be funny, to share wit, is beyond language. When I wrote *The Clean House* and began it with the joke in Portuguese that probably no one would understand, that was part of the impulse. But people do laugh. Some nights they don't; that's a night when we're in trouble'.[7] In this play, the ability to tell and to appreciate a good joke represents not just intelligence, but also love: Mathilde says that her father always said of her mother that they 'have never been apart since the day [they] met, because I always wanted to know the next joke' (p. 11). The joke-telling ties into the play's emphasis on issues of both literal and metaphorical translation. What we learn very quickly is that Mathilde, who has come to the United States from Brazil, is not particularly interested in being a cleaning lady for Lane, the woman doctor in whose house she works. Lane's inability to pronounce Mathilde's name correctly suggests her lack of awareness of how to connect with others – including, as we soon see, her own husband.

The 'clean house' of the title is set in what Ruhl calls a 'metaphysical Connecticut, [o]r, a house that is not far from the sea and not far from the city' (p. 7). Lane's failure to clean her own house implies, in a traditional Freudian sense, a lack of self-knowledge (as well as her social class limitations). But Lane's sister Virginia loves to clean, and so on the sly, Virginia comes over and does the cleaning for Mathilde while Lane is at work. Her love of cleaning is equally suspect, though, since she seems to use the obsessive need to tidy things up as a substitute for doing anything else with her life: 'cleaning my house—makes me feel clean' (p. 19). It is only when – as is more often the case than not in Ruhl's work – unexpected alliances form that the women are able to gain a new kind of strength in their lives. When Virginia – who is forming a friendship with Mathilde – finds a pair of underwear in the laundry basket that clearly belongs to another woman than Lane, they realize that Lane's husband Charles, also a doctor, is having an affair. We, as well as Lane, discover that his new love is an Argentinian woman named Ana whom he met when diagnosing her breast cancer. In a different sort of play, this would be the point at which the relationships fall apart – but instead, this is the point at which the unanticipated relationships among the characters continue to form, and the play becomes less and less dependent on a realist mode – in other words, less 'clean' in terms of the separation between illusion and reality.

As these borders break down, the characters move closer together. A strong bond forms in particular between Mathilde and Ana, as the latter reminds Mathilde of her own recently deceased mother – and they are even able to speak a mixture of Portuguese and Spanish with each other. In one scene, Ana and Mathilde throw apples off the balcony into the 'sea', which also – as the scenes have conflated – is Lane's living room. There is a kind of absurdity in the sight of Charles in Alaska, digging up a yew tree in a last-ditch effort to save Ana's life with its medicine, and at the end of the play we even see him drag the entire tree into the living room. The grand romanticism of the gesture, though, signifies the extent to which he is driven by true love. Confronted by Lane for her cleaning obsession, Virginia attempts to prove her wrong by dumping pots of dirt from plants into the living room. When Ana gets too sick to be alone, she moves in with Lane and Mathilde, and Lane says she can't hate Ana because Ana glows with love from Charles and she knows he 'never looked at me like that' (p. 91). As an image of their new unity, we see all of the women eating ice cream out of the same container together, a border-crossing that never would have happened earlier. Finally, on Ana's request, Mathilde helps her to cross into the world of the dead by telling her the same joke (which we don't hear, since she whispers it) that made her mother laugh so hard when her father told it that she died laughing. Reviewer Neal Weaver's comment on the Odyssey Theatre (Los Angeles) production seems to overlook the more complex sides of this seemingly happy ending: he calls the work 'so resolutely cheery and life-affirming that it strains credibility' (p. 47). Indeed, Mathilde's closing line to the audience sums up the alternatingly light and dark themes of the play: 'I think maybe heaven is a sea of untranslatable jokes. Only everyone is laughing' (p. 109).

Passion Play (2005)

Passion Play, a piece that – as stated earlier – Ruhl has reworked multiple times, is one of her most ambitious plays. It uses the medieval genre of the passion play (the enactment of Christ's crucifixion), but retells it in three different historical time frames: England in 1575 at the time that Queen Elizabeth was about to shut the passion plays down; Oberammergau, Bavaria (the traditional site of the annual passion plays) in 1934 Germany just at the beginning of the Nazis' rise to power (apparently Hitler saw the play that year and was a big fan); and South Dakota between 1969 (the Vietnam War era) and the present. The result is a piece that is epic in effect; in his review of Brooklyn's important Irondale Ensemble production directed by Mark Wing-Davey, David Sheward calls it 'the most exciting, stimulating, and thrilling piece of theater to hit New York since *Angels in America*'.[8] Also invoking Kushner, James Al-Shamma says that Ruhl 'investigates the potency of the theatrical gesture as metaphor, with theatricality defined as artifice in which, to paraphrase Tony Kushner, it is okay and maybe even beneficial if the wires show'.[9] Ruhl tells us in her Playwright's Note that she asked herself the following questions: '[H]ow would it shape or misshape a life to play a biblical role year after year? How are we scripted? Where is the line between authentic identity and performance? And is there, in fact, such a line?' (p. ix)

To respond to these questions, Ruhl in a sense repeats the same plot several times and cleverly triple-casts the actors in corresponding roles: Pontius/Satan and John/Jesus have a rivalry; the two Marys (Virgin Mary and Mary Magdalene) are in love with them; a Visiting Friar in Part One becomes the Visiting Englishman in Part Two and the V.A. Psychiatrist in Part Three; the Village Idiot is alternately tolerated and persecuted; and the political hegemony is represented by the same actor playing Queen Elizabeth, Hitler and Ronald Reagan. Ruhl emphasizes the play-within-a-play motif throughout: the characters play actors who play the characters in the passion play. For example, in Part One, Pontius, says, 'All my life I've wanted to play Christ . . . if only, I thought, they put me on a cross, I would feel holy, I would walk upright. And every year my cousin plays the Savior' (p. 16). The characters continually question their own similarities to and differences from the characters they play; again in Part One, Mary 2 remarks, 'Mary Magdalen was a whore because she pretended and that's like me—I'm a whore because I pretend things' (p. 23).

Moving further beyond these questions about identity and role-playing, though, Ruhl also emphasizes the political resonances and commonalities of the three periods, showing the cyclical nature of history and the rise to power. There is an eerie resonance to Part Two's setting in pre-World War II Germany, for instance, when Mary 2 talks about how, as a little girl, she was so moved by the play that she 'wanted . . . to run onstage and fight the Jews' (p. 99). In Part Three, P (Pontius), recently back from Vietnam, suffers enacting his role as his experience in the war causes him to question his character's motives: 'Pilate had good intentions—he *had* to kill someone innocent, it was all part of the big plan. He saved us all, didn't he, by being willing to be bad. But—a little girl's brains—there's no plan for that' (p. 207). In the last scene of the play before P delivers a closing speech, Ronald Reagan talks about his days as a baseball announcer when he wouldn't actually be at the game and would create an illusion for his audience, going on to claim that he 'feel[s] as though' he served in the military because he had 'one of the happiest times of my life' (p. 232) making training films for soldiers during World War II. Ultimately, then, Ruhl implies that while the distinction between being an actor and being a character is indeed a blurry one, not questioning the line between reality and illusion may also cause delusional interpretations of past history: playing a role requires a certain level of self-examination about how and where one steps in and out of that role.

Dead Man's Cell Phone (2007)

Ruhl has said that she wrote *Dead Man's Cell Phone* as the result of 'feeling constantly plugged in', pointing out that 'many, many people right now are losing the ordinary, we're so plugged in all the time' and that even for her, '[t]he theater's the only time when I turn my cell phone off'.[10] Here, too, Ruhl returns to her preoccupations with such themes as the afterlife and love triangles. In this work, a woman, Jean, is in a café when the man at another table, Gordon, dies. She pockets his cell phone and ends up having her life deeply entwined with Gordon's mother, his brother Dwight, his widow Hermia and the 'Other Woman' with whom Gordon was having an affair. Just as she does in the later play *In the Next Room*, Ruhl uses a piece of technology – here, the prop of the cell phone – as the link between worlds, which is also the role played by the letters in *Eurydice*. It is important to note that the play is not critical of the cell phone the way one might expect; rather, it is taken for granted but also to some extent, our reliance on it and trust in it is parodied. John Lahr calls the play 'a meditation on death, love, and disconnection in the digital age; like her other works, it inhabits a dramatic netherworld between personal suspense and suspended time'.[11] Ruhl tells Lahr that cell phones and other devices 'will change people in ways we don't even understand. We're less connected to the present. No one is where they are. There's absolutely no reason to talk to a stranger anymore—you connect to people you already know. But how well do you know them? Because you never see them—you just talk to them. I find that terrifying'.[12] As Gordon's mother says while the song 'You'll never walk alone' rises at the end of her eulogy, 'You'll never walk alone. That's right. Because you'll always have a machine in your pants that might ring. Oh, Gordon. *She sings too*' (p. 17). And Gordon (who, as we shall see, reappears in Part Two) laments the demise of the phone booth as it has been replaced by people talking into their cell phones. His words characterize not only what he hears as the result, but in a sense, what Ruhl does with the imagery of filaments and networks of communication in this play itself: 'People are yammering into their phones and I hear fragments of lost love and hepatitis and I'm thinking, is there no privacy? *Is there no dignity?*' (p. 39)

The irony of this line, of course, is that Gordon himself lives on, not only by means of Jean appropriating his cell phone, but also because he effectively comes back to life in the second part of the play. As in such works as *Eurydice*, Ruhl is intimately concerned with life after death and, as such, is willing to break the conventions of realism despite the play's ostensibly realistic contemporary setting. This becomes particularly evident when, unexpectedly, the opening scene of Part Two of the play shifts back to the last day of Gordon's life, and we hear from him directly. He says to the audience, 'I woke up that morning—the day I died—thinking I'd like a lobster bisque' (p. 39). As it turns out, though, a woman at another table – Jean – has just finished the last bowl of it. He begins to have a heart attack and first thinks about calling his wife, mistress or mother, but ends up preoccupied with Jean, whom she decides 'looks like an angel—not like a bitch at all' (p. 42), and just as he dies he decides he is glad that she got the last bowl of soup.

What Ruhl seems to be concerned with here is the surprising transmission of one fate to another, the mysterious ways in which we form connections to one another without knowing it. At first, Jean is only pretending to have known Gordon, but she finds herself drawn more and more deeply into the worlds of those who knew him, even falling in love with Dwight. She rescues Hermia's memories of Gordon (who had been selling human organs on the black market) by making up a story about how, the day he died, he was writing a letter to her on a napkin in the café about how connected he always felt to her. The play gets further into a kind of magic realist territory when the Other Woman (Gordon's mistress), disguised as a Stranger, gets into physical combat with Jean in Johannesburg when trying to get the phone back and hits Jean on the head with the gun. During Jean's blackout, we see a vision of her having a conversation with Gordon in the café as they discuss the day that they (briefly) met and Gordon died. Gordon tells Jean that they are alike because they 'both told lies to help other people' (p. 54). At the end of the play, Jean is reunited with Dwight but the mother has chosen to go to heaven to join her son. And as in so many of Ruhl's other plays, the action ends with a gesture of love – in this case, a kiss between Jean and Dwight as she asks that they 'love each other absolutely' (p. 63). What Ruhl seems to be asking here is whether, in a fragmented and technology-driven postmodern world, true love is possible – and the play implies that through the imagination and by taking leaps of faith/trust, it is.

In the Next Room (Or the Vibrator Play) (2009)

In the Next Room (Or the Vibrator Play) takes place in the 1880s and was inspired by Rachel Maines's book *The Technology of Orgasm*. Ruhl was interested in the early days of electricity during which it was 'discovered' that women's so-called hysteria and other problems could be treated by a device that brought them to orgasm. She tells Vogel that one doctor in Maines's book was quoted as saying 'that at least three-fourths of women had ailments that could be cured by the vibrator. Which is kind of stunning'.[13] As she remarks in her opening notes to the script, the two things that seem strangest in the play – the existence of this device and the commonness of hiring wet nurses – 'are all true', while '[t]hings that seem commonplace are all my own invention' (p. 6). From the point of view of realism, then, this work is more grounded in its historical use of setting than many of Ruhl's other pieces: we don't have flights of fancy into other worlds or alternate realities. As Heidi Schmidt puts it, 'Followers of Ruhl's work may . . . be surprised at the play's realist leanings: actors never address the audience directly, there are no raining elevators, and the primary source of magic is electric lighting—magical indeed, given the time period'.[14] Rather, what is emphasized is how constrained the characters are by their expected gender, class, and racial roles – and the extent to which the worlds of art and sexuality may be the keys to freeing up the constraints of these roles' expectations.

As in her other works, Ruhl is fascinated with creating unexpected and triangular relationships among her characters. Katherine E. Kelly calls the characters' amorous pursuits of one another 'a series of errors echoing *A Midsummer Night's Dream*, whose fairy dust has been replaced by electric vibrations'.[15] This play interweaves the lives of Catherine Givings, the wife of the electricity-bearing doctor (Dr Givings); Annie, the doctor's assistant; Sabrina Daldry, a patient; and Elizabeth, the African-American wet nurse who is hired to feed Catherine's baby. While Catherine remains in the dark for the first part of the play about what exactly her husband is doing to his women patients 'in the next room', she forms a bond with Sabrina's husband as they take a walk in the rain while waiting. The play builds into a continuing series of such unanticipated relationships: between Catherine and Sabrina when

Sabrina plays the piano for Catherine; between Sabrina (for whom the treatment really only works when Annie is there) and Annie. When Catherine becomes curious about what her husband is doing with his patients, Sabrina shows her the device while the doctor is out. At the beginning of the second act, we are introduced to a male patient, Leo, who is also treated with the doctor's electrical vibrator and who ends up, again, having a powerful conversation with Catherine when they are both in the living/waiting room. Leo, an artist, tells Elizabeth that he wants to paint a picture of her nursing Catherine's baby. And later, Catherine begs Leo to take her away to Paris with him, but he says that it is Elizabeth whom he loves, unreciprocatedly.

Key to this play is the tension between the overt emphasis on sexual pleasure in the action itself – it is rare to see a piece that so centrally preoccupies itself with the issue of orgasm, particularly female orgasm – and the characters' repression or lack of understanding of what they are experiencing or enabling. Kelly praises the humour that emerges from 'the characters' decorous pursuit of symptomatic relief and from the doctor's presumption of the separation of emotion and arousal'.[16] Dr Givings sees himself as a pioneer in a medical resolution to female 'hysteria', but claims to take a purely clinical attitude towards his 'treatments' of his patients; as Kelly puts it, his portrayal 'wryly captures the prejudice of nineteenth-century male physicians on the subject of women's sexuality. . . . Part of the play's humor arises from the gap between the characters' scientific explanation of the device's therapeutic effects and the audience's post-Freudian dismissal of that interpretation'.[17] He resists the idea of any connection between the orgasms he is inducing in these patients and any kind of pleasure; indeed, when Catherine becomes jealous of Elizabeth's growing attachment to the baby and demands that her husband use the device on her, he becomes distressed that she is using it for 'onanism' (p. 95). He is upset, though, when he then senses that she is attracted to Leo, and he tells Leo not to return. Elizabeth shocks both Catherine and Sabrina when she tells them that the sensations they feel from the machine are the kind that some women feel when they are 'having relations with their husbands' (p. 115). There is an implied potential lesbian relationship between Annie and Sabrina that is never fully acknowledged or played out; Annie continues to give

Sabrina lessons in Greek philosophy while she is 'treating' her. By the end, though many of these issues are left unresolved, there is at least a sense of optimism about the central husband and wife relationship insofar as Catherine and her husband reconcile and for the first time, are seen making love as they finally, in a magical garden setting, acknowledge each other's bodies. This, too, is the point at which the setting departs from realism: as Schmidt puts it, 'the walls of the living room and operating theatre fly slowly out of the theatre space, revealing snow-covered trees behind'.[18] Ruhl comments that at the Lincoln Center production, audience members were more shocked by the sexuality of the ending than by the use of the vibrators in the rest of the play: 'In this day and age, what's radical is human intimacy'.[19] Throughout the play, one expects to see the women characters nude, and yet the only nudity (at least in the Lincoln Center production) was that of the doctor in this closing scene. Schmidt aptly characterizes this as a Brechtian moment that calls attention to the constructs of staged representation: 'By reversing the traditional representation of male/female nudity, Ruhl reminds us that the representation of gender is constructed, and as such can be subverted and altered'.[20]

Summary

In all of Ruhl's works, she makes the boundaries of naturalism permeable: in other words, while each of her plays (except *Eurydice*) is grounded in the 'real' world (and even that play has trappings of the everyday such as an elevator), Ruhl constantly crosses between her ostensibly realistic settings and other worlds: the world of the dead in *Eurydice*, *The Clean House* and *Dead Man's Cell Phone*; the worlds of different historical periods in *Passion Play*. Ruhl tells her interviewer/mentor Paula Vogel, 'If you transform space and atmosphere, you don't have to connect the dots psychologically in a linear way'.[21] On a more literal level, her scenography encourages worlds to melt into one another: the various places of *The Clean House* (the doctor's balcony, Lane's house, Alaska) overlap, while *In the Next Room* creates the idea of secrets that are revealed and thresholds that are transgressed when characters cross over from the living room into the operating theatre. As John Lahr puts it, Ruhl 'writes in a poised, crystalline style about things that are irrational and invisible. [She] is a fabulist'.[22]

Just as Ruhl shows a visual and thematic preoccupation with border crossing in her settings themselves, her characters – who frequently turn and address the audience, in Brechtian fashion – are continually 'crossing over' in their own changing constructions of their identities: in Ruhl's worlds, identity is shaped through language and characters are never static because they seek the power to reshape their worlds by changing the roles they play. This is most obvious in *Passion Play*, where the characters' meanings change with history, but also where characters like Pontius/P struggle between the way they have been 'scripted' and the internal (or real) battles they fight. It is clear in *The Clean House*, where the sisters Lane and Virginia both face challenges to the preconceived notions they had of how they were going to live their lives. In *Eurydice*, the title character is unsure how to 'be' a wife or a daughter, while a character like Annie in *In the Next Room* does not fit into the expected roles for her gender, sexuality or education during the play's time period. And in *Dead Man's Cell Phone*, Jean creates a larger world of love around her by pretending to be someone (a close friend of the dead Gordon) that she is not.

Identity in these works is closely linked to issues of language and translation, most clearly in *Eurydice* where the inhabitants of the underworld and the living world do not speak the same language, but also in *The Clean House* where we learn to appreciate jokes through their tenor if not the actual language in which they are told. Ruhl tells Vogel, 'That's one of my peculiar monomanias—people speaking other tongues in the theater and the audience understanding them'.[23] The paternal medical discourse about women's bodies of *In the Next Room* competes with the language of those bodies themselves, or with the conversations between characters like Catherine and Leo about art, or between Annie and Sabrina about classical philosophy. The observers who come to the sites of *Passion Play* from outside – the Visiting Englishman, for example – enter a world of different discourse and must learn to 'translate'.

Possibly the strongest thematic link among Ruhl's works, though – and one not unrelated to those mentioned previously – is the repeated notion that relationships are continually evolving and can form and change where one least expects it. It is of course a staple of dramatic plots to have characters expressing illicit or unrequited love for other characters. But in Ruhl's plays, the active transitions of relationships (their multiplicities, their crossings of gender/sexuality, social class, race and even life/death) resonate profoundly throughout. Ruhl's early works *Melancholy Play* and *Late: A Cowboy Song* focus on characters who have to work out the repercussions of changing their minds about the subjects of their infatuations. Like Tilly in *Melancholy Play*, Eurydice is faced with the competing loves of Orpheus, her father and the Nasty Interesting Man. But relationships in such plays as *The Clean House*, *Dead Man's Cell Phone* and *In the Next Room* often land the characters in unexpected places. The ill Ana forms a close bond with Mathilde and moves into the home of Lane, her supposed rival for Charles' affection. Despite having their entire relationship initially based on the lie that she knew Gordon, Jean falls in love with his brother. And virtually every character in *In the Next Room* loves someone who is 'wrong': Leo loves Elizabeth, Catherine loves Leo, Sabrina loves Annie. Ruhl implies that when we think about love from a postmodern perspective, what gets dramatized rather than repressed is its complexity, its variability, its refusal to follow set rules and limits. The drama of the human heart, she suggests, lies in its refusal to stop beating.

Primary Sources

Works by Sarah Ruhl

The Clean House and Other Plays: The Clean House, Eurydice, Late: A Cowboy Song, and Melancholy Play (New York: Theatre Communications Group, 2006).

Dead Man's Cell Phone (New York: Samuel French, 2009).

In the Next Room (Or the Vibrator Play) (New York: Theatre Communications Group, 2010a).

Passion Play (New York: Theatre Communications Group, 2010b).

Two Plays I Didn't Write: Woolf's Orlando *and Chekhov's* Three Sisters [adaptations] (New York: Theatre Communications Group, 2011).

Secondary Sources

Al-Shamma, James, 'Review of *Passion Play*', *Theatre Journal* 63, 2 (May 2011a), pp. 262–4.

—, *Sarah Ruhl: A Critical Study of Her Plays* (Jefferson, NC: McFarland, 2011b).

Als, Hilton, 'It's a Man's World: The Theatre', *New Yorker* 86, 3 (October 2010), 105–6.

Hofler, Robert, 'Scribes' Survival Techniques', *Variety* 419, 1 (May 2010), A4.

Kelly, Katherine E., 'Making the Bones Sing: The Feminist History Play, 1976–2010', *Theatre Journal* 62, 4 (December 2010), 645–60.

Lahr, John, 'Surreal Life: The Plays of Sarah Ruhl', *The New Yorker*, 17 March 2008, pp. 1–6.

—, 'Mouth to Mouth: Sarah Ruhl on Attraction and Artifice', *New Yorker* 87, 15 (May 2011), 84–5.

Malone, Roger, 'Review of *Eurydice*', *The Stage*, 25 March 2010, p. 19.

Schmidt, Heidi, '*In the Next Room (Or the Vibrator Play)*', *Theatre Journal* 62, 4 (December 2010), 669–70.

Sheward, David, 'Sarah Ruhl's *Passion Play*', *Back Stage*, 12 May 2010, p. 40.

Strahler, Amy, 'Auditory Traces: The Medium of the Telephone in Ariana Reines's *Telephone* and Sarah Ruhl's *Dead Man's Cell Phone*', *Contemporary Theatre Review* 21 (2011), 112–25.

Vogel, Paula, 'Sarah Ruhl', *Bomb* 99 (Spring 2007), 1–12. http://bombsite.com/issues/99/aricles/2902.

Weaver, Neal, 'The Clean House', *Back Stage*, 27 May 2010, pp. 46–7.

Notes

1. Paula Vogel, 'Sarah Ruhl', p. 7.
2. John Lahr, 'Surreal Life: The Plays of Sarah Ruhl', p. 5.
3. Ibid., p. 4.
4. Paula Vogel, 'Sarah Ruhl', p. 1.
5. Roger Malone, '*Eurydice*', p. 19.
6. John Lahr, 'Surreal Life', p. 15.
7. Paula Vogel, 'Sarah Ruhl', p. 9.
8. David Sheward, 'Sarah Ruhl's *Passion Play*', p. 40.
9. James Al-Shamma, 'Review of *Passion Play*', p. 262.
10. Paula Vogel, 'Sarah Ruhl', p. 11.
11. John Lahr, 'Surreal Life', p. 4.
12. Ibid., p. 4.
13. Paula Vogel, 'Sarah Ruhl', p. 11.
14. Heidi Schmidt, '*In the Next Room (Or the Vibrator Play)*', p. 669.
15. Katherine E. Kelly, 'Making the Bones Sing: The Feminist History Play, 1976–2010', p. 659.

16. Ibid., p. 658.
17. Ibid., pp. 658–9.
18. Heidi Schmidt, '*In the Next Room*', p. 669.
19. Robert Hofler, 'Scribes' Survival Techniques', p. A4.
20. Heidi Schmidt, '*In the Next Room*', p. 670.
21. Paula Vogel, 'Sarah Ruhl', p. 5.
22. John Lahr, 'Surreal Life', p. 4.
23. Paula Vogel, 'Sarah Ruhl', p. 5.

16 JOHN PATRICK SHANLEY

Annette J. Saddik

Danny and the Deep Blue Sea; the dreamer examines his pillow; Beggars in the House of Plenty; Doubt

Introduction

John Patrick Shanley is probably best known for his Academy Award-winning screenplay, *Moonstruck* (1987), starring Cher, Nicolas Cage and Olympia Dukakis, and his Pulitzer Prize-winning play, *Doubt: A Parable* (2004), which was made into a 2008 film. *Doubt* was Shanley's Broadway debut, and was first staged off-Broadway in 2004, winning the Obie (off-Broadway Theater Award), the Lucille Lortel Award, the New York Drama Critics' Circle Award and the Drama Desk Award. It transferred to Broadway in 2005, and went on to win the Tony Award for Best Play and the 2005 Pulitzer Prize for Drama. The film version of *Doubt* was written and directed by Shanley, earning him an Oscar nomination for Best Adapted Screenplay.

Shanley's screen directing debut in 1990, his film *Joe vs. the Volcano* starring Tom Hanks, Meg Ryan and Lloyd Bridges, was unsuccessful at the box office, but has since become a cult favourite, and remains the only film besides *Doubt* that he has directed. He received an Emmy nomination for *Live From Baghdad* (2002), a teleplay for HBO that he co-wrote. Although he has approximately 13 films and teleplays to his credit, Shanley began his career as a playwright during the late 1970s, and continues to have a distinguished career in the theatre with over 30 plays, several of which he has also directed. His most recent play, *Sleeping Demon*, deals with questions of 'the relationship between spiritual experience and social action', and centres on 'a Bronx Borough President who is forced by the mortgage crisis into a confrontation with a local minister'.[1] The play is the final instalment of a trilogy called

Church and State, which began with *Doubt* and continued with *Defiance* (2006), a play set on a United States Marine Corps base in North Carolina in 1971.

Born 13 October 1950 in the Bronx in New York City to an Irish-Catholic family, Shanley is the youngest of five children. His father was an Irish immigrant who worked as a meatpacker, and his mother, a native of Brooklyn and the daughter of Irish immigrants, was a telephone operator. He grew up in a predominantly working-class Irish-Italian neighbourhood; his early schooling was fraught with discipline issues, but with the help of a priest who believed in his intellectual potential, he finally graduated from a New Hampshire prep school that was affiliated with the Catholic Church, and attended New York University (NYU) in 1968. He dropped out of college during his first year, however, and went into the Marines. After his discharge, he returned to NYU in 1974 and graduated as class valedictorian in 1977. Shanley's own biographical sketch, which appears on the back of the published text of *Doubt,* is typical of his playful sense of humour when discussing his life's journey:

> John Patrick Shanley is from the Bronx. He was thrown out of St. Helena's kindergarten. He was banned from St. Anthony's hot lunch program for life. He was expelled from Cardinal Spellman High School. He was placed on academic probation by New York University and instructed to appear before a tribunal if he wished to return. When asked why he had been treated in this way by all these institutions, he burst into tears and said he had no idea. Then he went into the United States Marine Corps. He did fine. He's still doing okay.

Before winning the Oscar for *Moonstruck,* Shanley worked several jobs while supporting his writing – elevator operator, house painter, furniture mover, locksmith, bartender – but storytelling was the only job that suited him. Shanley currently resides in Manhattan; he has been married and divorced twice, and has two children, Frank and Nick, whom he adopted with his second wife, Jayne Haynes.

Shanley began his work as a playwright writing for the off-Broadway theatre with *Saturday Night at the War* (1978), a collection of one-act plays. In 1982, a collection of short playlets, *Welcome to the Moon,* was staged by the Ensemble Studio Theatre. Although watching the audience respond to this production was an epiphany for Shanley when he realized that what the audience wanted was 'the truth', the critical reception of the play was essentially negative. In a review of *Welcome to the Moon* in *The New York Times,* Frank Rich called Shanley's insights 'sophomoric', claiming that his characters 'blur together' and that 'by evening's end, the audience is bored silly'.[2] It was *Danny and the Deep Blue Sea: An Apache Dance*, staged by the Actors Theatre of Louisville and the Circle in the Square Theatre in New York City in 1984, that became Shanley's breakthrough play. Mel Gussow's review acknowledged Shanley's linguistic 'choreography', calling the play a 'self-described "Apache dance," a vicariously theatrical if artificial pas de deux'.[3] In the notes to *Danny and the Deep Blue Sea*, Shanley specifies that the play 'does not take place in a realistic world', yet it is nevertheless 'emotionally real'.[4] He does, however, dedicate the play to 'everyone in the Bronx who punched me or kissed me, and to everyone whom I punched or kissed' (a group he also thanked in his acceptance speech when he won the Oscar for *Moonstruck*), and the influence of his Bronx background continues to be a strong influence in Shanley's work.

The Plays

Danny and the Deep Blue Sea: An Apache Dance (1983)

After a staged reading for the National Playwrights Conference at the Eugene O'Neill Memorial Theatre Center in 1983, *Danny and the Deep Blue Sea* received its professional premiere at Actors Theatre of Louisville in February 1984, and its New York production at the Circle in the Square in June of that year, playing to standing ovations. It starred John Turturro and June Stein, and was directed by Barnet Kellman. The play also marked Shanley's London premiere, receiving a London production later in 1984 when it was included as part of the travelling arm of the Louisville Festival that showcased the best new American plays. In a review in *The New York Times*, Mel Gussow called the play 'a Bronx variation on "Beauty and the Beast"', and described it as 'a factitious fairy tale'.[5] This 'Beauty and the Beast' motif is evident in *Moonstruck* as well, and, interestingly, Shanley's original title for the film was *The Bride and the Beast*. Shanley describes *Danny and the Deep Blue Sea* as an 'Apache dance', which he defines in the production notes as 'a violent dance for two people, originated by the Parisian apaches. Parisian apaches are gangsters or ruffians' (p. 11). The characters verbally spar and joust throughout the play; for her role as Roberta, Stein acknowledged that the play was 'hugely demanding both physically and emotionally; we got on the horse and rode it hard'.[6]

The characters, 31-year-old Roberta, who is 'physically depleted, with nervous bright eyes', and 29-year-old Danny, who is 'dark and powerful' and 'finds it difficult to meet Roberta's gaze', are both 'violent and battered, inarticulate and yearning to speak, dangerous and vulnerable' (p. 11). As in several plays that were to follow, Shanley brings out the conflicting and contradictory aspects of human beings' imperfect search for love and understanding – sometimes tender, sometimes violent, always difficult. Gussow described the experience of seeing the play as 'the equivalent of sitting at ringside watching a prize fight that concludes in a loving embrace',[7] and indeed the aggressive and defensive aspects of the characters' courtship comes across, as two desperate souls meet in a bar and dance around complex issues of trust, vulnerability, self-loathing and hope, beginning to form an emotional connection. The main aspect of the play is its authentic emotional quality, as Shanley indicates that the play is 'emotionally real, but does not take place in a realistic world' (p. 11).

Both Danny and Roberta are emotionally and physically devastated, holding onto secrets and lies, and feeling unworthy of love or compassion; they come to the bar to avoid people, but realize throughout the course of their chance encounter that they need each other to heal. The play opens with Danny entering the bar and trying to engage Roberta in reluctant conversation; almost immediately, both acknowledge that they 'don't like people' (p. 12). Danny, who shows up at the bar badly bruised and with one of his cheeks cut, reveals himself as a lost and angry soul, compulsively getting into fights because 'people fuck with [him]' (p. 14). Roberta tells him that she is divorced with a kid and lives with her parents, a situation that drives her to scream 'For no reason at all', while Danny is similarly 'jumping out of [his] fuckin skin' (p. 16) because 'Everything hurts!' (p. 19). Both know they can't 'stay the way [they are]' for much longer (pp. 14; 21). Danny emphasizes his displacement and sense of alienation, telling Roberta that the guys he works with call him 'the Beast' (p. 26). He is distraught because he thinks he might have killed someone in a fight, and Roberta, a victim of incest, believes that she 'did something so awful. I ain't even gonna tell you what. If I told you, you wouldn't even look at me' (p. 19).

Dissatisfied and frustrated, the two reveal their secret pain to each other, wanting desperately to break through their defences and connect. Eventually, Roberta decides at the end of Scene I that they are 'gonna love each other' (p. 26) and takes Danny back to her room, which is decorated in 'slate blues and dove grays', with a 'doll, dressed as a bride' on one of the shelves – spare, but hopeful. They make love on a mattress on the floor, and, during the course of the night, they fall in love and engage in romantic fantasies. Even though they insist that they are unworthy of their romantic dreams, they decide to take a chance and get married, a decision Roberta denies the next morning as just a crazy dream that 'don't make no sense' (p. 49). Danny, however, desperate and persistent, convinces Roberta to let go of her defences and let it happen, since they deserve at least one beautiful day, 'a weddin day', and 'Just cause it don't make no sense don't mean it ain't true. If you want it' (p. 49).

Danny and the Deep Blue Sea deals with the destructive, and self-destructive, results of loneliness and social isolation and the surprising power of redemption. Initially, the bond between the characters is the sense of alienation, shame and displacement that they share. Ultimately, however, Danny and Roberta move through Shanley's intense, honest language towards the resurrective powers of compassion and understanding to take a leap of faith and find 'a home' (p. 26). The play was the first in what Shanley later described as a four-play cycle; it was followed by *Savage in Limbo* (1984), *the dreamer examines his pillow* (1985) and *Italian American Reconciliation* (1988).

the dreamer examines his pillow (1985)

Originally presented as a staged reading at the 1985 National Playwrights Conference at the Eugene O'Neill Memorial Theatre Center, *the dreamer examines his pillow* was first produced by the Double Image Theatre in New York City in October 1986. Like *Women of Manhattan* (1986), the play deals, in part, with acknowledging and accepting what it is we want rather than what we think we should want (particularly when it comes to romantic and sexual relationships), the defences we develop to protect ourselves from losing ourselves in a union with the other, and the legacy of how we learn to love, 'how to be intimate with another human being'.[8] The fantastic 'plot' centres on Donna, who begins the play by chastising her ex-lover, Tommy, for sleeping with her 16-year-old sister; Donna and Tommy are trapped in a love/hate relationship that ensures they cannot be together, yet cannot stay apart. For Shanley, 'punching and kissing' seem to be two sides of the same coin, and the underlying, or sometimes overt, violence inherent in intensely passionate relationships surrounds the play.

Questions that deal with the instability of identity also drive the play, leading Donna to seek out her father – whose first response is 'Oh no no no no no no. It's my daughter come to make me a parent' – to ask him some questions and 'find out a few things' about herself.[9] After some heated monologues about the power of sexual connection and the impulse to sabotage that intensity, Donna realizes that, in her relationship with Tommy, she is repeating her mother's role in her parents' marriage, and Dad explains that he treated her mother badly because she 'was the love of my life' and 'I hid part a me from her to save somethin cause I was scared' (p. 204). Eventually Dad realizes that, despite the pain of this 'total fuckin mess' (p. 218), Donna and Tommy are also in love. This 'friggin fairytale' (p. 197) then ends in what seems like 'a moment of madness' (p. 199), but one that fulfils the truth of their relationship. Dad takes charge and forces their marriage at the end of the play, insisting that 'You gotta make the big mistakes. . . . But remember, too, that Sex does resurrect. Flyin in the face of the truly great mistakes, there is that consolation' (p. 218).

Beggars in the House of Plenty (1991)

Shanley's most directly autobiographical play, *Beggars in the House of Plenty* was first produced in 1991 by the Manhattan Theatre Club. The fragmentary staging and shifts in time are decidedly non-realistic; Robert Coe calls the play 'arguably his most successful work employing surrealistic elements, while also breaking from his usual intense dramatic focus to explore a more studied irony'.[10] The characters include an undisguised portrait of the artist as a young man named Johnny (played by an adult actor who represents the character from age 5 to 18), Ma, Pop, siblings Sheila and Joey, and Sister Mary Kate. The children are all begging for love in one way or another, yet their pleas seem to get lost in the spaces between language, and the dialogue is disjointed and disconnected.

The loosely constructed plot opens with Johnny beginning to tell the story of his youth to the audience, explaining how he 'discovered fire' when he was 'one, two, three, four, five freakin years' old, as he strikes a match, smiling. Rightaway we are thrown into the strange and chaotic idiosyncrasies of this family dynamic.[11] Joey, who is 'young, handsome, healthy as a dog' (p. 325), arrives home from the Navy for sister Sheila's wedding day, while Ma constantly complains of headaches and Pop is alternately threatening and berating his children. Johnny's sense of being trapped in an irrational nightmare sets the tone of the play, as he ironically announces that 'There's something fake about all this' (p. 324). The world of the play is indeed violent and surreal, and yet there is a sense that, emotionally, the play is realistic at its core. Johnny's acknowledgement that he is isolated in his rationality to the point of being invisible emerges in the moments where he pleads 'Can anybody hear me? . . . you better start payin attention to me!' (pp. 334–5). Time is not stable, and Pop predicts Joey's emotional future, telling him that 'You'll look for love to stop the starving thing in you that I put there, but nothing will stop the starving thing. I'll never approve of you' (p. 530).

Coe argues that this play is 'about how some siblings make it and others don't',[12] and while Johnny realizes that his salvation arrived when he learnt to substitute creativity for destruction – 'It's just very rare that

285

I start a fire now. . . . Now I have language . . . *at my disposal* (p. 339) – his brother is killed by his father at the end of the play, a literalization of his emotional violence. The ending serves as a rather direct catharsis with Johnny's final words:

> I will say this one thing more, my friends, and then I am through with this subject. My parents loved each other. How I do not know. We were alone. . . . Now I am some kind of man. I live in a city where it is difficult to survive. Nothing is new. Some of us walk. Some of us are lying on the ground. (*He strikes the match.*) When I was one, two, twenty, forty years of my life, I stopped to grieve for my fallen brothers (p. 370).[13]

Doubt: A Parable (2004)

Doubt, Shanley's only Broadway play to date, received its world premiere at Manhattan Theatre Club on 23 November 2004. It transferred to Broadway's Walter Kerr Theatre, where it opened on 31 March 2005. The play was directed by Doug Hughes, with Brían F. O'Byrne as Father Flynn; Cherry Jones as Sister Aloysius; Heather Goldenhersh as Sister James; and Adriane Lenox as Mrs Muller. With this play, Shanley felt that he was taking a different step in his writing: 'It's less about language and me as a writer, more about the plot, what these characters are going through and what questions that engenders in the audience'.[13]

Set in a Catholic church/school in a predominantly Irish and Italian working-class neighbourhood in the Bronx in 1964, the plot of *Doubt,* which involves a nun's quest to expose a priest's possible sexual involvement with a child, was inspired by the experience of one of Shanley's relatives who was molested by a priest. After the family went up the chain of command to a high-ranking Church official and was assured that the situation would be dealt with, the priest was promoted, and the family, shocked and disappointed with the results, left the Church for 10 years. When they decided to return and give it another chance, a monsignor at their parish gave a speech blaming parents, rather than the clergy, for the increasing molestation scandals, and the family left the Church once again in disappointment.[14] Later, when the Church scandals were becoming more widely known, Shanley realized that it was the nuns who were, in many cases, discovering what was happening; given the Church hierarchy, however, these women had to go through a formal chain of command, which often led nowhere but to cover-ups, a situation he saw as creating 'very powerful frustrations and moral dilemmas for these women'.[15] Yet Shanley's inspiration for the play came not only from these observations, but from his insights that, in America, 'debate has become the form of communication. . . . There is no room or value placed on doubt, which is one of the hallmarks of the wise man'.[16]

One of the related issues surrounding Shanley's respect for doubt comes out of his own experience. After a difficult time in the educational system, he thrived at the Church-affiliated Thomas Moore Preparatory School in New Hampshire, where he experienced the kindness of many caring teachers. Although he does acknowledge that they may have had ulterior motives for taking an interest in his progress, he asserts that there was never any sexual impropriety in his case. Shanley told *The New York Times* in 2004 that

> It was homosexual teachers for the most part who saved me. . . . The head of discipline at Thomas Moore was gay, and he was my friend and protector. Did he have his reasons for being interested in me? Everybody has their reasons. Passion fuels many things, and it's used in many ways. Many of these people never cross the line.[17]

In an interview in 2010, Shanley stated that at his high school reunion some students revealed to him that this particular teacher was 'a predator'. Since Shanley himself was never molested, he concludes that his particular experience with this man was a beneficial one, and yet the situation is not so clear-cut.[18] The complex questions of character, human motivation and the line between thought and action, particularly relevant in Catholic theology, defy neat categorization, and doubt is what we are left with. In an interview in the *Houston Chronicle*, Shanley remarked that 'The play's not so much about the scandal itself, but the philosophical power in embracing doubt . . . . If I'm proselytizing at all, it's to say, "Live with it, brother. Doubt is part of life"'.[19]

Shanley's observation that 'Everybody has their reasons' is echoed in *Doubt* by Mrs Muller in a conversation with the school principal, Sister Aloysius, about her son, Donald. After being called to the school to discuss her son, Mrs Muller notices that Sister Aloysius appears to be 'on the march'[20] to destroy Father Flynn, a progressive and friendly priest who has taken an interest in protecting Donald, a new student who is particularly vulnerable as the first and only African American child in the school during a changing racial climate, a time when 'the whole world seemed to be going through some kind of puberty'.[21] Sister Aloysius reveals her suspicions to Mrs Muller that Father Flynn's interest in her 12-year-old son may not be entirely professional. Mrs Muller, who is primarily concerned that Donald receive a good education so that he can get into a good high school and have more opportunities for college, insists that whatever the problem is, 'it's just till June' (p. 45). When she learns that Sister Aloysius has no proof of her suspicions, she is frustrated that Sister Aloysius is dragging her son into a situation that could interfere with his education and, even worse, could get him into trouble at home with her husband, a man who beats, and may one day kill, his son because he suspects he has homosexual tendencies. His parents' suspicion that Donald's 'nature' may simply be 'that way' (p. 48) adds another dimension to the conversation, as Mrs Muller implies that a sexually-charged relationship may not in fact be coerced or damaging, even though Donald is an adolescent. She is desperate to have Donald 'take the good and leave the rest' (p. 48) when he leaves the school in June, and finally tells Sister Aloysius to not exacerbate the situation:

> Things are in the air and you leave them alone if you can. That's what I know. My boy came to this school 'cause they were gonna kill him at the public school. So we were lucky enough to get him in here for his last year. Good. His father don't like him. He comes here, the kids don't like him. One man is good to him. This priest. Puts out a hand to the boy. Does the man have his reasons? Yes. Everybody has their reasons. *You* have your reasons. But do I ask the man why he's good to my son? No. I don't care why. My son needs some man to care about

him and see him through to where he wants to go. And thank God, this educated man with some kindness in him wants to do just that. (p. 49)

Mrs Muller continues to insist that 'Sometimes things aren't black and white' (p. 49).

For Sister Aloysius, however, things are precisely black and white, and doubt has no place in her agenda. Having no concrete evidence, her suspicions rest on a particular interpretation of actions that could be read in several ways, and her crusade is primarily driven by her conviction, which is fuelled by past experience. She is determined to get Father Flynn thrown out of the school, but, as a woman, is below him in the Church hierarchy, and is not permitted to accuse him directly. She enlists the aid of a young new teacher, Sister James, who is generous and kind, but slightly naive. While Sister James wants to believe in Father Flynn's innocence, she also wants to protect the students, and is pulled into Sister Aloysius' manipulations.

One prominent theme in the play involves the changing society and a clash between the old and the new ways of thinking and behaving. While neither view is necessarily given preference in the play, there is a suggestion that Sister Aloysius is trying to hold on to a way of doing things that is slipping away with the changing times, and her distrust of the more progressive Father Flynn is not unrelated to her distrust of modernization and her need to maintain control. Fundamentally, Sister Aloysius is 'old-fashioned' in her ideas of discipline and the role of the Church. She believes, first of all, that the clergy should not befriend the families in their parish and appear to be 'members of their family rather than emissaries from Rome', as Father Flynn proposes, but insists that they maintain a distance, claiming that 'The working-class people of this parish trust us to be different' (p. 30). Both Father Flynn and Sister James reject the harsh disciplinarian style of dealing with students, and can be seen as representatives of a younger generation and a changing Church during the 1960s that believed in relaxing strict doctrine in order to appeal to a wider group and teach with kindness, rather than threats of punishment. Sister James, however, as a new teacher and a woman, is under Sister Aloysius' control, unlike Father Flynn. Sister Aloysius objects to Sister James' teaching style on the basis that she shows too much 'enthusiasm' (p. 10) and is naively trusting of the students' motives, and she is appalled at the suggestion of Father Flynn and Sister James that the school introduce secular songs into the Christmas pageant. She resists any attempt at modernization, believing that ballpoint pens are the 'easy way out' (p. 9) and make the students 'press down, and when they press down, they write like monkeys' (p. 10). Father Flynn, who uses a ballpoint pen in her presence, keeps his nails long, and asks for three lumps of sugar in his tea, is the quintessence of a kind of casual attitude and self-indulgence that, in her mind, indicates a slippery slope to the sexual molestation of a child.

The philosophical themes in this play revolve around the power of language and its role in constructing truth; issues of interpretation and understanding; the epistemological questions concerning the meaning of knowledge; and the relationship between power and truth. Sister Aloysius claims that she 'must be careful not to create something by saying it', yet she does precisely that (p. 15). In a warning sermon on the dangers of gossip, Father Flynn tells the story of a woman who was afraid that her gossiping was a sin, and so went to her priest for council. He advised her to 'go home, take a pillow up on your roof, cut it open with a knife, and return here to me!' When she returned, explaining that the result was 'Feathers everywhere', he instructed her to 'go back and gather up every last feather that flew out on the wind!' She replies, of course, that this cannot be done, as she doesn't know where they went, 'The wind took them all over'. That, precisely, the priest explains, is gossip (pp. 36–7). When Sister James asks Father Flynn if he made up the story of the pillow, he responds by explaining 'Yes. You make up little stories to illustrate. In the tradition of the parable' (p. 38). Language, let loose, is a profound and uncontrollable force, and can create truth, regardless of the actual circumstances or facts.

Sister Aloysius' power in the play is also her tragic flaw: she has her conviction, her 'certainty' (p. 54), which is based on her prior experience and her own perceptions, rather than on any concrete evidence. What she 'knows' is based on her emotions, her beliefs, yet it may not be without merit. As Father Flynn tries to reason with her, he tells her that 'there are circumstances beyond your knowledge. Even if you feel certainty, it is an emotion, and not a fact' (p. 55). In the end, she tricks Father Flynn into a corner, telling him that she called a nun at his former parish, and suggests that she has evidence that will expose him. She threatens to destroy his reputation throughout the parish unless he resigns. She made no such call, however, and yet Father Flynn has his reasons for not wanting to challenge her. He admits to a transgression in his past, although we do not know the specifics. Finally, Father Flynn speaks to the bishop, who handles the situation by promoting Father Flynn to the position of pastor at another school. Therefore, in one sense, Sister Aloysius' truth prevails, as Father Flynn is removed from the school, which is what she wanted; on the other hand, the bishop does not believe Sister Aloysius (or decides to cover up the allegations) and promotes Father Flynn, so *his* truth can be seen as prevailing.

In this play, truth becomes a game that is connected to power, power that can either stem from surreptitious manipulation or from more formal institutional hierarchies. We never know whether Father Flynn was guilty of sexual misconduct with Donald, or perhaps with other boys in the past, or if there was some unrelated transgression in his past and he simply did not want Sister Aloysius casting doubt on his reputation through her accusations. Ultimately, the audience is left with doubt and unanswered questions, and the play ends with even the self-assured Sister Aloysius announcing to Sister James that she has 'such doubts!' (p. 58) Whether these are doubts concerning Father Flynn's guilt, about whether she has done the right thing, about the efficacy of the Church hierarchy or about the world that is changing all around her, is a question left to the audience's own interpretations.

Summary

The themes in Shanley's plays, particularly his earlier ones, often revolve around the difficulties of human relationships and the frustrations of communication, illustrating the complexities of emotional attachments through the plight of damaged souls searching for love and understanding. They address the tensions surrounding a desperate need to connect, countered by an inability to connect, or at least a lack of understanding concerning how to forge meaningful and functional relationships in a cold and confusing world. Yet these plays are wonderfully full of unsentimental (albeit bizarre and surprising) hope in their optimism that we can discover who we are and simply forge ahead to embrace life, finding moments of connection along the way. Playing with the boundaries between realistic and non-realistic representation, Shanley's titles are often tagged with descriptive subtitles that resist and blur the boundaries of style: *Danny and the Deep Blue Sea: An Apache Dance; Savage in Limbo: A Concert Play; Women of Manhattan: An Upper West Side Story; Italian American Reconciliation: A Folktale; The Big Funk: A Casual Play; Doubt: A Parable.* His plays are therefore often allegorical, presenting lessons that illustrate the essential truth(s) under the surface.

While in some of the early plays Shanley's characters might seem undifferentiated, reciting dialogue that resembles a therapy session or philosophical musings that take on explorations of life, love and human motivation, they often break through this to profound insights and powerful dramatic moments. In 1988, Craig Gholson described Shanley's style in the following way:

> Shanley chooses characters stretched to the breaking point between rage and love; characters whose dramatic arc begins by being afraid and moves towards a bravery and an exploration of personal courage usually signaled by the confession, "I'm scared. I love you". His are characters of obsessive passions who match those passions with hyper-melodic language.[22]

Dan Bacalzo has remarked that 'There is a consciousness to [Shanley's] style that cuts to the core of a character's emotions', pointing out that his use of language has been referred to as 'taut', 'muscular', and 'incendiary'.[23] Shanley's language is undeniably packed with emotion and aggressive truths, but in *Sailor's Song* (2005), written following a difficult 18-month period during which Shanley's father, mother and sister all died, language is subordinated to music and dance. In this play Shanley goes beyond the metaphorical dance of words and actions that characterized *Danny and the Deep Blue Sea,* more literally relying on non-rational expression. *Sailor's Song* is a philosophical and emotional piece that is more concerned with painting an image than telling a linear story, embracing a style and tone that led Charles McNulty of the *Village Voice* to write that 'the quirky piece fearlessly streaks its emotions across the stage'.[24]

At times, the tensions in Shanley's plays lead to an examination of the most primal and irrational psychological depths, particularly where sexual relationships are concerned. In *Psychopathia Sexualis* (1996), sexual fetishism is presented with humour and playful irony, and yet his explorations of unconscious desire in plays such as *the dreamer examines his pillow*, which honours the awesome power of sexual connection and examines the influence of the legacies we inherit in learning to forge romantic relationships, and *Where's My Money?* (2001), a sardonic account of the relationship between money, marriage and sex, take on a darker tone, touching on sadomasochism and the delusions of romantic connection. In *Dirty Story* (2003), an allegory written in response to the 11 September 2001 attacks, Shanley expands the sadomasochistic theme from the personal to the political sphere with regard to the Israeli-Palestinian conflict in the Middle East, and the result is an off-beat, yet powerfully balanced, exploration that is both disturbing and illuminating.

In his more recent plays of the new millennium, Shanley seems less concerned with closely examining personal issues, and has expanded to dealing more broadly with larger social issues. In 2004 he told Coe:

> I always said that if things went well I would spend the first half of my life writing about my problems, and the second half I would write about other people's problems, and that's sort of what happened—I'm able now to start turning *out*. Maybe that's why I was able to write *Doubt*, and why I was able to write *Dirty Story*. Of course they're personal plays, but they are about larger social concerns.[25]

Like *Doubt*, Shanley's 2006 play *Defiance* – his latest produced play to date – explores the relationships among power, loyalty and responsibility; both plays deal with issues surrounding the cost of doing the right thing, while realizing that we can never be completely sure what that is. In *Defiance*, however, the hierarchy is that of the military rather than the Church. Thematically, it fuses the personal explorations of identity that occupied much of Shanley's earlier work with the larger social questions of his later, more plot-driven plays; it moves from the necessity of finding out who we are and what we want, to deciding what is it we stand for and the imperative of acting on our beliefs.

Overall, however, whether he is addressing the social or the personal realm, epistemological inquiry remains, at some level, at the centre of Shanley's work: What do we really know about ourselves, each other, human motivations, our social institutions, and this thing called life in general? And how do we know, or think we know, these things? Finding specific answers is ultimately not the most important part of this journey. Rather, Shanley's work illustrates the need to begin to ask and explore the questions, then allow things to run their course. And, in the process, we must learn to accept an inevitable measure of doubt.

Primary Sources

Works by John Patrick Shanley

13 By Shanley: Collected Plays, Volume I (Danny and the Deep Blue Sea; Welcome to the Moon and Other Plays ["The Red Coat"; "Down and Out"; "Let Us Go Out Into the Starry Night"; "Out West"; "A Lonely Impulse of Delight"; "Welcome to the Moon"]*; Savage in Limbo; Women of Manhattan; the dreamer examines his pillow; An Italian American Reconciliation; The Big Funk, Beggars in the House of Plenty)* (New York: Applause Books, 1992).

Dirty Story and Other Plays (Dirty Story; Where's My Money?; Sailor's Song) (New York: Theatre Communications Group, 2007).

Doubt: A Parable (New York: Theatre Communications Group, 2005).

Psychopathia Sexualis (New York: Dramatists Play Service, 1998).

Romantic Poetry (New York: Dramatists Play Service, 2009).

Secondary Sources

Bacalzo, Dan, 'John Patrick Shanley'. In Garrett Eisler (ed.), *Dictionary of Literary Biography: Twentieth-Century American Dramatists, Fifth Series*(Detroit: Gale, 2008), pp. 191–9.

Coe, Robert, 'The Evolution of John Patrick Shanley', *American Theatre*, November 2004.

Evans, Everett, 'Shanley's award-winning play is opening doors: Basking in the shadow of a Doubt', *Houston Chronicle*, 22 May 2005.

Gholson, Craig, 'John Patrick Shanley', *BOMB Magazine* 24 (Summer 1988).

Gussow, Mel, 'Stage: "Danny and the Deep Blue Sea"', *The New York Times*, 8 June 1984.

McNulty, Charles, 'Ethnic Blending', *The Village Voice*, 9 November 2004.

Rich, Frank, 'The Stage: "Welcome to the Moon"', *The New York Times*, 24 November 1982.

Rightmyer, Jack, 'An Interview with John Patrick Shanley', *Writers Online Magazine* 15, 2 (Spring 2011).

Stein, June, 'John Turturro', *BOMB Magazine* Vol. 99 (Spring 2007).

Weber, Bruce, 'Shaky Marriages Sunk by Emotional Baggage', *The New York Times*, 12 November 2001.

Witchel, Alex, 'The Confessions of John Patrick Shanley', *The New York Times*, 7 November 2004.

Notes

1. Atlantic Theater Company 2011–12 season brochure.
2. Frank Rich, 'The Stage: "Welcome to the Moon"'.
3. Mel Gussow, 'Stage: "Danny and the Deep Blue Sea"'.
4. John Patrick Shanley, *Danny and the Deep Blue Sea: An Apache Dance*, in: *13 By Shanley*, p. 11. Subsequent references to the play will be cited parenthetically in the text.
5. Mel Gussow, 'Stage: "Danny and the Deep Blue Sea"'.
6. June Stein, 'John Turturro'.
7. Mel Gussow, 'Stage: "Danny and the Deep Blue Sea"'.
8. John Patrick Shanley, qtd. In: Robert Coe, 'The Evolution of John Patrick Shanley'.
9. John Patrick Shanley, *the dreamer examines his pillow*, in: *13 By* Shanley, p. 201. Subsequent references to the play will be cited parenthetically in the text.
10. Robert Coe, 'The Evolution of John Patrick Shanley'.
11. John Patrick Shanley, *Beggars in the House of Plenty*, in: *13 By Shanley*, p. 319. Subsequent references to the play will be cited parenthetically in the text.
12. Robert Coe, 'The Evolution of John Patrick Shanley'.
13. Everett Evans, 'Shanley's award-winning play is opening doors'.
14. Alex Witchel, 'The Confessions of John Patrick Shanley'; Robert Coe, 'The Evolution of John Patrick Shanley'.
15. Robert Coe, 'The Evolution of John Patrick Shanley'.
16. Alex Witchel, 'The Confessions of John Patrick Shanley'.
17. Ibid.
18. John Patrick Shanley, Interviewed by Thomas Keith at the Tennessee Williams/New Orleans Literary Festival (26 March 2010).

19. Everett Evans, 'Shanley's award-winning play is opening doors'.
20. John Patrick Shanley, *Doubt: A Parable*, p. 46. Subsequent references to the play will be cited parenthetically in the text.
21. John Patrick Shanley, Preface to *Doubt: A Parable*, p. viii.
22. Craig Gholson, 'John Patrick Shanley'.
23. Dan Bacalzo, 'John Patrick Shanley', p. 192.
24. Charles McNulty, 'Ethnic Blending'.
25. Robert Coe, 'The Evolution of John Patrick Shanley'.

17 WALLACE SHAWN

Martin Middeke

A Thought in Three Parts; Marie and Bruce; Aunt Dan and Lemon; The Fever; The Designated Mourner; Grasses of a Thousand Colours

Introduction

Wallace Shawn belongs to the most controversial, most experimental and most underrated playwrights of contemporary American drama. Many people do not even know about his career as a playwright, but know him primarily as an actor both for the screen and for the stage. The International Movie Database records 150 titles over more than 30 years. Cinema aficionados around the world recall art-house films such as *My Dinner With André* (1991, dir. Louis Malle), which Shawn co-wrote and acted in with his long-term collaborator André Gregory, or *Vanya on 42nd Street* (1994), an adaptation of Chekhov's *Uncle Vanya*. He translated Niccolò Macchiavelli's 1518 play *La Mandragola* (*The Mandrake*, 1978); most recently, he translated Henrik Ibsen's *The Master Builder* (1892) into English for a new film project tentatively named *Wally and André Shoot Ibsen* (2013, dir. Jonathan Demme).[1]

Wallace Shawn was born in New York City on 12 November 1943 as the son of William Shawn, the famous editor-in-chief of *The New Yorker*. He graduated from Harvard in 1965 and also holds degrees from Magdalen College, Oxford. His wealthy family background had Shawn surrounded by high-class literature, and his very few remarks about aesthetic influences mention, for instance, Maeterlinck, Strindberg, Beckett, Chekhov, Wilder, O'Neill and Robert Wilson.[2] As regards his 'preoccupation with the subject of sex', Shawn points to authors such as James Joyce and D. H. Lawrence, whose overt treatment of sexuality has succeeded in 'expanding the scope of literature and redrawing humanity's picture'.[3]

Shawn's work as a writer for the theatre started as far back as the 1960s when he was still at university. Until his first produced play, *Our Late Night* (1975), he had already written several plays that remained unpublished.[4] Since the late 1970s, Wallace Shawn has had his biggest successes in England; the Royal Court Theatre premiered most of his work up to the present. In May and June 2009, the Royal Court used the opportunity of the world premiere of *Grasses of a Thousand Colours* for a comprehensive retrospective of Shawn's work. In 1975 and 1986, Shawn was awarded Obie Awards for (Distinguished) Playwriting (*Our Late Night* and *Aunt Dan and Lemon*), and in 1991, *The Fever* earned him another Obie for the Best New American Play.

The Plays

A Thought in Three Parts (1977)

A Thought in Three Parts was premiered in London on 28 February 1977, and it was performed by the Joint Stock Theatre Company at the Institute of Contemporary Arts (ICA). Previously, the play had only seen a workshop run at the New York Shakespeare Festival, when the artistic director Joseph Papp decided to close it after devastating reviews. In England, it also caused a scandal even though censorship had come down in 1968. A vice squad was sent into a performance, and there were calls in the House of Lords to stop government funding for the ICA.

The play has a tripartite structure. 'Summer Evening' introduces David and Sarah, whom we encounter in a hotel room in a foreign country. Throughout the play the frantic speed of their speech and often overlapping dialogue indicate their disturbed communication. It is only through their asides and monologues that we become aware of their unquenched desires. Their prison-house of simulacra – clothes, hotels, drinks, food – can only momentarily be escaped by violent fantasies of transgression and excess. Sarah says she would 'stick a hot poker up my ass if I thought I would like it' (p. 14) and excels in dreams of boundless unconstraint: 'If I needed to pee I would pee in my bed, and my feet would get pretty wet in my bed' (p. 9); David, after pointing to the affinities of love and hate, has violent fantasies about her death.

Whereas 'Summer Evening' focuses on paralysis and *in*action, 'The Youth Hostel' – the notorious second part of the play and the bone of contention of the theatrical scandals in New York and London – features an overkill of sexual action. There are five youths in two separate rooms; the whole scenery is a farcically exaggerated chain of sexual intercourses, masturbation scenes and orgasms – a grotesque parody of both post-1968 sexual liberation, promiscuity and porn movies. What looks like a hedonistic, playful orchestration of casual sex just as well resembles regressive displacement and vacuum-activities driven by boredom and ennui.

The atmosphere of cold isolation is enhanced in the last part of the play, 'Mr Frivolous', a monologue by a man in his early thirties. Similar to the much older Krapp in Beckett's *Krapp's Last Tape*, freedom, lightheartedness, love and a momentary sense of belonging appear only as faint memories while the speaker is lying naked in his room imagining to be 'pulled, and looted, and ripped . . . , painted, like a placard, with . . . lipstick on my back, my legs, my ass, my asshole' (p. 53). The common denominator of these scenes, the eponymous thought behind the three parts, is the controversy between the absence as well as the thirst for a complete well-being in love, and Shawn 'forces us to pay attention to the workings of an argument by stripping his play of all the trappings of "theatre"'.[5]

Marie and Bruce (1979)

Marie and Bruce was first performed in the Theatre Upstairs at the Royal Court Theatre, London, on 13 July 1979. In the United States the play was premiered in the Newman Theatre at the Public Theatre in New York on 8 January 1980.

Marie and Bruce is another dark and 'morbidly entertaining'[6] look at love and marriage and continues the character constellation of *Our Late Night* and 'Summer Party'. From the first sentence of the play, in which Marie directly speaks to the audience, we witness a marriage in crisis: 'I'm fed *up* with this God damned fucking incredible pig' (p. 62). Marie's poison-tongued tirades, accusations and scoldings are encountered by merely passive, emotional distance from her husband, who seems either indifferent or well used to the routine of Mary's verbal abuses.

Again and again, slices of the conversations and, hence, dramatic immediacy are intercut and suspended by longer monologue passages, which not only give insight into the stream of consciousness of the respective speaker, but also bridge gaps of time in between the impressionist stations of a single day. The monologue passages diversify the tone of Marie's voice into a 'shocking range . . . from the ferociously profane to the lyrical and dreamlike'.[7] Marie remembers getting ready for an evening party at a friend's. On the way to the party, she is followed by a dog and falls asleep in a garden only to be woken up by a violent fantasy when 'a powerful impulse to have intercourse with the dog, a male, made my heart pound rapidly and my face flush hotly with blood' (p. 70). In a similar monologue Bruce speaks about his day before the party and his failure to masturbate in a hotel room when he is watching a woman cleaning her apartment in an opposite building, who eventually is getting undressed. The more gentle, hallucinatory tone of these monologue passages reveals the fragility, vulnerability and loneliness deep down in both characters. When both finally reach the party, the conversation of the party guests functions as filters through which the outside world reaches into their relationship. They leave the party and go to a restaurant, but eat in silence (p. 88). Even Marie's culminating provocation 'I never loved you. I never loved you' (p. 89) leaves Bruce entirely unperturbed. Marie brings Bruce home, makes him hot milk and puts him to bed. Like Joyce's Molly Bloom, she is a mother/wife figure, lost in her thoughts, finally falling asleep. The marriage, however, will relentlessly go on, making Shawn's play a disillusioning yet moving articulation of 'alienation, frustration, and angst of contemporary urban relationships'.[8]

Aunt Dan and Lemon (1985)

Aunt Dan and Lemon is Shawn's most successful and certainly most controversially reviewed play to this date. It marks a considerable change in Shawn's work, a shift to the more openly political, a definite turn towards reality and its correlation to the fictive and imaginary. Critics like Gaylord Brewer have pointed out that the turning point that procured this change was Shawn's film script for *My Dinner With André* (1980), which juxtaposes clashing ideas such as real-life orientation and meta-dramatic, meta-theatrical and aesthetic reflection.[9]

The play begins with a narrator addressing the audience. The narrator is Leonora, who since childhood has been called 'Lemon' by Danielle, a friend of her parents, whom she fondly remembers as 'Aunt Dan'. Of all of Shawn's, for the most part unreliable, narrators, Lemon is the most unreliable one. Identifying Lemon as unreliable both on the basis of her moral stance (as she clearly argues against all humanist common sense) as well as her restricted view (as all first-person narratives are restricted) prevents us from confusing her perspective with Shawn's own. In fact, it is the very point of unreliable narration not to fully and directly reveal the narrator's unreliability, but only to hint at it and to leave the readers to wonder how much the narrator should be trusted.

The play is set in London; Lemon is born in 1960 – thus, at the time when her narrative starts and she begins reflecting back on her past, she must be in her mid-twenties. She is weak and sick, apparently anorexic, as she can neither eat nor keep any food in her. The play opens and ends on two long monologues by Lemon; the present moment of this narrative frame is interspersed with different layers of interlacing memories – partly, again, in the form of monologues, partly in dialogue sequences (the Mindy episodes and diverse conversations between her parents and Aunt Dan) that flash back to different stages of her life and touch on key events that provide a fragmented storyline.[10]

In the opening monologue Lemon briefly reports about her family history and very casually mentions her bedtime readings that used to be 'mysteries' and 'detective novels' that she has nowadays discarded and replaced by 'reading about the Nazi killing of the Jews instead' (pp. 103–4). The very casualness by which she makes this transition, the shocking thriller description of how effective the Nazis had been in Treblinka, and her conclusion that the Nazis were 'certainly successful against the Jews' (p. 105) finish off her reliability right from the start of the play. Her deluded perspective is enhanced by her general indifference to the outside world; she does not listen to the radio, watches neither TV nor the news, does not read the newspapers, has no visitors, but spends most of her time 'just staring into space' (p. 105). Her behaviour has a prehistory that her memories highlight episodically: An American father, who tries to gain a foothold in England with his work ethic of performance at all costs; a weak mother who cannot even momentarily come out on top of either her husband or Aunt Dan. After Lemon has realized that her mother is a harmless 'saint', and her father 'a caged animal', whose 'teeth were rotten, his shit was rotten, and of course he stank. He stank to hell' (p. 111), Aunt Dan, in fact, takes over her education and, as it turns out, her misguidance and corruption. Aunt Dan – who 'resembles Muriel Spark's fictional teacher, Jean Brodie, a Pied Piper who advocates self-fulfillment'[11] – was 'one of the youngest Americans ever to teach at Oxford' (p. 116) and, for Lemon, represents everything that her parents are not. Dan's freethinking individuality cannot save her from almost reactionary political and moral disorientation, though. She holds a brutal Social Darwinist stance towards a just distribution of wealth and privilege, she adores Henry Kissinger and downplays his responsibility for the atrocities in the Vietnam War basically by saying that 'he was doing his job' – an argument boiling down to such realpolitik morals as 'you can't make an omelet without breaking eggs'. In much the same vein, Dan backs and literally excuses her sidekick and lover Mindy's frauds and even Mindy's murder of one of her 'clients'.

What is at issue here is what Hannah Ahrendt once notoriously phrased as the 'banality of evil'. It is exactly this 'banality of evil' which ultimately explains Lemon's completely deluded equation of the killing of Indians, Jews and cockroaches in her final monologue. It seems useful to recall that it was Shawn's father, William Shawn, who sent Hannah Arendt to Jerusalem to report on the Eichmann trial in Jerusalem for *The New Yorker*. Ahrendt readily accepted the mission and was taken aback by whom she met, who was, so it seemed to Ahrendt, no monster, no Richard III, but an ash-grey bureaucrat, a thoughtless and obscenely common executor, a tomfool, a morally deformed human being without imagination. But – I need to emphasize this from hindsight – Ahrendt was mistaken; in fact, she was (like everyone else in the courtroom) blinded and fooled by the show Eichmann put on to appear as a mere receiver of orders, when in fact – as the Sassen interview sufficiently proves – he had a destructively active and devilishly creative hand in the Holocaust.

Hence, when Wallace Shawn confronts us with such an alleged 'banality of evil', he seeks to prevent us from making the same mistakes twice. The unreliable narration *implies* the appeal to *contradict* the narrator: Whenever Lemon says 'we' instead of 'I' – as she crudely diagnoses that, for instance, 'an enjoyment of killing is in *us*' [my emphasis] (p. 153) – readers and audiences are meant to resist and to withstand such engrossing rhetoric.[12] Ahrendt was misled by Eichmann, Lemon is misled by Aunt Dan, we are not to be misled by either of them, but to identify rather than trivialize evil and, most of all, to see through the seductive, rhetorical mechanisms of such community building – no matter how seemingly well-crafted an argument is. The narrator, as has been shown, is not to be trusted because the more Lemon denies the significance of 'compassion' (p. 154), the more humanist compassion is exactly restored by the distance Shawn creates in between the narrator, her narrative and its reception. Thus, some critics' accusations that *the play* would rationalize the Holocaust, quite simply, seem absurd.[13] Shawn turns out a 'master of emotional syllogism'[14] in an important play, which is aesthetically complex and subversively ethical.

The Fever (1990)

'Compassion' is also a central theme in Shawn's beautiful and 'dazzling monologue'[15] *The Fever*, which pushes dramatic form to its limits. Like Samuel Beckett's later works, the script dissolves clear-cut boundaries between drama and prose fiction. Unlike Beckett's aesthetic minimalism, though, Shawn's self-reflection is ostensibly grounded in real life. 'I'm unable to totally forget the world', he asserts, 'but I still haven't (yet) become a compassionate enough person to leave my bed for more than a moment in or to devote myself to changing the world or alleviating the suffering of my fellow human beings'.[16] *The Fever* was first performed by Shawn himself in January 1990 in an 7th Avenue apartment in New York City. Before the monologue transferred to the Public Theater, it saw 70 more living room performances. The play has been revived many times both in London and in New York and was turned into a film (2004), starring Vanessa Redgrave.

 The play is set in an unnamed, presumably Latin American country, and a nameless speaker – who may either be a man or a woman (as, for instance, in the 1999 London production at the Almeida Theatre, in the 2012 revival at the LaMaMa in New York, or in the film version) – reflects upon his/her privileged upper-class life, the utter self-righteousness and complacency of the rich in the face of injustice, torture, unfair distribution of wealth, education and opportunities, and the destitution of the masses of the poor. Performing this monologue in cozy apartments was one attempt in 'theatrical conscience-baiting',[17] as was the sarcastic champagne reception preceding the 2007 production of *The Fever* at the Acorn Theatre in New York. The reaction to this confrontation has always been mixed: 'You'll never pass another homeless beggar in the streets of London', Lyn Garner wrote in 1991, 'without questioning why you have the money in your pocket and they don't'.[18] In contrast, Nicholas de Jongh abominated 'this narcissistic form of liberal conscience that parades its guilt with rapt self-absorption, pretending it gives us food for thought'.[19] For Benedict Nightingale the speaker is 'the Ancient Mariner at the feast, the puritan in the posh pulpit, the angry flagellant who aims his whip at all the privileged including himself'.[20]

 The eponymous fever, from which the speaker suffers in his seedy hotel room at night, may thus be real (and physical) and/or a metaphorical representation[21] of the (metaphysical) breakdown the speaker has to live through which, ultimately, leads him to some vision or epiphanic moment. Throughout the monologue Shawn alternates between the speaker's 'resignation and conviction'.[22] Likewise, the spiralling, hallucinatory, daydream-like stream of consciousness fluctuates between contradictory images and impressions of a totalitarian state and memories of luxury hotels, parties in fancy restaurants and the desire for violent sex. The speaker recalls how he was raised, how he was taught to shun the poorer quarters and how much he likes Beethoven. Reading Marx's *Capital* makes him question 'commodity fetishism' (p. 171) for a while, whereas a visit to a performance of Chekhov's *The Cherry Orchard*, another intertextual reference point for change and a mouldy inability to adapt to it, has no effect on the speaker: 'She [Madame Ranevskaya] would have to live in an apartment instead. . . . I couldn't remember why I was supposed to be weeping' (p. 176). His language hovers between self-accusation and self-justification, between his naturalistic (and sometimes condescending) picturing of poor housing conditions and time-stretching, poetic contemplations of rain in New York City. Throughout the monologue, the speaker is racked by violent fits of vomiting induced by the nausea of self-disgust until a culmination point is reached, when he realizes that 'every muscle of my body aches with the effort of constant lying' (p. 199). His monologue ends with his prospect of going home and a resolution which sounds like a prayer:

> Let everything filthy, everything vile, sit by my bed, where once I had my lamp and clock, books, letters, presents for my birthday, and left over from the presents bright-colored ribbons. Forgive me. Forgive me. I know you forgive me. I'm still falling.
> (p. 202)

Of course, he knows as much as we do that 'a sympathy for the poor does not change the life of the poor' (p. 200). Many critics have argued in this vein when they ironically suggest that Shawn had better surrender his worldly goods or have people spend their money on Oxfam rather than on theatre tickets. But Shawn's narrator is candid enough to admit how quickly all the twinges of remorse and conscience usually pass, the speaker's 'haunted, searching, incomplete voice',[23] therefore, serves as a humanist reminder, and his genuine pain 'presents an opportunity – for criticism or silent empathy, perhaps also the steady evolution of new impulses into thoughts of greater complexity'.[24]

The Designated Mourner (1996)

The Designated Mourner was first performed at the National Theatre, London on the Cottesloe stage on 18 April 1996 and was directed by David Hare. Its reception was altogether favourable: John Peter called it 'a bitter, difficult and brilliant play',[25] Bill Hagerty spoke of 'a superb, mind-challenging experience'.[26]

The play is set in an unnamed country, which quite unmistakably, however, is the United States sometime in the future. Shawn is taking the title of the play from a tribal custom, whereby, when the last member of a family dies, someone is designated as the mourner. The self-appointed designated mourner in Shawn's play is Jack, who introduces himself as 'a former student of English literature who—who—who went downhill from there' (p. 10). Jack is married to Judy, the daughter of Howard, a famous essayist and poet, a modern version of Chekhov's Aleksandr Serebryakov in *Uncle Vanya*. Howard once wrote an ardent essay rejecting anti-communist government politics and has since then been held in suspicion by the authorities.

Howard's precarious position becomes the linchpin of a three-level dystopian development of the storyline: On the level of *society* and *culture* the play depicts the downfall of the highbrow culture Howard (and his followers) represent. In the course of the play we hear of censorship and of demonstrations by the underclass masses, whose lowbrow culture makes Howard despise them as 'dirteaters' (p. 41). A stone is thrown through Howard's window, an economical crisis occurs, assassinations take place with 'ten thousand examples of "human remains"' (p. 52), Howard is attacked, and later Howard and Judy are arrested and put into prison for five years, then briefly released, before both are executed. By the end of the play, 'everyone on earth who could read John Donne was now dead' (p. 99). The second level of dystopia in *The Designated Mourner* concerns the *community* of highbrow people, symbolized by the family constellation and the fact that Howard, Judy and Jack live in the same house. Superficially kept together by Howard's highbrow standards, it becomes obvious that this community has always been a sham. When Howard becomes ill, Judy is taking care of him while Jack becomes increasingly insecure about his own position in the family. Realizing that he has 'always been a lowbrow at heart' (p. 92), he leaves the house and the relationship whereas Judy stays on. The third level of dystopian deterioration is the development of Jack's argument with his *personal self*. The ritualistic killing of his former (highbrow) self is sealed as follows:

> **Jack**   ... I put a book of poetry in the bathtub, and I urinated
>   on it. An interesting experiment. Then I left it in the tub,

and then, later, when I needed to shit—I hadn't planned this, it just came to me as an idea instead of shitting into the toilet, I shat on the book. Just to see, you know, if it could be done. And apparently it was possible, despite what anyone might have told me. So, like a scientist, I noted in my diary that night, "Yes, the experiment has been a complete success". (pp. 92–3)

Jack's self-chosen split from highbrow culture, however, does not entail the freedom that such self-realization might promise at first sight. Separated for good from Howard (and his world), he becomes an isolated self, alienated, solipsist, de-historicized and trapped in the doubtful escape of 'forgetting his name, forgetting him, and forgetting all the ones who remembered him' (p. 102). Such temporal and moral displacement in unison with his contemplation of murdering Judy with a mallet and the sardonic, indifferent tone with which he reports on Howard's and Judy's execution makes one wonder whether he has not in the end, in fact, lost his mind altogether. His peace of mind enjoying the 'sweet, ever-changing caress of an early evening breeze' (p. 103) is evidently traded off for moral, spiritual and cultural brutalization and detachment, by which Jack joins the long queue of Shawn's unreliable narrators.

Quite in contrast to this, these three strands of dystopian development indicate that Shawn understands that society, community and the development of a personal self belong together. (Western/American) Society is not to grow so abstract that communities (of an either high- or lowbrow bend) form and exclude each other; communities likewise are not supposed to be so exclusive that they become fetters and straitjackets for the individual or start to wage war against each other; individuals who set themselves apart from either society or communal togetherness end up in a solipsistic no man's land of moral, political and cultural arbitrariness and inertia. Hence, Shawn's devastating view of the Western world (and America in particular) 'as one of lapsed intellectual and moral rigor and creative failure'[27] describes a threefold deterioration process of society, community, and individual. The audience is left behind with the feeling of ineluctable and encompassing melancholia – that sociological (or psychological) state (of mind) which, according to Sigmund Freud, follows a mourning that has not been overcome.

In *The Designated Mourner*, all of this is less dramatized than narrated; for readers and audiences alike the play seems 'a more mental than kinetic experience, like following a story read aloud'.[28] Readers and audiences face an intricate Chinese-box of memories/monologues within the framework of Jack's stream of consciousness. Even though the play is the richest in plot of all of Shawn's plays, the narrative structure suspends a coherent chronology and blurs temporal layers. Hence, even the ontological status of some of the monologues is left opaque, and, again, Shawn relishes in contradictions and ambiguities. 'In its integrity of form and ambition', Bonnie Marranca rightly concludes, '*The Designated Mourner* is drama for a post-dramatic age. One of the most important works for the theatre in recent decades, it is unsparing in its portrait of a particular kind of social privilege and life of the mind in our time.'[29]

Grasses of a Thousand Colours (2009)

It took 13 years until Wallace Shawn's next play, the astonishing and fulminant *Grasses of a Thousand Colours*, was first performed at the Royal Court Theatre, London on 18 May 2009 – the New York premiere is scheduled for autumn 2013 at the Public Theater. Shawn once wrote that he saw writing 'as a sort of collaboration between his rational self ('me') and the voice that comes from outside the window, the voice that comes in through the window, whose words I write down in a state of weirded-out-puzzlement'.[30] He is obviously referring to the voice of the sub-conscious and also to the topic of sex uttered by that voice, which may be difficult to listen to, he acknowledges, but which he 'decided [he] was going to trust'[31] for the sake of artistic truthfulness. In no other play has Shawn done this as relentlessly (and honestly) as here.

Grasses is divided into three parts. Not only does the play interlace different temporal layers of monologues, it also intersects the real with the fictive and the imaginary to the point where the three become indistinguishable. Moreover, *Grasses* is a genre-hybrid: Set in the future, it is partly a dystopian satire of misdirected science and scientific arrogance. At the same time, it is a complex dream-play, a pornographic fairy tale in which male as well as female sexuality and carnality are cherished, yet also unmasked as insidious traps. 'Man has two basic needs—the need for food and the need for sex' (p. 14) – this assertion is the starting point from which Ben, another unreliable narrator, or rather memoirist, starts looking back on his life. Reminiscent of the literary topos of the mad scientist, Ben has brought it to fame because he has found the solution to the problem of food shortages in that he has systematically enabled animals (and, by logical extension, human beings) to live cannibalistically on their own species. In this future world, sex has become just like food, a trite matter of course: Just like the general public, politicians talk about their penises and vaginas, Ben's lover Rose has a picture of her vagina on her business cards (see p. 59), children masturbate in front of their parents, parents masturbate in front of their children, and incest between parents and children is accepted and, in fact, seems only a variant of the cannibalistic feeding practices. Likewise, Ben's obsession with his 'monstrous' penis – 'my best friend, and in a certain way, it's my only friend' (p. 26) – is hardly more than a variation of his hubris and self-centred arrogance as a scientist. These details are satirically heightened, exaggerated and often thoroughly amusing images and echoes of a permissive society, market cannibalism and (American) 'dog-eat-dog'-capitalism.[32] However, early in the first part of *Grasses*, Ben directs our attention to various bits of film in which his wife Cerise recalls terrifying, frightening images that unmistakably foreshadow how Ben's experiments have gone terribly out of control. He has disturbed the food chain, hundreds of dogs, for instance, press their muzzles 'into the ground, as if they were trying to bury themselves to stop the pain, as if their faces were covered with actual flames' (p. 18), and humans first suffer from attacks of vomiting and finally reach the exonerating moment 'when the vomiting doesn't stop' (p. 81) and they can die.

At the end of Part One, Ben tosses the manuscript of his memoirs into the wastepaper basket and starts reflecting on his adulterous love affair with Robin. The beginning of Part Two takes this up and further develops into a surreal dream sequence that plunges deeply into Ben's and the women's sexual imaginary. Ben leaves the bed and goes for a walk in the park, through a forest, mounting a horse that carries him to a castle where he is greeted by an evening society of cats and their leader, a white cat named Blanche. The intertextual reference point is Madame d'Aulnoy's late-seventeenth-century literary fairy tale 'The White Cat', in which the white cat Blanchette turns out a cursed princess ready to reward her prince. Even though the literary pre-text is already replete with erotic undertones, its treatment of sexuality remains altogether subliminal. In *Grasses*, Blanche, the white cat, becomes the cypher for the id, the subconscious, the female anima, lust. As the personification of the id, Blanche functions as a medium of the imaginary through which Ben's, Cerise's, Robin's, and later even Rose's subconscious desires and fears can be acted out. Quite symbolically, feasting with the cats for Ben entails sharing their animal appetites for mice and their animal lust, and vice versa, in order to be able to feel completely at ease in sexuality he has to let the animal side of lust have its way:

> **Ben**   At a certain point in the meal, I felt the white cat's paw move onto my leg. Playing with my testicles humorously and slowly, she watched me eating the ice, a drunken, drowsy expression wavering on her face. Then somehow her paw had extracted my member from inside my trousers, and my astonished penis was completely enclosed in a warm coat of indescribable coziness, such a travelers dream of on snowy nights. When I turned towards her, all of a sudden she stared into my eyes, penetrating me so deeply and fully that I felt turned inside out. My God—finally. Finally, to be known, I thought, as hot sperm flowed out of me, flowing over her paw as if it would never stop. (p. 37)

Throughout the play, Blanche remains an ambiguous, multifaceted image summarizing, as it were, the complex treatment of sexuality in Shawn's entire work. The image has enough *shock potential* for readers and audiences to fathom their own subconscious depths. The cat is the pivotal point of the *intersection of reality and dreams*, of the pleasure as well as the reality principle, as Blanche becomes the object of the characters' desires and, as a catalyst, also determines their everyday interaction. In her sheer elegancy Blanche is a (meta-dramatic) symbol of *the correlation between creativity, sex, beauty, and art* – an embodiment of the bliss involved in the erotic moment, which can teach us 'to love the meaningless and thereby turn it into the meaningful'.[33] Blanche, however, like sexuality, is also an image of *conflict*, which in *Grasses* touches on aspects of ownership and ardent jealousy – Robin cuts off Blanche's head, and later bestially hacks her to pieces (see p. 77). Most of all, though, the cat represents an *ecological* or even *eco-critical image*, which, at least in a utopian fashion, indicates an imagined harmony between (the) human and (the) animal. Such a carnivalesque counter-kingdom is envisaged especially in the castle scenes where animals and humans both from a male and female perspective form a carnal union which allows us, as the fictional epigraph of Ben's memoirs makes clear, to see 'grasses of a thousand colours, in which many rabbits, in absolute silence, were leaping and running like small horses' (p. 10). Part Three of *Grasses* corroborates this utopia when the human characters turn cat-like (Ben's hand is once referred to by Cerise as a paw), and in the end Blanche and Cerise transmogrify into each other.

Ben's hubris as a scientist has rebelled against nature, and nature has struck back against the human over-reacher. Sexuality is a vital part of nature, and writing about sexuality, for Shawn, is a variant of Wordsworth's 'writing about nature'.[34] Thus, *Grasses* is characterized by a complex appeal structure: Nature always fights back if humans cannibalize on themselves either economically or socially. Moreover, the play argues in favour of a natural ecology within our psychoanalytical households where the conscious and the unconscious, reality and dreams, have to be brought into some equilibrium, however unstable this may be. This, of course, means a lifelong fight on a battlefield, liberation from which can only be procured by death, which, in the end, may even appear as a relief:

> **Ben** Quote unquote "death" will actually feel no different from a dreamless sleep—although everyone else will notice that you're not waking up. . . . I found a very pleasant mossy spot, and I curled up pleasantly in a comfortable position, and—you know—what can I say?—I mean, don't be envious about it—I have to admit, it felt quite nice. (p. 90)

Summary

The critical reception of Shawn's plays is radically split into two camps: There have been critics (and audiences) who have for almost 40 years encountered Shawn's oeuvre with a fierce rejection, treating the plays as if they were nothing but abject symptoms of the diseased modern world that Shawn's plays depict. At the same time, however, for other critics Shawn's work has always had cult status. Scholars such as W. D. King, Bonnie Marranca, Marc Robinson and Gay Brewer have rated Shawn as one of the most experimental and impressive representatives of contemporary American drama. Especially Shawn's provocatively overt and unreserved treatment of human sexuality and his monologue-driven interest in introspection have been considered tasteless and self-indulgent by some, while enthusiastic critics like Jack Kroll have looked upon Shawn's unique voice as ranking 'with David Mamet and Sam Shepard' and even to outrival these in its ability to disturb 'our cozy assumptions'.[35]

From the beginning in the 1970s until today Shawn's plays have radically thwarted normative expectations both in their dramatic form and subject matter. Shawn himself has deplored that 'whenever I ventured out to see one of my own plays, I was always seized by the very strong suspicion that three quarters of the audience were actually sitting there under some awful misapprehension, wondering when the bears on bicycles were going to appear'.[36] The aesthetics of Shawn's drama appear much more fractured, disjointed, chaotic, his plays resemble

> a wonderful pile-up of bodies, lights, sets, gestures, clothes, nudity, music, dance, and running through it all and driving it all is a stream of words, sentences. Words and sentences are (to me) aesthetic materials, and a purpose that I think one would have to call aesthetic can certainly be the governing element in writing a play. One plays with sentences the way a child plays with matches—because they're unpredictable.[37]

Playfulness and inconclusiveness permeate his plays as they affect subject matter and formal structure at the same time: Dialogue intermingles with painstakingly crafted monologues; dramatic immediacy stands next to narrative distancing; time levels merge and, thus, temporal unities are completely displaced; the plays are for the most part plotless; they almost debunk traditional forms of characterization and frustrate the idea of closure and teleological development. 'Nothing unfolds neatly in the work of Shawn', Marc Robinson aptly points out, and 'nothing is final'.[38] For Shawn, such formal provocation is especially vital in the United States where, he feels, the theatre 'has simply never caught on in the way it has in England or on the European continent'.[39]

Important leitmotifs in all of Shawn's work are the nausea and the painful vomiting which are indicative of the psychosomatic self-reproach and self-disgust characters feel about themselves, their actions and their place in the world. These images go hand in hand with images of trance-like parties, indicating an exhausted state of mind in the emotional vacuum of that 'life after the orgy' which Jean Baudrillard once spoke of – a dystopian (post-) millennial climate of consumerism, fatigue, anticipation, panic and ecstasy in contemporary culture.[40] Shawn subdivided his collection of essays from 2009 into two sections, which he – quite programmatically for his entire oeuvre – called 'Reality' and 'Dream-World'. The first part of the volume contains essays with an openly political concern about, for instance, 9/11, patriotism, the Iraq War or on Israel's attack on Gaza. His essay on 'Morality'[41] acknowledges that self-restraint is a basis for moral behaviour, socialization and education. Nevertheless, Shawn admits 'a fantastic need to tear all that moral training of my heart one and for all so that I can finally begin to enjoy the life that is spread out before me like a marvelous feast'.[42] The dreamscapes of his plays often make it impossible to decide if what we read or witness is imaginary or not, thus, they rather engage reader and audience activity as they provoke an oscillatory communication process between text, stage and reception. No matter how agreeable or nightmarish they are, 'dreams', Shawn writes, 'can . . . agitate for change, or for a better world'.[43]

The theatre and the provocative transgression of established norms (both aesthetic and moral) 'provide a forum, a gathering place, where society can meet and discuss its own future, its problems, and its needs'.[44] Shawn insists that he had 'always somewhat hated being "me and only me"', that 'a playwright can spend a lifetime writing without ever speaking from his own location', and that writing, for him, means to 'lie down, dream, and become "someone else"'.[45] Such self-less writing inevitably can hardly be didactic or moral. Rather than that, Shawn's plays *reflect upon* morals and morality, and this reflection or introspection is devoid of a moral answer to the questions it raises. In fact, as Shawn himself puts it, his work is characterized by a 'skepticism, a certain detachment, when people in my vicinity are reviling the evil and alien Other, because I feel that very easily I could become that Other, and so could the reviler'.[46] Hence, the experimental openness and ambiguity of Shawn's plays lay bare their *ethical* rather than moral impact and concern. Questions such as 'How will the world change', 'Can we in the mansion of arts and letters play a part', 'Could we possibly use the dreams we create to lure our friends in another direction'[47] or 'Where do the dreams go, and what do they do, in the world of the real?'[48] are essential points of Shawn's ethics. At their heart lies the attempt to keep readers/audiences entangled in a continuous process of re-negotiating language, form, structure and meaning of the plays and thereby to make them reconsider the questions of who and what we are, how we live, what we should do, what human rights are, and whether or not there is a universal validity of these rights. Doing this, Shawn has created 'one of the few examples of the kind of serious intellectual drama of the sustained dramatic voice and compelling psychosocial dimension that has virtually disappeared from theatre in this country'.[49]

Primary Sources

Works by Wallace Shawn

Essays (Chicago, Ill.: Haymarket Books, 2009).

Grasses of a Thousand Colours (London: Nick Hern, 2009).

Our Late Night/A Thought in Three Parts (New York: Theatre Communications Group, 2008).

Plays: One (London: Faber and Faber, 1997).

The Designated Mourner (New York: Farrar, Strauss and Giroux, 1996).

Secondary Sources

Boles, William C., 'Wallace Shawn', *Dictionary of Literary Biography* 266 (Farmington Hills, MI: Thomson Gale, 2002), pp. 255–68.

Brewer, Gaylord, 'He's Still Falling: Wallace Shawn's Problem of Morality'. In Norma Jenckes (ed.), *New Readings in American Drama: Something's Happening Here* (Frankfurt am Main/New York, Washington, D.C., Berne, Brussels, Vienna, Oxford: Peter Lang, 2002), pp. 171–93.

Combs, Robert, 'Slaughtering Lambs: The Moral Universe of David Mamet and Wallace Shawn', *Journal of American Drama and Theatre* 13 (2001), 73–81.

King, W. D., 'Beyond "A Certain Chain of Reasoning": Wallace Shawn's *Aunt Dan and Lemon*', *Journal of American Drama and Theatre* 6 (1994), 61–78.

—, *Writing Wrongs. The Work of Wallace Shawn* (Philadelphia, Pa.: Temple UP, 1997).

Kroll, Jack, 'That Nice Mr Hitler', *Newsweek* 18 (1985), 90.

Marranca, Bonnie, 'The Solace of Chocolate Squares: Wallace Shawn in Mourning', *PAJ: A Journal of Performance and Art* 22, 3 (2000), 38–46.

Robinson, Marc, 'Four Writers', *Theater* 1 (1993), 31–4.

Notes

1. See Dave Itzkoff, 'Wallace Shawn and André Gregory Tackle Ibsen', *New York Times*, 28 February 2012.

2. See ibid., p. 104, and also: Boles, 'Wallace Shawn', pp. 255–68.

3. Shawn, 'Writing About Sex', *Essays*, pp. 153 and 154.

4. For an extensive overview, see King, *Writing Wrongs*, chapters 1–3.

5. Robinson, 'Four Writers', p. 34. See also Brewer, 'He's Still Falling', p. 171.

6. Angela Ashman, 'Infinite Sadness', *Village Voice*, 6 April 2011.

7. Brewer, 'He's Still Falling', p. 176.

8. Ibid., p. 176.

9. See Boles, 'Wallace Shawn', p. 263.

10. For an interesting psychoanalytical reading of the character constellation of *Aunt Dan*, see King, 'Beyond "A Certain Chain of Reasoning"', pp. 65ff.

11. Combs, 'Slaughtering Lambs', p. 78.

12. King is perfectly right to emphasize that the use of the collective 'we' 'has the rhetorical force of demonstrating that the Nazis are indistinguishable from anyone else'. See King, 'Beyond "A Certain Chain of Reasoning"', pp. 73–4.

13. See, for instance, Benedict Nightingale's review in *The Times*, 26 April 1996: 'Shawn used shock tactics to propose the unpalatable argument that there are parallels between cruelty to cockroaches and Hitler's extermination of Jews'.

14. Martin Hoyle, *Financial Times*, 13 January 1991.

15. Michael Coveney, *Financial Times*, 1 January 1991.

16. Shawn, 'Introduction', *Essays*, p. 13.
17. Charles Isherwood, 'The World's a Mess, and It's All Your Fault', *New York Times*, 30 January 2007.
18. Lyn Garner, *City Limits*, 24 January 1991.
19. Nicholas de Jongh, *The Guardian*, 11 January 1991.
20. Benedict Nightingale, *The Times*, 7 April 2009.
21. See Gerald Weales, 'Degrees of Difference', *Commonweal* 11 (1991), 18.
22. Brewer, 'He's Still Falling', p. 189.
23. Ibid., p. 190.
24. Robinson, 'Four Writers', p. 35.
25. John Peter, *Sunday Times,* 4 April 1996.
26. Bill Hagerty, *News of the World*, 28 April 1996.
27. Marranca, 'The Solace of Chocolate Squares', p. 44.
28. Ibid., p. 39.
29. Ibid., p. 46.
30. Shawn, 'Writing About Sex', *Essays*, p. 154.
31. Ibid., p. 156.
32. See George Hunka's insightful review of the play on the following website: http://www.superfluitiesredux.com/2011/02/11/grasses-of-a-thousand-colors-2009-by-wallace-shawn/.
33. Shawn, 'Writing about Sex', *Essays*, p. 158.
34. Ibid., pp. 158 and 161.
35. Jack Kroll, 'That Nice Mr Hitler', p. 90. See also Brewer, 'He's Still Falling', p. 171.
36. Shawn, 'Myself and How I Got into the Theatre', *Essays*, p. 108.
37. Shawn, 'Aesthetic Preferences', *Essays*, p. 122.
38. Robinson, 'Four Writers', p. 32.
39. Shawn, 'Myself and How I Got into the Theatre', *Essays*, pp. 108 and 109.
40. See Jean Baudrillard, 'Between Difference and Singularity: An Open Discussion with Jean Baudrillard', http://www.egs.edu/faculty/jean-baudrillard/articles/between-difference-and-singularity.
41. Shawn, *Essays*, pp. 33–48.
42. Shawn, 'Morality', *Essays*, p. 36.
43. Shawn, 'Aesthetic Preferences', *Essays*, p. 125.
44. Shawn, 'Myself and How I Got into the Theatre', *Essays*, p. 104.
45. Shawn, 'Introduction', *Essays*, pp. 9–10.
46. Ibid., p. 10.
47. Shawn, 'The Quest for Superiority', *Essays*, p. 25.
48. Shawn, 'Introduction', *Essays*, p. 10.
49. Marranca, 'The Solace of Chocolate Squares', p. 46.

18 SAM SHEPARD

Katherine Weiss

Chicago; The Tooth of Crime; Buried Child; True West; States of Shock, The Late Henry Moss

Introduction

Samuel Shepard Rogers was born in Fort Sheridan, Illinois in 1943 and later raised in South Pasadena, California. In 1961 he began his training in animal husbandry at a nearby two-year college, but soon became bored with the classes there. This led him to the college's theatre programme where he was cast in Mary Chases' *Harvey* and Thornton Wilder's *The Skin of Our Teeth*.[1] To this day, Shepard's interest in acting thrives. His stage performances include Slim in his play *Cowboy Mouth* (1971) and Salter in Caryl Churchill's *A Number* (2004). Additionally, Shepard has taken on more than 50 roles in films, most notably *Days of Heaven* (1978), *The Right Stuff* (1983), *Hamlet* (2000) and *Don't Come Knocking* (2005).

It is during his short college career that Shepard first read Samuel Beckett, the playwright who would most influence Shepard's writing. After three semesters, Shepard left college, running off to New York City with Bishop's Company Repertory Players.

He met Joe Chaikin, the 'experimental theatre director' who had recently founded the Open Theater.[2] Shepard admired Chaikin's willingness to veer from naturalistic acting. Chaikin's vision of acting was 'almost a spiritual quest with great eloquence and emotional directness'[3] – a style that fit Shepard's work of the sixties and seventies well.

Only a year after Shepard began writing, he won his first of eleven Obie Awards for the combined success of *Chicago*, *Icarus's Mother* and *Red Cross*. These early works are characteristically short plays in which the scenes and dialogue freely take on various topics and forms, reflecting Shepard's interest in French symbolism, European surrealism and the *avant-garde*, as well as lessons he had learnt from Chaikin. While in New York, he would go on to stage several more plays, publish his first book of plays and work with Michelangelo Antonioni on the film *Zabriskie Point*. Yet the Vietnam War, student protests, the Cuban Missile Crisis and the drug culture in America would finally wear Shepard down.

In 1971 Shepard fled the unrest in America, moving to London where his plays had preceded him. There he got his first taste of directing while working with Stephen Rea, Bob Hoskins and Ken Cranham on *Geography of a Horse Dreamer* (1974) at the Royal Court Theatre. In London Shepard wrote his most daring play, *The Tooth of Crime*, the title of which is taken from Stéphane Mallarmé's poem 'Anguish'.[4] The play premiered at the Open Space Theatre[5] in 1972 and won Shepard another Obie Award when it was staged off-Broadway. Despite this and its appeal to scholars, the play received devastating reviews from theatre critics both in England and America. This play about two duelling rock-stars was 'largely uncomprehended in London'.[6] The first American production at the Princeton University's McCarter Theater in 1972 and subsequent stagings of the play, such as the La MaMa revival in 1983, were met with equally disappointing reviews. Don Shewey argues that the 'real problem' with the play is Shepard's musical scores: 'It's all in basically the same style, a dated sort of late sixties blues-rock that fails to distinguish characters or attitudes. It's the weak link in an otherwise perfect play'.[7] Shepard rewrote the play in 1996, including a new musical score by T-Bone Burnett. The revised play, *Tooth of Crime (Second Dance)* premiered at Signature Theatre's year-long dedication to Shepard's work.

After three years abroad, the homesick Shepard returned to California to serve as playwright-in-residence at San Francisco's Magic Theatre from 1975 to 1984. One of the early plays Shepard wrote for the Magic Theatre was *Angle City*, his 1976 play about three screenwriters which was based on his experiences with Antonioni.[8] It is at the Magic Theatre, too, that Shepard began writing about dysfunctional families much like the one he grew up in. The violent and alcoholic men in plays such as *Curse of the Starving Class* (1978), *Fool for Love* (1983) and *The Late Henry Moss* (2000) haunt Shepard; they are, it has frequently been argued, veiled representations of his own father.[9]

For three decades Shepard wrote prolifically for the stage. After 1985 and the success of *A Lie of the Mind* (1985), however, Shepard had little left to say. Then there came another turn in his writing. After a six year hiatus, Shepard wrote his 'first overtly political play'.[10] The bizarre *States of Shock* testifies to Shepard's own state of shock at the first Iraq War and the conservative climate in America. Reviewers noted that the play was 'endless tedium' and 'strictly for those who remained convinced that Shepard is a genius'.[11] According to Wade, the play was overwhelmingly 'criticized for its heavy-handedness, propagandistic intent, [and] leaden symbols'.[12] Perhaps because of the devastating reviews, Shepard did not write another political play until 2004 when he rushed his anti-Bush play, *The God of Hell*, into production. Ben Brantley of the *New York Times* wrote that the play 'is neither smooth nor subtle . . ., at its best it has an absurd and angry vigor that brings to mind Mr Shepard's salad days as the ultimate wild young dramatist of the 1960's'.[13] The London premiere at the Donmar Warehouse in 2005 fared better, but was also criticized for being 'a squib: a series of images, sometimes vivid, mostly violent, entirely without an argument'.[14]

While Shepard's last family play was a box office success, *The Late Henry Moss* (2000) received mediocre reviews. The reviews and scholarly responses nitpicked this play for being merely a repetition of Shepard's earlier and better family dramas.[15] The financial success of the play, Rosen suggests, was largely due to 'the star power of the performers and the event status of the premiere'.[16]

His last two plays, *Kicking a Dead Horse* (2007) and *Ages of the Moon* (2009) were produced at the Abbey Theatre in Dublin and directed by Shepard. Regardless of the magnificent image of a dead horse on stage, *Kicking* was deemed a pretentious, self-reflexive play.[17] *Ages*, on the other hand, was heralded as 'a poignant and honest continuation of themes that have always been present in the work of one of this country's most important dramatists, here reconsidered in the light and shadow of time passed'.[18]

The Plays

Chicago (1965)

Chicago was staged with great success by Theatre Genesis, and shortly thereafter, by Café La MaMa. Shepard's experimental work about abandonment was successfully revived in 1996 by Chicago's Signature Theatre. Ben Brantley praised the play, stating that it was a 'compelling testimony to the abiding obsessions and evolving craftsmanship of a man who ranks, with David Mamet and August Wilson, as one of the great American dramatists of his generation'.[19] However, *Chicago*, like Shepard's other plays of the 1960s, is seldom written about perhaps because it is 'difficult to make rational sense of'.[20]

In a bathtub on an otherwise bare set, a young man named Stu begins his rhythmic monologue about someone looking for his dog. This search for the dog turns out to be futile because, as Stu reveals, 'yer dog is dead and ya' don't care anyhow' (p. 55). Difficult to make sense of because it has no apparent connection to this play about the inevitable breakup between him and his girlfriend, Joy, Stu's monologue does resonate on a symbolic level. Joy, whose name suggests that she is the joy in Stu's life, is leaving him to take a job in another city. Perturbed by the approaching loss of 'joy' in his life, Stu stews in a bathtub, thinking up scenarios that, no matter how outwardly different his tales may seem, reflect in some way Stu's emotional state.

During Stu's bathtub monologues, Joy serves biscuits as various friends arrive, each holding a suitcase and fishing pole. Stu is the only character who is not going anywhere. After being prodded, Joy tells Stu that she has gotten a job that will require her to leave; however, his enthusiasm 'I'm really, really glad' (p. 58) is immediately dampened by his anxious question, 'When are you going?' (p. 58) Unable to come to terms with the realization that his girlfriend will soon be leaving, Stu, with Joy in the tub, imagines a boat voyage. This fantasy soon evolves into a frightening trip in which Joy is surrounded by hungry barracudas. Food and eating becomes a central image in Shepard's theatre. In this early play, we see a tension between the enjoyment of the biscuits that

Joy bakes and the hungry barracuda that threaten to devour her. Like the barracuda, Stu does not want a 'hunk of dough that goes down and makes a gooey ball in your stomach' (p. 57). Claiming that 'Biscuits were invented to trick people into believing they're really eating food!' (p. 57), Stu, perhaps unknowingly, reveals that he feels tricked into believing Joy, who he turns into food for the hungry predators of the sea, was fulfilled and was fulfilling. Although content for a time, Stu finds himself hungry for her while she is slipping away.

After Joy leaves the tub, Stu continues with his monologues, now speaking of a train journey which results in a couple's infidelity while the train becomes invaded by the foul odour originating from the bowels of a glutton. His anxiety of being left is again apparent. The journey he is excluded from – Joy's journey to Chicago – leaves him envisioning a train ride in which relationships are betrayed. Gluttony, alcohol consumption and lust all emerge into a terrifying vision.

Stu's last fantasy about the 'bunch a' cowards' (p. 66) fornicating on the beach until they build a house changes into a stifling image of a community that turns on each other.

> They bump into each other because it's dark. They can't see so they hit and claw each other with their nails. They have long nails. They kick and scream and the sweat is rolling off them. They can't breathe and it's hot. They're screaming, see. (pp. 66–7)

Throughout this vision, Stu's feelings of fear and anxiety are intensified. His vision reveals human beings as primitives ready to devour each other in their sexual gluttony. As the lights dim and Joy leaves the stage, Stu increasingly expresses an overwhelming urge to flee the confines of the civilization his imaginary people have created as well as the confines of his own predicament. Yet, as the concluding story testifies, this is easier said than done because he fears the alternative – a community that has resorted to its primitive, violent nature, resulting ironically in confinement. Stu's longing for freedom, that which he sees Joy potentially heading towards, leads to a 'total, chaotic animalism'.[21]

The Tooth of Crime (1972)

The Tooth of Crime has impressed scholars and audiences, despite the poor reviews from theatre critics, for its radically new style; it is a play with musical numbers, but it is neither a musical nor an opera. Moreover, in it Shepard has invented a new lingo, much like Anthony Burgess does in *A Clockwork Orange*. Blending together fragments of rock'n'roll, blues, Old Westerns, gangster lure and mythology to make up this new lingo, Shepard creates a 'post[-]apocalyptic future world'.[22] In this world, rock-n-roll and fame is linked to drugs, violence and murder. During act one, Hoss, the aging rocker, who is desperately holding onto his rock-n-roll territory, consumes alcohol, shoots up heroin and snorts cocaine. America, for Shepard, is run by consumers, devouring anything they can get hold of, as shown in the way Hoss moves from one drug to the next. Along with his consumption of narcotics, Hoss insists that he is 'ready for a kill!' (p. 205)[23] and caresses several guns. Once he knows that some Gypsy's 'marked' him (p. 212), Hoss prepares for their duel:

> *Hoss picks up the knives and stalks the dummy. He circles it and talks to the dummy and himself. As he talks he stabs the dummy with sudden violent lunges then backs away again. Blood pours from the dummy onto the floor.* (p. 221)

When the duel begins, Hoss learns that rockers no longer kill with guns and knives; language is the new weapon of choice. Despite having none of Harold Pinter's economy, *Tooth* is a nod to the British playwright who so often stages language as the ultimate weapon, as seen in *The Dumb Waiter*.

Shepard shows that identity based on a fabricated image rather than actions is a lie of the mind.[24] The play opens with Hoss's song, 'The Way Things Are' which begins with the lyric: 'You may think every picture you see is a true history of the way things used to be or the way things are' (p. 203). Here, Shepard reveals that images and stories are not historical facts as we like to believe them to be, and as such they represent a mythical past and present. Identity, furthermore, as this play asserts, is based on territory. Hoss paints himself as a hero who has captured much of the American territory with his kills and his style. However, the game is changing and new blood has taken his land. Hoss is anxious about losing Las Vegas and the approaching Crow who threatens to usurp him. In his anxiety, he recognizes that he has no self 'to fall back on in a moment of doubt or terror or even surprise' (p. 225). Since identity in Hoss's world is a fabrication, 'the heroes', he sings, 'is dyin' like flies' (p. 203), foreshadowing his own death in Act Two as his identity is stripped away by Crow's ability to match his style. *Tooth*, thus, depicts the obsession in America for identity and territory as Hoss and Crow strive to gain land to establish who they are; however, this leads to their demise.

Buried Child (1978)

Buried Child, the 1979 Pulitzer Prize-winning play, depicts a family wasting away, yet it is not clear what their demise resulted from. Its cause is buried like the skeletal remains of a child on their farm. The mystery of who murdered and buried the child resurfaces reluctantly in dialogue upon the unexpected arrival of Vince, who is returning to his grandparents' home with his nosey girlfriend, Shelly. After a harrowing night, the buried child is brought on stage by Tilden, one of the family's disturbed sons. He is *'profoundly burned out and displaced'* (p. 18). Bradley, the second oldest son, is an angry, violent amputee.

The wasteland motif is central to *Buried Child*. The alcoholic Dodge, the family's impotent patriarch who was responsible for the child's death, has lost his authority over his family. He is, as he himself puts it, a 'corpse' (p. 15). In addition, Shepard draws on the Corn King myth from Sir James Frazer's *The Golden Bough*. In this myth, the Corn King, a strong and healthy man, 'is sacrificed in the Autumn to insure that fertility continues in the new solar year'.[25] However, Dodge, who represents the now decrepit Corn King, cheats death. When he was virile, he sacrificed the innocent child instead. In essence, Shepard remakes myths, exploring what happens when one element of the tale is altered.

Shepard not only details the structure of mythology,[26] but also comments on the American Dream as a myth fabricated by women like

Halie, the family's matriarch. Despite the incestuous relationship she had with her oldest son Tilden, which led to the birth of an illegitimate son, she dreams of restoring the family's honour with the resurrection of 'a statue of Ansel [their youngest son]. A big, tall statue with a basketball in one hand and a rifle in the other' (p. 27). Dodge and his sons' questioning of Ansel's prowess, however, reveal that the American Dream is merely a myth.[27] Although the family home looks 'like a Norman Rockwell cover' (p. 44), as Shelly laughingly characterizes it, the inside of the home and its inhabitants are rotting away. What the idealistic Vince, who wishes to reconnect with his 'heritage' (p. 44), discovers is that 'the family is a black hole that holds its off-spring in a deadly grip, eventually sucking them back into its vortex'.[28] When Dodge finally passes away, Vince inherits the family home only to continue the cycle of neglect, alcoholism and violence.

Buried Child's success with audiences is largely the result of the play's deconstruction of realistic family drama.[29] Both the San Francisco premiere and the 1996 revival by Chicago's Steppenwolf Theatre Company were huge successes. For the revival, Shepard revised the play's text, trimming some of the more repetitive and excessive dialogue. Shepard had found his niche. His postmodern family dramas keep audiences at the edge of their seats as they wait for bombs to drop on kitchen tables.

True West (1980)

Shepard's third family play, also written for the Magic Theatre, marks the return of duelling forces; this time, those forces are brothers who live different lives. The younger of the two, Austin, is a college graduate and successful screenwriter. Lee, on the contrary, is an uneducated petty thief who lives out in the desert. Many scholars have explored the possible worlds and ideologies that each represent. According to Hart, Shepard 'pits the rugged frontier individualist (Lee) against the urban socialite (Austin)'.[30] Others compare the brothers to Cain and Abel.[31] What these views on the play reveal is that the conflict between the brothers is one that is deeply rooted in all of us. It is another Dr Jekyll and Mr Hyde story – the struggle to ward off one's primitive instincts in order to be civilized. Revealingly, Shepard has said: 'I think we're split in a much more devastating way than psychology can ever reveal. It's not so cute. Not some little thing we can get over. It's something we've got to live with'.[32] Recognizing the inability to win such a battle, Shepard built into his play a role-reversal, a technique he would use again 20 years later in *The Late Henry Moss* (2000). While the play opens with Austin sitting at the typewriter and Lee drinking beer, in scene seven Lee is at the typewriter and Austin is '*sprawled out on kitchen floor with [a] whiskey bottle, drunk*' (p. 36). Unlike *Tooth*, *True West* does not end in victory for either brother.[33] The play closes with the reversal upset again; the lights fade out on the unsettling tableau of the brothers, both full of primitive instincts, '*caught in a vast desert-like landscape[;] they are very still but watchful for the next move*' (p. 59). The first to move will be slaughtered by the other.

Since its premiere, *True West* has been well received by audiences, theatre critics and scholars. Particularly productions 'take a lighter approach',[34] as the Steppenwolf's production with Gary Sinise and John Malkovich in 1982 and the Broadway revival in 2000 with John C. Reilly and Philip Seymour Hoffmann did. Even when the direction of the play has been critiqued as the 1980 New York Shakespeare Festival's production was for its 'sombre *pas de deux* showdown between rival brothers',[35] Shepard's writing was applauded.[36] Many have noted that this brilliant play puts Shepard on the same level as Samuel Beckett, Harold Pinter and David Mamet.[37] This play, furthermore, has influenced writers of a younger generation. One needs only to think of the bickering brothers in Martin McDonagh's *The Lonesome West* and rivalry of the brothers in Suzan-Lori Parks's *Topdog/Underdog*.

The Late Henry Moss (2000)

More than any of Shepard's earlier work, *The Late Henry Moss* depicts the devastating effects of domestic violence. Yet, unlike the dominant discourse of domestic violence in today's media and society, Shepard's focus and empathy lies with the husbands and sons haunted by their violent and impotent acts. Henry Moss, the dead father brought back to life in flashbacks,[38] recalls the day he fled his family: 'I remember the floor—was yellow—I can see the floor—and—her blood—her blood was smeared across it. I thought I'd killed her—but it was me, it was me I killed' (p. 112). After a brief interruption in which his oldest son, Earl, attempts to leave in order not to relive the past, Henry continues, describing his flight:

> I ran out into the yard and I remembered—I remembered this—death. I remember it now—Cut off. Everything—far away. Birds. Trees. Sky. Removed! Everything—out beyond reach. And I ran. I ran to the car and I drove. I drove for days with the windows wide open. The wind beating across my eyes—my face. I had no map. No destination. I just drove. (p. 112)

Henry reveals more than just the moment he fled the family; he reveals that he is haunted by the past and traumatized by his own violence. Yet his violence has deeper roots. Henry is a war veteran, who 'dropped bombs on total strangers!' (p. 79). The play 'picks up the figure of the war-traumatised father incapable of re-integrating into and fitting in the family, re-enacting the violence and brutality he saw and inflicted upon strangers within the home'.[39]

But Earl and his younger brother, too, are victims of trauma which become apparent when they re-enact their father's violence on the mother. In Act One, Earl turns on his brother: '*He overpowers him and sends him crashing across the stage into [the] refrigerator. Ray hits the floor. Earl crosses to him and kicks Ray in the stomach. Ray collapses*' (p. 45). Later, in Act Three, it is Ray who '*turns himself into [the] drunken Henry*' (p. 98) and is '*savagely kicking Earl all over the stage. Earl scrambles on this hands and knees but Ray is relentless*' (p. 99). Moreover, both brothers are haunted that neither stepped in to stop the attack on their mother despite Henry's claim that Earl could have stopped him. Although the past casts a shadow on the Moss men, they all insist that they live in the moment. Esteban recalls that Henry refused to reflect on his past: 'He say he have no past' (p. 86). Similarly, Earl in Act One and Ray in Act Three say they were 'never one to live in the past' (pp. 6, 113). As such, the brothers remain stuck in a cycle of violence, denial and fear.

The play closes with the opening lines, only the brothers' lines are now switched in a brilliant role reversal, revealing that the play will start over, but this time Earl will interrogate Ray's inability to act.

Summary

In a telling interview conducted the same year *The Late Henry Moss* was completed, Shepard told Roudané that the troubled male figures in his plays are based on the alcoholic and violent men who influenced him. These men, Shepard continued, were

> . . . like lost children, not knowing how to deal with it. Instead, they were plunked down on the desert not knowing how they got there. And slowly they began receding further and further and further away—receding from the family, receding from society. You see it with some Vietnam vets. It was the same thing, except these guys—my father's generation—were coming out of World War II. I can't help but think that these wars had something to do with the psychological states that they came back in.[40]

During rehearsals of *The Late Henry Moss*, Shepard again spoke of his father, drawing connections between the play and their relationship.[41] Such statements make it tempting to read Shepard's creative output biographically. However, Roudané reminds us,

> Shepard has never been "an autobiographical writer in the simple sense of dramatising his own experiences". In fact, the most remarkable feature about *The Late Henry Moss* is its compelling presentation of a series of events which suddenly broaden to encompass experiences felt by too many audiences.[42]

Instead, Shepard uses theatre as a way to work through issues many families face, and in doing so, he suggests that much domestic strife is rooted in war trauma. His plays repeatedly look at how political and historical violence shapes and scars family life, much like Bertolt Brecht's *Mother Courage*, the plays of David Rabe and Paula Vogel's *How I Learned to Drive*.

Even Shepard's earliest plays merge the private, domestic tensions and fears with historical and public violence. *Chicago*, for example, begins with

> *A Policeman com[ing] out in front of the curtain with a club. He beats the curtain several times with the club, then walks into the audience and up the center aisle. He goes to the back of the house and bangs his club three times on the back of a chair. Someone [is] reciting the "Gettysburg Address".* (p. 55)

The presence of the police officer's violent banging of his club reminds a 1960s' audience of the civil rights movement, student anti-war protests, the Cuban Missile Crisis, President Kennedy's assassination and nuclear threat.[43] By coupling twentieth-century police presence with the recitation of the Gettysburg Address in a play about separation anxiety, Shepard reveals that violence in American, violence which affects families as the assassination of JFK did, has deep roots. America is a nation founded on war and slavery, Shepard reminds us, and like the deadly barracuda that Joy fears, violence in America is ever present, ready to tear into the flesh of civilization.

In nearly all of Shepard's plays, images and recollections of wars are prevalent. The most obvious is Shepard's *States of Shock*. In a 1991 interview with Rosen, Shepard recalls his disgust at America's response to Desert Storm – George Bush's war on Iraq:

> I couldn't believe it. I still can't believe it. I can't believe that, having come out of the '60s and the incredible reaction to Vietnam, that voice has all but disappeared. Vanished. There's no voice anymore. This is supposed to be what America's about?[44]

However, in *States of Shock* Shepard goes beyond critiquing the Persian Gulf War. The play attacks a culture of war that destroys the bond between father (the Colonel) and son (Stubbs).

Fathers and sons are always fighting it out on Shepard's stage. The battles, Shepard reveals, are deeply connected to American warfare which has destroyed his male characters' ability to connect to their families. In *Curse of the Starving Class* (1978), Wesley describes his drunken father's attempt to enter the home as a battle. The family in this, and other plays, is full of violence much like Suzan-Lori Parks's brothers in *Topdog/ Underdog* who are inflicted by the past and, consequently, are full of impotent rage.

Shepard obsessively, and perhaps a bit fearfully, explores the inheritance younger generations receive from a failed patriarchy.[45] In *Curse of the Starving Class,* Weston passes on his drunken violence to Wesley, like a poison or a curse. In *Buried Child* the grandson Vince inherits the violence infesting the male members of the family. And, although Earl claims he 'is *nothing* like the old man!' (p. 83), the audience sees him waging a war on his brother as his father did years before.

Part of the trauma that these men inherit, according to Shepard, was

> . . . coming back into the Eisenhower fifties. . . . Where everything was wonderful, the front lawns were all being taken care of, there was a refrigerator in everybody's house. Everybody had a Chevy, and these guys had just been bombing the *shit* out of Germany and Italy and the South Pacific and then they come back; I mean it just must have been unbelievable. I mean nobody ever really talks about that. Back then it was taboo to talk about it.[46]

Viewed as heroes by the public, these men had no way to voice another version of events; the truth would threaten to shatter the carefully constructed world America built while soldiers destroyed homes and cities abroad. This silence, Shepard shows us, is what ultimately shattered the family as it became the weapon exposing the Dream as facade.

Like Tennessee Williams, Arthur Miller and David Mamet, Shepard is critical of the dreams we are sold. Such dreams, like the American flag cookies Welch attempts to sell Emma in *The God of Hell,* are merely sugar-coated lies engineered to make us forget the past. These dreams turn us into zombies, as Wesley aptly observes in *Curse of the Starving*

Class. At a crucial moment of *True West*, Austin recognizes, 'There's nothin' real down here, Lee! Least of all me!' (p. 49). Austin, Lee and their mother, like Struther in *Kicking a Dead Horse*, are searching for authenticity. In a deconstructive move, Shepard sends his characters out to find *truth* and *authenticity* so that the audience, and sometimes the characters, can discover how futile such a search is in the post-World War II era.

For over 50 years, Shepard has written for the stage. His *avant-garde* plays of the sixties and seventies testify to his interest in European playwrights, such as Jean Genet and Samuel Beckett as seen in the existential angst of his characters in plays such as *Chicago*, *Icarus's Mother*, and *Geography of a Horse Dreamer*. Shepard's existentialism is carried throughout his career. Henry Moss, for example, is grappling with being pronounced dead by Conchalla in *The Late Henry Moss* and Struther, in his penultimate play, is plagued with questions of what his life has amounted to. As such, these characters could easily be Stu (*Chicago*) 40 years later. The Beat poets, too, influenced Shepard's early career which is apparent in the rhythmic, jazzy quality of *Chicago, The Unseen Hand* and *The Mad Dog Blues*. To achieve this effect, Shepard's early plays often used 'a single, distilled theatrical image, a "found object" which would act as the visual anchor for the play's flights of rhythmic, imagistic language'.[47]

In the late 70s, Shepard moves away from the abstract aesthetics of his off-off Broadway plays. His new direction, utilizing the family in ways similar to Arthur Miller, Tennessee Williams and William Inge, however, is by no means a turning away from his existential, *avant-garde* roots. Shepard's family plays reel the audience in with the suggestion of conventional modes. Once invested, however, the audience discovers that Shepard's family plays do not abide by realism. In these plays, Shepard destroys the set, which is often a representation of a family home, revealing how fragile both the family structure and theatrical conventions are.

Shepard's two political dramas are *tours-de-force*, utilizing Brechtian alienation techniques and Beckettian absurdism. Both *States of Shock* and *The God of Hell*, written 13 years apart, were poorly received by theatre critics perhaps because Shepard is not seeking empathy as theatre in the nineties and beyond tends to do. In these works, Shepard distances the audience as Brecht does and unnerves them as Beckett does to shock them into action. Unfortunately, his audiences were not ready for such a jolt.

Despite the many shapes his plays have taken, Shepard's 'intensely voracious and fresh voice'[48] remains consistent. His monologues are full of 'fragments and often of verbal and visual glut',[49] as seen in Stu's fantasies, Wesley's opening description of the previous night of violence and Vince's monologue about his flight. These monologues express raw, painful emotions. Ultimately, the voices that speak out on Shepard's stage warn the audience not to forget the past. It is through the past, whether it is a personal, private family secret or a political, historical past, that we can potentially spiral outwards rather than inwards as his characters frequently do. Only Emma, who at the end of *The God of Hell* rings the school bell to awaken the audience, is fully aware and alert to the danger of ignoring the past as she once did.

Primary Sources

Works by Sam Shepard

Buried Child (New York: Vintage Books, 2006).
Kicking a Dead Horse (London: Faber and Faber, 2007).
Seven Plays (London: Faber and Faber, 1985).
The God of Hell (New York: Vintage Books, 2005).
The Late Henry Moss, Eyes for Consuela, When the World Was Green (New York: Vintage Books, 2002).
The Unseen Hand and other plays (New York: Vintage Books, 1996).
Tooth of Crime (Second Dance) (New York: Vintage Books, 2006).

Secondary Sources

Adler, Thomas P., 'Repetition and Regression in *Curse of the Starving Class* and *Buried Child*'. In Matthew Roudané (ed.), *The Cambridge Companion to Sam Shepard* (Cambridge: Cambridge University Press, 2002), pp. 111–22.
Bigsby, C. W. E., 'Blood and Bones yet Dressed in Poetry: The Drama of Sam Shepard', *Contemporary Theatre Review* 8, 3 (1998), 19–30.

Bloom, Harold, *Bloom's Major Dramatists: Sam Shepard* (Philadelphia: Chelsea House, 2003).

Bottoms, Stephen J., *The Theatre of Sam Shepard: States of Crisis* (Cambridge: Cambridge University Press, 1998).

—, 'Shepard and Off-Off Broadway: The Unseen Hand of Theatre Genesis'. In Matthew Roudané (ed.), *The Cambridge Companion to Sam Shepard* (Cambridge: Cambridge University Press, 2002), p. 42.

Brantley, Ben, 'Sam Shepard of Today, and of Many Days Ago', *The New York Times*, 8 November 1996.

—, 'No-Good Dad Whose Tale is Told Repeatedly', *The New York Times*, 25 September 2001.

—, 'That's No Girl Scout Selling Those Cookies', *The New York Times*, 17 November 2004.

—, 'It's Old Timers' Day at Shepard's Arena', *The New York Times*, 28 January 2010.

Clapp, Susannah, 'Torch Songs and Torturers', *The Observer*, 30 October 2005.

Clum, John M., 'The Classic Western and Sam Shepard's Family Sagas'. In Matthew Roudané (ed.), *The Cambridge Companion to Sam Shepard* (Cambridge: Cambridge University Press, 2002), p. 173.

Cohn, Ruby, *New American Dramatists 1960–1990* (New York: St. Martin's Press, 1991).

DeRose, David J., *Sam Shepard* (New York: Twayne Publishers, 1992).

Graham, Laura J., 'Sam Shepard'. In Garrett Eisler (ed.), *Twentieth-Century American Dramatists: Fifth Series* (Detroit: Gale, 2008), pp. 200–16.

Gussow, Mel, '*Angel City*: Sam Shepard Revival', *New York Times*, 22 November 1984. http://www.nytimes.com/1984/11/22/theater/stage-angel-city-sam-shepard-revival.html.

Hart, Lynda, *Sam Shepard's Metaphorical Stages* (New York: Greenwood, 1987).

Lanier, Gregory W., 'True West? Sam Shepard's Mythic Misdirections', *Text and Presentation* 12 (1992), 49–54.

McCarthy, Gerry, 'New Mythologies: Mamet, Shepard and the American Stage', *Connotations* 6, 3 (1996–97), 354–68.

Mottram, Ron, *Inner Landscapes: The Theater of Sam Shepard* (Columbia: University of Missouri Press, 1984).

Nash, Thomas, 'Sam Shepard's Buried Child: The Ironic Use of Folklore', *Modern Drama* 26, 4 (1983), 486–91.

Orbison, Tucker, 'Mythic Levels in Sam Shepard's *True West*', *Modern Drama* 27, 4 (1984), 507–19.

Putzel, Steven D. and Suzanne R. Westfall, 'The Back Side of Myth: Sam Shepard's Subversion of Mythic Codes in *Buried Child*', *Journal of Dramatic Theory and Criticism* 4, 1 (1989), 117.

Rád, Boróka Prohászka, 'Dramatic Representation of a Culture of Violence in Sam Shepard's *The Late Henry Moss*', *Acta Universitatis Sapientiae, Philologica* 2, 1 (2010), 43–61.

Rosen, Carol, *Sam Shepard: A 'Poetic Rodeo'* (New York: Palgrave/Macmillan, 2004).

Roudané, Matthew, 'Introduction', In Matthew Roudané (ed.), *The Cambridge Companion to Sam Shepard* (Cambridge: Cambridge University Press, 2002), p. 2.

—, 'Sam Shepard's *The Late Henry Moss*', In Matthew Roudané (ed.), *The Cambridge Companion to Sam Shepard* (Cambridge: Cambridge University Press, 2002), p. 281.

— (ed.), *The Cambridge Companion to Sam Shepard* (Cambridge: Cambridge University Press, 2002).

Schiele, Jinnie, *Off-Centre Stages: Fringe Theatre at the Open Space and the Round House, 1968–1983* (London and Hatfield: Society for Theatre Research and University of Hertfordshire Press, 2005).

Shea, Laura, 'The Sacrificial Crisis in Sam Shepard's *Buried Child*', *Theatre Annual* 44 (1989–90), pp. 1–9.

Shewey, Don, *Sam Shepard* (New York: Da Capo Press, 1997).

Taav, Michael, *A Body Across the Map: The Father-Son Plays of Sam Shepard* (New York: Peter Lang, 2000).

Tekinay, Aslÿ, 'Sam Shepard's *States of Shock*: Nihilism in Political Drama', *Journal of American Studies of Turkey* 3 (1996), 69–74.

Wade, Leslie A., '*States of Shock, Simpatico*, and *Eyes for Consuela*: Sam Shepard's Plays of the 1990s'. In Matthew Roudané (ed.), *The Cambridge Companion to Sam Shepard* (Cambridge: Cambridge University Press, 2002), p. 264.

Willadt, Susanne, 'States of War in Sam Shepard's *States of Shock*', *Modern Drama* 36, 1 (1993), 147–66.

Notes

1. Don Shewey, *Sam Shepard*, p. 23.
2. Ibid., p. 47.
3. Ibid., p. 48.
4. Ibid., p. 84.
5. Founded by the American expatriate Charles Marowitz, this off-West End theatre company opened in 1968 and closed in 1979. Jinnie Schiele, *Off-Centre Stages: Fringe Theatre at the Open Space and the Round House, 1968–1983*, p. 7.
6. From Marowitz's dispatch to the *Village Voice*, qtd. in Don Shewey, *Sam Shepard*, p. 85.
7. Don Shewey, *Sam Shepard*, p. 86.
8. Mel Gussow, '*Angel City*: Sam Shepard Revival'.
9. See, f. ex., Matthew Roudané, 'Shepard on Shepard: an Interview', pp. 67–72; C. W. E. Bigsby, 'Blood and Bones yet Dressed in Poetry: The Drama of Sam Shepard', pp. 25–6.
10. Susanne Willadt, 'States of War in Sam Shepard's *States of Shock*', p. 148.
11. For an excellent summary of the critical response to *States of Shock*, see Leslie A. Wade, '*States of Shock, Simpatico*, and *Eyes for Consuela*', p. 264.
12. Leslie A. Wade, '*States of Shock, Simpatico*, and *Eyes for Consuela*', p. 264.
13. Ben Brantley, 'That's No Girl Scout Selling Those Cookies'.

14. Susannah Clapp, 'Torch Songs and Torturers'.

15. For a great overview of the critical response to the play, see Boróka Prohászka Rád, 'Dramatic Representation of a Culture of Violence in Sam Shepard's *The Late Henry Moss*', pp. 44–5. Also see Ben Brantley, 'No-Good Dad Whose Tale is Told Repeatedly'; Carol Rosen, *Sam Shepard: A 'Poetic Rodeo'*, p. 201.

16. Carol Rosen, *Sam Shepard*, p. 203.

17. For a complete list of reviews, see http://www.sam-shepard.com/deadhorse.html, a website dedicated to keeping up with the career of Sam Shepard.

18. Ben Brantley, 'It's Old Timers' Day at Shepard's Arena'.

19. Ben Brantley, 'Sam Shepard of Today, and of Many Days Ago'.

20. Stephen J. Bottoms, 'Shepard and Off-Off Broadway: The Unseen Hand of Theatre Genesis', p. 42.

21. Stephen J. Bottoms, *Theatre of Sam Shepard*, p. 48.

22. Laura J. Graham, 'Sam Shepard', p. 209.

23. I will be quoting from the 1972 script reprinted by Faber and Faber in the collection *Seven Plays*.

24. Don Shewey writes, 'For Shepard, . . . stardom—based on a nebulous, self-projected image, as easily put on or removed as a bit of glittery makeup—is worthless. Yet it's so ingrained in contemporary culture that it's practically irresistible'. *Sam Shepard*, p. 84.

25. Steven D. Putzel and Suzanne R. Westfall, 'The Back Side of Myth: Sam Shepard's Subversion of Mythic Codes in *Buried Child*', p. 117. Also see: Thomas Nash, 'Sam Shepard's Buried Child: The Ironic Use of Folklore', pp. 486–91.

26. For more on Shepard's incorporation of mythology in his plays, see Laura Shea, 'The Sacrificial Crisis in Sam Shepard's *Buried Child*', pp. 1–9; Thomas P. Adler, 'Repetition and Regression in *Curse of the Starving Class* and *Buried Child*', pp. 111–22; Carol Rosen, *Sam Shepard*, pp. 222–3.

27. Thomas P. Adler, 'Repetition and Regression', p. 121.

28. David J. DeRose, *Sam Shepard*, p. 99.

29. Thomas P. Adler, 'Repetition and Regression', p. 116. For a similar argument see Harold Bloom, *Bloom's Major Dramatists: Sam Shepard*, p. 42.

30. Lynda Hart, *Sam Shepard's Metaphorical Stages*, p. 88.

31. See for example Gregory W. Lanier, 'True West? Sam Shepard's Mythic Misdirections', pp. 49–54; Ron Mottram, *Inner Landscapes: The Theater of Sam Shepard*, pp. 144–50; Tucker Orbison, 'Mythic Levels in Sam Shepard's *True West*', pp. 507–19.

32. Qtd. in Lynda Hart, *Sam Shepard's Metaphorical Stages*, p. 105.

33. Taav argues that 'What distinguishes the two plays . . . is that Lee's victory is nowhere nearly as complete as that of Crow's, nor is Austin's defeat as devastating as that of Hoss's'. *A Body Across a Map*, p. 70.

34. Carol Rosen, *Sam Shepard*, p. 137.

35. Ibid.

36. Frank Rich, reviewer for the *New York Times*, noted that despite the terrible direction of the first New York production, Shepard is 'one of the American theater's most precious natural resources'. Reproduced in Harold Bloom, *Sam Shepard*, p. 61.

37. See, for example, Ruby Cohn, *New American Dramatists 1960–1990*, pp. 160–84; Gerry McCarthy, 'New Mythologies: Mamet, Shepard and the American Stage', pp. 354–68; Carol Rosen, *Sam Shepard*, pp. 138–9.

38. 'Shepard ingeniously uses the theatrical convention of changing light-effects to merge present and past, and alternate between different layers of time', Rád points out, 'so that the father—a corpse in the present of the events, placed on the bed in the alcove—can come to life within the play not only as a verbal but as a physical actuality to testify "in the flesh" to his last days alive'. 'Dramatic Representation', p. 52.

39. Boróka Prohászka Rád, 'Dramatic Representation', pp. 45–6.

40. Matthew Roudané, 'Shepard on Shepard', p. 71.

41. See Michael Almereyda's 2004 documentary *This So-Called Disaster*.

42. Matthew Roudané, 'Sam Shepard's *The Late Henry Moss*', p. 281.

43. For more on the political relevance in *Chicago*, see Stephen J. Bottoms, *The Theatre of Sam Shepard*, pp. 39–40.

44. Carol Rosen, *Sam Shepard*, p. 235.

45. John M. Clum, 'The Classic Western and Sam Shepard's Family Sagas', p. 173.

46. Matthew Roudané, 'Shepard on Shepard', p. 71.

47. Stephen J. Bottoms, 'Shepard and Off-Off Broadway', p. 43.

48. Matthew Roudané, 'Introduction', p. 2.

49. Stephen J. Bottoms, *Theatre of Sam Shepard*, p. 2.

19 CHRISTOPHER SHINN

Stephen Bottoms

Four; Other People; Where Do We Live; Dying City; Now or Later; Picked

Introduction

When future generations ask what it *felt* like to live in the United States at the beginning of the twenty-first century, there will be few more reliable barometers than the collected plays of Christopher Shinn. Insistently contemporary, Shinn's dramatic realism is almost diaristic in its chronicling of small but significant details in the everyday lives of his characters. Whether tracing seemingly trivial debates about entertainment media (his plays frequently feature arguments about the latest topical movie, TV show or internet innovation) or exploring the impact of historic events such as the 9/11 attacks on New York or the American-led war in Iraq, Shinn focuses unerringly on the texture of the quotidian, and on a deliberately understated sense of personal bewilderment or trauma, rather than on 'the big picture' dominating the headlines.[1] His primary interest is in the intersection between sociopolitical circumstances and the subtleties of individual psychology: 'I think all my plays are about the difficulty of integrating who we are with the world we live in.'[2]

Shinn is one of a significant handful of American dramatists who have been more consistently supported and produced by theatres in Britain than at home. His first four plays all premiered in London. For Shinn, this warmth of response 'across the pond' is explained by the fact that British and Irish playwrights from Shaw to Churchill have continually demonstrated an 'integration of the social and psychological that we don't quite have, I think, in America, where the psychological is seen as separate from the social and political'.[3] Certainly a recurring problem for the reception of his plays in America has been a tendency to focus on the former to the exclusion of the latter. Yet this may be because Shinn's drama relies on nuance and inference, more than on explicit social statements. He recalls that, when he read O'Neill's *Long Day's Journey into Night* and Miller's *Death of Salesman* at school, he was compelled less by their commentary on the damage wrought by poverty and capitalistic aspiration than by the almost inarticulable sense of collective trauma underpinning them: 'the feeling of dread overpowered me'.[4] Similarly, when Shinn came to adapt Henrik Ibsen's naturalist classic *Hedda Gabler* for the Roundabout Theatre on Broadway, in 2009, he pared away much of Ibsen's explanatory verbiage – dusting off the Victorian cobwebs in order to permit both actors and audiences more freedom in reading between the lines of the play's psychosexual tensions. 'This dramatist's singular gift', the *New York Times'* Ben Brantley has memorably remarked, is 'for presenting human murkiness with precisely shaded clarity'.[5]

Born in Hartford, Connecticut, in 1975, Shinn grew up with an acute awareness of social and economic difference. His father was from a wealthy, upper-middle-class family, and worked as an investment manager, but by comparison, his mother's background was relatively modest. She worked within the public school system, and it was her enthusiasm for the arts that initially inspired Shinn to take up writing (initially short stories, at a young age). Tellingly, though, he also recalls parental influence of a different sort: 'My father, who was not particularly sympathetic towards the poor, nonetheless had a great interest in the different neighborhoods of Hartford, and we'd often go for early morning weekend drives through the city's streets. There I saw the most profound and unimaginable poverty—and only five minutes away from my middle-class town.'[6]

A concern to reflect on social contrasts and injustices manifested itself early on in Shinn's writing, and he recalls being bewildered by the apparent lack of interest in such matters displayed by his fellow students on the Dramatic Writing programme at New York University, where he studied during the mid-1990s. Undeterred, Shinn channelled his knowledge of Hartford's suburban geography into the writing of his first play *Four*, and after graduating in 1997 he sent the manuscript out to not-for-profit regional theatres all over the United States. When the play was met with indifference, Shinn looked further afield in search of a more sympathetic hearing. London's leading new-writing theatre, the Royal Court, was at the time pursuing a particularly aggressive policy of searching out raw, young dramatic voices, in the wake of its mid-1990s successes with 'in yer face' dramas such as Mark Ravenhill's *Shopping and Fucking*.[7] Shinn sent *Four* to the Court with an uncharacteristically cocky cover note asserting that his play was better than Ravenhill's, and the strategy paid off. In 1998, aged just 23, he became the youngest American playwright ever to be produced at the venue.

The Plays

Four (1998)

The deceptively simple title of Shinn's first play, like his writing more generally, is in fact deftly multi-layered. The action takes place among four characters, on the Fourth of July, and mostly constitutes a kind of awkwardly elaborate foreplay prior to two simultaneous sexual acts. These take place in different locations, but are juxtaposed using a split-scene dynamic perhaps inspired by Tony Kushner's *Angels in America* (Kushner had been one of Shinn's visiting tutors at NYU). As in *Angels*, the fluidity of the play's swift movement between different scenes and locations necessitates a minimal use of staging (e.g. the appearance of key pieces of furniture, rather than full sets). The stage directions also imply the use of a projection screen at the back of the stage, on which the 'garish, gorgeous assault' of Independence Day fireworks is finally made visible in an explosion of 'silent color' (p. 50). The soundlessness of the pyrotechnics underscores their anticlimactic impact in the uneasy aftermath of the dual sexual encounters. A sense of aching disappointment with life pervades the whole play, in counterpoint to the celebratory occasion.

Shinn was just 20 when he wrote *Four*, and there can be little doubt that June, the troubled, white, 17-year-old introduced in the play's first scene, is rooted in personal experience. June is a young gay man who is not yet 'out' to his parents or friends, and seems acutely uneasy with his sexuality in a main street America which – despite the advances of gay liberation in major urban centres – remains deeply homophobic. The play depicts his first, surreptitious encounter with a black, older man, Joe, whom he has met through an internet chat room. Joe is a literature professor and seems superficially ebullient, pontificating about American pop culture in honour of the occasion: '*I* love America. Movies. Fast food. Cars. Freedom! Hah' (p. 11). Underneath the bravado, however, and the attempts to play the role of beneficent mentor, bestowing on June his first sexual experience, it is clear that Joe too is nursing a profound sense of pain and alienation from the very society he celebrates. This appears to be rooted in both his sexuality and his ethnicity: African Americans have historically struggled to become integrated not only within the mainstream but within a predominantly white gay subculture. Joe rails at the way that gay men (historically denied the right to publicly endorsed monogamy) have so often prized external appearances and casual sex over sustained relationships: 'this disease is the best thing that could have happened to gay men', he declares of the AIDS epidemic and the new sexual caution it induced, 'because in a certain sense it's made us *human*' (p. 37). By the end of the play, however, following a sexual encounter in which, thanks to June's virginal hesitation, Joe becomes very much the active partner, there is a sense that neither one has found the 'human' connection he was seeking. As they drive back to where June was picked up by Joe, it is the latter who begins, silently and unprompted, to weep.

In the play's parallel narrative, Abigayle, a young African American woman, conducts a similarly unsatisfying liaison with Dexter, a half-white, half-Latino basketball player and small-time drug dealer. This thread too is circular: just as June is picked up and dropped off at an empty car lot, Abigayle is found at the beginning and end of the play in her family home, attending to a bedbound mother who – though unseen – is heard pounding on the walls for attention. Abigayle, it gradually becomes clear, is Joe's daughter, and his wife's unspecified illness (like Harper's pill addiction in *Angels in America*) is implicitly a consequence of the prolonged psychological torment induced by marriage to a closeted homosexual who has no real desire for her. The collateral damage of homophobia is thus seen to extend in many directions.

This is not, however, the central concern of the Abigayle narrative: despite the relational link between the play's two (by two) encounters, Shinn is more interested in thematic parallels than in causal connections. He demonstrates a shrewd awareness that the personal difficulties of young gay men such as June do not make them exceptional: 'because of homophobia, homosexuality is more likely to be entwined with all kinds of traumas', he has noted, but more generally, 'it's simply really challenging to come into one's sexuality, whether one is gay or straight or anywhere in between. Sexuality is traumatic'.[8] Clearly that is the case for Abigayle, who struggles with the familiar young woman's dilemma of whether or not to 'put out' to a cute but potentially unreliable male suitor. Despite deflecting his telephone overtures at the outset, Abigayle eventually decides to turn the tables on Dexter, at his house, by abruptly taking the sexual initiative. It is one of Shinn's many achievements in this beautifully melancholic play, however, that by the time Abigayle has mustered the courage to enact this putative moment of female sexual liberation, we have learnt enough about Dexter's own vulnerabilities and uncertainties to see even this (like Joe's advances on June) as a kind of inadvertent molestation. Dexter later confesses that he lost his virginity, at age 13, in a church basement, to a girl named Ladrica. 'She's dead now' (p. 46). That simple line, left hanging and unexplained, is one of the many unexploded emotional bombshells with which Shinn litters *Four*'s muted American landscape.

Other People (2000) and *Where Do We Live* (2002)

In Shinn's next two major plays, both of which also premiered at the Royal Court, Shinn's quasi-autobiographical focus shifts from Hartford to downtown New York City (where he now makes his home). *Where Do We Live* is explicitly a sequel to *Other People*, and both plays feature the same protagonist – a young, gay writer character named Stephen (a flawed, awkward figure who is painted by Shinn as a kind of pitilessly critical self-portrait). As with *Four*, the language of these plays shifts gear regularly between hesitantly negotiated dialogue and sudden bursts of monologue, but where *Four*'s longer speeches are usually composed of evocative recollections (vividly painted micro-narratives of suburban life, like a series of Raymond Carver-esque short stories), the New York plays acclimatize to context by insistently bursting into volleys of opinionated, rapid-fire chatter: 'Anyway, so this guy. The date. Café, nice, blah blah, we swap stories, walk around the East Village, blab about ex-boyfriends, look at some clothes, decide, what the hell, let's go see a show!' (p. 57). In this particular speech, Stephen continues almost without pausing for breath for two solid pages of text (only occasionally interrupted by interjections from his roommate Petra), yet the talking is mostly a kind of nervous white noise, spoken to avoid the fear of awkward silence on being reunited with Mark, his 'significant ex'. The torrent of language, as so often in Shinn, functions as a substitute for – but also a barrier to – real communication.

In both Stephen plays, Shinn continues the pattern, established in *Four*, of presenting relatively short scenes which shift location fluidly while cutting back and forth between dual, thematically juxtaposed narratives. *Other People* again revolves around a time of celebration (Christmas and New Year), and traces the vain attempts of both Stephen and Petra to find love and connectedness in the big city. As the title suggests, the play asks fundamentally ethical questions of our attitudes towards other people. 'How we treat people', observes Mark, 'sometimes makes them who they are' (p. 95). That thought is explored, for example, through Petra's attempts to resist being seen by others simply in terms of her sexuality – while also appearing to crave or need the attention that such objectification brings her. As if *becoming* the person other people want to see, she returns to her old job as a stripper, even though she does not need to financially. Yet this continuing looked-at-ness makes her distrustful of men who claim to see more in her. When she is eventually treated with kindness by a lonely, older man who offers to pay her to spend time with him, she confusedly seeks to respond to his interest in her *mind* by offering herself romantically (an offer which he politely refuses). The other key identity crisis depicted in *Other People* involves Stephen's ex, Mark, who has converted to evangelical Christianity in an attempt to 'repent' his troubled past as a cocaine addict. Mark's fragile salvation also involves trying to overcome his (once promiscuous) homosexuality, and so he avoids all physical contact with Stephen even while seeking sanctuary in his apartment. Stephen's distress at this turn of events is only exacerbated by Mark's confused attempts to extend Christian charity to Tan, an attractive, homeless rent boy who tries to pick him up in the East Village. Each of these characters seems, in their own way, to be desperate for trustful intimacy with another, but unable to find or retain it.

In *Where Do We Live*, the focus expands from the inhabitants of Stephen's apartment to the building in which they are located. In New York, people from very different social and economic backgrounds often find themselves living cheek by jowl, and Stephen is clearly disturbed by what he sees around him each day: 'People are dying in this building', he tells his new boyfriend Tyler: 'They are dying of poverty, of drugs, I see them every day, there are no jobs, I see their children, they go to schools that are falling apart' (p. 284). Tyler's response is strikingly blasé: 'Fine, but why does it upset you so much?' Everyone, he implies, should simply look after themselves, and Tyler's friend Billy even asserts that Mayor Giuliani's welfare bill has 'made the poor take responsibility for themselves', by withdrawing the state safety net (p. 281). Conversely, Billy derides Stephen's liberal attitudes to welfare as mere condescension of the poor.

These arguments are given focus in the play by the simple, ethical question of how Stephen should respond when his next-door neighbour Timothy, a crippled African American man, knocks on his door to ask for help in getting downstairs to the store. Stephen agrees, in the face of Tyler's warnings against becoming involved, in case the dependency escalates: 'you don't want to be a caretaker' (p. 237). The question of whether or not to provide aid is complicated by the fact that Stephen suspects Timothy's nephew Shed of selling drugs from the next-door apartment. He also feels assaulted by Shed's violently homophobic rap music, leaking through the thin walls. Stephen's prejudicial misapprehensions about Shed are mirrored by Shed's about Stephen, yet the play makes clear that each one also aspires to much more than stereotyped labels would imply. It is only in the aftermath of the attacks on New York, on 11 September 2001, that Shed and Stephen move from mutual suspicion towards a kind of tentative, though inarticulate rapprochement – as if drawn momentarily together by the city's shared trauma.

Of the 12 scenes in *Where Do We Live*, the first 10 take place sequentially between 9 August and 15 August, 2001. Then, at the opening of Scene 11, the screened date caption informs audiences that time has leapt forward to 27 September – more than two weeks after the World Trade Center fell. Tellingly, the attack itself is barely mentioned in the play, but the last two scenes provide evidence of its occurrence: people walk into apartments in breathing masks; jet planes roar past outside the window; Shed loses his new job in a hotel because of the collapse of the hospitality trade. Precisely because the characters do not or cannot speak about what has happened, a kind of gaping wound yawns in the dramaturgy of the play, to mirror the one at Ground Zero. More so than ever, then, the things being talked about by Shinn's characters clearly do not represent what is being *felt*.

Shinn claims that he began writing *Where Do We Live* on 12 September 2001, in the immediate aftermath of the attacks. He felt compelled to write, but had no idea where he was going (which may be partly why he fell back on pre-existing characters as a starting point): 'I was just terrified. It was like automatic writing.'[9] Despite this, the play is strikingly coherent in its multi-layered depiction of competing interest groups and subcultures in Mayor Giuliani's New York, and the tensions and misapprehensions between them are implicitly paralleled with the global hostilities that suddenly manifest themselves so violently on 9/11. 'I've been reading about Afghanistan', Stephen comments, referring to the source of the attacks: 'the chaos of the region. So many tribes—so many different groups . . . disconnected from each other. . . . Just—how fractured and isolated they are—like New York too, in some ways' (p. 302). What if, the play seems to ask, the differences between people – whether across the world, or right next door to each other – are far less pronounced than we imagine?

Dying City (2006)

Where Do We Live won Shinn a *Village Voice* OBIE Award for Playwriting, and significantly raised his profile in the United States. With his next two plays, he was finally able to write to American commissions: *What Didn't Happen* premiered at New York's Playwrights Horizons late in 2002, and *On the Mountain* at South Coast Repertory, in Orange County, early in 2005. The first deals with the inter-generational tensions and rivalries between a group of writers gathered at a remote retreat house in upstate New York; the second, loosely based on Henry James's novella *The Aspern Papers*, explores conflicts over the legacy of a Kurt Cobain-like rock star. In both, a troubled young girl named Jaime (same name, different character) functions as a kind of living ghost of past loves (*j'aime*).

Neither play, however, is entirely successful: the allusive lightness of touch in Shinn's earlier work is replaced at times by somewhat ponderous overstatement. This appears to be a side-effect of his attempts to ground the plays in single settings (the outside and inside of a house, respectively), and to write longer, more sustained scenes, rather than permitting rapid shifts of location: 'In *What Didn't Happen*, I wanted to write a play that was set in one place', he explains simply.[10] This decision was, in part, a conscious reaction against the quick-cut televisual aesthetic that he had briefly been contracted to produce: Shinn left a writing contract with a cable TV network in 2002 (a decision alluded to in fictional form in *What Didn't Happen*). The scene-shifting fluidity of his earlier plays had to some extent resembled that of screenplays, and indeed *Four* was eventually adapted as a successful independent movie in 2012. Distrusting the formulaic requirements of television writing, however, and fearing the loss of his distinctive, individual voice as a writer, Shinn turned his back on the media industry (which today sustains so many of his fellow American playwrights), and attempted to reaffirm his identity as a *theatre* artist.

With *Dying City* (2006), Shinn finally struck a telling balance between the fluidity of his earlier work and the use of a single dramatic location. Hailed as his 'most psychologically piercing and richly textured drama yet',[11] it intercuts scenes taking place in the same apartment in two separate time-frames, 18 months apart. In July 2005, we find Peter paying an unscheduled visit to his sister-in-law Kelly's apartment. Their awkward exchanges prompt Kelly's memories of another night in January 2004, when her husband Craig left for the war in Iraq – a journey from which he would never return. In the scenes depicting this disturbing evening, Craig is played by the same actor who plays Peter (switching roles in a series of quick, off-stage changes). The brothers are identical twins, and Peter's visit thus constitutes a kind of uncanny haunting for Kelly, as if she cannot escape the memory of her dead husband. Peter, a professional actor, speaks of having grown up wanting to mimic his admired brother – and now he seems almost to have become his shade, or doppelganger.

Dying City is the second play Shinn wrote using the device of identical twins played by the same male actor, following the 2001's *The Coming World* (a shorter, gentler play which premiered at London's Soho Theatre). 'It's a really simple way of saying the social world exists', Shinn explains of his interest in twins, who though genetically identical might end up (like Peter and Craig) as very different people, whether gay or straight, actor or soldier: 'I'm interested in the ways that the social world determines individual psychology as much as other factors do.'[12] Even if 'it's not just genes', though, Shinn creates a powerful sense that these individuals are connected and conditioned in ways that are beyond their conscious control, and in both *The Coming World* and *Dying City,* he invites connections with O'Neill's *Long Day's Journey into Night* – that classic American drama of familial determinism. In *The Coming World,* set on a windswept beach, the names of the brothers – Ed and Ty – suggest an allusion to O'Neill's Edmund and Jamie Tyrone. In *Dying City,* Peter is performing the role of Edmund in a New York production of *Long Day's Journey*. His fellow actors, he complains, have lost sight of the traumatic depths of the play, treating it simply like any other job: 'it turned out to be like Long Day's Journey to the Hamptons—actors constantly checking messages, luxurious spreads of pastries laid out at every rehearsal. . . . I wanted to scream! The play is like being in a war, these people are trying to kill each other–literally!' (p. 37) Peter sounds, not coincidentally, like a soldier disgusted with the population back home, who are ignoring or forgetting the terrifying reality of the protracted war in Iraq (which was at its bloodiest when Shinn wrote the play in 2005). Peter believes that his brother's death has induced, in him, a form of post-traumatic stress disorder, and he speaks of waking nightmares such as the moment he 'saw' a Black Hawk helicopter crashing through the roof of the theatre during a curtain call.

Yet while Peter feels haunted by his brother's death, he seems narcissistically unaware of the re-traumatizing impact his own presence in her apartment is having on Kelly. As eventually becomes clear in the flashback narrative, Craig effectively broke his marriage to her on the night he left, claiming that he no longer loved her. Having kept that devastating news to herself, and having dutifully performed the role of grieving widow, she now finds herself being expected somehow to comfort Craig's identical twin – who also insists on reading to her, out loud, from printouts of email correspondence that Craig had sent to him from Iraq. The emails raise the possibility that Craig may have taken his own life, and – equally distressing for Kelly – they suggest a disturbing confusion in his mind between military and sexual conquest. There are echoes here of the horrific, sexualized abuse of Iraqi prisoners at Baghdad's Abu Ghraib prison, at the hands of American service personnel, which came to light in 2004.

Craig, it seems, does not intend to hurt or anger Kelly in the reading of these emails. Careful reading of the dialogue and subtext suggests that he does so simply through ineptitude, and a misdirected urge to maintain some kind of family intimacy with his sister-in-law by sharing memories of his brother, her husband. But this, as Shinn explains, is precisely the concern of the play: 'the stated intent of the war was not to go in there and humiliate and sadistically torture Iraqis. Just as in a relationship between two people, hopefully the intent is never to betray them in a violent or sexual way. So I was interested in the idea of good intentions becoming perverted'.[13] That theme is also apparent, in different ways, in Shinn's next play, *Now or Later*.

Now or Later (2008)

Premiering at the Royal Court in the immediate run-up to the 2008 US Presidential election, *Now or Later* depicts the climax of a fictional presidential campaign. Set in the hotel room of the candidate's son on the night that election results are being announced on television, the play is sustained as an intense, single act over a real-time running length of about 80 minutes – as mounting crisis builds inexorably to a climactic confrontation. Although the political details recounted in the play locate it very much as contemporary to 2008, Shinn avoided depicting the kind of headline-grabbing 'first' represented by Barack Obama's election that year as the first African American president. Instead, he again focuses on the ramifications of America's confrontation with the Islamic world, and specifically the threat to freedom of speech posed by the fear of fundamentalist violence. The play alludes directly to the recent case of Danish newspaper cartoons of the Prophet Mohammad, which had given sufficient offense as to cause rioting and deaths in some parts of the world. In *Now or Later*, the campaign team are extremely agitated about just-released internet images of John, the candidate's son, dressed up as a parody of Mohammad at a college party. Appearing on the night of John Senior's likely election victory, the images seem calculated to derail the celebrations, prompt negative media headlines and perhaps invite violently hostile reactions internationally. John is thus under pressure to issue an immediate public apology for his actions, to take the sting out of the story.

The epigraph for *Now or Later* is taken from *Hamlet*: 'Be bloody or be nothing'. But just as the dramatic tension in *Hamlet* depends on the Prince's elongated delay in exacting revenge on Claudius for his father's death, in *Now or Later* John delays assenting to the apology, thereby accentuating the (perceived) danger of bloody reprisals. A series of campaign aides and family members pay an ever more agitated series of visits to John's room, but he stubbornly resists their demands that he 'go public' with an apology, because he resents the idea that any form of public expression deemed to cause offense to Muslims should be censored or retracted. He had dressed as Mohammad, in the first place, not merely as 'fancy dress', but as a way of mocking the cultural relativism of his peers: how can liberal Americans demand the right to gender and sexual liberation (as at the college 'naked party' John had gate-crashed), but simultaneously endorse the right of Islamic states to oppress women and homosexuals in the name of cultural 'difference'? Isn't that another case of good intentions (not to cause offense) becoming somehow perverted? Is it really 'cultural imperialism' to believe that American values *at their best* – such as the First Amendment right to freedom of speech and expression – should be enjoyed universally?

This is, then, a play about speech. Yet the brilliance of *Now or Later* lies in the way that Shinn again deftly balances what is *said* with what is left *unsaid*. These characters are highly intelligent, politically astute people who can (and do) argue vociferously over the finer points of America's position in the world. Yet there is a sense, throughout the play, that the debates over West versus East are in part a smokescreen hiding the much closer-to-home tensions of son versus parents (just as *Where Do We Live* had paralleled the tensions between next-door neighbours and global neighbours). 'Why can't you see how they see you?' asks campaign aide Tracy asks, referring to Muslims encountering the internet postings, to which John responds: 'I can see how they see me! That's the problem—they need to see me differently—as having a right to my opinion!' (p. 27). There is a slippage here around the word 'they' – a word that seems to refer *both* to the imagined Muslims *and* to his politically cautious parents. Indeed, part of his rationale for refusing to issue an apology is that he does not wish to live a life in the 'public eye', as an adjunct of to his parents' political ambitions: 'I want a normal life!' he insists, 'I want not to live in a bubble of insanity' (p. 15). The barely spoken of trauma lurking behind the play's action is the memory of John's teenage suicide attempt – apparently a result of confusion over both is parents' true feelings for him, and his own nascent homosexuality. He remains 'in the closet', even now, with his parents' tacit consent (a 'gay son' might not play well for them in middle America), and so their sudden demand that he 'go public' is all the more galling. The play builds inexorably towards a climactic scene in which John's father finally arrives to confront and persuade him – a scene in which their hesitant expressions of familial love are negotiated with all the awkwardness of a political summit. When John still refuses to back down, his father loses his temper and physically assaults him. In the shocked aftermath of this attack, the re-traumatized John finally assents to a public apology – on the grounds that he doesn't want anyone to be hurt because of his actions. The ironies here are palpable, and Shinn leaves us to ponder who, if anyone, was in the right.

Picked (2011)

Now or Later was a hit in London, enjoying an extended run at the Royal Court, after which – Shinn admits – 'I thought there would be a war between theaters here [in the United States] to do the play first.'[14] Yet the play was met with almost complete disinterest at home, and it took four years (and another presidential election campaign) to find an American premiere, at Boston's Huntington Theatre. Shinn speculated that the complexity of political debate in the play might have been the problem: 'we're obsessed with the human stories [at election time,] and yet really digging deep, getting under the skin of the political and social issues that define us somehow feels "un-American" because it reminds us of differences and divisions we don't like to think about'.[15] Like his characters in the play, however, Shinn may here be rationalizing a deeper sense of personal hurt: by his own account, he spent a lot of money on therapy trying to understand *Now or Later*'s rejection, and his next play *Picked* can be read as a direct reaction to it. Consciously cutting his reliance on the Royal Court in a bid to raise his profile at home, Shinn secured a premiere production at the Vineyard Theatre in New York.

Leaving aside the political concerns of Shinn's recent work, *Picked* is a kind of psychological mystery revolving around an actor, Kevin, who is suddenly plucked from obscurity to star in a major new Hollywood movie. The film's director, John, is a specialist in high-concept science fiction, modelled after James Cameron (the descriptions of his most recent film clearly allude to Cameron's 2009 spectacular, *Avatar*). John virtually seduces Kevin into the role with promises not just of stardom, but of an intensely personal creative process. Using brain scan technology, the film's narrative is to be built around his own deepest personal conflicts, and Kevin will, through the wonders of computer graphics, play both the film's human hero and its robotic villain.

Bit by bit, though, this Faustian bargain begins to unravel. During filming, John concludes that the doubled casting will not work, and introduces a second actor, Nick, to play the robot. 'This is not a rejection', John tells him, 'it's actually a testament to how powerful your captain is' (p. 28). It's the kind of flattering explanation that may be perfectly sincere, but is bound to provoke self-doubt in the listener. The anxieties are magnified when, with filming completed, it is Nick who quickly gets further work on another major film, while Kevin remains frighteningly unemployed. Meanwhile his girlfriend Jen, an actress who has long been unemployed herself, becomes understandably resentful of

Kevin's self-pity over the 'failure' of his big break. Yet after ending their relationship, she is cast in John's next movie.

In *Picked*, Shinn subtly succeeds in drawing the audience into sharing Kevin's increasingly paranoid sense that the world is somehow conspiring against him. Indeed we see the action very much through his eyes: the play is divided into 22 tightly scripted scenes, and the implied location shifts constantly, dictating a minimum of stage design. The one constant factor in this fluid narrative is Kevin himself, who remains central to every scene – the ruling consciousness of the play just as he was supposed to be in the film! Thus, it is with Kevin that the audience encounters John's high-tech psychobabble, the introduction of his strange doppelganger Nick, Jen's decision to leave him and the bewildering sense that people are avoiding speaking to him. Shinn cleverly weaves a sense of metaphysical conspiracy, or unsolved cryptogram, before leading us – finally – towards the realization that there never was a mystery other than life itself, and its strange twists of fate or chance. *Picked* is in part a study of the peculiar insecurity of the acting profession – with its contingent narcissism and helplessness, its reliance on personality chemistry and the whims of casting directors. Yet it is also, more broadly, Shinn's most piercingly consistent portrait to date of human 'murkiness', rooted as it apparently is in his own struggle to process the highs and lows of success and rejection, and the existential fear that one's best moments may already be in the past, rather than still to come.

Summary

'I'm really lucky that I got produced right away and felt that my uniqueness in particular was what was valued,' Shinn has commented in interview: 'Now, if those initial plays had been rejected, I wonder if I would have tried to write plays that were less specific.'[16] Arguably, Shinn's career tells us much about the peculiar pitfalls of being an American playwright in the early twenty-first century. Championed overseas in London, by a theatre that sought to celebrate the distinctive 'voices' of young writers, he proved less willing than some of his peers to accommodate his skills to the anonymizing, production-line demands of writing for television. And yet Shinn's insistence on writing sharply intelligent, politically provocative plays, often centring around gay male characters, has perhaps made it difficult for him to find the production opportunities at home that his writing richly deserves. True, *Dying City* was nominated for the Pulitzer Prize and has subsequently been produced in cities across the United States. Yet its appeal to producers lies not least in being mercifully cheap to stage (only two actors), and in its showcasing of a virtuoso role-doubling 'turn' from its male lead. Conversely, there is a sad irony in the fact that *Now or Later*, a play centrally concerned with issues around freedom of speech, should have been effectively silenced in the United States for four years after its world premiere.

At the risk of indulging in the kind of conspiracy paranoia that *Picked* both explores and ultimately doubts, it is worth noting that Shinn has probably, indeed, won himself powerful enemies in the American theatre world by refusing to toe the industry line. In 2006, he inadvertently became a spokesperson against self-censorship in American theatre when a blog article he wrote was picked up on by the mainstream press (just as the 'amorphous, gossipy stuff' in *Now or Later* goes from internet backwaters to international headlines). Shinn had decried the decision of the New York Theatre Workshop to cancel its scheduled production of Alan Rickman's documentary play *My Name is Rachel Corrie*, apparently for fear of offending members of the New York's Jewish community.[17] (Rachel Corrie was an American peace activist who had been crushed to death by an Israeli bulldozer while protesting against the occupation of Palestinian territories.) Shinn's analysis of the situation – to which *Now or Later* was a kind of response – was that the American not-for-profit theatre sector had become so reliant on funding from corporate sponsors and conservative subscribers that it had become pathologically cautious about causing offence.[18]

Such forthright biting of the hand that feeds will not have made Shinn popular in certain circles. Yet despite his diagnosis of caution and conservatism, he remains a passionate advocate for the potential of theatre as a public art form in these difficult times. As well as being a place for laughter and entertainment, he notes, 'theater is a place where you can be scared, where you can grieve, it's a place for fear, a place for mourning'. In its understated, allusive way, his own playwriting stands as compelling testimony to that conviction: 'Theater is one of those places where that traumatic space is still alive—and the only place where it's a communal event. Now is the time for theaters to step up, to provide what can't be provided anywhere else.'[19]

Primary Sources

Works by Christopher Shinn

Dying City (London: Methuen, 2006).

Hedda Gabler, adapted from the play by Henrik Ibsen (New York: Playscripts Inc., 2009).

Now or Later (London: Methuen, 2008).

On the Mountain (New York: Dramatists Play Service, 2006).

Picked (New York: Dramatists Play Service, 2012).

Where Do We Live and Other Plays: Four, Other People, What Didn't Happen, The Coming World, Where Do We Live (New York: Theatre Communications Group, 2005).

Secondary Sources

Armstrong, Mark, 'Staying Alive in a *Dying City*', *Brooklyn Rail,* February 2007, http://www.brooklynrail.org/2007/02/theater/staying-alive.

Bottoms, Stephen, 'The Canonization of Christopher Shinn: A Modest Proposal on Ethics', *Modern Drama* 55, 3 (Fall 2012), 329–55.

Brantley, Ben, 'Actors Live Their Double Lives, Both on the Screen and Off', *New York Times,* 20 April 2011, http://theater.nytimes.com/2011/04/21/theater/reviews/picked-by-christopher-shinn-at-vineyard-theater-review.html?_r=0.

Burton-Hill, Clemency, 'The laureate of intractable conflicts', *Spectator,* 10 September 2008, http://www.spectator.co.uk/features/2075081/the-laureate-of-intractable-conflicts/.

Corrie, Rachel, Alan Rickman and Katherine Viner, *My Name is Rachel Corrie* (London: Nick Hern, 2008).

Dapier, Jarrett, 'A Playwright's Traumatic Vision', *In These Times,* 7 March 2008, http://inthesetimes.org/article/3542/a_playwrights_traumatic_vision/.

Greenspan, David, 'Christopher Shinn', *BOMB* 81 (Fall 2002), http://bombsite.com/issues/81/articles/2522.

Hartigan, Patti, 'Christopher Shinn on politics, pain, and *Now or Later*', *Boston Globe*, 13 October 2012, http://www.bostonglobe.com/arts/theater-art/2012/10/13/playwright-christopher-shinn-politics-pain-and-now-later/fn1k6mdDZLGywGa1LYzTnJ/story.html.

Shinn, Christopher, 'It Starts With Us'. In Caridad Svich (ed.), *Out of Silence: Censorship in Theatre and Performance* (Roskilde: Eyecorner Press, 2012), pp. 58–63.

—, 'Market Rules', *Index on Censorship*, Winter 2008 www.indexoncensor ship.org/wp-content/. . ./12/shinn-winter08.pdf.

Sierz, Aleks, *In-yer-face Theatre: British Drama Today* (London: Faber, 2001).

Wallenberg, Christopher, 'A playwright looks inward to understand the reasons we act out', *Boston Globe*, 21 October 2007, http://www.boston.com/ae/theater_arts/articles/2007/10/21/a_playwright_looks_inward_to_understand_the_reasons_we_act_out/?page=full.

Notes

1. For a lengthier consideration of what I have called Shinn's 'traumatic realism', see Stephen Bottoms, 'The Canonization of Christopher Shinn'.
2. Qtd. in Wallenberg, 'A Playwright Looks Inward'.
3. Qtd. in Burton-Hill, 'The laureate of intractable conflicts'.
4. Qtd. in Greenspan, 'Christopher Shinn'.
5. Ben Brantley, 'Actors Live Their Double Lives'.
6. Qtd. in Dapier, 'A Playwright's Traumatic Vision'.
7. See Sierz, *In-yer-face Theatre*.
8. Qtd. in Dapier, 'A Playwright's Traumatic Vision'.
9. Qtd. in Greenspan, 'Christopher Shinn'.
10. Ibid.
11. Christopher Wallenberg, 'A Playwright Looks Inward'.
12. Qtd. in Armstrong, 'Staying alive'.
13. Qtd. in Wallenberg, 'A Playwright Looks Inward'.
14. Qtd. in Hartigan, 'Christopher Shinn on politics, pain'.
15. Qtd. in Burton-Hill, 'The laureate of intractable conflicts'.
16. Qtd. in Armstrong, 'Staying alive'.
17. For full context of this case see Christopher Shinn, 'It Starts With Us', pp. 58–63, and other material in Caridad Svich's *Out of Silence*.
18. See Shinn's articles 'It Starts With Us' and 'Market Rules'.
19. Qtd. in Armstrong, 'Staying alive'.

20 LUIS VALDEZ

Jorge Huerta

The Shrunken Head of Pancho Villa; *La quinta temporada (The Fifth Season)*; *Zoot Suit*; *I Don't Have to Show You No Stinking Badges*; *Mummified Deer*

Introduction

Luis Valdez is indisputably the leading Chicano (Mexican American) director and playwright: as the founder of the Teatro Campesino (Farm Workers' Theater) in 1965, he inspired a national movement of Chicana and Chicano theatre troupes dedicated to the exposure and analysis of sociopolitical problems that have plagued the Chicano and Mexican communities of the United States. Almost 50 years later, no other Chicana or Chicano playwright or director has generated as much critical interest as Valdez. His work includes plays, poems, books, essays, films and videos, all of which deal with the Chicano and Mexican experience in the United States. Valdez's work has inspired many articles, theses and dissertations and two books: a comparative analysis of Valdez's early work and the protest theatre of Amiri Baraka by Prof Harry Elam, Jr., as well as a critique and analysis of his work with the Teatro Campesino by Prof Yolanda Broyles-Gonzalez.

Luis Valdez was born to migrant farm worker parents in Delano, California, in 1940, the second in a family of 10 children. By the age of 12, he had developed an interest in puppet shows, which he would stage for neighbours and friends. While still in high school, he hosted his own programme on a local television station. After high school, Valdez entered San Jose State College where his interest in theatre continued to develop.

Valdez's first full-length play, *The Shrunken Head of Pancho*, was produced by San Jose State College in January of 1964, directed by the playwright. In 1965, after one year of working with the San Francisco Mime Troupe, Valdez returned to his hometown, Delano, California and proposed forming a theatre to the leaders of the incipient farm workers' union, Cesar Chavez and Dolores Huerta. He had been inspired by the Mime Troupe's bawdy, comical skits and messages of social justice performed for free in the parks of San Francisco. Valdez gathered a group of striking farm workers and together they formed the Teatro Campesino. The group performed at the edges of the fields, where they would stage what he termed 'actos', short comical sketches that demonstrated the need for a Union. Most importantly, the actos were created collectively, through improvisations that pitted the humble 'campesino' against the arrogant, greedy and despised 'Gringo' grower.[1] These brief, commedia-like sketches were modern 'morality plays', descendants of the Spanish religious folk theatre that has been performed in the American Southwest for centuries. Valdez became the Artistic Director as well as resident playwright for this raggle-taggle troupe of striking farm workers.

Within a matter of months, the Teatro Campesino was performing away from the fields, at universities and community centres, educating the general public about the farm workers' struggle and earning revenue for the Union. By 1967 Valdez and the Teatro left the Union in order to focus on his theatre rather than on the demands of a struggling labour organization. He needed the full attention of his company if he and the Teatro were to evolve both artistically and politically. In those formative years Valdez described his theatre as 'somewhere between Brecht and Cantinflas', alluding to the politics of the German director and playwright and to the physical humour of Mexico's Charlie Chaplin.[2]

Although he and his troupe were working collectively from the beginning, Valdez began to explore genres other than the acto. In 1967, he created what he termed a 'mito', or myth, titled *Dark Root of a Scream*, that condemned the Vietnam War.[3] This contemporary myth takes place during a wake for a Chicano who died in Vietnam, symbolic of all Chicanos who fought in a war that the playwright himself objected to. 'I refused to go to Vietnam', Valdez said 20 years later, 'but I encountered all the violence I needed on the home front: people were killed by the Farm Workers' strike'.[4] Valdez and his troupe gained international exposure at the Theatre des Nations festival in Nancy, France in 1969.

In only four years, the Teatro Campesino had become an international symbol of the Chicano and Mexicans' sociopolitical struggles.

In 1971 the troupe moved to its permanent home base in the rural village of San Juan Bautista, California's first capitol. In a strategic move that aided the Teatro in establishing a place in this politically conservative town, Valdez directed an adaptation of a centuries-old Mexican play about the appearances of the Virgin of Guadalupe to the humble Indian, Juan Diego, in 1531. Valdez incorporated his actors and the locals in this pageant honouring the Patron Saint of Mexico, performed in the eighteenth-century Spanish mission. The play, titled *La Virgen del Tepeyac,* has been produced in the mission every other year in December, alternating with a Spanish religious folk play, *La pastorela* (*The Shepherd's Play*), celebrated at Christmas in many Spanish-speaking parishes for centuries.

Next, Valdez and his troupe began adapting traditional Mexican 'corridos', or ballads, to the stage. A singer would sing the lyrics and the actors would act them out, adding dialogue from the corridos' texts. Sometimes the singer/narrator would verbalize the text while the actors mimed the physical actions indicated by the song. These simple movements were stylized, enhancing the musical rhythms and adding to the unique combination of elements. The corrido style was to appear again, altered to suit the needs of a broader theatrical piece, *La gran carpa de los Rasquachis* (*The Great Tent of the Underdogs*), scripted collectively and directed by Valdez in 1973. This is an epic mito which follows a Cantinflas-like Mexican character from his crossing the border into the United States and the subsequent indignities to which he is exposed until his death.[5]

For the next few years, Valdez continued to write and direct plays, leading to his most commercially successful play to date, *Zoot Suit,*[6] which opened in Los Angeles in 1978 and on Broadway in 1979.[7] The play was subsequently adapted into a motion picture written and directed by Valdez and released in 1981. Although the play did not win sufficient critical acclaim in New York to survive there,[8] it continued to run in Los Angeles and the film became an art film to the cognoscenti.

After so many years of battling the insensitivity of Hollywood, it was inevitable that Valdez's next major stage play, *I Don't Have to*

Show You No Stinking Badges! (1985) would expose the problems of stereotyping provoked by Hollywood.[9] While the Teatro continued to produce, Valdez began to focus his efforts on writing and directing films. In 1987 his most successful motion picture to date, *La Bamba*, the story of 1950s rocker Richie Valens, was released. In response to criticism that he was selling out to Hollywood, Valdez told an interviewer, 'I'm not selling out—I'm buying *in*'.[10] That same year he adapted the *Corridos* for public television, re-titled *Corridos: Tales of Passion and Revolution*.[11] Despite the critical and especially the financial success of *La Bamba*, Valdez was still swimming upstream in Hollywood. In 1994 he wrote the script and lyrics for his next major play, *BANDIDO!*, with music by Lalo Schifrin. The world premiere production, directed by José Luís Valenzuela, was co-produced by the Teatro Campesino and the Center Theatre Group's Mark Taper Forum in Los Angeles, California. Setting the tone for later plays, this is a melodrama within a play, centring on a historical figure, Tiburcio Vasquez, as a social rebel, contrasted with popular (mis)representations of the man as a villainous 'bandido' in the late nineteenth century.

Valdez returned to the theatre with *Mummified Deer* in 2000 and in 2005 Valdez and his son Kinan adapted the earlier *Corridos* re-titled *Corridos Remix*, produced by the San Diego Repertory Theatre. In 2011 Valdez directed *Zoot Suit* for La Compañía Nacional de Teatro de Mexico (The National Theatre of Mexico); the critically acclaimed production was awarded the 2011 Best Mexican Musical of the Year, an honour no Chicano play had ever earned. The production toured Mexico and was also performed in Colombia, the first Chicano play to be presented in Bogotá's Teatro Mayor, the most prestigious commercial theatre in the nation's capitol.

Valdez has won countless awards, including an Obie (1968); the Presidential Medal of Arts (1984); Peabody Award for excellence in television for *Corridos: Tales of Passion and Revolution* (1988); and, from Mexico, the Aguila Azteca award, the highest decoration bestowed by the Mexican Government on citizens of other countries (1994). Valdez has also been awarded several doctorates and Doctor of Fine Arts degrees from universities across the country.

The Plays

The Shrunken Head of Pancho Villa (1964)

The Shrunken Head of Pancho Villa takes place in a humble Mexican/ Chicano household that symbolizes immigrant disenfranchisement through distortion.[12] In his prefatory 'Note on style', Valdez prepares the reader and production team for what he envisions: 'The play therefore contains realistic and surrealistic elements working together to achieve a transcendental expression of the social condition of La Raza en los Estados Unidos [Mexicans/Chicanos in the U.S.]. . . . In short, it must reflect the psychological reality of the barrio.'[13] This play revolves around the central figure of Belarmino, a character 'who has no body' and claims to be the lost head of Mexican revolutionary icon, Pancho Villa. For Valdez, the Chicano reality could only be expressed through the surreal juxtaposed with characters and situations that are also extensions of reality.

One of the most perplexing images in this play is created by the cockroaches that grow ever larger, crawling all over the walls, in true expressionistic fashion. Worse, Belarmino's sister, Lupe, feeds these repulsive creatures to him and eventually eats them as well. Audiences gasp and gag at this exaggeration, literally voicing their repulsion of such an idea. This is precisely what the young playwright intended – you do not have characters eating cockroaches in your play without expectations. I believe this is Valdez's metaphor for what he terms 'the psychological reality of the barrio': confusion created by displacement.

The young writer employed exaggeration for political reasons. Belarmino (the decapitated revolutionary) politicizes the youngest brother, Joaquín, who represents the (revolutionary) Chicano. Joaquín is the most sympathetic character, the misunderstood 'vato loco', a disenfranchised street youth in constant trouble with the law and in conflict with his brother Domingo, who transforms into 'Mr. Sunday' ('domingo' is Sunday in English) in his total rejection of Mexican and Chicano culture.

After spending time in jail for robbing supermarkets to feed the poor, Joaquín comes home without a head. The juxtaposition of the bodyless head and the headless body is clear: combine them for a complete, revolutionary man. It is the playwright's hope that the confusion he perceives in the barrio will be replaced by a political consciousness, his 'psychological reality' more informed by an awareness of marginalization than by Freudian analysis. Valdez's characters and the situations in which they find themselves are representative of the playwright's dislocation, which, he believes, is universal to working class Mexicans and Chicanos. When Domingo rejects his culture, the audience laughs at the ridiculousness of his actions because they know people like him. Belarmino has the last word, calling for unity as an end to the Chicanos' cultural/political confusion. Years after the first production of the play, Valdez told an audience: '. . . people didn't exactly get it. . . . the horror, the horror of watching a brother become a stranger and the horror of watching somebody get their head cut off'.[14] Thus for the young playwright this play was a visceral response to the loss of a brother to total acculturation through denial of his Mexican roots and the loss of cultural identity through brainwashing/decapitation. In many ways, this experiment in playwriting set the tone for all of Luis Valdez's later works, none of which can be termed realism or realistic.

La quinta temporada (1966)

A good example of the farm worker acto is *La quinta temporada*, or *The Fifth Season*, created collectively under the sure hand of Valdez in 1966. As is usual in the typical acto, a character runs on to the stage or acting area to grab the audience's attention. He is wearing a sign around his neck that reads 'Campesino' and speaks directly to the audience:

> Oh, hello—*quihubole*! My name is José. What else? And I'm looking for a job . . . . You see, I just got in from Texas this morning and I need to send money back to my *familia*. I can do whatever you want, pick cotton, grapes, melons. (p. 29)

In an instant, we know who this character is, where he's from, why he is here and what he wants: a job. The sign around his neck also gives us his economic station: farm worker. Adding to the immediacy, when this acto was first created, the members of the Teatro Campesino *were* farm workers. This was not psychological realism, but reality served with a flourish of theatricality. When this acto was performed at the edge of the fields, with armed guards standing watch to make sure the members of the troupe did not step onto the grower's land, there was an urgency and palpable danger that few actors ever encounter. It was dangerous laughter being provoked when the second character walks on, introducing himself as 'Don Coyote' to the delight of the 'campesinos', who called farm labour contractors by this insulting name.

As the acto proceeds, we learn that Don Coyote is gathering farm labourers for the pig-faced Patrón, or boss. All of this is presented in broad strokes, with exaggerated movements and dialogue. While the incipient farm workers union was fighting for a union hiring hall and other improvements to their living and working conditions, the growers benefitted from 'coyotes', who sat in their air-conditioned trucks while the campesinos laboured under miserable conditions in the fields. Once the Campesino has agreed to work, the Patrón calls for summer. An actor walks on wearing the 'Summer' sign and with the back of his or her shirt covered with fake money. The campesinos laugh with glee at this visual representation of the economics of farm work: Summer is, indeed, 'covered with money'.

As 'Summer passes', the farm worker picks the money off 'Summer's' back and puts it into his back pocket; then the Coyote takes the money out of the farm worker's back pocket, stuffing *his* pockets with the money while the Grower takes most of the money out of the Coyote's back pocket. At the end of the season, the Campesino is left with no money while the Coyote and the Grower are flush. When the Campesino complains, the Coyote tells him that 'Autumn' is around the corner, 'Covered with money'. With no recourse, the Campesino agrees and the same pattern follows, again leaving the Campesino high and dry.

As the 'seasons' pass, the physical is made metaphorical and universal in this rendering of the farm workers' plight in the face of the greedy grower and Coyote. When 'Winter' arrives, the Campesino is left to fend for himself because there are no more crops to be picked. But 'Spring' arrives, offering hope to the Campesino by telling him to fight for his rights. When 'Summer' arrives the Campesino goes on strike and the Coyote and Patrón watch helplessly as Summer passes and nobody picks the crops. The same occurs when 'Autumn' passes and with the inevitable return of Winter, the cash-strapped Campesino survives with the help of 'The Churches', 'The Union' and 'La Raza' ('The People'), allegorical figures. They offer him money, food and spiritual support. The Patrón is finally forced to sign a Union contract and the acto ends in triumph for the farm worker and the Union.

As in all the actos that would follow, the basic action is to demonstrate a problem and offer a solution to that problem. Initially, the answer was 'Join the Union', but when the Teatro began to perform away from the fields, in schools, churches, community centres and universities, the solution was to boycott grapes and support the Union with donations and other kinds of material and emotional assistance. Most importantly, the actos demonstrated the power of unity against the growers and other.

Zoot Suit (1978)

Premiered in 1978, Zoot Suit played to sold-out houses for 11 months – breaking all previous records for Los Angeles Theatre. While the Los Angeles production continued to run, another production opened in New York on 25 March 1979. Although audiences were enthusiastic, the New York critics generally were not and the play closed after a four-week run. Hurt, but undaunted, Valdez could have the satisfaction that the success of the Los Angeles run enabled him to move more seriously into film-making and he adapted and directed Zoot Suit as a motion picture in 1981.[15]

In Zoot Suit Valdez combined elements of the earliest Teatro Campesino street theatre aesthetic and the 'mito' with 'Living Newspaper' techniques, professional choreography and Brechtian narrative that kept the action moving forward. Zoot Suit is the logical culmination of all that Valdez and his collective had written before, combining elements of the acto, mito and corrido in a spectacular documentary play with music. Unlike any of his previous plays or actos, however, Zoot Suit is based on historical fact, not a current crisis. The documentary form of the play is influenced by the Living Newspaper style; a documentary theatre that exposed current events during the 1930s. The giant backdrop of a newspaper front page is an effective metaphor for the all-pervading presence of the press. Zoot suiters were on the headlines of current newspapers and when El Pachuco symbolically cuts his way through the news and onto the stage at the top of the play he is taking possession of the stage and the audience. The giant switchblade he brandishes is a direct descendant of the exaggerated props in the actos.

Like the acto, *Zoot Suit* exposes social ills in a presentational style. It is a play that is closer to the docudrama form, owing more to Brecht than to Clifford Odets as the action reveals the events surrounding the infamous Sleepy Lagoon Murder Trial of 1942. By employing a narrator, Valdez makes direct contact with his audience. El Pachuco's almost constant presence underscores the central character, Henry Reyna's inner thoughts and tribulations, skilfully captivating the audience and serving as a continual commentator on the action.

El Pachuco even stops the action entirely in order to make a point, telling Henry (and the audience) to listen again when the judge rules that the 'zoot haircuts will be retained throughout the trial for purposes of identification . . .'. (p. 53) It is a kind of 'instant replay' that is only used once for maximum effect. In another example of narrative license and meta-theatre, El Pachuco stops the fight between Henry and a rival gang member, freezing the action. Then he says, '*Que mamada* ['What bullshit']. Hank. That's exactly what the play needs right now. Two more Mexicans killing each other. Watcha [take note] . . . . Everybody's looking at you', (p. 46) as he points to the audience. Countering the figure of El Pachuco is the allegorical character of The Press, a morality play device which descends directly from the acto as well.

Like the corrido form, there is a musical underscoring in *Zoot Suit*, placing the events in a historical context by employing the music of the period. El Pachuco sings most of the songs setting the mood through lyrics. In the scene at a dance, while El Pachuco and his trio of Chicana back-up singers sing, the actors dance to the rhythms he creates, transforming from youthful fun to vengeful intensity gone wild by the end of the scene.

Most importantly, this play places the Chicanos in a historical context that identifies them as 'American', by showing that they, too, danced the swing as well as the mambo. Valdez is telling his audience that the Chicanos' taste for music can be as broad as anyone's. He is also revealing a transculturation in the Chicanos' language, customs and myths. As Valdez so emphatically stated when this play first appeared, 'this is an American play', attempting to dispel previous notions of separatism from the society at large. He is also reminding us that Americans populate the *Américas*, not just the United States.

Valdez employs elements of the mito very subtly; when the Pachuco is stripped of his zoot suit by marauding US sailors and Marines, he remains covered only by an indigenous loincloth. This image suggests the sacrificial 'god' of the Aztecs, stripped bare before his heart is offered to the cosmos. It is a stunning moment in the play, when the cocky Pachuco is reduced to a bare nakedness in piercing contrast to his treasured 'drapes'. He may be naked, but he rises nobly in his bareness, dissolving into darkness. He will, and does return.[16]

The character of El Pachuco also represents the Aztec concept of the 'nahual', or other self, as he comes to Henry's support during the scene in solitary confinement. Henry is frightened, stripped emotionally bare in his cell and must rely on his imagination to recall the spirit of El Pachuco in order to survive. The strength he receives from his other self is determined by his ability to get in touch with his nahual.

Like most of Valdez's works, this play dramatizes a Chicano family in crisis. Henry Reyna is the central figure, but he is not alone. His 'familia' is the link with the Chicano community in the audience; a continuing reminder that the Chicano is a community. Unlike the members of his family, however, Henry's alter ego brings another dimension to this misunderstood figure. El Pachuco represents an inner attitude of defiance that determines Henry's actions most of the time. El Pachuco is reminiscent at times of the Diablo and Diabla, devil characters that permeated the corridos, motivating the characters' hapless choices as in Medieval morality plays. *Zoot Suit* is also a re-writing of history, the central issue in many of his plays, as Valdez delves even further into the Chicanos' historical experiences.

I Don't Have to Show You No Stinking Badges! (1988)

I Don't Have to Show You No Stinking Badges[17] was co-produced by the Teatro Campesino and the Los Angeles Theatre Center in 1988 under

363

Valdez's direction. After great success in Los Angeles, the play was co-produced with the San Diego Repertory Theatre and the Burt Reynolds Dinner Theatre in Jupiter, Florida, followed by a production in San Francisco, California. While he had tackled melodramatic portrayals of Chicanos in *Bandido!* and stereotypical representations throughout his playwriting career, this new play addressed a community with which he had now become all too familiar. *I Don't Have to Show You No Stinking Badges!* is unique in the development of Chicano dramaturgy as the first professionally produced Chicano play to deal with middle-class Chicanos rather than the usual working poor and working-class characters and situations that concerned most Chicana/o playwrights of the period. The Valdezian questioning of reality reaches its pinnacle in this play as the playwright presents us with a world that resembles a hall of mirrors, sometimes catching this picture, other times, another view; we never know for certain if what we are observing is real or an illusion. We now have Valdez exploring the different levels of reality between the world of the stage and the realm of television. Like *Zoot Suit*, this play was written for a fully-equipped theatre. Further, it requires a realistic set, designed to look like a television studio setting, including video monitors hanging above the set to help the audience make the transfer into a 'live studio audience'.

The play centres on Connie and Buddy Villa, the self-proclaimed 'King and Queen of the Hollywood Extras', who have forged a comfortable life for their two children and themselves playing (silent) Mexican maids and gardeners and other stereotypes for Hollywood. Hence, the title, a direct quote given by a Mexican 'bandido' in the 1948 classic, *The Treasure of Sierra Madre*, when asked for his badge by Humphrey Bogart. The major conflict arises when their son, Sonny, a Harvard honours student, drops out of the Ivy League to pursue a career in Hollywood. The parents, whose daughter is a medical doctor, are appalled and try to dissuade their brilliant son from 'ruining his life', but he is determined (as is the playwright) to break through the wall of Hollywood racism and indifference. In typical Valdezian fashion, Sonny (and the audience) begin to hear voices and he imagines events that take us into a surreal or even expressionistic mode as we ponder whether this is an all a dream/nightmare he is having. The set (and, if possible, the theatre) must look like a sitcom setting, complete with working appliances and running water in the sink, but with the inevitable television monitors and illuminated signs used for a live studio audience. There is even a laugh track under Sonny's 'visions', to enhance the feeling that this is all a sitcom gone awry.

Sonny is the central character in this play, a young, confused Chicano searching for his identity with parents that have lived invisible, silent identities all their professional careers. When Sonny chides his mother for always playing maids she counters with: 'As Hattie McDaniel used to say: "I'd rather play a maid than be one."' (p. 174)

As if in response to the types of roles he will be offered, Sonny robs a fast-food restaurant dressed as a 'cholo', or Chicano street punk, a descendant of the pachuco of the 1940s. Sonny's response to Hollywood is to give producers what they expect and he fulfils their fantasy/nightmare by becoming a thief rather than a lawyer. When the police try to communicate with Sonny through megaphones outside, we do not know if this is real, although his girlfriend, Anita, also hears their voices. But the initial set-up, the theatre-as-television-studio, has left all options open and we soon find ourselves on another level of reality with the director's face and voice coming on over the monitors as it would in a real studio situation. But the Director looks and speaks exactly like Sonny.

The audience is thus plunged into what appear to be multiple realities, similar to the juxtapositions *Bandido!* But while *Bandido!* transposed melodrama with realism, here we have the 'real' in contrast to and in negotiation with the video 'reality', which is, of course, not real at all. Yet, there are live actors on that stage and live audience members sitting next to you in the auditorium-cum-studio. All of this is designed to confuse and conflate realities we live with daily. Early in the play Sonny is recording his voice and asks: 'Are you real or are you Memorex?' (p. 166), a question that reverberates throughout the play.

Once the play becomes a live taping, anything can happen and it does. As the play/sitcom comes to a close, off-stage, Sonny and Anita are lifted in a space ship that is described as a giant Mexican 'sombrero' (hat) as Connie and Buddy revel in their son's decision to return to Harvard. In reality, the 'Happy Ending' is neither. Having entered the realm of the sitcom, we are left to ponder whether any of this represents real people in real situations and the intrusion of the fantastical exit leaves more confusion than conclusion.

Still, Valdez's play raises issues that are ultimately crucial to him and, by extension, to any other Chicanas and Chicanos – Latinas and Latinos who are fed up and frustrated with Hollywood's indifference to Latina-themed programming and Latino characters. By giving Sonny an existential moment of angst, the playwright raises themes that do not go away. Sonny tells his parents he did not belong at Harvard because he doesn't know where he belongs. In a major monologue on identity Sonny tells his parents: 'You see, in order to ACT TRULY AMERICAN, you have to kill your parents: no fatherland, motherland, no MEXICAN, Japanese, African . . . old-country SHIT!' (p. 207) Sonny is speaking metaphorically, but the declaration is real to many people struggling with their place in this society. Survival has always been at the core of Valdezian dramaturgy, whether economic, cultural or spiritual, and this play is no exception to that commitment. Regarding his trajectory to 1998, Valdez commented:

> For me, it's always a question of the path less traveled. I have to be, like Che, in the mountains. So I live in an isolated place (San Juan Bautista . . .). My focus is on trying to create pieces and plays. Theatre can only happen if there are enough pillars, and the pillars are the plays. That's what we pass on to the next generation. So when we get the play done, in any way possible, we continue to build a future. (REPorter 1998, p. 3)

Mummified Deer (2000)

Valdez told me in 1997 that he was eager to work on a play he had been developing for several years, initially titled *The Mummified Fetus*. He first began to think about the play that would become *Mummified Deer* in 1984, when he read a newspaper article about the discovery of a 60-year-old foetus in the womb of an 84-year-old woman.[18] Over the years, as he continued to think about that image, he determined that he would write a play centred on the character of an old Yaqui woman who has been carrying a foetus in her womb for 60 years. The play opened at the San Diego Repertory Theatre in April, 2000, directed by the playwright. This production was soon followed by a revised version of the play, directed by the playwright for the Teatro Campesino in their theatre in San Juan Bautista, California.

While preparing for the opening of this play, he told an interviewer, 'I immediately saw her in a hospital bed, surrounded by her family.'[19] He told me that he based the central character on his own Yaqui grandmother.[20] For Valdez, the mummified foetus becomes a metaphor for the Chicanos' indigenous heritage as seen through the lens of his own Yaqui blood. While the main action of the play is framed by a narrative presented to the audience that takes place in the present, or 1999, Valdez places this play in the year 1969. This was the beginning of the Chicano Movement, a time when Chicanas and Chicanos were questioning the power structure and demanding better conditions in the schools, in the workplace, on the streets and in the courts. The decade of the 1960s was also the era of the Chicanos' deepening interest in their indigenous roots, as evidenced not only in Valdez's mitos but in the poetry and visual culture of other Chicana and Chicano activists. Chicanos knew that they owed their culture to Mexico, but beyond that Mestizo (mixed-blood) nation they were more interested in what the Native Americans on both sides of the man-made border had to say to them.

As he began to picture the 84-year-old Yaqui woman in her hospital bed, Valdez also imagined a Yaqui deer dancer as her alter ego, a vibrant reminder of her own past and that of her peoples. Valdez names the Deer Dancer Cajeme, a legendary Yaqui rebel who fought against the Mexican government in the nineteenth century. Thus Cajeme becomes an integral part of Valdez's play, a symbol of the foetus in the old woman's womb. We see the visions in Mama Chu's mind because Valdez wants to contrast the Yaqui culture with that of the Mestizo. Thus the Mexican Circus clown, Cosme Bravo, appears as counterpoint to Lucas Flores, the resistance fighter, and as adversary to Cajeme. Cosme represents the 'torocoyori', who Mama Chu describes as '. . . a turn-coat Yaqui, who was slaughtering his own people like a rabid dog at the service of his Yori [Mexican] masters'. (p. 59) Every culture has its torocoyori, the vendido character that has his roots in Domingo/Mr Sunday in *The Shrunken Head of Pancho Villa*, pitted against and contrasted with the young social bandit, Joaquín, as discussed earlier.

When Mama Chu does finally die, Cajeme 'dances to a climax at the foot of the bed. With his deer head up in triumph, he collapses, lifeless' (p. 62). At the end of the play, Mama Chu has died and taken Cajeme with her, or does Cajeme die, taking Mama Chu with him? Most importantly, Cajeme dies dancing, with his head 'in triumph'. Both Mama Chu and Cajeme have endured beyond endurance and will now pass to the next stage of the cosmic Indio vision. They have served their purposes and the revolution will continue.

The action is framed by Mama Chu's granddaughter, Armida, a 24-year-old graduate student in Cultural Anthropology when the play opens in 1969, and a 54-year-old professor at the play's conclusion at the end of the twentieth century. Like the Pachuco in *Zoot Suit*, Armida speaks directly to the audience but only as a 'frame'; at the end of the play we are her students in a university lecture hall. Ironically, insensitive teachers and professors permeated early actos, including the classic *No saco nada de la escuela* (*I Don't Get Anything Out of School*) created under Valdez's guidance by the Teatro Campesino in 1969. Thirty years later we find a Chicana professor with integrity and intelligence on Valdez's stage with the final moments of this play celebrating the Chicanos' history through the image of the victorious deer dancer. This ending reveals no simple solutions but requires thoughtful action on the part of the audience, action that will hopefully result in change for the better, change that can only come through knowledge of one's past.

Summary

Luis Valdez has gone from the fields of Delano to the migrant labour of a theatre artist, to the even more complex world of Broadway, Hollywood and the regional theatres. But he has never forgotten his roots; has never abandoned the beauty of his languages, English, Spanish and the pachucos' argot, Caló. Nor has he forgotten about his people's troubles and triumphs. Ultimately, Valdez's plays present us with different aspects of the playwright himself. Valdez is the Pachuco of Broadway, the social bandit of the media, the brilliant student who will change the face(s) of Hollywood and the cultural anthropologist, lecturing her students. He may even be that Yaqui woman, carrying her foetus until it is time to let it live, free. He laughs at himself as much as at historians and Hollywood in his plays, exploding myths by creating others; transforming the way in which Chicanos and Chicanas view themselves within the context of this society. For each of his plays is finally about a search for identity through the playwright's quest for what is reality, past, present and future. 'How can we know who we are', he continually asks, 'if we do not know who we were?'

Primary Sources

Works by Luis Valdez

Garza, Roberto J. (ed.), *Bernabé. Contemporary Chicano Theatre* (Notre Dame, IN: University of Notre Dame Press, 1976).

Huerta, Jorge, *Necessary Theater: Six Plays About the Chicano Experience* (Houston: Arte Público Press, 1989).

Hurwitt, Robert (ed.), *West Coast Plays 19/20* (Berkeley: California Theatre Council, 1982).

Valdez, Luis, *The Shrunken Head of Pancho Villa. West Coast Plays 11/12* (Berkeley: California Theatre Council, 1982).

—, *Early Actos* (Houston: Arte Público Press, 1990).

—, *Zoot Suit. Valdez, Zoot Suit and Other Plays* (Houston: Arte Público Press, 1992).

—, 'El Teatro Campesino', *Ramparts* (July 1966), pp. 55–6.

—, *Mummified Deer. Mummified Deer and Other Plays* (Houston: Arte Público Press, 2005).

Secondary Sources

Anon., REPorter: San Diego Repertory Theatre Newsletter (1998), p. 3.

Bagby, Beth, 'El Teatro Campesino: Interviews With Luis Valdez', *Tulane Drama Review* 11 (Summer 1967), 70–80.

Broyles-Gonzalez, Yolanda, 'What Price "Mainstream"? Luis Valdez's *Corridos* on Stage and Film', *Cultural Studies* 4 (October 1990), 281–93.

—, *El Teatro Campesino: Theater in the Chicano Movement* (Austin: University of Texas Press, 1994).

de Poyen, Jennifer, 'Roots Rockero: Luis Valdez Reaches into His Family History to Create *Mummified Deer*', *San Diego Union-Tribune* 26 (October 2000), 4.

Diamond, Betty Ann, *Brown-Eyed Children of the Sun: The Cultural Politics of El Teatro Campesino* (Ann Arbor: University Microfilms, 1977).

Elam, Harry, Jr., *Taking it to the Streets: The Social Protest Theater of Luis Valdez and Amiri Baraka* (Ann Arbor: University of Michigan Press, 1997).

Faderman, Lilian and Omar Salinas (eds), *Dark Root of a Scream. From the Barrio* (San Francisco: Canfield Press, 1973).

Huerta, Jorge, *Chicano Theater: Themes and Forms* (Tempe: Bilingual Press, 1982).

—, *Necessary Theater: Six Plays About the Chicano Experience* (Houston: Arte Público Press, 1987).

—, *Chicano Drama: Performance, Society and Myth* (Cambridge: Cambridge University Press, 2000).

Kelly, Ken, 'The Interview: Luis Valdez', *San Francisco Focus* 52 (September 1987), 51–3; 93–102.

Kourilsky, Françoise, 'Approaching Quetzalcóatl: The Evolution of El Teatro Campesino', *Performance* 2 (Fall 1973), 37–46.

Lucas, Ashley, 'Prisoners on the Great White Way: *Short Eyes* and *Zoot Suit* as the First US Latino Plays on Broadway', *Latin American Theatre Review* 43, 1 (Fall 2009), 121–35.

Pizzato, Mark, *Theatres of Human Sacrifice: From Ancient Ritual to Screen Violence* (Albany: State University of New York Press, 2004).

Rossini, Jon D., *Contemporary Latina/o Theater: Wrighting Ethnicity* (Carbondale: Southern Illinois University Press, 2008).

Yarbro-Bejarano, Yvonne and Tomás Ybarra-Frausto, '*Zoot Suit* y el movimiento Chicano', *Plural* 9, 7(103) (April 1980), 49–56.

Notes

1. 'Gringo' is a pejorative term for Anglo-Americans used by Mexicans and Chicanos.
2. Luis Valdez, 'El Teatro Campesino', p. 55.
3. Lilian Faderman and Omar Salinas (eds), *Dark Root of a Scream*, pp. 79–98.
4. Ken Kelley, 'The Interview', p. 53.
5. See Françoise Kourilsky, 'Approaching Quetzalcóatl', pp. 37–46 for an excellent analysis of *La gran carpa de los Rasquachis*.
6. For an overview of the critics' responses to *Zoot Suit* in New York, see Yolanda Broyles-Gonzalez, *El Teatro Campesino*, pp. 189–205. See also Ashley Lucas, 'Prisoners on the Great White Way', pp. 121–35 for an interrogation of Miguel Piñero's *Short Eyes* and *Zoot Suit*, the first two plays on Broadway written and directed by Latinos. Lucas points out that both plays deal with incarcerated subjects.

7. See Broyles-Gonzalez, *El Teatro Campesino*, for the most thorough analysis of five versions of this controversial play. See also Jorge Huerta, *Chicano Theater*, pp. 174–84.

8. Broyles-Gonzalez in *El Teatro Campesino*, p. 195 points out that the following publications published positive reviews of *Zoot Suit* on Broadway: '. . . *Wall Street Journal, Variety,* the *Washington Post, Daily News, Newsweek,* to name a few'.

9. *I Don't Have to Show You No Stinking Badges!* is published in Valdez, *Zoot Suit*, pp. 155–214.

10. Kelley, 'The Interview', p. 52.

11. Valdez's staged and televised productions of *Corridos* created much controversy, especially for its depiction of women. See Broyles-Gonzalez, 'What Price "Mainstream"?', pp. 281–93; and her later, revised version of this article in *El Teatro Campesino*, pp. 154–63.

12. Published in *West Coast Plays 11/12*, pp. 1–61, and in Jorge Huerta, *Necessary Theater*, pp. 142–207. For more about this play, see Betty Ann Diamond, *Brown-Eyed Children of the Sun*, pp. 129–46; and Huerta, *Chicano Theater*, pp. 49–60.

13. Huerta, *Necessary Theater*, p. 154.

14. Luis Valdez, 'Keynote Address' (c. 1983), 'Eighteen years after the founding of El Teatro Campesino'. An unpublished typescript in my collection.

15. *Zoot Suit* and its director/playwright were not without their critics in the Chicana/o community. For an overview of these critiques, see Yolanda Broyles-Gonzalez, *El Teatro Campesino*, especially pp. 177–208.

16. For an interesting analysis of the Pachuco and violence, see Mark Pizzato, *Theatres of Human Sacrifice*. Pizzato compares El Pachuco to Tezcatlipoca (pp. 119–22) and the stripping of the zoot suit to the Aztec flaying of a sacrificed warrior's skin at the festival of the god, Xipe Totec (p. 114).

17. Published in Valdez, *Zoot Suit*, pp. 156–214.

18. Published in Valdez, *Mummified Deer*, pp. xv-62.

19. Jennifer de Poyen, 'Roots Rockero', p. 4.

20. In a telephone conversation with Luis Valdez, 15 March 2002.

21 PAULA VOGEL

Joanna Mansbridge

Desdemona; The Oldest Profession; The Baltimore Waltz; Hot 'n' Throbbing; How I Learned to Drive; The Long Christmas Ride Home

Introduction

Paula Vogel is a playwright's playwright. Her plays respond to and rewrite texts by authors such as William Shakespeare, Edward Albee, Sam Shepard and David Mamet, revising their plots, reformulating their conflicts and recasting their dramatis personae. Vogel shifts the focus away from an often universalized, truth-seeking male protagonist and places women at the centre of action, not as valourized heroines, but as complex, curious and flawed figures. Her highly meta-theatrical plays borrow not only from the traditional canon, but also from the wider spectrum of theatre history and cultural production, incorporating the lavish theatricality of the American musical and the bawdy comedy of vaudeville and burlesque, as well as elements from contemporary popular culture. Unabashed and irreverent in her blending of high and low culture, drama and comedy, pathos and Eros, Vogel writes plays that complicate and overturn hierarchies of gender, sexuality, class and cultural production.

Along with revising past texts, Vogel's work also confronts contemporary concerns, such as domestic violence, pornography, paedophilia and AIDS. She does not write 'about' AIDS, paedophilia and domestic abuse, however; she defamiliarizes these subjects in ways that encourage audiences to see them not as sensational 'issues' but as historical questions. To engage with the plays of Paula Vogel, then, is to engage in a two-way dialogue, communicating at once with theatre history and with contemporary culture.

Born in Washington, D.C. in 1951 to a Jewish father and a Catholic mother, Vogel identifies her beginnings as distinctly working class. After graduating from high school, she attended Bryn Mawr College, later transferring to Catholic University of America, where she finished her B.A. in Drama in 1974. After the Yale School of Drama rejected her application for graduate studies, Vogel applied to and was accepted into Cornell University, where she completed all of the requirements for her doctorate in Theatre Arts, except the dissertation. She taught intermittently at Cornell from 1977 to 1982. In 1985, Vogel began teaching playwriting at Brown University, where she remained for 23 years and trained some of the most exciting new playwrights in the country, including Nilo Cruz, Gina Gionfriddo and Sarah Ruhl. In July 2008, Vogel accepted a position as the Eugene O'Neill Professor of Playwriting and Chair of the Playwriting Department at Yale School of Drama, a satisfying turn of life events, no doubt.[1]

Vogel has written over 20 plays, 10 of which have been published. She has also written for television, including screenplays for *How I Learned to Drive* and *The Oldest Profession*. Vogel won her first playwriting award in 1976 at the American College Theatre Festival in Washington, D.C. for a play called *Meg*, a revision of Robert Bolt's 1960 play *A Man for All Seasons*. This award earned her some recognition, but more importantly, it landed her an agent at William Morris. Her first major professional success was with her 1992 play, *The Baltimore Waltz*, which won an Obie Award for Best Play and earned a Pulitzer nomination. In 1997, Vogel was nominated again and won the Pulitzer Prize for Drama for her most successful play to date, *How I Learned to Drive*. It made an almost clean sweep of off-Broadway awards for best play, winning Obie, New York Drama Critics, Drama Desk, Outer Critics, Lortel and Hull-Warriner awards. She was awarded the Susan Blackburn Award in 1998, and the Pen/Laura Pels Award for Playwriting in 1999. In 2005, Vogel received The Academy of Arts and Letters Award for Literature, and in 2006, she was inducted into the Academy of Arts and Sciences. Vogel was the 2010 recipient of the Inge Festival Distinguished Achievement in the American Theater award. And she has two awards named in her honour: the Paula Vogel Award, created by the American College Theatre Festival in 2003 and given out annually to 'the outstanding student-written play that celebrates diversity and encourages tolerance while exploring issues of disempowered voices not traditionally considered mainstream'; and the Paula Vogel Award in Playwriting, given annually by the Vineyard Theatre, since 2007. Its first recipient was Yale School of Drama alum Terrell McCraney.

The Plays

Desdemona: A Play about a Handkerchief (1979)

Vogel wrote the first draft of *Desdemona* in 1977, and it received partial production and a second place prize at the Actors Theatre's New Play Festival in 1979. It did not receive a full production, however, until 1993, when it was staged at Circle Repertory in New York City, with Gloria Muzio directing. *Desdemona* transforms Shakespeare's most idealized heroine into exactly the whore Othello imagines her to be. Maybe worse. Defamiliarizing stereotypes of female sexuality and class, Vogel depicts the aristocratic Desdemona as insatiably lascivious, the working-class Emilia as an emblem of piety and the prostitute Bianca as a proud woman secretly harbouring middle-class aspirations. Vogel reveals her impetus for writing the play:

> In the 1970s, when I had read *Othello*, I was struck by the fact that my main point of identification, of subjectivity, was a man who is supposedly cuckolded, that I was weeping for a man who is cuckolded rather than for Desdemona. And, of course, at that point in the seventies, in terms of women's studies, there was all the virgin/whore analysis coming out, and it wounded me a great deal that Desdemona is nothing but an abstraction and that I didn't find any way of identifying with her.[2]

Using negative empathy, Vogel created a Desdemona that audiences were invited to identify with, not as a victimized wife or idealized heroine, but as an impudent hussy.

Structured as 30 cinematic 'takes', *Desdemona* unfolds in a series of brief scenes that comprise a behind-the-scenes-burlesque of Shakespeare's

Othello. A parody of Othello's worst nightmare, Vogel's Desdemona spends time working at Bianca's brothel in order to alleviate the tedium of her patrician lifestyle. The dramatic conflict of *Desdemona*, however, is generated from the class tensions and simmering desires among the women, rather than the fears and fantasies of female sexuality circulated among the men of *Othello*. And yet, although the male characters never appear on stage, it is understood that they remain in the background, and thus influence, the relationships among the three female characters in Vogel's play. Emilia's description of female relationships provides the most salient summation of the female homosocial world of *Desdemona*. She tells Bianca,

> Don't be a fool hussy. There's no such creature, two-, three or four-legged, as a "friend" betwixt ladies of leisure and ladies of the night. And as long as there be men with one member but two minds, there's no such thin' as friends between women. An' that's that. (p. 200)

Emilia's theory of female friendship aptly captures the conflict in *Desdemona*. And yet, Vogel's playworld remains dictated by the male fears and fantasies that govern *Othello*. In the final scene, Emilia performs the nightly ritual of brushing Desdemona's hair 100 strokes, as they try to allay each other's anxieties regarding Othello's escalating anger as if aware on some level of its inevitable conclusion. The play's final blackout, however, occurs on the ninety-ninth stroke, thus refusing the tragic conclusion and catharsis of Shakespeare's play, and leaving Desdemona perpetually poised one brush stroke away from death. Vogel would continue to write plays that, like *Desdemona*, provocatively respond to a masculinist dramatic canon and place women centre stage and that, at the same time, are animated by a comic irreverence.

The Oldest Profession (1981)

First produced professionally by Theatre Network in Edmonton, Alberta, Canada, in April 1988, *The Oldest Profession* is a tribute to Vogel's late grandmother, an experiment with repetitive form, and a revision of

David Mamet's *The Duck Variations*. The play was substantially revised as a more pointed social critique of Reagan-era America for its 2004 New York premiere at Signature Theater, an off-Broadway theatre that devotes an entire season to the work of a single playwright. In 2004/2005 Vogel was the featured playwright, and *Profession*, *The Baltimore Waltz* and *Hot 'n' Throbbing* were staged during that season.

Equal parts Beckett, Vaudeville and *Golden Girls*, *Profession* depicts five elderly prostitutes struggling amid 1980s' Reaganomics and its effects on their business, their daily lives and their aging bodies. The characters are a vividly drawn quintet of varying dispositions: sweet-natured, 72-year-old Vera is the character modelled after Vogel's grandmother; 74-year-old Edna is the 'good-time girl'; 79-year-old Ursula is 'Germanic, bossy'; 83-year-old Mae is the group's leader and a 'self-made woman' (p. 130). As a quasi-Reaganite, Ursula is the most pragmatic of the bunch, arguing that 'Social Security has no place in a free market' (p. 135), while Mae is the most nostalgic, mourning the loss of security, warmth and community of their brothel Life. Mae articulates their differing dispositions: 'Ursula, you're a whore with the soul of a businesswoman. And I'm a businesswoman with the soul of a whore' (p. 143).

In *Profession*, Vogel works a double defamiliarization: she defamiliarizes the sexuality of elderly women by representing it as wholesome and ordinary, and she defamiliarizes prostitution by depicting it a as profession built on nurturing, compassion and love. Prostitution works as a metonym for different modes of production, and in this climate of competition and alienation, the women become increasingly at odds with one another, as well as with the new generation of 'Cheap amateur whores' (p. 138) encroaching on their Upper West Side territory. The women's increasing social invisibility, as aging senior citizens, produces a palpable vulnerability, and their recollections of the brothel in Storeyville, a place conjured throughout the play in the stories the women tell one another, contrast sharply with the hostile conditions of their present life.

The play's subtitle, *A Full-Length Play in Six Black-Outs*, reveals that form *is* content here, as the black-outs divide the scenes and signal the deaths of one of the women. As each scene opens with one woman fewer on the stage, a note of crisis seeps into the otherwise comic play. In the Signature Theater production, as each woman made her final exit, she would return 'home' to a mythic brothel heaven, a place where their bodies and labour are still one. Only Vera is left at the play's end, cold, hungry, and alone on a desolate street corner, a stark image of abjection in a culture that has stopped acknowledging the stories – and bodies – of the past.

The Baltimore Waltz (1992)

Vogel received national recognition with *The Baltimore Waltz*, which premiered in 1992 at New York Circle Repertory Theater, with Anne Bogart directing. Vogel wrote *Waltz* as a commemoration of her brother Carl Vogel, who died of AIDS in 1987. The play revolves around an imagined European trip, a premise that comes from Carl's invitation to Vogel to join him on a similar trip in 1986. She declined, not having the money and not realizing Carl was HIV positive. He died just over a year later, and Vogel wrote her play as a way to take that journey with him. With *The Third Man* as its main intertext, *Waltz* mobilizes a playful *noir* vibe, circular structure and dream-like *mise en scène* to take the audience on a wildly imaginative journey through Europe, with Anna, her brother Carl and the Third Man.

Waltz has a triangular structure, with three characters, three stage spaces, and three registers of action – fantasy, memory and reality. With 'Anna . . . dressed in a full slip/negligee and a trench coat' and 'Carl . . . in flannel pajamas and a blazer', it is quickly apparent that this is not the realism of Larry Kramer or Terrence McNally. Vogel's production notes suggest that 'The lighting should be stylized, lush, dark and imaginative, in contrast to the hospital white silence of the last scene' (p. 6), a juxtaposition that emphasizes the cold sterility in the first and last scene in relation to the fecund chaos of the fantasy scenes they frame.

Like a Viennese Waltz, the play moves seamlessly between the forward and backward movements of memory and fantasy. The play is a montage of scenes that alternate between travelogues, language lessons, Hollywood burlesques, riffs on psychiatric models of grief and political critiques regarding the lack of arts funding and the high cost of medical care. The play eschews sexual moralism in favour of an exuberant theatricality, and the pathology of AIDS and its associations with gay male sexual promiscuity are defamiliarized in the play through metaphorical displacement of its causes, symptoms and target demographic. In *Waltz*, it is Anna who is terminally ill with Acquired Toilet Disease (ATD), an incurable disease contracted primarily by single female schoolteachers and transmitted through contact with the toilets used by their young students. The doctor's declarative diagnosis at the start of the play – 'There's nothing we can do' (p. 9) – initiates Anna's fantasy as she attempts to flee the finality those words convey. And since ATD is not sexually transmitted, Anna attempts to 'fight the sickness of the body with the health of the body' by sleeping with every 'Thomas, Dieter, and Heinrich' (pp. 29, 42) she encounters in Europe.

The actor playing the Third Man performs a series of roles, including Anna's string of sexual partners, a language instructor, a sinister urine-drinking Viennese doctor and the *noir* villain, Harry Lime. In his dizzying array of roles, the Third Man disrupts any attempts to construct this playworld in binary terms. Moreover, by acting as the sexual partners of both Anna and Carl, he also disrupts the homo/hetero binary traditionally used to organize sexuality. As the play's whimsical adventure becomes increasingly edged with sinister notes of danger, however, we see the authority of Anna's fantasy being usurped by the reality of the Baltimore hospital. By the play's penultimate scene, the audience realizes that it is Carl who has died, and that what we have watched is Anna's fantastical escape from that moment of loss.

Hot 'n' Throbbing (1994)

Although its first draft was written in the mid-1980s, *Hot 'n' Throbbing*, like *Desdemona*, had to wait over a decade to receive a major production. In 1994, *Hot* was staged at the American Repertory Theatre, with Anne Bogart directing, and was revised in 1999 for the Arena Stage production, directed by Molly Smith. *Hot* has many thematic similarities to Vogel's earlier play, *And Baby Makes Seven* (1984), which revises Edward Albee's

Who's Afraid of Virginia Woolf? and features a lesbian couple, Anna and Ruth, about to have a baby with Peter, their gay best friend. Whereas *Baby* uses broad comedy and a vaudevillian structure to re-imagine 'family', *Hot* uses sharp-edged humour and cinematic jump-cuts to critique conventional family structures. Both plays interweave and often confuse fantasy and reality, creating play-worlds in which these two registers merge in the lives of the characters.

Unlike the playful fantasies that animate the lives of Anna, Ruth and Peter, however, *Hot* investigates the violent side of fantasy. Implicitly responding to a long tradition of male playwrights whose work, as David Savran states, 'romanticizes violence against women',[3] *Hot* stages violence in myriad ways: visually, through two distinct though related stage spaces – the white-lit reality of a lower-middle-class living-room and the red-lit area of a seedy strip bar; discursively, through intertextual references to writers such as James Joyce, Vladimir Nabokov and Shakespeare; and physically, through the abusive relationship between an ex-husband and wife. The action centres around Charlene Dwyer, a single working-class mother, who supports her two children, Leslie-Ann and Calvin, by writing erotic screenplays for a feminist film company called Gyno Productions. Her ex-husband, Clyde, intrudes into the family home, drunk and lonely, initiating the play's climactic act of violence. The remaining two characters, The Voice and the Voice Over (V.O.), move between the two stage spaces and act as conflicting aspects of Charlene's consciousness. As an embodied representative of discursive cultural authority, The Voice narrates passages from *Ulysses*, *Lolita* and *Othello*, which disrupts Charlene's own narrative voice, as she fights to meet a writing deadline. The V.O. is a female character and sex worker who directs and performs the script that Charlene is writing. The seductively clad V.O. represents the hypersexualized female body in popular culture, while The Voice represents the voice of literary history and dominant culture. Charlene is negotiating her place between these two traditions, trying to become an author of female pleasure and desire within a history that persistently positions women as object and spectacle.

Capturing the play's leitmotif – who controls and authorizes the discourses that define desire, sexuality, and violence? – the following

379

exchange between Charlene and Clyde is interrupted by The Voice, who narrates the words of nineteenth-century sexologist Richard von Krafft-Ebing, and by the V.O., who vocalizes Charlene's thoughts:

> **Clyde** . . . So where do all these words come from?
> **Charlene** I don't know. When I really get going, it's like a trance—it's not me writing at all. It's as if I just listen to voices and I'm taking dictation.
> **The Voice** "Case 103 continued. Subject, however, experienced constant excitation, due to what the subject described as inner 'voices' usually urging him to erotic acts."
> **Clyde** Doesn't that spook you? I mean, whose voices are these? Who's in control?
>
>
>
> **V.O.**
>
> But she was in control.
>
>
>
> **Charlene** Well, they're the characters speaking, or the script itself. I mean, it's me, but I have to get into it. At first it spooked me a little. But now I know when I hear them, it's a good sign. And I am in control. (p. 260)

The tension between fictional representations of sexuality and violence and the actualities of domestic violence is left unresolved in the play, and yet the violent act that concludes the play – Clyde strangles Charlene in an irrational moment of jealous rage – suggests that we urgently need to expand our vocabularies on these subjects. The material effects of literary history and the juxtapositions of sexuality and violence that are reinforced throughout the play culminate in this scene, as The Voice narrates Molly's soliloquy from Joyce's *Ulysses*, just as Clyde tightens his grip on Charlene's neck.[4] The original ending of the play shows Leslie-Ann taking her mother's place at the typewriter, implying that the cycle of violence will repeat itself in the life choices of Charlene's daughter. For the Arena Stage production, Vogel revised the ending so that the play flashed forward 10 years to show Leslie-Ann as a university professor, teaching her students to think critically about questions of sexuality, cultural power and narrative authority.

How I Learned to Drive (1997)

How I Learned to Drive premiered in February 1997 at the Vineyard Theatre, with Mark Brokaw directing and featuring Mary Louise Parker and David Morse in the lead roles. In April 1997, it moved across the street to the Century Theatre for a commercial run, where Jayne Atkinson (and, later, Molly Ringwald) and Brain Davison took over the lead roles. After 450 performances over a 15-month run, the play went on to be produced across the country and around the world. *How I Learned to Drive* (1998) was published as a companion play to *The Mineola Twins* (1996), a political farce featuring warring twins, Myra and Myrna Richards, whose polarized sexual dispositions as virgin and whore act as an allegory for America's political polarization between Right and Left. Collectively titled *The Mammary Plays* (1998), *Drive* and *Twins* work dialectically to satirize late-twentieth-century American culture, with a particular focus on women as both active, political subjects and sexualized, commodified objects of that history.

Drive is a delicately balanced play that unravels the dynamics of a 7-year relationship between a young girl, L'il Bit, and her Uncle Peck. Their sexually intimate though unconsummated relationship involves lessons in objectification and violation, but also in love and compassion. The play reorients conventional representations of sexual abuse to get at the complexity, historicity and humanity of this vexed topic. As with all of her plays, Vogel depicts characters, issues and ideas from multiple angles, and challenges reductive categories, such as victim and victimizer. Instead, *Drive* employs a *Lolita*-esque narrative of seduction told, importantly, from the point of view of a female narrator.

L'il Bit begins the play with a lure: 'Sometimes to tell a secret, you first have to teach a lesson' (p. 7). Drawing the audience in with the promise of an exposed secret recalls Michel Foucault's 'repressive hypothesis', a theory that defines modern sexuality, not as something 'consigned sex to a shadow existence', but rather something that is spoken of '*ad infinitum*' even as it is exploited as '*the* secret'.[5] In *Drive*, Vogel exploits the seductive allure of (private) secret, by subverting it with a (public) lesson, a lesson about the complexity of sexual desire and the contradictory cultural codes that define genders, sexualities and bodies. Moving, in turns, by exposure and concealment, the play teaches us the many complex ways we learn to desire and to be desired, and shows that the effects of those lessons are often shame, isolation and alienation.

Drive is not divided into traditional scenes and acts nor does it have a linear plotline. Instead, it has a recursive structure and mobilizes Brechtian strategies, such as scenes designated by road signs and gear shifts, which work to complicate conventional modes of spectatorship and, in this play, redirect traditional circuits of identification and desire. The play situates the relationship between Peck and L'il Bit, which many might automatically deem pathological, within the broader institutions of family and education – represented by the Male, Female, and Teenage Greek Choruses – and amidst the products of American culture – from the *Playboy* images to the popular songs that permeate the play. The lessons Peck teaches L'il Bit are, in this way, situated within a culture that persistently sexualizes young women.

With driving as the primary conceit, L'il Bit's recollections unfold in a series of lessons that can be read as lessons in gendering. Teaching L'il Bit how to 'drive like a man', Peck hopes to give to her the same sense of 'power' and 'control' that he feels behind the wheel (p. 50). When she asks why the car is a 'she', Peck responds, 'I guess I always see a 'she'. You can call her what you like'. To the audience, L'il Bit says, 'I . . . decided not to change the gender' (p. 51). L'il Bit identifies with this masculine position of power and control, even as she is taught elsewhere lessons in feminine passivity and shame. From her Uncle Peck, L'il Bit learns to be both an active subject and sexualized object, and in the play's most poignant irony, he teaches her how to protect herself from the very harm he imposes on her.

In this way, the play deftly avoids simplistically casting Peck as victimizer and L'il Bit as victim. We see Peck violate an 11-year-old L'il Bit in the front seat of the car, but we also we see them support one another and find refuge in their relationship from a world they seem equally, though differently, at odds with. The play ends as L'il Bit recalls that first encounter in the car with Peck, which she describes as 'the last day I lived in my body' (p. 90). Believing now in 'Things like family and forgiveness' (p. 91), however, L'il Bit gets into her car, acknowledging the spirit of Peck in the rear-view mirror, as he joins her on a journey with no clear destination.

The Long Christmas Ride Home (2004)

The Long Christmas Ride Home had its world premiere at Trinity Repertory Company in Providence, Rhode Island in May 2003, directed by Oskar Eustis, moving to the Vineyard Theatre in New York City in 2004, with Mark Brokaw as director. It is a family drama that is at turns poetic, poignant and disturbing. *Ride* fuses the techniques of Japanese Bunraku puppet theatre with the motifs in Thornton Wilder's one-act plays, *Long Christmas Dinner* and *Happy Journey to Trenton and Camden*. Vogel reveals, 'I chose Christmas because for us in America, whether or not we are Christian, it is the closest thing to myth we have'.[6] Translating the everyday into the poetic, the material into the abstract, *Ride* uses innovative narrative techniques, minimal set and props, and a recursive structure to stage a family car trip to Grandma's house for dinner on a 'very cold Christmas in a long and cold winter—decades and days ago' (p. 13).

The play's subtitle, *A Puppet Play with Actors*, suggests the importance of the puppets to the play's deconstruction of some of the fundamental dualities structuring Western theatre and culture: body-voice, actor-role, interiority-exteriority, past-present. The puppets stand in as the child-selves of the adult puppeteers, who actively observe the actions they make their puppet selves perform. In this way, the puppeteers act as a diegetic audience, watching the performance that they themselves are orchestrating, and in this way witnessing a re-enactment of their past from an objective perspective. The puppet-puppeteer relationship not only stages the dual consciousness of actor-role, but also positions that consciousness *in time* so that both the actor/puppeteer and the audience see the formation of identity as a process of remembering, observing and integrating the past as it is remembered in the present.

The play is structured as a journey, a car trip during which a mother and father – referred to generically as Man and Woman – argue in the front seat while their two daughters, Claire and Rebecca, and son,

Stephen, sit anxiously in the back seat. As the argument escalates, the car veers out of control, coming to a stop on the edge of a slippery cliff, just at the moment when the father raises his hand to hit the mother. The play suspends this moment, which has since crystallized into memory and returns every year to haunt each family member. Interrupting the linear flow of time and action, this suspended moment works in the play as a dialectical image, a convergence and recognition of the past in the present moment.[7]

The second half of the play flashes forward 25 years, depicting the now-adult children as they each continue to live in the aftermath of that long-ago moment in the family car. The sisters, at the end of failed relationships, hopeless and desperate, each contemplate suicide, but are suddenly filled by the memory of their brother, who pours his breath into his sisters' bodies, bringing them back to life. What the audience realizes is that Stephen has since died of AIDS, and returns every year on the day after Christmas, St Stephen's Day, to observe his sisters.

In the tradition of a Noh *shite* and the Wilder's Stage Manager, the Ghost of Stephen provides critical, aesthetic, spiritual distance in the second half of the play. Returning to that frozen moment in time on the edge of the slippery cliff at the play's end, the Ghost of Stephen says to the audience, 'There is a moment I want you to watch with me. A moment of time stopping' (p. 53). As he breathes life back into the puppets and resumes his place as puppeteer, the play begins again at the moment when the Man is about to hit the Woman, but, now, both the children and the audience understand the future implications of this moment. As '*the man backhands the woman*', a cascade of hopeful 'what if's' erupt from each family member: 'If I try harder' wonders the mother, 'If I dress a bit younger—If I say softer things' (pp. 55–6). And together, the Man and Woman wonder:

If . . .
But it is Rebecca who interrupts their speculation with:
Rebecca   And then our father thought of Sheila. (p. 57)

Re-reading her father's thoughts, his desire to see his mistress Sheila, Rebecca remembers the past critically, objectively. Assuming narrative authority, she looks at the past from a distance, and sees other possible outcomes of that moment decades ago.

The play concludes with the Man stating, 'let's go home', and Stephen narrating the final lines, in past tense: 'And so—we went' (p. 57). The journey in *Ride* is, in the end, a return home, and perhaps even a nostalgic longing for home. Ann Pellegrini argues that, as a whole, *Ride* 'reveals the fragility and the hope of human (re) connection', and the characters 'yearn for contact with each other, with the past, with lost parts of themselves'.[8] *Ride,* like *Waltz,* uses a recursive structure to construct a playworld without a definite beginning and without a search for final endings, hovering instead in the theatrical present-tense wherein what has been lost can be recovered, if only for a moment.

Vogel's most recent play, *A Civil War Christmas* (2008) takes the narrative of *Ride* and expands and applies it to pivotal moment in American history. Vastly different in style, tone and scope from her previous work, this Dickensian epic premiered at the Long Wharf Theatre in New Haven in November 2008, with Tina Landau directing. It weaves together a series of overlapping plot-lines and historical figures, all punctuated by period songs and narrated passages. Believing that America still lives in this moment – the eve of the end of the Civil War – Vogel invites audiences to revisit, remember and re-imagine this historic moment, and to feel its resonance in the present.

Summary

'Defamiliarization' is, for Vogel, 'the purpose of drama.'[9] Taking up Victor Shklovsky's notion of defamiliarization, a term adapted by Brecht and renamed *Verfremdungseffekt,* she uses non-realist forms, negative empathy and juxtaposition to confront such contentious topics as homophobia, violence and social marginalization. Vogel's artistic perspectives are eclectically informed by Russian Formalism, Kenneth Burke, playwrights such as Brecht, Artaud and Strindberg, along with 'all the songs of Judy Garland; every Broadway musical; and a gay brother, who, when I was seventeen, took me to see John Waters'.[10] Vogel considers Strindberg to be one of her greatest allies, for she sees in his plays a misogyny unparalleled in other playwrights, male or female. When asked who her prototype is as a feminist playwright, however, she cites 'Chekhov, Williams, and Guare', because in their female characters there is a 'complicated desire' and a 'psychological complexity equal to the male characters'.[11] Savran refers to Vogel as a male impersonator because her 'playwriting represents a revision and repossession of a highly masculinized textual practice'.[12] That she steals the tricks of a dramatic canon of predominately white, male playwrights suggests something of Vogel's crafty use of the very institutions that have marginalized her as a woman, feminist and lesbian. Indeed, as Pierre Bourdieu asserts, 'the strategy *par excellence* is the 'return to sources', which is the basis of all heretical subversion and all aesthetic revolution, because it enables the insurgents to turn against the establishment the arms which they use to justify their domination'.[13]

Vogel's dramaturgy is grounded in an understanding of history as a lived, embodied relationship to the past *in* the present, and her plays try to get at history 'in a visceral way'.[14] She outlines her understanding of history as follows:

> The connection I have with time is something that causes enormous emotional repercussions for me. . . . I don't think that there's a neat demarcation, politically, ethically, between history and the present moment. It's a continuum. History is simply a way of us being enough out of the picture to analyze shifting interconnections among politics, social history, economics, culture, gender. History is simply the name we give a discrete moment when we analyze those connections.[15]

History emerges in the choices, language, memories and bodies of her characters, as much as in the events and images that surround them. Juxtaposing bodies and voices, distant past and immediate present, thought and feeling, Vogel encourages her audiences to pay attention to the presence of history, and to ask questions of it.

As an avowed feminist, Vogel examines from multiple angles how we come to learn our genders and sexualities, and how some are defined as natural and legitimate, while others are deemed pathological, deviant or obscene. Her feminism is not an identity, but rather a mode of inquiry, and her characters both enact and question the social, historical and theatrical conventions through which normative gender and sexuality establish their authority. Unlike much of the feminist or queer theatre theorists of the 1980s and 1990s, Vogel has never been interested in developing a theory of theatre grounded in a feminist or lesbian aesthetic, creating an alternative female canon, or valourizing women on stage. She writes instead about subjects that disturb her, which has often meant 'fall[ing] between the different models of what feminist theatre is . . . or queer theatre'.[16] C. W. E. Bigsby explains Vogel's difficulty getting her plays produced in the 1980s, stating, 'Her plays were not offered as an antidote, still less as a palliative, but they were offered as an irritant. She aimed to disturb and for much of the 1980s she found herself operating in a theatre where that was not a priority'.[17] Finding her audiences in the 1990s, amid identity politics and theories of performativity, Vogel found her representations of gender and sexuality fit more comfortably within a context shaped by Judith Butler's highly influential theory of gender as, 'a stylized repetition of acts'.[18] Vogel's characters continually cite the acts and gestures of gender and sexuality authorized as legitimate, even as they challenge and, often, re-perform them illegitimately.

Vogel's playwriting voice is undeniably comic. Specifically, it is a unique fusion of camp and burlesque, both of which highlight the theatrical, the flagrant and the incongruous. And while burlesque captures Vogel's emphasis on the ubiquitous ways the female body has been eroticized in popular and high culture, camp describes her emphasis on language, wit and role-playing. Eve Kosofsky Sedgwick's theory of camp as a reparative practice in *Touching Feeling* works as perhaps the most apt theory through which to understand Vogel's dramaturgical techniques. Sedgwick writes:

> To view camp, as among other things, the communal historically dense exploration of a variety of reparative practices is to do better justice to many of the defining elements of classic camp performance: the startling, juicy displays of excess erudition, for example; the passionate, often hilarious antiquarianism, the prodigal production of alternative historiographies; the

"over"-attachment to fragmentary, marginal, waste or leftover products; the rich, highly interruptive affective variety; the irrepressible fascination with ventriloquistic experimentation; the disorienting juxtapositions of present with past, and popular with high culture.[19]

As a playwright, Vogel participates in just such 'prodigal production of alternative historiographies', 'juicy displays of excess erudition' and 'ventriloquistic experimentation', and her 'juxtapositions of present with past, and popular with high culture' culminate in a 'communal historically dense exploration' of sexuality and gender, of social and literary history, of the forgotten and the overexposed. As Alisa Solomon contends, Vogel is 'one of America's most daring and complicated dramatists',[20] and although her plays take up familiar American themes – family, politics, history, sexuality – her complex dramaturgy presents them in ways that foreground their contradictions and incongruities, inviting us to look at them differently, sometimes uncomfortably, and to imagine them otherwise.

Primary Sources

Works by Paula Vogel

Savran, David (ed.), *Baltimore Waltz and Other Plays* (New York: TCG, 1996).
—, *A Civil War Christmas: An American Musical Celebration* (New York: Dramatists Play Services, 2010).
—, *The Mammary Plays: The Mineola Twins and How I Learned to Drive* (New York: TCG, 1998).
—, *The Long Christmas Ride Home: A Puppet Play with Actors* (New York: Dramatist Play Service, 2004).
—, *Meg* (New York: Samuel French, 1977).

Secondary Sources

Benjamin, Walter, 'Central Park', *New German Critique* 34 (1985), 32–58.
Bigsby, C. W. E., *Contemporary American Playwrights* (New York, Cambridge UP 1999).

—, *Modern American Drama 1945–2000* (New York: Cambridge UP, 2000).

Bourdieu, Pierre, *The Field of Cultural Production* (New York: Columbia UP, 1993).

Butler, Judith, *Gender Trouble* (New York: Routledge, 1990).

Casey-Craig, Carolyn, *Women Pulitzer Playwrights: Biographical Profiles and Analyses of the Plays* (Jefferson, N.C.: MacFarland, 2004).

Foucault, Michel, *History of Sexuality, Vol. 1: Introduction*, trans. Robert Hurley (New York: Vintage, 1990).

Friedman, Sharon, 'Feminist Revisions of Classic Texts on the American Stage'. In Bárbara Ozieblo Rajkowska and María Dolores Narbona Carrión (eds), *Codifying the National Self: Spectators, Actors, and the American Dramatic Text* (New York: Peter Lang, 2006), pp. 87–104.

Geis, Deborah R., 'In Willy Loman's Garden: Contemporary Re-visions of *Death of a Salesman*'. In Enoch Brater (ed.), *Arthur Miller's America: Theatre and Culture in a Time of Change* (Ann Arbor: University of Michigan Press, 2005), pp. 202–18.

Green, Amy, 'Whose Voices are These? The Arts of Language in the Plays of Suzan-Lori Parks, Paula Vogel, and Diana Son'. In Alexis Greene (ed.), *Women Writing Plays: Three Decades of the Susan Smith Blackburn Prize* (Austin: University of Texas Press, 2006), pp. 143–57.

Kimbrough, Andrew, 'The Pedophile in Me: The Ethics of *How I Learned to Drive*', *Journal of Dramatic Theory and Criticism* 16, 2 (2002), 47–65.

Pellegrini, Ann, 'Repercussions and Remainders in the Plays of Paula Vogel: An Essay in Five Moments'. In David Krasner (ed.), *A Companion to Twentieth-Century American Drama* (Malden, MA: Blackwell, 2005), pp. 473–85.

—, 'Staging Sexual Injury: *How I Learned to Drive*'. In Janelle G. Reinelt and Joseph R. Roach (eds), *Critical theory and Performance* (Ann Arbor: University of Michigan Press, 2007), pp. 413–31.

Savran, David, *A Queer Sort of Materialism: Recontextualizing American Theater* (Ann Arbor: University of Michigan Press, 2003).

Sedgwick, Eve Kosofsky, *Touching Feeling: Affect, Pedagogy, and Performativity* (Durham: Duke University Press, 2003).

Shepard, Alan and Mary Lamb, 'The Memory Palace in Paula Vogel's Plays'. In Robert L. McDonald and Linda Rohrer Paige (eds), *Southern Women Playwrights: New Essays in Literary History and Criticism* (Tuscaloosa: University of Alabama Press, 2002), pp. 198–217.

Solomon, Alisa, 'Bump and Grind: Teasing Apart Sex and Violence in a Menacing Vogel Drama', *The Village Voice*, 30 March 2005.

Vogel, Paula, 'Interview with David Savran'. In David Savran (ed.), *The Playwright's Voice: American Dramatists on Memory, Writing, and the Politics of Culture* (New York: Theatre Communications Group, 1999), pp. 263–88.

—, 'Interview with Alexis Greene', In: Alexis Greene (ed.), *Women who Write Plays: Interviews With American Dramatists* (Hanover, NH: Smith and Kraus, 2001), pp. 425–48.

—, 'Interview with Ann Linden', In: Joan Herrington, *The Playwright's Muse* (New York: Routledge, 2002), pp. 253–60.

—, Foreword. *The Skin of Our Teeth: A Play.* Thornton Wilder (New York: Perennial Classics, 2003), pp. vii–xiii.

—, Foreword. In Robert Emmet Long (ed.), *Writing* (New York: Ginger/Continuum, 2008).

Notes

1. Biographical information has been taken from a personal interview that I conducted with Vogel in New Haven, Connecticut, on September 18, 2008. Any unnoted references to her life and work that follow herein are taken from this conversation.
2. Bigsby, *Contemporary American Playwrights*, pp. 299–300.
3. David Savran, *A Queer Sort of Materialism*, p. 181.
4. In the revised ending of *Hot 'n' Throbbing*, printed in the 1999 play-text published by Dramatists Play Service, The Voice narrates Othello's lines as he strangles Desdemona: 'Put out the light and then put out the light' (p. 73). Further, whereas in the original version, Clyde leaves the Dwyer home after killing Charlene, in the revised 1999 version, he goes to the bathroom and shoots himself.
5. Michel Foucault, *History of Sexuality*, p. 35.
6. Qtd. in Raymond, 'Puppets and Politics', p. 57.
7. I am invoking here Walter Benjamin's notion of dialectical image. See his essay 'Central Park', p. 49.
8. Ann Pellegrini, 'Repercussions and Remainders in the Plays of Paula Vogel: An Essay in Five Moments', pp. 482–3.
9. Paula Vogel, email to author, Friday, 22 July 2011.
10. Paula Vogel, 'Interview with Alexis Greene', p. 430.
11. Paula Vogel, 'Conversation between Paula Vogel and John Guare', 5 January 1998, 92nd Street Y, New York (Cassette Recording), accessed 27 September 2008.
12. David Savran, *A Queer Sort of Materialism: Recontextualizing American Theatre*, p. 191.
13. Pierre Bourdieu. *The Field of Cultural Production*, p. 84.
14. Paula Vogel, 'Interview with David Savran', p. 276.
15. Ibid., p. 283.
16. Paula Vogel, 'Interview with Ann Linden', p. 257.
17. C. W. E. Bigsby, *Contemporary American Playwrights*, p. 295.
18. Judith Butler, *Gender Trouble*, p. 192.
19. Eve Kosofsky Sedgwick, *Touching Feeling: Affect, Pedagogy, and Performativity*, pp. 149–50.
20. Alisa Solomon, 'Bump and Grind: Teasing Apart Sex and Violence in a Menacing Vogel Drama', p. 69.

22 NAOMI WALLACE

Pia Wiegmink

The War Boys; In the Heart of America; One Flea Spare; Things of Dry Hours; Fever Chart: Three Visions of the Middle East

Introduction

Naomi Wallace's theatre is innately political. Following Brecht's dislike for realism, Wallace's theatre experiments with the power of language and the corporeality of bodies on stage.[1] While her work is generally labelled 'political theatre' immediately, the respective politics presented and debated in her plays escape rash categorization. As Tony Kushner describes her work:

> Naomi Wallace commits the unpardonable sin of being partisan, and, the darkness and harshness of her work notwithstanding, outrageously optimistic. She seems to believe that the world can change. She certainly writes as if she intends to set it on fire.[2]

Naomi Wallace is not only a merciless commentator of contemporary American politics – her plays painfully document, for example, the physical and psychological effects of war with a sharpness and political poignancy that can rarely be found on American stages – but she also forcefully explores the history of interracial relations and conflict in the United States, radically questions the American dream, and addresses less popular political histories, such as labour history, communism and the Great Depression.

While many of her plays touch upon 'made-in-America' themes and conflicts, Wallace's work also transgresses the confines of the US American nation state in many ways. In *Fever Chart: Three Visions of the Middle East* (2008), American characters are entirely absent; instead, the play juxtaposes diverging views of Palestinian, Israeli and Lebanese characters on the conflict in the Middle East. *One Flea Spare* (1995) and *The Inland Sea* (2002) explore issues of class and sexuality in seventeenth-century London during the Great Plague and eighteenth-century Yorkshire respectively. Wallace's characters come from all classes, ages, races and social backgrounds and gender confines only exist in her work to be deconstructed throughout the course of a play. Although relationships – and how they echo and/or try to resist social power structures – play an important role in her work, they are hardly ever heterosexual or without conflict.

Born in Louisville, Kentucky in 1960, Wallace grew up on her father's cattle farm, but after her parents' divorce she also spent part of the year in Amsterdam, visiting her Dutch mother. While she was enrolled in the playwriting programme at the University of Iowa, she took a master class taught by Tony Kushner, who became interested in her work and who later directed a workshop production of her second play, *In the Heart of America*, at the Long Wharf Theater in New Haven, Connecticut in 1994.[3] Her early plays *The War Boys* (1993), *In the Fields of Aceldama (1993)*, *In the Heart of America (1994)*, *One Flea Spare (1995)* and *Slaughter City* (1996) all premiered in London, the first three in smaller fringe venues (like the Finborough Theatre and the Bush Theatre), while the last two were produced by the Royal Shakespeare Company. Soon thereafter, *Birdy* (1996), an adaptation of William Wharton's eponymous novel, premiered in the West End. Wallace's screenplay *Lawn Dogs* (1997), although filmed in Kentucky, was produced by a British entertainment company.

As Vivian Gornick observed, '[t]o American ears, Wallace's work can sound like Beckett rewriting Clifford Odets'.[4] Up until 1996, Wallace's work was largely ignored in the United States. However, in the following years, her work became well established on American stages. For *One Flea Spare*, a play about the London plague of 1665, Wallace earned several prestigious American awards, among them the Susan Smith Blackburn Prize, the Kesselring Prize and an OBIE Award. In 1998, *The Trestle at Pope Lick Creek* was the first of her plays to be commissioned for and premiere in an American theatre (the Actors Theatre in Louisville). The following year, Wallace received the MacArthur 'genius' fellowship, a prize which positioned her among American writers and artists such as Sandra Cisneros, David Foster Wallace, Guillermo Gómez-Peña and Anna Deavere Smith.

Her more recent plays circle around two major themes, the intersections of race and class in American society (*Things of Dry Hours*, 2004, *The Hard Weather Boating Party*, 2009, *And I and Silence*, 2011) and the wars in the Middle East and Afghanistan (*Fever Chart*, 2008, 'One Short Sleepe', 2008, *No Such Cold Thing*, 2009). In 2002, Wallace organized a one-week trip to the Middle East in which six American playwrights (among them Tony Kushner and Kia Corthron) visited Palestinian theatre artists in the Occupied Palestinian Territories.[5] This trip also led to a collaboratively written play *Twenty One Positions: A Cartographic Dream of the Middle East* (2008), which Wallace wrote with fellow traveller and Jewish American playwright Lisa Schlesinger and Palestinian theatre director Abdel Fattah Abu-Srour (2008).

Thus far, Wallace has published 19 plays. Among them are 14 full-length plays, several one-acts, a stage adaptation and two plays for children and young adults which she co-wrote with her husband Bruce McLeod (*The Girl Who Fell Through A Hole in Her Jumper*, 1994 and *In the Sweat*, 1997). In addition, Wallace has also published a collection of poetry (*To Dance a Stony Field, 1995*) and three screenplays: *Lawn Dogs* (1997), *The War Boys* (2009), which was an adaptation of her first play, and *Flying While Blind* (2012), the latter two works being co-written with McLeod.

The Plays

The War Boys (1993)

Wallace's first play, *The War Boys*, premiered at the Finborough Theatre in London (directed by Kate Valentine) in February 1993. The play is set in 'a place that could be the Mexico/Texas border' (p. 145). In this border zone, three amateurs help the official border patrol track illegal immigrants for extra bucks – white, college-educated David; white, working-class George; and Mexican American Greg. That night, they do not catch any border-crossers but instead play the 'War Boys game' (p. 147). In this disturbing, confessional role-play, which begins rather light-heartedly but soon becomes increasingly violent, the young men explore different power constellations between men and women, parents and children, American and immigrant, perpetrator and victim. By telling each other their most personal experiences of betrayal, shame, and self-discovery and performatively re-enacting these stories, the three men, who 'were always friends' (p. 195), come to terms with themselves but also painfully realize the social divides which separate them.

> **Greg** ... So tell me, David, how do you spell relief? (*Beat*) My story is about halves. (*Lifts shirt*) Will you look at this? Split down the middle. But which side is which? I mean, the moment I hit you, when the crisis struck, which did you choose, Hostess or Sara Lee? JVC or Sony? I mean, isn't that the simple beauty of it: who can afford to hire a maid and can't afford not to be one? (p. 194)

What begins as a playful showing-off of masculine clichés soon turns into a bitter recollection of one's own identity and an existential demand for cultural, social and personal recognition.

Stylistically, Wallace's first play is surprisingly experimental and self-reflectively makes use of the theatricality of the medium. Not only does the play dramatize several play-within-the-play situations, in which the characters switch between various roles, it also spatially features two playing areas which symbolically positions the audience within the in-between space of the border. While Naomi Wallace critically recollects her early work by acknowledging, '[so]me of the first plays I wrote, I probably couldn't write again. I had a certain innocence or naïveté about playing with the form of theater'.[6] Tony Kushner remembers his first encounter with Wallace's play quite differently:

> ... I was blown away. ... I said to myself: "Now take it slow. Don't overwhelm her." Then she walked into class the next day and I gushed: "This is one of the most astonishing plays I've ever read. And this the *most* astonishing play by a student I've

ever read." I came back to New York and took her play to my agent. I said to her: "This woman is going to be big someday. Please read her play and take her on." And she did. Naomi's language bowled her over, too.[7]

In the Heart of America (1994)

In the Heart of America was first performed in August 1994 in the Bush Theatre in London. Three months later, Tony Kushner directed a workshop production of the play at Long Wharf Theatre in New Haven, Connecticut. In a complex interweaving of different plots strands, places and times, the play gradually unravels the circumstances that led to the death of Remzi, a Palestinian-American soldier who was killed during the First Gulf War. When Remzi disappears without a trace, his sister, Fairouz, begins to look for her brother and unveils not only the troubled story of two siblings and their different ideas of Arab-American identity, but also the tragic love story between her brother and his fellow soldier and self-proclaimed 'White Trash, River Boy, Arab-kissing Faggot', Carver Perry (p. 114). Remzi, it is revealed in the end, was not killed during enemy combat but in 'friendly fire' (p. 136), that is beaten to death by his fellow comrades.

In this play, Wallace further develops her 'animosity towards "realism" on stage'[8] and continues her experimentation with language, the body and dramatic form. In what will become a signature stage direction for many of her plays and echoes her distaste for the 'kitchen sink drama',[9] the setting is 'minimal and not "realistic"' (p. 80). In addition, Wallace's theatre often refuses to present a linear sequence of events and instead makes frequent use of flashbacks, overlapping time-levels and the appearances of dead characters or even ghosts. In many of her plays, dead characters re-appear or ghosts travel across time and space. As *In the Heart of America* progresses, Fairouz's investigation of the death of her brother alternates with scenes from the past which depict the blossoming relationship between Carver and Remzi, as well as with scenes between Remzi and Fairouz discussing what it is like to be Palestinian in America. Furthermore, the play's complex portrayal of themes like (homosexual) love, national identity and belonging in times of war is further enhanced by Wallace's use of two characters from the past, time travellers who interact with Carver, Fairouz and Remzi. Lue Ming, a dead Vietnamese character who was killed during the Vietnam War, guides Fairouz in her search for her brother. Meanwhile, Lue Ming tries to find her murderer Lieutenant Calley, who reappears in the play as Boxler, Lieutenant Calley's soul, and who gives Carver and Remzi lessons in combat and torture.

In the Heart of America powerfully brings together two themes that loom large in Wallace's work: the polymorphism of language and the body as a socially defined but vulnerable entity. The love affair between the two soldiers takes place in the midst of war. Confronted exclusively with violence, destruction and weapons, for Remzi and Carver, the language of war inevitably becomes the language of love. Carver tries to convey this process to Fairouz:

> **Carver** Things get lost. People.
> **Fairouz** Get lost. But why not you? Why didn't you get lost?
> **Carver** Because I fell in love. In our bunkers at night, Remzi used to read the names out loud to us, and it calmed us down. He must have read that weapons manual a hundred times. All those ways to kill the human body. Lullabies. It was like . . . they were always the same and always there, and when we said them to ourselves there was nothing else like it: Fishbeds, Floggers and Fulcrums. Stingers, Frogs, Silkworms, Vulcans, Beehives and Bouncing Bettys. (p. 111)

The play not only exemplifies how language determines our experience of reality but, more importantly, how language, in its everyday use, can be transformed into a tool of resistance. Wallace comments on this procedure: 'My impulse is to break up the language, or highlight it so that it works against the purposes it was invented to work for'.[10] In a radical act of appropriation, Wallace turns the harsh rhetoric of mass destruction into its opposite, the soft and sensual experience of intimacy between two men.

The second major theme of the play, the body and how it is used, loved and mutilated, is closely connected to Wallace's exploration of the intricacies of war and love and how language impacts both. In *In the Heart of America*, none of the characters' bodies remains unharmed. The very first image visible on stage is Carver's body literally upside down: '*Lights up on Carver doing a headstand in a cheap motel room. Fairouz is standing in the shadows watching*' (p. 83). Fairouz cannot walk properly because in her childhood four boys smashed her foot with a hammer while her brother Remzi watched behind bushes, too scared of being hurt himself to help her. Lue Ming shows Fairouz her 'hunched over' walk, which makes her 'less of a target' (p. 91). Before Lue Ming lost her child in the My Lai massacre, her braid had been cut off by Lieutenant Calley. Calley, in turn, is the living dead, eking out a miserable existence because his soul – personified by Boxler – left his body a long time ago. As Beth Cleary observes, 'the play's characters are haunted, whether dead or alive, by the political and personal histories of war making that mark their bodies, trouble their memories'.[11] In a similar vein, Naomi Wallace recollects her motivation for writing this play:

> I wrote *In the Heart of America* because I was thinking about the body in war. We forget that these weapons are used to tear up as many bodies as possible. When they were dropping cluster bombs in former Yugoslavia, that was to kill as many Serbian soldiers as possible. The body that kills is the same body that loves. How do you use your body as a war machine and also to make love? What happens to the body in this process?[12]

These questions could have also been the pressing issues that led one of Wallace's British contemporaries to write the most controversial drama of the 1990s, Sarah Kane's *Blasted*: premiered at London's Royal Court Theatre in January 1995, only four months after the premiere of *In the Heart of America* at the Bush Theatre.

Content-wise, both plays explore the (im-)possibilities of corporeal intimacy and the physical atrocities people commit in times of war.

Aesthetically, both plays literally tear apart the foundations of realist representation on stage. As Helen Iball observes:

> In the bomb blast that rips apart the conventions of the box-set hotel room, *Blasted* also explodes the central tenets of realist form: the representation of a "slice of life" through a logical connection between characters and action which culminates in resolution. . . .[13]

Both plays interweave the local everyday life of the characters with war zones around the world. Like *In the Heart of America, Blasted* merges the home front with a violent, yet distant military conflict. However, except for some occasional racist remarks by Ian and the play's allusion to the war crimes committed in Bosnia, in Kane's play, cultural and racial contexts are entirely absent.[14] In *In the Heart of America*, Remzi is not killed by enemy troops but by his fellow American soldiers, exposing his belief that 'there is room for me here [in America]. Where I have my friends' (p. 95) as a lethal misjudgement. The play demonstrates how the war resonates with daily racism and homophobia, how Philippine, Korean and Vietnamese 'gooks' become Arab 'gooks' and how the military's 'don't ask, don't tell' policy criminalizes male love in its ranks.[15]

In *In the Heart of America* the memory of the Gulf War haunts Carver's life at home in Kentucky, but with the two characters of Boxler and Lue Ming, Wallace adds the Vietnam War as a historical comparative frame of reference. In a metaphorical embrace of these various pasts, at the end of the play, the surviving lover Carver identifies himself as 'a White Trash, ... Indian, Sandnigger, Brown Trash, Arab, Gook Boy, Faggot. . . . From the banks of the Kentucky River' (p. 136).

One Flea Spare (1995)

Like Wallace's previous plays, *One Flea Spare* first premiered on a London stage. At the same time, the play also marks the beginning of her lasting presence on American stages. Paradoxically, after the Actors Theatre of Louisville, Kentucky had rejected two of her plays, both of which explicitly referenced local characters and history,[16] it was this play about the London plague of 1665, which received its American premiere at the Humana Festival of New American Plays in February 1996 and won numerous awards. In the following year, the play's production at the renowned Public Theater won an OBIE Award for best play. However, although British reviews praised the play as 'an exquisite study in social tension' and 'the gritty poetry and startling images',[17] critics in New York described the play as 'stiff, schematic and surprisingly unaffecting'[18] and complained that the historic setting of the play 'translate[s] to present equivalents only very generally'.[19]

As the plague ravages London, four people – the wealthy, elderly couple William and Darcy Snelgrave, a young, orphaned girl, Morse, and the sailor Bunce – are captured in the Snelgrave's townhouse over a period of several weeks. The characters' only contact with the outside world is Kabe, a watchman who communicates with the residents through a window. Inspired by two very different events, the London Plague of 1665, or rather, Daniel Defoe's fictionalized account of this event (*The Journal of the Plague Years*, 1722) and the Los Angeles race riots of 1992, Wallace's play recreates 'a time of crisis' on stage.[20] Trapped inside the house and set apart from all social norms, the characters soon transgress the confines of gender and class in which they have lived all their lives.

While Bunce at first, although reluctantly, obeys Snelgrave's orders, in a Butlerian performative act of identity exploration, he soon playfully tries on his master's clothes.

> **Snelgrave** . . . What do you see?
> **Bunce** I see a master without his shoes. And his new servant.
>   He is wearing very fine shoes.
>   . . .
>
> **Snelgrave** Historically speaking, the poor do not take fine shoes. They never have and never will. . . .
> **Bunce** What if I kept the shoes? . . .
> **Snelgrave** That is not a historical question.
> **Bunce** No. It's a game question. You said this was a game, Sir. (p. 26)

In the course of the play, Morse, the 12-year-old daughter of the maid of a couple the Snelgrave's are friends with, becomes Darcy's confidante and finally assists her in her suicide. Morse's intellectual, social and moral capabilities go far beyond her age – a trait that seems typical for Wallace's female adolescent characters. Although Morse survives the plague, the first and last scene of the first act, as well as the very last scene of the play, shows her in yet another form of confinement: Suspected of the murder of her new masters, Mr and Mrs Snelgrave, it is Morse's imprisonment that frames the story.

The most explicit transgression of social confines in the isolation of the house is found in the burgeoning love affair between Darcy and Bunce. Since a tragic fire accident that mutilated her body at the age of 17, Darcy has never again been touched by her husband and covers her body under a thick layer of clothes ever since. Likewise, Bunce lives 'with a wound that doesn't heal' (p. 53). As Claudia Barnett observed, '[p]aradoxically, the plague frees them from these metaphorical manacles: When they are physically imprisoned, they are emotionally unfettered; in the absence of society, they unlearn society's rules'.[21] In other words, Wallace's theatre of incarceration allows the characters to physically reconnect with their bodies and with other people regardless of class, gender or age.[22]

Things of Dry Hours (2004)

In contrast to most of Wallace's plays, *Things of Dry Hours* did not premiere in London's fringe or New York's off-Broadway scene but in the Pittsburgh Public Theater in 2004. Inspired by Robin Kelley's *Hammer and Hoe* (1991), the play explores a widely neglected chapter of American history, the work of the Communist Party as a radical labour movement that transgressed the colour line in the American South. Set in Alabama during the depression era, *Things of Dry Hours* examines a time in which segregation was rarely challenged and the violent activities of the Ku Klux Klan peaked. Tice is an African American, unemployed, labour activist who lives with his widowed daughter Cali. While her father organizes political rallies, Cali works as a laundrywoman for white families and earns their daily bread. When Corbin, a white steelworker who could be both comrade and snitch, forces himself into their house, Tice embarks on the dangerous crusade of turning Corbin into a dedicated activist for the all-inclusive labour movement. Corbin, however, seems more interested in Cali than Tice's teachings from his two books of wisdom, the Bible and the *Communist Manifesto*.

Taking its cue from James Baldwin's statement that 'as long as you think you're white, there's no hope for you' (which is also the epigraph of the play), *Things of Dry Hours* is Wallace's most explicit exploration of American race relations (a theme, she continues to address very prominently in her most recent play *And I and Silence*, 2011). This process, as Wallace acknowledges, requires careful self-reflection:

> When I was writing this play, I was acutely aware that I was a white writer writing black characters—and that I had to write against my grain and a mind stewed since birth in racism. I had to challenge that all the time. It's about consciousness and how racism works in myriad ways. . . . Whiteness is not just biology, it is a ticket to power. . . .[23]

One way Wallace attempts to escape the potential traps that come with writing black characters as a white dramatist is the extensive research she does for her works. For *Things of Dry Hours*, Wallace researched not only American labour history and its racial composition, but also the long and troubled history of racial representation on the American stage. When Corbin woos Cali and tries to persuade her that he is 'a decent man' (p. 48), Cali invites him to a play that involves role-reversal in terms of both gender and race. Wrapped in a white blanket and his face painted with black shoe polish, Corbin is supposed to play a black female who tries to fend off the demeaning advances of a white predator (played by Cali using white porridge on her face) accusing her (Corbin) of being a temptress. Corbin is first reluctant, then plays along and finally loses his self-possession as he falls upon Cali. Stepping out of his assigned character, he '*pins CALI to the floor and kneels over her. He unbuckles his belt*' (p. 51). In a critical re-enactment of blackface minstrelsy, the first genuinely American theatre form, Wallace not only deconstructs its core female stereotype (the seducing wench) but also exposes white supremacist thinking that still lurks beneath Corbin's longing for Cali.

> **Cali**   . . . You want something? Here. (*She scrapes porridge from her face.*) You can have this. (*She roughly smears it across his mouth.*) But I tell you one thing, Corbin Teel. You will not dream on my body. (p. 51)

At the end of the play, Tice has failed with his experiment, Corbin has not turned into the faithful communist Tice wanted him to become but has snitched on Tice and Cali. Reminiscent of the historical ghosts of *In the Heart of America* or the frame of Morse's confinement in *One Flea Spare*, Tice, who has long ago died for his political cause, returns from the dead and closes the play with an utterly didactic monologue in which he turns the past into a teachable moment for the present: 'Read what it says on the inside. And then, get to work' (p. 79).

Fever Chart: Three Visions of the Middle East (2008)

Fever Chart is a trilogy of short plays and part of Wallace's larger dramatic exploration of various conflicts in the Middle East. Vision one, 'A State of Innocence', and vision two, 'Between this Breath and You', are two one-act plays with three characters each which address the Israeli–Palestinian conflict. Vision three, 'The Retreating World' is a monologue about an Iraqi man who was forced to sell his books and his pigeons to be able to buy food.

The first printed edition of *Fever Chart* also includes 'One Short Sleepe', a monologue by a young Lebanese man mourning the death of his sister who was killed during an Israeli jet attack. The trilogy premiered in New York's Public Theater (directed by Jo Bonney) in April 2008. At Chicago's Eclipse Theatre Company, which staged several of Naomi Wallace's plays in their 2011 season, *Fever Chart* became a four-part vision of the Middle East as *No Such Cold Thing* (2009), Wallace's play about a Chicano soldier and two Afghani sisters, was staged along with the three original visions.

Inspired by real events,[24] in vision one and two, Wallace presents two stories about Israeli and Palestinian characters whose fates are inextricably connected. 'State of Innocence' takes place in the surreal setting of the remnants of a zoo in Rafah (in the Gaza strip) which had been destroyed by Israeli forces. In the zoo, three characters encounter each other: Yuval, an Israeli soldier who guards the devastated zoo; Um Hisham, a Palestinian woman; and Shlomo, a Jewish architect hungry to transform the zoo into a Zionist settlement modelled on the historic precedent 'Homa Umigdal'. All three characters, it turns out, are ghosts and their stories interlace.[25] Um Hisham was not allowed to come close to her daughter while she died from an Israeli bullet, yet she held Yuval, who prevented his fellow soldiers from beating her husband to death, in her arms after a Rafah sniper had shot him. As an act of revenge for Yuval's death, her house was bulldozed to make room for Israeli settlements. As Yuval and Um Hisham allow themselves to feel empathy for each other, they overcome the political barriers that are supposed to separate them.

> **Um Hisham**   Everything I have despised, for decades – the uniform, the power, the brutality, the inhumanity – and I held it in my arms. . . . But it should have been your mother. . . . And every day I'll come here [to the zoo] and visit you, as I visit my daughter. (p. 23)

In a similar fashion, the second vision, 'Between This Breath and You', connects the fates of a Palestine father, Mourid, and a young Israeli nurse, Tanya. Israeli Defense Forces shot Mourid's son and he agreed to have his lung transplanted to Tanya whose cystic fibrosis threatens to kill her. Although Tanya refuses to acknowledge this connection at first, in the end, she allows Mourid to reconnect with his dead son by teaching her how to breathe with his son's lungs.

As one of only very few American playwrights, Wallace has actually visited the Occupied Palestinian Territories and her representation of the Israeli–Palestine conflict dissolves common dichotomies of victim and perpetrator, enemy and friend. Despite an emerging genre of

Middle-Eastern drama in American theatre, theatre critic Randy Gener observes that

> it is very difficult, at this moment, to grant ordinary Palestinians their humanity on U.S. stages without someone insisting that the words "suicide bomber" and "Hamas" need also be uttered in the same breath.[26]

However, refusing to focus on Palestinian characters as the perpetrators seems to come at cost. When the Guthrie Theater in Minneapolis commissioned Wallace's collaborative musical play *Twenty-One Positions: A Cartographic Dream of the Middle East* (which she co-wrote with Jewish-American playwright Lisa Schlesinger and the Palestinian director and refugee aid worker Abdel Fattah Abu-Srour), the dramaturg accused the three writers of 'supporting terrorism' and the play did not premiere at the Guthrie Theater.[27]

Despite such drawbacks, in Wallace's dramas about the Israeli–Palestinian conflict, enemy parties are connected to each other either by a shared experience of loss or by physical interdependence. As Neil Genzlinger recounts in his review of *Fever Chart*, '[i]t's a plot device you might find on the Lifetime channel, but the obligatory feel-good embrace, thankfully, never materialized. There are no easy solutions in Mrs. Wallace's world, just as in life'.[28]

Summary

Naomi Wallace has been writing for the theatre for almost 20 years now. However, her works have thus far received very little critical attention. Despite her rich and complex body of work, no book-length study of her plays has yet been published. There are only a sparse number of scholarly essays on Wallace's dramas and the authors usually only discuss her early plays with a narrow focus on one or two major themes or compare her work with that of other (female) playwrights.[29]

Although her most recent play, *And I and Silence*, received its world premiere at the Finborough Theatre in London, the same theatre which also produced Wallace's first play *The War Boys*, her work is usually produced on both sides of the Atlantic. While some theatre critics praise Wallace as 'an expert at mixing politics and poetry',[30] others find that her plays are too poetic and intellectual and complain that 'she diminishes the importance of character and story'.[31] Indeed, many of her plays, their titles, and major themes are inspired by poems – *One Flea Spare*, *Things of Dry Hours* and *And I and Silence*, for example, take their titles from the poems by John Donne, Gwendolyn Brooks and Emily Dickinson – and Wallace's creative process often begins with the writing of a poem which is then transformed into a play.[32]

Wallace herself acknowledges that she 'like[s] very bare stages . . . . On a clear stage, the body of the actor and the language, have a lot of space'.[33] In many of her plays, characters do not just speak their lines, but experiment with language in form of pauses, beats and uncommon punctuation. Comparable to Remzi's fascination with the language of weapons manuals which becomes a lover's code in *In the Heart of America*, these modifications de-familiarize everyday speech and result in a heightened perception of communicative processes. Likewise, for Wallace, a body on stage is not merely the representation of a character but also a means with which she inquires into larger political conditions. As Beth Cleary observes,

> [a]ll of Wallace's plays concern the body as a historically-produced, work-determined, polymorphously-desiring container of the conscious and unconscious states of human being. In all of her plays, the human, working, loving body struggles to produce, not be produced, yearns to remake, not be made.[34]

The corporeality of her characters – be that the physically injured bodies of *In the Heart of America*, the socially confined bodies of *One Flea Spare*, the polluted bodies of *A Hard Weather Boating Party*, or the labouring bodies in *The Trestle at Pope Lick Creek*, *Slaughter City* or *And I and*

Silence – thus always also functions as an indicator of broader social, economic and political processes. As Wallace explains,

> [w]hat fascinates me is how much the body and politics are connected. The body that labors is also the body that loves. . . . Social roles damage our body, labor damages our bodies. That affects how we love. From the day the body is born, our body is pulled and stretched in different directions through the political values of our society.[35]

In *And I and Silence*, for example, Dee and Jamie train their bodies to become good servants when they are released from prison. In the 1950s' segregated America, however, the labouring female body, as Wallace's play painfully illustrates, cannot be perceived independently from its racial and sexual signification.

In her objection to realist representation, Wallace's plays experiment with theatrical conventions. Characters are time travellers, linear dramatic structures are absent as different time levels and spaces interlace, and role-plays as well as rehearsal situations further enhance the theatricality of her plays. The combination of this stylistic ingenuity and her tenacious dissection of various discourses of power make Wallace one of the most remarkable and genuine political playwrights today. For Wallace, theatre serves as a means of exploring and thinking about power relations. She writes that

> . . . all theatre, as Brecht reminds us, is political, and by political we mean human and social in its interaction and impact. All theatre deals with questions of power. Who has it? Who doesn't? Who wants to get it and how? Who lost it and why? Who has killed for it? Who has died for it?[36]

As a white female dramatist from Kentucky, Wallace does not recoil from writing across and against the confines of class, race, gender and national belonging. In order to create her unique characters and to explore identities other than her own, she often 'write[s] outside [her] whiteness'.[37] Her characters comprise homosexual, African American,

Chicano, Vietnamese and Middle Eastern characters and Wallace never shies away from topics which many of her contemporaries would not dare to touch upon in this degree of radicalism and legibility, in particular not as a white female dramatist from the South. Ultimately, for Wallace, the personal is always political. The emotional bond between Carver and Remzi, Darcy and Bunce, or Callie and Tice transgresses the confines of sex, class and race. Thus, in Wallace's plays, politics is always also a form of personal interaction between individual characters whose actions result from and are informed by the institutional, historical and social dynamics in which they occur.

Primary Sources

Works by Naomi Wallace

In the Heart of America and Other Plays [*One Flea Spare, In the Heart of America, The War Boys, Slaughter City, The Trestle at Pope Lick Creek*] (New York: Theatre Communications Group, 2001).

Things of Dry Hours (New York: Broadway Play Publishing, 2010).

Fever Chart: Three Visions of the Middle East. (New York: Theatre Communications Group, 2009). [also includes 'One Short Sleepe'].

And I And Silence (London: Faber and Faber, 2011).

Secondary Sources

Baley, Shannon, 'Death and Desire, Apocalypse and Utopia: Feminist Gestus and the Utopian Performative in the Plays of Naomi Wallace', *Modern Drama* 47, 2 (2004), 237–49.

Barnett, Claudia, 'Physical Prisons: Naomi Wallace's Drama of Captivity'. In Thomas Fahy and Kimball King (eds), *Captive Audience: Prison and Captivity in Contemporary Theater* (New York: Routledge, 2003), 147–65.

—, '*Things of Dry Hours* by Naomi Wallace. Directed by Israel Hicks. O'Reilly Theater, Pittsburgh Public Theater, Pittsburgh, 22 April 2004', *Theatre Journal* 56, 4 (2004), 670–72.

Brantley, Ben, 'Prisoners in the Home, Facing the Twin Ravages of Plague and Power', *New York Times*, 10 March 1997, p. 11.

Butler, Judith, 'Performative Acts and Gender Constitution: An Essay in Phenomenology and Feminist Theory'. In Sue-Ellen Case (ed.), *Performing Feminism, Feminist Critical Theory and Theatre* (Baltimore: Johns Hopkins UP, 1990), pp. 270–82.

Cleary, Beth, 'Haunting the Social Unconscious: Naomi Wallace's *In the Heart of America*', *The Journal of American Drama and Theatre* 14, 2 (2002), 1–12.

Clum, John M., *Still Acting Gay: Male Homosexuality in Modern Drama* (New York: St. Martin's Griffin, 2000).

Corthron, Kia, Tony Kushner, Robert O'Hara, Lisa Schlesinger, Betty Shamieh and Naomi Wallace, 'On the Road to Palestine: Six American Playwrights Come upon the Checkpoints—Both Military and Metaphorical—That Define the Daily Realities of Palestinian Life', *American Theatre* 20, 6 (July/August 2003), 28–32.

Cummings, Scott T., 'Naomi Wallace', *Twentieth-Century American Dramatists* (Detroit: Gale Group, 2002). http://go.galegroup.com/ps/i.do?id=GALE%7CH1200010521&v=2.1&u=wash43584&it=r&p=LitRC&sw=w.

Gardner, Lyn, 'The Enemy Within', *The Guardian,* 5 February 2007, p. 28.

Gener, Randy, 'See Under: Homeland, on U.S. Stages, Israeli and American Artists Espouse Humanism in a World of Violence', *American Theatre* 25, 5 (2008), 32–3, 77–9.

Genzlinger, Neil, 'Enemies Face to Face, Exchanging Tales of Loss', theater review, *New York Times*, 10 May 2008, p. B14.

Gornick, Vivian, 'An American Exile in America', *New York Times Magazine*, 2 March 1997, pp. 27–31.

Haagensen, Erik, '*Things of Dry Hours* at New York Theatre Workshop', *Back Stage* 50, 24 (2009), 22.

Hemings, Sarah, 'Shades of "The Servant"—London Fringe Theatre', *Financial Times*, 1 November 1995, p. 21.

Howe Kritzer, Amelia, 'Enough! Women Playwrights Confront the Israeli-Palestinian Conflict', *Theatre Journal* 62, 2 (2010), 611–26.

Iball, Helen, *Sarah Kane's Blasted* (London: Continuum, 2008).

Joseph, Rajiv, *Gruesome Playground Injuries; Animals Out of Paper; Bengal Tiger at the Baghdad Zoo: Three Plays* (Berkeley: Soft Skull Press, 2010).

Kane, Sarah, *Blasted & Phaedra's Love* (London: Methuen, 1996).

Over, William, 'Performance Review: *One Flea Spare*. By Naomi Wallace. The Joseph Papp Public Theatre, New York City. 14 April 1997', *Theatre Journal* 50, 2 (1998), 254–7.

Ozieblo, Barbara, '"Pornography of Violence": Strategies of Representation in Plays by Naomi Wallace, Stefanie Zadravec, and Lynn Nottage', *The Journal of American Drama and Theatre* 23, 1 (2011), pp. 67–79.

Sierz, Alexs, '"Looks like there's a war on": Sarah Kane's *Blasted*, political theatre and the Muslim Other'. In Larens de Vos and Graham Saunders (eds), *Sarah Kane in Context* (Manchester: Manchester UP, 2010), pp. 45–56.

Wallace, Naomi, 'In the Heart of America: Forging Links; Interview with Naomi Wallace' by John Istel, *American Theatre* 12, 3 (1995), 25.

—, 'Poetry, Plays, Politics, and Shifting Geographies'. In Robert Vorlicky (ed.), *Tony Kushner in Conversation* (Ann Arbor University of Michigan Press, 1998), pp. 255–65.

—, 'Interview with Naomi Wallace' by Alexis Greene. In Alexis Greene (ed.), *Women Who Write Plays: Interviews with American Dramatists* (Hanover: Smith and Kraus, 2001), pp. 449–71.

—, 'Intimate Histories: Naomi Wallace in Conversation with Claire MacDonald', *PAJ: A Journal of Performance and Art* 28, 3 (2006a), 93–102.

—, 'Naomi Wallace'. In Barbara Baker (ed.), *The Way We Write: Interviews with Award-Winning Writers* (London: Continuum, 2006b), 199–213.

—, 'On Writing as Transgression', *American Theatre* 25, 1 (2008), 98–102.

—, 'The Ethics of Ethnic', *The Dramatist* 13, 1 (2010), 30–1.

Notes

1. Naomi Wallace, 'Interview with Naomi Wallace', p. 470.
2. Tony Kushner, qtd. in Lyn Gardner, 'The Enemy Within', p. 28.
3. Scott T. Cummings, 'Naomi Wallace'.
4. Vivian Gornick, 'An American Exile in America', p. 31.
5. For an account of the trip see Naomi Wallace et al., 'On the Road to Palestine', pp. 28–32.
6. Naomi Wallace, 'Interview with Naomi Wallace', p. 458.
7. Tony Kushner, qtd. in Vivian Gornick, 'An American Exile in America', p. 28.
8. Naomi Wallace, 'Intimate Histories', p. 100.
9. Naomi Wallace, 'Interview with Naomi Wallace', p. 470.
10. Ibid., p. 465.
11. Beth Cleary, 'Haunting the Social Unconscious', p. 1.
12. Naomi Wallace, 'Interview with Naomi Wallace', p. 465.
13. Helen Iball, *Sarah Kane's Blasted*, p. 2.
14. See, in this context, Alex Sierz's discussion of references to Muslim characters in Kane's play and subsequent performances. Alex Sierz, 'Looks like there's a war on', pp. 45–56.
15. See Naomi Wallace, 'Forging Links', p. 25.
16. Naomi Wallace, qtd. in Vivian Gornick, 'An American Exile in America', p. 31.
17. Sarah Hemings, 'Shades of "The Servant"', p. 21.
18. Ben Brantley, 'Prisoners in the Home', p. 11.
19. William Over, 'Performance Review: *One Flea Spare*', p. 257.
20. Naomi Wallace qtd. in Vivian Gornick, 'An American Exile in America', p. 31.
21. Claudia Barnett, 'Physical Prisons', p. 154.
22. A variation of this theme is taken up in Wallace's most recent play *And I and Silence* which premiered in London in May 2011. Set in segregated America in the 1950s, the play depicts the friendship, love and finally shared suicide of two female characters, Dee (white) and Jamie (African American). The scenes of the play alternate between 1950, when both characters were in prison, and 1959 after they have been released from prison and struggle to make a living together. During their incarceration, the two women coach

each other to become good employees. However, despite all training, once released from prison, Dee and Jamie are stricken by hunger, sexual harassment, unemployment and racism. Comparable to Darcy's suicide in *One Flea Spare*, Dee and Jamie's mutual killing at the end of the play symbolizes not a mental collapse but an escape from the confines of class, race and heterosexuality.

23. Naomi Wallace, qtd. in Lyn Gardner, 'The Enemy Within', p. 28.

24. In an interview with Claire MacDonald, Wallace acknowledges that she was inspired to write 'State of Innocence' by the destruction of a children's zoo in Rafah and the account of a Palestinian mother holding the Israeli soldier who was shot at her door and died in her arms, see Naomi Wallace, 'Intimate Histories', pp. 93–4. Amelia Howe Kritzer points out that 'Between This Breath and You' is also based on a real occurrence, the death of a Palestinian boy by Israeli soldiers and the willingness of his parents to give his organs to Israeli people in need of a donor. See Howe Kritzer, 'Enough!', p. 623.

25. Although set in Baghdad instead of Rafah, the elements of a destroyed zoo, a wandering ghost and the interlacing of the fates of three main protagonists powerfully reoccurs in the 2010 Pulitzer finalist *Bengal Tiger at the Baghdad Zoo* by Rajiv Joseph. Directed by Moises Kaufmann, the story evolves around a Tiger ghost of the Baghdad zoo who is guarded by two American soldiers, Kev and Tom.

26. Randy Gener, 'See Under: Homeland', p. 79.

27. See ibid., p. 80 and Naomi Wallace, 'Intimate Histories', p. 100.

28. Neil Genzlinger, 'Enemies Face to Face', p. B14.

29. See, e.g. Claudia Barnett, 'Physical Prisons'; Beth Cleary, 'Haunting the Social Unconscious'; John M. Clum, *Still Acting Gay*, pp. 300–9; Amelia Howe Kritzer, 'Enough!'; Shannon Baley, 'Death and Desire'; or Barbara Ozieblo, 'Pornography of Violence'.

30. Claudia Barnett, '*Things of Dry Hours*', p. 670.

31. Erik Haagensen, '*Things of Dry Hours*', p. 22.

32. Naomi Wallace, 'Interview with Naomi Wallace', p. 456.

33. Naomi Wallace, 'Naomi Wallace', p. 206.

34. Beth Cleary, 'Haunting the Social Unconscious', p. 1.

35. Naomi Wallace, 'Poetry, Plays, Politics', p. 258.

36. Naomi Wallace, 'On Writing as Transgression', pp. 98–9.

37. Naomi Wallace, 'The Ethics of Ethnic', p. 30.

23 WENDY WASSERSTEIN

Frazer Lively

Uncommon Women and Others; Isn't It Romantic; The Heidi Chronicles; An American Daughter; Third

Introduction

Wasserstein was born in 1950 in Brooklyn, the youngest of five children in a high-achieving Jewish family. Both parents were Polish immigrants. Her father invented a lucrative ribbon process. A sister became an upper-level bank executive, a brother a Wall Street financier. When Wasserstein was 12, the family moved to the Upper East Side in Manhattan. Her mother, a dance enthusiast, sent her to June Taylor School of Dance and to Broadway plays, of which Wasserstein later said: 'I remember going to them and thinking, I really like this, but where are the girls?'[1] She attended private girls' schools, majored in history at Mount Holyoke College and earned a master's in creative writing from City College of New York, where she studied with Israel Horowitz and Joseph Heller. Playwrights Horizons produced her first public reading, *Any Woman Can't* (1973). She later called the play 'awful',[2] but it afforded her entrance to the Yale School of Drama, where she received her Master of Fine Arts in playwriting in 1976.

At Yale, Wasserstein met lifelong friend and colleague Christopher Durang, as well as actors Meryl Streep and Sigourney Weaver. Wasserstein and Durang co-wrote a farce, *When Dinah Shore Ruled the Earth*. Wasserstein was the only woman playwright in her year. At the first reading of her thesis play, *Uncommon Women and Others*, Wasserstein recalled: 'This guy . . . said "I can't get into this, it's about girls." And it was amazing to me that someone would really say this and not be embarrassed. And I thought, I spent my life getting into *Hamlet* and *Laurence of Arabia*, so why don't you try it . . . . I was quite angry.'[3]

Wasserstein found an early artistic home at Playwrights Horizons under the aegis of André Gregory, who produced almost all her plays. She was generous in giving interviews and appeared frequently on television talk shows, successfully promoting her work and becoming known as a social critic. Her humorous writing appeared in newspapers and magazines; some of these pieces were published in two collections of essays, *Bachelor Girls* (1990) and *Shiksa Goddess* (2001). While the pieces are witty, they reveal some of Wasserstein's loneliness. Nevertheless, like many of the characters in her plays, she led an active social life among the famous and the well-to-do. She was close to several gay men, whom she called her 'husbands'. Despite pressure from her mother to get married, she never did so, but she gave birth through in-vitro fertilization when she was in her late forties. Wasserstein described this process in her most moving essays.[4]

Wendy Wasserstein's plays 'spoke for a generation',[5] the baby boomer generation of upper middle class women to which she belonged. Her commercially successful, intelligent comedies show women characters trapped between convention and modernity. She used a comedic lens and a realist style to approach issues of gender roles, history and Jewish identity.[6] Wasserstein achieved critical and commercial success with many of her pieces, especially the Pulitzer prize-winning *The Heidi Chronicles* (1988), the first play on Broadway to attempt a history of the women's movement.

Wasserstein's carefully crafted comedy about Jewish roots, *The Sisters Rosensweig* (1992), was a popular success and also won numerous awards.

More overtly political is *An American Daughter* (1997), which examines the downfall of a woman in public life in a media-driven culture. Several critics who had disparaged her earlier comedies praised *An American Daughter,* but it failed at the box office, perhaps because it attacked the media and criticized a liberal president, or perhaps because audiences expected lighter fare.

After her child was born, Wasserstein wrote two full-length plays, *Old Money* (2000) and *Third* (2005), before her death. Her lesser-known pieces include *Tender Offer* (1983), the musical *Miami* (1986), *The Man in a Case* (1986), *Workout* (1995) and *Welcome to My Rash* (2004). The

Elements of Style, a posthumously published novel, satirizes the heedless rich of New York City.

Wasserstein received negative press for what Robert Brustein called her 'witticism habit'[7] and playgoers sometimes compared her work to situation comedy. Her plays are not simply commercial products, however. She called them 'serious plays that are funny'.[8] She explained that 'there is a strength in being comedic. It's a way of getting on in the world, of taking the heat out of things. Humor is a life force'.[9] To some extent a social critic, Wasserstein wrote characters like herself: clever, well-to-do, driven Americans, Ivy League educated, whose unhappiness arises from confusions over gender expectations in the late twentieth century.

The Plays

Uncommon Women and Others (1977)

Uncommon Women and Others ran for just three weeks off Broadway, but it had over a thousand college and regional theatre productions after a public television broadcast of the play. Wasserstein said, 'I wrote *Uncommon Women* because I wanted to see an all-female curtain call there. I wanted to see those college girls on stage, because I thought they were play-worthy. And, by the way, for a woman to be play-worthy she doesn't have to be insane or desperate or deliriously crazy.'[10]

As in all Wasserstein's work, *Uncommon Women*'s specific historical moment matters. Most of the play takes place in 1972, the graduation year for seven seniors at Mount Holyoke College, one of the 'Seven Sisters' elite women's schools linked to Ivy League institutions which were all-male until the 1970s. The main characters in the play are confused about their futures. The students' directives when they first entered school have changed: now, instead of or in addition to marrying well, they feel pressure to pursue their own careers and dreams.

The students spout the names of Kate Millet, Germaine Greer, Simone de Beauvoir and Virginia Woolf, but the feminist writers serve mainly as fodder for jokes. The play is hardly a political tract. Rather, it is a diffuse, ironic portrait of a group of women, caught at a moment of change, who deflect their fears or sadness with humour. There is emotional action, but no plot, other than the seasonal movement from autumn to graduation. Fourteen loosely linked vignettes in the dorm are framed at the beginning and end of the play by two scenes in a restaurant in 1978, where five graduates meet to catch up on their lives since college.

The five characters at the reunion are the 'uncommon women' of the title. Wasserstein provides more detailed character descriptions here than in any of her later plays, as if she did not yet trust her own dialogue to provide depth. Rita, the nascent artist, the instigator of games and predictor of future success, 'refuses to live *down* to expectations'. Holly, overweight, rich and insecure, has 'devised strong moral code of warmth for those you love and wit for those you're scared of'. Samantha, the 'classic' woman, is also 'a closet wit'. Beautiful Kate 'always walks with direction, and that's why it's fun to make her stop and laugh'. Muffet, 'attractive, wry and cheerful', is rethinking her younger beliefs that 'men were just more interesting than women'.[11]

Four additional characters, the 'others' of the title, appear only in the college scenes.

A taped Man's Voice punctuates each scene with pompous rhetoric, taken by Wasserstein primarily from a Holyoke catalogue. He gives patronizing descriptions of the qualities the students are expected to embody. The Voice says:

> The college produces women who are persons in their own right: Uncommon Women who as individuals have the personal dignity that comes with intelligence, competence, flexibility, maturity, and a sense of responsibility. This can happen without a loss of gaiety, charm, and femininity . . . . The college makes its continued contribution to society in the form of graduates whose intellectual quality is high, and whose responsibility to others is exceptional. (p. 7)

Part of the irony of the play depends upon the gap between the students' lives and the Voice's pronouncements. The Voice's praise of 'the spirit of systematic disinterested inquiry' is followed by Kate's question, 'Did you ever have penis envy?' (p. 57) After the Voice announces that the college encourages 'strenuous and sustained effort in any area of endeavor', Rita puts on a male persona, asking Samantha, 'Hey, man, wanna go out and cruise for pussy?' (p. 52)

Rita plays the part of the outrageous radical, a playful feminist who complains that 'this entire society is based on cocks' (p. 34) and who claims liberation because she has tasted her menstrual blood. She is unabashedly promiscuous. The women are affected by the sexual revolution as much as they are by feminism; men dominate their consciousness, and all except Samantha have had multiple sexual experiences. Only Samantha opts for a traditional engagement, to a man who is 'better than me and he'll love me' (p. 26). Kate, the most successful academic, 'sneaks trashy novels' and says she has slept with more men than Rita has. Muffy, embarrassed she lacks Rosie the Riveter's courage, says 'I would really like to meet my prince . . . . I just don't know suddenly why I'm supposed to know what I want to do' (p. 25).

In the most touching scene of the play, Holly places a desperate phone call to a man who has forgotten meeting her. She giggles her way through confessions of inadequacy and need ('I couldn't very well call you up and tell you to move me to Minneapolis and let's have babies, could I?'), before she admits:

> I like my friends, I like them a lot. They're really exceptional. Uncommon women and all that drivel. Of course, they're not risky. I'm not frightened I'll ruin my relationship with them. . . . Often I think I want a date or a relationship to be over so I can talk about it to Kate or Rita. I guess women are not as scary as men and therefore they don't count as much. *Begins to cry.* I didn't mean that. I guess they just make me feel worthwhile. (p. 63)

The women's friendship outweighs their competition in the play. While women friends in Wasserstein's plays never admit any possible repressed homoerotic desire, here the characters do share exuberant physicality, admiring each other's dance moves and celebrating uncomplicated affection. Chirico believes that the dance 'permeates the drama's structure' and 'suggests that the group's sense of togetherness is a constant force' (p. 88). To Susan Carlson, 'it is almost as if Wasserstein knew her play could not end this way, so she indulged her dreams and her characters' dreams of togetherness in this wish-fulfilling pseudo-ending.'[12]

A lasting women's community remains elusive in the play, in part because after graduation, the utopia of the all-female world at college will end. The loss of the women's community looms, and even though feminist ideas have become part of the characters' thinking, they do not know how these ideas will play out in their lives outside of college.

The graduates discuss those options in the final scene of the play, when five characters come together six years after college. None of the women is content. Samantha is happily married and pregnant, but says she is intimidated and has not done anything important. Kate, a lawyer with an important job, is experiencing the numbness she feared law school would bring her, and a relationship has failed because the man wanted someone 'not quite so uncommon' (p. 69). Former radical feminist Rita, supported by a wealthy husband, has not begun writing her novel and is having panic attacks. Muffy is earning a living in a job she dislikes. Holly's parents call her to ask 'Are you thin? Are you married to a root canal man? Are *you* a root canal man?' but she has made no choices and is still 'in transition'. (p. 71)

Uncommon Women and Others was nevertheless 'one of the first proto-feminist realist plays', according to Jill Dolan.[13] The play captures the angst and confusion that existed in the early 1970s among American undergraduates. That Vietnam, presidential elections and civil rights struggles never appear in the play may seem regrettable. Wasserstein removed references to Vietnam from an early draft, choosing to focus more specifically on women.

In *Uncommon Women and Others*, Wasserstein showed situations that had never before appeared on stage. She announced ideas she would approach in future plays: friendship and competition between women, music as a way of establishing female bonding as well as historical moment and limited slots for women. Wasserstein's criticisms of the feminist movement deepened in her next two plays, culminating in *The Heidi Chronicles*.

Isn't It Romantic (1981, revised 1983)

Isn't It Romantic received mixed reviews in 1981. Even critics who found it amusing compared it unfavourably to *Uncommon Women and Others*. Gerald Gutierrez directed the 1983 version; Wasserstein gave him credit for helping her to excise unnecessary jokes, shave 45 minutes from the original and focus on the protagonist. The revised play still received attacks in print, but most reviewers praised it.[14] *Isn't It Romantic* ran for nearly two years Off Broadway and went on to be performed successfully in regional theatres. Wasserstein said the play made her 'financially and emotionally secure'. For the first time, she earned her living as a playwright.[15]

Isn't It Romantic could serve as a sequel to *Uncommon Women and Others*. The later piece shows two women a few years older are now out in the world, having to make a life. Both plays are episodic, but *Romantic* is more tightly structured, with a clear plot. Like the earlier play, it consists of short scenes, separated by taped voices of people who are never seen. While the one authoritarian male speaker in *Uncommon* provides an ironic commentary, the voices in *Romantic* (added in the 1983 revision) are multiple answering machine messages. The play as a whole concerns voice, especially how Janie Blumberg searches for her voice as an independent woman. She must separate from meddling parents, refuse a man who belittles her and choose her own life over the ones chosen for her. In addition, the play shows a close female friendship that falls apart. Wasserstein called it 'a serious play . . . the story of one woman's liberation, put into a comedy'.[16]

The schematic nature of the play places Janie and her best friend Harriet in relation to their mothers, Tasha Blumberg and Lillian Cornwall, and to their respective boyfriends, Marty and Paul. Janie is a bright writer, a plump young Jewish woman given to witticisms to deflect her insecurity; she says that compared to Harriet, she looks 'like an extra in *Potemkin*' (p. 82). Wasserstein told an interviewer:

> Janie Blumberg's humor gives her the ability to distance herself from situations. But she simultaneously endears herself to people by being amusing. The play is about her difficulty in

communicating. She is so verbal, and yet she can't talk. It's a play about speech—about the ability to speak and not to speak at the same time, which comes from the pressure women are under to be a good girl, a smart girl, and a warm girl simultaneously.[17]

Harriet appears to have no doubts about her worth and is already a success in the business world, while Janie cannot even unpack the boxes in her new apartment. Of the two, Harriet speaks like the more liberated woman: she advises Janie that 'no matter how lonely you get or how many birth announcements you receive, the trick is not to get frightened. There's nothing wrong with being alone . . . . I never respected women who didn't learn to live alone and pay their own rent'. (p. 104)

Each young woman reacts to a strong mother. Tasha, a dance enthusiast, invades Janie's apartment at 7 a.m., urges her to get up and dance, pressures her to marry and sings the wedding song from *Fiddler on the Roof* to her answering machine. Lillian, a high-ranking corporate executive, has little interest in Harriet's personal life, but requires a business analysis of her work. Perhaps predictably, each young woman chooses the opposite of what her mother prescribes. Harriet accepts the first man to propose to her, abandoning the importance of women's friendship. Janie eventually refuses 'her mother's dream come true', a Jewish doctor.

Marty nicknames Janie 'Monkey' and makes decisions for her, even renting an apartment for them both without consulting her. He tries to convince Janie to concentrate on him, not her new job as a writer for Sesame Street, because he needs 'a great deal of attention'.

Marty has signalled what Janie's life would be like with him. She feels suffocated, but as Wasserstein explained, 'Janie is a character who has a problem expressing her feelings and she desperately wants to be liked'.[18] Until Harriet encourages her to do so, Janie cannot call off the relationship. Finally she tells Marty: 'I can't move in with you. If I did, I'd always be a monkey, a sweet little girl.' (p. 139)

Wasserstein called this her 'most autobiographical play', admitting that she had modelled the characters on herself, her mother and her sister Sandra (as the corporate executive mother).[19]

The gap Wasserstein described between the feminist ideals of the 1970s and the selfish focus of the 1980s would resurface in later plays. The problems between Harriet and Janie prefigure one of the main issues of *The Heidi Chronicles*.

The Heidi Chronicles (1988)

The Heidi Chronicles, Wasserstein's best known and most controversial play, attempts a history of the women's movement from 1965 to 1989. The play was developed at the Seattle Repertory Theatre and directed by Daniel Sullivan before opening in New York. After it transferred to Broadway, it won numerous awards: the Susan Smith Blackburn Prize, the Drama Desk Award, the Hull-Warriner Award, the New York Drama Critics Circle Award, the Outer Critics Circle Award, the Tony Award and the Pulitzer Prize. The general public perceived Wasserstein's plays as feminist, but *Heidi*'s lavish honours perturbed many feminist critics, who argued that *Heidi* distorted what they had fought for. Jill Dolan, for example, wrote that the play 'narrates the uncomplimentary view of the feminist movement promoted by the dominant culture'.[20] Wasserstein said:

> I wrote this play because I had this image of a woman standing up at a women's meeting saying, "I've never been so unhappy in my life." . . . Talking to friends, I knew there was this feeling around, in me and in others, and I thought it should be expressed theatrically.[21]

Once again, as in her first two major pieces, the play is episodic. Wasserstein explained that she used this structure partly because of her difficulty in telling stories.

Each of the two acts begins with a prologue set in a Columbia University lecture hall in 1989 (the present) where Dr Heidi Holland gives art history lectures. The other scenes show 23 years in Heidi's history, with the scenes usually jumping forward by two or three-year increments. The structure is inventive: Czekay says that 'on a formal level, *The Heidi Chronicles* is Wasserstein's most complex play'.[22] Wasserstein is concerned with the effect of historical events on individuals and how the individuals respond to them. A problem with her structure, identified by Christopher Bigsby, is that 'the effect of the rapid jumps between scenes, each one taking place several years after the preceding one, is to eliminate psychological development'.[23]

In her prologue lectures, Heidi attempts to rectify the absence of women's art from the canon by teaching her students (the audience) about little-known women artists. Both lectures are entertaining, but not especially academic. She tends to speak of the people pictured as personal friends (e.g. 'hello, girls'). After the prologue, the first two scenes of Act I take place in the 1960s. Wasserstein introduces the two men with whom Heidi will interact throughout the play. A fourth character, Susan, is also introduced. In scene one, at a 1965 high school dance, Susan wants to attract boys, but Heidi remains on the periphery, where she meets and has an ironic flirtation with Peter Patrone. When he asks her to marry him, she says 'I covet my independence'. Scene two takes place in 1968 at a Eugene McCarthy rally; Heidi is now a Vassar student who meets Scoop Rosenbaum, a 'charismatic creep' (p. 181) with whom she wrangles about women's rights. With no clear reason to be attracted to him, she acquiesces to an on-again, off-again affair that will last several years. The rest of Act I brings Heidi with Susan to a 1970 feminist consciousness raising group, treated by the playwright with a heavy dose of mockery, but a turning point for Heidi; to her 1974 demonstration for 'women in art' at the Art Institute of Chicago, where Peter comes out as gay; and to Scoop's 1977 wedding to another woman. Act I ends with Heidi and Scoop in each other's arms, dancing to Sam Cooke's 'You Send Me'.

Act II pursues the 1980s decade of materialism, where the characters become increasingly alienated from the idealistic impulses a few of them felt in their youth, and the scenes become increasingly brittle, almost surreal. A 1980 baby shower for Scoop's wife Lisa shows women lying to one another; no one tells Lisa that Scoop is cheating on her. A 1982 appearance on a television show becomes the place where Scoop, now the editor of *Boomer* magazine, and Peter, the best paediatrician in New York under 40, dominate the conversation, giving Heidi no chance to speak, even when the interviewer asks her questions. In 1984, at a restaurant, Heidi meets her old friend Susan, but she is unhappy to learn this is a business lunch, not a chance to reconnect; Susan wants her to consult on a TV series. Susan says, 'I'm not political anymore. I mean, equal rights is one thing, equal pay is one thing, but blaming everything on being a woman is just passé' (p. 226). Heidi gives a 1986 talk, the emotional centre of the play, on 'Women, Where are we going?' which is a flood of regret, apology and unhappiness. Finally, she says, 'I feel stranded. And I thought the whole point was that we wouldn't be stranded. I thought the point was that we were all in this together' (p. 232). A year later, on Christmas eve, 1987, Heidi drops off donations to Peter's AIDS clinic for children. She plans to leave New York for a teaching job, and has felt 'sad' for some time. Peter tells her 'A sadness like yours seems a luxury' (p. 237), in comparison to the losses he has experienced from AIDS. She decides to stay in New York, for his sake. In the final scene of the play, in 1989, Heidi is in her new, empty apartment; Scoop appears to explain that he is entering politics. Heidi has adopted a baby. She foresees a time when her daughter and Scoop's son will meet, and 'Maybe things will be a little better' (p. 247). After Scoop leaves, she holds Judy and sings 'You Send Me' to her. A final art slide shows Heidi holding Judy beneath a banner of the Georgia O'Keefe retrospective.

Nothing in the play has suggested that Heidi wants a baby; the adoption scene feels grafted on. Heidi is in some ways a faceless as well as a voiceless character. The two men, Scoop and Peter, have the more vibrant roles. Helene Keyssar says that 'For much of the play, Heidi is dominated, dramaturgically, by the wit and strong presence on stage of the two men in her life.'[24] The consciousness raising scene in Act I is problematic in that Fran, the lesbian character, is a figure of fun, and the entire enterprise is trivialized, yet, the scene is also the only women's community in the play. 'Ultimately, the struggle for male homosexuals is valued more than feminism's struggle for gender equality.'[25]

An American Daughter (1997, revised 2003)

Wasserstein's next major play was the popular *The Sisters Rosensweig* (1992), about three middle-aged sisters who come to terms with their

Jewish identity. Some critics complained that *Rosensweig* was too safe and not disturbing enough. It was in reaction to *Rosensweig* that Robert Brustein wrote, 'I had hoped, after *The Heidi Chronicles,* that my very gifted former student was shaking her witticism habit.'[26] Wasserstein wrote that her friends and her own inner critic asked when she was going to show her anger and her 'dark side'.[27]

An American Daughter is, in fact, her darkest, angriest and most overtly political play; it was developed in a workshop in Seattle in 1996, with Daniel Sullivan directing and Meryl Streep in the leading role. The play then opened directly on Broadway in 1997 with a different cast. The production closed after a short run, but although it received mixed reviews, some critics praised it as the one of the finest plays Wasserstein had written. Glenda Frank analysed it as Wasserstein's 'linguistically richest play, employing complicated tropes and allusions'.[28] Wasserstein herself called it her best play.[29] A revised version appeared at the Arena Stage in 1999.

The play is not episodic, but a realist well-made play. It has two acts, with four scenes in each, and takes place in September in 'the present'. The protagonist, Lyssa Dent Hughes, lives in Georgetown, in Washington, DC. She is the daughter of a Republican senator, and a descendant of Ulysses S. Grant. A prominent physician, she supports national health care and women's freedom of choice, in contrast to her father's beliefs. Her husband Walter, a professor of sociology, has written a once well-known book on liberalism, but he resents how Lyssa's success surpasses his. Their two sons are never seen, but their voices are heard calling from upstairs, asking for attention from Lyssa.

An unnamed Democrat president has nominated Lyssa to be Surgeon General. She is qualified for the position, and no problem is expected with her confirmation. She is initially characterized by a television commentator as 'a popular choice with both pro-choice soccer moms and more conservative fast-food dads' (p. 16). However, after her husband says in front of an ambitious journalist that she once threw away a jury notice, and their friend Morrow repeats the allegation on camera, she is attacked by the media in what gets called 'jurygate'. In addition, also on camera, she has called her late mother 'the kind of ordinary Indiana housewife who took pride in her icebox cakes and cheese pimento canapés' (p. 45). Indiana housewives are outraged and women across America contribute to the media frenzy against her. The president fails to defend her. Eventually she chooses to withdraw her nomination.

Lyssa's close friend Judith, an African American Jewish oncologist, mirrors Lyssa's public journey with her own private despair and anger over not being able to conceive a child. Quincy Quince, Walter's former student, a young neo-feminist and opportunistic media star, uses Lyssa to gain notoriety for herself, and also makes a successful play for Walter. Morrow, Lyssa's politically conservative gay friend, resembles Quincy in his self-absorbed focus on his own career. The cynical journalist Timber Tucker seizes his chance to use the jury story. Alan Hughes, Lyssa's senator father, stands by his daughter despite their political differences.

Wasserstein, who referred to herself as a 'New York playwright liberal', told an interviewer that she had been wanting to write a play 'about the liberal establishment' for some time, and she expected she 'would make some people uncomfortable'.[30] *An American Daughter* provides an alternative to what she called 'the political claustrophobia of American theatre' (p. x) in which ideas and people on the left are all presented as good, and those on the right as bad.

The unnamed Democrat president who fails to stand by the Surgeon General he nominated clearly suggests President Bill Clinton's desertion of Zoë Baird and Lani Guinier. Wasserstein explained that her idea for the play arose from the 'Nannygate' incident in Clinton's first term, and also from the way Hillary Rodham Clinton was treated by the media. Baird's nomination for attorney general was derailed when it was learnt that she had failed to pay Social Security taxes for domestic help. She withdrew her nomination after weeks of controversy. During Bill Clinton's first campaign, Hillary Rodham Clinton made the mistake of saying she did not want to 'stay home and bake cookies'. After a national furore, in her next public appearances, she was holding her husband's hand and wearing a headband. Wasserstein wrote:

> In other words, we hadn't come such long way, baby. In my mind, there was a connection between the image of the chastened first-lady-to-be and the attorney general who tried so hard to do it all that she missed a glaring detail. They were both accomplished

professional women who seemed completely prepared for life's obstacles. Whereas their contemporary femininity seemed at first their strength, it became their downfall. (p. ix)

In attempting to turn the story to her advantage, Lyssa is persuaded by a spin expert to dress in conservative feminine attire, including a headband, for her final television interview. Unlike Heidi, who was unable to talk when sandwiched between two men who dominated the television talk show, Lyssa speaks eloquently on her own behalf:

There's nothing quite so satisfying as erasing the professional competency of a woman, is there? Especially when there's such an attractive personal little hook to hang it on. Oh, we all understand it now! She must have hated her mother! That's why she's such a good doctor. She must be a bad cold person. That's why she achieved so much! And anyway, it would be all right if she were a man and cold. . . . (p. 92)

Claudia Barnett makes the valid criticism that Lyssa 'articulates every nuance of her position, making it unnecessary for her audience to ponder the character or the issues'.[31] However, after Lyssa is entrapped by the slick newscaster, and after her relatively calm demeanour through most of the play, there is some thrill in seeing her rage, despite the fact the monologue spells out a little too clearly Wasserstein's central idea.

After future audiences have forgotten the Zoë Baird and Hillary Rodham Clinton controversies, the play's relevance may continue in its withering portrayal of the media and the press. Wasserstein mounts a strong attack on what Walter Shapiro called 'the tart-tongued TV culture of Washington',[32] where sound bites and the self-serving careers of journalists debase public discourse and destroy public servants.

The revised version of the play intensifies this attack by showing several television commentators. The revision also sharpens Lyssa and makes her relationship with her husband more precarious. At the end, instead of going upstairs to comfort her sons (as in the original), she turns off her husband's Beach Boys album, puts on Mozart, and sits down to work.

Third (2005)

Like *An American Daughter,* Wasserstein's final play interrogates liberalism, but it is not an angry piece. Her most sparely written play, *Third* sounds a new note of forgiveness in Wasserstein's oeuvre. *Third* appeared at the outset as a one-act at the Arena Stage, paired with *Welcome to My Rash,* a comedy about a woman's struggle with a mysterious illness from which she eventually recovers. Daniel Sullivan persuaded Wasserstein to expand *Third* for the New York production he directed. The public and many of her friends were unaware that Wasserstein had been suffering from lymphoma for some time. She managed to attend previews and the opening night on 24 October 2005. She died on 30 January 2006. *Third* serves in part as her valediction. It also makes a plea for understanding across political lines in America in an era of escalating mistrust.

Third focuses on 54-year-old professor Laurie Jameson, a pioneering feminist at her elite New England college, and her dispute with a student who calls himself Third (Woodson Bull III). The play takes place over the course of the 2002–03 academic year, as the Iraq war begins. A confrontation over plagiarism is the ostensible topic. Third, an athlete on a wrestling scholarship, turns in a cogent, publishable paper on *King Lear.* Without any evidence, Laurie brings him up on plagiarism charges before the Academic Standards committee.

In the dynamic lecture on *King Lear* which opens the play, Laurie addresses the audience, proclaiming her classroom a 'hegemonic-free zone'. She argues that 'Goneril and Regan were right!' The true tragedy of the play is 'the girlification of Cordelia'.[33] After class, she meets Third. To her, his status as an athlete and his prep school background represent the patriarchy she abhors; she assumes him to be a rich Republican (this turns out to be an incorrect assumption). At home, Laurie screams at the television coverage of the upcoming Iraq war; he can barely greet her daughter Emily. Her father appears; he is losing his mind, but sometimes remembers her as his favourite daughter. She is, in life, the Cordelia to his Lear.

Wasserstein gives no back story or subtext to her characters, but Laurie's monologues tell the audience her thoughts and feelings while 'protecting her' from the other characters, as Jill Dolan points out.[34] During the plagiarism hearing, Laurie's second monologue is a fantasy sequence; the lights change while the other characters freeze. She calls Third 'a walking red state' (p. 80), wishing to hold him accountable in place of the president and vice president. She ends her fantasy as Third finishes successfully defending his paper, both saying 'Nothing will come of nothing'.

Act II begins during spring break as the US invasion of Iraq has begun. Emily meets Third, and learns from him what her mother did. Third's revelation propels her to confront Laurie: 'You decided he plagiarized because you needed that to be true. Just like they decided there were weapons of mass destruction because they needed *that* to be true'(p. 83). Jack, soon before his death, apologizes to Laurie: 'Listen to me. Sometimes, you just need to say, I'm sorry.' In the final scene, she follows her father's advice, making amends to Third.

The plot deals with plagiarism, but the play is never about plagiarism. It is about the hardening of liberal feminist views into bigotry, and the necessity to transcend that hardening. *Third* attacks certainty and self-righteousness, suggesting that intellectual arrogance is what is wrong with America at the beginning of the twenty-first century.

Summary

At the ends of these plays, the main characters are alone. The plays all have moments of camaraderie (often involving songs) but the typical stance of the protagonist is similar to the figures Heidi describes in her second art lecture: 'What strikes me is that both ladies seem slightly removed from the occasions at hand. They appear to watch closely and ease the way for others to join in' (*The Heidi Chronicles,* p. 206). It is this quality of seeming to be on the outside that gives to some of Wasserstein's heroines the appearance of neutrality or blandness in comparison with the more colourful peripheral characters, although this is not true for all the plays.

People in Wasserstein's plays separate themselves from others through their inveterate wit and cleverness. The witty remarks light up the stage, but can prevent characters from going as deeply as they otherwise might. Wasserstein said, 'The real reason for comedy is to hide the pain. It is a way to cope with it. A way of staying "up."' You are there, and you are not there.'[35] In some of her early plays, language is used to keep feelings at bay, and an over-topical reliance on brands and famous personalities becomes a shorthand for establishing character. In her later plays, especially in *An American Daughter*, the humour becomes more integral to character.

Despite a sense of being a perennial outsider, Wasserstein created a place for women in the popular theatre, and she began this project at a time when there were few others. She told an interviewer:

> Feminism gave me the perspective to see that there weren't enough women's voices being heard. It gave me the belief that my own voice was worth hearing. . . . When I started writing, there were so few women characters. Women were underestimated, ignored, or invisible.[36]

She remains the only woman to have had most of her plays produced on Broadway during her lifetime. After her death, critic Frank Rich wrote that 'A woman of her generation didn't have her career in the theater, especially the commercial theater, without fighting for it.'[37] Her comedies and comedy-dramas are plays about women's survival. She had the courage to see that her side had blinders. Her work as a whole charts a history of her generation.

Primary Sources

Works by Wendy Wasserstein

An American Daughter (New York: Harcourt Brace, 1998).
An American Daughter, rev. edn (New York: Dramatists Play Service, 2001).
Bachelor Girls: a Collection of Essays (New York: Knopf, 1990).
Old Money (New York: Samuel French, 2002).
Seven One-Act Plays (New York: Samuel French, 2000).
Shiksa Goddess, or, How I Spent My Forties (New York: Knopf, 2001).

The Elements of Style, a Novel (New York: Knopf, 2006).

The Heidi Chronicles and Other Plays (*Uncommon Women and Others, Isn't It Romantic, The Heidi Chronicles*) (New York: Harcourt Brace, 1990).

The Man in a Case [Adaptation of the Anton Chekhov short story], *Orchards* (New York: Knopf, 1986).

The Sisters Rosensweig (New York: Harcourt Brace, 1993).

Third (New York: Dramatists Play Service, 2006).

Third. American Theatre April 2006, pp. 72–87.

Secondary Sources

Aronson, Amy, 'Yes, I am a feminist', *MS Magazine*, September/October 1997, p. 44.

Barnett, Claudia, 'Review of *An American Daughter*, by Wendy Wasserstein', *Theatre Journal* 49, 4 (December 1997), pp. 520–1.

—, 'An Interview with Wendy Wasserstein'. In Claudia Barnett (ed.), *Wendy Wasserstein: a Casebook* (New York: Garland, 1999), pp. 179–87.

Bigsby, Christopher, *Contemporary American Playwrights* (Cambridge: Cambridge University Press, 1999).

Brustein, Robert, 'Review of *The Sisters Rosensweig*', *New Republic*, 7 December 1992, p. 34.

Carlson, Susan L., 'Comic Textures and Female Communities 1937 and 1977: Clare Boothe and Wendy Wasserstein', *Modern Drama* 27, 4 (1984), 564–73.

Christiansen, Richard, 'Writing Not All Giggles for Wendy Wasserstein', *Chicago Tribune*, 17 October 1985.

Coen, Sarah Blacher, *Making a Scene: The Contemporary Drama of Jewish American Women* (Syracuse: Syracuse University Press, 1997).

Czekay, Angelika, 'Interview with Wendy Wasserstein'. In Joan Herrington (ed.), *The Playwright's Muse* (London: Routledge, 2002), pp. 17–44.

Dolan, Jill, *Presence and Desire: Essays on Gender, Sexuality, and Performance* (Ann Arbor: University of Michigan Press, 1993).

—, 'Feminist Performance Criticism and the Popular: Reviewing Wendy Wasserstein', *Theatre Journal* 60 (2008), 433–57.

Finn, William, 'Sister Act', *Vogue Magazine*, September 1992, pp. 360, 366.

Frank, Glenda, 'Three American Daughters: Wendy Wasserstein Critiques Success'. In: Claudia Barnett (ed.), *Wendy Wasserstein: A Casebook* (New York: Garland, 1999), pp. 161–77.

Franklin, Nancy, 'The Time of Her Life', *New Yorker*, 14 April 1997, pp. 62–71.

Gussow, Mel, 'New "Romantic" by Wendy Wasserstein; Review of *Isn't It Romantic*', *New York Times*, 16 December 1983, p. C3.

Isherwood, Charles, 'Wendy Wasserstein Dies at 55: Her Plays Spoke to a Generation', *New York Times*, 31 January 2006.

Keyssar, Helene, 'When Wendy Isn't Trendy: Wendy Wasserstein's *The Heidi Chronicles* and *An American Daughter*'. In Claudia Barnett (ed.), *Wendy Wasserstein: A Casebook* (New York: Garland, 1999), pp. 133–60.

Lewis, Jan, 'Bodies and Souls: Constructing Jewish Women on the Twentieth Century American Stage', Diss. University of California Santa Barbara, 2001.

Marks, Peter, 'An Outsider Goes Inside the Beltway', *New York Times*, 23 March 1997.

Munk, Erika, "'Tis the Reason . . .; Review of *Isn't it Romantic*'. *Village Voice*, 27 December 1983, pp. 109–10.

Nightingale, Benedict, 'There Really is a World Beyond Diaper Drama; Review of *Isn't It Romantic*', *New York Times*, 1 January 1984, p. II2.

Oliver, Edith, 'Rev. of *Uncommon Women and Others*', *New Yorker*, 26 December 1983, p. 68.

Ouderkirk, Cathleen Stinson, 'Human Connections—A Playwright's View: Wendy Wasserstein Discusses *The Heidi Chronicles*', *Christian Science Monitor*, 10 October 1989, p. 11.

Rich, Frank, 'Everybody's Wendy', *New York Times*, 31 December 2006.

Savran, David, *The Playwright's Voice* (New York: Theatre Communications Group, 1999).

Shapiro, Walter, 'Wendy Wasserstein: Chronicles of Frayed Feminism', *Time*, 27 March 1989.

—, 'In Washington, Life Imitates Art; Review of *An American Daughter*', *USA Today*, 16 April 1997.

Sirkin, Elliott, 'Review of *Isn't It Romantic*', *The Nation*, 18 February 1984, p. 202.

Wasserstein, Wendy, 'Interview with Kathleen Betsko and Rachel Koenig'. In Kathleen Betsko and Rachel Koenig (eds), *Interviews with Contemporary American Playwrights* (New York: Beech Tree Books, 1987), pp. 418–31.

—, 'Interview with Leslie Jacobson'. In Jackson R. Bryer (ed.), *The Playwright's Art: Conversations with Contemporary American Dramatists* (New Brunswick: Rutgers University Press, 1995), pp. 257–76.

Whitfield, Stephen, 'Wendy Wasserstein and the Crisis of (Jewish) Identity'. In Jay Halio and Ben Siegel (eds), *Daughters of Valor: Contemporary Jewish American Writers* (Newark: University of Delaware Press, 1997), pp. 226–46.

Winer, Laurie, 'Wendy Wasserstein: the Art of Theater XIII', *The Paris Review* 142 (1997), 164–8.

Notes

1. Laurie Winer, 'Wendy Wasserstein', pp. 164–8.
2. Ibid.
3. William Finn, 'Sister Act', p. 360.
4. See Wasserstein, *Shiksa Goddess,* pp. 187–235.
5. This phrase is frequently found in descriptions of Wasserstein's work. See Nancy Franklin, 'The Time of her Life,' p. 68, and Charles Isherwood, 'Wendy Wasserstein Dies at 55'.

6. For explanations of the Jewish content of Wasserstein's plays, see Jan Lewis's dissertation, 'Bodies and Souls: Constructing Jewish Women on the Twentieth Century American Stage', as well as Sarah Coen, *Making a Scene*; Glenda Frank, 'Three American Daughters'; Stephen Whitfield, 'Wendy Wasserstein and the Crisis of (Jewish) Identity'.

7. Robert Brustein, 'Review of *The Sisters Rosensweig*', p. 34.

8. Wendy Wasserstein, 'Interview with Leslie Jacobson', p. 258.

9. Wendy Wasserstein, 'Interview with Kathleen Betsko and Rachel Koenig', p. 419.

10. Cathleen Stinson Ouderkirk, 'Human Connections—A Playwright's View, p. 11.

11. Wasserstein, *Uncommon Women and Others*, In: *The Heidi Chronicles and Other Plays*, pp. 4–6. Further references will be taken from this edition.

12. Susan L. Carlson, 'Comic Textures and Female Communities 1937 and 1977', p. 570.

13. Jill Dolan, 'Feminist Performance Criticism and the Popular', p. 444.

14. See Nightingale, Munk, and Sirkin for examples of negative reviews, and Oliver 1983, Gussow 1983, and Kerr for positive ones.

15. Richard Christiansen, 'Writing Not All Giggles.'

16. Ibid.

17. Wendy Wasserstein, 'Interview with Kathleen Betsko and Rachel Koenig', p. 420.

18. Ibid., p. 419.

19. William Finn, 'Sister Act', p. 366.

20. Jill Dolan, *Presence and Desire*, p. 50.

21. Walter Shapiro, 'Wendy Wasserstein: Chronicles of Frayed Feminism'.

22. Angelika Czekay, 'Not Having It All', p. 29.

23. Christopher Bigsby, *Contemporary American Playwrights*, p. 347.

24. Helene Keyssar, 'When Wendy Isn't Trendy', p. 142.

25. Jill Dolan, *Presence and Desire*, p. 52.

26. Robert Brustein, 'Review of *The Sisters Rosensweig*', p. 34.

27. Wendy Wasserstein, *An American Daughter*, p. viii. Further references will be to this edition.

28. Glenda Frank, 'Three American daughters', p. 161.

29. David Savran, *The Playwright's Voice*, p. 299.

30. Peter Marks, 'An Outsider Goes Inside the Beltway'.

31. Claudia Barnett, 'Review of *An American Daughter*', p. 521.

32. Walter Shapiro, 'In Washington, Life Imitates Art'.

33. Wendy Wasserstein, *Third. American Theatre*, p. 72. Further references will be from this edition.

34. Jill Dolan, 'Feminist Performance Criticism and the Popular', p. 452.

35. Wendy Wasserstein, 'Interview with Kathleen Betsko and Rachel Koenig', p. 425.

36. Amy Aronson, 'Yes, I am a feminist', p. 44.

37. Frank Rich, 'Everybody's Wendy'.

24 AUGUST WILSON

Sandra G. Shannon

Gem of the Ocean; Joe Turner's Come and Gone; Ma Rainey's Black Bottom; The Piano Lesson; Seven Guitars; Fences; Two Trains Running; Jitney; King Hedley II; Radio Golf

Introduction

Frederick 'Freddy' August Kittel was born on 27 April 1945, the fourth child and first son of Daisy Wilson, a black domestic worker and daughter of southern sharecroppers, and Frederick A. (Fritz) Kittel, a white German immigrant baker whom his son remembered as a 'wine drinker Muscatel by the gallon' – and couldn't keep a job'.[1] August Wilson, as he would later rename himself during one of the most volatile and restless decades in American history, recast himself in a calculated effort to disown his wayward father's European heritage and to affirm his mother's ties to the south and to her African American racial and cultural identity: 'The only father-son experience Wilson remembers,' according to John Lahr, 'was being taken downtown by Fritz in a blizzard to get a pair of Gene Autry cowboy boots.'[2]

August Wilson was a native of Pittsburgh, Pennsylvania's Hill District, an ethnically mixed, predominately African American neighbourhood, one of the poorest, most beleaguered areas of the city. Memories of his Pittsburgh childhood not only included an emotionally and physically distant father, but also the squalid living conditions he and his siblings faced in the cold-water flat behind Bella's Market on Bedford Avenue. Known to residents as simply The Hill, the 1.4-square-mile cluster of neighbourhoods perched above downtown Pittsburgh was home to jazz greats like Stanley Turrentine and Art Blakey and was once the home of the Negro National League baseball team that fielded Satchel Paige, Josh Gibson and James 'Cool Papa' Bell. Harlem Renaissance poet

Claude McKay called the Hill District 'the crossroads of the world', referring to The Hill's heyday between 1930 and 1950. But political and social change that followed pitched The Hill into a downward spiral. Once vibrant businesses deteriorated into crumbling shells. The Hill underwent monumental changes from nearly two decades of urban renewal and the devastation from the riots, in 1968, ignited by the assassination of Martin Luther King, Jr. A once-vibrant, culturally rich and diverse community was rapidly descending into blight, isolation and dislocation.

Despite these bleak circumstances, Wilson and his family thrived in this notorious section of Pittsburgh under the watchful care of Daisy Wilson, who saw to it that her children were well fed, clothed and schooled. As her first-born son after a succession of older sisters, Freddie was the favourite – and, for a time, the only son – in the Kittel household. Due, in large part, to the grounding he received from Daisy Wilson while under the watchful care of elderly men from his neighbourhood, August was able to navigate his way through the troubling circumstances of his boyhood in Pittsburgh and to set himself on a trajectory that would open up new opportunities for the fledgling poet.

Wilson's big break on the long road to becoming a 'serious' playwright came in the form of an invitation from Claude Purdy, a former Pittsburgh resident, theatre director and friend, to visit the Twin Cities. After a decade of writing poetry and fostering art and education in Pittsburgh, Wilson accepted Purdy's call to work with him at an African American theatre company in St Paul, Minnesota. In an interesting twist of fate, playwriting became Wilson's day job as well, when the Science Museum of Minnesota hired him to write short plays for its anthropology section. At 33, Wilson had pulled up his Pittsburgh roots.

> I left Pittsburgh but Pittsburgh never left me. It was being in St. Paul, being away from the environment I was most familiar with, that I began hearing the voices.[3]

Wilson's evolution into a first-rate playwright continued when – upon the advice of playwright, poet, social activist and professor Robert Lee 'Rob' Penny – he submitted a play script to be workshopped at the Eugene O'Neill Theatre Center. *Jitney* became the first attempt to become a 'serious' playwright. 'I sat down to write it and the characters just talked to me. In fact, they were talking so fast that I couldn't get it all down'.[4] Set among jitney drivers and numbers runners in an unlicensed taxi station on the Hill, *Jitney* evoked the rhythms of the life he knew in Pittsburgh. The play was not an immediate success, though he did get it staged at the Allegheny Repertory Theater in Pittsburgh.

At a workshop, Wilson met Lloyd Richards, who, 25 years earlier, had directed Lorraine Hansberry's ground-breaking African-American drama, *A Raisin in the Sun,* on Broadway. The veteran director took the playwright under his wing, teaching him dramaturgy and stagecraft and introducing him to a powerful network of theatre practitioners and financiers. Their theatrical partnership would bring Wilson's first six published plays to regional and Broadway stages.

The Plays

In a remarkable run over the next two decades, Wilson had 10 plays produced – nine of which made their way to Broadway, winning the author a Tony, two Pulitzer Prizes and the National Humanities Medal from President Bill Clinton. His plays, alternately called the Century Cycle or the Pittsburgh Cycle, comprise

- 1904 – *Gem of the Ocean,* (first produced in 2003)
- 1911 – *Joe Turner's Come and Gone* (1988)
- 1927 – *Ma Rainey's Black Bottom* (1984)
- 1936 – *The Piano Lesson* (1990, winner Pulitzer Prize)
- 1948 – *Seven Guitars* (1995)
- 1957 – *Fences* (1987, winner Pulitzer Prize)
- 1969 – *Two Trains Running* (1991)
- 1977 – *Jitney* (first produced in 1982—revised and re-staged in 1996)
- 1985 – *King Hedley II* (1999)
- 1997 – *Radio Golf* (2005)

While each play has its own autonomous story line, collectively, the 10 plays boast a much more sweeping narrative – one that chronicles the

African American presence from post-Civil War America to the Clinton years. The epic storyline traces the struggles of 'sons and daughters of newly freed African slaves'[5] through several watershed moments in history to the threshold of the twenty-first century, complete with various measures of both triumph and tragedy.

With the exception of *Ma Rainey's Black Bottom,* which is set in a Chicago recording studio, all of the 10 plays in August Wilson's decade-by-decade twentieth-century cycle take place in Pittsburgh's Hill District. And while it is, for the most part, a continuing saga of a community, culture and people, the characters, families and settings and the play's ultimate focus change from one play to the next. Though each is set in a significant watershed moment in history, none of the plays owes allegiance to any concomitant historical events. History, in fact, serves as backdrop to Wilson's plays, usurped only by the stories of the triumphs and tragedies of his characters. As such, the cycle plays depict changes in their attitudes and circumstances, their sometimes questionable courses of action, threats to their cultural memory and the struggle to survive with dignity. According to Wilson, 'I was trying to focus on what I felt were the most important issues confronting black Americans for [each] decade', Wilson said, 'so ultimately they could stand as a record of black experience over the past hundred years presented in the form of dramatic literature'.[6]

The plays set earliest – *Gem of the Ocean* (1904) and *Joe Turner's Come and Gone* (1911) – are inhabited by a generation that has moved north but that vividly remembers and struggles with the ghosts of slavery and the arguably worse form of trauma that followed during post-Reconstruction South. *Ma Rainey,* the cycle's focus upon the 1920s, explores the deep conflicts brought on by modernity and commercial exploitation and commodification of music produced by African American culture bearers. As Wilson's fictional version of the real-life pioneering blues singer Gertrude 'Ma' Rainey, says:

> They don't care nothing about me. All they want is my voice . . . As soon as they get my voice down on them recording machines, then it's just like if I'd be some whore and they roll over and put their pants on . . . If you colored and can make

them some money, then you all right with them. Otherwise, you just a dog in the alley.[7]

In *The Piano Lesson,* the 1930s play, Wilson uses a 135-year-old family heirloom to pose a complex question: 'Can one acquire a sense of self-worth by denying one's past?'[8] Siblings Berniece and Boy Willie battle over whether to keep the piano that stands as the only monument to their family's long history as slaves and craftsmen, or to sell it so they can buy back land that was stolen from their forebears. As Alan Nadel points out in *May All Your Fences Have Gates,* 'Berniece, we could say, wants to hide from history and Boy Willie wants to get rid of it'.[9] Legacy and opportunity, past and future come into conflict in the 1930s.

At the centre of Wilson's play for the 1950s is the towering, tragic figure of Troy Maxson, a roaring lion of a black man and one of American theatre's most indelible characters since Willy Loman and Stanley Kowalski. *Fences* revolves around a once-great Negro League ballplayer, Troy, who grapples with the mid-century changing racial landscape and who is caught between his furious resentments of the opportunities denied him and the prospects tentatively opening for his son, Corey, in the decade of Jackie Robinson and Brown versus the Board of Education. As in other Wilson plays, such as *The Piano Lesson* and *Radio Golf,* a generational family battle reveals the psychological toll that racism has exacted on characters who still struggle to partake of some portion of the American Dream. By design, *Two Trains Running's* depiction of the 1960s alludes only obliquely to the tumultuous events of that turbulent decade, but, like *Fences,* it explores the dissolution of black culture and community in the wake of integration, as well as the economic insufficiencies of civil rights. Although the play is set in 1969, it is basically a smouldering reaction to a series of unforgettable cataclysmic events that occurred in 1968. In a *New York Times* interview, August Wilson provides some clues as to the secondary position that history occupies in his dramatic agenda:

> Since I was not a historian but a writer of fiction, I saw as my task the invention of characters. These personal histories would not only represent the culture but illuminate the historical

context both of the period in which the play is set and the continuum of black life in America that stretches back to the early 17th century.[10]

The characters in *Jitney*, in the 1970s, bear witness to the demise of the soul and spirit of the black community under the wrecking-ball of urban renewal, while *Radio Golf*, set in the 1990s, explores the consequences to African American culture and community when its 'talented tenth' takes flight to the middle and professional classes, abandons their legacy only to regard it as a marketable commodity.

August Wilson's 10 play narratives provide ample evidence of his skill at weaving or stitching together an ambitious albeit understated storyline that runs intermittently throughout the cycle. This unity coalesces around characters from one play who resurface later in others, around a familiar Pittsburgh neighbourhood that becomes the epicentre of conflict for more than one of the Cycle Plays, around the same wise community healer who shows up to dole out advice to clients from several different plays, or around the looming presence of the wrecking ball on behalf of urban renewal. In each scenario, Wilson manages to achieve a certain organic unity within his loosely connected network of dramatic instalments.

The community healer and long-time Pittsburgh resident Aunt Ester Tyler, for example, makes her presence known in four of Wilson's Cycle plays: *Gem of the Ocean*, *Two Trains Running*, *King Hedley II* and *Radio Golf*. From the time her name is first uttered onstage in *Two Trains Running* to her cataclysmic offstage death in *King Hedley II* and to her challenged legacy in *Radio Golf*, Aunt Ester's role as the spiritual centre of August Wilson's dramatic universe takes on increasing significance. *Gem of the Ocean*'s 'reintroduction' of Aunt Ester has much to do with Wilson's manipulation of time in that he disrupts the order in which he reveals her story. His use of Aunt Ester throughout the cycle, moreover, subordinates the importance and boundaries of time in order to render her timeless, ageless and possibly immortal. In the preface to *King Hedley II*, Wilson explains that 'Aunt Ester has emerged for me as the most significant persona of the cycle. The characters, after all, are her children'.[11]

Another subtle linking of storylines in individual plays within the Cycle can be observed in the relationship between *Seven Guitars* (set in 1948) and *King Hedley II* (set in 1985). An unborn male child (later to be named King Hedley II) is first introduced in *Seven Guitars* by his mother Ruby. In *King Hedley II* this one-time infant re-emerges as a fully grown man seething with anger. He is incensed with his biological mother Ruby for handing him over to another woman to raise. He is furious with Purnell for slashing his face in a longstanding, arguably petty, dispute. He is enraged at the man whom he later discovers killed his biological father, and he is seething at the white power system for ignoring his right to be treated fairly and humanely. This anger erupts and ultimately leads to his accidental shooting death at the hands of Ruby. By all accounts, then, the seed that Ruby transports within her on her long trek from Birmingham, Alabama to Pittsburgh, Pennsylvania fails to take root in this northern landscape. As August Wilson often noted,

> We were land-based agrarian people from Africa. We were uprooted from Africa, and we spent 200 years developing our culture as black Americans. And then we left the South. We uprooted ourselves and attempted to transplant this culture to the pavements of the industrialized North. And it was a transplant that did not take.[12]

The plight of the tragic figure, King Hedley II as well as that of countless other justifiably angry African American men is highlighted in the generational connections revealed between the two sequel plays, *Seven Guitars* and *King Hedley II*. One may infer from King's belligerence that abandoned black male babies grow up to be angry, vengeful black men incapable of love and destined only for self-destruction. These texts provide evidence to support direct correlations that emerge between the dysfunctional circumstances of King's upbringing, his fits of anger, his ultimate embrace of street justice and his decision to avenge by murder.

Wilson establishes more common ground among the separate stories in his Pittsburgh Cycle in the form of the character Canewell, who emerges first in *Seven Guitars* as a fast-talking harmonica player and who later morphs into the scripture-spouting, newspaper-hoarding Stool Pigeon in *King Hedley II*. Clues as to Canewell's transition and metamorphosis are embedded in the dialogue of *Seven Guitars*, but take on new meaning some 40 years later when, at first, he appears to have randomly lapsed into a state of madness.

For the Hill District native and visionary playwright, the imposing spectre of demolition equipment sent to flatten once thriving establishments along Wylie Avenue in the name of urban renewal was nothing short of traumatic – so much so that the image of the wrecking ball found its way into his Cycle Plays as a symbol of wide-scale cultural devastation and erasure for all African Americans. Deeply moved by certain annihilation and collateral damage in store for the targeted communities, Wilson wrote three plays that display the resilience and resistance of a community under assault disguised as gentrification. In *Two Trains Running* (set in 1969), *Jitney* (set in 1971) and *Radio Golf* (set in 1997), Wilson demonstrates the power of community to rally against that which threatens its cohesiveness. By doing so, he captures the essence of resistance, resilience and nobility that he later discovered in his fellow Hill District residents.

Ironically, it is the ominous threat of a wrecking ball waiting in the wings to level Memphis Lee's business in *Two Trains Running* that invites us to understand the power of this African American Hill District community and the communal bonds that have been formed and nurtured within its confines. In an archetypal David versus Goliath type showdown, Memphis vows to fight Pittsburgh's powerful City Hall. Memphis Lee has the will to fight, the support of the community and the sage advice of community leader Aunt Ester: 'They give white folks a good price', he tells one of his regular customers.

> Most time that be who they buying it from. Well, they gonna give me just like they give them. I bought it eight years ago for fifty-five hundred dollars and I ain't taking a penny less than twenty-five thousand (10).

Memphis not only comes out the victor in the showdown, but is rewarded many times over in City Hall's payment for his establishment.

The conflict in *Jitney* also hinges upon an imminent wrecking ball. A still-functioning cab station in the heart of Pittsburgh's Hill District is its target. Not only does this communal space serve as the station owner's well-run and successful business establishment, but it also doubles as a home away from home and – against the station owner's rules – a numbers running station for several jitney drivers who use this space to make an extra hustle. Although several subplots compete for attention in this play, arguably the most dominant one involves the uncertain course these lives will take once Becker's station becomes rubble. Wilson leaves us to only imagine the fate that awaits these men whom he credits for 'making something out of nothing'.

It is not until all options are exhausted, that Jim Becker calls the community of men in his station to action:

> I say we stay here. We already here. The people know we here. We been here for eighteen years . . . and I don't see no reason to move. City or no city. I look around and all I see is boarded up buildings. Some of them been boarded up for more than ten years. If they want to build some houses that's when they can tear it down. When they ready to build the houses. They board this place up the first of the month and let it sit boarded up for the next fifteen . . . twenty years.

Becker is not only angry about the prospect of losing his own business, but he is also disgusted about a pattern of neglect that he has witnessed in the wake of the city's previous demolition crusades. Years after the wrecking ball did its work, homes and businesses and entire neighbourhoods remain in ruins.

Radio Golf completes the trilogy of Pittsburgh Cycle plays that highlight the strength of community under assault from the harbingers of urban development. Set in 1997, *Radio Golf* raises complex questions of how African Americans can strive for financial and political success at the end of the twentieth century without leaving behind their past and community. Its central conflict revolves around plans to demolish Old Joe's house. Tearing it down would signal the demise of the blighted Hill District of Pittsburgh.

Radio Golf draws attention to the alarming prevalence of cultural erasure that has the Hill District community within its grips. It is a new day, and the sons and daughters of W. E. B. Du Bois's Talented Tenth now seem to have been cured of the anxieties of double consciousness. As such, the play reveals a correlation between increased access to the American Dream on the part of the black middle class and a retreat from morals and ethical values that are a part of their cultural history. In the Hill District of 1997, where once was community cohesiveness is now blind, selfish ambition. August Wilson lays the blame for this humanitarian lapse squarely at the feet of the black middle class.

August Wilson was never one to shy away from an interviewer's question about his playwriting process. With remarkable consistency and over the course of years of countless backstage interviews and hotel restaurant and barroom conversations, he meticulously outlined the details of his mission to write 10 plays chronicling the African-American experience during the twentieth century. From these interviews, one can glean first-hand information on his early literary and artistic influences, the idiosyncrasies of his writing process, his abiding emphasis upon Africa and the ancestors, his embrace of West African Sankofa principles and his commitment to chronicling themes of separation, migration and reunions. One such testament to his willingness to talk about his craft can be found in the collection *Conversations with August Wilson* – edited by Jackson R. Bryer and Mary Hartig – a compilation of interviews that 'cover the full range of Wilson's career'.[13]

Once Wilson accepted the mantle of a 'serious playwright' in the mid-1980s, he, just as seriously, began to define the principles that would guide his work. To simplify matters, he selected a series of alliterative terms to convey the influences that are most prevalent in his playwriting: The Blues, Romare Bearden, Amiri Baraka and Jorge Luis Borges. 'My four B's', as he referred to them, were his essential artistic, political and spiritual influences.

As early as 1987, August Wilson had already conceptualized a blues-driven aesthetic that would inform each play. In an interview with David Savran that same year, he revealed his rationale:

> Blacks do not have a history of writing–things in Africa were passed on orally. In that tradition you orally pass on your entire philosophy, your ideas and attitudes about life. Most of them were passed along in blues. You have to make the philosophy interesting musically and lyrically, so that someone will want to repeat it, to teach it to someone else as soon as they've heard it. If you don't make it interesting, the information dies. I began to view blues as the African American's response to the world before he started writing down this stuff.[14]

August Wilson traces the source of his artistic vision to 1965 – the year he was introduced to the blues. Perhaps it was providence that led him to purchase a three-dollar record player and to discover among some old seventy-eights he had bought Bessie Smith's 'Nobody Can Bake a Sweet Jelly Roll Like Mine'. As he listened to the record, he was mesmerized by the emotions that Smith's sassy delivery stirred in him. The effect on the 20-year-old Wilson was profound: He had discovered the universal language of the blues. He had tapped into a non-verbal means of understanding the gamut of emotions locked up inside him.

This can be seen, implicitly and explicitly, in plays such as *Ma Rainey Black*, *Seven Guitars*, and *Fences*. In *Ma Rainey's Black Bottom*, its influence is on multiple levels. The play is not just about the blues recording industry. If regarded as a blues composition presented as a play, *Ma Rainey's Black Bottom* becomes infinitely more understandable. Like a blues song or jazz rendition, the play is a slow-building, repetitive, unpredictable ride on an emotional roller coaster. Ma does not appear until well into Act I, yet the goings-on during the pre-rehearsal session are analogous to a lengthy musical prelude leading up to the vocal accompaniment. Levee's recurring complaints against Ma and the other band members function as the refrain to this blues play;

and the competing stories of Ma and her band echo the interwoven improvisations of blues and jazz performers. Corresponding to the emotion-charged lyrics of the blues song are the characters' tortured testimonies of survival. Both Ma and Levee, though constantly at odds with each other at some point in the play, turn inwards to reveal the source of their private pain.

Collagist and fellow Pittsburgh native Romare Bearden, who participated in the migration as a young boy, influenced August Wilson's thinking as an artist on multiple levels. At 32, Wilson was introduced to the work of the world-famous artist. He saw Bearden's work as expressing visually what blues lyrics stirred inside of him. In a foreword to a study on Bearden, Wilson writes,

> What for me had been so difficult, Bearden made seem so simple, so easy. What I saw was black life presented on its own terms, on a grand and epic scale, with all its richness and fullness, in a language that was vibrant and which, made attendant to everyday life, ennobled it, affirmed its value, and exalted its presence. It was the art of a large and generous spirit that defined not only the character of black American life, but also its conscience.[15]

For Wilson, Bearden and the blues are provocative instances of communicating the otherwise incommunicable triumphs and tragedies of African American life: 'In Bearden I found my artistic mentor and sought, and still aspire to make my plays the equal of his canvas'.[16] In his collages, Bearden took disparate objects from the everyday world – photos, print, fabric and wood – to create compositional portraits of black life and experience. His collages, while carefully and intricately designed, appear improvisational, akin to jazz. Wilson reimagined Bearden's technique for the stage as well as finding direct inspiration in the work. Bearden's *Mill Hand's Lunch Bucket* (1978) planted the seed for *Joe Turner's Come and Gone,* just as Wilson's *The Piano Lesson* grew out of Bearden's collage of the same name. Bearden's imagery infuses the sets, lighting and blocking of Wilson's plays.

The inspiration that Wilson derived from black playwright, Amiri Baraka, resulted from his fascination with his politically charged poetry and his collection of one-act revolutionary plays. Baraka awakened in Wilson a sense of social awareness and provided another means of affirming his own racial identity. Baraka used his writings to accuse and attack, to boldly dramatize black power and identity in the face of being defined by white society. 'Amiri Baraka has said that when you look in the mirror, you should see your God', Wilson told Bill Moyers. 'If you don't, you have somebody else's God'.[17]

Finally, the complexly structured stories of Argentine fiction writer, Jorge Luis Borges, also contributed to Wilson's approach to drama. In particular, he was intrigued by Borges's non-linear style of starting his narrative at the end and then going back to trace the path that brought the character to that juncture. Though Wilson employs this technique sparingly in his work, Borges opened his eyes to the structural possibilities of storytelling.

Summary

The amount of serious critical attention given to August Wilson as a playwright veered sharply upwards following the late 1980s Broadway production of *Ma Rainey's Black Bottom*. Seemingly, in one stroke, this play marked Wilson's transition from novice to celebrity and allayed any of his lingering doubts that he was a 'serious playwright'. What followed was Wilson's meteoric rise accompanied by movie deals, two Pulitzer Prize awards and recognition for his playwriting skills on both national and global levels. Beginning in the mid-1990s, a network of scholars based at various institutions throughout the United States turned their attention to Wilson's growing list of critically sophisticated plays and, collectively, launched what is now more formally known as 'Wilson Studies'. Harry Elam, Marilyn Elkins, Joan Herrington, Alan Nadel, Sandra Richards and Sandra Shannon, for example, created a body of solid scholarship in the form of a succession of essays, books and collections on Wilson's plays that appear in leading journals and with prestigious publishing houses. In doing so, they did much to cultivate and introduce his works to an academic audience.

Over the span of more than two decades, August Wilson essentially clinched the title of America's premier playwright. Even before his sudden death in October 2005, his resounding achievements in the realm of theatre had forged him a place in the canon of American letters. Sentiment in some circles saw him poised to receive the Nobel Prize for Literature following the completion of his 10 now-classic plays depicting twentieth-century African American life. This recognition would have been the logical next step after the Pulitzer Prize Committee twice voted to award Wilson its top honour for the startling realism and classic resonance captured in *Fences* in 1987 and in *The Piano Lesson* in 1990. Further attesting to the calibre of his work is an array of other awards ranging from the New York Drama Critics' Circle and Drama Desk Awards to the coveted Tony Award.

As if to further underscore the importance of Wilson's work, several public gestures solidify his legacy. On October 16, 2005, 14 days after August Wilson's death, a Broadway theatre was renamed in his honour. In 2007 the Theatre Communications Group packaged and published all 10 of his cycle plays in an attractively bound package titled *The August Wilson Century Cycle*. September 2009 marked the opening of Pittsburgh, Pennsylvania's August Wilson Center, which honours the playwright's life and legacy while at the same time functioning as

> a hub for people celebrating and experiencing the on-going contributions of African Americans—in music, theater, dance, science, athletics, business and many other aspects of American life.

Other noticeable indicators of Wilson's legacy and the staying power of his plays, particularly the frequency with which they are staged throughout the world and the steady increase in scholarship on his work attest to the enduring nature of Wilson's plays before a new generation of theatre goers.

Primary Sources

Works by August Wilson

August Wilson Century Cycle (New York: Theatre Communications Group, 2007).
Fences (New York: New American Library, 1987).
Gem of the Ocean (New York: Theatre Communications Group, 2006).
Jitney (New York: Overlook Press, 2000).
Joe Turner's Come and Gone (New York: New American Library, 1988).
King Hedley II (New York: Theatre Communications Group, 2005).
Ma Rainey's Black Bottom (New York: New American Library, 1985).
The Piano Lesson (New York: Plume, 1990).
Radio Golf (New York: Theatre Communications Group, 2008).
Seven Guitars (New York: Dutton, 1996).
Two Trains Running (New York: New American Library 1993).

Secondary Sources

Bloom, Harold (ed.), *August Wilson* (Broomhall, PA: Chelsea House, 2002).

Bogumil, Mary L., *Understanding August Wilson* (Columbia: University of South Carolina Press, 1999).

Booker, Margaret, *Lillian Hellman and August Wilson: Dramatizing a New American Identity* (New York: Peter Lang, 2003).

Bryer, Jackson R. and Mary C. Hartig (eds), *Conversations with August Wilson* (Jackson: University of Mississippi Press, 2006).

Clark, Keith, *Black Manhood in James Baldwin, Ernest J. Gaines, and August Wilson* (Urbana: University of Illinois Press, 2002).

Crawford, Eileen, 'The Bb Burden: The Invisibility of *Ma Rainey's Black Bottom*'. In Marilyn Elkins, *August Wilson: A Casebook* (New York: Garland, 1994), pp. 31–48.

Glasco, Laurence A. and Christopher Rawson, *August Wilson, Pittsburgh Places in His Life and Plays* (Pittsburgh: Pittsburgh History & Landmarks Foundation, 2011).

Lahr, John, 'Been Here and Gone: How August Wilson Brought a Century of Black American Culture to the Stage', *New Yorker*, 16 April 2001, pp. 50–65.

Moyers, Bill, 'August Wilson: Playwright'. In Jackson R. Bryer and Mary C. Hartig (eds), *Conversations with August Wilson* (Jackson: University of Mississippi Press, 2006), pp. 61–80.

Nadel, Alan, 'Boundaries, Logistics, and Identity: The Property of Metaphor in *Fences* and *Joe Turner's Come and Gone*'. In Alan Nadel (ed.), *May All Your Fences Have Gates: Essays on the Drama of August Wilson* (Iowa City: University of Iowa Press, 1994), pp. 86–104.

Pereira, Kim, *August Wilson and the African American Odyssey* (Urbana: University of Illinois Press, 1995).

Rothstein, Mervyn, 'Round five for the Theatrical Heavyweight', *New York Times*, 15 April 1990, p. 1+.

Savran, David, 'August Wilson'. In Jackson R. Bryer and Mary C. Hartig (eds), *Conversations with August Wilson* (Jackson: University of Mississippi Press, 2006), pp. 19–37.

Shafer, Yvonne, *August Wilson: A Research and Production Sourcebook* (Westport, Conn: Greenwood Press, 1998).

Shannon, Sandra G., *The Dramatic Vision of August Wilson* (Washington, D.C.: Howard University Press, 1995).

—, *August Wilson's Fences: A Reference Guide* (Westport, CT: Greenwood Press, 2003).

Wilson, August, 'Characters behind History Teach Wilson about Plays', *New York Times*, 12 April 1992, p. H5.

—, 'Foreword'. In Myron Schwartzman (ed.), *Romare Bearden: His Life and Art* (New York: Abrams, 1990), p. 8.

Wolfe, Peter, *August Wilson* (New York: Twayne, 1999).

Notes

1. John Lahr, 'Been here and gone', p. 35.
2. Ibid., p. 36.
3. Laurence A. Glasco and Christopher Rawson, *August Wilson*, pp. 14, 23.
4. Ibid., p. 14.
5. August Wilson, *Joe Turner's Come And Gone*.
6. Ibid.
7. August Wilson, *Ma Rainey's Black Bottom*, p. 63.
8. David Savran, 'August Wilson', p. 25.
9. Alan Nadel, *May All Your Fences Have Gates*, p. 3.
10. August Wilson, 'Characters behind History Teach Wilson about Plays', p. H5.
11. August Wilson, *King Hedley II*, p. x.
12. Mervyn Rothstein, 'Round five for the Theatrical Heavyweight', p. 1+.
13. Jackson R. Bryer and Mary Hartig (eds), *Conversations with August Wilson*, p. viii.
14. David Savran, 'August Wilson', p. 26.
15. August Wilson, 'Foreword', p. 8.
16. Ibid.
17. Bill Moyers, 'August Wilson: Playwright', p. 77.

25 WILLIAM S. YELLOW ROBE, JR.

Birgit Däwes

Sneaky; The Independence of Eddie Rose; The Star Quilter; Better-n-Indins; Grandchildren of the Buffalo Soldiers

Introduction

Indigenous theatre is North America's oldest form of cultural expression. It is, in Ojibway playwright Drew Hayden Taylor's words, 'as old as this country, as old as the people who have been here for thousands of years, as old as the stories that are still told today. It is merely the presentation that has changed'.[1] This change of presentation occurred mainly in the 1960s and 1970s, when Native American and First Nations authors increasingly merged aboriginal performance traditions with Western stages and dramaturgies in order to present their work. With productions such as Kiowa playwright Hanay Geiogamah's *Body Indian* (1972) in the United States and Ojibway writer George Kenny's *October Stranger* (1977) in Canada, and with the formation of theatre companies such as the American Indian Theater Ensemble (1972) and Spiderwoman Theater (1975) in New York, Red Earth Performing Arts in Seattle (1974), the Native Theater School (1975) and Native Earth Performing Arts (1982) in Toronto and De-Ba-Jeh-Mu-Jig Theater Company on Manitoulin Island, Ontario (1984), a movement was initiated that would soon gain remarkable popularity and academic attention. Plays by Tomson Highway (e.g., *The Rez Sisters* [1986], *Rose* [1999] or *Ernestine Shuswap Gets Her Trout* [2005]), Drew Hayden Taylor (e.g., *Someday* [1995], *alterNatives* [1999], or *The Berlin Blues* [2007]), Marie Clements (e.g., *The Unnatural and Accidental Women* [1999] or *Burning Vision* [2003]), Diane Glancy (e.g., *Weebjob* [1987], *The Woman Who Was a Red Deer Dressed for the Deer Dance* [2005], or *Salvage* [2008]), or Larissa FastHorse (e.g., *Average Family* [2007] or

Hunka [2012]) are by now internationally known, and in the decade between 1999 and 2009, the publication of eight major anthologies substantially contributed to the increasing visibility of indigenous North American drama.[2]

While the production of plays was initially less burdened with difficulties for First Nations artists in Canada, with more opportunities for funding, better access to educational and cultural institutions and a stronger public presence,[3] Native American playwrights in the United States have also recently benefited from improving conditions, with more organizational support and an increasing number of venues and commissions. Festivals celebrating indigenous plays (such as Native Voices at the Autry, the Tulsa Indian Art Festival, or The Native Theater Festival at New York's Public Theater) as well as theoretical and practical infrastructures at universities and museums (e.g. the Native American Women Playwrights Archive in Miami, Ohio, the Native American Playwright website at Haskell Indian Nations University, Project HOOP at the University of California at Los Angeles or the Smithsonian National Museum of the American Indian) anchor Native drama and performance within the American cultural landscape of the twenty-first century.

Next to Hanay Geiogamah and Spiderwoman Theater, one of the pioneers of Native American drama in the United States is William S. Yellow Robe, Jr., a playwright, poet, actor, director and teacher of Assiniboine/Nakota and African American descent. Yellow Robe names his indigenous heritage as his major cultural influence: 'I am 3/8 African American and 5/8 Assiniboine. A lot of people think I am a full-blood Native, and I was raised to be a full-blood'.[4] Born in 1960 on the Fort Peck Indian Reservation in north-eastern Montana, where he lived until he was 18 years old, Yellow Robe studied history, journalism and performance at the University of Montana. In the 1990s, he taught playwriting at the Institute of American Indian Arts in Santa Fe, New Mexico, one of the most influential institutions in shaping what Hanay Geiogamah has termed the 'New Native American Drama' – the hybrid mix of different cultural influences and performative traditions. In 1997, he also founded (and served as artistic director of) the Albuquerque-based Wakiknabe Intertribal Theater Company. Like Drew Hayden

Taylor, William S. Yellow Robe considers Native American storytelling traditions a rich resource for his work:

> Well, playwriting does not exist within the Assiniboine language. A lot of theatrical concepts such as "play", "acting", and "directing" do not exist in indigenous languages. So my process has always been the process of trying to bridge or finding elements that are already in existence within the Native culture and then trying to form a bridge with the Euro-American style of theater; one such element is story telling. I have found elements of traditional story telling that I can incorporate into my writing.[5]

He has written 48 plays to date,[6] 10 of which were published in the two major collections of his work, *Where the Pavement Ends* (2000) and *Grandchildren of the Buffalo Soldiers* (2009). His unpublished plays include, among many others, 'Wink-Dah' (1984), 'The Breaking of Another Circle' (1985), 'The People' (1989), 'A Coyote's Tale' (1989), 'A Broken Bottle, a Broken Family' (1999), 'The New Forest Order' (2001) and 'Native American Paranormal Society' (2007). Yellow Robe has received a number of prestigious awards, including a National Endowment for the Arts Playwriting Fellowship (1991), a Princess Grace Foundation Theater Award (1990), the Native Writers Circle of the Americas' First Book Award for Drama (1992), as well as the New England Theatre Foundation's Special Award for Excellence (2004), and he was named a Native Achiever by the Smithsonian National Museum of the American Indian in 2010.

The Plays

Sneaky (1987)

Sneaky was written in 1982 as Yellow Robe's first more widely received play. It premiered at the New World Theatre (University of Massachusetts, Amherst) in October 1987 and received further readings and productions at the Public Theater, New York (1995), the Taos Arts

Association in Taos, New Mexico (1999) and in Providence, Rhode Island (2003). Like the later *Grandchildren of the Buffalo Soldiers,* it is a play centred on a conflict between three Assiniboine brothers: Frank, Eldon and Kermit Rose. The first of three scenes opens with a fire, which the brothers have started in order to burn the private belongings of their recently deceased mother. As they begin to plan the funeral, Frank advocates the idea of burying their mother traditionally, without the assistance of the local mortician. This tradition requires the family 'to bury their own' (p. 136) by placing the body in a tree: 'We can find an old tree and place wood around it and set them on fire' (p. 136). In order to convince his sceptical brothers, he asserts that it was their mother's will 'to be buried near the place she grew up at. She wanted to be buried in the traditional way' (p. 137). When Eldon reminds him of the legal restrictions, and the opposition they would face from the priest and the mortician, their discussion becomes a site of negotiation for larger conflicts. The differences between the brothers take centre stage: whereas Eldon lives in a functional family, with a regular income and an affinity towards the Christian faith, Kermit, the youngest of the three, severely suffers from alcoholism. He is drunk for most of the play, but he also most strongly identifies with his indigenous heritage: he speaks Assiniboine (pp. 131, 162, 165), knows how to perform a traditional grass dance (p. 141) and angrily charges Eldon with being 'an apple, red on the outside' but 'white all over' (p. 152) because of his successful business. Frank, the eldest, serves as a mediator between the two: he too used to join the ritual drinking with his father and brother, but he has accepted the responsibility for his own family now. He is also the one who most distinctly remembers their grandparents' cultural knowledge. Thus, when he suggests they secretly remove their mother's body from the funeral home to bury it 'in the Indin way [sic]' (p. 161), his younger brothers follow him.

Through the adventure of 'steal[ing] Momma' from the morgue (p. 139), the brothers are forced to confront their differences and come together in their shared grief over losing their mother. Even though it seems, at first, as if the symbolism of the burial pits indigenous traditions against non-Native commodity culture – with an unprivileged Assiniboine family offering resistance to a profit-oriented white mortician – it turns out that the conflict is much more complex. In the morbidly funny scene of the dead body's abduction, with drunk Kermit having to hide 'in a garbage bin' (p. 145) and mistaking the corpse for a potential lover, the brothers have to face their animosities: While Kermit mocks Eldon as an arrogant 'Mr. Chamber of Commerce' (p. 153), his brother justifies himself by an understandable desire for health and stability: 'Just because I didn't drink with you guys didn't mean I was too good for you guys. It just meant I was sober' (p. 154). Even though the play identifies the living conditions on the reservation as long-term consequences of colonization, perpetuated into a vicious cycle of social injustice, poverty, alcoholism and violence, the line of conflict cannot be clearly drawn between Natives and non-Natives. This is further emphasized by Jack Kence, the mortician, who finds out about the stolen body but allows the brothers to proceed with their plan, in spite of 'laws' and 'health codes' (p. 161).

In the end, all characters realize that death and loss are universal human experiences: 'They all have one thing in common', as Jack Kence cynically notes about the dead, 'after a certain amount of time, they rot and they're forgotten' (p. 162). In the end, the three brothers prepare the traditional funeral by a hybrid ceremony of burning sweet grass and reciting an adapted version of the Lord's Prayer ('Give us our . . . daily fry bread' [p. 167]). The play concludes shortly before the lighting of another fire – resuming the symbolism of the first scene in a cyclical structural gesture – as the brothers 'hold arms, and sing' (p. 169). Even though the temporary harmony remains fragile, it also encloses the seed for change, joining the brothers in the spirit of community.

The Independence of Eddie Rose (1986)

Even more openly than *Sneaky, The Independence of Eddie Rose* presents life on the reservation as characterized by poverty, unemployment, addiction and domestic violence. First produced at the University of Montana's Playwriting Festival in Missoula in June 1986, this play – Yellow Robe's 'signature piece',[7] according to Mimi Gisolfi D'Aponte – turns a spotlight on a highly dysfunctional family on a Montana reservation. Its protagonist, a teenager of some 15 years, is trying to cope with his unemployed, alcoholic mother Katherine and her violent boyfriend Lenny while feeling responsible for the protection of his younger sister Theia. Expelled from the local school for his regular use of controlled substances (p. 48), Eddie Rose is supposed to continue his education elsewhere but refuses to attend a boarding school. David Krasner, who characterizes the play as a 'Native American Bildungsdrama', argues that its 'dramatic conflict is unambiguous – Eddie either stays or leaves'[8] – but there is much more to *The Independence of Eddie Rose* than this spatial decision.

Again, as in *Sneaky*, the protagonist's situation microcosmically represents larger communal and cultural conflicts. The play – much like Hanay Geiogamah's *Body Indian* – is an indictment of the violence dominating Native communities: Eddie's immediate environment is dangerously dysfunctional. His father, who was also an alcoholic, 'threw him against the wall' (p. 59) when he was a baby, and mother Katherine and her boyfriend alternately attack Theia, Eddie and each other. In addition to the constant outbreaks of verbal and physical violence, both Eddie and Theia are subject to sexual abuse: Katherine makes incestuous passes at Eddie, and the play culminates in the brutal rape of Theia by Lenny (p. 91). In Native North American drama, the motif of rape is often employed (e.g. in plays by Margo Kane, Shirley Cheechoo or Tomson Highway) as a metaphor of colonialist conquest, since it graphically captures the aggressive intrusion of patriarchal (European) culture upon the dominantly matriarchal American continent. In *The Independence of Eddie Rose*, too, sexual violence symbolically evokes the institutionalized abuse of executive power – especially through the character of Eddie's friend Mike, who is repeatedly forced to extend sexual favours to his detention officer in jail (p. 67). Similarly, Eddie's stepfather Lenny admits that he too was once raped by a white guard in a drug rehabilitation centre (p. 90), a fact that suggests the epidemic perpetuation of (colonial) violence. Like *Sneaky*, the play thus subtly probes the historical roots of domestic violence, making easy accusations or solutions impossible. Therefore, in spite of the fact that, as one character in *Better-n-Indins* puts it, 'most of our problems in this part of the hemisphere are due to colonization' (p. 267), Eddie's loyalties and affiliations do not run along ethnic lines. Quite on the contrary, his process of initiation – or rather, 'denitiation'[9] – requires a particularly courageous act of separating himself from his biological roots.

In this bleak domestic environment, the adolescent's only solace is his hope for escape – first through drugs, and eventually through a physical change of place. Quite tellingly, it is Aunt Thelma, who represents the lost link to Eddie's cultural heritage, who helps him with his decision: in a traditional sage-burning ceremony conducted at the cemetery where Eddie's grandparents are buried, she accompanies his rite of passage into adulthood. The play ends on a note of hope: Aunt Thelma takes over the child custody for Theia, and Eddie decides to begin a new life, away from the existential threats of his home. Leaving the reservation, he takes along the cultural knowledge communicated to him by his aunt and begins to affiliate with a family of choice, promising to his friend Mike that 'I will pray for you like Indins [sic] do': 'We'll always be brothers' (p. 82). Cultural identity becomes a dynamic process: instead of being fixed by categories of blood quantum or genetic heritage, it depends on the individual's affiliations, mobility and choice.

Furthermore, by exposing a harsh reality of social and economic injustice, *The Independence of Eddie Rose* most efficiently pursues Yellow Robe's declared aim of countering classic 'Indian' stereotypes, especially those projecting Native people as harmoniously spiritual and holistic. 'I don't do Sundance 101 in my plays',[10] Yellow Robe states, and the 'kitchen-sink naturalism'[11] of *Eddie Rose* will certainly disrupt any audience expectations of this kind. This aspect has been seen as one of the play's primary strengths, as one reviewer notes: 'At last here is a Native American play that refuses to beat the tom-toms of political and historical issues or cater to white fascination with Indian spirituality'.[12] Furthermore, the play tells us, contemporary Native identity does not simply come with a status card: it is a complex process of orientation among various historically conditioned coordinates, and thus an ongoing quest.

The Star Quilter (1988)

While most of Yellow Robe's plays highlight the complexities of identity by closely interweaving intra- and intercultural differences, *The Star Quilter* most densely focuses on the conflict between Native and non-Native cultures. First produced at the Crystal Theater in Missoula, Montana in 1988, the four-scene play microcosmically intertwines the personal and the political in an encounter of two women. Mona Gray, an Assiniboine housewife and mother in her thirties, uses her sewing skills to 'brin[g] some extra money into the house when things get tight' (p. 9), when LuAnne Jorgensen, a neighbour of German and English descent, intrudes upon her life. In a scene that openly echoes the history of colonization, LuAnne – who has become rich through an oil well on Assiniboine land – enters Mona's house on a Montana reservation without knocking. Wanting to present a local gift to the Senator of Montana, with whom she recently dined at the tellingly named Custer Hotel,[13] she tries to persuade Mona to sell one of the eponymous star quilts. Even though Mona initially hesitates, she agrees to make a quilt for 80 dollars. The play then follows the two women's economic connection across three decades: LuAnne starts a business, the 'Princess Light Sleeps Company' (p. 25), to distribute indigenous quilts. She tricks Mona and other neighbours into working for her, but it turns out that the Native women are shamefully taken advantage of, while LuAnne and her agent in New York resell the quilts for 800 dollars apiece without sharing the profit.

In spite of this synecdochal re-enactment of colonial exploitation, the play ends on a conciliatory note. As a side effect of their various discussions about tribal elections, Wounded Knee, land leases, diabetes and giveaway ceremonies, Mona educates LuAnne about Native American life and history, countering the racist stereotypes that the European-American woman has internalized. When LuAnne has to admit that she only ever came to Mona's house when she wanted a quilt, she feels 'empty and cold' (p. 42), but Mona wraps a shawl around her: 'Warm yourself, LuAnne. At least it could be a start' (p. 42).

The star quilt is the play's central symbol: as Deborah Weagel summarizes, it 'can be affiliated with family history, autobiography, and love'.[14] Most crucially, it stands for Mona's Assiniboine heritage and her dignity, both of which are unmarketable:

> Star quilts are beautiful, because they have one color and all the different shades of that color lead them to the center, the heart.

That's why I made these quilts—they came from my heart. I wanted to share this gift with people, because it really made different ones happy. How can you sell something that comes from your heart? It has to be given. (p. 41)

It is only when LuAnne understands that the quilts are not commodity articles that a friendship between the ageing women becomes possible. As in *Rez Politics* and *Grandchildren of the Buffalo Soldiers,* the play invites a critical investigation of historical injustices and cultural divides, but it also emphasizes that human decency does not reside in ethnicity, gender, religion or class. Mona summarizes this in an ethical credo in the end, when she tells her antagonist that 'I don't want to let our differences become a barrier. I really wanted to know who and what you were. And that's because we both live here, in this world. Deer, badgers, even a grasshopper will live near one another, though they are not the same, but each is valuable and necessary in completing the circle' (p. 41). In this holistic perspective on cultural diversity, the respect for otherness and an inclusive understanding of community matter all the more.

Better-n-Indins (2004)

First produced at the University of Maine in November 2004, *Better-n-Indins* is William S. Yellow Robe, Jr.'s most humorous and most bitingly satiric play. The play's form breaks most openly with Yellow Robe's characteristic mode of realism. Reminiscent of Hanay Geiogamah's *Foghorn* (1973), Spiderwoman Theater's *Winnetou's Snake Oil Show from Wigwam City* (1988) and LeAnne Howe's *Indian Radio Days* (1996), this comedy employs 32 characters and a variety of media to contrast stereotypical non-Native expectations with both intra-cultural tensions and colonial practices. In a *tour d'horizon* of revisionist historiography, it criticizes the 'Assimilating Institutions' (p. 296) that have systematically exploited indigenous cultures – from the Bureau of Indian Affairs to the Hollywood film industry. Like *Pieces of Us,* in which a Chorus of Governance and a Chorus of Academia alternately claim the right to define what an 'Indian' is, *Better-n-Indins* centrally revolves around the question of indigenous identity. This is most pointedly displayed by the final of 10 episodes: a TV game show features two 'unaware, uninformed, and just plain uncaring citizens' (p. 328) who have to 'correctly identify people in the photographs we present as Indian or not Indian' (p. 322). The show exposes the absurdity of judging people by their outward appearance: the candidates mistake a Chinese child and even a science fictional character – 'an admiral in the Romulan fleet from *Star Trek*' (p. 326) – for 'Indians'.

Yet again, as in Yellow Robe's other plays, the divide separating people is not easily drawn along ethnic lines: *Better-n-Indins* mocks non-Native impostors just as much as indigenous fundamentalists (through characters such as Brent Big Shoulders, a vain opportunist) or activists (such as Russell Means)[15] who are mostly concerned with their own fame. The intra-communal mechanisms of exclusion are again exposed here: Janelle, for instance, a Native woman who brings a Gothic fancy dance costume to a powwow, is ridiculed and humiliated by the indigenous community because of her unorthodox creativity.

Without reducing the question of cultural difference to the distinction between 'white' and 'Indin', the largest part of the play deals with the selling-out of Native American culture. Tellingly set at a museum, it presents a hippie who speaks for 'all the elders of Turtle Island' (p. 277), a history teacher denying one of his students' ethnicity and a non-Native healer's workshops and 'magical retreat[s]', such as 'Chanting for Cleansing and Internet Purification' (p. 288) or 'Sun Dancing for Non-Turtles of Turtle Island' (p. 288). The first part's series of satirical scenes culminates in the appearance of 'Sam, the Sacred Shaman' who has 'all kinds of sacred and ceremonial objects for sale' (p. 293), and whose business features a tanning salon and an optics centre ('if you need to hide those blue or green eyes, we have eye contacts in brown, dark brown, and "O-my-god-how-much-peyote-did-you-eat-because-all-I-can-see-is-your-pupils-darkest brown"' [p. 294]).

This practice of what Spiderwoman Theater call 'plastic shamanism'[16] – the commercial exploitation of indigenous spirituality – is effectively disrupted by the recurrent appearance of the museum's director, representatively named Adam Redman, who announces the scenes, comments on the action, and directly addresses the audience. Assisted by a plurality of 'Moccasin Telegraph voices' (p. 265), this authorial presence not only provides the play with a ritualistic structure, but, in the tradition of epic theatre, it dismantles the 'fourth wall' between stage and audience and perforates the boundary between reality and fiction. Through this technique, as well as through extradiegetic comments, and the inclusion of audience members as characters, audience expectations are lastingly disturbed. Combined with announcements of time and reminders that 'the following people are still Native' (pp. 267, 277, 308) – with references to actual indigenous people such as Chief Joseph, Tomson Highway, Sherman Alexie or the playwright's mother, Mina Forest Yellow Robe – the director's comments prevent a fixating colonialist gaze and remind the audience that 'Yes, we do shop at Wal-Mart, have lawns, have bank accounts, and have served in every war of and by this government. We are individual nations within a nation' (pp. 328–39).

Grandchildren of the Buffalo Soldiers (2005)

Grandchildren of the Buffalo Soldiers is like a reprise of *Sneaky*, since here, too, the author's signature themes of multiracial identity and contested cultural affiliation are translated into a conflict between three brothers. One of Yellow Robe's most recent and most well-received plays, *Grandchildren* was first produced in September 2005 at the Penumbra Theater in St Paul, MN, as a cooperation between Penumbra and the Trinity Repertory Company.[17] Again, like *The Independence of Eddie Rose* and the other 'blood quantum plays'[18] – which also include *Rez Politics* (1997), *Mix Blood Seeds* (2002) and *Pieces of Us* (2006) – this play foregrounds the challenges of a mixed cultural heritage, in this case with a particular focus on African-Native interrelations.[19] This long neglected facet of hybrid identity is introduced by the play's title: 'buffalo soldiers' was the nickname given to the members of the first exclusively African American regiment in the US Army. Established by Congress in 1866, six regiments took a central role in the settlement of the American frontier. As Frank N. Schubert notes, '[t]hese African Americans who served in the Regular

Army between the Civil War and World War I fought in some of the most difficult wars against western Indians.'[20] *Grandchildren* not only takes up the economies of exclusion resulting from these intercultural encounters, but it also addresses the challenges of recovering a silenced historical heritage.

The plot is triggered by the return of the protagonist, Craig Robe, to his home on the reservation in Montana. Having come back for the traditional naming ceremony of his niece, August, he soon finds himself struggling with his younger brothers Brent and Elmo over their differences in relating to their cultural heritage. Since Craig lived in the city for a long time, Elmo, who has just been left by his wife, charges him with having 'been hanging around white people too long' (p. 107). When Craig wants to hug his brother, for instance, Elmo reprimands him: 'We don't hug here like white people do in the big cities, Craig. We just shake hands. Indins aren't like that. We keep it simple, enit, Brent?' (p. 110). Thus, even expressions of affection are restricted by cultural or ethnic codes; and since Craig is no longer familiar with all aspects of '[p]owwow etiquette' (p. 110), his position is continuously questioned.

In *Grandchildren*, the suspicion towards 'urban Indins' (p. 133) – a common motif in contemporary Native literature – is then crucially explored in connection to the Robe family's heavily contested African American heritage. Craig tells his niece in the very first scene that their grandfather, a nineteenth-century African American soldier, fell in love with their Native American grandmother. Their love story, which is introduced by a non-verbal prologue set in 1885, is socially stigmatized from the very beginning: Grandma Phyla's father 'disowned her', and Private Chauncey Haul was dishonourably discharged from his unit 'for marrying a savage' (p. 102). The dynamics of this racism reverberate well into the present generation: Brent's father-in-law, for example, denies the family its access to tribal financial support because of their 'being part colored' (p. 111), and the brothers are also frequently faced with racial slurs and even physical attacks. Brent has therefore found his own strategy to cope with the hostility: he denies his father (p. 159) and claims that 'I'm a fullblood. I don't have any nigger blood in me' (p. 159). Craig is appalled by this behaviour, and in a statement that substantially summarizes Yellow Robe's ethics of cultural identity, he tells his brother that

> We aren't fullblood in any blood quantum. It doesn't say that on our enrollment papers, and it never will. . . . We are part black. I've never said at any time, we have to try to behave, or act black. All I've been trying to say is that we should respect, honor, and love that about ourselves, because it's a part of us. . . . We aren't breeds, we aren't half a tribal person, or half a human, and that's because we have these things put into us by the creator. We are good—"was-te." (p. 169)

Attempting to unite the family, Craig, Elmo and their sister Sugar finally invite Brent to join a ceremony of playing the family drum, but Brent merely turns his back on them: 'I am not ha-sapa [dark-colored]. I have no family' (p. 171).

Even though the drum, as a symbol of their traditional indigenous heritage, cannot overcome the fraternal differences, the play nevertheless ends on a literal note of hope, in another musical symbol. Craig reminds the family of a 'French Canadian jig/reel' (p. 120) that their father taught them 'to make us happy, to give us a smile when we were down' (p. 168), but Brent and Elmo reject it because '[i]t wasn't Indin' (p. 119). Their opposition to a cheerful and positive cultural activity is particularly ironic, since their African-American grandfather learnt the dance from 'a Northern Cree who shared his fishing camp' (p. 120), and thus indeed from an indigenous person. In the play's final scene, August performs the hybrid dance 'in memory of Grandpa' and 'for all our relations' (p. 176): '*She turns on the tape recorder and as the music plays, AUGUST begins to dance a reel. CRAIG laughs. Blackout*' (p. 176). Whereas the traditional Native family drum does not succeed in reuniting the brothers, the dance – as a symbol of cross-cultural encounters and an inclusive optimism unlimited by ethnic boundaries – is handed on to the next generation. The memory of the 'buffalo soldiers' is thus honoured and maintained by August's performance, and not least, of course, by Yellow Robe's play at large.

Summary

In *Grandchildren of the Buffalo Soldiers,* protagonist Craig and his niece discuss their mixed cultural heritage:

August "So it isn't a bad thing to be a breed, enit?"
Craig "No. It means you have more ways of helping your people. If you can learn how to do it." (p. 124)

This statement is programmatic of William S. Yellow Robe's work in general. While his plays centrally revolve around questions of mixed cultural heritage, particularly located at the crossroads between African American, Native American and European American influences, they also promote an ethics of respect and understanding, regardless of the characters' genetic backgrounds. As plays such as *Rez Politics, Mix Blood Seeds,* and *Grandchildren of the Buffalo Soldiers* demonstrate, subject positions – and especially Native/African-American ones – are never easily claimed. Contemporary Native American identity involves confrontations with both history and the ongoing challenges of colonization, but it is also a site of negotiation, dialogue and reconciliation. Yellow Robe's plays are thus part of a larger movement towards a more differentiated perspective on ethnicity: refusing to take sides either with the strategies of separatist essentialism or with the harmonizing lure of assimilationism, they liberate indigenous identity from the grip of ontological categories and emphasize its dynamic processes instead. In the 'shift of emphasis away from notions of a melange in the direction of a simultaneity of—often conflicting—positions, loyalties, affiliations and participations' that Helmbrecht Breinig and Klaus Lösch have described in the terminology of 'transdifference',[21] the concept of identity becomes a self-reflexive work-in-progress, allowing for multiple identifications in heterogeneous communities.

In spite of these contested sites of difference and sameness, William Yellow Robe's plays are also humorous and often optimistic, celebrating the survival of indigenous North American people. When asked about his motivation, the author once answered that 'I do plays to show the Assiniboine are still alive, and that we are a part of the great Lakota

Nation, and that I honor and celebrate the fact that my people are still alive today'.[22] Even though realism – in the tradition of Eugene O'Neill or Sam Shepard[23] – is his signature format for this purpose, plays such as *The Council, Pieces of Us,* or *Better-n-Indins* also explore mythical, magic realist or satirical strategies.

In the field of contemporary Native American theatre, William S. Yellow Robe, Jr. is certainly one of the most visible and most frequently produced artists. The first issue of *The Native Playwrights' Newsletter*, a magazine dedicated entirely to this genre, featured him on its cover, and Hanay Geiogamah praises his colleague's 'courageous determination to dramatize some of the harsher truths of American Indian life' – especially those that are not immediately visible: 'His plots are often based on highly sensitive aspects of contemporary Indian life that are likely to be ignored or denied by tribal traditionalists and academic purists.'[24] As one of the few early contributors to the genre, he continues to write and stage successful plays to the present day: his most recent production, entitled 'Wood Bones', premiered on 7 March 2012, at Playwrights Horizons in New York City. While his *oeuvre* captures a wide range of characters, styles, and themes, the one element at its heart is the dedication to an intercultural ethics. What matters in the end, in the words of a character from *Pieces of Us,* is that 'we can be just "people"' (p. 369), regardless of exterior labels.

Primary Sources

Works by William S. Yellow Robe, Jr.

Where the Pavement Ends: Five Native American Plays (The Star Quilter, The Body Guards, Rez Politics, The Council, Sneaky). (Norman: University of Oklahoma Press, 2000).

Grandchildren of the Buffalo Soldiers and Other Untold Stories (A Stray Dog, Grandchildren of the Buffalo Soldiers, Mix Blood Seeds, Better-n-Indins, Pieces of Us: How the Lost Find Home) (Los Angeles: UCLA American Indian Studies Center, 2009).

The Independence of Eddie Rose. In Mimi Gisolfi D'Aponte (ed.), *Seventh Generation: An Anthology of Native American Plays* (New York: Theatre Communications Group, 1999), pp. 39–100.

The Pendleton Blanket. In *Frank: An International Journal of Contemporary Writing and Art* No. 16–17 (1999), pp. 105–8.

Secondary Sources

Bellamy, Sarah, '"Your Blood Ain't Redder Than Mine"': Hybridity, Legacy, and the Creation of America', *Penumbra Theatre Company Study Guide: Grandchildren of the Buffalo Soldiers* (2005), 4 January 2012 http://penumbratheatre.org/downloads/studyguides/GOTBSStudyGuide2005.pdf, pp. 21–38.

Bonnett, Alistair, 'Shades of Difference: African Native Americans', *History Today* 58, 12 (2008), 40–2.

Breinig, Helmbrecht and Klaus Lösch, 'Introduction: Difference and Transdifference'. In Helmbrecht Breinig, Jürgen Gebhardt, and Klaus Lösch (eds), *Multiculturalism in Contemporary Societies: Perspectives on Difference and Transdifference*, (Erlangen: Universitätsbibliothek, 2002), pp. 11–36.

Brinster, Freddie, 'Drama's enemy is poverty, alcohol', *Native Playwrights' Newsletter* 8 (1995), 72–3.

Brooks, James (ed.), *Confounding the Color Line: The Indian-Black Experience in North America*, (Lincoln: University of Nebraska Press, 2002).

D'Aponte, Mimi Gisolfi, 'Introduction'. In Mimi Gisolfi D'Aponte (ed.), *Seventh Generation: An Anthology of Native American Plays*, (New York: Theatre Communications Group, 1999), pp. ix–xxiii.

Däwes, Birgit, 'An Interview with Drew Hayden Taylor'. *Contemporary Literature* 44, 1 (Spring 2003), pp. 1–18.

—, *Native North American Theater in a Global Age: Sites of Identity Construction and Transdifference* (Heidelberg: Winter, 2007).

Field, Ron and Alexander Bielakowski, *Buffalo Soldiers: African American Troops in the US Forces, 1866–1945* (Westminster, MD: Osprey Publishing, 2008).

Forbes, Jack D., *Africans and Native Americans: The Language of Race and the Evolution of Red-Black Peoples* (Champaign: University of Illinois Press, 1993).

—, 'The Tricky Business of Racism: Comments Upon Reading *Grandchildren of the Buffalo Soldiers*', *Penumbra Theatre Company Study Guide: Grandchildren of the Buffalo Soldiers* (2005), 4 January 2012, http://penumbratheatre.org/downloads/studyguides/GOTBS-Forbes_essay.pdf.

Geiogamah, Hanay, 'Courage, Truth, and Commitment: The Theater of William Yellow Robe, Jr.', *Penumbra Theatre Company Study Guide: Grandchildren of the Buffalo Soldiers* (2005), 4 January 2012, http://penumbratheatre.org/downloads/studyguides/GOTBS-Courage_Truth_and_Commitment.pdf.

Haugo, Ann, 'American Indian Theatre'. In Joy Porter and Kenneth M. Roemer (eds), *The Cambridge Companion to Native American Literature* (Cambridge: Cambridge University Press, 2005), pp. 189–204.

Huck, Ed, 'Penumbra Theatre Company, *Grandchildren of the Buffalo Soldiers*', *Talking Broadway.com* (2005), 4 January 2012, http://www.talkinbroadway.com/regional/minn/minn130.html.

Huhndorf, Shari, 'American Indian Drama and the Politics of Performance'. In Eric Cheyfitz (ed.), *The Columbia Guide to American Indian Literatures of the United States Since 1945* (New York: Columbia University Press, 2006), pp. 288–318.

Johnson, Wayne, 'Violence and Grim Truth Meet in Native American Drama', *The Seattle Times*, 6 July 1990.

Katz, William Loren, *Black Indians: A Hidden Heritage* (New York: Atheneum, 1986).

Kosmider, Alexia, 'Killing the Indian: A Review of William S. Yellow Robe's *Grandchildren of the Buffalo Soldiers*', *Penumbra Theatre Company Study Guide: Grandchildren of the Buffalo Soldiers* (2005), 4 January 2012, http://penumbratheatre.org/ downloads/studyguides/ GOTBS-Killing_The_Indian.pdf.

Krasner, David, 'Coming-of-Age on the Rez: William S. Yellow Robe's *The Independence of Eddie Rose* as Native American Bildungsdrama'. In Steve E. Wilmer (ed.), *Native American Performance and Representation* (Tucson: University of Arizona Press, 2009), pp. 171–81.

Lewis, R. W. B., *The American Adam: Innocence, Tragedy, and Tradition in the Nineteenth Century* (Chicago: University of Chicago Press, 1955).

Lukens, Margo, 'Introduction'. In Margo Lukens (ed.), *Grandchildren of the Buffalo Soldiers and Other Untold Stories: Five Plays by William S. Yellow Robe, Jr.* (Los Angeles: UCLA American Indian Studies Center, 2009), pp. xiii–xxx.

Mayo, Lisa, 'Appropriation and the Plastic Shaman', *Canadian Theatre Review* 68 (Fall 1991), 54–5.

Onion, Pat, 'Rev. of *Where the Pavement Ends,* by William Yellow Robe', *Studies in American Literature* 13, 2/3 (Summer/Fall 2001), 114–17.

Pulitano, Elvira, 'Telling Stories Through the Stage: A Conversation with William Yellow Robe', *Studies in American Indian Literatures* 10, 1 (Spring 1998), 19–44.

Rathbun, Paul Roland, 'Meet the Playwright: William S. Yellow Robe, Jr.', *Native Playwrights' Newsletter* 1 (Spring 1993), 1–2.

—, 'Interview with William S. Yellow Robe, Jr.', *Native Playwrights' Newsletter* 8 (Summer 1995), 75–82.

—, 'Interview with William S. Yellow Robe, Jr.'. In Hanay Geiogamah and Jaye T. Darby (eds), *American Indian Theater in Performance: A Reader* (Los Angeles: UCLA American Indian Studies Center, 2000), pp. 342–58.

Rooks, David, 'The Real Thing: Identity and Cultural Authenticity are Dramatic Fodder for William S. Yellow Robe Jr.', *American Theater* Vol. 22 (July-August 2005), 4 July 2005, www.tcg.org/am_theater/at_articles/AT_Volume_22/JulyAugust2005.html.

Saunt, Claudio, *Black, White and Indian: Race and the Unmaking of an American Family* (Oxford: Oxford University Press, 2007).

Schubert, Frank N., *Voices of the Buffalo Soldier: Records, Reports, and Recollections of Military Life and Service in the West* (Albuquerque: University of New Mexico Press, 2003).

Stanlake, Christy, *Native American Drama: A Critical Perspective* (Cambridge: Cambridge University Press, 2009).

Stoudt, Charlotte, 'Border Crossings: Theatre, Tribalism and Twenty-First-Century America. Luis Valdez at San Diego Repertory Theatre and William Yellow Robe, Jr., at Trinity Repertory Company'. In Charlotte Stoudt (ed.), *Stages of Transformation: Collaborations of the National Theatre Artist Residency Program* (New York: Theater Communications Group, 2005), pp. 56–67.

Sze, Arthur, with William S. Yellow Robe, 'Speaking With Yellow Robe'. In *Frank: An International Journal of Contemporary Writing and Art* No. 16–17 (1999), pp. 101–4.

Taylor, Drew Hayden, 'The Re-Appearance of the Trickster: Native Theatre in Canada'. In Albert-Reiner Glaap and Rolf Althof (eds), *On-Stage and Off-Stage: English Canadian Drama in Discourse* (St. John's, Newfoundland: Breakwater, 1996), pp. 51–9.

Uno, Roberta, '*MELUS*-Interview: William Yellow Robe', *MELUS* 16, 3 (Fall 1989–90), pp. 83–90.

Ward, Pamela and Jason Harber, 'An Interview with the Playwright: William S. Yellow Robe, Jr.', *Penumbra Theatre Company Study Guide: Grandchildren of the Buffalo Soldiers* (2005), 4 January 2012, http://penumbratheatre.org/downloads/studyguides/GOTBSStudyGuide2005.pdf, pp. 8–13.

Weagel, Deborah, 'The Quilt as (Non-)Commodity in William S. Yellow Robe Jr.'s *The Star Quilter*', *Western American Literature* 46, 1 (Spring 2011), pp. 47–61.

Weinen, Alexander, *Buffalo Soldiers: Die Rolle der Schwarzen in den amerikanischen Streitkräften des 19. Jahrhunderts* (Wyk auf Föhr: Verlag für Amerikanistik, 1992).

Weinert-Kent, Rob, 'In the Trenches: William Yellow Robe', *Theatre Communications Group Circle* (17 May 2010), 21 January 2012, http://www.tcgcircle.org/2010/05/in-the-trenches-william-yellow-robe/.

Wilmer, Steven E. (ed.), *Native American Performance and Representation* (Tucson: University of Arizona Press, 2009).

Zuzek, Ashley, 'Playwright Discusses Biracialism', *The Dartmouth.Com* (18 January 2008), 24 February 2012, http://thedartmouth.com/2006/01/18/news/playwright/print.

Notes

1. Drew Hayden Taylor, 'The Re-Appearance of the Trickster: Native Theatre in Canada', p. 51.
2. These are, in chronological order: Mimi Gisolfi D'Aponte (ed.), *Seventh Generation: An Anthology of Native American Plays* (New York: Theatre Communications Group, 1999); Hanay Geiogamah and Jaye T. Darby (eds), *Stories of Our Way: An Anthology of American Indian Plays* (Los Angeles: UCLA American Indian Studies Center, 1999), Heather Hodgson (ed.), *The Great Gift of Tears: Four Aboriginal Plays* (Regina, Saskatchewan: Coteau Books, 2002), Monique Mojica and Ric Knowles (eds), *Staging Coyote's Dream: An Anthology of First Nations Drama in English* (Toronto: Playwrights Union of Canada Press, 2003), Jaye T. Darby and Stephanie Fitzgerald (eds), *Keepers of the Morning Star: An Anthology of Native Women's Theater* (Los Angeles: UCLA American Indian Studies

Center, 2003), Shirley A. Huston-Findley and Rebecca Howard (eds), *Footpaths and Bridges: Voices from the Native American Women Playwrights Archive* (Ann Arbor: U of Michigan P, 2008), Ann E. Armstrong, Kelli Lyon Johnson and William A. Wortman (eds), *Performing Worlds Into Being: Native American Women's Theater* (Miami, OH: Miami UP, 2009) and the second volume of Monique Mojica and Ric Knowles (eds), *Staging Coyote's Dream* (Toronto: Playwrights of Canada Press, 2009). All of these anthologies contain four or more plays by Native American or First Nations dramatists. In addition to these, there are 11 collections of three or more plays by individual playwrights, such as Joseph Bruchac, Hanay Geiogamah, Diane Glancy, Joan Shaddox Isom, Bruce King, Yvette Nolan, Lynn Riggs, E. Donald Two-Rivers and William S. Yellow Robe, Jr. A collection of plays by Lynn Riggs has been re-edited in 2003. These do not yet include the large number of plays published individually or in journals, or those published in more generally oriented anthologies.

3. As William Yellow Robe puts it: 'The most difficult thing in being produced . . . is the economics. It's very hard to have original work produced in this country because of the price tag that goes with it' (Sze, p. 102). Drew Hayden Taylor explains why 'the Native voice is much more prevalent in Canadian society: we have very strong political representation, and we have very strong cultural and artistic representation in the larger Canadian mosaic. And I think Native people are the constant and predominant non-white presence available in Canada, whereas in the States, it's the complete opposite' (Däwes, 'An Interview', p. 6).

4. Pamela Ward and Jason Harber, 'An Interview with the Playwright: William S. Yellow Robe, Jr.', p. 10.

5. Ibid., p. 8.

6. Cf. Margo Lukens, 'Introduction', p. xxix.

7. Mimi Gisolfi D'Aponte, 'Introduction', p. xix.

8. David Krasner, 'Coming-of-Age on the Rez', p. 172.

9. R. W. B. Lewis, *The American Adam: Innocence, Tragedy, and Tradition in the Nineteenth Century*, p. 115.

10. Roberta Uno, '*MELUS*-Interview: William Yellow Robe', p. 89.

11. Wayne Johnson, 'Violence and Grim Truth Meet in Native American Drama'.

12. Freddie Brinster, 'Drama's enemy is poverty, alcohol', p. 77.

13. General George Armstrong Custer was a US cavalry commander who became infamous for ferociously fighting against Native American tribes after the Civil War. He was defeated in the Battle of Little Bighorn in 1876, but he continues to be celebrated as a national hero who sacrificed his life for his country.

14. Deborah Weagel, 'The Quilt as (Non-)Commodity in William S. Yellow Robe Jr.'s *The Star Quilter*', p. 60.

15. Russell Means is an Oglala Lakota activist. He was a prominent leader of the American Indian Movement (AIM) in the 1970s, but the organization distanced itself from him because of his acting career. Means appeared in Michael Mann's adaptation of *Last of the Mohicans* and played a Navajo character in Oliver Stone's movie *Natural Born Killers*.

He was particularly criticized for his appearance in, and endorsement of, Walt Disney's *Pocahontas*. In *Better-n-Indins*, an arrogant white movie director praises him: 'Russell was so good in *Natural Born Killers*. And the voice work in *Pocahontas*, man, he was in a zone' (p. 315).

16. Lisa Mayo, 'Appropriation and the Plastic Shaman', p. 54.

17. It was also staged at the Mashantucket Pequot Museum and Research Center in Connecticut in March 2007 and at the Smithsonian National Museum of the American Indian in Washington, D.C. from 22 April to 2 May 2010, in the context of a groundbreaking exhibition on African-American and Native-American interrelations, entitled *IndiVisible: African-Native American Lives in the Americas*.

18. Lukens, 'Introduction', p. xxvi.

19. Yellow Robe underlines the autobiographical impetus of his play: 'I was called "nigger" for the first time when I was in the third grade by a very good friend of mine. So I went home and asked my mother: "Am I part nigger?"' (David Rooks, 'The Real Thing'). Sharing this heritage, he 'was sort of isolated—I couldn't run to the white community. . . . There was no African-American community to hide with. But within that process, I had a chance to see both sides, and I've never hated either' (David Rooks. 'The Real Thing').

20. Frank N. Schubert, *Voices of the Buffalo Soldier: Records, Reports, and Recollections of Military Life and Service in the West*, p. 1.

21. Helmbrecht Breinig and Klaus Lösch, 'Introduction: Difference and Transdifference', p. 21.

22. David Rooks, 'The Real Thing'.

23. Cf. Paul Roland Rathbun, 'Interview' (1994), p. 32.

24. Hanay Geiogamah, 'Courage, Truth, and Commitment: The Theater of William Yellow Robe, Jr.'.

CONTRIBUTORS

Susan S. W. Abbotson is Professor of Modern and Contemporary Drama, Rhode Island College, Providence, RI, USA.

Jochen Achilles is Professor of American Studies at the University of Würzburg, Germany.

Tom Adler is Professor Emeritus of English at Purdue University, West Lafayette, IN, USA.

Klaus Benesch is Professor of North American Literary History at the LMU Munich, Germany.

Ina Bergmann is Assistant Professor of American Studies at the University of Würzburg, Germany.

Stephen Bottoms is Professor of Contemporary Theatre and Performance, University of Manchester, UK.

Annalisa Brugnoli is an Honorary Fellow at the University of Venice, Italy.

Scott T. Cummings is Associate Professor of Theatre, Boston College, Chestnut Hill, MA, USA.

Birgit Daewes is Junior Professor of American Studies at the University of Mainz, Germany.

James Fisher is Professor of Theatre at the University of North Carolina, Greensboro, NC, USA.

Deborah Geis is Associate Professor of English at DePauw University, Greencastle, IN, USA.

Jorge Huerta is Professor Emeritus of Theatre at the University of California at San Diego, CA, USA.

Christopher Innes is Distinguished Research Professor of Performance and Culture at York University, Toronto, Canada.

Frazer Lively is Associate Professor of Theatre at Wesleyan College, Macon, GA, USA.

Joanna Mansbridge is Lecturer in the Department for Gender Studies at Simon Fraser University, Vancouver, Canada.

Martin Middeke is Professor and Chair of English Literature at the University of Augsburg and Visiting Professor of English at the University of Johannesburg, South Africa.

Matthew C. Roudané is Regents' Professor of American Drama, Modern Drama, and American Literature at Georgia State University, Atlanta, GA, USA.

Ilka Saal is Professor of American Studies at the University of Erfurt, Germany.

Annette J. Saddik is Professor of English and Theatre at the New York City College of Technology and the CUNY Graduate Center Doctoral Program, New York City, NY, USA.

Kerstin Schmidt is Professor of American Studies at the Catholic University of Eichstätt-Ingolstadt, Germany.

Peter Paul Schnierer is Professor of English Literature at the University of Heidelberg, Germany.

Sandra G. Shannon is Professor of Drama at Howard University, Washington, D.C., USA.

Ken Urban is a Playwright and Director and teaches at Harvard University, Cambridge, Mass., USA.

Russell Vandenbroucke is Professor of Theatre at the University of Louisville, Louisville, KY, USA.

Katherine Weiss is Associate Professor of Modern Drama at East Tennessee State University, Johnson City, TN, USA.

Pia Wiegmink is Assistant Professor of American Studies at the University of Mainz, Germany.

Toby Zinman is Professor of English at the University of the Arts, Philadelphia, PA, USA.

The editors are grateful to all of the above, to the efficient and patient staff at Bloomsbury Methuen Drama, and many others. Once again, we wish to convey our greatest debts of gratitude to Lisa Haubeck, Georg Hauzenberger, Adriana Lopez, Julia Peter, Nadja Rehberger, Tim Sommer, and Katja Utz for their diligent work on the manuscript during various stages.

INDEX

INDEX